The 6th
United States Cavalry
in the Civil War

The 6th United States Cavalry in the Civil War

A History and Roster

DONALD C. CAUGHEY and
JIMMY J. JONES

Foreword by Eric J. Wittenberg

McFarland & Company, Inc., Publishers
Jefferson, North Carolina, and London

Frontispiece: Regimental colors, 6th U.S. Cavalry
(courtesy of the U.S. Cavalry Museum, Ft. Riley, Kansas).

Library of Congress Cataloguing-in-Publication Data

Caughey, Donald C., 1967–
The 6th United States Cavalry in the Civil War : a history and roster /
Donald C. Caughey and Jimmy J. Jones ; foreword by Eric J. Wittenberg.
p.   cm.
Includes bibliographical references and index.

ISBN 978-0-7864-6835-5
softcover : acid free paper ∞

1. United States. Army. Cavalry Regiment, 6th.   2. United States —
History — Civil War, 1861–1865 — Regimental histories.   3. United
States — History — Civil War, 1861-1865 — Cavalry operations.
4. United States — History — Civil War, 1861–1865 — Campaigns.
.   I. Jones, Jimmy J., 1977–   II. Title.
III. Title: Sixth United States Cavalry in the Civil War.
E492.56th.C38 2013   973.7'4 — dc23   2013008979

British Library cataloguing data are available

On the cover: print entitled *Battle of the Wilderness–Desperate fight
on the Orange C.H. Plank Road, near Todd's Tavern, May 6th, 1864,*
Kurz & Allison,1887 (Library of Congress); United States Cavalry emblem

Manufactured in the United States of America

*McFarland & Company, Inc., Publishers
Box 611, Jefferson, North Carolina 28640
www.mcfarlandpub.com*

This book is respectfully dedicated to the brave troopers of the 6th U.S. Cavalry who have answered the nation's call and followed the guidon in every conflict since its inception. And to those brave men and women who continue to serve in the regiment's active squadrons today, at home and abroad.

Table of Contents

Acknowledgments

The interpretations set forth in this book are our own, and we accept full responsibility for them. If there are errors in the telling the story of the regiment, they are ours and we ask the reader's indulgence.

A work such as this would not be possible without help from others. We were consistently thrilled and amazed at the assistance we received from complete strangers throughout the project. We have a number of people to thank for their support, and we hope we haven't missed anyone. If we have, please understand that it was simply through oversight and not a lack of appreciation for your assistance.

Cavalry historian Eric Wittenberg has been of invaluable assistance as friend and mentor throughout the book's formation. Indeed, it may not have reached publication without him.

Blake Magner drew the majority of the maps for this book before his untimely passing in October 2011. An experienced cartographer, he was gruffly patient in dealing with rookie authors whose notes and sketches were not always legible. We feel that the classic look of his maps will greatly enhance the reader's understanding of the regiment's many long marches and campaigns. Thank you, Blake: you are missed.

Steven Stanley was kind enough to step in on very short notice and provide the battle maps for the Beverly Ford and Fairfield chapters. A consummate professional, he expanded both of our original maps into sequences which will make it much easier for the reader to follow these confusing engagements.

Researcher Karen Higgins, for assistance in obtaining material from the L. Henry Carpenter Papers at the Historical Society of Pennsylvania, as well as the staff of the society for their assistance. This huge collection of letters was invaluable to our record of the regiment.

Our thanks also go to the following:

Patty Millich, descendant of one of the regiment's soldiers, for countless hours spent locating obscure soldier enlistment records and transcribing sections of the L. Henry Carpenter letters.

The staff of the U.S. Cavalry Museum, Fort Riley, Kansas, who not only provided access to a set of the regiment's actual Civil War colors, but also provided the photo of them included in this book.

Cavalry historian J.D. Petruzzi, for several rare pieces of information and numerous helpful comments throughout the process.

Conrad Bush, for permitting use of material from his previously unknown collection of the letters and newspaper articles of B. Nathaniel Owen. We look forward to seeing them in print on their own someday soon.

Bev Applegate at the Beaver County Historical Society, for bringing the Robert Steel letters to our attention, and descendant Alta Musgrave, for permission to use them in this book.

   Alice Gayley, for assistance in obtaining material from the National Archives, and Lori Dodson, for her assistance in obtaining material from the Library of Congress.

   Finally, we express our appreciation and devotion to our wives, Gina Caughey and Twyla Jones. They've invested as much in this book as we have, including too much lost time with our families, mountains of books and paper clutter, hours of animated discussion about people long dead, and countless weekend and evening hours in front of a computer researching and writing. We could not have done this without them.

Foreword by Eric J. Wittenberg

While there have been thousands of books published on the American Civil War, few of them have dealt with the service of the small core of professional soldiers who made up the regular army. Nearly all tell the story of the Regular Army infantry and artillery regiments without telling the story of the Regular horse soldiers. This book begins to address that notable deficit.

When the war broke out in the spring of 1861, the regular army numbered only about 16,000 men serving in ten regiments of infantry, four regiments of artillery, two regiments of cavalry, two regiments of dragoons, and one regiment of mounted infantry. The strength and combat readiness of these Regular Army units decreased dramatically when Southern officers resigned to serve their states and other noncommissioned and commissioned officers resigned in order to accept commissions as officers in Union volunteer regiments, thereby leaving a drastic shortage of men to fill the ranks. Consequently, President Abraham Lincoln put out a call for 75,000 volunteers after the fall of Fort Sumter.

After the outbreak of hostilities, the Union high command decided that it needed a third regiment of cavalry, which was raised in western Pennsylvania and eastern Ohio. Originally designated as the 3rd U.S. Cavalry, its name changed shortly after its organization when all regular army mounted units, whether cavalry, dragoons, or mounted infantry, were redesignated as cavalry. These units were then numbered in accordance with their age. The oldest units (the 1st and 2nd Dragoons) received the lowest numbers. As the newest unit, the new cavalry regiment was redesignated as the 6th U.S. Cavalry, a designation the unit carries to this day.

The study of cavalry operations has always been a niche area of scholarship, but it is the one I have always found most interesting. The scarcest regimental studies are those dealing with the U.S. Army's regular cavalry regiments. Until the publication of this book, there was no monograph dedicated to the study of the operations of the regular army cavalry units in the Civil War. While the 2nd, 5th, and 6th U.S. Cavalry regiments have unit histories, they are just that: unit histories that cover the entire career of the regiments that are their subjects up to the date of their publication. These books certainly contain coverage of the Civil War, but the Civil War makes up only a portion of these books, and they largely lack detail. The 1st, 3rd, and 4th U.S. Cavalry regiments do not have published unit histories at all.

The 1st, 2nd, 5th, and 6th U.S. Cavalry regiments served in a single brigade attached to the Army of the Potomac's Cavalry Corps that was called the Reserve Brigade. In 1863, the 6th Pennsylvania Cavalry formally joined the Reserve Brigade, and I have spent years researching and telling the story of the 6th Pennsylvania. Along the way, I came to appreciate the all too often overlooked service of the U.S. Regulars, and lamented the fact that so little good information is available on the honorable service of these regular regiments in the Civil War.

Hence, this work, by Donald C. Caughey and Jimmy J. Jones, is an unprecedented study. It focuses on the formation of the 6th U.S. Cavalry, and then follows its service during the Civil War in great detail. It features plenty of good maps and an ample selection of images that help the reader to follow these events in detail. More important, this volume tells you stories of the men of the 6th U.S. Cavalry, often in their own words. The authors have deeply researched this work, and they have left no stone unturned in doing so. I am confident that where primary source material on the 6th U.S. Cavalry exists, they have found it.

When taken as a whole, the story of the 6th U.S. Cavalry is a compelling tale, filled with the terror of hand-to-hand combat and the mundane, boring days spent on picket duty. Caughey and Jones have told this story well, and I commend their effort to you as a necessary addition to any study of Civil War cavalry operations. The regimental roster alone is worth the purchase price of the book. It will occupy a prominent place in my personal library, and it likewise should occupy a prominent place in yours.

Eric J. Wittenberg is a Civil War historian, author and attorney. He has written more than a dozen books focusing on the cavalry in the Civil War and numerous articles in popular magazines, and he was the winner of the 1998 Bachelder-Coddington Literary Award. He is also active in battlefield preservation.

Preface

As we celebrate the 150th anniversary of the Civil War, there are numerous accounts of volunteer regiments and their battles. State veterans associations and local historical societies are fertile grounds for histories of volunteer regiments. The same is not true for the regiments of the regular army who fought in the war. These men, recruited regionally rather than by state, fought side by side with their volunteer brethren, yet seldom are their equally compelling stories told. Only recently have scholars looked at the regular army, and then usually from a large-scale view of operations as a whole.

The 6th U.S. Cavalry was a unique regiment in many ways. Of the 272 regiments which fought in the Civil War, it was the only new regular cavalry regiment. It participated in every campaign in the eastern theater during the war. Since its nominal commander, David Hunter, did not serve a single day with the regiment during the war, it was commanded in battle by the senior officer present. These ranged at various times from its lieutenant colonel to a mere second lieutenant. One of these interim commanders was relieved during a campaign, for treason.

For an organization that had not been conceived when Fort Sumter was attacked, its members were very successful during the war. Four of its officers were promoted to major general by the end of the war and two more to brigadier general. One of its assistant surgeons would eventually become the country's surgeon general, and one of its privates would become the first man to rise from the rank of private to chief of staff of the army over the course of his career.

The regiment's initial cast of officers was a unique collection of individuals who included two grandsons of former president Zachary Taylor, two cousins of the governor of Pennsylvania, the son of a powerful Radical Republican senator who opposed Lincoln, and a cousin of the Confederate president, Jefferson Davis.

The enlisted men were no less remarkable. Twenty-eight of them would earn commissions as officers during the war, some in volunteer regiments and others remaining with the regulars. One of these was a Philadelphia blueblood and another the nephew of General Joseph Hooker. Several of those who made the leap to appointments as commissioned officers were immigrants. Two of the regiment's soldiers won the Congressional Medal of Honor for their service during the war. Three eventually became generals after the war. In the army's history, only three men have held both of the highest officer and enlisted ranks, sergeant major and general. Two of these were from the 6th Cavalry, and both of them served during the Civil War.

Although actively recruited in four states, 2,130 men and at least one woman from 29 states and 14 countries served in the regiment during the war. The woman, who enlisted to

stay with her husband, remained with the regiment and finished her enlistment even after
he was wounded and discharged early. The demographics provide a good cross section of
the Union's population: 1,182 of the enlisted personnel were native-born, while nearly 900
were immigrants. Forty of forty-six officers were native-born.

This book is the first scholarly history of this regiment's service in the Civil War. Two
works were previously published which discuss the regiment during the war, both now out
of print. Private Sidney Morris Davis' postwar memoir, *Common Soldier, Uncommon War*,
provides a detailed and entertaining glimpse into the life of a private soldier, but its viewpoint
is limited by its very nature and the story is entirely anecdotal. William H. Carter's *From
Yorktown to Santiago* chronicles the regiment's history from its creation at the beginning of
the Civil War through the end of the Spanish-American War. Carter served the majority
of his forty-year career as an officer in the regiment, and his narrative reflects an under-
standable bias. The primary difficulty with Carter's book is that there are no references for
any of the contents. Original reports are easily identified, but no other sources are provided.
The story is again told from a single perspective, and in this case the work is a secondary
source.

Our book relies heavily upon primary sources to tell the regiment's story in the words
of the participants from as many viewpoints as possible. These include diaries and letters
of officers and enlisted men alike, several of which are previously unpublished. We have
delved deeply into archives and letter collections to locate as many different viewpoints as
possible of the regiment's service. Official reports are excerpted when appropriate to provide
the commander's view of the regiment's performance. No book this size can relate everything
about the activities of a thousand soldiers over a four-year period, so the end notes are as
detailed as possible to aid the reader in search of more information.

This reliance on primary sources contributes greatly to the book's format. Our narrative
focuses heavily on the first three years of the war. In our eyes and the eyes of the participants
after the war, the battle of Fairfield was the summit of the regiment's service, so it is treated
in as much detail as possible. Due to the effects of that battle and the expiration of initial
enlistments in the summer of 1864, there are almost no primary accounts remaining of the
regiment's service during the last year of the war. We have chosen to cover this period in
much less detail, relying on secondary accounts to summarize the regiment's participation
in the final campaigns.

We have spent the last five years piecing together the story of the 6th U.S. Cavalry,
and are confident that this is the most comprehensive account possible of the regiment's
service. We have attempted to use our experience as cavalry officers to remove bias while at
the same time examining why some decisions were made by leaders at various points.

We hope you find their tale as engrossing as we have.

Introduction

Atop a small ridge in southern Pennsylvania on a hot July afternoon, men prepared for their biggest moment of the war. To their front, a broken wave of Lieutenant Colonel Thomas Marshall's Seventh Virginia Cavalry reeled down the hill back to their lines in disarray, their charge broken. Farther to the west, a fresh regiment of Confederate cavalry was emerging around the wagons that were the goal of the expedition, and a battery of cannon began to unlimber in a wheat field on the opposite ridge.

On the left, Lieutenant Adna Chaffee's squadron was dismounted as skirmishers in an apple orchard. They checked the loads on their carbines, every fourth man to the rear holding the reins of his squad's horses. To the right, Lieutenant Tattnall Paulding's squadron was dismounted behind a stone wall, their horse holders a safe distance to the rear as well. Both squadrons had used their carbines to effect in breaking the enemy charge down the fence-lined lane to their front. To the rear, the regiment's newest officer, former first sergeant Joseph Bould held his squadron in reserve. The regimental colors floated at the front of this, the largest squadron in the regiment. To their rear, the regiment's two surgeons were already working on the wounded. In the center, Lieutenant Christian Balder's small squadron remained mounted in the road, looking to the regimental commander for instructions.

Major Paddy Starr observed the enemy's withdrawal from the center of his line. The combative former dragoon was in a difficult situation. The regiment was alone miles behind enemy lines, and missing two of its six squadrons. His forces were solidly deployed on the most defensible terrain in the area. As a third regiment began to emerge past the wagons while the enemy battery went into action, he realized he was both outgunned and badly outnumbered. The nearest friendly units were miles away defending the Union left flank at Gettysburg. The object of the raid, a train of enemy supply wagons, was now safely behind the ranks of an entire brigade of enemy cavalry with artillery support.

Starr needed time and space to extract his command. The next defensible terrain was miles to his rear at Fairfield Gap. Already the commands of the next enemy regiment's officers carried up the hill as they prepared to charge. A cavalry force was at its most vulnerable and disorganized following an unsuccessful charge. The fences lining the lane would help to reduce the effects of the disparity in numbers. If he could blunt this second attack, he might be able to slow his enemy and make them more cautious as he withdrew the regiment by squadron.

Starr dispatched his adjutant, Lieutenant L. Henry Carpenter, with orders for Paulding to withdraw his men, as Starr was about to charge and would be driven back. After Balder, Paulding was the senior and most experienced officer present. Paulding's tired troopers began to thin the line along the stone wall and race back to their horses.

Major Starr drew his saber and ordered Balder's small squadron to charge. He rode at the head of about seventy troopers as they thundered down the narrow lane to meet the charge of a fresh Confederate regiment, Major Cabell Flournoy's Sixth Virginia Cavalry.

The wisdom of the day held that it took one to two years of training to prepare a cavalry regiment for combat. Two years before, this newest of the Regular Army's cavalry regiments hadn't existed. Its officers worked from recruiting stations across several states to raise the regiment, which hadn't yet been assigned a single horse. A long winter of training under a firm taskmaster and a solid leavening of professional noncommissioned officers had prepared the regiment for its first campaign.

Now, two years later, they were as experienced as any cavalry regiment in the Army of the Potomac. They served as part of the advance guard of McClellan's army throughout the Peninsula campaign, even taking a handful of casualties in the ill-fated charge at Gaines Mill. After the battle of Antietam, hundreds of volunteers had chosen to leave their former units and join their ranks. They were the only horsemen to enter Fredericksburg during the battle there, and they had endured a long winter of picket duty along the Rappahannock fords. They acquitted themselves well during Stoneman's Raid in the spring on their first raid behind enemy lines. The previous month they had more than held their own at Brandy Station, and realized on the skirmish-filled march north to Pennsylvania that they had at last reached parity, at least, with their opponents.

Their initial officers now commanded brigades and divisions. At Fairfield the regiment was led primarily by officers promoted from its own talented ranks. These ranks, which included former farmers, clerks, and confectioners from twenty-eight states, and at least one woman, were now filled with veteran soldiers.

This is their story, the history of the troopers of the 6th United States Cavalry during the Civil War.

PART I: REGIMENTAL HISTORY

Chapter 1

Raising the Regiment

As the guns of Fort Sumter fell silent on April 12, 1861, the U.S. Army's mounted service was in disarray. Only five of the army's nineteen regiments were mounted, and none of these were close to full strength. They were spread from the Mississippi to the Pacific and from Canada to Mexico in small one- and two-company posts. The majority of the 1st and 2nd U.S. Cavalry regiments narrowly avoided capture as they hastily evacuated seceded territory in Texas and the Indian Territory. The commanding officers of four of the five regiments resigned.

These five regiments were spread across three mounted arms: two of dragoons, one of mounted riflemen and two of cavalry. Each arm had separate promotion systems and traditions. With the exception of the Mounted Riflemen, the scattered companies of these regiments made their best time to the Union armies forming east of the Mississippi. The Mounted Riflemen would focus on the defense of the New Mexico and Colorado territories for the first year of the war. In the meantime, volunteer cavalry units were actively discouraged by the War Department and commanding general Winfield Scott. Only a few ill-equipped and poorly trained volunteer companies were available for service.

On May 3, 1861, President Lincoln issued a proclamation directing the expansion of the regular army by ten regiments: eight of infantry, one of artillery, and one of cavalry. This was the only expansion of the regular army during the war.

The following day, in accordance with the president's proclamation, the Adjutant General's Office issued General Order No. 16, which announced the expansion and prescribed the plan of organization for the new regular regiments. The new mounted regiment was designated the 3rd U.S. Cavalry.[1] The order provided additional details such as how officers would be selected, where the regiment's initial headquarters would be, and when it should start recruiting.

This order was the beginning of a long road which would eventually result in a trained regiment prepared for battle. The biggest question initially facing the War Department was who would command this new regiment. As mentioned previously, resignations had decimated the top positions in the existing mounted regiments. There simply were no senior cavalry leaders available. There was, however, someone available with whom the president was familiar.

David Hunter graduated from the U.S. Military Academy in 1822 and served as a dragoon, infantry and paymaster officer. In 1860, while stationed as a major at Fort Leavenworth, he began a correspondence with Abraham Lincoln, focusing on Hunter's strong antislavery views. The relationship had long-lasting political effects, the first of which was an invitation to ride on Lincoln's inaugural train from Springfield, Illinois, to Washington, D.C., in February of 1861. During this duty, Hunter suffered a dislocated collarbone trying to protect Lincoln from a crowd pressing in on the president-elect at Buffalo, New York. The injury further cemented the friendship with the new president, and Hunter consequently received the honor of becoming the inaugural colonel of the nation's newest regular cavalry regiment.[2]

While Hunter hadn't served as a dragoon since he was a lieutenant, his inexperience with mounted soldiers was expected to be balanced by the experience of his second in command. Lieutenant Colonel William Emory was an old army veteran who had won fame in his own right. Ironically, a series of unfortunate events for this man resulted in extreme good fortune for the fledgling regiment.

A native of Maryland, William Helmsley Emory, graduated 14th in his class from the U.S. Military Academy in 1831. He served as an artillery officer and later a topographical engineer, winning great acclaim as the chief surveyor for an expedition to establish the boundary between Texas and Mexico in the 1850s. He was appointed a major in the 2nd U.S. Cavalry when it was formed on March 3, 1855, then transferred to the 1st U.S. Cavalry two months later. He was promoted to lieutenant-colonel of this regiment on January 31, 1861.[3]

Information on national politics reaching the frontier on the eve of the war was both out of date and often inaccurate. While serving with his regiment, Emory received the news of the attack on Fort Sumter, as well as a number of other radical rumors, some true, others false. These included the supposed resignation of the country's greatest living military hero, Maj. Gen. Winfield Scott, the abandonment of Washington, D.C., and even the breaking up of the government. In a moment of desperation, he submitted his resignation, addressing it to his brother in Maryland so that he could turn it in for William in case matters were as bad as rumored. Emory would then be able to return to Maryland, under no obligations to the government, to protect his family.

The day after Lt. Col. Emory mailed his resignation, his command was threatened by the secessions of Arkansas and Texas, and as the senior officer present he deemed it necessary to withdraw his unit from seceded territory to avoid the difficulties that had proved so disastrous to the army in Texas. He at once decided to recall his resignation, and telegraphed friends in Washington, D.C., to intercept it. He sent his telegrams and letters by an Indian to the nearest telegraph office at Fort Smith, Arkansas. Unfortunately, secessionists had seized the fort, and Emory's telegrams never reached Washington, D.C.

Lt. Col. Emory had meanwhile marched out of the seceded territory and consolidated his troops at Fort Leavenworth, Kansas. Although continually threatened by bodies of secessionists along the way, he did not lose a single man or piece of equipment throughout the month-long march to safety. Upon reaching the fort, Emory discovered that his resignation had been received and accepted.[4]

His command safe, he immediately went to Washington, D.C., to try to recall his resignation. Gen. Winfield Scott wrote a letter to Secretary of War Simon Cameron on Emory's behalf, expressing his perfect satisfaction at the faithful manner in which Emory had carried out his instructions, and recommended that he should be restored to his command, if possible. If it was not, he went on to recommend that Emory receive an appointment in one of the new regiments then being organized.[5]

Since another officer had been promoted to his position in the regiment in the same order announcing his resignation, the secretary of war was unable to restore him to his old command. Emory was thus appointed lieutenant-colonel of the newest regular regiment, the 3rd U.S. Cavalry.

Appointments

Adjutant General's Office General Order No. 33 officially appointed the regiment's officers on June 18, 1861, with an effective date of rank for all appointments of May 14, 1861. The new regiment's initial complement of officers was appointed the same way the officers had been appointed to its two sister cavalry regiments at their creation in 1855. A third of the officers were appointed from currently serving officers, a third from the civilian populace, and a third from deserving noncommissioned officers in existing regiments.

The theory behind the civilian appointments was that these young men's pedigrees and upbringing, along with their education, training, and social and political connections, would provide quality fresh blood to the army and not overly deplete the officer ranks within existing regiments. As one might expect, the civilian appointments were somewhat politicized, and were generally apportioned to wealthy or politically well-connected families. The remaining one-third was taken from among the sergeants of existing regiments, on the recommendation of their regimental commanders. This one-third, after the completion of the regiment's organization, was to be appointed to one-half of the vacancies in the lowest grade of commissioned officer, second-lieutenant. The appointment of noncommissioned officers as junior officers ensured a backbone of experience to assist in raising the new regiment. The following officers were appointed by the order, with their status at the time of their appointment[6]:

Colonel
    David Hunter   Major, Paymaster.
Lieutenant-Colonel
    William H. Emory   Lieutenant-Colonel, 1st Cavalry.
Majors
    Daniel H. Rucker   Captain, Assistant Quartermaster.
    Edward H. Wright   Civilian appointment, New Jersey.
Captains
    Isaiah N. Moore   Captain, 1st Dragoons.
    August V. Kautz   1st Lieutenant, 4th Infantry.
    Andrew W. Evans   1st Lieutenant, 7th Infantry.
    William S. Abert   1st Lieutenant, 4th Artillery.
    David McM. Gregg   1st Lieutenant, 1st Dragoons.
    Joseph H. Taylor   1st Lieutenant, 1st Cavalry.
    John I. Gregg   Civilian appointment, Pennsylvania.
    John Savage   Civilian appointment, Pennsylvania.
    George C. Cram   Civilian appointment, New York.
    Charles R. Lowell   Civilian appointment, Massachusetts.
1st Lieutenants
    John K. Mizner   1st Lieutenant, 2d Dragoons.
    William W. Averell   2d Lieutenant, Mounted Riflemen.
    Herbert M. Enos   2d Lieutenant, Mounted Riflemen
    Ira W. Claflin   2d Lieutenant, Mounted Riflemen.
    Sewell H. Brown   Civilian appointment, Pennsylvania.
    Benjamin T. Hutchins   Private, Co. A, National Rifles, D.C.
    Hancock T. McLean   Civilian appointment, Kentucky.
    Tattnall Paulding   Civilian appointment, New York.

Frederick Dodge	Civilian appointment, Nebraska.
John B. Johnson	Captain, 11th Pennsylvania Infantry.
James F. Wade	Civilian appointment, Ohio.
Mark F. Leavenworth	Civilian appointment, New York.
2d Lieutenants	
John W. Spangler	1st Sergeant, Co. H, 2d Cavalry.
Peter McGrath	1st Sergeant, Co. I, Mounted Riflemen.
Hugh McQuade	1st Sergeant, Co. F, Mounted Riflemen.
Curwen B. McLellan	Sergeant, Co. H, 2d Cavalry.

There was no advance notice of the appointments, so currently serving officers and non-commissioned officers served blissfully unaware with their assigned units until news of their promotions reached them. Since these units were without exception on the frontier, it would take them time to join their new regiment. One of the appointees was in Washington Territory and another in California when they received notification of their appointments. The war quickly took its toll on the initial complement of officers, presenting the regiment with its own unique set of challenges before the initial officers even began to assemble to recruit their men.

An appointment as an officer of volunteers did not negate one's commission in the regular service. As a result, the regiment lost its commanding officer before he even reported. David Hunter was promoted to brigadier general of volunteers just three days after his appointment as colonel of the regiment. He continued to serve in his volunteer rank throughout the war, while still holding the colonelcy of his regular regiment. He retained the title of colonel of the 6th U.S. Cavalry until he retired on July 31, 1866, having never served a day with his regiment.[7]

Major Rucker declined his appointment, choosing to remain a quartermaster.[8] Major Wright was appointed to General Winfield Scott's staff on June 14, and never joined the regiment.[9] When they were eventually notified, Captain Moore and Lieutenant Mizner also declined their appointments, busy commanding their squadrons of the 1st and 2nd Dragoons, respectively. Captain William P. Sanders was appointed to replace Captain Moore.

Several others would either arrive to the regiment late in the war or not at all. Captain Evans was in New Mexico when he received his appointment, and served in campaigns there until September 1863.[10] William Averell received his appointment in error, and was actually appointed to the Regiment of Mounted Riflemen, soon to be redesignated as the 3rd U.S. Cavalry.[11] Herbert Enos remained in the western theater in various capacities throughout the war.[12] Congress did not approve Mark Leavenworth's appointment before it expired on August 6.[13]

Two of the enlisted appointees died before they could join their new regiment. Second Lt. Hugh McQuade was appointed a captain of volunteers in June 1861 while away from his unit on leave. He was wounded and captured while leading his Company F, 38th New York Infantry, during the battle of Bull Run in July. After losing his leg from amputation, he died in Libby Prison before the end of the year.[14] Second Lt. Peter McGrath was still serving as a first sergeant of Mounted Riflemen when he died on May 1, 1862, of wounds received during the battle of Apache Canyon, New Mexico.[15]

William Price "Doc" Sanders was born in Lexington, Kentucky. He was the son of wealthy attorney Lewis Sanders, Jr. and the cousin of the Confederate president, Jefferson Davis. William entered the U.S. Military Academy in 1852 and was far from a model cadet.

Among his many transgressions as an underclassman was a fistfight with upperclassman Jeb Stuart that left the future Beau Sabreur hospitalized.[16] He was recommended for dismissal by superintendent Robert E. Lee, but he was saved by his cousin, then secretary of war Jefferson Davis. After graduating with an unimpressive 41st ranking in the class of 1856, he served the next five years in the 1st and 2nd U.S. Dragoons.[17]

August Valentine Kautz was born in Ispringen, Baden, Germany. His family immigrated to America and settled in Ohio during the first year of August's life. During the Mexican War, he served for a year as a private in Company G, 1st Ohio Infantry, before receiving an appointment to the U.S. Military Academy. He graduated 35th in the class of 1852, where he was close friends with Phillip Sheridan and George Crook. He served the nine years leading up to the war with the 4th U.S. Infantry in the Washington and Oregon territories.[18]

William Stretch Abert was born in Washington, D.C. He was the son of Colonel John J.

David Hunter, 1861 (Library of Congress).

Abert, the U.S. Army's chief of topographical engineers. This probably helped William secure a direct commission as a lieutenant in the 4th U.S. Artillery in 1855.[19]

David McMurtie Gregg was the grandson of Senator Andrew Gregg and the cousin of Andrew Gregg Curtin, Pennsylvania's wartime governor. David graduated from the U.S. Military Academy an impressive 8th in the class of 1855. Upon graduation, he served the next six years in the 1st Dragoons.[20]

Joseph Hancock Taylor was born in Jefferson County, Kentucky. He was the son of Joseph Pannill Taylor, the army's commissary general of subsistence and nephew of former president Zachary Taylor. Joseph was also the son-in-law of Brigadier General Montgomery C. Meigs, the army's quartermaster-general. He graduated 31st in the U.S. Military Academy class of 1856. He served in the newly organized 1st U.S. Cavalry after graduation until receiving his new appointment.[21]

A native of Pennsylvania, John Irvin "Long John" Gregg was also a grandson of Pennsylvania Senator Andrew Gregg, and related to Pennsylvania's governor Andrew Gregg Curtin. In fact, he and David McMurtrie Gregg were first cousins. John served as both an enlisted man and an officer in a volunteer Pennsylvania unit and the 11th U.S. Infantry during the Mexican War. He then entered the iron industry with the family firm of Irvin, Gregg & Co. His nickname derived from his height of 6' 4" at a time when the average American stood only 5' 6" tall. At the outbreak of the Civil War, he was appointed lieutenant colonel of the 5th Pennsylvania Cavalry, but resigned his volunteer commission to accept his appointment as a captain in the 3rd U.S. Cavalry.[22]

The native son of a prominent Philadelphia family, John Savage listed his occupation as a "gentleman" at the time of his appointment.[23]

George Clarence Cram was the son of Jacob L. Cram, who was a distinguished lawyer and proprietor of the prestigious New York law firm Cram and Cram. George was working as a lawyer at his father's firm when he received his appointment.[24]

Charles Russell Lowell, Jr. was a member of the prominent Lowell family of Massachusetts, which included Francis Cabot Lowell, statesman and federal judge John Lowell, and Abbott Lawrence Lowell, president of Harvard University. Charles graduated from Harvard University as the class valedictorian in 1854. He worked as a railroad executive after graduation, managing the Mount Savage Iron Works in Cumberland, Maryland. At the outbreak of the war, Charles requested an appointment in the regular army, noting his qualifications: "I speak and write English, French and Italian, and read German and Spanish; knew once enough of mathematics to put me at the head of my class at Harvard, though now I may need a little rubbing up; am a tolerable proficient with the small sword and single-stick; and can ride a horse as far and bring him in as fresh as any other man. I am twenty-six years of age and believe that I possess more or less of that moral courage about taking responsibility which seems at present to be found only in Southern officers."[25]

Ira Wallace Claflin was born in Windsor, Vermont. He was the son of Ira Claflin, the Van Buren County, Iowa, surveyor and county commissioner, and the grandson of Nathan Claflin, a member of the Vermont legislature of 1829. Ira graduated from the U.S. Military Academy 27th in the class of 1857. Upon graduation, he was assigned to the Regiment of Mounted Riflemen, and served in New Mexico Territory until notified of his appointment.[26]

William Helmsley Emory (Library of Congress).

Sewell Handy Brown was the son of the famous Philadelphia attorney, forensic orator, and playwright, David Paul Brown. After an unsuccessful application to West Point when he was 16, he worked as an engineer instead of following his father and two of his brothers into the legal profession.[27]

Benjamin Tucker Hutchins, a native of New Hampshire, was descended from many senior officers. He spent one year at Brown University before obtaining a job as a clerk in Washington, D.C. At the outbreak of war, he enlisted as a private in Company A, National Rifles, a three-month volunteer unit raised in Washington, D.C.[28]

Hancock Taylor McLean was born in Kentucky. He was the grandson of Judge John McLean, associate justice of the Supreme Court, and the grandnephew of former president Zachary Taylor. He was a cousin of Company F's commander, Joseph H. Taylor, and was eventually assigned to his cousin's company.[29]

Tattnall Paulding was born in Huntington, Long Island, New York. He was the son of Rear Admiral Hiram Paulding, and the grandson of John Paulding, who had assisted with the capture of Major Andre and exposed the traitorous plot of Benedict Arnold. Tattnall was established in business in New York when the war broke out. Believing the war would be over quickly, he initially enlisted in the 7th New York Infantry as a private in April 1861, a three-month volunteer regiment.[30]

Frederick Dodge was born in Indiana. He was the grandson of Israel Dodge, Sr., the state's first governor. Many members of the Dodge family were engaged with Indian affairs. Frederick was nominated by President

August Valentine Kautz (Library of Congress).

David McMurtie Gregg (Library of Congress).

Buchanan to be a major, special Indian agent, and was assigned to the western Utah Territory. He served there from 1858 to 1860 when he traveled to Washington, D.C., to petition for Indian rights.[31]

John Bucher Johnson was born in Harrisburg, Pennsylvania. He was the son of David M. Johnson, superintendent of Indian Affairs in North America and Susan Dorothy Bucher, the daughter of associate judge John Jacob Bucher, who sat on the Pennsylvania legislature for nine consecutive terms beginning in 1803. As the war began, he was appointed captain of Company F, 11th Pennsylvania Infantry, serving until he received his regular army commission in the 3rd U.S. Cavalry.[32]

James Franklin Wade was born in Jefferson, Ohio. He was the eldest son of powerful congressman Benjamin Franklin "Bluff" Wade, a fierce critic of the Lincoln administration.[33]

John W. Spangler was born in Owen County, Kentucky. He enlisted on July 11, 1855, as a private in Company H, 2nd U.S. Cavalry, and was promoted to first sergeant of his company over the next few years. He was cited for bravery during an engagement with Comanches in Texas on May 12, 1858, where he killed six enemy and was wounded himself.[34]

Curwen Boyd McLellan was born in Merton Hall, Wigtonshire, Scotland. His family owned extensive lands in Glasgow. After coming to the United States, he served an enlistment in Company B, 3rd U.S. Infantry, before joining Company H, 2nd U.S. Cavalry, in 1856.[35]

John Irvin Gregg (courtesy Medford Historical Society).

These were the initial appointments to the regiment, a fine mix of weathered veterans and prominent American youth. (The regiment's remaining officers, the majority of its second lieutenants, were appointed later.) Together, these men lent a solid foundation of leadership for the new regiment.

Organization

Although generally similar in composition to the existing regiments, the 3rd Cavalry was authorized twelve companies rather than the usual ten. At full strength, this would amount to nearly two hundred additional soldiers, for a total of nearly 1,200. The regimental headquarters was authorized a colonel, a lieutenant colonel, two lieutenants to serve as the regimental adjutant and quartermaster, two chief buglers, and sixteen musicians for the regimental band. Three battalion headquarters were authorized, each consisting of a major, a battalion adjutant, a battalion quartermaster, a sergeant major, a quartermaster sergeant, a commissary sergeant, a hospital steward, a saddler sergeant, and a veterinary sergeant. Each battalion would consist of two squadrons of two companies each, with no additional personnel. Maximum aggregate strengths were 95 for a company, 389 for a battalion, and a total of 1,189 for the regiment.[36]

In actuality, the regiment normally operated by squadron or regiment. Although authorized, the battalion organization was not used except for a brief period in 1864 when the regiment was suffering severe shortages of both personnel and officers. The battalion headquarters billets were never filled during the war, with the exception of the three majors. A regimental sergeant major was appointed, and squadrons were led by the senior company commander present and his first sergeant.

The companies, the basic units of operation for the regiment, were designated A through M. Each was authorized three officers: a captain, a first lieutenant, and a second lieutenant. Each was also authorized a first sergeant, a company quartermaster sergeant, four sergeants, eight corporals, two buglers, two farriers, a saddler, a wagoner, and up to 72 privates.[37]

Noncommissioned officers were to be appointed by the colonel of the regiment, upon the nomination of the captain, and approved by the major commanding the battalion. The first-sergeant of each company was to be taken from the other sergeants of the same company by the captain. Sergeants were taken from corporals, and corporals were taken from the enlisted men.[38]

Noncommissioned officers "were chosen with care from the enlisted men by the captain of the company who recommended them for appointment to the colonel or the commanding officer of the regiment, who appointed them to the posts recommended, and announced his decision to the regiment drawn up in line through an officer called an adjutant."[39] One veteran described the responsibilities of the noncommissioned officers.

> The first sergeant out-ranked all other warrant officers of the company. Very many of the duties of the captain have by custom fallen to the sergeant to do. The captain is responsible but the first sergeant relieves him of a great many burdens, or rather of the performance of many duties. The first sergeant becomes a quite important person in a company and enjoys a great many privileges. The discipline of the company is largely his work.
>
> The four other sergeants are "duty" sergeants who serve with the company always in all of its duties. The sergeants usually have command of small working parties, and may have one or more corporals with them. The sergeants perform important parts in drills, and are very necessary under officers. The corporals rank below sergeants, and take rank among themselves from first to eighth. Often a sergeant or a corporal may be such only in name, not having received an appointment. This is often done to reward a specially good enlisted man when there is no vacancy to be filled, or when the captain may wish to more fully acquaint himself with a soldiers [*sic*] capacity before finally determining to appoint him to the position.[40]

Even though the regimental officers were assigned to their respective capacities, many of them frequently changed duties; being temporarily assigned to other companies to fill in losses, assigned to work in staff positions of higher commands, or even never serving with the regiment at all. In the subsequent years of the war, the regiment at one point had only two lieutenants left to command on the battlefield.

The old mounted regiments were not authorized the new twelve-company organization until July 17, 1862.

Recruiting

In compliance with General Order No. 33, the newly appointed officers immediately began recruiting. Five recruiting offices were opened for the organization of the regiment — one for each of the first five squadrons. Since no officers had yet reported for the sixth squadron, no additional recruiting office was opened. Offices were initially opened in Pittsburgh, Philadelphia, Rochester, Columbus and Cleveland.

Military notices were soon published daily in the local newspapers, such as the following recruitment advertisement posted July 25, 1861, in the *Pittsburg Post*:

United States Cavalry Recruits:
Wanted immediately, 850 able-bodied men, between the ages of 18–35, to enter the Third Regiment of United States Cavalry. Men accustomed to horses will be given the preference. Each man will be furnished by the United States a good horse and equipments, ample clothing and substinence [*sic*] of the best quality. The pay ranges from $12 to $21.00 per month, according to the rank and service of the soldier and so complete in the provision made by the Government for all his wants, that he can save every cent of his pay if he chooses, leaving him in the end of his enlistment from $860.00–$1,200.00. Attention is called to the fact that the government have wisely commenced to promote officers from the ranks, and advancement is therefore open to all who enlist. H.T. McLean, First Lieut., Third Cavalry, Recruiting Station, National Hotel, Water Street, Pittsburgh, Pa.

A similar article appeared in Philadelphia newspapers:

Recruiting for the Regular Army — Several stations for enrolling recruits for the regular army have been opened in different parts of the city. Recruits for the regular service, however, are not obtained as fast as for the volunteer regiments. By an act recently passed, the term of enlistment for the regular service is changed from five to three years, and every soldier who serves that time is entitled to $100 bounty from the Government. The same amount is also allowed to those in the volunteer service.

A few days since, Lieut. F. Dodge, of the Sixth regiment United States cavalry, regular service, by order of the War Department opened a recruiting office at the Girard House, where he is now busily engaged in enlisting men. Every man, before being sworn in, undergoes a strict examination by the doctor. If he passes the examination, he is at once furnished with a complete an durable uniform, and his pay commences. The men are also provided with good lodging and board at a hotel in Eighth street, below Chestnut. Lieut. Dodge intends to recruit only ninety-two men, or one company, about half of whom have already been obtained and will be sent to Bladensburg. The command of this regiment will be assumed by Major General Hunter of the United States army.[41]

Although the appointments were effective in May, the army did not notify the regiment's officers until the order was published on June 18, and many were a great distance from their new regiment.

With Gen. Hunter absent, the task of raising the regiment fell to Lt. Col. Emory. Upon arrival at the regiment's assigned headquarters location in Pittsburgh on June 28, 1861, he quickly secured permission to establish a camp of rendezvous for the recruiting officers at Lynden Grove, a former picnic area. He named it Camp Scott, in honor of Winfield Scott, perhaps as a small token of honor for Scott's helping secure his commission back into the army. He also wrote a letter requesting authority to buy horses, but did not receive it, that responsibility belonging to the quartermaster department.[42]

The regimental headquarters and recruiting offices in Pittsburgh were initially established at the National Hotel.[43] Companies D, F and M were almost entirely recruited here.

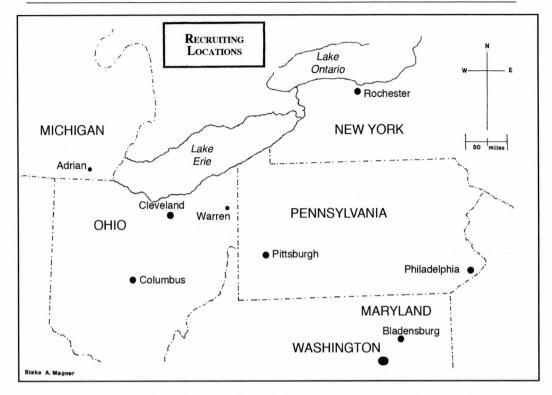

In Cpt. Taylor's absence, Lt. McLean immediately started recruiting and enlisted every soldier save one in Company F by the end of July. Lt. Brown, whose commander still served in the 4th U.S. Artillery, subsequently recruited most of his Company D from the same offices before the end of August.

The experiences of recruits varied depending on the location of the recruiting office. Sidney Morris Davis of Company F described the process in Pittsburgh:

> Prospective recruits were guided to the recruiting offices of the Third U.S. Cavalry in Pittsburgh, catching their first glimpse at a stack of sabers standing in the corner, or a pistol holster hanging on the wall near the door, undoubtedly sparking excitement in their minds, as they knew these would be the tools of their future profession.
>
> Upon entering the recruiting office, an orderly would usher the potential recruit into an inner room, and with great formality, introduce them to their recruiting officer. In company "F's" case, it was 1LT Hancock T. McLean; a handsome gentleman, about 24 years of age, with very black eyes and short black curly hair. He would proceed to ask them, in a slow, modulated voice, "Well, sir, do you wish to join the army?" If the recruit responded with "yes," he would go on to ask them basic questions, such as how old they were, their place of birth, etc.
>
> Upon the recruit passing the initial introduction, he would be ushered into the presence of the surgeon for examination. The surgeon would then administer a series of tests, making the recruit conduct a remarkable series of kicks, jumps, coughs, twists and turns, all while in the nude. If he were pronounced an able-bodied man, he would be issued a certificate to that effect.
>
> The final process ushered the recruit into yet another room, where he would raise his right hand, and swear to serve a period of five years; to uphold the laws of the Constitution of the United States; to obey the President of the United States and all officers appointed over themselves; and to defend the United States against all her enemies, so help them God.
>
> Within the hour, the recruit would be dressed in his "Union blues," and taken to his quar-

ters at the National Hotel, who had the contract to house the regulars, as Camp Scott had not yet been built."[44]

Not all of the Pittsburgh recruits experienced the thoroughness of Pvt. Davis' physical examination. Martha Parks Lindley followed her husband, William, to war, enlisting in Company D under the unimaginative alias of Jim Smith. Two days after her husband enlisted, Martha arrived in Pittsburgh wearing his clothes and was mustered into the regiment on August 11, 1861. She was described on the muster roll as twenty-seven years old, five feet eight inches tall, with brown eyes, black hair, and a dark complexion. She told the recruiter that her former occupation was soldier. In truth, she was a wife and mother who left her two children in the care of her sister and, despite her husband's pleas, would not return home to them. In a postwar newspaper interview, Martha Lindley expressed her feelings about joining a Union cavalry regiment. "I was frightened half to death," she said, "but I was so anxious to be with my husband that I resolved to see the thing through if it killed me." It did not kill her, and apparently those with whom she served did not detect either her fear or her gender. Rather, her "comrades ... never knew that the ... chap, whom everyone liked so well, was not a handsome boy, but a brave and determined woman who loved her husband so well that she refused to be separated from him." Their fellow soldiers thought that Jim Smith and William Lindley were "chums."[45]

Once enlisted, the recruits were introduced to the rudiments of military discipline and drill in their quarters. Pvt. Sidney Davis described the duty:

> Guards were posted at several places, in charge of one thing or another, with elaborate instructions to resist imaginary enemies. At night, patrols were organized, to pick up those who proved they could not navigate the labyrinth of streets and alleys back to their prospective quarters at the hotel on the count of their frequent potations. Such occasions were found very amusing to all concerned, and the sergeant in charge had no difficulty finding volunteers for the duty. The punishment for offenders was very slight, although they were notified that they would be put in the Black Hole — a hideous prison supposed to be located beneath the floor of the bar-room. Of course, this threat was so often made, and the delinquents so often pardoned, that the recruit quickly figured out that the dreaded Black Hole was a figment of their imagination.[46]

Philadelphia, the second largest city in the country after New York, was naturally a lucrative recruiting area, even with the number of volunteer units simultaneously recruiting there. Like the Pittsburgh office, it also passed along from officer to officer as each filled his company and departed with his recruits.

Cpt. Savage, a Philadelphia native, opened the office at the Girard House on Chestnut Street and began recruiting his Company H as soon as he received his appointment. He recruited all 90 men for his company between July 5 and August 19, then departed with them for the camp at Bladensburg, Maryland. Since no officers had yet reported for duty with Company A, Lt. Dodge remained behind and inherited the office. He enjoyed as much success as his commander, filling all of Co. A and even 15 men for Co. I by mid–October, when they in turn departed for Camp East of the Capitol. Lt. Stephen Balk then assumed command of the office and recruited exclusively for Co. C until February 22, 1862, when he closed the office and led his recruits to Washington to join the regiment.

It is probably no accident that recruiting in Ohio centered on Columbus and Cleveland, despite the fact that their combined size was only a third of the capital of Cincinnati.[47] James F. Wade lived in Columbus, which was also the seat of his father, powerful Ohio senator Benjamin F. Wade. Upon receiving his appointment, Lt. Wade began recruiting

Co. B in Columbus, and spent the next several months rotating between there and Cleveland filling companies for the regiment. Once Co. B was filled and had departed for Bladensburg, he continued to recruit for Cos. E and A. By the time he arrived at the regiment's camp in mid–October, Wade had enlisted a total of 223 men, or roughly 25 percent of the regiment.

Many of Wade's recruits were quite young; he enlisted the majority of the regiment's teenaged buglers, some as young as 14. Among his many recruits were the Oby brothers. New York natives George and David Oby were working as sailors when they enlisted two days apart in late June 1861. Another was 16-year-old confectioner Edson Cook, who Wade enlisted as a bugler for Co. I.[48]

Cpt. Lowell opened another Ohio recruiting office in Warren, part of the Western Reserve. Warren was much more rural than other Ohio cities, with a prewar population of only 2,400.[49] Lowell opened his office in the second-story rooms above a store, and arranged to board his recruits by the meal in the nearby Eagle Hotel. After two days in Warren, the frustrated Lowell wrote home to lament:

> I write out of sheer dullness; a mounted officer without a horse, a captain without a lieutenant or a command, a recruiting officer without a sergeant, and with but one enlisted man, a human being condemned to a country tavern and familiar thrice a day with dried apples and "a little piece of beefsteak"— have I not an excuse for dullness? I am known here as the agent of that cavalry company — and the agent's office is the resort of half the idle clerks and daguerreo-type artists in town — but those fellows don't enlist.... I am afraid the colonel will object to many of my recruits, that they are to [sic] youthful, but I cannot help the tendency.[50]

On the very same day he wrote the above letter, however, his fortunes changed. A young man named Adna Romanza Chaffee happened upon Cpt. Lowell on his way home. Chaffee later wrote of his recruiting experience:

> I was en route from my home to Columbus, Ohio, to enlist in the 23d Ohio Volunteers. Walking along Main Street, in Warren, I observed a recruiting poster on the wall of a building, with a picture of a mounted soldier. I stopped for a moment to take in the situation and read, "Recruits wanted for the United States Army." Standing in a near-by door was a fine-looking man in uniform, and he said to me, "Young man, don't you wish to enlist?" I told him of my intention to join the 23d Ohio. He at once set forth the advantages of the cavalry service *and the Regular Army* in such fascinating terms that within fifteen minutes I determined to accept his opinion of what was best for me to do. I enlisted in his troop — K, Sixth Cavalry — and served as an enlisted man until May 12, 1863. While I was not the first, I was one of the first dozen enlisted by Lowell at Warren, Ohio, in the summer of 1861, my hand being held up on the 22d of July.[51]

Lowell soon began to gather recruits, many enticed by the attractive handbills the enterprising captain scattered around town. Another of Lowell's early recruits, Henry McQuiston, remembered the enlistment experience: "... [O]ne would climb a rickety pair of rear stairs of a two-story building to the recruiting office, being conducted their [sic] by a little dry-goods clerk. This little clerk was always conveniently on hand to offer himself as an escort to the would-be recruit, as there was a fee of two dollars a head for as many as he could conduct to the recruiting officer occupying rooms over the store in which the clerk was employed."[52]

The young captain lost no time in preparing his new recruits for their duties. Pvt. McQuiston served as one of the first drill instructors for his fellow recruits: "Capt. Lowell undertook to have his recruits instructed in marching, through me. He gave me a volume of cavalry tactics, and marked in the book what he wished me to teach them. The instruction was very simple, mainly designed to keep them at the depot and to furnish them with a little exercise. Twice a day I drilled them. There was no trouble with them because they were all attentive and anxious to learn."[53] The recruits didn't remain in Warren very long. By the beginning of August, Cpt. Lowell had recruited 30 men for his company, and transported them via wagon and rail to Camp Scott. He left them there and shifted to Rochester, New York, to recruit the rest of his company.

The Rochester recruiting office was generally manned by the same officers throughout its existence. Cpt. Cram recruited 57 men for his Company I between July 24 and September 29. Lt. Dodge added 15 men from Pennsylvania, and Capt. Lowell added 12 more once he finished his own company. Lt. Wade added the final three men to Company I from his offices in Ohio. Among those enlisted by Cpt. Cram in New York were Beriah N.L. Owen, who regularly corresponded with the local newspaper, and Charles F. Miller.[54] Cpt. Lowell arrived in Rochester after dropping off his Ohio recruits for Co. K in Pittsburgh. Lt. Paulding added another 25 men from the Franklin and Butler areas of Pennsylvania in July and August. Lowell recruited the final third of Co. K in Rochester, as well as assisting Cos. I and G.

Once Cram and Lowell completed their own companies, many Rochester recruits went to fill Co. G's ranks. The two captains and Lt. Hutchins recruited 29 men for the company, and Lt. Tucker even added one recruit during a brief stop at the Rochester office on August 10.

Cpt. J. Irvin Gregg had difficulties similar to those of Capt. Lowell. In almost seven weeks of recruiting in Erie County, Pennsylvania, he was able to recruit only 35 men for Co. G. His efforts were further hampered when Lt. Leavenworth resigned after recruiting for only four days. Other officers from the Rochester office recruited the remainder of the company.

Cpt. David Gregg was sick in a New York hospital after eating some bad oysters, so recruiting for Co. E didn't start until late August. This placed a large recruiting burden on the shoulders of a newly promoted lieutenant in the regiment, who was fortunately more than equal to the task. Stephen S. Balk had served since 1845 as a musician and in the general mounted service prior to receiving his appointment, so he was well suited to his task. Initially assigned to Co. K, he was ordered to recruit for Co. E, then the regimental band, and finally for Co. C. Not assigned to a squadron recruiting office as most of the other officers were, Lt. Balk was the most well travelled recruiting officer in the regiment. By the time he finished his travels, only Lt. Wade had enlisted more soldiers into the regiment.

Balk's first stop was Adrian, Michigan, where he recruited 35 men for Co. E in only ten days. One of these recruits was a young farmer named James H. Cory. From Michigan, he travelled to Cleveland, where he recruited another 18 men by September 20 to complete Co. E. Moving on to Lancaster County, Pennsylvania, in October, he had the good fortune to enlist the Mount Joy Brass Band in its entirety, solving the regimental band issue at one fell swoop.[55] With November came orders to change his focus to Co. C. While other officers hurried to join their new companies, Lt. Balk remained on recruiting duty until February 1862. He recruited an additional 64 soldiers into the regiment during that time, achieving a total of 138 men. When he finally turned his last batch of recruits over to form Co. C on Washington's birthday, he assumed duties with Co. D.

In all, soldiers enlisted from four different states, with origins in half a dozen more. A large number of them were immigrants, particularly in the Pennsylvania companies. Lt. Balk recruited the oldest, 48-year-old Swiss immigrant Emanuel E. Gates, to lead the regimental band. Lt. Wade enlisted two fourteen-year-olds to serve as buglers, and Balk added another to serve as a private in Co. E in September.[56]

Not all of the recruits reached the regimental rendezvous at Camp Scott. Adam Eberle was the first death in the regiment. He died of unknown causes on August 19, just six days after he enlisted into Co. E.[57]

Camp Scott

The *Pittsburgh Evening Chronicle* reported on July 27, 1861, "We understand that Col. Emory has secured permission to establish a cavalry camp here, and that he has selected Linden Grove for the purpose. The location is a good one, and so easy of access that when the camp goes into operation, we doubt not that there will be plenty of visitors."[58] The regiment's soldiers generally agreed with Lt. Col. Emory's choice. "The camp of the regiment was on the right bank of the Monongahela River about four miles from Pittsburgh, situated on an elevated ridge running back from the river, gently sloping on the right and left side to woods," one of them later described the location.[59]

On July 29, 1861, the regiment received orders to move to its new camp. The following day the fledgling 3rd U.S. Cavalry marched out along Fourth Street during an oppressively hot summer afternoon. The tired and dusty men immediately began work on the camp.[60] Pvt. Sidney Davis remembered the details of establishing the camp even decades later:

> Though the men were very much fatigued, and hungry, priorities of work prevailed, and the men began immediately pitching their tents. The officer quarters were built first, followed by the tents of the men. Lines were drawn, stakes driven into the ground, and one by one, "A" frame tents were erected. As this was unaccustomed work for the men, it was slow business, and the canvas houses were taken down several times by the men and realigned. The officers offered their part in making the task at hand even more uncomfortable for the men, as they demanded exactness in the precision of erecting the tents, to within less than one inch of each other, correcting deficiencies if even the slightest off-center.[61]

Once the officers were satisfied with the placement of the tents, company areas were designated. Each squad of four men was assigned a tent, and they busily installed

Henry Blake Hays (courtesy Medford Historical Society).

wooden floors over the next several days with wood secured by the regiment. Soon afterward, they transferred their belongings inside and made their new homes as comfortable as possible. Due to an issue with the contract to provide food to the camp, the men did not receive a hot meal the first night in camp, instead receiving only bread.[62]

A soldier of Company K described his first night in the new camp: "I remember the very curious feelings I had when I spread out a blanket to lie upon the ground for the first time. The earth appeared to be smooth. Before morning my tent-mate and I found it rough enough and hard. Our sleep was very disturbed."[63] The next morning at dawn, reveille sounded, and the men arose very sore from the previous day's work to a breakfast consisting of a piece of bread, a piece of meat and a pint of coffee. The regiment was assembled at 9:00 A.M., and a series of orders were read aloud, one of which officially designated the new camp as Camp Scott.

Joseph Hancock Taylor (public domain).

Over the next few weeks the regimental companies recruited away from Pittsburgh arrived at the camp and pitched their tents. "The camp in general was a model one in all respects. The tents were new and bright looking, each pitched in line, and drawn with mathematical precision. Each company swept its streets twice daily with brooms improvised from the boughs of trees. In time, the men grew used to their hard beds, sleeping soundly from tattoo to reveille. At headquarters, a large American flag floated from a staff, giving completeness to the picture," as Henry McQuiston of Co. K described the camp.[64]

The soldiers quickly grew accustomed to the regular duties of camp life. Orders were issued establishing regular hours for drill, fatigue, and police duty. Guard mount took place daily at 9:00 A.M., with soldiers performing guard duty on various portions of the camp for a 24-hour period under ser-

William Monroe Notson (courtesy National Library of Medicine).

geants or corporals. Regulations and the Articles of War were read every second Sunday by the regimental adjutant. According to Pvt. Davis, the adjutant's "diction was not elegant, but his faultless emphasis upon the words 'court-martial' and 'shot,' tapering of[f] delicately on the barely understood phrase — 'or such other punishment as the court shall direct' — always left the men with the shock of extreme punishment upon their susceptible nerves."[65]

Mornings at the camp consisted of reveille at dawn, followed by formation, with each company aligned in front of its respective area. The company first sergeants then called the roll, reporting those present and absent to their waiting officers. Any new information would be issued to the ranks, then the formation would be dismissed to prepare for breakfast and daily duties.[66]

The initial difficulties of feeding the regiment were quickly solved. The National Hotel had contracted to continue to feed the regiment once it occupied Camp Scott, but it was unable to overcome the challenges of the sheer volume of food now that multiple companies were present and the distance to the camp. The hotel employees attempted to serve the men restaurant-style, with companies rotating through a set of tables three at a time. As one recruit recalled, "We would form in order and march to the tables, get our food and march away. Sliced tomatoes is [*sic*] the only thing I can now remember that we had, I presume we had potatoes, a variety of meat and bread, and we were actually waited upon by waiters. I suppose the waiters supplied tea or coffee. I wish I could remember now what we did have; because this manner of feeding soldiers is contrary to the regulations of the Army."[67]

Lt. Col. Emory changed this policy when he learned of it and cancelled the contract with the National Hotel, work details of soldiers constructed sheds to serve as kitchens. The regiment purchased provisions, and cooks detailed from each company prepared

William Henry Forwood (courtesy National Library of Medicine).

Henry Augustus DuBois (courtesy National Library of Medicine).

meals, the same way they would operate once they reached the field. At mealtimes the companies were marched to the kitchens. The men quickly learned to manage their food, as for the first few weeks the day's supply of bread for each soldier was issued at breakfast. An unwary soldier might consume his whole loaf at breakfast, then be hungry until dinner. The regiment later adjusted this while still outside of Pittsburgh to cut the loaves into thirds and issue one piece at breakfast, another at noon and the last in the evening.[68]

Henry McQuiston recalled yet another physical examination after the recruits reached Camp Scott:

> While in this camp one after another of us appeared before Dr. Irish of Pittsburgh who was in camp to examine the recruits as to their physical fitness for the duties of a soldier. Capt. Lowell had examined each of his recruits at the place of enlistment, each recruit being divested of the greater part of his clothing. Dr. Irish, the hospital steward, and an officer I believe were in the tent at the time. Each man in turn was entirely stripped of his clothing. This was the only examination to which we were subjected. In time of peace, a very much more thorough examination, indeed three or four of them, is made of each recruit before he is at last assigned to a company.[69]

Martha Parks Lindley once again managed to avoid the examination.

The evenings at Camp Scott were pleasant for the recruits, as the full rigors of training for war had not yet started. The white tents, illuminated from the outside by the city lights, presented an almost ghostly appearance. With the forest surrounding the camp, the glimmer of the river below it, and the city glare above it, it must have looked quite picturesque.[70]

In August of 1861, the whole command was marched out upon the parade ground to listen to orders read by the inaugural regimental sergeant major, Samuel M. Whitside. A Canadian by birth, he was a veteran of three years in the general mounted service at Carlisle Barracks when he joined the regiment. He had been appointed sergeant major earlier that same morning.

In order to simplify matters for the large number of volunteer units being formed during the war, Congress had decreed on August 3, 1861, that all mounted regiments should be known as cavalry, instead of three separate arms of cavalry, dragoons and mounted rifles. General Order No. 55, August 10, 1861, prescribed the following:

> The six mounted regiments of the army are consolidated in one corps, and will hereafter be known as follows:
>
> | | |
> |---|---|
> | The 1st Dragoons | as the 1st Cavalry. |
> | The 2nd Dragoons | as the 2d Cavalry. |
> | The Mounted Riflemen | as the 3d Cavalry. |
> | The 1st Cavalry | as the 4th Cavalry. |
> | The 2nd Cavalry | as the 5th Cavalry. |
> | The 3rd Cavalry | as the 6th Cavalry.[71] |

The substance of the order was a surprise for the majority of the recruits, as they were formally announced to be the 6th Regiment of Cavalry, United States Army. The remainder of the news in the order was even more welcome: their terms of service were shortened from five years to three, their pay was increased from $12 to $13 a month, and they were to receive an additional $100.00 bounty.[72]

Meanwhile, several additional officers received their appointments and joined the regiment. 1st Lt. Joseph Crain Audenried of Pottsvillle, Pennsylvania, received his appointment upon his graduation from West Point in the second class of 1861 on June 24. He was the son of Pennsylvania senator William Audenried, the founder of the U.S. public school system, and the grandson of Louis Audenried, a Pennsylvania coal magnate. He did not join the regiment for some time, however, as he was appointed an aide-de-camp for Brig. Gen. David Tyler prior to the battle of Bull Run and remained on his staff until late in the fall.[73]

On August 5, 1861, the regiment added three more new officers to its ranks. Henry Blake Hays was born in Allegheny County, Pennsylvania, the son of James Harden Hays, the pioneer of bituminous coal mining in western Pennsylvania. He was also the son-in-law of William Jordan Howard, the mayor of Pittsburgh. He was working at the family coal mining business in Allegheny County when he received his appointment as a captain in the new regiment. Hays' original appointment had been disapproved by Congress for some reason. The subsequent delay in his effective date of rank resulted in his assignment to Co. M instead of Co. L, since James Brisbin was appointed in the interim.[74]

James Sanks Brisbin was a native of Boalsburg, Centre County, Pennsylvania. He was the son of Ezra D. Brisbin, an orator in his local county, and the grandson of Dr. William Brisbin, a Revolutionary War veteran. James worked as a teacher and was admitted to the Pennsylvania bar before purchasing the *Centre Democrat* newspaper. He became prominently known as an antislavery orator. He was initially appointed a lieutenant in the 1st U.S. Cavalry in May 1861, and was wounded twice during the battle of Bull Run in July while leading a detachment of recruits to join their artillery battery on the battlefield. James was appointed the regiment's final company commander.[75] Another native of Pennsylvania, Henry Tucker, a descendent of many Revolutionary War veterans and political figures, was appointed a lieutenant.[76]

With enough officers now assigned and present for duty, on August 15, 1861, Regimental Order No. 1 was published, assigning officers to companies and companies to squadrons.[77] The squadrons were organized in the order that the companies completed their recruiting. Cos. B and H comprised the first squadron, which was also designated as the flank squadron. This was the only squadron initially equipped with carbines in addition to the sabers and pistols common to the rest of the regiment's soldiers. It was their task to provide skirmishers and serve as the advance guard for the regiment. The remaining squadrons were comprised as follows:

2nd Squadron	Cos. D and K
3rd Squadron	Cos. E and I
4th Squadron	Cos. F and G
5th Squadron	Cos. A and M

The sixth squadron would consist of Companies C and L, but recruiting for these companies would not be complete until the following spring. Initially there were no officers present to command the squadron, and the men assigned were used to fill vacancies in the other companies, as were the squadron's mounts. It would be the following fall before the entire squadron would join the regiment in the field.

It wasn't long after Camp Scott was established

Adna R. Chaffee (courtesy Dr. Ken Lawrence).

that Pittsburgh's residents began to visit daily to watch the regulars. Under the training of the sergeants and the officers, the regiment gradually mastered the art of drill and assumed a soldierly appearance on parade. The company and regimental officers appointed the sergeants and corporals for each company, generally choosing those with prior military experience. As McQuiston recalled, "The position of first sergeant was given to an ex-soldier of the British Army who had served during the war in the Crimea in an Irish cavalry regiment. The captain evidently thought this man's military experience bid well to make him a better first sergeant than my better education and habits. At least he appointed the old soldier and I remained first duty sergeant and company clerk until promoted to a lieutenancy in the regiment."[78]

Once the majority of the companies and their officers arrived at Camp Scott, the regiment was ready to move to its camp of instruction, where it would progress beyond basic drill and learn its trade as a cavalry regiment.

Chapter 2

Learning the Trade

On August 22, 1861, the regiment, now numbering over 400 men, received orders to leave Camp Scott and depart via rail for Bladensburg, Maryland. The following days were busy ones for most of the men. Friends and families of recruits from the local area came to wish them goodbye. Rations for three days were distributed and personal belongings packed for the move. Articles which would not fit in the men's baggage were sent home by express or left behind. Tents and the kitchens were packed up and placed on wagons.

Early on Monday morning, August 26, the regiment formed its ranks and departed Camp Scott, marching into the city to the train station. As they neared the Pittsburgh depot, they found the streets crowded with people. Loud cheers greeted them as the men filed up to the waiting train and boarded under supervision of their corporals, sergeants and officers.

At length the engine's shrill whistle sounded, and the cars began to move. The regiment rode the Pennsylvania Central Railroad all day and reached Johnstown just after dark. After a brief stop, the train continued through the night. By morning, it was running along the banks of the Susquehanna River, arriving in Harrisburg before noon.[1] At Harrisburg, the command changed rail cars, and the conditions worsened tremendously. As one trooper later described it, the regiment "occupied box-freight cars which had been used for transporting cattle, whose floors were still heavily covered with manure. Possibly rude seats made of plank had been put into the cars. The men were indignant without redress."[2]

The lumbering train continued its travels and, as it neared Maryland, the troopers observed armed sentries on duty along the railroad to protect the track and keep open communication with the capital. As the train dashed by, the guards halted on their beats, faced the train, and presented arms. The regiment responded with loud cheers.[3] The train reached Baltimore sometime after dark, and the men disembarked from their disagreeable quarters. Since the next train was not scheduled to depart for Washington for several hours, the men found the opportunity to stretch their fatigued bodies out on any available point at the depot to sleep. Some citizens even furnished provisions to the waiting soldiers.

Co. K formed the exception to this rule. While the other company commanders permitted their men to break ranks and roam the depot at will, Cpt. Lowell ordered his men to remain in formation. Lowell's men found this galling. As one of the troopers noted, "Capt. Lowell, while he remained in the company constantly imposed more restrictions than any other officer in the regiment. His company became noted in this disagreeable respect."[4]

The men loaded the railcars upon their arrival, and started south, where two hours later the train halted about half a mile from Bladensburg. Here the men found Company H, who had arrived several days before, snugly ensconced in tents along the banks of a fine brook. The site was a very pleasant one for a cavalry camp. A meadow skirted on the south by the brook and woodlands, which formed the limits of the camp on that side. Several of the forts for the defense of Washington were in plain view. The railroad was not far from camp and several trains passed daily to and from Washington.[5] The camp quickly became a bustling place. Within a short time tents were pitched, company streets established and kitchens built. Recruits were arriving daily and the companies were fast filling.

The soldiers' duties during this period were light but incessant. First, reveille aroused the slumbering raw recruit, and then roll was called. This was followed by lessons in saber exercise, which gave the men an appetite for breakfast. After this meal came a drill in field maneuvers, followed by dinner, then another drill in the afternoon. At 5:00 P.M. the labors of the day were closed with a final formation. At sunset and 9:00 P.M. the men had retreat and tattoo respectively, at which they simply fell in under arms and answered to their names at the roll call in the company street.

In addition to this daily routine, there was guard mount, details for camp, cook's police, and fatigue parties. The soldier who came off guard one morning went on camp police the next, and was expected and required to keep the company streets and grounds around the officers quarters swept clean. On the succeeding morning he was detailed as cook's police, and was obliged to carry water, split wood, and otherwise assist with the pots and kettles.

Late one night, just after the regiment arrived in Bladensburg, a bugle in the camp struck up a shrill, nervous call, quite different from any the men had previously heard. Almost instantaneously following this came the voices of officers, ordering their companies to "turn out, fall in." A few minutes later, amid great shouts of laughter, the men returned to their tents. Company H's Capt. John Savage, believing some of his men were absent without leave, had ordered his bugler to sound "assembly," in order to discover if such were the case. The inexperienced trumpeter sounded "to arms" instead, alerting the entire camp.[6]

Training initially focused on dismounted drill and saber exercise, as the regiment had the equipment for this already in hand. This drill was initially conducted by the company officers, and later by the sergeants. Several of the more experienced officers figured prominently in this training. One trooper later recalled the following:

> In giving command each officer had some peculiarity by which he was easily identified. In some, the peculiarities were more pronounced than in others. Capt. Kautz' voice was high-pitched, shrill and penetrating. Instead of the word "march" he always said in a high prolonged voice "Parch." On foot it was usual for the commanding officer of the company to say "left" just as the left foot reached the ground in order to mark the time distinctly. Kautz was accustomed to say "hep," "hep." Captain Taylor on the other hand affected a deep, base [sic]voice, and used to say "left," "left," "left," with as much sonorousness as the deep bay of a hound.[7]

Since copies of the cavalry tactics manual were very scarce, the noncommissioned officers were required to memorize the lessons in order to drill their troops. Officers were appointed to hear the company noncommissioned officers recite in cavalry tactics in the evenings under a tent fly by candlelight. "A sergeant Chaffee and I were good friends and much of the time tented together. We kept up the study of tactics until none excelled us in the regiment in the knowledge of cavalry tactics," Henry McQuiston wrote years later.[8]

On September 6, 1861, during the command's stay at Bladensburg, the regiment received its first assistant surgeon. A native of New Hampshire, John A. Bell was the son of the Honorable Samuel Dana Bell, chief justice of the U.S. Supreme Court, and the grandson of Samuel Bell, governor of New Hampshire. After studying medicine at Dartmouth and the University of Pennsylvania, he initially practiced in his home state before taking his practice to New York City. At the war's outbreak he volunteered his services and was assigned to the 6th U.S. Cavalry.[9] The following day two new majors received appointments. James Henry Carleton was appointed a brigadier general of volunteers and assigned to command the Department of New Mexico the same month, so he never served with the regiment.[10]

Lawrence Abert Williams was working as an aide-de-camp on McClellan's staff at the time of his appointment. His father had served as the army's chief of engineers when he was killed at the battle of Monterrey during the Mexican War. Lawrence was also a cousin of Confederate general Robert E. Lee, and a close family member of the Lees and the Custises. He graduated 35th in the U.S. Military Academy class of 1852, and served in the 7th and 10th U.S. Infantry regiments prior to the war.[11] One of his soldiers described him: "Major Williams was rather tall and slender. He wore a close-fitting jacket and top boots to his knees which fitted him nicely. He had a nice horse which he rode splendidly. He was a very conspicuous figure on horseback, and was known for his fine riding in which he evidently took pride."[12] While the appointments of Majors Carleton and Williams nominally filled the regiment's complement of field officers, only Lt. Col. Emory and Maj. Williams were actually present.

The regiment's horses began arriving shortly after the establishment of the camp. Horse equipment also began to appear at regimental quartermaster Lt. John Spangler's office — a great pile of nosebags, bridles and saddles. Nosebags were an item the government issued for the horses instead of troughs. These were fastened up to the mouth by the means of a strap passing up over the head and behind the ears. It took the animals a short time to learn how to eat out of the bags, but they soon became accustomed to them.

After the men had been furnished with all their equipments they were numbered off as their names appeared alphabetically on the roster of each company. The number stood for, respectively, the number at which he fell alphabetically in his company, the company designation, and regiment. The number of Private Davis, Company F, for example, was 28F6Cav. All of his equipment was then marked with this number. This system ensured that although there were duplicate names within the ranks, there would never be a duplicate number.[13]

The horses are described by troopers' memoirs and letters as generally above the average in quality, which differs drastically from the accounts of men in regiments raised later. A couple of factors worked in the regiment's favor here. First, very few regiments of cavalry were as yet forming and receiving their mounts, so units could be selective in their choices. Second, the regimental quartermaster was a veteran cavalryman and former first sergeant with sufficient experience and expertise to carefully inspect prospective mounts. In relatively short order, all of the regiment's horses arrived in their corrals, ready for assignment. Rank had its privileges in this as in all things, so officers chose their mounts first, followed by the regimental staff, then the company noncommissioned officers in order of rank. In accordance with cavalry tradition, companies had the same color mounts wherever possible. Company C had sorrels, for example, while Company K's were black.[14]

A lottery system was adopted to make horse assignments for the common troopers to prevent confusion and arguments among the men. Paper tickets were cut and numbered, and corresponding numbers were marked upon the halter-straps of the horses as they stood hitched to the picket line. The tickets were thrown into a hat and well shaken. Each soldier would select a ticket from the hat, then proceed down the line until he found his mount.[15]

The regiment's daily duties changed materially with the assignment of the horses.

Immediately after roll call following reveille, the bugle sounded "stable-call," and each company mustered in the stables to feed and groom their horses. This lasted one hour, after which a commissioned officer would inspect each horse to see that the work was properly done and that the animals of the soldiers absent on guard duty and other duties were not neglected.

The company stables were simply four heavy posts set deep into the ground on a line along each company's street, in front of the tents, at intervals of approximately 20 feet. A strong rope known as the "picket line" passed through a bored hole in the top portion of each post, where it was drawn as tight as possible to prevent it from becoming slack. The horses were tied to this rope, each sergeant's squad together on opposite sides of the picket line.[16]

The drills now shifted, as described in the cavalry tactics manual, to the "School of the Trooper, Mounted." The officers began moderately with the training. First, they instructed the men as to the proper mode of saddling and bridling up, rolling up and strapping on to the pommel and cantle of the saddles their overcoats and blankets, as well as how to carry forage and rations upon horseback.[17] They then progressed to riding fundamentals. "When we first began to drill with horses, we rode round a ring with the Capt. in the middle. Only a few could drill at a time in this manner under one instructor," one soldier remembered. Another description follows:

> Many of the soldiers were utterly ignorant of equestrianism, perhaps never being astride a horse prior to their enlistment. Once the basics were covered, troopers were required to "cross the stirrups" to ensure they could control their mounts with their knees, as they would need to do in a fight. This involved throwing the stirrups over the horse's neck so they couldn't be used, then trotting and galloping the horse. At first consideration an odd drill, it taught the riders confidence in the saddle, as well as sparing their mounts. Inexperienced riders instinctively grabbed the saddle horn and turned their toes out while trying to grip the horse with their legs, inadvertently raking the horse with their spurs. Once riders were trained not to grip the horse with their feet, they were much less likely to accidentally use their spurs while trying to keep their seats.[18]

Inevitably, men began to test the speed of their horses and establish their reputations as riders as their confidence grew. The result was impromptu races when taking the horses to water under the charge of one of the sergeants. The watering area was a mile away and out of sight of the camp, providing a rare opportunity for such a frolic. While the ride to the site was usually peaceful, quite often a stampede occurred on the ride back to camp as men attempted to gallop their horses with only watering bridles and saddle blankets. One of the noncommissioned officers would eventually restore order. On one of these forays an unfortunate incident befell Michael Conway of Co. F when his mare carried him into a tree. The projecting stump of a limb struck him in the side, throwing him heavily to the ground and injuring him internally. He never recovered from the injury and died three months later, on January 1, 1862.[19]

Once notified of a pending grand review of all of the cavalry in Washington shortly after they received their horses, the regiment's officers hurried the lessons along in company and squadron drills. Their purposeful energy was perhaps commendable in the officers, but severe on the men and horses. Preparations focused on mounted maneuver and formations rather than weapons training and dismounted drill. The reputation of the new regiment and its officers would be established by their performance in the review.

The most dreaded of all the movements was the company or squadron wheel. Unless remarkable care was taken, the men on the marching flank would move too fast, or the men in the center would move too slowly. Both produced the same results, and the inevitable consequence was the curving of the front of the element instead of its remaining straight. When this occurred, the front of the company or squadron would emerge from the maneuver in a crescent shape, with the two wings projecting far beyond the center. Then a crushing of legs followed as the center forced itself into alignment by sheer strength.[20]

On October 8, a grand cavalry review was held on the plain east of the nation's capitol, approximately three-quarters of a mile from that building. To the inexperienced eyes of most of the men, it was certainly a grand affair. Over 6,000 mounted men, according to newspaper reports, marched in review by column of companies before the president, cabinet members, General Winfield Scott, foreign diplomats, and other dignitaries. The regiment returned to the camp at Bladensburg in the late afternoon, tired, hungry, and muddy after an entire day in the saddle. The newspapers spoke very highly of the apparent state of discipline among the regiment, furnishing a theme of conversation for some time among the men.[21]

Camp East of the Capitol

Several days later, on October 12, orders came down to break up the camp at Bladensburg and move to Washington, D.C. Early the following morning the regiment packed their tents and broke down the camp. The regiment's new camp was located near where they had marched in the late grand review, close to the city workhouse and the Congressional Cemetery, and not far from the Eastern Branch of the Potomac River. It was named in regimental orders "Camp East of the Capitol." In most respects, it was a desirable spot for the regiment's purposes, surrounded by a large plain upon which to drill; the river furnished water for the horses. "From our camp we have a very good view of Washington — Prominent above all other objects towers the unfinished dome of the Capitol," one soldier wrote to a family member.[22]

The men quickly established the new camp in the same manner as their previous one: "There was a row of tents, and then a row of horses and so on until the last. Within a short time a long shed, gabled, with open sides was provided for the horses who were arranged in two long rows facing one another with a double manger between their heads. One end of this shed was enclosed for keeping forage and equipments not in use. The men occupied A-tents and the officers wall-tents. I think there were four men in each tent. My tent was occupied by another sergeant and myself."[23]

At the edge of the new camp lay "Laundry Row." The wives of enlisted men, a maximum of four per company, were quartered here in wall tents. A guard was posted in front of their quarters to protect them from insult or injury. They washed the clothes of the soldiers of their husbands' companies, at a usual rate of five cents for shirts and underclothing, and ten cents for pants. This practice was discontinued once the regiment took the field.[24]

Interestingly, Pvt. Sidney Davis of Co. F corroborated part of Martha Parks Lindley's story of service in his memoirs, mistaking her for one of the laundresses, and noting, "A laundress attached to company D donned a uniform and followed her husband all through the Peninsular campaign, remaining with the wagon train while the soldiers were marching and fighting, rejoining them when they encamped. The men seemed to somewhat be proud of her, although she was not at all good looking."[25]

Around midnight of the same night the regiment arrived at the camp, a messenger arrived at Lt. Col. Emory's tent. A few minutes later, his orderly quickly moved to each of the company officer's tents. These officers soon mustered their companies. The men were armed, ordered to pack their clothing, and saddle up. Prior to mounting, they were commanded to "load your arms." For a time, confusion reigned supreme as men aroused from a sound night's sleep prepared to move, but the regiment soon marched down Pennsylvania Avenue past the capitol and through Georgetown to the Chain Bridge. Upon reaching the bridge, the column halted, dismounted and stood to horse until after sunrise. A few hours later, bugles sounded "to horse," the regiment mounted, and countermarched slowly back to camp.[26]

Camp routines were quickly reestablished. Guard duty, whether perimeter posts or stable guard, was an incessant daily detail from each company. It was customary in the mornings following guard mount that the men retire above the guardhouse and discharge their weapons. They were allowed to do so at will, but it was the sergeant major's responsibility to ensure all weapons were empty prior to releasing the guard.

The structure of the daily routine remained unchanged. Officers conducted morning and afternoon training sessions of various sizes to continue training men and mounts. Recitations in cavalry tactics continued in the evenings for officers and noncommissioned officers alike.

Weekly, there was both undress and dress parade. Undress parade, normally held on Wednesday afternoons, consisted of assembling in a two-rank line of battle before the commander's quarters. The adjutant then announced to the formation the official news of the week, all appointments, promotions, demotions and results of any courts-martial from the preceding week. On Sunday mornings, the regimental commander personally inspected his men, "drawn up in line of battle; colors waving, band playing and officers and men in uniform dress."[27]

Monthly, the regiment was "mustered." This involved formations to account for every single soldier in the regiment by name, as well as all assigned equipment. It was a massive undertaking for the companies, since every page had to be prepared by hand. One soldier described the process:

> All the individuals in the company capable of writing a good hand are hard at work at present in making up the papers required at the end of every month. A descriptive roll has to be prepared of each one, every month with the amount of pay due each for the receipt of the paymaster. An inventory of company property has to be made out and sent to the quartermaster general. Registration of rations have to be sent to the quartermaster of the regiment to secure our Government allowances in the way of food. And various other papers which it would be interesting to describe.[28]

Training continued apace. The entire regiment was initially equipped as light cavalry with sabers and pistols. While every trooper did not initially have a weapon, there were sufficient numbers of both weapons to conduct training. Dismounted saber drill became mounted saber drill once leaders could be confident the men wouldn't hack off their horses' ears or injure themselves. As with horsemanship, many of the new soldiers had never handled or fired a pistol, so marksmanship training began with dismounted firing.

In his memoirs, Pvt. Davis related an amusing event which occurred during one of Company F's first target practices. The company was formed into lines, with the commander moving down each line issuing firing commands to each trooper in turn. Things went smoothly until he reached Pvt. James Gargan, who was visibly nervous as he approached the firing line and drew his weapon:

> He obeyed the subsequent commands with evident dread, as though expecting an order to shoot himself instead of the target. Finally, when the words, "Aim; fire!" were uttered, there was no response, or discharge. He stood still, pointing the pistol at the target.

Capt. Taylor asked him sharply why he did not obey, and Pvt. Gargan lowered his pistol carefully and examined it, then went through the motions again with a similar lack of success.

"What do you mean sir?" asked Cpt. Taylor. "Why do you not fire?"

"I can't get it off," tremblingly replied Pvt. Gargan.

The captain took the revolver and upon examining it, pronounced it all right, and handed the pistol back to the soldier.

Gargan tried again, with no better success; the hammer would not fall he explained to his displeased commander.

Capt. Taylor again examined the weapon, but could find nothing wrong with it. The cylinder revolved and the hammer operated as well as any of the other pistols. He handed the pistol back to Gargan and ordered him again to fire, watching him closely.

Once more the unfortunate private attempted to shoot, and the countenance of the captain's face broke into a brief smile, before quickly regaining a severe expression. "Why you damned fool, no wonder the hammer won't fall. You are holding it back!" Indeed, Pvt. Gargan had securely held the hammer back with his thumb, while pressing on the trigger with great vigor. A loud laugh burst forth at the unfortunate soldier's expense, and training continued.[29]

Once comfortable firing their weapons on terra firma, the men conducted target practice mounted, in order to accustom their mounts to the sounds of firing. Although somewhat hazardous due to the prancing movement of the horses and awkwardness on the part of some of the riders, no serious incidents were recorded.

Mounted drills continued as well. Now safely past the pressure of the grand review, training focused on conducting the various drills at speed. The men were soon charging over the plain by company, then squadron, then regiment. At each session there were always a few unfortunates who tumbled into the mud or whose horses fell floundering on top of them. Fortunately no one was injured more seriously than the occasional broken limb.

Cpt. Abert of Company D provided an admirable example of coolness during a charge by his company. They moved off at a walk, then a trot, then a gallop, and finally charged at full speed across the plain. While leading his company at the front of the charge, his horse fell and the company dashed over them both. As the end of the company cleared the tangle of horse and rider, the captain raised his head and shouted, "Attention, company! Gallop; trot; walk; halt!" The company promptly obeyed these successive orders, and Capt. Abert remounted his horse and rejoined the company, his dignity intact.[30]

As training intensified, so did the various modes of punishment employed in the army for the preservation and enforcement of discipline. Each company's noncommissioned officers handled minor offenses directly. Failure to follow instructions often resulted in extra duty details or assignment to the "cordwood brigade." This involved the offender marching with a log on his back or shoulder, depending on the severity of the offense, for hours under the supervision of a corporal or sergeant. More serious punishments involved stringing a soldier up to a post by his thumbs, his toes barely touching the ground. The weight of the body rested almost entirely upon the thumbs, and the suffering was intense.

The last resort for the sergeants before resorting to the guardhouse was to "buck and gag" the offending soldier, a method generally used if soldiers became violent or threatening. "Bucking and gagging" consisted of seating the offender on the ground, tying his hands together by the wrists in front, and then forcing his knees up between the arms and running a stout stick under the knees and over the elbows, rendering all struggle impossible. A wooden stick was then inserted between the teeth like a bridle-bit and fastened securely behind the head by a rope or strap.

More serious infractions resulted in courts-martial, with those convicted serving their punishments in the regimental guard house until they were completed. By common consent, the prisoners in the guardhouse were jokingly referred to as "Company Q." One example is cited here: "One man named Sherry was tried by court martial for striking a corporal. His sentence was this: 'To carry a log weighing 30 lbs for 30 days from "Reveille to Retreat" (from sunrise to sunset). Then to be confined in close custody 60 days with a ball weighing 30 lbs attached to his left leg by a chain 3 feet long.'"[31]

Nor were the noncommissioned officers immune from punishment. Appointed by their lieutenants and captains, they could be reduced to the ranks just as quickly as they had been promoted. One letter home reported an unfortunate corporal in Co. C reduced to the ranks for striking a private: "He ordered the cook to do something which the man was slow in performing. This enraged Albert and he struck and kicked the fellow. The matter came to the Lieutenants [sic] ears and the Corporal was broken."[32]

"One Third" for Appointments

The remainder of the regiment's officers arrived in two waves during the last months of the year as they were notified of their appointments.

On October 15, 1861, 1st Lt. Dodge arrived from Philadelphia with a sufficient number of recruits for Company A. Along with a number of Lt. Tucker's Pottsville recruits and Lt. Wade's Columbus recruits, the company was organized that day. Neither Captain Sanders nor Lt. Mizner had yet reported to the camp for duty.[33]

Elements of the 1st U.S. Cavalry had recently arrived in Washington from the Department of the Pacific, and two of its noncommissioned officers were selected for appointments as new officers in the regiment. First Sgt. Isaac M. Ward was a bootmaker in Kentucky prior to enlisting in the 1st Dragoons in 1857. His enlistment documents describe him as being 5' 6" tall, with hazel eyes, light hair, and a fair complexion. Upon notification of his appointment, he immediately took command of Co. A.[34]

Sgt. Christian Balder was born in Loeheim, Germany. He originally enlisted in Company A, 1st Dragoons, and was described in his enlistment records as being a previous soldier, with grey eyes, brown hair, fair complexion, and being 5' 6" tall. He was assigned to Co. F as a second lieutenant.[35]

The exchange of noncommissioned officers for lieutenants worked both ways. Sergeant Byron Kirby of Company B left the regiment on November 29, 1861, to serve as a second-lieutenant in the 6th U.S. Infantry. By the war's end he had achieved the rank of brevet brigadier-general of U.S. Volunteers for gallant and meritorious service during the war.[36]

Two days later, two more appointments were made, one of them again from the 1st U.S. Cavalry. A native of Ohio, Sergeant Albert Coats served five years in Company C, 1st Dragoons. Upon his appointment, he was assigned to Company E. A native of County Clare, Ireland, Joseph Kerin was a veteran of both the 2nd Dragoons and the General Mounted Service when he received his appointment. He was assigned to Company H.[37]

On November 1, 1861, Cpt. Hays arrived from Pittsburgh with a sufficient number of recruits to officially organize Company M. Hays was originally intended to command Company L, but his appointment had initially been rejected without explanation by Congress, then subsequently approved, delaying his arrival.

The regimental band also officially organized when they arrived from Mount Joy on November 1. One new private opined, "It will be a fine addition to the regiment."[38] The week also saw two more junior officer appointments, both from within the ranks of the regiment.

Born in Liverpool, England, Daniel Madden had previously served as a soldier before he enlisted in the regiment on August 14. His enlistment documents described him as 5'7½" tall, with blue eyes, brown hair, and a fair complexion. He was almost immediately promoted to Regimental Quartermaster Sergeant, and later appointed a second lieutenant on November 4.[39]

Andrew Stoll originally enlisted in Company K, 1st U.S. Cavalry, on May 5. He transferred to the 6th U.S. Cavalry, where he quickly became the first sergeant of Co. F before his appointment as a second lieutenant on November 5.[40] This completed the initial appointments of second-lieutenants within the regiment.[41]

Preparing For Winter Camp

In November, a large force of men were set to work building stables for the horses and barracks for the men, and these were occupied by mid–December. The long, L-shaped buildings, each large enough for a company, were constructed of rough lumber and topped with slanted roofs. One member of Co. K left the following description of the interior: "The soldiers occupied as quarters the perpendicular portion of the L, and as dining room and kitchen the horizontal part. There was a room partitioned off for the first sergeant for stores and quarters for himself. The soldiers slept in wooden bunks, capable of holding four persons, two tiers high, with a narrow passage way between them. The barracks were rather poorly lighted, but if I can accurately remember, they were sufficiently ventilated."[42]

The soldiers did their best to make their quarters comfortable. Each man was issued an extra blanket and a bed tick, which they filled with straw. Large stoves were installed at one end of each barracks for heating and cooking. Pine bough chandeliers hung from the ceilings at intervals of perhaps twenty feet, and from these a number of tallow candles shed their dim light. Additional candles burned at almost every bunk or berth.[43]

With fewer hours of daylight, there was more leisure time in the evenings before tattoo. Solitary soldiers would take advantage of the better light in upper bunks to read, repair clothing, or write letters home. The more open area around the stove was the social center of the barracks, where groups would gather for singing, stag dances and occasionally boxing matches.[44]

"I wish you could have a picture of this barrack, as it appears at present," wrote Nathaniel Owen of Co. I as he described a typical December evening:

> I am stationed at one end, in the *"upper story,"* as we call it (the bunks being two tiers high) where I can look down the row. Right at my feet, on the floor, is a set playing euchre, and their noisy shouts proclaim them all awakened and excited. Right across the two feet passage is a young urchin who in spite of my repeated threats of shortening his days persists in squawking on a fife, till my ears feel as though there was a *"bumble-bees"* nest in them. One is mending stockings, others reading, and in the middle of the floor is a full set dancing a cotillion. To be sure, there are no ladies present, but one of the fellows doffs his cap, and his partner pays him the most assiduous attention, striving to fancy him some *"faire ladye love"*— casting at him tender glances, hugging him genuinely, and between the sets politely serving him, not with wine, I would have you know, but with a drink of cold water. It is rare sport, I dare say, but requires too great a stretch of the imagination to make it enjoyable for me. We are all cold water men, not so much, some of us, from principle, as from necessity.[45]

Not all were "cold water men" of necessity. Inevitably, imaginative troopers found ways to smuggle into the camp, despite the penalty of a lengthy stay in the guardhouse or worse if caught.

The barracks were completed just in time, as the rainy season had commenced about the middle of November. The exposure to the cold and wet weather and having to sleep on the damp ground since the tents had no flooring began to have its effect, evidenced by the rapidly filling hospitals. Some troopers recovered and returned to their companies. Others perished.

Pvt. John W. Manson, Company K, died on November 6. Pvt. George Schiede, Co. F, died in the hospital the next day. Pvt. Samuel Brocker, Co. D, died on the 10th. Pvt. James Gargan, Co. F's master of the revolver, died of the fever on December 3. Pvt. Joseph H. Blakely, Co. D, also died of the fever two days later. Pvt. Harrison Hardy, Co. B, was the regiment's last casualty of the year, dying of smallpox on December 13. All of them were buried with the honors of war in the Congressional Cemetery.[46]

An army funeral was a ceremony of considerable form to show respect to the dead. Six pallbearers were selected from the company of the deceased. The remainder of the company not on duty elsewhere formed the escort, marching dismounted with sabers and revolvers. The coffin was draped with the American flag and carried upon a handbarrow. The regimental band preceded the remains, playing a mournful dirge, followed by the pallbearers carrying the body. Behind them followed the horse of the deceased, saddled and bridled, with crepe attached to each side of the bridle-bit, while the deceased's boots hung reversed from the stirrups. The escort formed the rear of the procession to the grave site.

As regular army regiments did not have chaplains, one of the officers normally volunteered to read the Episcopal funeral service and appropriate Bible verses. Several soldiers and officers noted that Lt. Tattnall Paulding performing these services on multiple occasions. Paulding, one wrote home following a funeral, "seemed to be the most active in this work and I was impressed with the idea that he is truly a religious and good man."[47]

The coffin was then carefully lowered into the grave while the escort presented sabers. A few shovelfuls of earth were thrown on the coffin while the escort ordered sabers. A firing detail then fired three volleys over the grave, and the procession re-formed to depart. After marching a short distance in silence, the band again played a dirge. If the band did not attend, the company buglers took their place. As the earth was thrown in, they sounded the appropriate call of "extinguish lights."[48]

On December 8, 1861, it was discovered that Sergeant Major James F. Jackson had earlier enlisted as Charles Jackson and deserted from the General Mounted Service to join the regiment on August 21, 1861. He apparently performed his duties well, as no charges were pressed against him and he was "returned to duty without trial." He was, however, demoted to the rank of private and assigned to Co. K, and later Co. L, until October 1, 1862, when he deserted the regiment. Upon Jackson's embarrassing discovery, Sgt. John Lee of Co. K was promoted to the position of regimental sergeant-major.[49]

December also saw the departure of assistant-surgeon Bell, who was transferred to a hospital in Georgetown. Assistant surgeon James Henry Pooley joined the regiment in his place. Born in Cambridgeshire, England, the 22-year-old's father was a well respected surgeon of the same name. James had graduated from the Columbia College of Physicians and Surgeons in 1860. He was appointed an assistant surgeon on August 26, 1861, and worked in various hospitals in Washington, D.C. before his transfer to the regiment.[50]

Due to the absence of its assigned officers, Company C did not form until December

23. Second Lt. McLellan relinquished his position as regimental adjutant to take command of the newly organized company. Second Lt. Audenried then assumed duties as the regimental adjutant.[51]

Guard Duty

Guard duty for the men during the winter of 1861–62 was very severe. Quarters for the prisoners and reliefs consisted of a small barrack room built some distance away from the regimental quarters and were not large enough to accommodate the entire force. One diminutive fire was all that was allowed to keep the men warm or to dry their clothing.

"The worst thing that we have to do is to stand gard around the camp," wrote one trooper.[52] The posts, or beats, extended around and through the entire camp. The orders usually were, for those on the outside to prevent any soldier or horses from passing out of the camp and for those stationed between the barracks to watch for fights or fires. All the guards when on post were expected to salute all officers according to rank.[53]

About the middle of December, upon conclusion of dress parade one Sunday, Lt. Col. Emory announced to the regiment that, because of their uniform good conduct and efficient discipline, the secretary of war had detailed them as a guard for the capital city. The next day a squadron was sent out with two days' rations and forage for this duty. This squadron presented a rather comical appearance, mounted on their horses with haversacks full of bread and meat hanging by their side, and a bag of oats and a bundle of hay stowed upon the cantles of their saddles. The men did not like this feature as it detracted from their soldierly appearance, and the horses constantly attempted raids on each other's forage.[54]

Speculation abounded about the new duty, some claiming it was guarding the capitol building or the White House itself. "When the initial squadron was relieved and returned to camp two days later, the men were besieged for information. To the men's great disgust it turned out to be a sort of police service — to arrest drunken soldiers, strip all negroes of government clothing, and to prevent all fast driving of wagons and carriages."

Many of the men found duty in the city greatly demoralizing, soldiers and officers alike. The patrol quarters were established in Sibley tents on Maryland Avenue, much less comfortable than their warm barracks in winter weather. Liquor was too easily procured, resulting in painfully frequent courts-martial with successively more severe penalties. At times as high as two full squadrons, by the middle of January the provost guard requirement was reduced to one company, but the duration was extended to fifteen days. The regiment continued on this duty until mid February.[55]

Remaining Months at Camp

Shortly after the new year, the regiment was assigned to the Cavalry Reserve Brigade commanded by Brig. Gen. Philip St. George Cooke. The brigade consisted of three regiments: the Fifth and Sixth U.S. Cavalry, and the Sixth Pennsylvania Cavalry (Rush's Lancers), numbering in aggregate about 2,500 men.[56]

A veteran dragoon, Cooke was well aware of the amount of training necessary to produce competent cavalrymen. Determined to have his regiments prepared for the spring campaign, he decreed his troops would drill mounted twice per day, rain or shine, with at least one brigade drill per week. The new regimental drill routine consisted of squadron drills in the mornings and regimental drills in the afternoons. Only on the rarest of occasions would drill be cancelled, as inclement weather and poor conditions on the drill field were not considered impediments.[57]

While excellent preparation for the rigors of campaigning that lay ahead, the drills were at times wildly unpopular with soldiers and officers alike. "There is more of the cavalry that gitts [sic] throwed off their hourses [sic] and gets killed and their arms and legs broke than the Secesh will kill," commented Pvt. Robert Steel in a letter to his family.[58] Cpt. Lowell agreed, writing of the conditions: "It is particularly hard on cavalry, encamped on a clay bank — the horse splashed with wet clay after three hours' drill is not a cheerful spectacle to the recruit who has to clean him — it opens the eyes to some of the advantages of infantry."[59] Cpt. August Kautz of Co. B was of a similar opinion and noted it in his journal on January 17: "Notwithstanding the condition of the drill ground, General Cooke had a brigade drill and even had our regiment to charge in echelon. We were covered in mud by the time drill was over. Many of the horses fell, and though there were some narrow escapes, no one was seriously injured...."[60]

In addition to their martial benefits, the drills also prepared the brigade for monthly mounted reviews. The regiment was reviewed by President Lincoln in January and February. Cpt. Kautz wrote of the January review: "By 12 o'clock we reached the President's house and were marched around the President taking a position on the left of the portico. The officers were afterwards presented, each in his turn. We were then paraded in front of the Secretary of War's quarters, presented to him afterwards and took a drink with him. We then returned to camp."[61]

As the winter progressed, preparations for the upcoming campaign intensified as the army waited for the weather to

Frederick Knapp, Co. E (courtesy the Sandra K. Smith Collection).

break. Soldiers were constantly occupied with preparations. "All the 'guidons' or company colors are being painted to represent the America flag instead of being red and white bars, as they were before. This is by order of the secretary of War," noted a soldier. "Our old steel bits and combs have been condemned & have all been handed over. In their place we are supplied with brass curbs. They can be brightened so as to shine almost like gold and look elegantly upon the horses."[62]

Other preparations were more warlike. "For the last two or three days every odd minute that we get is occupied in putting and edge on our sabers. We have wore one small grindstone almost up. We grind until Tapps [*sic*] eight oclock."[63]

As late as February, the regiment still struggled to obtain necessary supplies such as carbines, pistol cartridges, and saddle blankets. Not only were the carbines unavailable, but a trip by Cpt. Kautz to the War Department failed to produce even a manual for the weapons.[64] On February 24th, the flank squadron finally received its carbines. One soldier described the new weapons: "They are Sharps shooters and will kill a man at the distance of 800 yards or nearly half a mile. It is expected that all the companies will be supplied with the same arms." The other companies would not receive their carbines until September.[65]

Pvt. William Lloyd, Co. H, February 1862 (courtesy Dr. Ken Lawrence).

Later that afternoon, a terrific gale of "wind increased to a hurricane and blew down several of the stables and damaged all of them more or less. Portions of the roof in several cases were carried many yards."[66] The orderly bugler sounded "assembly" to turn out the men to rescue their horses from several collapsed stables. "When we got there we found that the stables had been blown down as flat as possible. Boards, beams and all came down on the backs of the horses and they were nearly buried. Every fellow 'pitched in' and proceeded to release the poor animals tortures. None were hurt seriously."[67] Several days of labor under the direction of the regiment's sergeants and carpenters repaired the structures, and campaign preparations resumed.

By the end of February, the regiment stood with 42 officers assigned and 966 enlisted men. Of these, only 28 of the officers and 781 men were present for duty; 42 of the regiment's men were serving on extra duties away from the regiment, mostly as teamsters for the Quartermaster Department. A harsh winter was also taking its toll, as 76 troopers were sick in the camp and an additional 11 were sick and absent in hospitals stretching from Pittsburgh to Washington, D.C.[68]

Disease was a concern in the camps all winter, and various illnesses at times ran rampant among the cramped quarters of large numbers of soldiers. Earlier that month, a soldier noted, "The measles are very prevalent in this camp at present and there are many cases in the hospital."[69]

The shortage of assigned officers was exceptionally galling to the regiment. Many officers sought positions of higher rank with volunteer units, and the regiment received no replacements for them. Just the month before, a frustrated Lt. Col. Emory had written:

> The unremitted instruction given this regiment is all in vain without the presence of officers to retain and enforce the instruction. A few tours of detached service or inclement weather interfering with the exercise effaces the labors of a month.
>
> The best old cavalry requires more officers in proportion to the men than are with this, a regiment of a few months' standing. Without proper officers, no effort can make good cavalry, and all military authorities agree that bad cavalry is worse than useless.
>
> It is not only the positive inconvenience resulting from the absence of these officers, but it is the discontent fastened in the minds of those left behind, who are equally desirous of obtaining high commands in the volunteer forces.[70]

Lt. Col. Emory made adjustments to the enlisted staff of the regiment as well. In an effort to improve the condition of the horses, Sgt. Hellings of Co. K was appointed veterinary surgeon and assigned to the regimental staff.[71] The quartermaster sergeant, Frank Gormley, was dismissed due to "irregularities" and reduced to the ranks. Sgt. Rousseau, also of Co. K, was promoted to fill the vacancy. On March 1, Charles Gilliams of Co. M was appointed the regiment's 2nd chief bugler.[72]

On March 7, the regiment had its only interaction of the war with its nominal commander, Maj. Gen. David Hunter. Hunter, his family, and Lt. Col. Emory's daughter reviewed the brigade from a carriage. The parade went well, with the regiment charging past by squadrons. Departing the review, however, the carriage's axle broke in the field's deep mud. Two of the regiment's troopers were quickly able to extricate the carriage and make repairs.[73]

Reconnaissance, and to Alexandria

In the drizzling rain of March 10, the regiment's much anticipated marching orders arrived during breakfast. By 9:00 A.M. regimental adjutant Lt. Audenried was rushing from company to company to notify them. One of the sergeants recalled, "He told me that orders had arrived for the regiment to march immediately and that Company 'C' must be ready at 11 o'clock. It was then just nine. I instantly ordered every man to pack up his effects. I then went to the Quartermaster's store and obtained rations for three days."[74] By 11 o'clock the regiment had formed in line on the parade ground, eleven of twelve companies present. Co. L had still not formed. The sergeants and officers conducted final inspections of men, horses and arms.

One soldier later recalled a dramatic end to this final formation at the camp. After the first sergeants made their reports to the adjutant and the company officers gave their customary salute, Lt. Col. Emory called for the regimental standard-bearer. Taking the banner in his hand and holding it aloft, he said, "Soldiers, we are to take the field. I want no man to abandon this flag."[75]

The bugle call "lead out" sounded, and the command broke by fours to the front. In a few moments the soldiers of the Sixth U.S. Cavalry bade farewell to their camp and marched in column of platoons along Pennsylvania Avenue towards the capitol. They soon turned off in the direction of the Long Bridge, crossing the Potomac in the rain. "When we reached the other side the regiment was halted and the men dismounted in order to allow the 5th Regular Cavalry to pass us. When the last man had passed we were formed and again we were on the line of march," recalled one sergeant. The rain soon ceased as they spent the afternoon marching through a deserted countryside, halting only once to water their heavily burdened horses.[76]

Arriving at Fairfax Court House about 5 o'clock, the regiment halted in a large field next to an orchard in a column of companies, and spent a cold, shivering night on the wet ground. The wagons with their tents and forage for the horses were still on the road behind them, so many of the men spent the night on pallets made from their horses' saddle blankets and fence rails.

As for the soldiers' rations on this first march, one sergeant later described them as "hard-bread in cakes about three inches square and about ⅜ of an inch thick. The haversack held somewhat I think over two dozen of these pieces. We carried some coffee and some brown sugar. Perhaps a few soldiers may have taken some pork." Inexperienced with the need to make their food last, many soldiers ate the greater portion of their rations on the first day.[77]

The shrill notes of a bugle aroused the men while the stars still glittered in the clear, cold sky. The bivouac fires, which had burned low, were started up with fresh vigor. Regimental quartermaster sergeant Rousseau arrived at sunrise with forage for the hungry horses. Mounts were fed and groomed, and the men quickly consumed a breakfast of pork, crackers, and coffee.[78]

At 7:00 A.M. "boots and saddles" rang out, and the regiment prepared to move. Unfortunately, not all would continue the march. As the men of Company C mounted, "an orderly came riding up to Lieut. McLellan and delivered an order to him. I was close enough to hear. It was a direction to return with our company to Washington in order to guard our old camp and to assist in guarding Washington. I never felt so bad in my life."[79]

General Cooke ordered the company back to Washington for two reasons. They had received their last recruits only two weeks before, and their last mounts just the previous week. Many needed more mounted drill. Although eager to remain with their comrades, the company was not yet ready for war. They were also to assist in training the sister company in their squadron, Company L. Short of officers, it was at last nearly to its full complement of recruits and mounts. So while the regiment marched south, the men of Company C retraced their steps back to the capital.[80]

The remainder of the regiment continued south to examine the abandoned Confederate works at Centerville. One trooper described them as "built to be strongly fortified, but for want of guns some of the port holes were filled with logs, painted black, and marked on the butt '12 pounder.' How far they would shoot was not mentioned."[81]

After making a quick examination of the works, the men rode a wide loop of many miles searching in vain for the departed Confederates. Their long miles and hours in the saddle were rewarded with only a solitary drunken Confederate prisoner and a sighting of pickets in the distance. Not until 9:00 P.M. did they reach Centerville once more, very sore, hungry, and tired. The regiment posted guards and went into camp in the abandoned Confederate works. They remained in place the next day, providing both mounts and men with much needed rest.[82]

The following morning, the flank squadron under Cpt. Kautz accompanied a brigade of infantry on a reconnaissance down the Orange & Alexandria Railroad toward the Rappahannock. Other than a brief skirmish with pickets on the south bank of Cedar Run in which no one was hurt, they found no enemy. It was a miserable trip, as the men had taken only three days' provisions for themselves, and little forage for the horses. Rain swollen streams held them in place the next day, and they didn't return to Fairfax Court House until the afternoon of the 17th.[83]

At Fairfax they found rations and forage for their hungry mounts, as well as one of their own officers. Cpt. Joseph Taylor, formerly of Company F, was there on detached service as chief of staff for Gen. Sumner. He would not return to the regiment during the war.[84]

The majority of the regiment started toward Alexandria on the 14th, camping that night at Fairfax Station, on the Orange and Alexandria Railroad. Towards morning, a cold, drizzly rain began to fall, and by daylight, the men were soaked to the skin. They started for the Potomac at 9:00 A.M., marching all day through the storm. Upon their arrival at Alexandria, the disgruntled troopers were covered from head to foot in mud.

The end of the day's march brought no improvement to their plight. Their rations and forage were exhausted, and wood was scarce for fires. After the men spent a very uncomfortable night, the trains rejoined them in the morning with rations, forage, and the regiment's tents. The needs of men and mounts addressed, a new camp was established between Alexandria and the Protestant Episcopal Theological Seminary, where Kautz' squadron rejoined them on the 18th.[85]

Meanwhile, back at Camp East of the Capitol, the sixth squadron's officers drilled their men relentlessly. Lt. McLellan was ordered to rejoin the regiment a week later, turning Company C over to Lt. Stoll. The 1st Rhode Island Cavalry in the meantime occupied much of the now vacant camp while they awaited the remainder of their mounts. The men hoped daily for orders to rejoin the regiment while they drew the remainder of their horses.[86]

On the 18th, the regiment was notified of its third commander. Like his predecessor, Lt. Col. Emory was appointed a general of volunteers. He was assigned to command the 1st Brigade, Cavalry Reserve, consisting of the 5th U.S., 6th U.S., and 6th Pennsylvania Cavalry regiments. Brig. Gen. Cooke moved up to command both brigades of the army's Cavalry Reserve. Maj. Williams assumed command of the regiment.[87]

Said one trooper of the departed Emory in later years, "Of Lieutenant Colonel Emory I suppose there was but one opinion among the common soldiers in the Sixth Cavalry — that he was a good-hearted man and a lion-hearted soldier. Although a strict disciplinarian, he was free from the mean caprices which curse the character of so many of our commissioned officers." The same soldier noted that the new commander was "distinguished for his rigorous discipline and haughty bearing. Though intensely hated by the men, he seemed to have the welfare of the regiment, as far as its military reputation was concerned, at heart."[88]

The regiment remained encamped near the seminary at Alexandria for nearly a week, awaiting their turn to embark for Fortress Monroe. Several officers secured passes to visit Washington and settle their affairs and excess company property. Lt. Dodge went on a drunken binge and refused to return to camp. It was apparently not the first such incident. He resigned his commission on the 24th.[89]

On March 27, the regiment marched down to the wharves at Alexandria. After much delay, the flank squadron led the boarding, with Company B embarking on the two-masted schooners *North Halifax* and *Kasbee*. In general, half a company filled a transport. Once loaded, the transports moved out into the river to allow empty ships their turn at the docks. Only a portion of the regiment boarded that afternoon; the remainder camped that night on the wharves.

The following morning, the rest of the regiment embarked. Steamers, also loaded with troops, began to take the schooners in tow in the early afternoon. In an oversight, no attention was paid to unit integrity in the orders to the steamer captains, leaving companies, squadrons and regiments spread randomly throughout the fleet. Cpt. Kautz was fortunate enough to have his two schooners towed by the steamer *Long Branch*.[90]

The conditions aboard ship were miserable for the cavalrymen. Cooking arrangements were too limited to accommodate the soldiers, so rations were limited to cold pork, crackers and water. The horses were picketed on deck, and the men were crowded away into dark holds upon the ballast of coal. Men slept where they could, listening to the tramp of their mounts on the deck above them. To make matters worse, heavy rains set in on the 28th, turning to snow the next day.[91] Despite the snow, a favorable wind enabled the ships to reach Hampton Roads on the 30th.[92]

Chapter 3

The Tip of the Spear

Upon arriving at the peninsula, the regiment found the water covered with innumerable boats of all descriptions, loaded with military troops and stores. Most of the companies disembarked as the various vessels arrived and safely anchored in the magnificent Hampton Roads harbor, off Fortress Monroe. Some companies, however, were forced to wait an additional day or two to reach dry land, as arriving infantry units had priority, at the limited docks, for unloading over the cavalry and artillery.

In the case of the cavalry, this led in some cases to a rather comical mode of disembarkation. Unable to find dock space and eager to leave the ships, the cavalrymen used their ingenuity to develop a solution. The ships' boats were used to ferry men ashore, and the horses were pushed over the side and forced to swim to shore. Cos. F and G were the only ones fortunate enough to unload on the docks, though persuading their horses to walk down the narrow gangways was nearly as trying as forcing them to swim. The muster rolls show no men or mounts lost to drowning from this exercise. As companies reached shore, they were marshaled and marched just beyond the town of Hampton to camp.[1]

The flank squadron lost its commander as soon as it arrived. Cpt. Kautz contracted typhoid fever on the voyage south, and was admitted to a hospital established in the Hygeia Hotel next to Fortress Monroe. Co. H's Cpt. Savage assumed command of the squadron.[2]

Once the entire regiment was ashore, they drew rations and marched on April 4 as the rear guard of the army. They moved slowly westward up the peninsula over the next week, on the road from after breakfast until long after dark. One night they went into camp after midnight in a valley filled with a horrible stench. At dawn they discovered they had camped next to a pond used by the Confederates as a slaughterhouse to feed their troops.[3]

Another temporary camp was established near the aptly named Shipping Point on the York River, where large details spent long hours each day unloading forage from schooners for the army's horses. The forage, heavy sacks of feed and bales of hay, had to be offloaded and moved to the waiting wagons by hand. The rest of the regiment drilled daily, working horses and riders back into shape following the voyage.[4]

The regiment shifted camp again on April 11, moving several miles closer to the front to occupy a large clearing surrounded by pine forest. The men happily abandoned their work as stevedores to focus on preparations for combat. The officers took advantage of the respite from work details to intensify their training with a

series of drills, mounted and dismounted, by company and by regiment, and of such frequency as to take up the entire day. Each company had hunted up an available field, made ditches, erected poles, put up posts to represent men, with bags stuffed with hay for their heads, at each ditch and pole, and at intervals between, and went through such a course of exercises as they had never before experienced. First, the men had to ride at a walk, avoiding the pole and ditches, and strike off the heads on the posts; then this was repeated at a trot and then at a gallop. After this, the men galloped around the ring, learning to jump the poles and ditches, and then to strike off the heads while their horses were in the act of leaping, and in the succeeding intervals, being obliged by the latter requirement to recover themselves instantaneously from the shock. These performances were repeated with revolver in hand; and then, instead of striking, they would shoot at the heads.[5]

Camp Winfield Scott was officially established on the 21st, and during this latter part of April the regiment continued to train. Cannonading from the siege of Yorktown could be heard in the distance. The regiment had been in service nearly a year and had been put through its paces by some of the finest drillmasters of the old army, but it had not yet seen action. This spurred some men from the older regular regiments to chaff the men as volunteers. Upon one occasion, this became an issue when Sgt. Myron Palmer of Co. B allowed his resentment to lead him into difficulty with the camp guard of the 1st U.S. Cavalry. The result of the investigation is shown in the following extract from a letter to the commander of the 1st Cavalry:

> [T]he Major Commanding directs me to say, relative to Sergeant Palmer, that he has investigated the case and finds from an ex parte statement of the Sergeant, who is a very quiet and reliable man, that the Sergeant of the guard of your camp used very abusive language towards him, calling him a "damn recruit and volunteer," drawing his sabre upon him and threatening to cut him down; this without his having refused to obey an order. It is difficult to arrive at the truth of these matters except before a court. If you desire it, the major Commanding directs me to say, that on the presentation of the charges against him, Sergeant Palmer shall be brought to trial.[6]

Cpt. Kautz was released from the hospital and rejoined the regiment on the 29th, though not yet recovered enough for full duty. He learned of difficulties between Gen. Emory and Maj. Williams from the regiment's officers and Emory himself, noting in his diary, "General Emory and Major Williams continue to have difficulty. The General has put the Major in arrest...."[7]

The men of the 6th U.S. prepared for their usual Sunday inspection on May 4, and had just marched onto the parade field when they received orders to move immediately to the front. Fortunately, the weekly inspection consisted of men and mounts fully equipped and prepared for movement. Accordingly, the head of the column turned onto the road and advanced toward Yorktown.[8] Following the Confederate abandonment of the works at Yorktown, chief of cavalry Brig. Gen. George Stoneman was assigned a composite force of combined arms and the assignment to pursue and harass the rear of the retreating enemy as the advance guard of the Army of the Potomac. His force consisted of Hays' brigade of four batteries of horse artillery, four cavalry regiments, and Barker's squadron of cavalry.[9]

Stoneman's advance guard on the Yorktown road consisted of the 1st and 6th U.S. Cavalry regiments and Cpt. Gibson's Company G, 3rd U.S. Artillery, commanded by Brig. Gen. Cooke. The 6th U.S. joined the rest of the command at Yorktown about noon, and they set forth down the Yorktown-Williamsburg road. Captain Magruder's squadron of the 1st U.S. Cavalry rode about half a mile in advance of the column, with Captain Savage's squadron of the 6th U.S. acting as flankers. Cpt. Kautz, still recovering from illness, remained in camp.[10]

Six miles from Williamsburg, according to Stoneman's report, the force encountered and quickly drove off Confederate pickets. Two miles farther down the road, the column made contact with the Confederate rear guard, "about two companies, at a defile of a mill and dam and a breastwork across the road." A section of the battery deployed and fired, and the Confederates retreated before a charge could be made. After crossing the defile, Brig. Gen. Emory was sent across to the Lee's Mill road with a regiment and a battery to cut off any force retreating on that road. Cooke's command continued down the Yorktown road. Over the course of the advance, Lt. Kerin's platoon of 6th Cavalry flankers captured Captain Connell of the Jeff Davis Legion and five privates.[11]

Two miles from Williamsburg, at the junction of the Yorktown and Lee's Mill roads, Cooke's force discovered a strong earthwork flanked by redoubts about three o'clock in the afternoon. The area was ill-suited for the battery due to thick forest and marshy ground, but Gen. Cooke ordered Gibson's battery to shell the position, with Lt. Col. Grier's 1st U.S. Cavalry in support.

Unbeknownst to the Federals, the rear guard of the Confederate army was in the process of abandoning the works as they approached. Confederate commander Joseph E. Johnston himself was at the works when he received word of Cooke's advance. He immediately ordered Semmes' brigade of Brig. Gen. McLaws' division and an artillery battery to reoccupy the works, and summoned Kershaw's brigade and a second battery to assist them.[12]

Cpt. Gibson's men manhandled their guns into position, and the 1st U.S. occupied a small ravine to support the battery. As soon as they opened fire, however, they were answered by two Confederate batteries. Cpt. Savage's flankers had located a track through the woods which led to the Confederate left flank, and they reported unoccupied works there. Cooke ordered Maj. Williams to take the 6th U.S. down the trail and attack the enemy's left flank. Stoneman deployed the remainder of his force in a clearing half a mile to the rear.

By now the earthworks, named Fort Magruder by the Confederates, were manned by

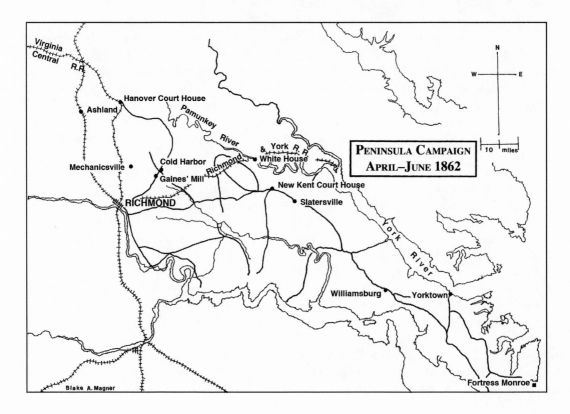

three regiments of infantry, a regiment of cavalry and two batteries of artillery. After an artillery duel of 45 minutes, Stoneman ordered his forces to withdraw. Inability to silence the enemy guns, increasing activity from the Confederate regiments to his front and a lack of infantry support led him to believe that he could not hold his position. The battery retired by piece, and the 1st U.S. was ordered to cover its withdrawal and assist in evacuating the wounded.

Emboldened by the Union withdrawal, Lt. Col. Williams Wickham was ordered to charge with his 4th Virginia Cavalry and attempt to take the guns. As the charging Confederates approached, Cpt. Benjamin F. Davis wheeled the 60 men of his trail squadron of the 1st U.S. and countercharged, repulsing the Confederate attack. Lt. Col. Grier charged to their support with the rest of his regiment and Cpt. Savage's squadron of the 6th U.S. Cavalry. Lt. Col. Wickham was wounded in the side by a saber and the 4th Virginia's colors were seized in the melee around the guns.[13]

Meanwhile, the 6th U.S. Cavalry proceeded nearly half a mile at a trot down the forest road, across a ravine, and up to the left flank of the Confederate earthworks. The ravine could be crossed only by file, and as the regiment reformed on its far side, Lt. Madden was dispatched with his platoon to reconnoiter the earthworks. The remainder of the regiment "proceeded at a trot, with drawn sabres, in column of companies," wrote one of the soldiers later. "The regiment marched as if going through a drill, the officers constantly looking to see if the men were keeping their alignment and retaining their proper distances from the companies in front of each other.[14]

Madden found an empty redoubt with a ditch and rampart. As he passed the rear of the structure, he discovered several regiments of infantry and cavalry close at hand advancing

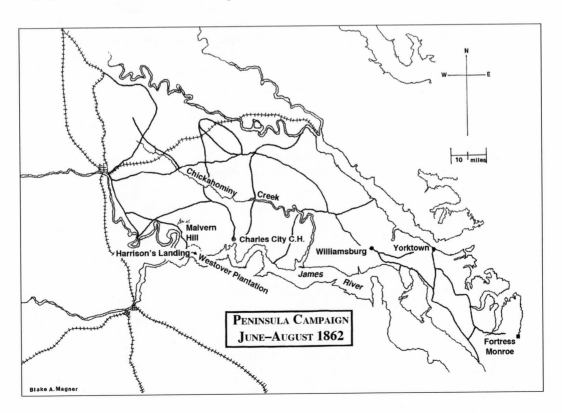

PENINSULA CAMPAIGN
JUNE–AUGUST 1862

Blake A. Magner

to occupy it. "At first they were supposed to be our own men, so close were they and so confident in their advance; but the mistake was soon discovered and our guns opened on them with shell," Gen. McLaws wrote in his report.[15] Madden wheeled his platoon and raced back to report as the first shells began to fall around the exposed 6th Cavalry. Outnumbered, Major Williams ordered his force to withdraw by platoons across the narrow ravine, harassed the entire way by enemy fire. Cpt. Sanders' squadron of Cos. A and M trailed the regiment.

"Our cavalry coming up, I directed Colonel Davis, commanding, to charge that of the enemy, which he did in gallant style," wrote McLaws.[16] Col. Davis led the cavalry of the Hampton and Wise legions in pursuit while the Confederate artillery continued to fire as the 6th Cavalry filed back through the ravine. Lt. McLellan of Co. A was seriously wounded in the leg when a shell burst near him. As the gray cavalry closed with the troopers in blue, the artillery ceased its fire.[17]

"While in the worst part of the ravine the cavalry appeared on the edge and opened a destructive fire from carbines and pistols. I hurried across as fast as possible and formed platoons. The enemy followed across the ravine and up the hill," Cpt. Sanders wrote later in his report.[18] Hearing the firing to his rear, Maj. Williams turned to their regiment to answer the attack. Reaching the top of the hill, Sanders wheeled his squadron and immediately ordered them to charge. "The men all acted bravely and turned at the command, after having been subjected to a very severe fire while retiring across the ravine, and charged gallantly," Sanders continued. Part of Cpt. J.I. Gregg's squadron, under Lts. Paulding and Ward, rushed back to their comrades' aid.[19]

The troopers in blue "swept upon them, with glittering sabres, like an irresistible avalanche, and crushed them back into the marsh with considerable loss. Hoarse shouts of vengeance went up as the sabres flashed and the strokes fell rapidly in all directions."[20] A brief, bloody fight ensued in the ravine, and the Confederates were driven back and forced to retreat.

Maj. Williams re-formed the regiment and withdrew to join the rest of the command. Gen. Stoneman consolidated his forces in the clearing half a mile away and waited for infantry support. The skirmish was over.

Rejoining the rest of the column, the various units involved re-formed and counted their losses. "The lines were carefully dressed, the men counted off by fours again, and the roll was called amid profound silence. When one did not answer to his name, his comrades were asked if they knew anything about him, and if one could tell of their friend's fate, they would respond."[21] Pvt. Suel Merkle of Co. E was the regiment's first battle casualty, and the only soldier killed in the engagement. The majority of the 20 wounded were from Sanders' squadron, with two from those of Gregg's squadron that rushed to their support in the defile.[22]

The regiment acquitted itself well in its baptism of fire, with many members singled out for gallantry in various reports. General Stoneman singled out Major Williams, Captain Sanders and his squadron.[23] Sergeant John F. Durboran of Co. M reportedly killed two Rebels in the engagement, and was praised in General Cooke's report. First Sergeants Joseph Bould of Co. A and Michael Cooney of Co. M received mention from Cpt. Sanders, while Cpt. Gregg praised First Sergeant Andrew F. Swan of Co. G and Sgt. Emil Swartz of Co. F as "especially deserving of praise for their gallant bearing."[24] All of the first sergeants mentioned received commissions as officers in the next year. "The Sixth did its duty that day," noted a trooper from another regiment present at the skirmish. "The impetuosity and boldness of the charge caused the enemy some confusion, but it was for a minute, for although the men crossed sabres, and steel clashed against steel, and the fierce conflict raged until the stoutest heroes lay dead on the ground, still grasping the bloody sabre they had so manfully disputed for life, they were forced to give way before the fast accumulating force of the enemy. But there was no sign of a rout, no disorder."[25]

The Confederates reoccupied Fort Magruder in force, and there was a major battle the following day, but the 6th U.S. Cavalry played no part more significant than supporting a battery of artillery, joined by the 8th Illinois Cavalry.

On the morning of May 7, "MAJ Williams announced that, on account of the regiment's meritorious and praiseworthy conduct during the battle of Williamsburg on Sunday, the regiment had been assigned the post of honor, and should lead the advance on Richmond."[26] In all likelihood, this was more likely due to the presence of the flank squadron's carbines, as the other regular regiments were still armed only with pistol and saber. Even so, for the next several weeks they formed the advance of the Union army as it pressed steadily westward. This meant a great deal of work for the flank squadron, as it led the advance and accompanied every regimental patrol for the support of its firearms. The regiment stayed close to the Confederate rear guard, and several engagements ensued between the advance and small groups of cavalry with a cannon or two in support.

On May 11, the regiment collided with the Confederate rear guard. As the regiment approached Slatersville, Maj. Williams received a report of a detachment of enemy cavalry in front of the town. He posted the carbineers with two other companies along the edge of the woods directly in front of the enemy's line and deployed skirmishers to engage their attention. He then ordered three companies, Cpt. Lowell's squadron, consisting of 55 men, and Cpt. Sanders' company of 32 men, down a forest path leading around the right side of the town to cut off their escape.[27]

Unfortunately, soon after the column started, an enemy vidette posted in the edge of the woods spotted them and signaled his company, which wheeled away from Williams' distraction toward the new threat. Cpt. Lowell, leading the column, immediately ordered his squadron to the gallop and charged. The enemy retreated into the village with Lowell's men in hot pursuit.[28]

A squadron of Confederate cavalry emerged on Lowell's left, but Cpt. Sanders charged them immediately with his company. Sanders' charge caused the enemy to retreat in confusion, but Sanders could see yet another squadron approaching from behind the village. Thinking quickly, he wheeled his small company and charged the newcomers as well, forcing them to retreat.[29] Obviously outnumbered at this point, Cpt. Sanders ordered the recall sounded. He quickly gathered his company and took the forest path back to the regiment. Cpt. Lowell's squadron, however, had pursued through the town beyond the sound of the bugle. Sighting still more troops beyond the town, he managed to withdraw before the enemy had recovered sufficiently to pursue.[30]

Lts. Hutchins, Whitside and Coats were commended for their conduct in this affair. While the initial reports from the regiment show a loss of four killed, eight wounded, and three missing, regimental returns show only two killed in action: Pvts. Able Irish and Charles O'Harra of Co. E.[31]

News of this skirmish made it all the way back to New York, where one of the local newspapers reported: "Lieut. Whiteside, of Co. I, Sixth Cavalry, dashed into the woods with sixteen men, and put to flight a whole squadron of the enemy's cavalry. They scampered off in a most hasty manner yelling at the top of their voices '*The Yankees, The Yankees.*'

Lieut. Whiteside returned with one prisoner and two horses."[32] That evening, Cpt. Kautz rejoined the regiment at Cumberland and resumed command of the flank squadron. He found the regiment's officers "all well and glad to see me. The hard work they have had seems to agree with them."

The officers, however, were not very happy with their commander. Kautz wrote they were "very much dissatisfied with Major Williams. They complain that he is constantly absent and never to be found when wanted. He was present when I arrived, but I did not see him again until retreat, after half of the officers had reported to me under the impression that he had not returned. His time appears to be spent on the gunboat which is lying opposite the White House. He is said to be taking great interest in the protection of the property of his cousin, General Lee."[33]

On May 12, the command reached New Kent Court House, near the Chickahominy River. The same day, Sgt. Maj. John Lee was appointed a second lieutenant, relinquishing his old position to 1st Sgt. Tullius C. Tupper of Co. E. Tupper, an Ohio native, had worked his way up from private to first sergeant of his company since the previous July.[34]

On May 14, 1862, the flank squadron was sent on reconnaissance to Dr. Macon's house, and on the 15th to scout in the direction of Hanover Court House. This advance guard captured 75 mules and three six-mule teams belonging to Windsor's Confederate brigade at Hawe's Shop.[35]

Late in the day of 15th, the regiment encamped at White House on the Pamunkey River, not far from Cumberland. This large plantation was soon occupied by a large force of infantry and transformed into a Union supply depot. The enemy withdrew to Tunstall's Station, on the York River Railroad, leaving a few cavalrymen to watch Union movements.

The regiment's pickets were posted on a line stretching across the broad open fields from the river, which protected their right flank, to the woods on the left. Here they connected with the 1st New York Dragoons, the latter extending off towards the mouth of the Chickahominy.

The duties of the cavalry during these days were very arduous. The cavalry force was so small and the extent of the country to be guarded was so great that the men were obliged to picket roads singly and at distances from each other varying from one mile to four miles. Sometimes they were obliged to sit on their horses for 12 hours at a time without relief or food.[36] Pvt. Owen noted the following in a letter home to the local newspaper: "We have had the advance of the army, marching in front all day, deploying as skirmishers, running through brush, driving in the enemy's pickets, and then standing picket guard all night. At one time I only had two hours sleep in four nights. Our men get so worn out that when we would halt to rest, while on the march some of our men would drop asleep and fall off their horses. To add to this, we only had hard crackers to eat."[37]

On May 15th, Maj. Williams, the regiment's commanding officer, was arrested for alleged communication with the enemy. As previously noted, Williams was a relative of the Lee family and had relatives in the vicinity of White House. Several days previously, he had been warned back inside the picket line by Lt. Madden. He was subsequently arrested outside the lines in front of the 1st U.S. Cavalry's pickets on the night of the 15th. After a Confederate mail carrier was captured with a letter allegedly from Williams to Confederate General J.E.B. Stuart, Gen. Stoneman ordered Williams placed under arrest and confined in his tent under a strong guard.[38] He was sent to Gen. McClellan's headquarters under arrest the following day. Two days later, Williams wrote a letter to Gen. Stoneman requesting an investigation:

HEADQUARTERS 6TH CAVALRY, *May* 17, 1862.

Assistant Adjutant General,

Advance Guard of the Army.

SIR: On the evening of the 15th instant, I was placed in arrest as a prisoner of the state, a guard of four of my own men put over me, and with orders to shoot me if I attempted to leave the tent. A procedure so extraordinary in itself, independent of the humiliation and disgrace which it must impose on a soldier of spirit and a gentlemen of pride, could only have been resorted to from reasons of the gravest importance. The General commanding the advance-guard believed the information which subjected me to this mortifying restraint sufficient to justify his order no doubt, but, as the fact of my arrest is known to the men of my regiment and the army generally, and as the arrest casts an imputation upon my fidelity as an officer, I respectfully request that a Board of Examination be appointed by the General Commanding to investigate the circumstances.

I am, sir, very respectfully, your obedient servant,

LAWRENCE A. WILLIAMS,

Major, 6th Cavalry.[39]

Gen. Stoneman forwarded the request to Gen. McClellan's headquarters the same day, and Maj. Williams was ordered released from arrest and returned to command of his regiment that evening.[40]

Maj. Williams' conduct had been noted by several of his subordinates as very suspicious prior to his arrest. Cpt. Kautz mentioned such behavior in his diary several times in the days leading up to the arrest, noting two days earlier,

> Major Williams was asleep at reveille. He was about camp for a short time during the morning but disappeared in the afternoon and was not seen again by me during the day. This is very annoying as he goes off without turning the command over to me, and I don't know whether I am to act or not. I had some conversations with him about the enemy. He thinks there is little or no danger. He says he is here among old acquaintances, the servants of the White House know him and he says he could send any message he chose to friends in Richmond.[41]

Although cleared of guilt and returned to duty, suspicion continued to follow Maj. Williams as he led the regiment for the remainder of the campaign. In the meantime, the bulk of the army moved up to White House, and Cpt. Kautz ordered the surgeon and trains up to the regiment's camp.[42]

Maj. Williams resumed command of the regiment the next morning, May 18. About noon, the regiment advanced cautiously about six miles, to Cold Harbor, and reached Dr. Gaines' Mill after a brief skirmish the following day in which no one was injured.

On the 20th Cpt. Sanders' squadron reconnoitered New Bridge, a bridge across the Chickahominy. Co. A lost three men in the skirmish, Corp. John Manice, killed, and Pvts. William Dickson and James Brennan, wounded. The squadron withdrew to the regiment's camp at Gaines' Mill.[43] After two days in camp, six companies advanced to reconnoiter the Chickahominy, check enemy dispositions and secure a lodgment on the far side if possible. The regiment's advance guard of five soldiers was ambushed half a mile from the bridge, and Corp. McAleese of Co. M was killed. Co. M's blacksmith and two horses were also injured, and the party was forced to retreat on foot. Satisfied the enemy's infantry held the river line, the companies returned to camp. Maj. Williams posted pickets and patrols on all roads in the vicinity until relieved by the arrival of Gen. Porter's V Corps on the 21st.[44]

The regiment marched again as part of Gen. Stoneman's advance guard on May 23, Cpt. Kautz' flank squadron once again in the lead. The regiment was accompanied by Cpt. Benson's battery and one or two infantry regiments. They encountered a small force of the enemy with artillery outside of Mechanicsville, who withdrew after a brief artillery duel. The regiment camped in a nearby orchard and picketed the roads leading west from Mechanicsville, in the rain, the next two days.[45]

In the evening, Kautz' squadron was ordered out to Shady Grove Church on picket. He noted in his diary, "The pickets are very much extended. There is plenty of forage and provisions in the neighborhood, which makes the duty rather pleasant." They remained there until just before midnight the following night, when they were ordered back to camp. Once again there were problems with Maj. Williams, as Cpt. Kautz noted: "The major was quite drunk when I reported to him and apparently unconscious of what I said to him."[46]

On May 27, the regiment "turned out without breakfast or feeding" to lead the Union advance on Hanover Court House. After chasing in the enemy's pickets, they spent the remainder of the battle in support of Cpt. Benson's Battery M, 2nd U.S. Artillery. Maj. Williams formed the men in close column of squadrons to the rear of the guns with drawn sabers.[47] Cpt. Kautz was less than pleased with the dispositions. "Williams again put us in dense columns of squadrons behind Benson's Artillery and we were in great danger," he wrote in his diary.[48] One trooper left the following account of the battle: "Our part was to support the artillery, which brought us in range of the enemy's guns, as we had to take our position directly in rear of our guns. For over an hour we stood with the shells bursting all around us, coming so near we could distinctly feel the air of the balls as they passed over our heads. It made us rather '*skery*' you may be assured. One ball goes a foot above your head, and you imagine how easy it would be for the next one to fall a foot lower — and then the consequences."[49]

The regiment suffered only three wounded in the engagement, Pvt. H.C. Smith of Co. H and two horses. The regiment pursued the retreating enemy to Hanover Court House following the battle, but it was quickly recalled after reports of enemy cavalry in the Union rear. The attack thwarted with no additional loss, the regiment went into camp in a pine forest just north of Mechanicsville for the night.[50]

The regiment spent the next several days destroying bridges. On the 27th, four squadrons marched down the Fredericksburg road as far as the farm of Confederate colonel Williams Carter Wickham. Col. Wickham, at home convalescing from the saber wound received from Cpt. Sanders in the skirmish at Williamsburg, was captured and paroled. Lt. Kerin's platoon destroyed the nearby railroad bridge in about three hours. That evening, Lts. Kerin and Coats and a platoon from Co. B burnt another bridge about 200 yards above the railroad bridge. Cpt. Cram's Co. I also completed the destruction of a bridge fired by the 6th Pennsylvania Cavalry the day before.[51]

The next day, the regiment was ordered to destroy the Virginia Central Railroad bridge across the South Anna River. Since the enemy was reported to be in the area in force, a section of Benson's battery under Lt. Peter Hains and four companies of the 17th New York Infantry accompanied them. After securing the approaches to the bridge, Cpt. Abert's squadron and a platoon from the flank squadron destroyed the 300-foot long bridge in about an hour.[52]

The command returned to camp in the afternoon, only to receive orders for the regiment to immediately march to Walnut Grove Church. They reached the church about midnight, "having been in the saddle eighteen out of the twenty-four hours," according to Maj. Williams' report.[53] The tired men spent the next morning replenishing haversacks and grooming mounts. Ready to march once again by noon, they heard the distant roar of cannon and musketry to the south. They listened to the sounds of the battle of Fair Oaks

Battle of Williamsburg, Virginia (*Harpers Weekly*).

that day and the next, but received no orders to join the distant battle and remained in camp.[54]

The first month of active campaigning had been hard on the regiment. Five troopers were killed in action, and four more died of disease in the hospital at Yorktown. Despite vaccinations for nearly all in the regiment prior to moving south,[55] fifty troopers were sick in camp at month's end, with another 106 sick in hospitals away from the regiment. Only 23 officers and 670 men remained present for duty.[56]

Although quiet for the army as a whole, the next several weeks were busy ones for the army's limited force of cavalry. While the majority of the regiment remained in camp, each day details of patrols, companies and squadrons rode forth to cover the ground between the army's right wing and the Pamunkey River. Generally sent out with two days of rations, patrols and pickets frequently lasted three or four days, causing much wear and tear on men and mounts.[57] It should also be noted the term "camp" is used rather loosely, as the regiment hadn't seen its tents or slept under canvas since departing Yorktown. In most cases, the men simply tied their horses to trees, made a short shelter out of their blankets, and slept on pine boughs they had gathered.[58]

Cpt. Kautz conducted one such patrol on June 2, proceeding with the flank squadron and two squadrons of the 6th Pennsylvania Cavalry, "Rush's Lancers," to "burn the ferries and destroy all communications across the Pamunkey above Pipingtree to Doctor Wormley's Ferry, to arrest Doctor Wormley and to ascertain all I could about a force organizing in King William County."[59] They arrived that evening to find the ferry to Wormley's destroyed.

Battle of Hanover Court-House, Virginia (*Harpers Weekly*).

Kautz dispatched one squadron of Lancers to Pipingtree and the other to Basset's Ferry, and encamped with his squadron for the night.

The following morning, according to Kautz' report, "Through information obtained last evening and the aid of a slave recently escaped I was enabled to find the ferry-boat belonging to Dr. Wormley's ferry concealed in a creek nearby on the north side of the river, together with the sloop Golden Gate, about 25 tons, from Norfolk, eight wooden boats, and one metallic life-boat would carry two teams with their horses. All these were rendered entirely useless. The sloop was burned."[60] Lt. Balder crossed the Pamunkey with six men in a small canoe and arrested Dr. Wormley, who was conducted back to the army's provost marshal general. Finding no evidence of organized enemy forces across the river, Cpt. Kautz and his men returned to camp.[61]

The strains of the campaign began to take their toll on the regiment's mounts. Frequent rains in early June made the roads nearly impassable, creating poor marching conditions for the patrols and making it difficult to get wagons to the camps with adequate forage. Additionally, there was a shortage of horseshoes and nails, as the regiment's small store had long since been exhausted. The condition of the men was not much better. As one company commander noted, "The men are not in uniform and poorly clothed."[62]

On the afternoon of June 13, "they "got orders to '*saddle up*' and leave everything behind — the enemy were coming in our rear! We bustled about, and in ten minutes were under way."[63] The 5th U.S. Cavalry had made contact with a Confederate cavalry force under Gen. J.E.B. Stuart, and Gen. Emory ordered forth his regiments in pursuit.

Other than a brief contact with Stuart's rear guard that afternoon, the regiment rode all afternoon and a good part of the night in fruitless pursuit, as they made no further contact with Stuart's force. The regimental quartermaster, Lt. John Spangler, at Garlick's Landing with the regimental trains, briefly sighted the enemy in the afternoon, but the trains fortunately escaped detection. After a night of standing to horse awaiting another sighting of the enemy, the regiment learned he had escaped across the Chickahominy and returned to its camp near Cold Harbor.[64]

The regiment's soldiers received their first pay since departing Washington on June 17. Cpt. Kautz noted his pay for March, April and May totaled $574.10, a goodly sum for the time.[65] The enlisted soldiers were not as happy. One disgruntled trooper noted in a letter home,

> We do not draw no 14 dollars a month, we only get 13 and two of that is withheld and the shilling kept for the benefit of the soldiers hospital makes the pay we draw payday for two months only $21.75. Then our wash-bill takes $1.50 of that knocking it down to twenty dollars. Then we have to keep some in our pocket for postage stamps, pens, ink, paper, etc. which leaves only 10 or 15 dollars to send home. Then the government requires each man to have at inspection needles, thread, shoe blacking, and other things which we have to buy ourselves and take it all in all.[66]

After over a week of picket duty near Hawes' Shop, two squadrons at a time, the regiment was once again detached from its brigade and assigned to Gen. Stoneman, on June 25. Acting on rumors that a Confederate force under Gen. Jackson was approaching from Northern Virginia, they moved toward the South Anna River once again. The next day they were ordered "to block up all the roads and burn all the bridges on the streams and destroy ferries" in order to slow the suspected enemy advance.[67] Over the course of the day they withdrew to Hanover Court House, and the following day to Tunstall's Station, arriving at dusk. On the 26th, Maj. Williams fell ill and left the regiment for the hospital. He never returned to the regiment.[68]

They were on the army's far right during the battle of Gaines' Mill, out of sight of the fighting but able to hear "the most terrific cannonading."[69] They learned from stragglers that evening that Gen. Porter had been attacked by a large force under Jackson, and had crossed the Chickahominy. Not all of the regiment escaped the battle unscathed. Lt. Stephen Balk and two privates, serving with the brigade's provost guard, were wounded in the fighting. Another soldier who was serving as an orderly to Gen. Cooke, Pvt. Benjamin F. King of Co. D, was commended by the general in his report "for serving above that position as an orderly with intelligence, bravery, and promptness."[70]

The regiment withdrew to White House the next morning, where they rejoined Gen. Emory. Everything that couldn't be carried from the depot had been burned. That evening the regiment began to withdraw toward Yorktown. The two squadrons guarding the rear of the brigade, those of Sanders and Lowell, had occasional brushes with enemy pursuers, but took no casualties.

The next day they reached Yorktown. After two days there without rations or forage, they continued the march toward Fortress Monroe. The regimental trains withdrew toward the bulk of the army following the battle of Gaines Mill, traveling overland to Harrison's Landing on the James River. The regiment in the meantime changed from Gen. Stoneman's command to Gen. Emory's, and neither had requested supplies for it. They camped just outside of Fortress Monroe on July 2, and moved into the cavalry stables there two days later.[71]

On the afternoon of the 27th, the regiment's headquarters and trains were ordered to move immediately to Woodbury Bridge on the Chickahominy. Once there, they joined the rest of the army's trains and moved to the vicinity of Harrison's Landing on the York River by way of Savage Station, Bottom Bridge and Malvern Hill.[72]

An Interlude

Meanwhile, back in Washington, the Sixth Squadron continued to prepare for war. Since the officers of Co. L were still recruiting, their men were forwarded to Camp East of the Capitol and consolidated with Co. C to train until Co. L could be formed. There was a great deal of resentment between the two groups, as the men of Co. C blamed the recruits for being left behind in Washington.[73]

The remaining barracks at Camp East of the Capitol were empty only a matter of days, as space in Washington was at a premium. The 1st Rhode Island Cavalry occupied the camp for several days before moving south, neither the regulars nor the volunteers very impressed with one another. When the 1st moved south, several batteries of artillery from Maine joined the camp. Co. C continued to drill twice a day, with frequent inspections of men and equipment. Cpt. Brisbin arrived on April 18 to organize Co. L, and Lt. Tucker commanded Co. C.[74]

On June 5, the squadron received its Sharps carbines from the Washington arsenal. One of the sergeants noted, "The boys are overjoyed with their new arm. Indeed it is a splendid weapon, bright and new and warranted to carry 1000 yards. When we are on horseback the rifle is carried to a sling or band which crosses the shoulder."[75]

In mid–June, in an interesting reversal, Cpt. Brisbin exercised his prerogative as the squadron commander and transferred many of the more experienced soldiers and noncommissioned officers from Co. C to Co. L.[76] Two weeks later, on July 2, Co. L was ordered south to join the regiment on the James River. Co. C, short of personnel following the transfers, once again remained behind. It is certain that the men of Co. C did not appreciate the irony. Co. L marched to Alexandria the next day, and embarked in three ships for the James on the 5th. They disembarked at Fortress Monroe on the 10th, where they joined Cpt. Sanders' squadron.[77]

On the James River

The majority of the regiment boarded transports on the 7th at Fortress Monroe and sailed around the end of the peninsula to rejoin McClellan's army near Harrison's Landing on the James River. Due to the huge amounts of men and materiel there, the cavalry camp was established several miles downstream at the plantation of Westover. The transports received musket fire from guerrillas not far from Harrison's Landing, but no one was hurt. The trains and headquarters soon joined them in the new camp, and the other three companies arrived from Fortress Monroe on the 11th.[78]

The camp left a great deal to be desired. Established in one of the plantation's wheat fields, there were no trees to provide respite from the hot summer sun. Flies pestered the men during the day and mosquitoes hunted them by night. The 6th Pennsylvania Cavalry and the 5th U.S. Cavalry occupied neighboring areas on either side of the camp. The few springs were insufficient for the number of troops using them. Pvt. Samuel Hamilton of Co. F devised a solution. He and a work party of nine men dug a 27-foot deep well, which met the company's water needs. The other companies quickly followed suit.[79] "The water is cool and tastes well but somehow or other it will not get clear. It is always of a muddy tint," noted one soldier.[80]

The regiment's soldiers at least had the minimal protection provided by their tents, which had finally caught up with them. "Each company occupies 4 Sibley tents placed in line. The tents of the different companies are arranged parallel that is by sets of fours. The officer's tents are in a line with the respective companies," noted one sergeant in a letter home.[81]

Though based at Westover, the various cavalry regiments alternated duties picketing the army's front and flanks. Multiple squadrons at a time performed picketing and patrolling duties. The 6th U.S. Cavalry picketed the army's extreme left, toward Haxall's Landing[82]

The army's cavalry was reorganized once again while at Harrison's Landing. Gen. Stoneman attempted to keep the regular cavalry regiments together, but he was overruled. Much to Cpt. Kautz' chagrin, the regiment was initially assigned to the brigade of former captain — now colonel of volunteers — David McM. Gregg. "This is the most unpleasant stroke of all. After having adhered to the regular service so long to be made a Volunteer of, in spite of myself," he wrote in his diary.[83] Only months before, Gregg was junior to Kautz in the same regiment. The brigade also consisted of the 8th Pennsylvania Cavalry and 8th Illinois Cavalry. Brig. Gen. Alfred Pleasonton assumed command of the brigade on August 2.

While here, the regiment finally learned of the deaths of Lts. Hugh McQuade in Libby Prison and Peter McGrath in New Mexico. Several officers were detailed as aides to various generals as well, among them Cpt. Lowell to Gen. McClellan's staff, adding to the officer shortages.[84] These losses, as well as those suffered by the other regular regiments during the campaign, resulted in orders for nominations of deserving noncommissioned officers for commissions. As regimental commander, Cpt. Kautz accordingly interviewed sergeants nominated by his company commanders.[85]

One of the sergeants described the interview in a letter home:

> He then asked me what was my age. I told him 23 when I had entered service Nov 1. 61. What had been my education. I explained the point that I studied astronomy. Yes. What do you know about the solar system? I explained. Have you studied history? Yes, sir. When was America discovered? In 1492 by Chris. Columbus a native Geneva in Italy. The Capt. then asked if I knew anything of Germany and Trigonometry. I told him a little. If I could draw. I told him yes both mechanical & sketching from nature. He told me that was enough and that I might send Sergt. Van Reed to him, whom he catechized in very much the same style. There were about 5 sergeants of the whole regt. in all that were called to his tent.[86]

Health issues continued to be a concern. At the end of July, 62 soldiers were sick in camp and another 96 sick in hospitals away from the regiment. When Cpt. Kautz held an inspection and review on July 27, Co. L had only 15 men fit for duty.[87] Dr. Pooley had remained at a field hospital at Rip Raps outside Fortress Monroe, and was replaced by Dr. Henry DuBois. DuBois was joined by Dr. D.L. Rogers on July 18.[88]

The mounts suffered as well. Cpt. Kautz noted in his diary the day of the inspection, "The horses are dying very rapidly from some cause unknown. They stop eating for a day or two then go down and never get up again. It seems a kind of fever. The disease seems to attack the fittest horses."[89]

The regiment suffered a rude surprise the night of July 31. The Confederates had stealthily emplaced several batteries of artillery on the south side of the James River, and had taken advantage of the darkness and a temporary absence of Union gunboats to shell the Union encampments. "We had quite an excitement last night. The enemy's batteries opened upon us from the opposite side of the river about 1 o'clock at night and fired very rapidly and wildly into our camps for half an hour," wrote Cpt. Kautz.[90] "The sight was splendid I assure you," one soldier wrote two nights later. "Balls of lighted turpentine to give them a view of our whereabouts, and set fire to combustible matter, were continually sent over our heads lighting up the whole camp, and followed immediately by the whiz of a ball. Several pieces have range of our camp, and the thing was a little serious. If their balls had been two feet lower they would have completely riddled our camp."[91]

The absent gunboats returned a short time later, and the Confederates withdrew. Several horses had to be put down, but no men were seriously wounded. The cavalry regiments moved out of the camp farther inland to protect the horses for the remainder of the night. They did the same thing the following night, but there were no further attacks.[92]

As neither army sought to advance during the beginning of August, relations between the opposing pickets were relatively cordial, as evidenced by the following encounter:

> From our outpost on the left the enemy could be seen near a mill about 100 yards distant. We showed ourselves to them and expected them to fire, but instead of doing so, one of them helloed to us and asked if we had any coffee and sugar to exchange for tobacco. We said "no." He then asked us to come down and get a drink of water. I asked him to meet me halfway with a cup of water and he did so. I went to him alone, drank the water and asked him for the news. He said that there was none and that he heartedly wished the war was at an end. I agreed with him and inquired what regiment he belonged to. He said the 4th Virginia Cav. I then left him and joined our party.[93]

The regiment advanced from their camp on the evening of August 4, moving several miles toward Haxall's Landing and standing to horse the rest of the night. They resumed the march before the dawn the next morning and were soon joined on the march by the 8th Illinois Cavalry, which assumed the lead. Driving in the enemy's pickets, each regiment supported a light battery in an artillery duel as the Federal infantry approached. The 6th U.S. was once again drawn up in close column behind its battery.[94] "The shells burst very close but principally above our heads. One fragment passed within an inch or two of a private named Sherman and buried itself in the ground close behind me. A round shot stuck the fence just back of us, shattered it to pieces and then rolled a few yards along the ground. One shell burst in front and threw the dirt all over us."[95]

After a brief but spirited exchange, the Confederates withdrew up New Market Road toward Richmond. Both cavalry regiments spurred in pursuit, the heads of each column colliding with the Confederate rear guard. The lieutenant colonel and two men of the 8th Illinois were wounded, but the two regiments took 86 prisoners before the pursuit was halted.[96]

Advancing past the abandoned Confederate position, the 6th U.S. Cavalry threw out a strong force of pickets. Since there was no further contact before sundown, the flank squadron was sent forward to reconnoiter. Lt. Curwen McLellan commanded the squadron, as Cpt. Savage was absent, and Cpt. Kautz commanded the regiment.

The squadron had advanced only a short distance beyond the pickets when they were ambushed by a force of Confederate infantry, who stood and delivered a full volley. Undeterred, McLellan wheeled the squadron into line and vigorously returned fire with its Sharps carbines. The Confederates fled, but three men of the squadron were killed and two wounded, one mortally. McLellan gathered his casualties and withdrew back inside the picket line.[97]

The affair confirmed that the Confederates had not abandoned the field after all, and the regiment withdrew to the woods at the far edge of the field. Pickets were posted at the edge of the woods, with the flank squadron on line perhaps 30 yards to their rear. The remainder of the regiment formed in close column farther under cover.[98]

Daylight disclosed no visible enemy, and the regiment continued to picket the New Market Road. Two squadrons reconnoitered the road as far as the Confederate entrenchments near Bailey's Run and returned unscathed. That evening, however, Kautz ordered the regiment to withdraw to Haxall's Landing after the pickets under Lt. Hutchins were again driven in. Unfortunately, Cpt. Brisbin's Co. L was cut off by the enemy during the withdrawal. Thinking quickly, he devised a creative solution:

> My men all have grey shirts. I had on the grey shirt you made me. I made my men all take off their blue coats and tie them behind their saddles. It was moon-light but in their grey shirts they looked for all the world like rebels. The men set out & pretended as though we were rebels and looking for the "Yankees." I soon came up with a co. of rebel infantry but as we were going the same way, they were and had on our skirmishers they evidently thought we were their own cavalry and so paid no attention to us.[99]

After several near misses with Confederate units and his own regiment's pickets, Brisbin safely rejoined the regiment without losing a man. The regiment was replaced on the picket line the following morning, acting as the brigade reserve.[100]

Cpt. Savage rejoined the regiment the following day, bringing the unexpected news that the army was ordered back to the Potomac. Although the brigade continued to rotate regiments on picket on the roads around Haxall's for the next several days, the enemy showed no signs of advancing.[101]

By the 13th, the army's rear guard was composed of Pleasonton's reduced brigade of the 1st and 6th U.S. cavalries, and Benson's and Robertson's horse artillery batteries. With a picket line over fifteen miles wide to cover the army's retreat, the brigade was stretched thin. The men stood to horse the next two nights, anticipating Confederate probes that never came. On the 14th, Gen. Pleasonton appointed Lts. Spangler and Ward to his staff, depriving the regiment of two more officers. Cpt. Kautz protested the move in writing, but was overruled.[102] On the afternoon of the 15th, the tired men of the brigade finally began to withdraw. After a long, dusty march, they reached Charles City Crossroads on the 16th to find Gen. Sumner's corps still there. They spent the day there while the infantry continued their march eastward, rotating companies on picket to shield the withdrawal.[103]

The following afternoon, the brigade resumed their march. That morning, Cpt. Brisbin's Co. L and a company of the 1st U.S. Cavalry were detached to escort the brigade's trains to Williamsburg as the advance and rear guards respectively. The brigade departed their camp about 6:00 P.M. The pickets still out near Charles City Crossroads were driven in shortly after darkness fell and joined the brigade on the march. They reached the western bank of the Chickahominy at midnight and went into camp.[104]

They crossed the pontoon bridge at first light the next morning, the 18th, the 6th U.S. providing cover with one of the batteries while the engineers picked up the bridge. The regiment remained in camp here for the day as the rear guard, taking advantage of the opportunity to rest and clean men and mounts. The brigade trains reached Williamsburg that night.[105]

On the 19th, the regiment marched to Williamsburg, linking up with the forage left for them there by the brigade quartermaster, Lt. Spangler, under the supervision of Sgt. Carpenter of Co. L. After pausing several hours to feed the regiment, they resumed the march at 6:00 P.M., and reached Yorktown before midnight.[106]

The regiment remained in camp near Yorktown for the remainder of the month, await-ing their turn on transports back to Alexandria. The wait was a pleasant one. "While at Yorktown we lived in style," one soldier wrote home. "The farming people round about preferred Richmond shinplasters to our own currency. So we would buy up secesh notes at two or three cents on the dollars, get a pass, and obtain full price in produce at the houses round about. So we lived on chicken pot-pies, biscuit and butter, &c. for a few days."[107]

Brittle relations between Cpt. Kautz and Gen. Pleasonton did not improve. On the 23rd, Pleasonton observed Corp. Mulkay of Co. L mistreating a horse and ordered the man tied up. He sent a note to Cpt. Kautz ordering him to reduce "that man" to the ranks, and ordered his adjutant general, the 6th Cavalry's Lt. Isaac Ward, to follow up on the matter on the 26th. Kautz considered the matter too arbitrary and indefinite, as the offender was identified by neither rank, name nor company, and took no further action. When the adju-tant general inquired about the matter, Cpt. Kautz responded with a note stating the man had not been reduced, as army regulations recognized only two provisions for reducing non-commissioned officers to the ranks. One was by application of the company commander, and the other was by sentence of a court-martial.

While Kautz was technically correct in the matter and held the moral high ground, Gen. Pleasonton was not amused. He charged Kautz with "Disobedience of Orders and Highly Insubordinate Conduct" and had him arrested pending a court-martial on the charges.[108] Cpt. Sanders assumed command of the regiment.

On the 29th, the regiment moved down to the landing at Yorktown to load transports but found none available. They camped on the sandy beach that night and the next before embarking on the afternoon of the 31st.[109]

Among those few specially recommended by Gen. Pleasanton in his report for favorable notice were Cpts. Sanders and Gregg and Lts. Spangler and Ward, 6th U.S. Cavalry. Cpt. Kautz was the only regimental commander not specifically praised.[110] In closing his report of the operation of covering the withdrawal and the performance of very arduous duties as rear guard, Brig. Gen. Pleasanton said:

> I respectfully request of the General commanding that an appreciation of the gallant bearing of the men if this command may be evinced by permitting the following named regiments and batteries to inscribe on their colors "Malvern Hill, August 5th, 1862": the Sixth Regular Cav-alry, the Eighth Pennsylvania Cavalry, the Eighth Illinois Cavalry, Robertson's battery of horse artillery and Benson's battery of horse artillery. These were the only troops that were actually engaged with the enemy on that day; the only troops that followed in pursuit, and that were the last to leave the field when the army was withdrawn. They victoriously closed the fighting of the Army of the Potomac on the Peninsula.[111]

The regiment, in its first campaign, won the right to emblazon upon its standard the names of ten engagements. The gallantry and ability of its officers had marked many of them for higher commands, to the detriment of the regiment in some cases. Losses had begun to thin the ranks, but the men who rode the transports north were now veterans and no longer regulars in name only.

Chapter 4

To Maryland and Back

The regiment disembarked from its transports at Alexandria on the evening of September 2 and went into camp to the rear of Fort Albany. Cpt. William Sanders continued to lead the regiment. One of the men described him as "a large, red-faced man — a cross looking individual at all times. His cheek was disfigured by a large scar, and this added to his savage appearance when angered. A meerschaum pipe swung from his lips in an easy careless manner."[1] Cpt. Kautz never received his court-martial, accepting a promotion to colonel of volunteers and command of the 2nd Ohio Cavalry effective the same day he arrived at Fort Albany.[2]

On the 3rd, Cpt. Cram's Co. I and Cpt. Brisbin's Co. L were assigned to Gen. Sigel's corps and advanced to Dranesville. The squadron advanced from Dranesville on the 6th, losing saddler Robert McElroy, who was killed in a skirmish near the crossroads.[3]

On the morning of the 4th, the rest of the regiment marched to Falls Church on the Leesburg Turnpike. After a brief skirmish with enemy cavalry in which Pvt. William Boynton of Co. G was killed and several wounded, they were ordered to withdraw from Fall's Church and proceed to Tenallytown.[4]

They reached Tenallytown just before midnight, but remained only a few hours before continuing the march to Darnestown by the river road. They reached the town by noon, but stood to horse until evening before establishing camp on the Rockville Road. The regiment remained stationary here the next two days.[5]

On the 8th, the regiment marched to Dawsonville, and once again stood to horse the remainder of the day. The 1st Massachusetts Cavalry had the advance, and the regiment saw no action. The following morning the 6th U.S. Cavalry led the advance of the VI Corps to Poolesville and continued the march to Barnesville, where they bivouacked that night. Pvt. Davis later wrote of that evening: "[The regiment] turned off the road close to Barnesville and into a field that extended up a rather steep hill at the top of which they found several batteries of artillery parked for the night. Everything seemed to be quiet, and in a short time, the men kindled their fires, made themselves some strong coffee, roasted some pickled pork on a stick, fried their crackers in grease and sugar, unfastened, fed and groomed their horses, and spread out their blankets and laid down."[6]

Three miles to the north of Barnesville, Sugar Loaf Mountain rose to a commanding height, with clear views of the surrounding area. Gen. McClellan ordered Gen. Pleasonton to seize it, and Pleasonton in turn gave the mission to Cpt. Sanders.[7] Pleasonton assembled a demi-brigade under Sanders, consisting of the 6th U.S., 8th Pennsylvania, 8th Illinois and 3rd Indiana cavalries, as well as a section of Battery M, 2nd U.S. Artillery, commanded by Lt. Peter Hains.[8]

Unbeknownst to Sanders, the mountain was defended by two regiments of Col. Thomas Munford's brigade, specifically the 2nd and 12th Virginia cavalries and Chew's Battery. The Confederate force numbered about 500 men and four cannon and were in a strong position with rail barricades.[9] Cpt. Sanders' force left camp at 9:00 A.M., approaching the mountain on two roads. Arriving at the base of the mountain, Sanders posted pickets and supports for the artillery section before proceeding with the advance guard. Lt. Hains posted his guns on a knoll half a mile from the base of the mountain.

Squadrons of the 8th Pennsylvania and 8th Illinois dismounted and approached through the woods as skirmishers, while Hains' guns fired several shells at suspected enemy locations to draw fire. The Confederates were not fooled and held their fire.

Cpt. Sanders next led the flank squadron of the 6th U.S. Cavalry up the slope mounted in skirmish order. They quickly drove in the enemy's pickets, but had not proceeded far when Chew's cannons opened fire, followed immediately by a volley of musket fire from the Confederates. Fortunately for the bluecoats, the majority of the enemy fire was high, failing to account for shooting downhill. Outnumbered and outgunned, Sanders ordered the squadron back.

Now that he could see the enemy's location, Lt. Hains shelled the Confederates for half an hour with his two guns. Cpt. Sanders again attacked with the flank squadron, and was again repulsed. Realizing the position was strongly held and the terrain unsuitable for cavalry, he posted videttes and withdrew the majority of his force to Barnesville. The Confederates held their positions overnight, withdrawing the next morning before an advance by a brigade of infantry from VI Corps.

The regiment suffered only two casualties in the engagement, both from the flank squadron. Corp. William Alexander of Co. H was killed, and Pvt. Marshall Gibby of Co. B was wounded in the right arm.[10] Col. Munford's report makes no mention of the skirmish, mentioning only that his men held Sugar Loaf Mountain for three days.[11]

The regiment remained in place the next day, leaving camp on the evening of the 12th to advance on another night march via Greenfield Mills and Licksville to Middletown, Maryland. Arriving after midnight, they stood to horse until dawn before continuing their march to Jefferson. Cpt. Sanders reported his impression that Gen. Jackson was advancing on Harpers Ferry and was directed to push scouts in that direction.[12] Also on the 13th, Cpt. Cram's squadron scouted toward Petersville, driving the enemy from the town after a brief skirmish with no losses.[13]

The regiment's headquarters remained stationary near Jefferson for the next week, extending patrols to protect the VI Corps' flank and keeping the line of communication open with Washington. This involved constant patrols by the companies. They had very little involvement in trying to catch Stuart on his second ride around the Army of the Potomac, only receiving an order to proceed to near Gettysburg, which was quickly rescinded when it was discovered that he had escaped again. They heard the sounds of battle from the engagements at Harpers Ferry, South Mountain and Antietam, but saw no action.[14]

This did not mean their service during the campaign so far had been unappreciated, as VI Corps commander Gen. Franklin noted in his report on the battle: "Captain W.P. Sanders, Sixth Cavalry, was temporarily on my staff during the action, and rendered efficient service. I also commend him to the notice of the commanding general on account of the able manner in which the cavalry under his command guarded and watched the country on the left and front of Jefferson, and filled up the void left by the advance of the infantry column."[15] Gen. Pleasonton's report also praised Sanders, as well as Cpts. Cram and Hays and Lts. Coats, Ward and Spangler.[16]

On the 20th, the regiment was ordered to rejoin the main part of the army at Antietam. They found marks of the battle frequently along the march and saw burial parties still working as they approached the battlefield proper. They camped on the north bank of the river, near where the army's right wing had fought, for the next three days.[17]

Although the troops were stationary, these were busy days. The regiment was notified of several promotions on the 22nd, which resulted in a number of personnel moves. The interviews with Cpt. Kautz on the peninsula had borne fruit at last, as six of the regiment's sergeants received appointments as lieutenants. The promotions were effective July 17, but word didn't reach the regiments until September.

Sgt. Maj. Tullius Tupper was promoted and replaced by Sgt. Martin Armstrong of Co. M as regimental sergeant major.[18] Regimental quartermaster sergeant John Rousseau was replaced by Pvt. Edward Swift of Co. E.[19] First Sergeant Nicholas Nolan served in the artillery and 2nd Dragoons before he was assigned to Co. B in the 6th Cavalry the year before.[20] Similarly, First Sergeant John Irwin served in the 4th U.S. Cavalry before reenlisting into Co. E, 6th Cavalry, in May 1862.[21] L. Henry Carpenter of Co. L was a Philadelphia blueblood who had enlisted in the regiment the previous year in hopes of receiving a commission. He had served in Cos. C and L, earning the rank of sergeant prior to joining the regiment on the peninsula in June.[22]

On the 23rd, the rest of the regiment's companies were issued Sharps carbines. Not only was this good for morale, but it also greatly decreased the burden on the flank squadron and Co. L to constantly provide the advance guard and skirmishers for the regiment.[23] One pleased soldier wrote to his hometown newspaper: "Our Regiment is now fully equipped; there were a few companies which had not received their carbines until to-day, and we have been out on drill to see who were the best marksmen."[24]

The following day the regiment marched a short distance south to Knoxville, Maryland, two miles down the Potomac from Harpers Ferry, and established a more permanent camp. Replacement clothing and equipment were issued, and remounts arrived almost daily.[25] The respite was brief, however. Early on the morning of the 24th, the 5th and 6th U.S. cavalries and Robertson's Batteries B and L, 2nd U.S. Artillery, conducted a reconnaissance down the Charlestown Road from Harpers Ferry to drive in the pickets in front of Gen. Sumner's corps and determine the nearest force of Confederates. The enemy pickets retired before the column without firing until near Charlestown itself. Here their resistance stiffened, with several cannon firing in support. Their mission accomplished, the Union soldiers returned to their camp.

On the 27th, one squadron was sent across Loudon Heights to Hillsboro. The following day the regiment was sent on a second reconnaissance to Charlestown, where five prisoners were captured. The next day they captured three more prisoners at Hillsboro.[26]

Two days later, the 6th U.S. Cavalry and Robertson's Battery led Brig. Gen. Nathan Kimball's infantry brigade and another artillery battery on a reconnaissance in force from Harpers Ferry to Leesburg. The force conducted a rapid march over difficult terrain, covering 43 miles in as many hours with no significant enemy contact. The regiment, serving as the advance guard for the brigade, captured six enemy pickets during the march and suffered no casualties.[27]

On October 6th, the regiment ventured to Charlestown again, this time engaging in a sharp skirmish outside the town. Corp. John H. Erb of Co. D was killed in the skirmish, and Bugler John Sullivan captured.[28] In the same skirmish, Cpt. Sanders sent Co. F as skirmishers to flank the enemy on the left. After a rapid gallop across some difficult terrain, they emerged onto a road on the enemy's flank. Rounding a turn, they surprised a Con-

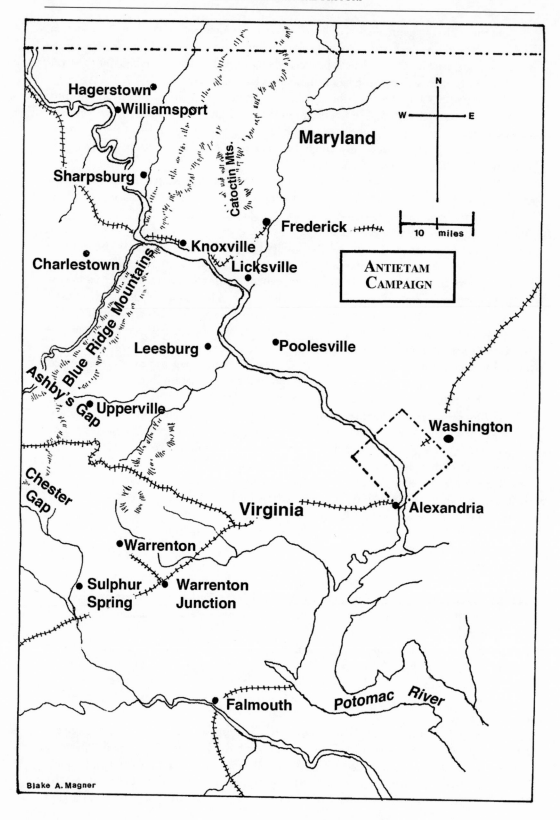

Blake A. Magner

federate lieutenant who had been checking his pickets. Pvt. August Poppenhager brought his cocked carbine to bear upon the unfortunate lieutenant, who promptly surrendered. As Pvt. Poppenhager conducted his prisoner to the rear, they encountered Lt. Hancock McLean marching at the head of the reserve. The Confederate asked Lt. McLean for an escort of equal rank, asserting that this was one of the courtesies of war. McLean denied the request, remarking that in his estimation a private in the Union army was of higher rank than any officer in the Confederate service.[29]

On October 16, Gen. Winfield Hancock led his division on a reconnaissance from Harpers Ferry to Charlestown. His advance guard was composed of the 2nd, 5th and 6th cavalries, under the command of Maj. Charles Whiting. According to Maj. Whiting's report, the regiment numbered only 300 men for the mission, but was still larger than the other two regiments combined.[30] The advance guard drove in the Confederate pickets before the town and pursued, to discover additional enemy forces with cannons on the high ground in front of the town. This force was Col. Munford's Confederate cavalry brigade again, specifically the 12th Virginia Cavalry and the guns of Chew's Battery.[31]

Chew's Battery opened fire on the advance, forcing the Union batteries to deploy and return fire. The cavalry dismounted to the front and flanks as skirmishers while waiting for the infantry to come up. According to Col. Munford's report, the Union advance was held up for four hours, and his force retired only after his artillery exhausted its ammunition.[32]

Gen. Hancock's force seized the town, capturing and paroling a hospital containing about 100 sick and convalescing Confederate officers and men. The infantry occupied the town overnight, while the cavalry picketed the roads into the town. The next afternoon they returned to camp. The regiment suffered no losses.[33]

The cavalry was again reorganized on October 21, with the regiment now assigned to Gen. Pleasonton's command, with the 3rd Indiana, 8th Illinois, 8th New York and 8th Pennsylvania.[34]

On October 24, the Army of the Potomac issued an order which would significantly affect all of the regular regiments in the army. General Orders No. 167 permitted members of volunteer units to enlist in regular army regiments for the remainder of their enlistment.[35] To the short-handed regular regiments depleted by constant campaigning, this order was a godsend. The cavalry regiments assigned recruiting officers, and a brisk trade in new soldiers was conducted from the camp at Knoxville. Lt. Claflin and Lt. Coats recruited for the 6th U.S. Cavalry. "This new law about recruits from volunteers is in full force and we are receiving about 80 recruits a day. We will soon fill the regiment," wrote Lt. Carpenter.[36]

Volunteers from infantry units, particularly those hard hit during the most recent battle, flocked to what they perceived as easier duty in the cavalry and artillery. The 14th Indiana Infantry provided 17 men to the 6th Cavalry, eleven from its Co. D alone. The 3rd Wisconsin Infantry provided another 19. Other regiments with large numbers of "defectors" included the 28th and 45th Pennsylvania infantries. In all, the regiment received nearly 500 replacements from this order over the course of the next month.[37]

As a result, there were finally enough men to officially organize Co. C on October 25, 1862, at Knoxville. Unfortunately, they were of little immediate use, as they had to be mounted and trained before they would be ready for service. The more enterprising among them perhaps had thought of this, since their enlistment period was still ticking away. So the regiment was at full strength with all twelve companies for only a day. When the regiment departed the next day, the new recruits were transported to Washington by train under the command of Lt. Claflin.[38]

On the morning of the 26th, the regiment marched from camp with three days' rations as part of the brigade column. They marched down the Potomac to Lovettsville, where Co. H was detached for duty at brigade headquarters.[39] "From this time until November 1 the brigade was occupied in scouting the country to Leesburg, Aldie, Middleburg, Philomont, and in gaining information of the enemy's movements," Gen. Pleasonton wrote later in his report.[40]

The next day the brigade caught up to the Confederates at Union. The regiment lost four soldiers wounded in stiff fighting that lasted until after dark. In stiff fighting the next day, B Co. lost two more wounded, Sgt. William Lepper in the left arm and Pvt. William H. Murray in the right hand.[41]

The regiment was sent with the 8th Pennsylvania to support an attack by Col. Averell's 1st Brigade on November 4, but saw no action. The same day, Cpt. Sanders, frustrated over the continued absence of officers and men from the regiment, submitted a letter to the Army of the Potomac's adjutant general.

> Headquarters 6th Cavalry,
> Camp at Upperville, Virginia, November 4th, 1862.
> GENERAL:— I have the honor to request that, in justice to my regiment, the 6th U.S. Cavalry be relieved from duty with General Pleasanton's brigade.
> General Pleasanton now has three officers from my regiment on his staff, one company and its officers as provost marshal, and almost every detail of men is made from this regiment. I am willing to go on any duty where the regiment will be justly treated. I have also the honor to request that some of the officers and men on duty at brigade headquarters be relieved.
> Very respectfully,
>   Your obedient servant,
>   W.P. Sanders,
> Captain, 6th U.S. Cavalry, Commanding[42]

No action was taken; the regiment remained under Gen. Pleasonton's command, and no soldiers or officers were returned to the regiment during the remainder of the campaign.

On the 5th, Pleasonton's 2nd Brigade advanced through Markham to Barbour's Crossroads and fought a large force of Confederate cavalry with artillery. It was Gen. Stuart with Hampton's and Fitzhugh Lee's brigades. Col. Gregg was sent with the 6th U.S. and 8th Pennsylvania to flank the enemy position on the left. Lt. Carpenter wrote of the battle:

> About noon we encountered the enemy in force near Barby's [sic] Cross Roads. The squadron I am in and that is commanded by Capt. Brisbin were deployed as skirmishers and ordered to advance. We did so and in a few minutes were in the midst of a heavy fire from the rebel infantry skirmishers who were opposed to us. Our boys went into it with a right good will and Nolan's Company B and mine on the right together with McQuiston's and Brisbin's drove the rebels from their position in the woods.[43]

The move was successful, forcing the enemy guns to withdraw. Stuart's brigades covered their withdrawal toward Chester Gap. The regiment suffered three soldiers wounded.[44]

Pleasonton was unable to advance through Chester Gap, Stuart being supported there by Jackson's Corps, and proceeded instead toward Orleans. The regiment advanced to Amissville on the 7th and Newby's Crossroads on the 8th, engaged each day in light skirmishing with enemy cavalry but suffering no losses. While on picket near Little Washington, the regiment captured a wagon, 12 horses and two prisoners from the 5th Virginia Cavalry near Newby's Crossroads.[45]

The next day, the brigade occupied a position at Corbin's Crossroads. That night, Lt.

Balder's squadron crept inside the Confederate lines toward Culpeper, capturing a captain of the 4th Virginia Cavalry, 5 pickets and a wagon of forage.[46] The advance on Culpeper was ordered stopped on November 10, the same day Gen. Burnside assumed command of the Army of the Potomac from Gen. McClellan. The regiment moved to the vicinity of Warrenton. Cpt. Sanders fell ill and received a 30-day leave of absence to go to Kentucky. Cpt. Brisbin assumed command of the regiment as the senior officer present.[47]

The regiment marched six or seven miles toward Sulphur Springs and established pickets along the river for several miles on the 16th. A heavy rainstorm hit them the first night on picket, followed the season's first snowstorm the next day. A probe toward the Rappahannock by two squadrons on the 17th made contact with Confederate infantry, but they escaped without loss.[48]

The rest of the regiment, meanwhile, shifted their camp into a thick pine forest nearby. Those companies not on the picket line built fires of fence rails, making coffee and roasting their rations on sticks. They made their beds on pine boughs.[49]

The Confederates advanced from the river on the 18th, driving in the pickets and shelling the camp. Lt. Hamilton's section of Pennington's Battery deployed in response, with the regiment in support. After a brief artillery duel, the Union forces withdrew to the east.[50]

The march toward Falmouth continued on the 19th. The regiment camped that evening in a dense pine forest near Hartwood Church, an area soon to become very familiar to them.[51]

A Detail Complete

The regiment's battle at Malvern Hill in August had cost Battery M, 2nd U.S. Artillery, the loss of its commander, Cpt. Henry Benson, and numerous others in the unit. Lt. Pennington, now commanding the battery, requested through Gen. Pleasonton a detail of 10 men from the 6th U.S. Cavalry to help man his guns. This request was granted, and a detail under Pvt. George Platt served with the battery throughout the entire Maryland Campaign, participating in every engagement with the battery. As the battery reached the vicinity of the Rappahannock at the end of the campaign, the men requested to return to their regiment. Platt, as their spokesman, approached Lt. Pennington on the matter and was told that since Gen. Pleasonton had ordered them assigned to the battery, only he could release them. Undeterred, Pvt. Platt walked the quarter mile to brigade headquarters. Finding the general outside his tent on a camp stool, he saluted and asked that he and his comrades be returned to their regiment. After a brief discussion, the general agreed to order their release.

Lt. Pennington rode to headquarters in person to appeal the order but was overruled. Returning to the battery, he ordered the men relieved so they could return to their regiment. After Platt lined up the men to bid Lt. Pennington farewell, the lieutenant toasted their health and sent them on their way.[52]

The regiment's campaign from the Potomac through Maryland to the Rappahannock was made up of almost constant fighting and marching, during day and night, and in sunshine, rain, and bitter cold and snow. On the whole, the men bore up well; they had by this time become enured to the hardships and dangers of campaign life.[53]

Gen. Pleasonton apparently did not hold a grudge against Cpt. Sanders for his letter, praising him in his official report for "distinguished gallantry and good conduct throughout the campaign." Lts. Coats, Kerin, Spangler, Wade and Ward were recognized by name as well.[54]

The muster rolls for the end of November 1862 show only 13 officers and 444 enlisted men present for duty. This number did not include the volunteer recruits still training in Washington. Cpt. Brisbin commanded the regiment, and lieutenants every squadron and company. Three companies were without officers altogether, and the year's campaigning was not yet over.[55]

Chapter 5

On the Rappahannock

On November 20, the regiment arrived near Falmouth and went into camp. They found Gen. Sumner's II Corps occupying the country on the north side of the Rappahannock, while the Confederates covered the heights on the other side. Lying between them on the broad bottoms south of the river was the town of Fredericksburg. Cos. B and E were immediately detached for escort duty with Gen. Sumner. With Co. H still detached on provost duty for the cavalry division and Co. C in Washington, the regiment was short a third of its companies.[1]

Like Cpt. Kautz a few months earlier, Cpt. Sanders received an appointment as colonel of volunteers. He was soon busy training his new regiment, the 5th Kentucky Cavalry, in its home state. Cpt. Brisbin assumed command, as Cpt. Cram had been absent sick in Washington for quite some time.[2] They established their initial camp near the mouth of the Potomac, seven miles from Falmouth. Lt. Madden's squadron marched back to Hartwood on the 24th, ordered to picket Richards and United States fords.

The picket posts were a long march from camp. Companies going on picket first marched to Falmouth, then proceeded ten miles toward Warrenton on the Warrenton and Falmouth Turnpike. The "town" of Hartwood consisted of an old brick church and "two or three miserable tumbled down shanties" at the intersection of the road to the fords and the turnpike. This marked the right flank of the Army of the Potomac, manned at the time by two squadrons of the 3rd Pennsylvania Cavalry. Turning left, the road to the fords ran three miles farther west through dense woods past Hartwood before it forked to the right and left toward the fords. The total distance from camp to picket was over sixteen miles.[3]

When Madden's men reached the fords, they found Confederate pickets guarding the opposite bank, but neither side appeared inclined to initiate hostilities. An uneasy truce was soon mutually agreed on.[4]

Squadrons, commanded by lieutenants, rotated duty at the fords every two days. The regiment shifted its camp on the 24th to Belle Plain to shorten the march to the fords. Within a few days, the regiment's trains arrived with their tents, and rations and forage became abundant as the army began to concentrate around Falmouth.[5]

Officer shortages continued to be a problem for the regiment. As Lt. Carpenter noted in a letter, "We feel very much the absence of officers in the Sixth. Not over 11 or 12 are on duty with the regiment and Captain Brisbin nearly the junior Captain is in command. Genl. Pleasonton alone has 4 officers belonging to the 6th on his staff. 5 or 6 Captains are Colonels of volunteers. Emory is a Brigadier General. The remainder are off on leave of absence for one reason or another."[6] The situation worsened the following day, when Gen. Pleasonton placed Cpt. Brisbin under arrest for an unknown offense. Lt. James Wade assumed command. Since the regiment had received no answer to Cpt. Sanders' letter of the 4th in the intervening three weeks, he again addressed the issue of the regiment's detachments in a letter to headquarters: "Previous to making a similar request to that of Captain Sanders, I would state that, in my opinion and that of every officer of the regiment, more than a fair portion of duty is assigned it. I am now compelled to send my companies sixteen miles on picket and relieve them myself. On account of the numerous heavy details ordered by your office from the 6th Cavalry, it is impossible for me, with the limited number of men left, to do the full duty of a regiment." As with Sanders' letter, there was neither response nor relief from the assigned duties from Gen. Pleasonton's headquarters.[7]

Lt. Carpenter relieved Lt. Madden at the fords on November 26. Not trusting the vigilance of the unit to his rear, he posted videttes to the north of his position on the road leading to the ford as well at both fords. He established his reserve at the intersection where the road branched toward the two fords.[8] It was well that he did so. The next evening, Confederate Gen. Wade Hampton crossed the Rappahannock with a force of cavalry at Kelly's Mill and marched east. He surprised and captured both squadrons of the 3rd Pennsylvania at Hartwood, proceeding to within eight miles of Falmouth. Hampered by his large number of prisoners, he was forced to turn back toward his own lines before daylight. He recrossed the Rappahannock at Ely's Ford, seven miles upstream from Carpenter's men at Richards. He said in his report, "A part of my plan was to have cut of the force at Richard's Ferry, but though I got completely in their rear, I found my number so reduced that I was forced reluctantly to abandon my design. The Sixth Regiment Regulars was on post there, and I had to leave them for another time."[9]

Carpenter was surprised to hear of the attack the next evening, as his troops had seen no sign of Confederates other than their counterparts across the ford. He was relieved the next day by a squadron under Lt. McQuiston with no further incident.

On December 1st, Lt. Claflin arrived in camp with his company and the recruits from Washington. His Co. C were all mounted on black horses. The recruits were quickly divided among the companies, and drilled at every opportunity.[10] Around noon on the same day, tragedy struck the regiment. A gunshot was heard, following by a multitude of shouts. Lt. McQuiston's squadron had just returned to camp from the picket line. After unsaddling their horses, two soldiers of Co. K, Pvts. David A. Thoburn and Carl Papke, began horseplaying and chasing one another around their tent. Papke saw a carbine leaning against a tree and grabbed it as he went by. Wheeling, he brought it to his shoulder, aimed at his pursuer and fired. Much to his surprise, it fired, striking Pvt. Thoburn in the heart and killing him instantly.[11]

"As usual in such cases the gun was not supposed to be loaded," McQuiston recalled later. The Sharps carbines were breechloaders and were kept unloaded in camp to minimize the chances of an accidental discharge. Papke was arrested on the spot, and Lt. Wade conducted an inquiry which resulted in the acquittal of Papke of any intentional wrongdoing. He was released and returned to duty.[12] Although Papke was absolved of responsibility, Sgt. Maj. Armstrong was not. Apparently ensuring the carbines of companies returning from picket were unloaded immediately upon arriving in the camp was one of the sergeant major's responsibilities, for he was reduced back to sergeant in Co. M the same day. Sgt. Hercules G. Carroll was appointed in his place.[13]

The regiment shifted its camp closer to Falmouth on December 7, just east of the road from Belle Plain to Falmouth and about four miles from Gen. Burnsides' headquarters. The previous camp did not have sufficient room for the regiment after the addition of the recruits from Washington. The same day, they were ordered to conduct drills twice a day when in camp, mounted in the morning and dismounted in the afternoon, in order to train the recruits as fast as possible. The regiment was also ordered to conduct daily drills as skirmishers[14]: "I drilled 'L' company today as Captain Brisbin still remains under arrest and there is no one to attend to his company. I was quite pleased with the facility the new men acquired for drill. These men have as a general thing served already over a year in the Volunteer service, and have acquired many of the habits and ideas of old soldiers. Teaching them merely the cavalry tactics will be easy enough."[15]

On the morning of December 11, the regiment was ordered to march to Falmouth with three days' rations. They halted and dismounted in a close column of squadrons to the rear of Gen. Sumner's headquarters, a large mansion known as the Lacy House on a hill overlooking the town and valley. The 8th Pennsylvania Cavalry formed to their left with a similar task. Ostensibly positioned to support the batteries atop the hill, the two regiments provided little support, as there were no Confederates on the north side of the river. They observed artillery shelling of Confederate positions in the town and the laying of the first pontoon bridge across the river before returning to camp that evening.[16]

The following morning they returned to the same position. The cannonade commenced just after dawn despite the foggy morning; long lines of infantry crossed the bridge under its cover. The regiment held its position near the guns, undisturbed but for an occasional artillery shell.[17]

About 3:00 P.M., the 2nd Squadron was ordered across the river to perform a reconnaissance of the enemy lines. Accordingly, Lt. Wade led his Co. K and Lt. Sewell Brown and his Co. D across the pontoon bridge and through the town. Reaching the field behind the town, they closed with the Confederate lines until they opened fire with their cannons. He then turned to the right and proceeded rapidly down the line to develop the situation. As the enemy fire increased, he quickly turned back into the town and withdrew in good order to report to Gen. Sumner at headquarters. The squadron resumed its position with the regiment following Lt. Wade's report, having suffered no losses.[18]

Their reconnaissance was noted by the infantry crossing the bridges. Shortly before Wade's advance, enemy shells had routed the 12th New Hampshire Infantry as they attempted to cross. An observing Massachusetts soldier noted that despite the falling artillery shells, the cavalrymen crossed "in perfect order," and that "the contrast was magnificent" compared to the unfortunate New Hampshire troops.[19]

Wade's squadron may have been selected by Gen. Sumner's chief of staff, Lt. Col. Joseph H. Taylor, former captain of Co. F, or one of his aides, Cpt. Audenried, the former adjutant.[20] Just before dark, the regiment mounted and moved about a mile to the north of Sumner's headquarters, where they camped for the night.

The next morning, the 13th, they resumed their position at dawn, supporting the Union batteries as the battle raged across the river. One officer wrote to his parents:

> I stand on the hill at Sumner's headquarters directly opposite the town of Fredericksburg, at a very considerable elevation and can see everything very distinctly. After a little the enemy were driven from the town and then the battle began in earnest at the base of the 1st line of heights. The roar of cannon and the rattle of musketry are terrific, and mingled with the crash of falling walls in the town. Genl. Burnside, Sumner and Hooker are all present on the portico of the house in which Sumner had his headquarters.[21]

A soldier noted, "The only part we took in the affair was standing in line each day, on a bluff opposite, near Falmouth, in full view, but out of range. It was a reckless waste of life. Our whole army could not have taken them."[22] At nightfall they returned to the previous night's camp.

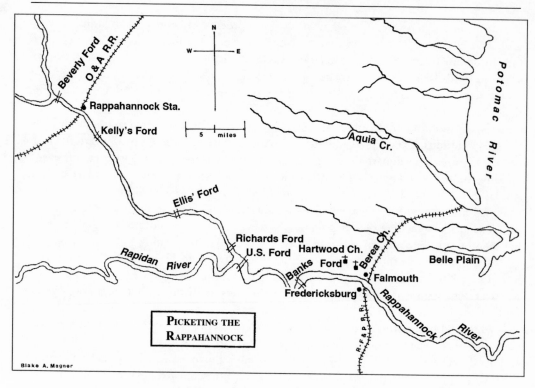

PICKETING THE
RAPPAHANNOCK

Blake A. Magner

The bulk of the regiment spent the 14th as they had the previous several days. In the afternoon, Lt. Carpenter and his company were detailed as provost guard and were ordered to allow no troops to cross the pontoon bridge. Seizing the opportunity to cross the bridge into town, he noted, "Every house is literally riddled with bullets and torn by cannon balls. The two fine church steeples are nearly ruined by shot and shell." The following morning the men rejoined the regiment in camp.[23] After several days of fruitless patrolling on the army's right flank in case Confederate cavalry crossed the river on another raid, the regiment occupied its old camp north of Falmouth.[24]

In late December, Cpt. George Cram returned from a leave of absence for illness to assume command of the regiment. One of the troopers described him as "a curious, capricious man, seeming to almost delight when the men most feared him." The same trooper continues his explanation:

A little hatred towards him was developed throughout the entire regiment. Whenever a soldier had occasion to speak of him, his name was invariably coupled with uncomplimentary phrases. The universal desire was often thus briefly expressed, except for the religious:
"Damn Cram!"
Thus religious wore off the round edge of a curse:
"Darn Cram!"
While the young men from the country, who still retained a wholesome fear of profanity, contended themselves with:
"Gol darn Cram!"[25]

While Cram was definitely an unpopular officer, it must be noted that Beriah Owen, a prolific correspondent, notes nothing derogatory about Cram in any of his letters, despite being assigned to Cram's company.

The shortage of officers in the regiment was a growing concern, despite the end of active campaigning. The colonel, lieutenant colonel, and all three majors were assigned away from the regiment. Similarly, only Cram and Brisbin remained of the regiment's twelve captains, and both of them had been civilian appointments the year before. Eight lieutenants were also detached from duty with the regiment. Although most of the lieutenants at this point had been promoted from within the ranks and were veterans themselves, the shortage of officers left the regiment with only a shell of its assigned leadership.[26]

Shortly after Cpt. Cram assumed command, he shifted the regiment's camp, as it became apparent there would be no more campaigning that winter. Six of the regiment's companies were once again on picket at Richards and United States fords at the time. As Lt. Carpenter described the move, "We removed our camp the day before yesterday about 200 yards to a spot well wooded and convenient for water. Captain Cram now commands the regiment and he is somewhat of a martinet. The whole force has been turned out to clear away all the brush and everything except the large timber. All the tents are exactly in a line. Officers are required to pitch their tents precisely 30 paces in rear of their command and in a line. Commanding officer has his marquis 120 paces in rear to an inch." Unpopular or not, the shift gave the men a good location to establish their winter camp. Indeed, Carpenter noted within days of his previous comments that "our camp is getting to be more and more attractive in its appearance. Some officers from the 1st Dragoons which were here today pronounced it to be the finest camp in the Army of the Potomac, and others have said the same thing so we feel quite proud of it ourselves."[27] Measures were undertaken to assure the comfort of both men and mounts when they were fortunate enough to remain in camp.

About a dozen men lived in each Sibley tent. They elevated their tents a couple of feet from the ground to increase headroom, constructing short walls for the sides from split logs with the round side facing out. Camp kettles were suspended from tripods and turned into stoves by punching holes in the bottom to create a draft for the fire. These field expedient stoves tended to make the tents smoky, despite an opening at the top of the tent for the smoke to escape. Those without camp kettles built a small fire on a raised platform of dirt. While the elevation for draft assisted the fire, it was of no help keeping feet warm. Soldiers were forced to either elevate one foot and then the other, or prop them both up on a rock or a box.[28]

Similar care was taken with the stables. Each company densely packed pine brush around their stables to break the cold winds, and roofs were constructed of log poles with more pine brush used as thatch to protect them from rain and snow. Extended periods of exposure and poor forage on picket was hard on the regiment's mounts. When a horse became ill, it was sent to a separate corral to be treated by the regiment's enlisted veterinary surgeon.[29]

Meeting the demands of picket duty was a constant challenge for the regiment. Six companies were tasked with securing Richards and U.S. Fords for a week at a time. Three companies were detached for service with Gen. Sumner's and Gen. Pleasonton's headquarters, leaving only three companies in camp to escort provisions to those on picket and perform other duties necessary to maintaining their camp. Additionally, they received other tasks. In late January, for example, they were assigned to keep all of the bridges in repair along a stretch of road near the river.[30]

A rotation at the fords was quickly established within the brigade. The 6th U.S. Cavalry would relieve squadrons of the 8th Pennsylvania at their posts, then be relieved in turn by the 6th New York six days later. A grand reserve of four companies would remain near Berea

Church, with one company picketing each of the fords and their approaches. They were opposed in early January by the 1st South Carolina Cavalry at Richards Ford and the 4th Virginia Cavalry at U.S. Ford.[31]

There was some excitement for the regiment in mid–January, with preparations for artillery positions and a planned pontoon bridge at U.S. Ford for an advance by the army, but heavy rains and miserable road conditions halted Gen. Burnside's "mud march" before it was well underway. It may have been just as well that the weather intervened. The regiment had observed and reported increased Confederate activity across the ford, as the cavalry pickets were replaced with infantry regiments and eventually an entire brigade. After the ill-fated march, things remained quiet for the pickets until late February.[32]

Life was difficult for those on picket that winter. The companies at the fords were forbidden to unsaddle their horses, and the majority of the men were expected to remain mounted. Posts were manned for two hours on and four hours in the picket reserve. While on post, the soldiers were required to be mounted with their carbine or revolver in hand and resting on their thighs. At the picket reserve, men could dismount, sleep and build small fires, but horses remained saddled and men clothed to be ready for action on short notice.[33]

Although fires were permitted in the grand reserve, the men had no tents. Horses could be unsaddled and brushed here, tied to exposed picket lines. Forage was very poor on those occasions when the regiment's wagons couldn't reach them because of road conditions. The men were able to find and slaughter animals from nearby farms when this happened, after compensating the owners, but their horses were reduced to eating bark and limbs from trees.[34]

At times, picket duty was preferable to life in camp, despite its hardships. The men's camp duties were very similar to those experienced the previous year at Bladensburg and Camp East of the Capitol. In addition to the normal ennui of camp details, drill and training continued as the regiment's leaders sought to prepare the fall's volunteer recruits for the rigors of the upcoming campaign.[35]

"We are drilling twice a day now and have been doing so for the last two weeks," an officer wrote home in January. "The men have been chiefly exercised in the manual of arms, both carbine and sabre and other minutiae of the dismounted drill. All of this is intended to perfect our recruits as much as possible during the leisure that we have and as the calm sometimes proceeds a storm, it is well that we should be prepared."[36] Strangely, equipment became a problem once again, as the regiment sought arms for the hundreds of recruits it received during the fall. Cpt. Cram at one point even obtained excess sabers and revolvers from Pennington's battery to arm some of his troops.[37]

One point of enjoyment in the camp was the presence of the regiment's band. The soldiers from Mount Joy were a source of pride and enjoyment to the regiment. "No one can tell without having experienced it how enlivening to the spirits is the effect of music," wrote one trooper. "Every morning and evening where it is at all possible some excellent music is discoursed in the Sixth and all the volunteers near envy us not a little in the possession of our privilege.[38]

In the evenings between "retreat" and "tattoo," the men's time was their own. Just as during the previous winter, time was spent as best suited the casts of the soldiers. Some played poker, while more religious soldiers played checkers or other games. Others wrote letters, discussed the day's experiences, or speculated about the probable duties of the next day. Another popular pastime was playing practical jokes on one another. These generally revolved around tormenting someone unwise enough to fall asleep before his fellows near the fire.[39]

In late February, the regiment's picket posts were changed from the army's right flank to its left. Their new posts were near Corbin's Neck, on the lower Rappahannock below Fredericksburg.[40] The primary changes the troopers noticed were in their counterparts across the river. No longer opposed by cavalry units, they faced the bedraggled "foot cavalry" of Gen. Jackson's corps. "The river here is narrow and deep, and it is interesting to sit on our horses and watch the movements of the rebels, in plain sight. They are all infantry — not a cavalry picket have I seen since we have been stationed here," one of the pickets wrote.[41]

The shift was part of a larger reorganization in the Army of the Potomac. After succeeding Gen. Burnside in command of the army, Gen. Joseph Hooker reorganized its cavalry into a cavalry corps. One of the results was that the 6th U.S. Cavalry was moved from the 2nd Brigade to the Regular Reserve Cavalry Brigade, or "Reserve Brigade" as it soon became known. The brigade was a consolidation of the four regular cavalry regiments and, a short time later, the 6th Pennsylvania Cavalry.[42]

As the senior regular officer present, Cpt. Cram initially received command of the new brigade, but he was replaced the following month by the arrival of Brig. Gen. John Buford. Buford, formerly the army's chief of cavalry on Hooker's staff, requested to command the Reserve Brigade under this reorganization. Cpt. Cram returned to command of the regiment, commanded by Cpt. Brisbin in his absence.[43]

Command of the new corps was initially given to Brig. Gen. George Stoneman, who had been in charge of the army's advance guard during the Peninsula campaign. "He is a splendid officer," one soldier wrote home, adding of the change, "You have probably heard of the organization of all the Cavalry into one Corps, commanded by General Stoneman. It is one of the best changes Hooker has made. You may look for 'big doings' from this branch of service when the army moves again, and especially from the 6th."[44]

As the weather finally began to improve, preparations intensified for the spring campaign. Gen. Stoneman was determined to take the fight to the Confederate cavalry. In order to do so, they needed a more aggressive spirit. A successful skirmish between Brig. Gen. Averell and Fitzhugh Lee's Confederate cavalry brigade near Kelly's Ford in mid–March raised expectations. Averell's force went head to head with the Confederates for several hours, and withdrew to the river at the end of the skirmish under no pressure.

The other thing his force needed was to increase its speed on the march. Stuart's cavalry had been able to easily evade its Union counterparts, partly because the Confederates were not tied to wagon trains. Accordingly, orders were issued to turn in all regimental wagons in the Cavalry Corps other than ambulances and replace them with mules. A sound idea in theory, the plan ignored practicalities such as the availability of trained mules and pack saddles for the trains or troopers trained in handling them. As one soldier commented, "How the arrangement will work remains to be seen. The plan does not strike me favorably. I shall wait to see how a bale of 350 lbs. of hay or a barrel of pork or sugar is to be packed on a mule."[45]

The winter on the Rappahannock had taken its toll on all the Union cavalry, including the 6th U.S. Cavalry. During the winter camp, 13 men died of disease, one died from an accidental gunshot, 17 deserted, and 59 were discharged for disability. Five recruits from volunteer units the previous fall were returned to their regiments for various reasons. One of them, Sgt. Benjamin Whiteside of Co. I, received a commission as a lieutenant in the 105th New York Infantry. In all, the regiment lost 96 men over the winter, nearly 10 percent of its assigned strength.[46] Those who remained, however, had been hardened in the forge of the tough winter duty. The previous spring they had left their camp as well-drilled but inexperienced soldiers. This spring they took the field as veterans. The change in attitude was contagious throughout the Cavalry Corps. This campaign they would take the fight to the enemy.

Chapter 6

Stoneman's Raid

President Lincoln visited the Army of the Potomac in early April, prior to the start of the spring's campaign. A series of reviews were held over several days for him to see all of the army's formations. He reviewed the Cavalry Corps on April 6, 1863, at the Sthreshley family farm known as Grafton. The Reserve Brigade was third in the procession, following the Second and First divisions, with Brig. Gen. Buford at their head. The brigade column was organized by seniority, so the 6th U.S. Cavalry was next to last, just in front of the 6th Pennsylvania Cavalry.[1]

Just a few days later, on the 11th, Cavalry Corps headquarters issued orders to be ready to move on Monday, the 13th. Accordingly, they marched forth with three days' rations and forage, reaching the familiar location of Hartwood Church that evening. The mule train was organized with six for each company, two for the hospital and two for the band.[2] They reached Kelly's Ford the following day and Rappahannock Station on the 15th. Heavy rains had started on the 14th and continued for a week, preventing fording of the Rappahannock. The regiment marched that night to Deep Run, finding it too deep to ford. Waiting until daylight to build a raft, they ferried over their supplies and swam the mules and horses across with no significant losses. They then marched to Morrisville, where they guarded the brigade's trains for the next several days.[3]

It did not take long for word of their eventual destination, or at least speculation, to reach the enlisted men. One soldier wrote home on the 20th: "We have just got orders to provide ourselves with six days rations and forage — every horse that is not able to march day and night for six days to be left — to go, report says on a scout down in the region of Gordonsville." The letter was published in the local paper on the 30th, during the raid.[4]

On the 22nd, the regiment moved to Bealeton Station on the Orange, Alexandria and Manassas Railroad, and proceeded the following day to Warrenton Junction. They rejoined the rest of the brigade at Hartwood Church on the 24th and waited with them for the river level to drop.[5]

After standing to horse in the rain for most of the previous night, the column finally crossed the Rappahannock at Kelly's Ford on the 29th. It was a difficult crossing due to the rains, and Kelly's wasn't one of the easier fords to cross at the best of times. The command swam their heavily laden mounts across, losing only a few of the mules. Each trooper carried thirty pounds of grain on his horse, and the packs on the mules averaged two hundred pounds each, carrying an additional three days' rations for the men and two for the horses.[6]

The crossing took the command the majority of the day, the only fighting occurring with Confederate pickets on the Stevensburg road. They camped that night in line of battle in a freshly ploughed field as the rain continued. No fires were permitted, since the enemy's location was unknown. The 9th and 13th Virginia Cavalry regiments under W.H.F. "Rooney" Lee were known to be nearby. One of the raiders later described the night as "dark and dreary in the extreme."[7]

At daylight the command started its march south, the Reserve Brigade in the lead with the 6th Pennsylvania in the advance. They reached Morton's Ford on the Rapidan River about 11 o'clock, where the advance guard captured eleven prisoners from the rear guard of a Confederate cavalry regiment to their front. The brigade crossed here, while the majority of the column crossed at the larger Raccoon Ford nearby.[8]

The command camped for the night on a plateau overlooking the ford. Pickets were pushed out in all directions to provide early warning. It was another miserable night, wet soldiers and mounts standing to horse in the mud. Horses were fed grain by their troopers, but were not permitted to be unsaddled for the second consecutive night. Fires were forbidden, and a thick fog settled in after dark.[9]

The march resumed about 2:00 A.M. on May 1, its slow speed a combination of fatigue, dark and fog. Gen. Gregg's division had the advance that day, followed by the Reserve Brigade. They moved southwest through Orange Springs and Orange Court House, sending out parties to destroy railroad tracks and telegraph lines as they were encountered along the way. They finally crossed the North Anna River and joined Gregg's men on the south bank of the river about 3:00 A.M. on May 2.[10]

For the first time since crossing the Rappahannock, unsaddling of horses and building of fires was permitted. Troopers ministered to their mounts, then ate what little remained of their rations. The mules were cared for as well. Consuming rations eased the burdens of the mules, but poorly packed and poorly fitted saddles had left many of them with sore backs.[11]

The march resumed at 7:00 A.M., and the column reached Louisa Court House about noon. To the surprise of the troops, the important town was undefended. They spent the next several hours destroying Confederate supplies and materiel, principally focused on the Virginia Central Railroad, which passed through town. Their rations exhausted or ruined by the rain, foraging parties were sent out to gather supplies. One such patrol under Lt. Tullius Tupper captured Stuart's chief quartermaster.[12]

They continued their march south at 3:00 P.M., and continued until they reached Thompson's Crossroads on the South Anna River about 10:00 P.M. Thompson's Crossroads was a strategic location. The main road from Gordonsville to Richmond ran through town, as well as a road to Spotsylvania and Fredericksburg. A large bridge crossed the South Anna River there as well.

At midnight, Gen. Stoneman assembled his brigade commanders and revised his plan. Using Thompson's Crossroads as a rally point, columns would spread out like a bursting shell into the surrounding countryside, doing as much damage to the Confederate infrastructure as possible. Stoneman himself would remain at Thompson's Crossroads with part of the Reserve Brigade as a reserve. Other than a squadron detached on a short raid under Lt. Claflin, the 6th U.S. remained with Stoneman.[13]

Using orderlies to maintain contact with his scattered forces, Stoneman shifted his location to Shannon Hill on May 4, and to Yanceyville on May 5. Other than a brief scare when the 5th U.S. was attacked by a superior force and withdrew to the reserve, they were undisturbed. "The 6th was drawn up in column of squadrons to charge them when they appeared and two pieces of cannon were trained to take the road but the enemy did not see fit to show himself, and we missed the fun," lamented one soldier.[14]

As word of the raiders spread, Confederate forces began to gather around the Confederate capital. Brig. Gen. Wade Hampton's brigade of cavalry was recalled to reinforce Richmond's defenses and find Stoneman's force. Other units converged on the capital as well. Due to Stoneman's shell-burst plan, they had no one place to focus their efforts, but pressure was mounting.

On May 5, Stoneman decided that he had achieved his objectives and turned his attention to withdrawing his force from Confederate territory. Other than small groups of Hampton's cavalry, the biggest threat to their withdrawal was a large concentration of troops near Gordonsville, including the two cavalry regiments under Rooney Lee. The best course for escape appeared to be to make straight for the Rapidan and Rappahannock crossings to return to the army, but the forces at Gordonsville could cut them off if left undisturbed.

Stoneman's solution was a diversion. Brig. Gen. Buford and a handpicked force would advance on Gordonsville in a feint to draw the enemy's attention, while the main body withdrew north. Buford's force was selected from those with the strongest horses in the Reserve Brigade, numbering 646 in total. The 6th U.S. Cavalry's contingent was led by Lts. Wade and Carpenter.[15]

They crossed the Yanceyville bridge across the South Anna River and tried to strike west cross-country to Gordonsville south of the railroad. It was a miserable march. Dense forest forced them back onto the roads, which rapidly deteriorated as the rains commenced again. The command turned north to Louisa Court House in search of better roads. Arriving in town, they found telegraph service restored, so they destroyed it again and seized the mail from the post office.

Buford then moved his men west along the railroad line to Trevilian Station, six miles from Gordonsville. Units here destroyed tracks, railcars and water tanks while the head of the column continued a cautious advance toward Gordonsville. The head of the column struck a large force of infantry and cavalry two miles east of Gordonsville. Although they were able to force the Confederates back temporarily with skirmishers, continuing the advance was no longer an option. They had achieved their purpose. Confederate attention was now on Gordonsville.[16]

The exhausted troopers turned north to attempt to rejoin the main body. Many men and mounts reached the limits of their endurance from fatigue and the muddy roads. Some troopers abandoned their horses when they foundered, simply removing their saddles and continuing the march on foot. Others slept on the backs of their horses, trusting them to remain with the column. They forded the rapidly rising North Anna River at Mallory's Ford. The river was so high that the rear guard was forced to cross the river on rafts. They halted briefly to feed and rest their mounts near Orange Springs.[17]

Stoneman and the main body, meanwhile, rested at Yanceyville until sundown. They burned the bridge behind them as they left and marched north all night. Stoneman and Gregg allowed a brief halt just after sunrise to quickly feed horses and men before continuing the march all day on May 5. They continued through the night as it rained heavily once again. Stoneman was very concerned about the column's escape being cut off by the rising rivers and being captured by the Confederates. He, Gregg and other commanders strove to push the column along. They forded the North Anna early on the 6th, discovering Buford's command not far on the other side.

The reunited command rested for several hours before continuing the march toward the Rapidan late in the afternoon. As they neared Raccoon Ford, the 1st U.S. Cavalry was sent forward to ensure the ford was unguarded and, more important, still fordable. Fortu-

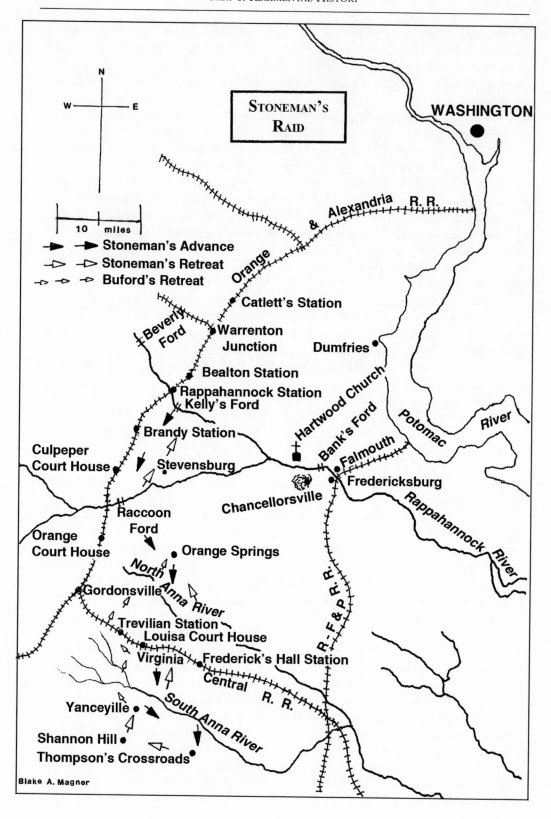

Blake A. Magner

nately that was the case, but it was fully dark by the time the column reached the river. It took from 2:00 A.M. to 4:00 A.M. for the exhausted command to make the crossing.[18] Realizing his force could go no farther, Stoneman halted the column on the north side of the river at dawn and ordered the horses unsaddled and fed. Fires were permitted for the men to cook whatever rations they might still have. The exhausted troopers rolled themselves in their blankets and slept, some without bothering to eat.[19]

After a halt of six hours they resumed the march late in the morning, aiming for Kelly's Ford. The command reached Kelly's Ford that night but found the water too high to attempt to cross. They posted pickets on all approaches to the ford and stood to horse until daylight. The Reserve Brigade led the crossing on the morning of the 8th, losing two horses but no men. Once across, the command moved to Rappahannock Bridge to draw forage, moving to Bealeton the following day for supplies. Stoneman's Raid was over.[20]

Although no soldiers were killed during the raid, the regiment's mounts suffered terribly. During the raid, 93 horses gave out, 51 were killed, and seven were lost to the enemy through capture. The regiment captured 29 horses and 13 mules. Most of the horses were brood mares or draft horses, unsuitable for anything other than transporting a trooper north of the Rappahannock.[21]

The regiment performed well in its first extended raid. Due to the tempo and conditions, the only personal accounts are letters and diaries after the fact. The regiment's official report was unfortunately lost. What is clear is that it was a tremendous exertion on the part of both men and horses. The normally unflappable Gen. Buford remarked in his official report, "During the whole expedition the roads were in a worse condition than I could have supposed to be possible, and the command was called upon to endure much severe discomfort. The men's rations were destroyed almost as soon as issued. No fires could be lighted to cook or dry by, and the dark, cold, wet nights that the men were compelled to march wore them out; but all, without exception, were full of enthusiasm, ready for any emergency, and did their duty with a hearty good-will."[22]

There was to be little rest for the tired troopers, however. They started the return march to their camps at Falmouth on May 10, and had only reached Deep Run when the Reserve Brigade received orders to picket the Rappahannock from Rappahannock Bridge to Falmouth. The regiment's share of the burden was a twelve-mile stretch of river, centered on Banks Ford. Their camp was near Hartwood Church. Five companies pulled the duty for two days at a time before rotating.[23]

On May 12, 1863, while in camp at Hartwood Church, Cpt. Cram, the regimental commander, accompanied by assistant surgeon William H. Forwood and two enlisted orderlies, rode to Gen. Buford's headquarters, about a mile and a half distant. That evening, as they rode back to camp, they were suddenly surrounded and compelled to surrender by about thirty of Mosby's partisans.[24]

It was a daring ambush, laid in the midst of the Cavalry Corps, on a piece of road supposed to be covered by patrols and pickets, yet resistance would have been foolhardy. The unfortunates were conducted through the forest to a house, where the band's leader, a Lt. Fairchild, offered to release them if they would give their parole. Cpt. Cram and the enlisted men were released on parole, minus their horses and equipment, and started to camp.

Since medical officers on both sides had the right to be released without parole if captured, assistant surgeon Forwood declined to sign the parole. He instead insisted upon his right, as a medical officer, to be released. This was refused, and he was turned over to a guard to be taken away as a prisoner. That night he was placed on foot between mounted guards in front and rear. While passing through a dense growth of pines, the gallant surgeon dashed into the undergrowth and escaped without injury from the carbine and pistol shots fired after him into the darkness. He floundered through the woods until daylight, when he discovered the rest of his party on the road near Gen. Buford's headquarters once again.[25]

The ordeal caused Cpt. Cram considerable embarrassment, and cost him his position temporarily. As a paroled prisoner, he could not return to active duty until exchanged. He and surgeon Forwood were sent to the camp of the Reserve Brigade's dismounted men, near Dumfries. As the only other captain serving with the regiment, Cpt. Brisbin assumed command. He also was apparently not a fan of Cpt. Cram. In a letter to his wife, he commented, "I am now again in command of the Regt much to the delight of all in it. The Rebles [sic] got Cram body and breeches — I am only sorry that they did not kill the son of a bich [sic], but we are rid of him and that is all we need care for."[26]

Considerable controversy arose over this capture, and the result was a general order published by the War Department forbidding the acceptance of parole under circumstances where parole was offered in friendly territory simply because the enemy lacked the ability to guard or secure them.

On the 17th, the regiment and the rest of the brigade moved their camps to near Brook's Station on the Acquia Creek Railroad, about four miles from the creek itself. While here, they learned of new officer appointments which had taken place on May 1. The first was First Sergeant Adna Chaffee of Co. K. The second was Joseph Hooker Wood, a nephew of Gen. Hooker. Since civilian appointments to regular regiments were not authorized by the secretary of war after the new regiments were filled in 1861, Wood had taken a novel approach to receiving his commission. Three weeks before, he had enlisted in the 2nd U.S. Cavalry, then his family lobbied the secretary of war for his appointment to a different regiment.[27]

There were losses as well as gains. They learned at the new camp that Lt. Sewell Brown and Maj. Wright both had resigned their commissions. Wright had never served with the regiment. Cpt. Samuel Starr of the 2nd U.S. Cavalry was promoted to major in his place.[28]

As the end of May approached, the Confederate cavalry and Mosby's partisans became increasingly active. The Union forces were very wary of another raid by Stuart and his Confederate cavalry. Encouraged by what he perceived as the success of Stoneman's raid, Cpt. Ulric Dahlgren, an aide-de-camp on Gen. Hooker's staff, proposed a bold counterpunch. If the Confederates launched a major cavalry raid, he proposed, it would be possible for a small force to take the same route Stoneman had and reach Richmond itself. The unit he proposed to lead on this raid was the 6th U.S. Cavalry. The plan was not adopted, as no raid was launched by the Confederates.[29]

On the 26th, the Reserve Brigade shifted camps to near Dumfries, ostensibly to recruit up its horses and mount as many of the remaining dismounted men as possible. Rumor had it that Gen. Buford said they would remain there a month. Several of the married officers in the brigade even made plans to send for their wives. Three days later they were surprised and dismayed to learn they would depart at 6 o'clock the following morning. As one philosophical soldier remarked, "Of course there was nothing to do, but to act as soldiers generally do. Obey orders and grumble."[30]

The next morning they marched to Bealeton Station on the Orange and Alexandria Railroad, where they found the rest of the Cavalry Corps. Learning of an attack on a train by some of Mosby's men, they proceeded down the tracks through Warrenton Junction until they found the train near Catlett's Station. After a brief pursuit, the brigade established camps near Catlett's Station. Gen. Buford was assigned command of all of the cavalry in the vicinity as the senior officer present. Accordingly, Maj. Whiting of the 5th U.S. Cavalry assumed temporary command of the Reserve Brigade.[31]

With June came several changes. Cpt. Cram was exchanged and returned to command the regiment. Gen. Pleasonton was assigned to command of the Cavalry Corps, replacing the popular Stoneman. Pleasonton continued to be a thorn in the regiment's side, this time by commandeering their band. As one outraged officer described events, "No sooner had he taken command then he ordered our Band to report to him on special duty at his headquarters. Now our Band is one of the finest in the Army of the Potomac; and all of the instruments were purchased by the Officers of the Regiment, and very naturally we wish to enjoy the music. No one ever heard of such a thing as detaching a Band from a regiment; and it is considered as rather arbitrary proceeding to treat us in this manner."[32]

It is unclear whether Pleasonton actually had a vendetta against the regiment. There clearly had been issues during his first command in the Maryland campaign and during the winter with the various regimental commanders, but many regiments had problems that winter with supplies and felt they were overtasked on their picket duties. What is clear is that the 6th U.S. Cavalry's band became a permanent fixture at Cavalry Corps headquarters, remaining there even after Gen. Sheridan assumed command of the corps the following year.[33]

The Union cavalry was very busy the first week of June attempting to locate the Confederate cavalry. Reports finally confirmed that the majority of Stuart's cavalry was concentrated near Culpeper Court House, just across the Rappahannock from Rappahannock Station. Gen. Hooker ordered Pleasonton to take his corps and disperse Stuart's forces, destroying them if possible. He provided Pleasonton with two select brigades of infantry, gathered from across the army, to support the attack.[34]

Gen. Pleasonton proposed an ambitious plan to Hooker. He would split his force in order to approach Culpeper Court House from multiple directions and prevent Stuart's escape. On the left, two divisions under Gregg and Duffie would cross the Rappahannock at Kelly's Ford. Once across, Gregg would proceed directly to Brandy Station, while Duffie would move first to Stevensburg, then approach Culpeper from the east. On the right, Buford's First Division, which now included the Reserve Brigade, would cross at Beverly Ford and move toward Brandy Station. There he would link up with Gregg's Second Division and advance to destroy Stuart's forces at Culpeper. Gen. Pleasonton would accompany the right wing. A select brigade of infantry was assigned to each wing to secure the fords after crossing and provide support as needed. It was a sound plan, if the Confederates were actually in Culpeper, and if Pleasonton could keep the two wings synchronized.[35]

Buford's division marched on the afternoon of June 8 with three days' rations, arriving near the ford about midnight. They established camp behind a dense forest on the north side of a hill to ensure they weren't detected by Confederate pickets. Although ordered to stand to horse, "one by one, the men drove stakes into the ground, or sought out bushes, until the whole party had managed to tie their horses to something, and crouched down upon the ground to sleep. It was clear enough to the men that the enemy was not far distant, and reflections of the coming morn were fraught with some solicitude."[36]

Thus the stage was set for a major confrontation south of the Rappahannock.

Chapter 7

Beverly Ford

At 2 o'clock in the morning of June 9, the command "to horse" was carried across the command by whispering orderlies and buglers. The command was far too close to Beverly Ford to risk alerting the Confederate pickets with bugle calls. After quickly brewing coffee, Buford's troopers silently mounted and stealthily advanced on the ford before dawn.[1]

Buford's portion of General Pleasonton's plan was relatively simple. One brigade of cavalry would seize the ford and enough space beyond it for the remainder of the division to cross. The other two brigades would expand the bridgehead, and the infantry would advance to secure the ford. Freed from securing the ford, the cavalrymen would advance to meet Gregg's division at Brandy Station.[2]

Colonel B.F. Davis' 1st Brigade led the advance, followed by the Reserve Brigade under Major Charles J. Whiting, Colonel Kellogg's two regiment 2nd Brigade, and Brigadier General Adelbert Ames' brigade of infantry. Three squadrons of the 5th U.S. Cavalry under Captain James Harrison led the Reserve Brigade, followed by the 6th Pennsylvania Cavalry under Major Robert Morris, the 6th U.S. Cavalry under Captain George Cram, and then the 2nd U.S. Cavalry under Captain Wesley Merritt.[3] The 1st U.S. Cavalry under Captain Richard Lord picketed the north side of the river to protect the flanks of Buford's crossing. Since the Federals were unsure of the exact location of Stuart's force, Buford dispatched Brisbin's squadron of the 6th U.S. Cavalry to scout his right flank toward Manassas Gap.[4]

Exchanged a few days previously, Captain Cram commanded the regiment. Major Samuel Starr, recently appointed to the regiment from the 2nd U.S. Cavalry, was expected to join any day from recruiting duty. Lieutenant Kerin accompanied Cram as his adjutant, while quartermaster Lieutenant Irwin remained north of the ford with the regimental trains.

With one exception, the detached squadron under Brisbin, lieutenants commanded all of the regiment's squadrons. Other than Cram, only two of the officers initially appointed to the regiment remained, Captain Brisbin and Lieutenant Wade. Without exception, however, the remainder of the officers were former enlisted men of the regiment, and veterans of the previous year's fighting.

The senior squadron commander, Capt. Brisbin, led the men of Cos. L and E, assisted by Lt. Henry McQuiston. Lt. James Wade commanded Cos. D and K, assisted by Lt. Albert Coats. Lt. Christian Balder commanded Cos. F and G, while Lt. Isaac Ward led Cos. A and M. Former first sergeant Lt. Andrew Stoll commanded Cos. I and C, assisted by Lt. L. Henry Carpenter. Former regimental sergeant major Lt. Tullius Tupper led the final squadron, Cos. B and H, assisted by former first sergeant Lt. Nicholas Nolan.[5]

The rigors of the previous month's campaigning still affected the regiment. Only 12 officers and 254 enlisted men crossed the Rappahannock. Of the regiment's enlisted men

334 languished without mounts in the brigade's dismounted camp at Dumfries, under the command of Lt. Adna Chaffee. Others served on detached service, while some of the volunteers received during the winter hadn't yet completed their training. Lt. Carpenter's Company C mustered only 20 men for the fight. Asst. Surgeon William Forwood remained with the dismounted portion of the regiment, while assistant surgeon William Notson accompanied the rest into battle.[6]

As dawn began to lighten the mists near the ford, shots rang out from the front of the column. Davis' advance guard surprised and scattered the Rebel pickets, forcing them back upon their reserve. Beckham's horse artillery barely escaped with its guns, its cannoneers fighting their way clear with pistols and ramrods.

By 4:30 A.M. Davis' command had seized the ford and pushed the Confederates back 500 yards. Resistance quickly stiffened as the rest of his brigade surged across the ford. Advancing rapidly up the Beverly Ford road, Davis' troopers were met by Confederate general William E. "Grumble" Jones charging at the head of the 6th Virginia Cavalry. Davis advanced to the front to rally the troopers of his own 8th New York Cavalry and was slain in hand-to-hand combat by Lieutenant Allen of the 6th Virginia.[7]

Davis' death momentarily stalled the advance. Major McClure of the 3rd Indiana Cavalry assumed command of the brigade, ordering a charge by the 8th Illinois Cavalry which forced back the Confederates temporarily. He deployed the 8th New York and the 8th Illinois on the left side of the road, with the remainder of his small brigade on the right side. He threw forward skirmishers to attempt to clear the woods to his front.[8]

General Buford was conferring with Cavalry Corps commander General Pleasonton at the ford as the Reserve Brigade crossed the Rappahannock. When he received word of Davis' death, he immediately spurred his mount to the front. He ordered McClure's brigade to clear the woods to their front and hold the ground from the road left to the bank of the river. He deployed the Reserve Brigade to the right of the road, giving Major Whiting responsibility for the right flank until the remainder of the division arrived.

General Jones meanwhile was busily organizing the Confederate defensive line. While the 6th and 7th Virginia continued to stubbornly contest the woods against McClure's brigade, all four Confederate horse artillery batteries massed atop the ridge between St. James Church and the Gee house, oriented down the Beverly Ford road. He formed the remainder of his brigade, the 11th, 12th and 35th Virginia cavalries, along the edge of the woods to the left of the artillery. As McClure's men finally reached the far edge of the woods, Confederate General Wade Hampton's brigade began to arrive to the right of the guns.[9]

The Reserve Brigade quickly crossed, and formed ranks in the clearing south of the ford. A continuous rattle of carbine fire was clearly audible to their front. Once they had formed, Maj. Whiting immediately threw skirmishers forward and attempted to secure his flanks. His lead regiment, the 5th U.S. Cavalry, was ordered to secure the right flank. The 6th U.S. Cavalry was initially assigned to support Lt. Samuel S. Elder's Battery E, 4th U.S. Artillery, which immediately unlimbered when it arrived in the clearing.

Colonel Kellogg moved the two regiments of his 2nd Brigade to the far right of the division's line as soon as they crossed, securing the line from Ruffins Run right of the 5th U.S. to the Rappahannock. General Ames' lead two regiments of infantry quickly passed through the Reserve Brigade and at last forced the Confederate skirmishers out of the woods to their front. They halted at the edge of the woodline, and reported a new enemy defensive line to their front on the high ground.[10]

His initial dispositions complete, Buford was now able to take the fight to the enemy.

Although he did not know their strength, the largest concentration of the enemy visible was the force around the guns near the church. It would not be an easy position to crack, as the open field, crisscrossed with ditches, extended 800 yards to the plateau, but Buford knew if he could take Beckham's guns it would put Stuart at a huge disadvantage. Since Ames' infantrymen now secured their front, Buford ordered the Reserve Brigade to advance up the Beverly Ford road and charge the enemy guns. Couriers immediately spurred their way to the regimental commanders.[11] His intent was for the entire brigade except the 5th U.S. to participate in the charge. Couriers were dispatched separately to the regiments of the brigade and to Maj. Whiting.

"General Buford sends his compliments to Major Morris, and directs him to clear the woods to his front," one of the couriers reported to the commander of the 6th Pennsylvania Cavalry before galloping down the line to the commanders of the other regiments.[12] Unfortunately, it took longer for the couriers to locate Maj. Whiting, who in the absence of orders had continued to fight his brigade. Since the Confederates continued to apply pressure on Major McClure, Maj. Whiting detached Lt. Tupper's squadron of the 6th U.S. Cavalry to maintain contact with the river and secure the left flank. The regiment's most experienced squadron remained there until the close of the day, eventually withdrawn by Buford after most of the brigade had recrossed the river.[13]

Whiting was most likely on the right flank in the vicinity of the 5th U.S. Cavalry when Buford's order was issued. Seeing the pressure building on Harrison's men, he ordered two squadrons of the 2nd U.S. to move to the right flank in support. These orders reached Capt. Merritt just after Buford's order to charge. Accordingly, Merritt dispatched the squadrons of Captains Canfield and Rodenbough to the right flank and moved the remainder of his regiment in that direction for support.[14] The consequence of this miscommunication would have devastating effects upon the attempt to seize the guns. Instead of three regiments attacking in unison, only thirteen understrength companies made the attempt.

Maj. Morris, meanwhile, immediately advanced his five companies into the woods as the courier relayed the order to Capt. Cram. Pvt. Sidney Morris Davis of the 6th U.S. Cavalry later recalled the event: "All eyes were bent upon them as they held their brief interview. Then the soldier rode rapidly away, whereas Captain Cram wheeled the head of his horse towards his regiment and issued a command that, even though many of the men couldn't distinguish the exact words over the barrage of fire on the field, as if by instinct the men seemed to understand it all, and in the next instant there was a gleam of steel in the air and a rattle of sabres as they were swept from their sheaths." The regulars then urged their mounts into the woods after the Pennsylvanians.[15]

An intimidating sight awaited the 6th Pennsylvania as they cleared the woods. The cleared fields sloped upwards over eight hundred yards toward the Confederate guns and supporting cavalry positioned atop the ridge. Four deep ditches cut laterally across the fields, wide enough to disrupt a mounted advance. A line of skirmishers stood dismounted a short distance before the guns, with mounted Confederate units to both sides of the artillery.

Undeterred, Maj. Morris ordered his regiment to advance. The Rebel skirmishers scampered back to their lines, and the artillery began to fire. The troopers in blue sorted themselves into two waves as the charge progressed. "We dashed at them, squadron front with drawn sabres, and as we flew along — our men yelling like demons — grape and canister were poured into our left flank and a storm of rifle bullets on our front."[16]

The 6th U.S. Cavalry in turn cleared the timber and, quickly dressing its lines, spurred in support of its sister regiment. "The clear notes of our bugle, sounding the charge, broke upon our ears, and the regiment dashed wildly forward." As the regiment left the timber, each man could see a thick gray line of Confederates to their front. To the left of this gray line, a mass of Confederate artillery thundered shells at the advancing bluecoats.[17]

Lieutenant Stoll's squadron led the charge of the 6th U.S. Cavalry. "When we emerged from the woods, the enemy were firing grape & canister, as thick as hail, from 3 or 4 pieces which they had placed on our left. The command was given to 'charge' and away we went," one of the squadron's officers later recalled. "As we went along at headlong speed, cheering and shouting, it seemed to me that the air was perfectly filled with bullets & pieces of shell. Shells burst over us, under us, and along side."[18]

The Confederate batteries increased their rate of fire as the two regiments closed. There was no respite for the charging cavalrymen. "Shell and shrapnel tore gaps in their ranks, but still they advanced," recalled one of the Confederate gunners.[19] Among others affected by the cannon fire, Lt. Daniel Madden was struck in the back by a piece of shell and taken to the rear.

Lt. Col. Elijah White led his 35th Virginia Cavalry Battalion in a countercharge to save the guns as the bluecoats approached within 200 yards, but was rolled back by momentum and superior numbers. As the Pennsylvanians neared the cannons' muzzles, Jones' regiments charged into their right flank. "Now the enemy on our right begin to close on us: our commander has fallen. Major Whelan assuming command, attempts to withdraw us from our terrible position. But how are we to retreat? The enemy have completely surrounded us — all is lost! Not yet, thank Heaven! The 6th United States Cavalry has been ordered forward to our support, and just at this moment their yell, as they charge upon the enemy, is heard. They turn to receive them: this is our time. The rebels give way on our right, and a way of escape opens."[20]

The Regulars reached the beleaguered Pennsylvanians just after Jones' Confederates, and a wild melee ensued around the guns. "When within twenty yards of the guns, double shotted with canister, we delivered their last fire into the mass of Federals and Virginians alike," noted one of the gunners.[21] The outnumbered Federals held their position by dint of heavy pistol and carbine fire for several minutes, but the arrival of additional charging Confederates forced them to withdraw under pressure.

"As we turned, a rebel made a dash close to me; I cut at him twice and missed him; as he passed he threw his sabre at me. One of my men almost thrust his carbine against the breast of the rebel & shot him to death. We captured in my company four or five prisoners, but were forced to leave them," Lt. Carpenter wrote to his parents after the battle. In the wild hand-to-hand melee, the regimental adjutant, Lt. Joseph Kerin, was captured from Cram's side. As the two regiments continued their retreat, the pursuit slackened, but not the fire from the enemy

Joseph Kerin (courtesy Dr. Ken Lawrence).

guns: "All this time the grape, canister, & the bullets were whistling & singing through the air like a hornet nest."[22]

Although unsuccessful, the charge was impressive. A sketch of the charge by Alfred Waud accompanied the *New York Times* account of the battle. "The grandest charge was made by the 6th Pennsylvania Cavalry, supported by the 6th United States, when they dashed upon a whole brigade of the enemy, and were taken in flank by another brigade; then, though surrounded, they fought their way out."[23] Their opponents were equally impressed. One of the battery commanders recalled after the war, "Never rode troopers more gallantly than the steady Regulars, as under a fire of shell and shrapnel, and finally of canister, they dashed up to the very muzzles."[24] The historian of Lee's artillery compared it to the famous charge of the Light Brigade at Balaclava, noting of the Union charge, "the latter possessing the additional feature that it was premeditated and not the result of an accident."[25]

The survivors withdrew through the lines of Ames' infantry in the woods to the field where they had started the charge. General Pleasonton had witnessed the charge with his staff from the edge of the woods. "Here we meet General Pleasonton, who commands his bugler to sound the "rally." Companies and regiments are all mingled in confusion, all flying for life. But the well-known sound recalls them to thoughtfulness; and in a few minutes the men of the two Sixes crowd again into column and await orders."[26]

The officers and sergeants quickly restored order. Captain Cram ordered Lt. Albert Coats to resume duties as adjutant, a position he had relinquished just three weeks before. The wounded were sorted and moved to the rear as the regiment re-formed in support of Elder's battery. One of the wounded was Corporal Miller of Company F. A squad mate, Pvt. Sidney M. Davis, attempted to assist him. When asked where he was hit, Miller replied, "In the back — gone clear through me."

Disbelieving, Davis told him to halt so he could check the wound. They halted for a moment, and Miller turned his back towards his comrade. Davis saw a small round hole, with an edging of crimson, appearing about the center of Miller's blouse, apparently having been cut by the bullet from a revolver. Miller then opened his shirt, and Davis' eyes fell upon what appeared to be an extra teat about an inch below Miller's left nipple. It projected outward about half an inch, and proved to be the conical point of a ball that was lying just underneath the skin.[27] Fortunately, Pvt. John W. McKibben, serving as one of the regiment's hospital stewards, happened upon the pair and assisted Davis in moving Miller across the Rappahannock to the field hospital. Miller survived the wound and later returned to duty with the regiment. At the hospital, they found several of the regiment's wounded men, Lieutenants Wade and Madden among them.

The regiment remained in the field in support of Elder's battery for several hours. Protected by the woods and line of infantry to their front, there was little for the troopers to do but remain ready and attempt to avoid enemy cannon fire directed at the battery. Cram took advantage of this respite to rotate his regiment by company to a small pond in the rear of their position to water their horses. Due to the size of the pond, only a squad or two could water their horses at a time. During Company F's rotation, an enemy cannonball ricocheted and struck Pvt. Spencer Viall, carrying away the upper portion of his head and killing him instantly.[28]

New orders arrived about noon, directing the Reserve Brigade to move to the right flank to relieve pressure on the 5th U.S. Cavalry and Colonel Kellogg's small brigade. The 2nd U.S. led the advance, followed by the 6th Pennsylvania and then the 6th U.S.[29] The

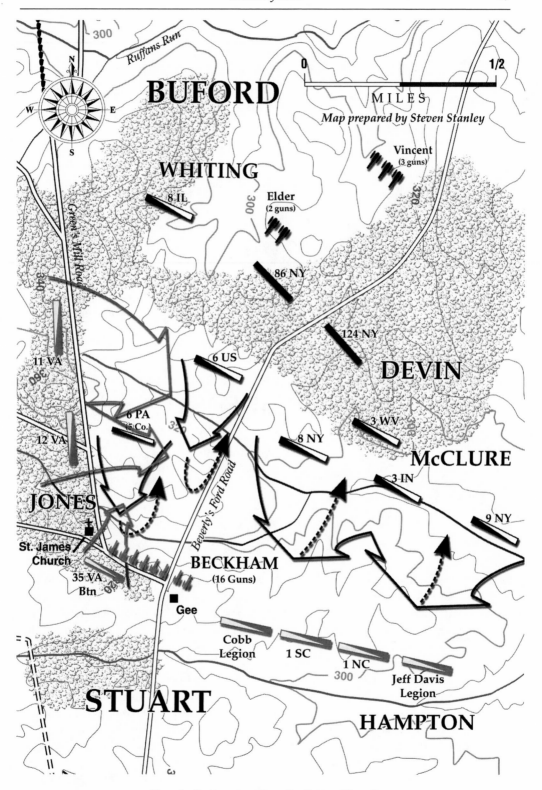

Brandy Station, attack at St. James Church

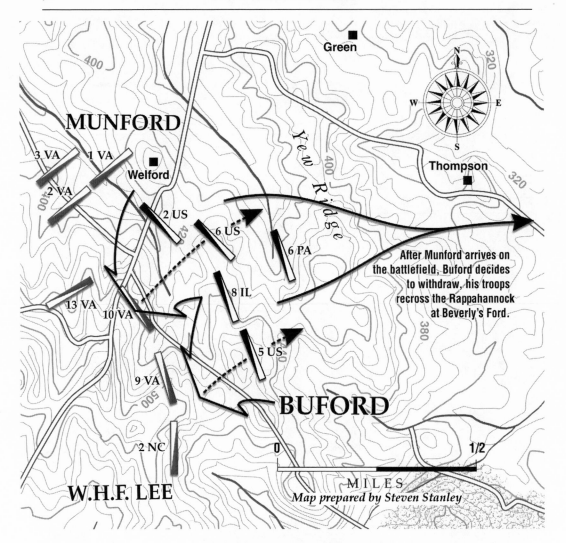

Brandy Station, the fight for Yew Ridge

brigade arrived to find Capt. Harrison's 5th U.S. and Kellogg's small brigade hotly disputing ownership of that portion of the field with Confederate General W.H.F. "Rooney" Lee's brigade. The Union cavalry fought from behind a stone fence on the eastern edge of the field, while the Confederates fought from behind a stone fence on the western edge. The 6th U.S. received unexpected reinforcements here, as Brisbin's squadron arrived just after they moved into position.

"Only a few rods back from the river we came to the front line of my regiment, and in fact the front line of our troops. My regiment lay stretched out, dismounted, behind a fence near a farm house. Capt. B.'s Company and my own were ordered to extend our line to the right which we soon did. Four hundred yards away was a rail fence behind which the enemy lay. This fence stretched away to our left, but joined another perpendicular to it in front of my company," wrote Lt. Henry McQuiston many years later.[30]

At this point, Buford's men were able to at last hear the guns of General Gregg's division near Brandy Station. With little pressure now on McClure's and Ames' brigades to his left,

Buford decided to advance to meet Gregg. The right side of his line offered the best route for an advance, but Lee's stubborn defenders had to be removed first. Buford enlisted the aid of two of Ames' infantry regiments, the Third Wisconsin and the Second Massachusetts, to break the impasse. The advancing infantrymen took Lee's line in the flank of the gray sharpshooters, sending them reeling back.[31]

Sensing an opportunity, Buford ordered a mounted charge by his two brigades. He left only the 5th U.S., completely out of carbine ammunition after the long battle at the fence, and a section of Graham's battery to hold the right flank. The Reserve Brigade with Elder's and Vincent's guns was the main effort, advancing down Ruffins Run towards Yew Ridge and the northern end of Fleetwood Hill. Kellogg's regiments followed and protected their right flank.[32]

Lt. Ward's small squadron was ordered forward to seize a point of dense forest in order to protect the right flank of the brigade's advance. Forcing their way through the thick foliage, they emerged to find themselves almost directly in the rear of the 9th Virginia Cavalry. Ward promptly charged the much larger force, his men cheering wildly as they swept forward. The Confederates halted a moment, gave a startled look backward, and then broke westward to flee to the rear. Audacity worked greatly in Ward's favor, as the Confederates did not realize how few men actually opposed them. A member of the 9th Virginia Cavalry who participated in this action was later quoted as saying, "From the noise you men made, we thought it was a whole brigade coming out of those woods."[33] Although it relieved pressure on the advance of the Reserve Brigade, the squadron's charge had one unfortunate result. Lt. Ward was shot in the chest as he was contesting for the flag of the 9th Virginia.

The remainder of the Reserve Brigade forced its way through the woods on the right side of Lee's line, turning his flank. The 6th U.S. moved into the timber, deploying two squadrons as skirmishers to the front. They connected with the 2nd U.S. line and acted as a reserve for the 2nd U.S. and 6th Pennsylvania as they advanced. They drove the enemy from the edge of the woods to a ridge in a plowed field between the Thompson and Welford houses.[34] As Buford later reported of the action, "A portion of the Reserve after much difficulty forced its way through a dense forest and became engaged, after exhausting the little ammunition it had left, out flew the sabers and most handsomely were they used. The enemy although mostly superior in numbers was fought hand to hand and was not allowed to gain an inch of ground once occupied."[35]

The Confederates attempted to flank the blue advance through the woods, but they ran into Ward's and Balder's squadrons, mounted in support of the skirmishers. "We rallied, drove them again to near the edge of a wood, they firing a shower of bullets at us and we at them, being only about 30 yards apart," Balder later recalled. The Union squadrons maintained pressure as the Confederates were forced from the woods into the fields beyond. "The rebs contested every inch of ground manfully, and the fight grew beautifully larger and larger," Balder wrote days later to a companion who missed the battle.[36]

The two sides charged and fired upon one another repeatedly as the fight progressed west through the fields towards the Welford house. During one of these charges, Lt. Balder had a very close call: "All of a sudden, a rebel officer came dashing at me, at full speed, making a tremendous right cut at me, but fortunately, I just perceived him in the nick of time. I parried his cut successfully and striking his sabre clean out of his hand. He fled by me, and one of my men shot him through the heart."[37]

Once the rebels were forced from the woods, the skirmishing squadrons remounted and rushed to join the fray. "Once on the top of the ridge, assured that the enemy had drawn back further, we were ordered to our horses to follow the enemy. Our progress was slow, and never very fast because the enemy stubbornly resisted our progress," Lt. McQuiston later wrote to his sister.[38]

Charges and countercharges flew across the fields, both sides seeking advantage. Firing could be continually heard, as units passed into and out of each other's sight due to the undulating terrain until they reached Yew Ridge. "At last my own Company and that of Capt. Brisbin were taken slowly through an open piece of wood, up a gentle slope and past other horsemen, until we emerged on the summit of a ridge with open fields forming each slope. The ridges continued in view two or three hundred yards, when upon our side the slope became much steeper."[39]

As Brisbin's squadron progressed down the south side of the ridge, they were engaged once again. "The fire of the enemy became more rapid, and I was exposed to a cross fire which I did not heed until my horse was shot in his right flank, the ball penetrating under the skin several inches," wrote McQuiston. "A rebel bullet struck the second soldier from me just where the visor joins the cap. The noise of course of the contact was heard. The soldier gradually dropped his head, and I could see the blood trickling down his forehead. He was led out of the ranks, and taken to the rear. The next day I learned that the bullet had penetrated the scalp just at the summit of the forehead and had passed between the scalp and skull to the back of his head from which position it had been dislodged. He was doing duty in camp next day."[40]

Buford's troopers fought Lee's brigade for some time in the open fields, gradually forcing them over Yew Ridge and onto the northern portion of Fleetwood Hill. Lt. Stoll's squadron reached the ridge as the fighting intensified again. One of Lee's regiments turned at bay and dismounted to oppose the pursuing squadron. "After remaining about an hour, in the hottest fire that I ever was in, an orderly arrived with orders for Stoll to withdraw. I waited ten or fifteen minutes on the right side of the line; Stoll having taken position on the left, and having no orders to withdraw, I rode to the centre, and took the responsibility upon myself of ordering the line to fall back slowly," Lt. Carpenter wrote.[41]

Unbeknownst to Carpenter, Stoll had been shot in the chest while leading his end of the squadron line. His men attempted to bring him off the field as the squadron was pushed back, but they were unable to do so, as the enemy targeted the casualty bearers. After Pvt. Brennan of Company C was wounded while trying to reach him, Stoll called to the others, "Go on, never mind me."[42] Stoll's successor continued to maneuver the squadron:

> I ordered my men therefor [sic] to pour in a rapid fire for a few minutes, and then ordered them to wheel to the right about, and to gallop at full speed. The men did just as I told them. The minute we commenced to retreat, the rebels arose in multitudes, as if by magic & poured in a dreadful fire. The next minute however I had gained the knoll with my squadron, and just behind it, I ordered them to stop and give it to the rebels. We were completely protected by the ground, and as the enemy had followed us in considerable numbers from the protection of the woods, we had a fine opportunity to pour in a raking fire on them. I saw a number drop, and the remainder retreated in great haste.[43]

At about this time, roughly 4:00 P.M., Confederate Colonel Thomas Munford's brigade reached the battle. Lt McQuiston saw their approach: "A considerable body of the enemy's cavalry came rapidly upon the other extremity of the ridge, in a column of four abreast and preceded by a color-bearer who was urging them on. They came within about a hundred feet of us and stopped. The color bearer came a few feet closer, calling on the others to follow. We began to shoot at them when they turned and left as hastily as they had come."[44]

Munford's men soon returned to join the fight, however, increasing pressure on the Reserve Brigade. As Gregg's division began to withdraw toward Kelly's Ford, the men of Jones and Hampton were free to join Lee's embattled brigade as well.

With more fresh Confederate troops arriving on the field and word arriving that Gregg had been repulsed, Pleasonton ordered Buford to withdraw his division. Cram was ordered to act as the rear guard for the Reserve Brigade. Stoll's (now Carpenter's) and Tupper's squadrons were ordered to act as skirmishers to cover the withdrawal. Captain Brisbin's squadron was ordered to once again support Elder's battery. "In compliance with order from the Brigade Commander and the Brigade returning I at the close of the engagement withdrew my command from the woods retiring slowly as skirmishers and keeping the enemy in check and acting as the rear guard of the Brigade," wrote Cram in his report the next day.[45]

The skirmishing squadrons withdrew slowly, desultory fire kept up by both sides. There were no means of carrying off the bodies of the outnumbered soldiers who were killed occupying the rear skirmish line due to proximity of the enemy, but the withdrew in good order. Lt. Tupper was later commended in the regimental commander's report for "the skill and deliberate manner in which, at the close of the engagement, he withdrew his skirmishers, his squadron being the extreme rear guard of the brigade, checking the enemy at every step as he retired and suffering more than any other squadron."[46]

As they exited the trees near Beverly Ford, Elder's battery went into action on a small hill to cover their withdrawal. The Confederate horse batteries advanced with their troops, and the opposing guns soon exchanged shots. One of Brisbin's officers recalled the exchange:

> The rebels opened on us with cannon to which our Artillery men replied. The sun was, or had just sunk behind the trees, but the sky was still brilliant above the trees with his light. I remember that the rebel battery with the green of the trees and yellow sky for a background the shallow valley and gently sloping greenly clad hill for a foreground with the smoke curling about the guns, made a pretty sight. The shot could be seen coming like large black balls from the guns. My troop was exposed to their view as it was resting behind the battery.[47]

One of the enemy cannonballs plunged amongst the battery's horses, disabling three of them. The teams had been secured too close to the battery in the open. "Capt. Elder was angry, scolding the riders for stopping so near the battery and in such an exposed place," wrote McQuiston.[48]

The battery recrossed the Rappahannock without further incident, soon followed by Tupper's and Carpenter's squadrons just before sunset. The 1st U.S. Cavalry under Captain Lord relieved the regiment at the ford, and the tired squadrons went into camp in a section of woods near their previous night's camp. The following day they returned to Catlett's Station.[49]

During this all-day engagement, the regiment lost four officers out of 12 who went into action: Lt. Ward, killed; Lt. Stoll, missing and thought dead; Lt. Madden, severely wounded; and Lt. Kerin, taken prisoner. Out of 254 enlisted men actually engaged, seven were killed in action or mortally wounded, 23 severely wounded, 22 disabled and 9 missing, making an aggregate loss of 65 officers and men. Lt. Ward's squadron had the most casualties, losing one man killed and 12 wounded. Lt. Carpenter's Company C suffered the worst, with five wounded of 20 engaged.[50]

Captain Cram's report of the battle commends in the highest terms the officers and men who participated in this hotly contested battle in the forests and clearings bordering the Rappahannock. Each of the squadron commanders was mentioned by name for acts of meritorious service, particularly the fallen Ward and Stoll. Lt. Stoll was even mentioned in General Buford's report on the division's fight, noting that he and his squadron "won my admiration."[51] Lieutenants Coats and Carpenter were also mentioned in Cram's report. The former was praised for "the energy and quiet courage under the most galling fire that he [displayed as he] discharged the hazardous duties of Adjutant," while Carpenter was commended for "skillfully bringing out the lamented Stoll's squadron after he was shot."[52]

Cram concluded, "The conduct of the men was remarkable for the indomitable endurance that marked it and their unflinching and dashing readiness to follow their officers. A commendation all the more deserved and to be appreciated when it is known that owing to the paralyzing system of absenteeism of officers, so fatal to this regiment and under the loss of the day. Three companies were during the engagement left without an officer and where it is the presence of a full compliment [sic] of officers so essential to success as in a Cavalry combat."[53]

The two captured officers were confined in Libby Prison. Lt. Joseph Kerin was one of those who escaped by means of the celebrated tunnel, only to be recaptured making his way to friendly territory. He was then confined in Macon, Georgia, then moved to Charleston, South Carolina. Here he escaped again during the move, by jumping from a moving train carrying prisoners, but he was recaptured once again. Confined to Columbia Prison, he escaped a third time, only to be recaptured with the aid of dogs. This gallant officer remained a prisoner until paroled in March 1865 at the close of the war.[54]

Lt. Stoll was not so fortunate. He survived his wound and the journey to Libby Prison and was later transferred with Kerin to prison in Charleston. He eventually died there of dysentery on September 28, 1864.[55]

Chapter 8

The Road North

The Cavalry Corps spent two days at Catlett's Station readying for their next mission. Cpt. Cram appointed Lt. Carpenter as adjutant to replace the captured Lt. Kerin. Lt. Coats took command of Co. K. On June 10, Maj. Samuel H. Starr, promoted from the 2nd U.S. Cavalry, reported to the regiment. No field grade officer had been present for duty since Maj. Williams left the regiment the year before.[1]

Unfortunately, Starr didn't initially serve with the regiment either. He was immediately given command of the Reserve Brigade, so Cpt. Cram retained command of the regiment. Maj. Starr displaced the 5th U.S. Cavalry's Maj. Charles Whiting, whom he ranked by a year's seniority. "Old Paddy" brought a solid reputation of dependability through long years of regular dragoon experience, but was known for a violent temper, which he unleashed against his own men as often as he did against the enemy.[2]

Starr was also a strict disciplinarian and rigidly exercised it towards both officers and enlisted men. His favorite method of punishment was to place the offender astride a fence, tie his feet together below, his hands behind his back, and place his horse's feedbag atop his head. This original composition won him the nickname "Old Nosebag."[3]

Maj. Starr's most redeeming feature in the eyes of his enlisted men was the poorly concealed fear he inspired in the regiment's officers. Cpt. Cram in particular seemed prone to draw Starr's ire, perhaps because he commanded his regiment. Whenever Cram was in his presence, Cram appeared very ill at ease. This was very gratifying to those who had been subject to Cram's foibles during the previous winter's camp. Despite his strictness, Maj. Starr was rather liked for his uniform application of the regulations and the articles of war to all, officers and enlisted men alike.[4]

The following day, Maj. Gen. Pleasonton reviewed the Cavalry Corps, reporting afterwards that his men were "in fine spirits and good condition for another fight."[5] Although he had already requested replacements for men and mounts lost in the Brandy Station fight, most regiments were down to 300–400 effective men from their authorized 1,000.[6] The same day, he reorganized the corps, assigning the 6th Cavalry's parent Reserve Brigade permanently to Buford's 1st Cavalry Division.[7]

There is a dearth of internal sources on the regiment's march north to Pennsylvania. Long days in the saddle, harsh weather, and a constant requirement to be ready to fight at a moment's notice precluded many letters home during this period. One regular later wrote of this march: "While the history of these days is disposed of a in a few sentences, it must not be imagined that the work was not severe. Every day and many nights we marched and countermarched, through good weather and bad, over mountains and through woods, subsisting as best we could on the army ration, when it was possible to obtain it."[8]

On the 13th, word reached Army of the Potomac commander Maj. Gen. Hooker that Lee's troops had reached Winchester in the Shenandoah Valley. Incensed, Hooker ordered Brig. Gen. Pleasonton to move his Cavalry Corps at once to locate the enemy main body and determine its intentions. Pleasonton responded by ordering Buford's division from Catlett's Station toward Thoroughfare Gap in the Bull Run Mountains, and Gregg's division due north to try to get in front of the Confederates.[9]

Late that afternoon, the regiment was in the saddle moving to the northwest. The long night march which ensued was full of delays due to road conditions, poor visibility, and the brigade's position in the column. One private later described the march: "The halts are just long enough to permit one to become sound asleep where one drops down in one's tracks, and the 'forwards' are just long enough to half waken one. Between them, they make up the most miserable of campaign experiences."[10] The regiment continued its weary march all night, reaching Thoroughfare Gap the following morning.

On the western side of the pass, two small valleys open to the west, with a large hill between them. A railroad winds through one of the valleys, and the road toward Salem through the other. The lead company, Co. I, advanced a line of skirmishers down both valleys. Co. F followed in support as the reserve, with part of the company in each valley. As the two valleys broadened and lengthened, the spaces between skirmishers increased until the men could no longer see one another. A prudent commander might have stopped at this point and moved more skirmishers forward, perhaps a company down each valley, but the advance continued.

Suddenly a shot rang out, and two mounted men in civilian dress dashed up the hill between the skirmishers and their support. They had evidently been concealed in the woods or tall corn as the skirmishers passed. They galloped after one of the skirmishers, who, finding himself cut off from the reserve, tried to escape by the Salem road towards the west. In order to reach the road, he had to gallop to the right down a steep hill. A stone fence about four feet high edged the field bordering this road, which was cut into the side of the hill at this point, making a clear fall of perhaps fifteen feet from the top of the wall to road surface. The rider did not hesitate to make this desperate leap, but the Confederates fired a second shot as he was high over the road. The soldier dropped lifeless to the road, and the Confederates galloped off toward Salem after a moment's halt beside the body.[11]

The slain soldier was Co. I's B. Nathaniel Owen, killed instantly by a shot to the head.[12] He was an author of articles for several western New York newspapers about his army experiences. One of these newspapers wrote of his death: "He was a brave, generous, upright young man and a gallant soldier, and his loss falls with crushing weight upon his family and friends, and is deplored by the community in which he lived."[13] Owen's infuriated comrades conducted a search of the area, discovering that the two men were the sons of an old farmer who lived atop the hill where the attack took place. Lt. Balder led a dismounted detail from Co. F up the hill to surround and search the farm, but the search was fruitless. After some delay, the body was turned over to the regimental surgeon and the march continued.[14]

A few miles farther west, the regiment halted, ordered to picket the Salem road. Companies rotated periodically on this duty, while the remainder of the regiment lay in an open field under an excessively hot sun. During their company's rotation, two soldiers of Co. F observed two suspicious looking men lurking in the woods to their front. They fired on them, but the men fled. The regiment never learned what happened to the attackers.[15]

The regiment remained here on picket for the next two days. While here, Lt. Wade's squadron of his own Co. D and Lt. Coats' Co. K were detached as provost guard to Cavalry Corps headquarters. Late on the evening of the 15th, they were ordered to collapse the picket line and rejoin the brigade at Manassas Junction. They reached their destination without incident at dawn after another long night march.[16] They stayed there on the banks of Bull Run until the 17th, rotating companies on picket while replenishing supplies for men and horses and bathing in the stream.[17]

On June 17, the regiment was again in the saddle with the rest of the Regular Brigade and moved towards the Blue Ridge Mountains. The June sun was exceptionally hot, and the long columns of horsemen raised clouds of dust. One trooper recalled times when the regiment did not lead the march: "It was customary to send a man ahead to the next farm house to fill as many canteens as he could carry and to meet the company as it came up." They marched slowly throughout the day, halting that evening just east of Aldie, where Gregg's division had fought Stuart's cavalrymen earlier in the day.[18]

They heard of the battle only through rumor and were ordered to stand to horse all night in case the Confederates reappeared. "All night long we lay, holding our bridles in our hands, speaking in subdued tones, without fires and suppose without much food, ready in a moment to mount our horses which stood ready saddled in line. This we were accustomed to do. It must have been awfully tedious and tiresome."[19]

The weary regiment resumed the advance in the morning, passing detritus from the previous day's battle for several miles. The morning's march proceeded uneventfully, other than sightings of small groups of grayclad pickets in the distance.

A brief delay ensued in the afternoon when the rear of the column was attacked by a small group of Confederate cavalry. Cpt. Cram galloped the regiment a short distance forward before facing about and deploying the regiment behind a stone wall. The attackers were chased off in short order, with the loss of only one man wounded, Pvt. Michael Bakeman of Co. E.[20]

The regiment garrisoned the stone wall until dark. About one-third of the command was detailed for picket duty that night, while the remainder stood to horse, ready to support the pickets. A tremendous rainstorm deluged the poor troopers that night, and continued for most of the next day.[21] "We held our horses as we had done the night before, and did not dare to build fires to make coffee. Our poor animals stood part of the day and all of the following night with their saddles on and with bridles in their mouths. This was two days and two nights under arms ready for emergency."[22]

The 19th consisted of a long march through the rain, disturbed only by a brief skirmish in which no one was injured. The regiment remained in place at the site of the skirmish through the night, again standing to horse in a wet field. Lt. Henry McQuiston described the experience.

> In a rain the felt hat would shed the water to the overcoat, where it would gradually run down and drop from the ends of the skirts. If the skirts descended below the boot tops, the water dropped upon the boots, and if the skirts did not reach below the boot tops the water drained directly into the boots or on to the trouser legs and thence much of it into the boots or shoes. It was a very common thing for the boots to fill with water. The soldiers dislodged the water by raising the foot higher than the knee by which maneuver much of it would run out.[23]

The regiment spent the following day in the same field, finally receiving a much needed rest.

In the meantime, larger events were unfolding which would impact the regiment on the 21st. Brig. Gen. Gregg's division had found Stuart's main body near the town of Upperville, and Pleasonton was maneuvering his corps and a division of infantry to attack him there. Pleasonton's plan was relatively simple. He would use his artillery batteries and infantry to force Stuart out of his initial positions, then hold his attention with Gregg's division from the front while Buford's division maneuvered around his left flank.[24]

Sunday, June 21, opened bright and clear, with warm sunshine drying roads and fields.[25] The 1st Division marched forth after breakfast, the Reserve Brigade third in the order of march. The regiment numbered 12 officers and 242 enlisted men in the ten companies present.[26]

They marched in fits and starts throughout the day as Buford's lead elements sought passage around the end of Stuart's line. Unfortunately, Gen. Jones' Confederate brigade had done an excellent job of tying their defenses into the edge of Goose Creek. A frustrated Buford was forced to countermarch and cross the creek in order to flank the position.

In the meantime, the opening moves of Pleasonton's gambit went well. Stuart was forced out of his initial positions and retreated back to a second defensive line behind the town of Upperville. Gregg's cavalrymen pushed the fight, engaging the Confederates in hand-to-hand combat in the streets of the town. Pleasonton requested more troops from Buford, who dispatched first the 6th U.S. Cavalry, then the remainder of the Reserve Brigade to assist.[27]

Cpt. Cram deployed his skirmishers and began his advance toward Upperville. A wrong turn was quickly identified and, reversing course, the regiment moved at a trot and then a gallop for three miles toward the sound of cannonading to the north. Shortly afterward, Cpl. Michael Slattery accidentally discharged his carbine, shooting himself through the right foot. He fell out of ranks and was placed in charge of the surgeon as the advance continued. They eventually emerged on a small plateau behind Gregg's forces, the entire battlefield in view before them.[28]

The Confederate line was crescent shaped with the convex front toward their opponents, extending some two miles from north to south and crossing the Upperville road at right angles. The left flank rested near the edge of the Blue Ridge and tied into the creek, as Buford's troops had already discovered. Their extreme right was located in some timber two hundred yards from the road. Directly in front of the enemy's line was the matching concave Federal line. The regiment rode onto the field and formed on the right side of the road, where it waited for orders.[29]

On the opposite side of the road, a Union force with Brig. Gen. Kilpatrick at the head of the column charged the Confederates. After initial success, a countercharge drove them back past the regiment's position. The Confederate charge pushed past the watching cavalrymen, exposing their left flank and rear. Inexplicably, Cpt. Cram did not order them to their comrades' support, and they held their position as Maj. Starr reached the field.[30]

Pleasonton reached Starr before Starr could reach Cram, and there ensued among the three "a short consultation, gesticulating wildly all the while. It was said among the men that he was denouncing the captain for disobedience of orders — which the latter, when the enemy had exhausted their strength upon the advance of the Federal troops, was to have attacked vigorously."[31]

As the general rode away, the regiment wheeled by fours and deployed into a column with a two-squadron front. One officer noted, "Our companies were very small. The four companies in line made just about the front of two companies." The other six companies fell in to their rear. As soon as they were formed, they were ordered to draw sabers.[32] "Forward — trot — gallop — charge!" rang out the commands, and in the same regular succession, the calls were obeyed. Sabers flashed above the men's heads as they rode forth with a loud cheer.[33]

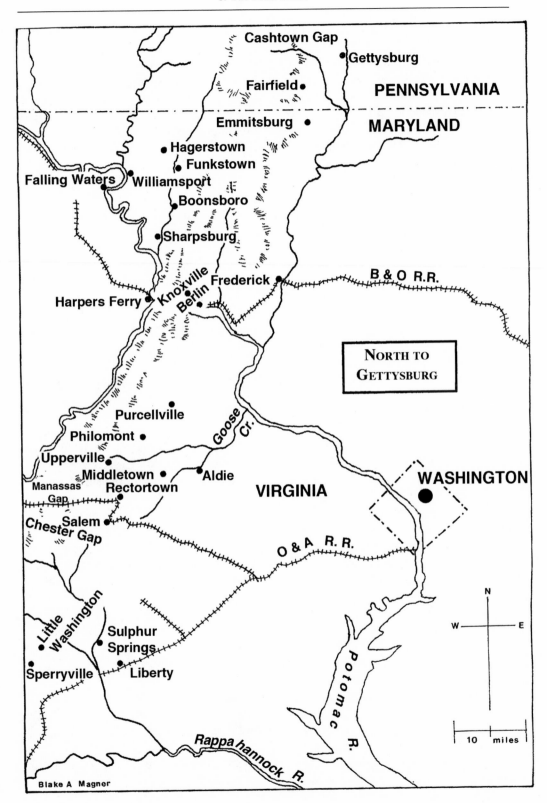

Cashtown Gap
Gettysburg
Fairfield
PENNSYLVANIA
MARYLAND
Emmitsburg
Hagerstown
Funkstown
Falling Waters
Williamsport
Boonsboro
Sharpsburg
B & O R.R.
Knoxville
Berlin
Frederick
Harpers Ferry

NORTH TO
GETTYSBURG

Purcellville
Philomont
Goose Cr.
Upperville
Middletown
Aldie
Manassas Gap
Rectortown
VIRGINIA
WASHINGTON
Salem
Chester Gap
O & A R.R.

N
W E

Little
Washington
Sulphur
Springs
Sperryville
Liberty

Potomac R.

10 miles

Rappahannock R.

Blake A Magner

Unfortunately, Cpt. Cram, in his haste to execute Maj. Starr's orders, failed to examine the terrain. Between the regiment and the enemy line lay a nearly 700-yard uphill stretch of open marshy ground, intersected by a rail fence and a large ditch. On mounts already tired from a day's march, it was too far for a gallop. Undeterred, the men went forward with a will. "Our squadrons advanced with steady, unbroken front over the fence, up the gentle slope to the woods, and here just at the very edge of the woods the squadrons halted," wrote one lieutenant after the battle.[34] As Cram later wrote in his report, "The charge was unsuccessful, the most of the horses being so blown that it was impossible to bring or keep them for such a distance at a charging pace."[35]

As the troopers rallied their tired mounts, Confederate Gen. Wade Hampton advanced a regiment from his brigade against them, and sharpshooters began to fire from the trees as well. The regiment turned to withdraw from this new threat, incapable of forward movement.[36] "The officers were in front advancing, and of course were in the rear on the retreat. I had scarcely turned when I felt a shock, and numb feeling in my hip, my left leg became useless, my saber dropping down but I did not loose my grasp upon it," wrote Lt. Henry McQuiston of Co. E. Two of his soldiers held him in the saddle as he was hurried to the rear. Several other troopers were wounded as well.[37]

After returning near their start point, Maj. Starr rode up and issued the command: "Dismount — prepare to fight on foot!" There was a sudden emptying of saddles and springing into line as the "fours" rushed the mounts to the rear. To the rear, the remainder of the Reserve Brigade arrived on the field. A battery of artillery galloped up to the right of the regiment and unlimbered, as Starr ordered the 2nd and 5th U.S. cavalries both to dismount and advance as well. In short order a crackling of carbines, accompanied by the thunder of the accompanying battery, was directed toward the enemy.[38]

The force before them, however, was Hampton's rear guard. Confusing the advancing dismounted troopers for infantry, Hampton ordered Maj. Lipscomb's 2nd South Carolina Cavalry to cover his rear as he withdrew his brigade from the field. The Reserve Brigade mounted and pursued, but Lipscomb's men were able to withdraw with the aid of artillery fire from a hidden battery.[39]

The men were pretty thoroughly disgusted with the entire affair. The regiment received a tongue lashing in front of one their sister regiments from an infuriated Maj. Starr, who charged them with cowardice during the first part of the conflict. As one soldier recalled, "Of course, this was severely resented by the men, and the fervent longing for the return of Cpt. Sanders and the old gallant days of 1862 found expression on the march, while on picket, and around the bivouac fires."[40]

The regiment returned to Aldie in the evening following the battle. As an advance from the enemy was possible, a section of artillery was unlimbered and trained down the road towards Upperville. The regiment was ordered to support the cannons, standing to horse with tightened girths once again during the night.[41] Given the extent of Starr's ire, it is entirely possible there was no enemy threat.

The regiment's casualties were relatively light. Lt. McQuiston's hip wound was severe, and he would not return to service with the regiment. In addition to Slattery's self-inflicted wound, Pvt. Charles Roemer of Co. A was seriously injured in the shoulder, five others were wounded less seriously and three were listed as missing.[42]

Cpt. Cram attempted to justify his regiment's performance during the charge in his official report:

In closing this report, out of justice to my regiment, I would respectfully call attention of my superiors to the dispiriting circumstances attending the unsuccessful charge, before described. The men were exhausted and worn out by the recent imposition of incessant picket duty in their position near Middleburg. They were taken from behind stone walls, which they had been guarding all night and the day before, mounted on horses as famished as themselves, and immediately marched with the column, and at the end of a fatiguing day were ordered to charge over ground almost impracticable in its nature.[43]

Given the nature of the campaign to this point, the 6th U.S. Cavalry was in no worse shape than the other regiments around it. The fault lay with Cpt. Cram himself. As the commander, it was his responsibility to know the condition of his unit. He exercised poor judgment in immediately ordering his unit to the charge. They were not under artillery fire as they had been two weeks earlier at St. James Church. They could have proceeded at a more reasonable pace that would have enabled them to fight once they reached their objective.

The regiment remained at Aldie the next day, picketing to the west of the town. That evening, Sergeant Major Hercules G. Carroll was captured while making his rounds inspecting the picket posts. He was hurried off undetected and sent to Libby Prison. No one knew what happened to him, and he was therefore listed on the muster rolls as a deserter until he was later exchanged. This led to the appointment of Patrick Cusack as sergeant major. Cusack transferred from the 4th U.S. Artillery — which supported the Reserve Brigade — to the regiment effective the same day. Cusack remained the regimental sergeant major until January 19, 1865, when he was appointed a captain, 9th U.S. Colored Troops.[44]

On the 24th, the regiment marched from Aldie via the Leesburg road. The march was a frustrating one of fits and starts, the road clogged by units, batteries and wagon trains. After a slow and very dusty ride, they camped at midnight in a meadow beside the road about a mile past Leesburg.[45] Buford's division guarded the front, left flank and rear of Gen. Reynolds' wing as it crossed the Potomac and entered Maryland. The Reserve Brigade was tasked to guard the rear, resulting in interminable marches for the troopers.[46]

The march resumed late the following morning, and they reached the pontoon bridge across the Potomac at Edward's Ferry before noon. They waited an hour for their turn to cross, then proceeded to Point of Rocks, where they bivouacked for the night. This was a rare night without picket duty or battery support, and the horses were unsaddled and thoroughly groomed for the first time in many days.[47]

The regiment started early the following morning, continuing its slow, monotonous march in the rear of the trains. This movement continued until far into the night, finally ending at the base of Sugar Loaf Mountain, near the scene of the regiment's skirmish the year before. The next two days consisted of long, slow, dusty marches toward Frederick via a long detour to the south and west of the city.[48]

The long marches were beginning to take their toll on men and mounts. "As we were on the march in a vigorous campaign we probably had for supper the usual fare under such circumstances, that is, hard bread and coffee and possibly brown sugar," one trooper later recalled.[49] "The cavalry horses were getting pretty badly used up, especially during their terrible trials of these historic days. For two months they had been in the saddle almost constantly, both day and night, marching and countermarching and picketing, occasionally for days without food, until in their ferocious hunger they bit at food, or clothing, or ate of each other's manes and tails," wrote Pvt. Davis.[50]

On June 29, newly promoted Brig. Gen. Wesley Merritt took command of the Reserve

Brigade, relieving Maj. Starr. Starr in turn assumed command of the regiment, and Cpt. Cram returned to command of Co. I and his squadron.[51]

The regiment started its march early, reaching Frederick by noon only to wait several hours for wagon trains to clear the way. They resumed the march in late afternoon, and reached Middleburg just before midnight.[52] The march was an ordeal. "They had to endure rocky, sloping terrain, a blistering sun, and clouds of dust so thick a man could not clearly discern those who rode beside or before him. Progress was aided, not slowed, by several rest halts."[53]

The day after winning his star, Brig. Gen. Merritt called on the regular army officers over whose heads he had been promoted and inspected the brigade's camps. One can only imagine Maj. Starr's reaction to this turn of events.[54] The same day, over Buford's objections, the Reserve Brigade was detached from his division and assigned to guard the army's supply trains at Mechanicstown.[55]

Only July 1, they resumed the march, making their way to Emmitsburg in the afternoon. While on this march, one of the junior officers accidentally discharged his revolver. Maj. Starr promptly had him put under arrest. This greatly amused the men in the ranks.[56] All day they were able to hear the sound of cannon and musketry from the northeast. They camped that night in Emmitsburg. They remained in Emmitsburg the next day, guarding the trains and chafing at their inaction while units hurried past them to the sound of the guns.

Chapter 9

Fairfield

On the morning of July 3, the 6th U.S. Cavalry and the rest of the Reserve Brigade awoke early to the distant rumble of cannon and musketry in the direction of Gettysburg. Late that morning, an old farmer rode into the brigade's lines and was soon taken to speak to General Merritt. He reported the presence of a large Confederate wagon train corralled on his farm near the town of Fairfield, about eight miles behind the Confederate main lines. The civilian reported that the wagon train "camped all night near Fairfield without a guard of any strength"[1] and added that the moment offered "a right smart chance for you'ns to capture it, the soldiers are all over at the big fight."[2] Merritt sensed an opportunity and ordered a single regiment, the 6th U.S., to capture the train by moving "upon the road between Fairfield and Gettysburg to keep any supports which might be sent to Gettysburg by the enemy."[3]

While possibly a questionable move on the surface, several factors likely influenced Merritt's decision. Major Starr was his senior subordinate. Indeed, he had relinquished command of the brigade to Merritt only a week before. The 6th U.S. was also one of the largest regiments in the brigade, particularly after the 6th Pennsylvania sent a detachment of 100 men south to Greencastle earlier that morning. Moving his entire brigade without authorization most likely exceeded his authority with a major battle raging nearby. Had he done so, he would have been badly out of position to obey the orders received a few hours later to advance on the left side of the Union lines near the Round Tops.

In fact, not all of the 6th U.S. went on this mission. Its largest squadron, consisting of the 127 men of Cos. D and K under Lt. Wade, served as escort for General Pleasonton's Cavalry Corps headquarters and was already in Gettysburg. Earlier that morning, General Merritt had dispatched Captain Claflin and a detail of 30 men to dislodge Confederate pickets at Union Bridge to open communications lines. These two detachments removed over 150 men from Starr's force, leaving him about 400 men.

Command and composition of the remaining squadrons differed somewhat from the fight at Beverly Ford nearly a month before. The first squadron, Cos. I and B, consisted of 72 men under Captain Cram and Lieutenant Nolan. Lieutenant Paulding's squadron, Cos. G and A, consisted of 87 men and 2nd Lt. Tullius Tupper. Lieutenant Balder commanded his Co. F and Lt. Joseph Hooker Wood's Co. L, a total of 74 men. A single officer commanded each of the remaining two squadrons. 2nd Lt. Adna Chaffee led the 102 troopers of Cos. M and E. Captain Claflin's departure left former first sergeant and newly promoted 2nd Lt. Joseph Bould in command of the 96 remaining men of Cos. C and H.[4]

Late in the morning, the regiment sounded "to horse" and assembled mounted for duty at Reserve Brigade headquarters. The idea of seizing a wagon train was tremendously popular among the men. "All was excitement, and you will not wonder when you imagine capturing a hundred wagons laden with spoils for confiscation, and the plundering and destruction of the same."[5]

Major Starr and the farmer rode at the head of the column. One trooper recalled, "The man seemed to be somewhat excited, emphasizing his conversation by gestures with a rawhide which he held in his right hand."[6] Along the way, the men saw no Rebels except a small picket post on the side of a mountain a mile or so from the road.[7] After a pleasant hour's ride, the regiment entered the valley south of Fairfield, and Starr called a halt approximately two miles from the village.

Starr dispatched Captain Cram's squadron to search for enemy foragers the farmer reported to be in the area. Cram was to follow the course of an unfinished railroad, which ran north and south at the foot of the South Mountain range on the western side of the narrow valley.[8] Cram's detachment reduced Starr's force by about 70 men. The rest of the regiment continued on toward the town, Lt. Christian Balder's small squadron now in the lead

As the command reached the streets of the town, men fanned out to search for the wagon train. The men of Co. F saw no male citizens, but a throng of women "swarmed into the road around us in a state of intense excitement, and manifesting great joy at our timely arrival," noted Pvt. Sidney Davis. "They stated that a train of eight wagons, loaded with supplies they had taken had just left, and at that moment must be within a mile of the village."[9]

"Arriving at Fairfield we found no train, but a few wagons which had been at the neighboring barns had left the town a few moments prior to our entering," noted Lt. Tattnall Paulding.[10] Eager to capture the wagon train, Starr sent Balder's squadron in pursuit of the wagons while he followed with the remainder of the regiment. Balder in turn posted a small advance guard, a squad of four men under Sergeant Brown, about 200 yards in front of the squadron.[11]

After proceeding some distance, Lt. Balder's little column passed a small schoolhouse just before reaching a fork in the road. After a quick halt to orient himself, Balder turned the column's head to the left fork and continued on the Fairfield-Orrtanna road. About a mile farther on, they approached a farmhouse.

Balder spotted a man in the yard of the house and called out to him, "Have you seen any rebels about here lately?"

The man did not answer right away, clearly debating the merits of responding and becoming involved. Undeterred, Balder repeated the question. This time, the man responded: "Six passed here a few minutes ago."

"What direction did they take?"

"Out that way, and up the road towards Cashtown," the man replied, pointing north, up the Fairfield-Orrtanna Road.

As the Federals moved off, the man stopped Balder, warning, "You had better be careful, Captain. There are many of them about here just now."

Balder responded harshly. "Is this Pennsylvania?"

"Yes, sir."

"And you farmers of Pennsylvania allow six rebels to ride unmolested about your state, and rob you just as they have a mind to?" retorted Balder. As the Federals marched off, the man gave an unintelligible reply.[12]

Balder's small command advanced down the road, flanked on both sides by post and rail fences. The country was open but subdivided into farm fields and orchards lined by well-built fences. Eventually they spotted the escaping wagons and galloped in pursuit.

It is unclear to this day how many wagons were involved, since the 6th U.S. did not capture a single one. General Jones noted in his report that the 6th was "en route to capture our cavalry division trains, which must have fallen an easy prey but for our timely arrival." In the same report, he mentioned that "many wagons in quest of forage were already within a few hundred yards of the enemy."[13]

After pursuing for a mile or so, Balder's men had nearly reached them when they saw a large column of Confederate cavalry approaching on the same road, its first companies coming into view as they passed the wagons.

In the approaching Confederate column rode the men of General W.E. "Grumble" Jones' brigade. The brigade at this time consisted of three veteran regiments. The 7th Virginia Cavalry, commanded by Lieutenant Colonel Thomas Marshall, led the brigade. Formerly Turner Ashby's regiment, the 7th Virginia was one of the best in the Confederate cavalry. Next in line was the 6th Virginia Cavalry, commanded by Major Cabell E. Flournoy. Colonel Lunsford Lomax's 11th Virginia Cavalry completed the brigade. The brigade's strength as of June 30th was 1,478 men.[14] Each of his three regiments was larger than the 6th U.S. Cavalry. Captain Preston Chew's five-gun battery of veteran horse artillery accompanied Jones' brigade, with 4 officers and 95 men.[15] Behind them rode General Beverly Robertson's brigade of North Carolinians, but the head of that column still lay north of Orrtanna, too far away to provide much support.

Jones' men had departed Chambersburg about 1:00 A.M. that day en route to Cashtown. They rested there for about an hour before receiving orders from General Lee to move "at once to the vicinity of Fairfield, to form a line to the right and rear of our line of battle."[16]

Quickly realizing how badly the approaching enemy outnumbered his small command, Balder wheeled his men about to return to the main body of the regiment. The Virginians spotted Balder's little column. "We had gone but a short distance when we met a squad of about thirty mounted Federal cavalrymen," recalled a trooper of the 7th Virginia, "who turned and ran through a lane with post and rail fence on either side."[17] Seeing an opportunity, the 7th Virginia spurred in hot pursuit of Balder's retreating men.

Cresting a low ridge at the narrowest point in the valley, Starr could see Balder returning and the pursuing Confederates. It is unlikely that he could see how many enemy approached, only that it was a fairly large column of horsemen. True to his somewhat pugnacious reputation, Starr chose to stay and fight. He occupied high ground, and as yet had no firm knowledge of the enemy's strength. The closest defensible terrain was Fairfield Gap, two miles to his rear.

Starr ordered his troops to deploy into line of battle atop the ridge. He ordered Lt. Chaffee's squadron to dismount along the northern edge of a large apple orchard to the left of the road. Lt. Paulding's squadron was posted to the right, dismounted behind a post and rail fence. Lt. Wood's Co. L and Balder's returning Co. F occupied the road in the center, still mounted. Lt. Bould's squadron formed the regimental reserve, remaining mounted in column behind the apple orchard to the rear of the position.[18]

One man in four from the dismounted squadrons rushed to the rear with the horses, reducing their effective strength by a further 25 percent. This left perhaps 75 effectives in the orchard with Lt. Chaffee and about 60 behind the fence with Lt. Paulding. The position offered good fields of fire for the defenders. While the terrain would normally be ideal for mounted operations, the strong fences bordering the road and adjacent fields made it difficult to approach the position in anything but a thin column. Starr's troopers needed every available advantage. It is unlikely that the thin blue defensive line extended more than 150 yards to either side of the road. As Starr's men finished making their dispositions, the 7th Virginia came into sight near the Benjamin Marshall house, about 300 yards away.

Jones spotted the Union line of battle and immediately ordered the 7th Virginia to charge, an order its veteran men happily obeyed. One of the Union troopers later described them as "Ashby's pet regiment, composed of really good and well-trained soldiers, charging with drawn sabers."[19] Grumble Jones later reported, "No estimate could be made of the opposing force, but knowing a vigorous assault must put even a small force on a perfect equality with a large one until a wider field could be prepared, I at once ordered the 7th Regiment, which was in front, to charge."[20]

The men of the 7th Virginia gave a wild Rebel yell, drew their sabers, and charged the regulars' position. Starr's dismounted troopers on the flanks, armed with breechloading Sharps carbines, opened a severe fire, and blunted the 7th Virginia's attack. Hemmed in by the strong fences, "too strong to be broken without an ax," the 7th Virginia suffered severely.[21] The regiment's commander, Lt. Col. Thomas C. Marshall, reported: "Moved up at a charge, and found the enemy strongly posted, a portion of their column in the lane, and their other forces disposed on either flank, protected on one side by an orchard and on the other by a strong post and rail fence in front. They opened a galling fire upon us driving us back and killing and wounding a good many."[22]

The men of the 7th Virginia were forced to fight their way out of the trap created by the flanking fire and strong fences. "Shattered and broken the head of the charging column faltered, the men behind it halted, and soon the whole regiment returned in spite of the strenuous efforts of its officers to force it forward," wrote the historian of Jones' Brigade.[23] One Union trooper recalled that the fight with the 7th Virginia was "a cruel, close one, where every shot from determined men told upon their opponents, who were thus jammed up between to [sic] fences and literally harmless."[24] The flanking fire of Starr's dismounted troopers was terribly effective against this initial charge. The brigade historian declared the failure of the 7th's charge was "clearly due to the fire from the ... men on the flanks, who, being unmolested, shot with deadly effect into the charging column."[25]

Capt. John C. Shoup and his brother Lt. Jacob G. Shoup both fell while trying to rally the men of the 7th. Captain Shoup was seriously wounded, and Lieutenant Shoup was killed outright.[26] Lt. Col. Marshall's horse was killed in the charge, and his adjutant's was wounded. Thirteen of the regiment's horses were killed and eight wounded in the charge.[27] Several members of Balder's squadron were wounded in the melee, among them Company L's Lt. Wood, nephew of Union general Joseph Hooker.

Although Jones blamed the failed charge on the regiment in his official report, his own reckless order caused the repulse. He failed to reconnoiter the position or "develop the situation" with skirmishers, as the tactics of the day dictated. The dismounted men behind fences were clearly visible before the 7th Virginia charged, as mentioned in his and Marshall's reports. He provided no opportunity for the regiment's commander to close his ranks prior to the charge, and gave his men no chance to remove any of the fences that caused the 7th Virginia so much suffering. Thus, he is responsible for the disaster that befell the 7th Virginia. "The bravest mounted troop that ever flashed saber in sunlight now are exceedingly chary in attacking an unknown number of dismounted men, especially when they are secreted behind fences or anything that affords immunity from a cavalry charge," observed Lt. John H. Connell of the 7th Virginia. "Every brave man who has been engaged in the mounted arm of the service will testify to the truth of this statement."[28]

"The regiment did not at this place, and time, close up as promptly as it should, in this manner, no doubt, making our losses greater than it would otherwise have been," Colonel Marshall later wrote in his report."[29] Still furious when he submitted his official report on July 30, Jones declared the 7th Virginia's "leading men hesitated; the regiment halted and retreated, losing more than a glorious victory would have cost had the onset been made with vigor and boldness. A failure to rally promptly and renew the fight is a blemish on the bright history of this regiment."[30] The 7th Virginia fell back 300 or 400 yards and tried to regroup once clear of the fences.[31]

The 6th Virginia, next in line in Jones' column and trailed by Chew's Battery and the 11th Virginia, arrived on the field in time to watch the rout of the 7th Virginia. As they arrived, the men of the 6th Virginia heard "the carbines and revolvers of the 7th ... already making music on quick time."[32] Jones ordered Chew's guns to deploy in a wheat field east of the road. Quickly going into action, the rebel gunners opened fire on the Union position, several hundred yards away. "We immediately put our guns in battery and opened on them, and our cavalry also opened with small arms, and for a while the conflict was fierce and hot," recalled Sgt. George M. Neese of Chew's Battery. "We had our guns in position in a wheat field where the wheat was standing thick, and nearly as high as my head, and dead ripe. It looked like a shame to have war in such a field of wheat."[33]

As Starr's men had no artillery of their own, the rebel gunners were able to go about their business unmolested. Charles F. Miller of the 6th U.S. later observed that "the shot and shell from five pieces of artillery made us think that we would better get out of there, and some of the boys made good time, too."[34] Private George Cooper of Co. E recalled differently: "The artillery fired two or three rounds of solid shot, but, their own men being endangered thereby, desisted."[35]

Although Sgt. Neese believed the battery's fire was very effective, it's not mentioned in any of the official reports. Cooper's account is the most likely of the three to be accurate. It is very doubtful that the battery would have had time for more than a handful of rounds, given the time available between charges, without endangering their own men. Such fire, though not effective, certainly would have had an effect on the nerves of the outnumbered and now outgunned Union troopers.

Major Starr observed the enemy's withdrawal from the center of his line. The combative former dragoon was in a difficult situation. His regiment was alone miles behind enemy lines, and missing two of its six squadrons. His forces were solidly deployed on the most defensible terrain in the area. As the enemy battery went into action and now a third regiment began to emerge past the wagons, however, he realized that he was both outgunned and badly outnumbered. With the supply wagons now behind enemy lines, there was no way to accomplish his assigned mission. He doubtless realized that his decision to stay had been a poor one.

Starr needed time and space to extract his command. The next defensible terrain was miles to his rear at Fairfield Gap. Already the commands of the 6th Virginia's officers carried up the hill as they prepared to charge. His dismounted squadrons would need time to move to the rear and remount their horses. A cavalry force was at its most vulnerable and disorganized following an unsuccessful charge, as he'd just witnessed. The fences lining the road would help to reduce the effects of the disparity in numbers. If he could blunt this second attack, he might be able to slow the enemy and make them more cautious as he withdrew his regiment by squadron.

Maj. Starr dispatched his adjutant, Lt. L. Henry Carpenter, with orders for Paulding to withdraw his men, as Starr was about to charge and would be driven back. The other officer from Paulding's squadron, 2nd Lt. Henry Tucker, assumed Carpenter's position as adjutant.[36] After Balder, Paulding was the senior and most experienced officer present. Paulding's tired troopers began to leave the fence and race back to their horses. "After my men were posted behind a fence by which they were to act, I saw the enemy in great numbers forming beyond us & very soon recd an order from Maj. Starr to withdraw my men as he was about to charge and would be driven back," scrawled Paulding in his diary. "The men were brought in as rapidly as possible but being much tired could not go fast & before they could reach the horses our men ... charged."[37]

Maj. Starr drew his saber and ordered Balder's small squadron to charge. He rode at the head of about seventy troopers as they thundered down the narrow lane to meet the charge of Major Flournoy's 6th Virginia Cavalry.

While Starr's decision appears foolhardy at first blush, his options were limited. With no artillery of his own, it was a matter of time before he would be driven off the ridge since he couldn't range the enemy guns with carbines. Had he intended his charge to be anything but a diversion, he would have added the weight of Bould's larger mounted squadron to his attack. Hindsight proved the decision a poor one. "It was very unfortunate that the scattered squadrons were not withdrawn instantly from the front of such superior forces for more favorable ground. The regiment paid dearly for this error, as Starr's unsuccessful charge unhinged the Regulars' defense," wrote Lt. Paulding after the battle.[38]

As soon as the 6th Virginia cleared the departing wagons, Major Flournoy immediately formed his regiment in column of squadrons.[39] Jones, irate over the 7th Virginia's failure, continued to push the tempo of the engagement. "Shall one damned regiment of Yankees whip my entire brigade?" he asked the 6th Virginia. The men replied, "Let *us* try them!" Jones ordered Flournoy to charge immediately.[40] In turn, Flournoy reportedly told his troopers, "Men, I want every one of you to do your duty; the men that you will meet are worthy of your steel; it is the 6th Regulars, the best regiment the Yankees have."[41] Flournoy's speech "rekindled some of our fire, for we did not feel very good after seeing the condition the Seventh was in," Private E. H. Vaughn of the 6th Virginia later recalled.[42] Eager to avenge their comrades, the men of the 6th Virginia spurred ahead, Captain Richards' squadron in the lead. "The men, with a wild yell, went forward splendidly," Flournoy later recalled."[43]

As the charge of the 6th Virginia gained momentum, some of the rallied elements of the 7th Virginia joined them and also moved against both flanks. With sabers flashing, the Rebel troopers swarmed toward the small advancing Union squadron.

The wave of the reinforced Confederate charge engulfed Lieutenant Balder's isolated squadron. Caught spread out in the midst of their own charge with their flanks uncovered, the enemy closed in on the regulars from three sides. Blue and gray troopers alike hacked with sabers and fired revolvers in a wild melee on the road between the fences. The maneuver quickly turned into a rout as the badly outnumbered Federals scampered back toward their main line of battle. Starr gave the order to retreat, ensuring that he was the last man withdrawing through the defile created by the fences. Brought to bay by pursuing Confederates, he was knocked from his saddle by a bullet through his right arm and a saber slash to his head from Lt. R.R. Duncan of the 6th Virginia Cavalry. Duncan went on to saber four more regulars, "running his saber entirely through one, and twisting him from his horse."[44]

Another member of Balder's squadron, Pvt. Joseph Charlton, nicknamed "the Pittsburgh boy," was wounded in the 6th Virginia's charge. A bullet tore into the left side of his chest, passed through his body, and lodged in his right side.[45] Trying to use a fence to dismount, the unfortunate trooper slipped and fell on the fence, breaking three ribs. In intense pain and weak from his wounds, Charlton was unable to stand. Private Jacob Schilling rescued him from the fence and carried him down the road to a nearby farmhouse, where he was left for treatment.[46] Corporal Peter Flory and Private Albert McCullough of Co. L were killed. Six other members of Co. L were wounded, as was Private Sebastian Gross of Co. F and acting adjutant Lt. Tucker with a leg wound.[47] With only 22 men engaged, Co. L's losses exceeded 40 percent.

The tide of the Rebel charge pushed the remnants of Balder's squadron up the road and through their defensive positions. The remainder of the regiment was now caught badly spread out, and a line of flankers overlapped both ends of the thin Union line as well. Divided by a road now filled with Confederate horsemen, each squadron was forced to fight on its own.[48]

Due to Starr's order to mount, the Rebel charge caught Lt. Paulding's squadron at its most vulnerable. Their defensive line had been further thinned as men raced for their horses. The few dismounted skirmishers still at the wall were quickly overwhelmed. Mounted Confederates ran down the dismounted regulars, using their sabers "mercilessly," scattering Paulding's command "through the field on the right of the road or on the left as we were now going, and being pursued by the mounted foe were soon captured."[49]

The majority of the squadron's troopers were caught grouped around their horses in the process of remounting and were unable to resist the Rebel attack. "Many jumped off their horses and concealed themselves in the tall grass; but this strategy was soon detected as we had a great many more horses than prisoners, so we commenced a search, and I shall never forget how ludicrous the soldiers looked as they popped up out of the grass as we approached them," recalled Lt. John B. Connell of the 7th Virginia."[50]

"The Sixth Virginia Cavalry charged down on the Sixth U.S. Cavalry, and they being dismounted, and having deployed in fighting the Seventh Virginia Cavalry, were taken at great disadvantage," noted one regular, "as most of them were unable to reach and remount their horses, and, as a result, it became a desperate hand to hand struggle."[51] So disadvantaged was the squadron that it sustained few casualties, with most of its men captured outright. Corporal William Guigan of Co. A and Pvt. Francis Cawley of Co. G were wounded, and Pvt. Henry Borden of Co. G was killed outright.

Nevertheless, the beleaguered Federals continued their resistance, occasionally inflicting serious damage on the pursuing Confederates. "Just as we entered the wheat field where the dismounted Federals were a bullet struck me a little below the right corner of my mouth and penetrated deep enough to knock out two of my teeth and break my jawbone," wrote Sgt, T.J. Young of the 6th Virginia after the war.[52]

Another Regular, Pvt. Sidney M. Davis, had a similar story. Out of cartridges for his carbine, he hid the weapon in the tall grass and drew his revolver. Seeing the futility of flight, Davis feigned a serious wound and leaned against a fence in hopes of being overlooked. A Rebel trooper eventually saw him and called to him, "Take off those belts!" Instead, Davis raised his revolver and tried to fire. His cartridges spoiled by dampness, the revolver failed to fire. Davis had no choice but to comply when his adversary demanded, "Come across the fence, and give up your arms."[53]

Lt. Adna Chaffee's squadron in the apple orchard held out the longest. Unlike their sister squadron across the road, they were well placed and prepared for the Rebel attack. They received no order to remount, and the trees of the orchard made it difficult for their mounted enemy to approach. Unfortunately, the squadron's fire was poorly aimed and inef-

"Medal of Honor" (courtesy www.donstivers.com).

fective in stopping the charge: "wasting ammunition, and emptying their arms, most of their shots passed over our heads."[54] The fight quickly transformed into a melee of close-range pistol shots and saber strokes as the Confederates swarmed the beleaguered regulars.

Lt. John Blue of the 6th Virginia noted, "As we neared the orchard we became convinced that something more than apples were to be found in that orchard." The advancing Rebels were ordered not to fire until they were face-to-face with the enemy.[55] The 6th Virginia's adjutant, Lt. John Allan, was shot and killed at the head of his regiment's charge. Lt. Allan apparently had anticipated that the next fight would be his last. He wrote a note the night before, asking that his body be delivered to his father in Baltimore and promising that anyone who did would be paid a reward of $500. "We delivered his body, together with the note, to a citizen and afterwards learned that he carried out the request and received the money," reported Pvt. John Opie.[56]

Opie described how "the boys rode, sabre in hand, right into the Sixth Regulars, sabering right and left as they went.... A great many of the enemy were knocked from their horses with the sabre but succeeded in escaping through the tall wheat, which had not yet been harvested."[57]

Lieutenant Blue noted that the Regulars were "stubborn fighters, rather inclined to be mulish and hard to drive."[58] Although their rapid-firing carbines held off the Rebels for a short time, they were vastly outnumbered and easily flanked. "We finally persuaded them to follow the rest of their line, which had already been driven back some distance by the

7th regiment on our right," recalled Lieutenant Blue. "When they left the orchard their line was badly broken and we gave them no time to reform and soon had them on the run on the road leading in the direction of Fairfield. Their running qualities were fully equal to their fighting."[59] Chaffee fell among his men with a ball in his thigh. His troopers evidently never received orders to mount or try to escape and were simply overwhelmed by the charge.

"Out as flankers to the left of the road were flanked & surrounded and had to Cut our way out run the gauntlet in fine style & most of us succeede in gett-out," recounted trooper Ran R. Knapp of Co. E.[60] Sgt. John Pattinson of Co. M and Pvt. Augustus Nelson of Co. E were killed, and Pvt. Christian Hildebrandt of Co. M was mortally wounded. Sgt. Martin Armstrong of Co. M received a saber wound to the head which resulted in his death four months later, and three other members of Co. E were wounded.[61]

The Confederates tried to parole Lt. Chaffee, but the young Ohioan refused a parole in the field, obeying a recent War Department directive that Union soldiers not give their paroles if captured.[62] The frustrated Confederates, concerned about managing a large haul of prisoners, left Chaffee behind with the other wounded. One of his men, Pvt. John W. McKibben, found Chaffee lying on the ground in the orchard, a "neatly cut crimson edged hole in his blue pantaloons over the front part of his thigh. He was quite cheerful."[63] He was evacuated to the Marshall house with many of the regiment's wounded, and assistant surgeon Forwood "very skillfully extracted the ball from Chaffee's thigh."[64]

Seeing the 6th Virginia's charge burst through the thin blue line and recognizing the danger to his comrades, former first sergeant Joseph Bould ordered his squadron to charge from behind the orchard into the approaching melee as it swirled closer. Lt. Paulding later wrote in his diary about the charge: "I saw Bould make a fine charge up the road with the rear guard which if we had not been so greatly outnumbered would perhaps have changed the fortune of the day. The color bearer with the regimental flag was at the head of the squadron.[65] Instead of relieving the pressure, however, this move only provided the Rebels with more prisoners. Pvt. Patrick Kelly of Company H made an unsuccessful effort to capture the colors of the 6th Virginia before Bould's gallant squadron was overwhelmed.

The 6th U.S. might have lost its own regimental colors in this charge but for the quick action of Pvt. George C. Platt. The color bearer's horse was shot and went down, pinning the soldier and the flag under it. Seeing the regimental color bearer shot at the head of the column, Platt called to his squad to save the colors and charged to retrieve them. He grabbed the flag from the color bearer and "sticking close to the fence, put spurs to his horse," rescuing the colors from certain capture.[66] He took "several severe saber cuts over the head" and rammed the flagstaff through a Confederate trooper as he cut his way through the melee and rode to safety. The rest of his squad were all either killed or captured.[67]

Pvt. James McDowell of Co. H described the fight for the flag as "all hand to hand work." He saw "the Flag Bearer and his Horse go down when there was a rush for

George Crawford Platt. The regiment's first Congressional Medal of Honor recipient (public domain).

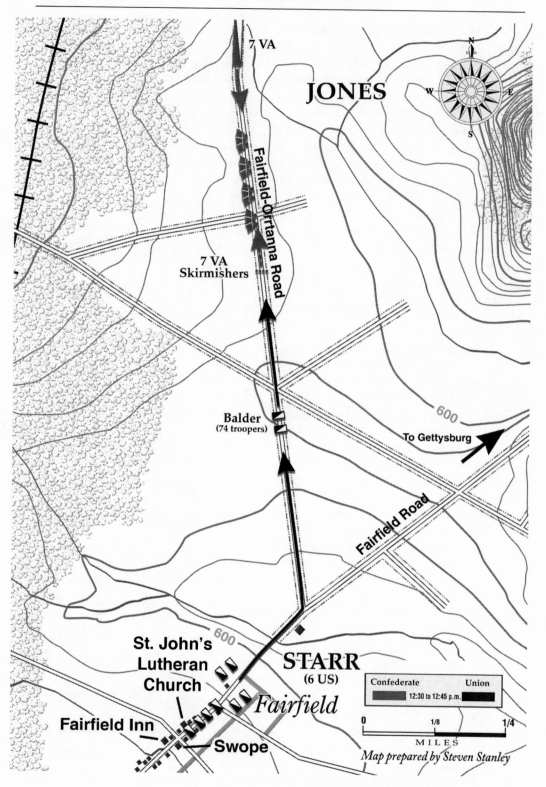

Battle of Fairfield 12:30 P.M.

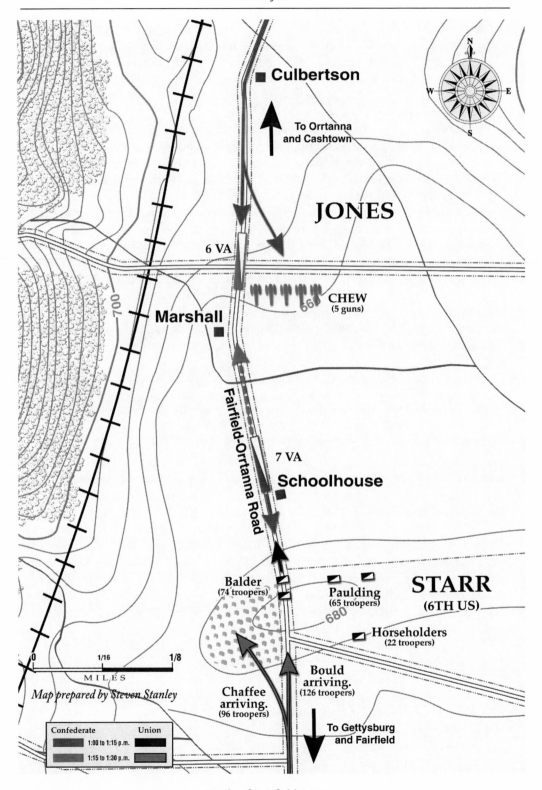

Culbertson

To Orrtanna
and Cashtown

JONES

6 VA

199 CHEW
(5 guns)

Marshall

7 VA

Schoolhouse

Fairfield-Orrtanna Road

Balder
(74 troopers)

Paulding
(65 troopers)

STARR
(6TH US)

Horseholders
(22 troopers)

680

Bould
arriving.
(126 troopers)

Chaffee
arriving.
(96 troopers)

To Gettysburg
and Fairfield

0   1/16   1/8
MILES

Map prepared by Steven Stanley

700

Confederate	Union
1:00 to 1:15 p.m.	
1:15 to 1:30 p.m.	

Battle of Fairfield 1 P.M.

the flag. They got it but at the same time I saw Geo. C. Platt grab the staff. There was a savage contest for it." He saw Platt rip the colors from the staff, stuff the flag into his shell jacket, and gallop off. McDowell lost sight of Platt and the flag when he was unhorsed by a saber stroke to the skull and was captured.[68] Co. C privates William R. Reynolds and William D. Masters were killed in the charge, as well as Pvt. William Mottern of Co. H. Seven other members of Co. H were wounded.[69]

As charging Confederates overran the apple orchard and the regimental reserve, Captain Cram's squadron finally reached the field, using the railroad bed to approach the battle from the southwest. Hearing the nearby battle raging, Lt. Nolan saw one of the enemy charges. The regulars rode to the sound of the guns, but they were, in Nolan's estimation, two miles away. As they approached the battlefield, they spotted Starr's routed troopers fleeing toward Fairfield. In an attempt to relieve the pressure on the rest of the regiment, Cram ordered his men to charge into the enemy's right flank.

The attack was futile. Initially met by Cpt. Owen's squadron of the 6th Virginia, the Rebels were soon joined by others as the regiment's resistance collapsed. The Confederates quickly absorbed Cram's command. Bugler Edson Cook was killed, and the other Company I bugler captured. Cram's horse was shot out from under him, and the rebels captured him once again, leaving Lt. Nicholas Nolan as the senior Union officer on the field. Sgt. Michael Gorman of Company I extricated Lt. Nolan from the enemy's hands, or he would have been captured as well.[70] Pvt. Charles F. Miller of Co. I, 6th U.S. Cavalry recalled the event:

> Two comrades and myself, through sheer, reckless excitement, not bravery, not even thinking our lives were in danger, confronted twice our number at no more than 15 yards distance, and exchanged salutations with them with Colts navy revolvers. We were not an easy prey as they had anticipated, as two of their number fell on the spot, and the other four putting spurs to their steeds fled. Looking around, we found ourselves alone; the whole command had vanished and we were being flanked, so we dashed on after the retreating column.[71]

Unfortunately, Miller's horse was shot out from under him before he could reach safety. Thrown to the ground, he crawled to a nearby fence for cover. With the last round for his carbine, he "leveled my piece on a rail, and taking slow and deliberate aim I fired. This delay was disastrous on my part for if I had taken to my heels as soon as my horse fell, possibly I might have escaped, but now they were too close upon me. I did, however, run until my breath was exhausted, unmindful of the shots which struck around me, and the commands to halt, surrender, etc." Miller reached his company, but his efforts were in vain. Unable to escape the press of overwhelming Confederate numbers, the bulk of the company was soon forced to surrender.[72] Privates John Ackerman and James Stroupe of Co. B were wounded, and Miller was initially reported killed in action. He rejoined the regiment months later after he was paroled from Belle Isle prison.

"I being the only officer then left with the squadron, took command," reported the 28-year-old Nolan, who was slightly wounded in the melee. "I found I was completely cut off from the regiment, and had the enemy on both flanks and rear of me."[73] Desperate for information on the rest of the regiment, he sent Sgt. Martin Schwenk to cut his way through to the rest of the regiment.[74] Schwenk somehow made it through the lines but was unable to locate any other officer.[75]

Overwhelmed by superior enemy numbers, Nolan rallied about 50 survivors of the rash charge and "commenced retreating, disputing every inch of ground with the enemy. Finding the enemy in force, I gradually fell back in the direction of Mechanicstown, where I found the regiment, and also ascertained that the commanding officer was wounded and

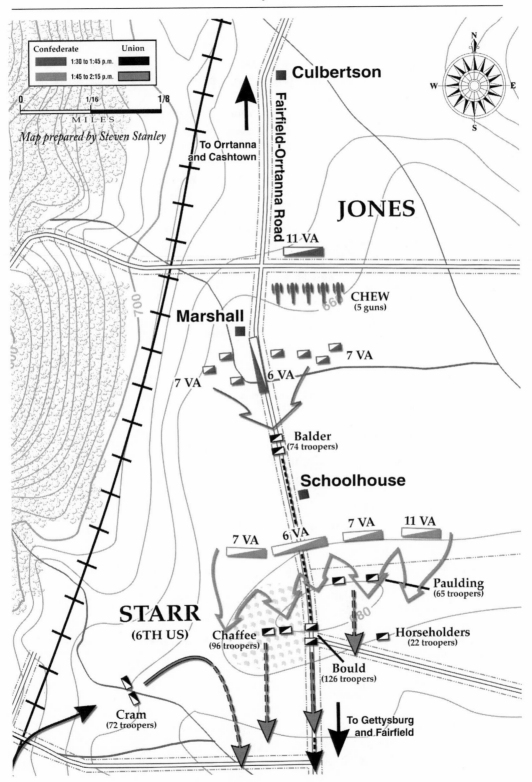

Battle of Fairfield 1:30 P.M.

in the hands of the enemy."[76] At this point the resistance of the 6th U.S. collapsed, the survivors of its routed squadrons fleeing toward Fairfield with the Confederates in hot pursuit. A private in Chew's Battery recalled, "We are having a sharp fight, the enemy is on the run. This is a beautiful engagement. The cavalry are picking up prisoners rapidly, prisoners are passing us by the hundreds."[77]

Lieutenant Paulding tried to escape on his horse but found his retreat hindered by the same fences that initially caused the Confederates such difficulties. "Finding it impossible to get away with my horse I left him between a ditch and a fence both impassable and climbing the fence took it on foot through the field pursued by half a dozen of the enemy's mounted men," he recounted. "They were soon on each side of me & being much blown by hard running & seeing no possibility of escape I surrendered to a man who was vociferously demanding my surrender & who at once robbed me of my field glass." The Confederates marched Paulding to the rear. When he arrived at the Marshall house, Paulding found a number of the regiment's officers lying wounded, including Starr.[78]

"At the fight near Fairfield, I thought several times that I was destined to be an inmate of Libby Prison," recalled Lt. Louis H. Carpenter, acting adjutant of the 6th U.S. "But I made up my mind that I would be badly wounded first at any rate. At one time I was entirely surrounded in the town itself, but I managed to cut my way out."[79] Carpenter lost his saber and his bridle while cutting his way to freedom, but was fortunate enough to capture a replacement bridle during the melee.[80]

The remnants of Balder's squadron were pushed up the road and through their defensive positions by the tide of the rebel charge. He attempted to rally his men several times as they were pushed back toward Fairfield, with little effect. Finally surrounded on the outskirts of town, Balder refused a demand for surrender and charged the rebels. They swarmed around him, firing their pistols. Although mortally wounded during this attack, Balder broke away and rode into the town. There, two citizens helped him from his horse and onto their porch, where he sat in a chair, his face pale, his eyes closed, and suffering intense pain. After the battle, Corporal James Donaldson of his company found him there and asked if he was hurt. Balder replied, "Corporal, tell the men to save themselves."[81]

Although Davis and his fellow prisoners thought Balder lingered in agony for several days, he died later that same afternoon. Assistant surgeon Forwood witnessed his passing:

> The Doctor saw Balder after he himself was taken by the enemy, dash almost alone though the town, cutting right & left with his sabre Numbers ran out into the road yelling to him to surrender but he leaned forward and with one slashing right cut the rebels fell back firing their pistols at him. He escaped unhurt until he met about 2 squadrons of the enemy toward the rear of the town. They called to him to surrender but his horse sprang into their midst and at the first cut he laid open one man's face. In a second he had wounded several others and the rebels had fallen away from him aghast, leaving a path. He had nearly got off in safety when a pistol bullet struck him in the back. He reeled, fell from his horse and crawled to a porch near by. As soon as possible the Doctor rushed to his assistance but the wound was fatal and he soon expired. A more gallant man than Lt. Balder never lived, and there was no better officer in the 6th Cavalry.[82]

The regiment's remaining men fled through Fairfield Gap toward Mechanicstown. "I rallied the men 3 times, within half a mile, checking the enemy and finally repulsed and drove him back, about a half mile this side of Fairfield," wrote Lt. Carpenter to his father several days later.

The battle of Fairfield was over. Of the 400 men who rode into Fairfield searching for the Confederate supply train, 232 were killed, wounded or missing. All five officers commanding squadrons were killed or captured, including the regimental commander. Major Starr's arm was amputated that afternoon by assistant surgeon Forwood, also a prisoner. The regiment's other assistant surgeon, William Notson, was shot through the body in the apple orchard and captured as well, though he later recovered. And Lieutenant Balder was killed. Only three officers, all lieutenants, were present for duty with the regiment the following morning at roll call. The Confederates did not escape unscathed. The two regiments reported losses of 12 killed, 40 wounded and 6 missing.[83]

The wounded were initially treated at the Marshall farmhouse by Forwood and the surgeons of the Confederate regiments. Forwood amputated Starr's shattered arm with the assistance of hospital stewards Benjamin Rees and Louis Frobin, who were both also captured. Once the Confederate brigade moved into Fairfield that evening, Forwood and Virginian Dr. Rice made a joint hospital in the Lutheran church, with the wounded reportedly "laid on boards across the backs of pews." Confederate wounded were on the left side and Union wounded on the right.[84] Wounded prisoner George Cooper also recalled details of the medical dispositions: "As a result of our fight, the enemy left 18 wounded men, unable to travel, in Fairfield, and left a nurse and an Assistant Surgeon of the 6th ... to attend them. They left 12 of my regiment, wounded, at a farmhouse and in the town, and detailed one Jacob Goode, of the 7th Va. Cav., to attend them."[85]

The wounded remained in Fairfield to recover, including their grievously wounded commander. Starr and several others were taken to the home of Susan Blythe, where she refused payment for their care. He spent several weeks recuperating there before he was well enough to return home to Philadelphia. In a gracious note penned several months later, he noted, "Surely my dear Madam, you have heaped obligations upon my head, like coals of fire, that they might burn into my brain and heart and fix your image eternally there."[86] He didn't return to the regiment until November.

The prisoners were brought initially to the Marshall house, then consolidated under guard at the nearby Culbertson house. Sometime in the evening, those able to march were ordered into ranks and marched toward Cashtown, the beginning of the long walk to Libby Prison and Belle Isle, which would take several weeks. It would be months before many of them would rejoin the regiment, and many wouldn't return at all. The oft-captured Captain Cram did not complete the journey with these men. Despite the specific orders from the War Department concerning voluntary paroles resulting from his last capture, he accepted a parole on July 7 or 8, citing as cause the gout in his feet from the tremendous amount of marching forced on the prisoners.[87]

The battered survivors of the regiment consolidated at Emmitsburg while the few remaining officers tallied their losses. The campaign was far from over, and the men quickly went about the business of preparing the regiment for its next fight. First Sergeant John Krepps of Company M later wrote, "When I called the roll in the evening of July 3, 1863, John Heckert and Henderson Donley answered 'Here' out of 45 men who had answered that morning."[88]

Ironically, the worst defeat in the regiment's brief history became one of its defining moments to the survivors of the battle. After the war, several regimental reunions were hosted by the Marshall family for the survivors of the battle, Union and Confederate alike. Several myths began concerning the regiment's defeat. One member later suggested that the old man who reported the presence of the Rebel wagon train was in fact the infamous Confederate spy William Richardson, bent on setting a trap for the 6th U.S.[89] Another later claimed that he overheard a Confederate tell another prisoner that the small train was a decoy, intended to lure the Yankees into a trap.[90] There is no official evidence from either side to support either contention.

Since Major Starr did not return to service for several months, no official report was ever submitted for the battle. Lt. Nolan's report covered his squadron's actions only, since he wasn't present for the majority of the fight. In 1868, Cram applied for a brevet to lieutenant colonel with part of his justification that he had commanded the regiment during the fighting after Starr fell. As was the custom of the time, the War Department forwarded the letter to Starr, still commanding the regiment at that time, for comment. Starr vehemently denied that Cram had commanded the regiment, even denying that he had seen him on the field. His badly outnumbered regiment, he noted, "was much cut up, routed, and disorganized, it is true, but was reformed several miles from the field by Lt. Louis H. Carpenter."[91]

Lieutenants Chaffee, Carpenter and Nolan received brevet promotions for their conduct in the battle.[92] Sgt. Martin Schwenk later received the Medal of Honor for his "bravery in an attempt to carry a communication through the enemy's lines" and for rescuing "an officer from the hands of the enemy."[93] George Platt was later awarded the Medal of Honor for seizing "the regimental flag upon the death of the standard bearer in a hand-to-hand fight and prevented it from falling into the hands of the enemy."[94]

Chapter 10

Headquarters Duty

The Long March to Belle Isle Prison

From Cashtown, the prisoners began their long march south on the afternoon of July 4. During the march they were consolidated with the rest of the Federal prisoners from the battle of Gettysburg the following day. The large number of prisoners and a scarcity of guards provided opportunities for escape, and many did so, including Lt. Bould.[1]

They reached Mountain Home on the 7th, where it was rumored that they would be paroled. Here Cpt. Cram's legacy caught up to them, however, and the officers warned them that in order to be paroled, prisoners had to be processed through the official exchange point at City Point, Virginia. In the meantime, their duty was to tie up as many Confederate troops guarding prisoners as possible, so they could not participate in the fighting. This did not prevent Cpt. Cram from once again giving his parole the following day, however. Pvt. Miller of Cram's Co. I described the officer's departure. "My Captain, a man reared in luxury and unused to such hardship, was complaining bitterly. He had not had his ration of commissary for three days, and his feet were so badly swollen he had to carry his boots in his hands, consequently he could not march and was released on his parole of honor."[2]

The prisoners spent the next two weeks on the march, suffering from frequent rains and infrequent rations. They finally reached Harrisonburg on July 21, where they were informed they would be moved by rail the remaining distance to Richmond. The following morning the prisoners were once again searched, and the officers separated from the enlisted men. They were then shipped to Richmond over the next several days. "For lack of transportation, only one squad of about seven hundred could be taken from camp in one day," wrote Miller. The day and a half ride to Richmond via Gordonsville was uncomfortable, "made mostly at night in boxcars with no seats," but this was still greatly preferable to marching.[3]

Upon reaching Richmond, the prisoners were marched from the train station to Castle Thunder, a former tobacco warehouse used as a prison. Here they were again searched, then issued rations and marched to Belle Isle Prison, on an island in the James River.[4]

The misery of life as a prisoner at Belle Isle is well chronicled, and the experiences of the men of the 6th U.S. Cavalry here were no different than those of other Union troops. Fortunately for the members of the regiment, the majority of them were paroled over the next several months.

The first lot, the men of Co. M and a mix of men from various other companies, was paroled within a month. A second batch of the regiment's men was released in November, and a third, consisting of mostly of men from Co. A, in December. Another 32 men were released in January, mostly from Co. C. In February of 1864, most of the men of Cos. F and G were paroled. From March to May another 17 were paroled, and the remainder who survived the experience over the course of the year were paroled.[5]

Many of the parolees became very ill from the effects of privation and disease in that place, and subsequently were checked into various hospitals around Annapolis, Maryland, where parolees were assigned before they returned to their regiments. Some never recovered, one of whom was former regimental sergeant major Martin Armstrong.[6]

Due to overcrowding at Belle Isle, some of the regiment's men were shipped to Andersonville Prison in Georgia, where conditions were even worse. Five of them died of disease and are buried in the cemetery there.[7]

The Pursuit

The remainder of the regiment, meanwhile, consolidated near Emmitsburg, and rejoined the brigade the next day. They pursued the retreating Confederates to South Mountain and engaged the rear guard at Williamsport on July 6. Sgt. Miles L. Teneyck of Co. E was killed in the engagement.[8]

The following day the regiment again encountered the 7th Virginia Cavalry, this time on a reconnaissance to Funkstown, Maryland. Late in the afternoon, the regiment, numbering only 146, reached the outskirts of the town and chased in the enemy's pickets. Receiving a report of additional forces in the town, Cpt. Claflin deployed the main body before moving 150 yards ahead to his advance guard to reconnoiter.[9]

The 7th Virginia, about 700 strong, were picketing the town and its approaches. When the picket was driven in, Lt. Col. Marshall rode to their support: "After examining their position, which was very much obscured by woods and the crest of an intervening hill, I ordered Companies F and G to advance upon them, and moved forward at a rapid trot. Their advance gave way before us, and fell back upon their reserve. I then ordered up our reserve at a charge."[10] What ensued was "another terrific hand to hand fight."[11] Cpt. Claflin was shot in the shoulder as the Confederates advanced, and Lt. Nolan assumed command of the regiment for the second time in four days. "I then made preparations to meet them, but, being overwhelmed by superior numbers, was forced to fall back; inflicting, however, great damage to the enemy in a running fight of 4½ miles," he reported.[12]

Marshall had taken advantage of his greater numbers and sent elements around both flanks of Nolan's line. "Our column pressed upon them with great rapidity, overtook, killing and wounding a great number," Lt. Col. Marshall wrote after the skirmish. The two regiments intermingled as the running fight continued down the road.[13]

Lt. Nolan tried to extract his command from the press, he, the color bearer and chief bugler Jacob Schuck fighting their way through to their comrades. Sgt. John McCaffrey of Co. A shot the 7th Virginia's standard bearer but wasn't able to reach the colors to seize them.[14]

Lts. Nolan, Carpenter and Tupper finally rallied the regiment near the outskirts of the Reserve Brigade's camp. Hearing the approaching noise, the 1st U.S. Cavalry advanced to support them. Lt. Col. Marshall tried in vain to halt his unit's charge, and by the time the fresh Union regiment reached the fray, the Confederates' mounts were exhausted. The pursuit turned in the other direction with two regiments chasing one, and the 7th Virginia lost 10 men and 15 horses in the ensuing chase.[15]

Brig. Gen. Merritt, in his report on the campaign, wrote that during the campaign, "there were some dashing, telling charges made, mounted. I mention, particularly, one made by the Sixth U.S. Cavalry, followed up by the First U.S. Cavalry, on the Boonsboro and Hagerstown road. In both of these the enemy was severely punished, and captures were made in hand-to-hand conflicts."[16]

The 6th U.S. Cavalry lost five killed, nine wounded and 45 prisoners in the fight. Lt. Carpenter wrote two days later "the regiment now numbers 87 men for duty. Lieut. Nolan, Lieut. Tupper & myself are the only officers left. 14 have been killed, wounded & captured since the 9th June last."[17]

The regiment was again engaged near Boonsboro on the 8th and 9th, but sustained no further casualties.

Escort, HQ, Cavalry Corps

The hard-fought battles of Brandy Station, Upperville, Fairfield and Funkstown had almost extinguished the 6th U.S. Cavalry. Accordingly, on July 11 the regiment was ordered to report for escort duty at Cavalry Corps headquarters. On the 13th, Lt. Wade's squadron of Cos. D and K rejoined the regiment, increasing its numbers to 256 for duty.[18]

The march continued over familiar ground from the previous year's campaign to Berlin, Maryland, where Cpt. Brisbin rejoined the regiment and assumed command. The march then continued south into Virginia via Lovettsville, Markham, and Warrenton Junction to near Germantown.[19]

When the regiment reached Piedmont, they received information from a mulatto boy that Mosby's men had concealed a large number of horses in a field a short distance away in the mountains near Manassas Gap. Cpt. Brisbin immediately requested and received permission from Gen. Pleasonton to investigate the matter. They found the field between two forested ridges. Lt. Carpenter later wrote of the raid: "Capt. Brisbin and Lt. Coats with about 60 men advanced around one side of the mountain and I moved on the other side with nearly the same number. We rapidly passed through the woods until we arrived at the field. Brisbin entered one end and I came in at the other. We found a force of guerrillas but after a short skirmish they fled precipitately into the woods. We captured 6 of them and succeeded in bringing off over 150 horses."[20] The regiment was able to remount some of its men on the best of the horses, and turned the remainder over to the quartermaster before continuing the march.

On the 28th, Cpt. Brisbin departed again on sick leave, but this time with an additional motive. As Lt. Carpenter noted,

> Captain Brisbin left two days since on Surgeon's Certificate of Disability. He has been troubled with a gathering in the neighborhood of the right eye. His leave gives him 10 days but I do not expect to see him at the expiration of that time. He has a great idea of commanding a negro brigade and he is about to visit Philadelphia to attend to some business related to the affair. He showed me a letter from Senator Wade of this, in which he was assured that the writer had recommended him to the War Department and that at that time they held his name under consideration.[21]

Although Cpt. Brisbin would rejoin the regiment later in the campaign, this letter from Senator Wade later resulted in the departure of many men from the 6th U.S. Cavalry to receive commissions in the 5th and 6th U.S. Colored Cavalry Regiments.

The regiment lost another officer while in Warrenton, as Lt. Stephen Balk applied to be admitted to the Invalid Corps the following day. A soldier who had initially joined the army as a bugler 25 years before, he was no longer able to meet the demands of active campaigning.[22]

Also while staying at the Glacey House in Warrenton, Cavalry Corps headquarters received a new flag by way of some officers who had been absent in Washington. An officer provided the following description of the new flag: "It consists of a white Maltese cross in the midst of a blue ground. The letter 'C' in the middle of the cross stands for 'Cavalry.' The old flag was a white piece of bunting with a Cross Sabres in the middle." It is not known whether the colors were designed by Gen. Pleasonton or someone else.[23] The regimental colors had by this time "become very tattered and torn and hardly anything is left except shreds and ribbons. The flag has been in 36 engagements." A new set was requested from the War Department.[24]

August proved to be an uneventful month for the regiment. The unit at large guarded headquarters and provided a provost squadron during movements, but it saw little other action than the occasional patrol to look for Mosby's guerrillas. For the men not on duty, the month was a return to garrison life, with daily dress parades and drills. Several of the regiment's officers remained detached for service on Gen. Pleasonton's staff, while others were tasked for duty at Reserve Brigade headquarters with Brig. Gen. Merritt. Lt. Nolan was serving as an assistant inspector general on Merritt's staff when he was wounded on August 1 in fighting at Culpeper.[25]

Lt. Thomas Simson finally joined the regiment in early August. A western theater veteran of the 4th U.S. Cavalry, he had been appointed to the 6th Cavalry in March, but was badly wounded at Franklin, Tennessee, in early April before he could report. After a long stay in the hospital, he reported for duty with the regiment, but he never fully recovered from his wounds. He was detached for recruiting duty the following April, and medically retired in February 1865 for incapacity of wounds received in battle. Simson died of complications from those wounds six months later. He was the last officer to join the regiment during the war.[26]

Mid-August brought a slight reorganization for the regiment. There were far too few officers present to have one per company, or even one per squadron. All of the regiment's billets were full, the officers were simply serving elsewhere. As a result, the regiment was organized into one squadron and two "divisions," an unofficial designation of convenience for the regiment's remaining officers. Still the largest of the squadrons, Cos. D and K served as the provost guard. The remaining ten companies were split evenly between the two divisions, with an officer in command of each. The new organization was temporary, until more men and officers returned for duty.[27]

Oddly, given their numbers, the 6th U.S. Cavalry did not accompany the Reserve Brigade when it was ordered to Giesboro Point to refit in August, nor was it sent later with a different brigade. It was the only regular cavalry regiment not to visit the facility during the war.[28]

September saw no relief in activity for the regiment. "Dress parades, drills, inspections and guard mounting have taken the place for the present of long, forced marches and hand to hand sabre fights," lamented one trooper.[29] However, many men had rejoined the regiment from the dismounted camp and from the parole camp at Annapolis, Maryland. The regiment mustered eight officers and 460 men ready to take the saddle by the end of the month.[30]

Notably, one of these returnees was not Cpt. Cram. After receiving his second unauthorized field parole after Fairfield, he was granted 20 days of leave starting on July 24, 1863, by reason of being a paroled prisoner. He then extended his leave for 60 days, and subsequently was assigned as an inspector of cavalry horses, first in Washington, D.C., and later in New York. He did not rejoin the regiment during the war.[31]

The regiment remained in camp near Germantown until September 12, 1863, when it marched with Cavalry Corps headquarters in fighting between the Rappahannock and the Rapidan near Culpeper, taking no casualties. On the 14th, it returned to camp near Culpeper, where it remained until October 11, 1863.[32] Skirmishing among the forward units continued, however, and the regiment provided orderlies daily to staff officers carrying orders to these units. Sgt. Frank Schweigus of Co. K was killed during one of these skirmishes, on September 29.[33]

The Confederate advance on Culpeper in early October caused the army to withdraw north across the Rappahannock. In a sudden attack near Brandy Station, the regiment once again assumed line of battle facing the Confederates. The 6th New York Cavalry, providing skirmishers to their front, suddenly withdrew to some woods to the regiment's rear, leaving

(Left to right) Maj. Gen. Alfred Pleasonton and Staff, Warrenton, Virginia. Standing: Lt. Ira W. Trask, 8th Illinois Cav.; Lt. George W. Yates, 4th Michigan Inf.; Lt. James F. Wade, 6th U.S. Cav.; Lt. Henry Baker, 5th U.S. Cav.; Lt. Leicester Walker, 5th U.S. Cav.; Capt. Charles C. Suydam, A.A.G.; Lt. Daniel W. Littlefield, 7th Michigan Cav.; Unknown; Lt. Curwen B. McLellan, 6th U.S. Cav.; Unknown; Lt. G. Irvine Whitehead, 6th Pennsylvania Cav. Seated: Lt. Col. Albert S. Austin, Chief Commissary; Col. George A. H. Blake, 1st U.S. Cav.; Maj. Gen. Pleasonton; Lt. Col. Charles R. Smith, 6th Pennsylvania Cav., Chief of Staff; Capt. Henry B. Hays, 6th U.S. Cav., Ordnance Officer. On ground: Lt. Woodbury M. Taylor, 8th Illinois Cav.; Capt. Enos B. Parsons, 8th New York Cav.; Capt. Frederick C. Newhall, 6th Pennsylvania Cav.; Lt. Clifford Thomson, 1st New York Cav.; Surgeon S.L. Pancoast, U.S.V.; Lt. B.T. Hutchins, 6th U.S. Cav. (Library of Congress).

its front and flanks exposed. Recognizing the danger, Maj. Morris was in the process of adjusting his lines when a Confederate column entered the opposite side of the field. Outnumbered, Maj. Morris rapidly turned and moved his company toward the woods with the Confederates in pursuit.

Passing the edge of the woods, a heavy fire of skirmishers poured into the head of the column. The 6th New York Cavalry had mistaken them for the advancing Confederates, who then caught up to the regiment's rear. During the fighting, one soldier was killed, seven wounded and 18 captured. The slain soldier, Sgt. William Ellsworth, had lost his brother, Cpl. Alonzo Ellsworth, just weeks before in the fighting at Funkstown. Among the wounded were surgeon William Forwood, Lt. Chaffee, just returned from his wound at Fairfield and commanding Co. I, and Sgt. Michael Gorman of Co. I. There's no record of which casualties were shot by the 6th New York Cavalry and which by the Confederates, but Co. I was leading the regimental column. Ironically, the 6th New York Cavalry was the regiment the 6th U.S. Cavalry had failed to aid during the battle of Upperville.[34]

The Cavalry Corps covered a great deal of ground over the following month and a half, and the regiment was again exposed in small groups as guards or orderlies. On October 13, Co. H's Cpl. Henry T. Keene was wounded and Pvt. Henry Eisle killed by guerrillas while serving as orderlies for a corps staff officer. Two days later, Lt. Nolan was again wounded near Broad Run while carrying dispatches. The same day, Pvt. Samuel Penney was wounded near Warrenton. During October, the regiment received nearly 100 men from parole and hospitals.[35]

Unfortunately, the regiment also lost one of its most beloved leaders in October. Col. William P. Sanders of the 5th Kentucky Cavalry, still a captain in the 6th U.S. Cavalry, was mortally wounded in fighting near Knoxville, Tennessee, and died on the 18th. One of the regiment's officers wrote of Sanders on learning of his death, "I question whether any other officer of the 6th Cavalry ever had the confidence and esteem of both officers and men to such an extent as Captain Saunders [sic]."[36]

On November 9, Pvts. John Harington, Harmon Place, and John Sweeney of Co. C were captured by guerrillas near Auburn. Also on the 9th, former sergeant major Hercules Carroll transferred to the General Service from the 6th U.S. Cavalry. He had been paroled from Libby Prison two days before. Three days later, Pvt. Penney's brother William, also of Co. D, was wounded near Rappahannock Station.[37]

Winter Camp Near Brandy Station

On December 1, 1863, the regiment left Robertson's Tavern, recrossed Germanna Ford and went into camp about two miles south of Brandy Station. The men were at once put to work building huts and stables for the winter. They were located near Cavalry Corps headquarters, located in the Green House near Beverly Ford. Parolees continued to return to the regiment, and by the end of the month there were 13 officers and 615 men present for duty.[38]

The regiment remained in this winter cantonment for five months. Although it was another long, cold winter, the regiment's burdens were much lighter than the winter before. There would be no extended rides to isolated picket posts this year! Cos. D and K continued on duty as provost guard at Cavalry Corps headquarters until February, when Co. L replaced Co. K. The other companies trained and drilled as much as the conditions would permit in preparation for the spring campaign, and the men suffered daily dress inspections from their officers.

Despite the easier duty, the regiment's mounts suffered greatly during the winter from a shortage of hay. The trouble was exacerbated by the issue of extra grain to attempt to make up for the absence of long forage, causing digestive issues.[39]

The opportunity was even offered for officers and men to go home for a few days each, a privilege gladly used after such a long period of continuous field service. Cpt. Brisbin did not return from his leave in January, however, instead accepting a volunteer commission as colonel of the 5th U.S. Colored Cavalry.[40]

Regimental numbers continued to build over the winter. The month of February saw 37 more men gained from parole, and 80 brave men reenlisted upon the expiration of their terms of service. Fourteen more men reenlisted in March, and included the regimental quartermaster and chief bugler. Officers returned as well, with Surgeon Forwood and Lt. Nolan both returning from their wounds in December.

The lighter comparative duty resulted in far fewer losses at winter, and the ability to construct log huts rather than dwelling in tents doubtless helped as well. Although 17 men died of disease in various hospitals, many probably the result of their time as prisoners of war, desertions were down to a handful of men.[41]

One notable desertion case drew a great deal of attention, however. Pvt. Jacob Knowl of Co. G deserted August 3, 1862, and was later apprehended on October 28, 1863. He received a death sentence from his court-martial — to be shot to death for desertion — in General Order No. 103, dated November 20, 1863, Headquarters, Army of the Potomac. Originally scheduled for December 4t the sentence was suspended by the commanding general. Pvt. Knowl spent the majority of the winter in irons in the regiment's guardhouse. During his two weeks in command before his appointment as colonel of the 11th Maryland Cavalry, Cpt. Evans attempted to intercede on his behalf in January. Pvt. Knowl's sentence was eventually mitigated in March to imprisonment at the Dry Tortugas, Florida, for the duration of the war.[42]

While in winter camp, the regiment's officers also attempted to locate the grave of Lt. Irwin from the June engagement there, combing the area and speaking to local inhabitants. It took several weeks, but a local farmer eventually showed them the grave in January, and Irwin was subsequently disinterred.[43]

In March, the regiment was surprised to learn that the secretary of war had relieved Gen. Pleasonton of command of the Cavalry Corps. As provost guard, Lt. Carpenter's squadron escorted him to Brandy Station on the 26th to catch the train north: "Before the General left I had quite a long talk with him. He said that he was very sorry to be obliged to leave the cavalry of the Army of the Potomac, that he had been identified with it ever since its organization, and know [*sic*] that it was capable of performing everything that could be expected of it, but that he left his old command with the satisfaction of knowing that it was in excellent condition."[44]

It is ironic that the 6th U.S. Cavalry was the unit to escort Gen. Pleasonton away from the corps, given its numerous difficulties with him the preceding winter.

Gen. Gregg assumed command of the corps that afternoon, but it was known among the headquarters staff to be temporary. "General Sheridan is now to be on his way from the west in order to assume command of the Cavalry Corps," wrote Lt. Carpenter several days later.[45]

As warmer weather finally approached, the regiment once again turned its attention to active campaigning.

Chapter 11

Campaigning with Sheridan

On April 6, 1864, Maj. Gen. Philip Sheridan assumed command of the Cavalry Corps, Army of the Potomac. He reviewed his command over the next several days and was not at all pleased with its condition. Although the regiment had light duty over the winter, the remainder of the corps had not been so fortunate. Constant picketing of miles of river bank in the winter weather had taken its toll. The cavalry's horses "were thin and very much worn down with excessive and, it seemed to me, unnecessary picket duty, for the cavalry picket-line almost completely encircled the infantry and artillery camps of the army, covering a distance, on a continuous line, of nearly sixty miles, with hardly a mounted Confederate confronting it at any point."[1]

He immediately set about having the cavalry relieved from much of the arduous and harassing picket duty, arguing that infantry units were more plentiful and just as capable of guarding fords and their own camps. Gen. Meade complied, reducing the picket burden by over half. This afforded an opportunity to give a brief rest to the horses and fit out the various commands for the spring campaign. Sheridan's intentions were very simple. He intended to use the army's cavalry to defeat Stuart's cavalry and deprive Lee of that cavalry's use.[2]

The regiment remained on duty as escort for Cavalry Corps headquarters, under the command of Cpt. Claflin. This entailed one squadron to guard the headquarters train as a provost guard while the other men served as orderlies and escorts for aides and the commander himself.[3]

With the coming of warmer weather, losses began to whittle down the regiment's numbers. During April, 12 men deserted and 33 chose not to reenlist at the end of their terms and were discharged. These were some of the volunteers who had joined the regiment after the battle of Antietam. This was a growing concern for the regiment's leadership, as the enlistment of every soldier in the regiment would expire over the summer and early fall. Additional losses were six men discharged for disability, four men transferred, one dropped, and one dying from disease, making an aggregate loss of 57 men in this month alone, all just before the spring campaign.[4]

The loss of so many regimental personnel, and continued duty at headquarters, greatly affects our tale of the regiment's service. As the spring campaign begins, personal accounts of service dry up. There is significantly less information of service unique to the regiment.

On May 4, 1864, the regiment left winter quarters to reconnoiter Germanna Ford, Mine Run and United States Ford, finding no enemy. They returned in time to accompany Gen. Sheridan during the Wilderness campaign. The campaign took a dramatic turn on May 8, when, following a dispute between Gen. Sheridan and Gen. Meade, Sheridan received permission to seek out and defeat Stuart's cavalry. The result was a whirlwind of fighting and marching that resulted in Stuart being mortally wounded at Yellow Tavern. The cavalry corps then moved to Haxall's Landing for supplies. Though very active during the fighting and long march that led to Yellow Tavern, they suffered no casualties.[5]

The regiment remained with the column until it arrived at Bottoms Bridge, when it was detached on May 14 and ordered to Fort Monroe to hurry forward supplies. The regiment marched 50 miles to Williamsburg on the 15th and delivered Gen. Sheridan's dispatches the next day, requesting supplies be sent forward to the corps. They remained there until the 21st, and then marched to rejoin the corps at White House. The cavalry corps rejoined the army on the 24th near Chesterfield Station, on the Richmond and Fredericksburg Railroad.[6] May also saw the departure of two more officers from the regiment. Lts. Carpenter and Wade departed to accept commissions as the lieutenant colonels of the 5th and 6th U.S. Colored Cavalry Regiments, respectively.[7]

At Hawes' Shop and again at Cold Harbor at the end of the month, they troopers were again present as observers. The end of the month saw 31 discharges and seven deserters. On June 4, they were sent to White House, and then they moved to New Castle Ferry to escort the trains back to meet the corps.[8]

On June 7, Gen. Sheridan set forth on his second raid, this one to cut the Virginia Central Railroad near Charlottesville. The regiment marched with three days' rations and two days' grain on the saddles. Several skirmishes occurred during the advance. The skirmishes culminated in the battle of Trevillian Station on the 11th, where the regiment was once again active but suffered no casualties. Burdened with a large number of wounded and prisoners, Sheridan's column started back toward the main army.

On the 16th, Gen. Sheridan dispatched Lt. Daniel Madden and 22 men from the regiment with a report on his progress and a request for supplies. A reporter from the *New York Herald* and a staff officer accompanied them. In the town of Bowling Green, they captured a Confederate officer who informed them that the Army of the Potomac had abandoned White House and crossed the James River. Deciding that Gen. Sheridan needed this information, Madden turned his party back with the prisoner.[9]

That night, Gen. Sheridan dispatched the entire regiment under Cpt. Claflin to establish contact with Gen. Meade's army. They were ambushed by home guards crossing a narrow bridge near Stephensville, where Pvt. George Beckert was killed and several wounded. Outnumbered, Claflin withdrew to Walkerton, where he met men from Gen. Custer's brigade. Leaving the bulk of the regiment with Custer, he seized a boat. Accompanied by the reporter, two staff officers and two enlisted men, Claflin attempted to sail the boat 30 miles to West Point. Upon reaching the town at noon on the 18th, they telegraphed Sheridan's dispatches to Gen. Meade.[10]

By the 21st the regiment had rejoined Gen. Sheridan's headquarters and the main column. They marched via New Baltimore to Wilcox Landing on the James River on the 26th. After a skirmish at Dabney's Mills the next day, they arrived near City Point on June 30. Between the two raids, the cavalry corps had been marching and fighting for 56 consecutive days. The men were placed in camp near Light House Point to rest and refit. The month of June closed with a loss of 75 discharges, 7 deserters, 8 missing in action, and three dead, two of these from disease: an aggregate loss of 93 men.[11]

The majority of the month of July was spent refitting the regiment. There was a rapid march to assist Gen. Wilson's division and several days at the end of the month spent on the north side of the James supporting Gen. Hancock's corps, but they saw no further fighting. The end of July saw another 137 men discharged at the expiration of their term of service.[12]

On August 1, 1864, Gen. Sheridan was relieved from duty with the Army of the Potomac and assigned to command the Middle Military Division. Co. L was detached from the regiment and accompanied the general as his escort, while the remaining portion of the regiment performed various duties as messengers, orderlies, guards, etc.[13]

The remaining companies embarked from Light House Point on the 12th. They landed the next day at Giesboro Point and camped that night near the Navy Yard Bridge. They departed on the 15th and marched via Rockville, Frederick and Knoxville to Harpers Ferry, where they encamped at Bolivar Heights on the 19th. The following day, the regiment proceeded to Berryville and joined the corps headquarters. Their hopes of active service were dashed, as they were once again ordered to headquarters escort duty. They remained near Berryville until mid–September.[14]

One reason for continued headquarters duty was undoubtedly their shrinking numbers. Another 256 men, a quarter of the regiment's authorized strength, were discharged upon their expiration of service in August.[15]

Gen. Sheridan spent August and the first half of September monitoring Confederate activity in the valley without actively seeking battle. Without all of his forces in place, he was outnumbered slightly by the Confederates, and they had more infantry than he did. There was also the expectation that Grant's pressure on Lee's forces around Petersburg would cause the withdrawal of some of Gen. Early's forces to help defend Richmond.[16]

By mid–September, all of Sheridan's troops had arrived in or near the Shenandoah Valley. Learning that the Confederates had withdrawn the infantry troops of Gens. Anderson and Kershaw back towards Richmond, Gen. Grant ordered Gen. Sheridan to drive the Confederates from the Shenandoah Valley.

Seizing the initiative, Gen. Sheridan began a general advance early in the morning of September 19. Crossing Opequon Creek, he advanced on Gen. Early's troops at Winchester. The long bloody day of fighting was roughly a stalemate until late in the afternoon. A mounted charge by the First and Third Cavalry divisions against the Confederate left flank coincided with an infantry frontal assault, and the Confederates were driven through Winchester and up the valley in disarray. It was the largest single cavalry charge of the war. The fall of darkness finally stopped pursuit.[17]

The pursuit continued at dawn, and the Confederates were finally brought to bay at Fisher's Hill on September 22. The Confederates were again flanked out of their defensive position, this time by Gen. Emory's 8th Army Corps. The 6th U.S. Cavalry was briefly released from headquarters duty to assist Col. Devin's brigade in the pursuit and escort prisoners to the rear, which occupied them until they reached Harrisonburg on the 24th.[18]

After a pause of several days, Gen. Sheridan received Gen. Grant's order to lay waste to the Shenandoah Valley to deprive the Confederacy of the support of its countryside. On the return march down the valley, everything that could be considered rations or forage was seized or destroyed. Gen. Early's Confederates had been badly beaten in the previous two battles and were unable to do much more than slowly follow Sheridan's forces back up the valley.

On October 12, 1864, Gen. Early conducted an early-morning surprise attack against the Union army. Gen. Sheridan was miles away in Winchester at the time. The Confederates drove the Union forces from their camps in disarray by dawn. Despite considerable confusion, the regiment hastily saddled and formed into line. Their camp was fortunately located to the left rear of the Union line.

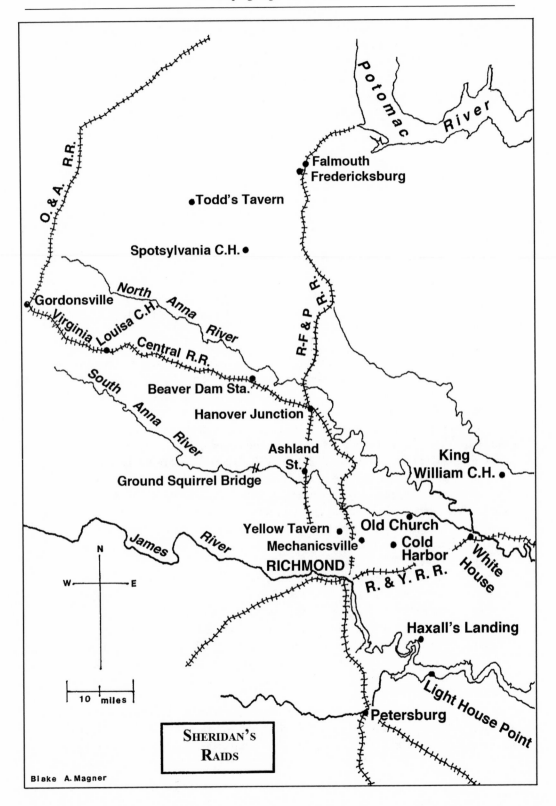

O. & A. R.R.

Potomac River

Falmouth
Fredericksburg

•Todd's Tavern

Spotsylvania C.H. •

R-F & P R.R.

North Anna River

Gordonsville

Virginia Louisa C.H.

Central R.R.

South Anna River

Beaver Dam Sta.

Hanover Junction

Ashland St.

King William C.H. •

Ground Squirrel Bridge

James River

Yellow Tavern •

Old Church •

N

Mechanicsville

Cold Harbor

White House

W — E

RICHMOND

R. & Y. R.R.

Haxall's Landing •

10 miles

Light House Point

Petersburg

SHERIDAN'S
RAIDS

Blake A. Magner

With daylight, the Union commanders on the scene were able to restore some order, and they stubbornly withdrew down the valley as the Confederates aggressively pursued them. A defensive line was established about two miles to the rear of their camps, and the cavalry skirmished on the advancing enemy's flanks. Notified of the impending disaster, Gen. Sheridan mounted his horse and made his famous ride to rally the army. Ironically, given the amount of time spent at his headquarters, the 6th U.S. Cavalry missed this ride, as the 17th Pennsylvania Cavalry had escorted the general to Winchester.[19]

By mid-afternoon, Sheridan had rallied his army, and ordered a general assault at 4:00 P.M. The cavalry was ordered to charge the Confederate flank. The tide turned with the general advance and the Confederates were routed, losing not only their gains of the morning, but 25 artillery pieces as well, all of their ambulances and ammunition wagons, and over 1,500 prisoners.[20]

During the charge, another favored son of the regiment fell in battle. Charles Russell Lowell, now a colonel of volunteers and on this day in command of the Reserve Brigade, was mortally wounded by a bullet while at the head of a brigade charge. He died later that afternoon, shortly after receiving notification of his appointment as a brigadier general of volunteers. His division commander, Gen. Merritt, noted in his official report that Lowell had been "the brightest star among the many good officers," and that his death had cast a pall on the entire command.[21]

The battle of Cedar Creek effectively ended the Shenandoah Valley campaign. Sheridan's forces conducted a half-hearted pursuit of Early's broken forces before returning to their camps at Cedar Creek. There was still work to be done chasing guerrillas and completing the devastation of the valley, but the Confederate force was broken beyond repair by the battle.

For a variety of reasons, none relevant to the regiment, Gen. Sheridan elected not to pursue Early's forces out of the valley and attack now unprotected sites such as the Virginia Central Railroad at Gordonsville or Charlottesville. Instead, he chose to keep his command in the valley, thus marking the end of the fall campaign for all intents and purposes.[22]

Still on duty at Gen. Sheridan's headquarters, the regiment remained in the vicinity of Cedar Creek until mid–November, when they moved to Kernstown. The regiment continued to hemorrhage men through the fall as their enlistments expired. The September regimental returns showed the discharge of another 96 men. October saw the loss of 61 and November 17 more.[23]

Toward the end of November, Cpt. Claflin received a leave of absence from commanding the regiment to travel home and marry his betrothed. While traveling with his friend Cpt. George Sanford of the 1st U.S. Cavalry and an escort from the 17th Pennsylvania Cavalry, they were ambushed near Bunker Hill by a band of Mosby's partisans. "The road," Sanford later wrote, "at this time was considered so excessively dangerous, that all travelling was done at night, the danger being regarded as less in the dark, as the guerrillas were then unable to perceive a command at great enough distance to complete their plans for an ambush in time."

In this case, the darkness wasn't enough to prevent the attack. Fortunately the two officers and the Pennsylvanians were equal to the task, and the partisans were repulsed with only a few men wounded. Claflin proceeded home unharmed for his impending nuptials.[24]

Chapter 12

In at the Death

The regiment made up for a relaxing November with an active December. Early in the month, they marched to Stephenson's Station and formed a part of Gen. Merritt's command on his raid into Loudoun Valley, returning on the 10th. On the 19th, they were back in the field, this time with Gen. Torbert's command on the raid to Gordonsville, and returned on the last day of the year, when they went into winter camp at Kernstown. The weather was intensely cold during these operations and both men and horses suffered severely.[1]

Despite the intensity of the year's campaigning, the 6th U.S. Cavalry ended the year relatively unscathed. Only two soldiers were killed in action, while three others died of wounds. Five others died of disease or while prisoners of war. Expiring enlistments were of course a different story. The close of this year saw the loss of nearly 800 men within the previous nine months. The December 1864 monthly return showed only 4 officers and 225 men present for duty — less than a quarter of its authorized strength — and many of those were sick.

However, winter camp provided the regiment an opportunity to fill its depleted ranks with recruits from the army's recruiting depots. In this way, 89 recruits were gained in December, 82 more in January, and 43 more in February. Conversely, January also saw the loss of 61 battle-hardened veterans. These included the gallant Sgt. Martin P. Schwenk, who would later be awarded the Congressional Medal of Honor for his actions at Fairfield, and the loss of Sgt. Maj. Patrick Cusack, who received an appointment as captain, 6th U.S. Colored Cavalry. In February, 18 more of these veterans were lost, making the aggregate gain for the time spent at winter camp 135 recruits — not enough to show even an appreciable gain. Yet fortunately, and unbeknownst to the regiment, the war had little more than a month of hard fighting left for these recruits to prove their merit on the battlefields.[2]

In February 1865, Gen. Sheridan received largely discretionary orders from Gen. Grant. He was to destroy the Virginia Central Railroad and the James River Canal, capture Lynchburg if practicable, and then either join Gen. William T. Sherman's army in North Carolina or return to Winchester. Sheridan interpreted Grant's orders rather liberally, and instead of heading to North Carolina in March 1865, he decided to rejoin the Army of the Potomac at Petersburg. He wrote in his memoirs, "Feeling that the war was nearing its end, I desired my cavalry to be in at the death."[3]

On February 27, 1865, winter camp was broken and the regiment marched from Winchester with the cavalry corps. The arrival of recruits had not helped the regiment much except on paper. Since the new recruits were not yet trained, they were sent to a remount camp near Frederick, Maryland, along with the regiment's headquarters. Only three officers and 62 enlisted men, the majority of them consolidated in Co. L, rode south under the command of Lt. McLellan.[4] Their small number did have one benefit, however. Now too small for headquarters duty, they were returned at last to the Reserve Brigade.

For the majority of the march, they were paired for duty with their old comrades of the 6th Pennsylvania Cavalry, generally securing bridges in advance of the column. They marched on terrible roads in brutally cold weather, proceeding via Staunton and Rockfish Gap to Ivy Depot on the Virginia Central Railroad, where they burned the depot and destroyed a warehouse full of tobacco and stores. They reached Charlottesville on the 5th and halted a day there to rest their mounts and lighten their loads before marching the 21 miles to Scottsville. Here they remained until midnight wreaking damage on the locks, boats and bridges of the James River Canal.[5]

The march continued to the southeast, the column destroying all infrastructure and supplies in its path. At one point, according to the brigade commander's official report, they marched "fifty-six miles in thirty-six hours." They finally reached White House on the 19th. Fortunately supplies from Gen. Grant's army were awaiting them when they arrived. The following morning they crossed the river and went into camp not far from Harrison's Landing.[6]

Although the brigade reported only three men killed and two wounded in 23 days of fighting and marching, the regiment did not escape unscathed. Three soldiers went missing in action along the march, and Pvt. William Vanderender was killed in a skirmish at Hanover Junction.[7]

On March 27, 1865, the cavalry joined the Army of the Potomac near Petersburg and on the 29th proceeded to Dinwiddie Court House. The next day they engaged the Confederates and drove them back into their works at Five Forks, holding the position for three hours against repeated attacks and until their ammunition was exhausted. The entire day a steady downpour turned the roads to mud, slowing the advance. The enemy flanked the regiment on its right under cover of dense woods, and when the line was withdrawn for ammunition, the Confederates charged the flank, capturing Lt. Nolan and 18 men.[8]

The battle continued the following day, the 29th, when Confederate infantry attacked and drove the Cavalry Corps back to Dinwiddie. Next morning the regiment occupied the extreme right in the memorable battle of Five Forks and connected with the Fifth Corps when it came into action during the afternoon, the regiment wheeling to the left and resting on the right of the enemy's works. An advance was ordered in the afternoon, and the Confederates were forced back.[9]

They were not the only badly under-strength unit in the brigade. At Five Forks, when the 6th Pennsylvania, "dismounted to fight on foot, there stood in the ranks but 48 men with carbines." The regiment was reassigned to Cavalry Corps headquarters the next day.[10]

On April 2, the Cavalry Corps once again caught up to the rear guard of the Confederates and dogged their heels for the next several days. The pursuit was continued incessantly and with great loss to the enemy until April 6, when they were forced to make a stand to save their trains near Sayler's Creek. Pressed hard on their flank by Union cavalry, their infantry was forced to form. This delayed their march long enough for the VI Corps to arrive, and a combined infantry and cavalry assault resulted in the capture of about 10,000 enemy soldiers.[11]

During this action, the regiment was ordered to take possession of some log huts. It is recorded in the regimental archives that the few men left in the ranks hesitated, believing it was a suicidal mission. Lt. McLellan faced them and said, "Men, let us die like soldiers!"

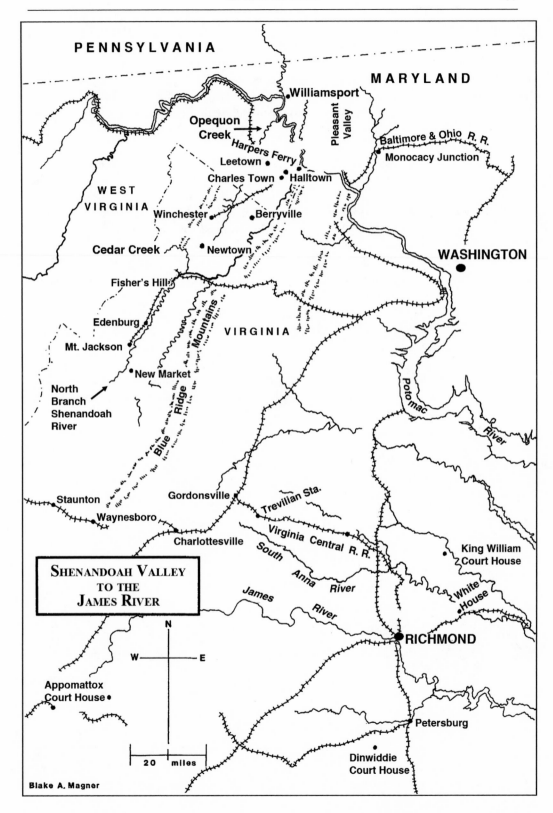

PENNSYLVANIA

MARYLAND

Williamsport

Opequon Creek →

Harpers Ferry

Pleasant Valley

Baltimore & Ohio R. R.

Leetown

Monocacy Junction

WEST VIRGINIA

Charles Town

Halltown

Winchester

Berryville

Cedar Creek

Newtown

WASHINGTON

Fisher's Hill

Blue Ridge Mountains

Edenburg

VIRGINIA

Mt. Jackson

New Market

North Branch Shenandoah River →

Potomac River

Staunton

Gordonsville

Trevilian Sta.

Waynesboro

Virginia Central R. R.

Charlottesville

South Anna River

King William Court House

White House

James River

SHENANDOAH VALLEY
TO THE
JAMES RIVER

RICHMOND

N
W — E

Appomattox Court House

Petersburg

20 miles

Dinwiddie Court House

Blake A. Magner

Every one of the little band rushed the huts through a hail of Confederate lead and seized them with a loss of but three men wounded.[12]

The pursuit was pressed into the night. While trying to force a passage across the creek after dark, a shell burst in the midst of the regiment's remaining soldiers, wounding three, one of them mortally. Pvt. James King died the next day from his wounds. This was the regiment's last fight, though they continued the pursuit with the rest of the Cavalry Corps — which culminated on April 9 in the surrender of the Army of Northern Virginia at Appomattox Court House.[13]

The following day, the cavalry started for Petersburg and after a brief rest resumed the march to North Carolina to join Sherman's army. They had only reached Danville on the march, however, when they received word that Gen. Johnston's army had surrendered as well. They immediately turned back and proceeded to Petersburg. They were joined there before the end of the month by Maj. Morris, who assumed command of the regiment.[14]

The regiment left Petersburg on May 10 and marched via Richmond and Alexandria to its former camp at Bladensburg, Maryland. After a review by Gen. Sheridan in Washington, it reached its camp on the 21st. Here they were soon joined by the detachments from the remount camp near Frederick.[15]

On May 23, 1865, the regiment rode at the head of the Reserve Brigade in the Grand Review held in Washington, D.C., followed by the 2nd Massachusetts Cavalry and the 6th Pennsylvania Cavalry.[16] They mustered only eight officers and 169 enlisted men — a mere shadow of the full organization which had so proudly marched down Pennsylvania Avenue three years before. The official close of hostilities was never declared, but for the 6th U.S. Cavalry, who again marched proudly during that long awaited day, the Civil War was finally over.[17]

PART II: REGIMENTAL ROSTER

Through years of research, the authors have attempted to identify every soldier who served in the 6th U.S. Cavalry during the Civil War. In doing so, we compiled statistics that are somewhat different than both Carter's *From Yorktown to Santiago* and Fox's *Regimental Losses in the American Civil War*. This additional research also disclosed many unknown statistics that would have been painstaking and therefore impractical to record before the computer age.

A total of 60 officers were appointed to the regiment, 14 from within the ranks. There were also 3 officers who declined their appointments, 2 officers who never joined, and 2 more who were assigned to another regiment, but attached for long enough to be listed on the regimental morning reports. Three officers were killed in action outright, 2 died of wounds received in action, 2 died as prisoners of war, 1 from disease and 1 from a steamboat accident, for a total of 9. Of the remaining officers, 21 were recorded wounded in the line of duty, and many received multiple battlefield injuries. A total of 30 officers were killed or wounded in action, or 50 percent of those assigned.

A total of 2,084 men and 1 known woman enlisted in the regiment. Of these, 29 received a commission, 15 outside the regiment; 914 were honorably discharged and 230 received discharges for disability; 43 were assigned but never joined; another 14 were recruits for some time, yet rejected for one reason or another; and 3 were confined and released by civil authority. There are 72 men who have no known information. Only 99 reenlisted after their initial tour, nearly all in February and March 1864, and 36 of these men later deserted. An additional 508 during their initial enlistment, and 1 was shot dead for desertion.

Enlisted casualties were 54 killed in action, 2 permanently missing in action and 148 wounded in action. Additionally, 384 went missing in action during one of the many battles, many of these captured by the enemy and later paroled. There are 242 men known to have been prisoners of war at some point, most of these from the battle of Fairfield. Another 27 died as prisoners of war, 74 died of disease, 2 died from accidental gunshot wounds, 1 drowned and 13 died from unknown causes — the most likely culprit being disease. This totals 172 dead, 148 wounded, 2 permanently missing in action and 384 missing in action at some point, totaling 706 casualties, or roughly 70 percent aggregate force.

The following roster lists every known soldier who enlisted in the regiment during the war. It contains as much additional information as space permits concerning volunteer enlistments, incarcerations, wounds received, etc. All were honorably discharged unless otherwise noted. Names that were spelled incorrectly in the original source have been corrected using brackets.

Ackerman, James Oscar. Mustered: Pvt. Co. E, 3rd WI Inf. 3 May 1861. Transferred: 1st Sgt. Co. C, 6th U.S. Cav. 24 October 1862 (age 21 in Knoxville, MD)–29 June 1864. B: 19 November 1841, Morristown, St. Lawrence Co., NY. Blue eyes, black hair, florid complexion, 5′5.

Ackerman, John. Mustered: Pvt. Co. E, 28th PA Inf. 6 July 1861. Transferred: Pvt. Co. B, 6th U.S. Cav. 25 October 1862 (age 23 in Knoxville, MD)–6 July 1864. WIA/POW, Fairfield, PA. Paroled at Baltimore, MD, 25 August 1863. B: 1838, Colesville, Sussex Co., NJ, lawyer. Hazel eyes, light hair, ruddy complexion, 5′10. D: 22 August 1914.

Ackerman, John E. (alias Evans, Charles M.) Mustered: Pvt. Co. B, 3rd WI Inf. 20 Apr 1861. Transferred: Pvt. Co. C, 6th U.S. Cav. 24 October 1862 (age 21 in Knoxville, MD)–29 June 1864. B: Allegheny Co., NY. Blue eyes, light hair, light complexion, 5'9. Mustered: Pvt. Co. A. 1st MD Potomac Home Brigade (PHB) Inf. 9 February 1865. Transferred: Co. A. 13th MD Inf. 8 Apr 1865–29 May 1865. Mustered out at Baltimore, MD.

Acton, William H. Rct. 2 November 1864 (age 21 at Cleveland, OH)–21 November 1864. B: Montreal, Quebec, CAN, grocer. Blue eyes, brown hair, fair complexion, 5'6. Sub for G. Kall. Deserted.

Adams, Benjamin F. Pvt. Co. F, 21 November 1864 (age 20 at Cincinnati, OH)–15 October 1865. B: Montreal, Quebec, CAN, blacksmith. Grey eyes, light hair, fair complexion, 6'. Deserted.

Adams, Benjamin F. Pvt. Co. M, 26 November 1861 (age 30 at Pittsburgh, PA)–7 January 1865. WIA, Williamsburg. Discharged at Camp Russell, VA. B: Farmersville, Cattaraugus Co., NY, farmer. Grey eyes, brown hair, light complexion, 5'1½.

Adams, Charles. Pvt. Co. C, 22 August 1864 (age 19 at Rochester, NY)–29 January 1865. B: Danville, CAN, laborer. Blue eyes, light hair, ruddy complexion, 5'4. Deserted.

Adams, George R. Pvt. Co. A, 19 September 1861 (age 23 at Philadelphia, PA)–27 April 1862. B: Weymouth, Atlantic Co., NJ, moulder. Lt. blue eyes, dark hair, dark complexion, 5'5½. Deserted.

Adams, John. Pvt. Co. A, 22 December 1864 (age 21 at Cleveland, OH)–10 May 1865. B: Allegheny Co., PA, book maker. Grey eyes, brown hair, fair complexion, 5'8½. Deserted.

Adams, John W. Pvt. Co. A, 19 September 1861 (age 21 at Philadelphia, PA)–19 September 1864. B: Millville, Cumberland Co., NJ, moulder. Blue eyes, brown hair, light complexion, 5'8. Discharged at Harper's Ferry, VA. Also served in Co. K, 4th U.S. Art. and the U.S. Coastal Art. D: 2 July 1902.

Adams, Thomas. Pvt. Co. L, 14 December 1864 (age 18 at Cleveland, OH)–27 January 1865. B: Niagra Co., CAN, farmer. Hazel eyes, Brown hair, dark complexion, 5'4½. Deserted.

Addis, Edward F. (S). Pvt. Co. B, 9 August 1861 (age 18 at Cleveland, OH)–27 April 1863. Disability discharge at Alexandria, VA. B: Nelson, OH, engineer. Grey eyes, light hair, sallow complexion, 5'4¾. WIA (gunshot wound of left tibia), Barber's Crossroads. Mustered: Pvt. Co.

D, 5th NJ Inf. 22 September 1864. Transferred: Pvt. Co. D, 7th NJ Inf. 6 November 1864, Mustered out 10 December 1864 at Ft. David, Petersburg, VA.

Adelmeyer, John H. M as Pvt. Co. E, 3rd WI Inf. Promoted to Eighth Cpl. Transferred: Farrier (CPL), Co. C, 6th U.S. Cav. 24 October 1862 (age 24 at Knoxville, MD)–24 April 1864. B: GER. Blue eyes, black hair, florid complexion, 5'5. Mustered as Cpl. Co. E, 1st WI Cav. 28 September 1864–19 July 1865. Mustered out at Edgefield, TN.

Ager, John. Enlisted: Pvt.—1st Sgt. Co. I, 4th U.S. Inf. 9 October 1857–9 October 1862. Enlisted: Pvt. Co. C, 6th U.S. Cav. 29 March 1864 (age 25 at Washington, DC)–29 March 1867. B: Wurttemberg, GER, cutler. Brown eyes, dark brown hair, florid complexion, 5'10. Discharged at Waco, TX.

Agnew, James R.. Pvt.-Saddler. Co. M, 10 September 1861 (age 31 at Pittsburgh, PA)–24 May 1864. B: IRE, shoemaker. Brown eyes, black hair, dark complexion, 5'4½. MIA, Brandy Station. D: 24 May 1864 from chronic diarrhea in General Hospital at Annapolis, MD.

Albert, John Henry. Pvt. Co. C, 25 November 1861 (age 25 at Philadelphia, PA)–19 February 1862. B: Harrisburg, Dauphin Co., PA., sailor. Grey eyes, brown hair, dark complexion, 5'10. Deserted.

Albrecht, Rudolph. Mustered: Pvt. Co. E, 1st OH Inf. 16 April 1861–1 August 1861. Enlisted: Pvt. Co. A, 6th U.S. Cav. 4 October 1861 (age 21 at Cleveland, OH)–4 October 1864. B: 1841, Baden, GER, bartender. Blue eyes, brown hair, fair complexion, 5'7¾. Discharged at Harrisburg, VA. D: 29 September 1866.

Albright, Henry William. Pvt. Cos. G & B, 12 August 1861 (age 28 at Rochester, NY)–9 February 1867. B: GER, teamster. Brown eyes, light hair, fair complexion, 5'8¼. Reenlisted: 10 February 1864 at Brandy Station. Discharged at Austin, TX. D: 23 November 1886.

Albright, James. Pvt. Co. L, 1 February 1862 (age 18 at Cleveland, OH)–26 May 1862. B: 30 November 1842 Stark Co., OH, boatman. Hazel eyes, sandy hair, ruddy complexion, 5'6¾. Disability discharge at Washington, DC. Mustered: Pvt. Co., 45th OH Inf. 26 January 1864–20 August 1865. D: 3 May 1922. Note: Grave is spelled "Allbright."

Alden, Alanson B. Cpl. Co. G, 31 June 1861 (age 20 at Erie, PA)–31 June 1864. B: 16 September 1841 Pine Grove, Schuylkill Co., PA, carpenter. Grey eyes, light hair, fair complexion, 5'5½.

Discharged at Lighthouse Point, VA. Note: Alanson and Rinaldo were brothers.

Alden, Rinaldo. Bugler. Co. G, 31 June 1861 (age 19 at Erie, PA)–31 June 1864. B: August 1843 Pine Grove, Schuylkill Co., PA, laborer. Grey eyes, light hair, fair complexion, 5' 5½. POW, Fairfield, 3 July 1863–17 February 1864. Paroled, reported at Camp Parole. Discharged at Lighthouse Point, VA. D: August 7, 1910.

Aldrich, William. Mustered: Pvt. Co. F, 3rd WI Inf. Transferred: Pvt. Co. F, 6th U.S. Cav. 25 October 1862 (age 21 at Knoxville, MD)–29 June 1864. B: Saratoga Springs, Saratoga Co., NY, harness maker. Grey eyes, brown hair, fresh complexion, 5' 8½. MIA, Fairfield, PA.

Alexander, James. Bugler. Co. H, 29 October 1861 (age 18 at Philadelphia, PA)–6 September 1871. B: Co. Down, IRE, clerk. Grey eyes, light hair, light complexion, 5' 7½. WIA, Funkstown. Reenlisted: 14 March 1864 in the field. Tried by GCMO 26 September 1865 at Frederick, MD. Deserted 7 October 1866. Apprehended 3 February 1867. Discharged 6 April 1867 by General Court Martial. Reenlisted: Pvt. Co. I, 18 August 1869, Philadelphia, PA. Deserted 14 May 1870. Apprehended 15 May 1870. Deserted 6 September 1871.

Alexander, James. Pvt. Co. A, 25 September 1861 (age 19 at Philadelphia, PA)–30 August 1862. B: Dundee, SCO, laborer. Hazel eyes, dark hair, dark complexion, 5' 4¾. WIA, Williamsburg. Brought to the Seminary Hospital, Hampton, VA, 11 May 1862. Discharged for disability at Philadelphia, PA.

Alexander, William. Pvt.-Cpl. Co. H, 17 August 1861 (age 18 at Philadelphia, PA)–10 September 1862. B: Co. Down, IRE, plasterer. Blue eyes, brown hair, fair complexion, 5' 7. WIA, Sugar Loaf Mountain. D: 10 September 1862.

Allen, Charles W. (alias Force, Preston S.) Cpl. Cos. C, L, 1 December 1861 (age 18 at Bristol, PA)–1 December 1864. B: Berks Co., PA, farmer. Grey eyes, red hair, ruddy complexion, 5' 8. POW, Fairfield, 3 July 1863–21 June 1864. Paroled. Discharged near Winchester, VA. Enlisted: Pvt. Co. A, 2nd U.S.V.V. Inf. And 3rd U.S.V.V. Inf.

Allen, James. Pvt. Co. M, 3 November 1864 (age 22 at Harrisburg, PA)–21 November 1864. Deserted. B: Co. Tipperary, IRE, boatman. Blue eyes, fair hair, fair complexion, 5'10. Sub for C. Brown.

Allen, James. Pvt.-Cpl. Co. M, 7 September 1861 (age 20 at Pittsburgh, PA)–10 July 1862. B: IRE, drayman. Grey eyes, sandy hair, light complexion, 5' 8½. WIA, Williamsburg. Disability discharge at Philadelphia, PA.

Allen, Logan. Mustered: Pvt. Co. C, 14th IN Inf. 6 July 1861–23 October 1862. Transferred: Pvt. Co. C, 6th U.S. Cav. 23 September 1862 (age 20 at Knoxville, MD)–23 April 1864. B: 7 January 1843, Daviess Co., IN. Grey eyes, brown hair, light complexion, 5' 6. D: 18 January 1900, Raglesville, Daviess, IN.

Allen, Wilbur R. Pvt. Co. E, 13 September 1861 (age 25 at Adrian, MI)–28 May 1862. B: Genesee, NY, painter. Blue eyes, light hair, sallow complexion, 5' 9¾. Disability discharge at Washington D.C.

Allen, Zimri H. Mustered: Pvt. Co. C, 14th IN Inf. 7 June 1861–23 October 1862. Transferred: Pvt. Co. B, 6th U.S. Cav. 27 October 1862 (age 28 at Knoxville, MD)–15 January 1863. B: 22 March 1835, Lawrence Co., IN, cooper. Grey eyes, brown hair, ruddy complexion, 5' 8. Disability discharge at camp at Falmouth, VA. D: 23 April 1883, Lawrence Co., IN.

Alpstag, John R. Pvt. Co. I, 2 August 1861 (age 28 at Rochester, NY)–9 February 1867. B: GER, farmer. Blue eyes, brown hair, fair complexion, 5' 5. WIA/MIA, Funkstown. Reenlisted: 8 February 1864 at Brandy Station. Discharged at Jacksboro, TX. D: 1923, Rochester, Monroe, NY.

Alton, Henry M. Pvt. Co. D, 19 August 1861 (age 21 at Pittsburgh, PA)–19 August 1864. B: London, ENG, miner. Brown eyes, brown hair, dark complexion, 5' 9½.

Amarine, Valentine. Mustered: Pvt. Co. D, 11th OH Inf. 22 April 1861–21 August 1861. Enlisted: Pvt. Co. E, 6th U.S. Cav. 4 September 1861 (age 22 at Columbus, OH)–3 March 1863. B: Miami Co., OH, rail roader. Grey eyes, brown hair, sallow complexion, 5' 6. Disability discharge at Washington D.C. Mustered: Pvt. 15th IN Art. Batt. (Light), 7 July 1863. D: 26 October 1863.

Ames, Almon Samuel. Mustered: Pvt. Co. I, 136th PA Inf. 8 August 1862–29 May 1863. Enlisted: Pvt. Co. D, 6th U.S. Cav. 26 January 1864 (age 16 at Meadesville, PA)–25 January 1867. B: 18 March 1847 Meadesville, Crawford Co., PA. WIA (GSW in right side), Wilson's Creek, 1864. Discharged at Jacksboro, TX. D: 5 January 1923, Roulette Twp., Potter, PA.

Anderson, Dalton. Pvt. Co. L, 19 September 1864 (age 24 at Rochester NY)–19 September 1867. B: Grange Co., TN, farmer. Blue eyes, brown hair, sallow complexion, 5' 8½. Discharged at Camp Wilson, TX.

Anderson, Edward F. Pvt. Co. C, 1 December 1861 (age 18 at Bristol, PA)–26 April 1862. B: Albany, NY, sailor. Grey eyes, brown hair, ruddy complexion, 5'5. Deserted.

Anderson, John. Pvt. Cos. A, L, 1 November 1861 (age 22 at Washington, DC)–4 November 1864. B: Riga, GER, butcher. Blue eyes, brown hair, ruddy complexion, 5'4½. Discharged at Cedar Creek, VA.

Anderson, William R. Mustered: Pvt. Co. G, 38th PA Inf. (9th Reserves), 4 May 1861. Transferred: Pvt. Co. M, 6th U.S. Cav. 28 October 1862 (age 26 at Knoxville, MD)–28 May 1864. B: Beaver Co., PA, butcher. Blue eyes, light hair, fair complexion, 5'9.

Andrews, Peter. Enlisted (age 14 at New York, NY), Co. B, 1st Dragoons, 1 October 1857–1 October 1862. Discharged near Sharpsburg, MD, musician (band). Break in service. Enlisted: Chief Bugler. Cos. L, F&S, 6th U.S. Cav. 1 April 1863 (age 19 at New York, NY)–14 June 1874. B: New York, NY. Hazel eyes, brown hair, dark complexion, 5'3¾. Discharged at Ft. Richardson, TX, as Chief Bugler. Reenlisted: 1 April 1866. Discharged 1 April 1869 as Chief Bugler. Reenlisted: 14 June 1869. Discharged 14 June 1874 at Ft. Hays, KS, a Pvt.

Annis, Samuel. Pvt. Co. B, 1 August 1861 (age 20 at Cleveland, OH)–1 August 1864. B: 1841, Cleveland, Cuyahoga Co., OH, farmer. Hazel eyes, brown hair, ruddy complexion, 5'5. Discharged at Lighthouse Point, VA. D: 28 September 1917, Willoughby, OH.

Antes, John W. Enlisted: Pvt. Co. K, 84th PA Inf. 1861. Deserted. Transferred: Pvt. Co. A, 6th U.S. Cav. 28 October 1862 (age 23 at Knoxville, MD)–6 November 1864. B: 1 October 1839, Clearfield Co., PA. Brown eyes, dark hair, light complexion, 5'7. Discharged at Cedar Creek, VA. D: 18 May 1910, Clearfield, PA.

Applebaugh, Charles Edwin. Mustered: Pvt. Co. B, 110th PA Inf. 5 September 1861–5 September 1862. Transferred: Co. D, 6th U.S. Cav. 28 October 1862 (age 25 at Knoxville, MD)–28 August 1864. B: 15 May 1837 Lewistown, Mifflin Co., PA. Grey eyes, light hair, light complexion, 5'6. WIA (slight) and listed MIA at Beverly Ford, VA, 9 June 1863. Discharged at Bolivar Heights, VA. Enlisted: Co. C, 76th PA Inf. 21 February 1865–18 July 1865, Sgt. Maj. D: 4 April 1929. Note: Charles and John were brothers.

Applebaugh, John Ealor. Enlisted: Pvt. (promoted to Cpl.) Co. B, 110th PA Inf. Transferred: Sgt. Co. D, 6th U.S. Cav. 28 October 1862 (age 21 at Knoxville, MD)–28 August 1864. B: 27 January 1840, Lewistown, Mifflin Co., PA. Grey eyes, light hair, light complexion, 5'6. POW (11 days and paroled), Beverly Ford, VA, 9 June 1863. Discharged at Bolivar Heights, VA. Reenlisted: Pvt. Co. B, 88th PA Inf. 20 March 1865. Promoted to Cpl. on 17 June 1865. Mustered out on 30 June 1865 at Washington, D.C. D: 24 April 1925.

Archible, John. Pvt. Co. F, 29 July 1864 (age 29 at Rochester, NY)–24 July 1865. B: Philadelphia, PA, shoemaker. Black eyes, black hair, dark complexion, 5'6. Deserted.

Armbruster, Jacob. Pvt. Co. F, 30 July 1861 (age 25 at Pittsburgh, PA)–9 July 1864. B: Wurttemberg, GER, blacksmith. Brown eyes, auburn hair, dark complexion, 5'9. POW, Coal Harbor, 8 July 1862–? Paroled. MIA Youngsville,12 May 1863–? Discharged at Lighthouse Point, VA. Enlisted: Pvt. Co. C, 5th PA Cav. Mustered out as a Farrier. D: 14 October 1888.

Armstrong, Ludlow. Pvt. Co. L, 11 November 1864 (age 18 at Cincinnati, OH)–11 November 1867. B: Rising Sun, IN, farmer. Hazel eyes, dark hair, dark complexion, 5'3. Discharged at Camp Wilson, TX. Enlisted: Pvt. Co. K, 3rd U.S. Cav. 1 August 1871. Deserted 9 July 1872.

Armstrong, Martin. Sgt.-Sgt. Maj. Co. M, 7 September 1861 (age 31 at Pittsburgh, PA)–4 October 1863. B: 1828 Chesterfield, Chester Co., PA, farmer. Hazel eyes, dark hair, dark complexion, 5'4½. WIA (severe), Williamsburg, VA. Brought to the Seminary Hospital, Hampton, VA, 11 May 1862. WIA (saber wound to the head), POW, Fairfield, 3 July 1863–20 August 1863. Paroled. Reported Annapolis, MD. D: of typhoid fever at Annapolis, MD 4 October 1863.

Arnold, James H. Mustered (Fentonville, MI): Pvt. Co. B, 7th MI Inf. 4 January 1862. Transferred: Pvt. Co. B, 27 October 1862 (age 19 at Knoxville, MD)–1 April 1865. B: Chew's Hollow, NY, farmer. Blue eyes, light hair, light complexion, 5'6. Discharged at Petersburg, VA.

Arnold, James L. Pvt. Co. I, 27 October 1862 (age 30 at Knoxville, MD)–23 April 1864. B: Steuben Co., NY, printer. Grey eyes, brown hair, fair complexion, 5'8. Discharged at Brandy Station, VA.

Arnold, Lorenzo Dow. Mustered: Musician, Co. A, 8th OH Inf. 22 April 1861–28 May 1861 (3 months). Reenlisted: 28 May 1861. Transferred: Pvt. Co. I, 6th U.S. Cav. 27 October 1862 (age 19 at Knoxville, MD)–23 April 1864. B: 1 July 1832 Tyrone, Schuyler, NY, printer. Grey eyes, brown hair, fair complexion, 5'5. Discharged at Brandy Station, VA. D: 15 March 1880, Tiffin, Seneca, OH.

Arthur, Philip D. Pvt. Co. I, 3 August 1861 (age 31 at Indiana, PA)–29 September 1862. B: Taylorsville, PA, farmer. Grey eyes, brown hair, light complexion, 5'8¼. D: 29 September 1862 at Harper's Ferry.

Arthur, William Wesley. Enlisted: Pvt. Co. D, 14th IN Inf. 6 July 1861–29 October 1862. Transferred: Cpl. Co. C, 6th U.S. Cav. 24 October 1862 (age 21 at Knoxville, MD)–18 January 1864. B: 5 August 1841, Green Co., IN. Blue eyes, black hair, light complexion, 5'8. D: 12 January 1912, Bement, Piatt, IL.

Atlee, Joseph Boude. Musician, F&S. 15 October 1861 (age 24 at Mount Joy, PA)–26 March 1862. B: 1 September 1837, Middletown, Dauphin, PA, carpenter. Hazel eyes, brown hair, light complexion, 5'7½. Disability discharge at Washington D.C. D: 1915, Ft. Madison, Lee, IA.

Auchincloss, James. Enlisted: Pvt. Cos. E, F, 2nd U.S. Cav. 29 September 1858. Transferred: Pvt. Cos M, B, 6th U.S. Cav. 1 August 1863 (age 30 at Germantown, PA)–1 August 1866. B: Galoway, SCO, musician. Grey eyes, brown hair, fair complexion, 5'8½. Discharged at Austin, TX. Reenlisted: Sgt. Co. L, 7th U.S. Cav. 14 September 1866. D: 6 April 1867 from disease at Ft. Morgan, Morgan, CO.

Austin, Benjamin P. Mustered: 8th Cpl. Co. C, 60th NY Inf. 10 September 1861 at Ogdensburg, St. Lawrence, NY. Transferred: Pvt. Cos. L, C, 6th U.S. Cav. 25 October 1862 (age 26 at Knoxville, MD)–15 October 1865. B: Centre, PA. Grey eyes, brown hair, dark complexion, 5'9. MIA, Brandy Station. WIA/POW, Fairfield, PA 3 July 1863–21 December 1863. Paroled, reported at Brandy Station. Reenlisted: 4 August 1865. Deserted 15 October 1865. D: 26 August 1885, Sparta, Monroe, WI.

Ayers, William H. Pvt. Co. E, 10 September 1861 (age 34 at Columbus, OH)–8 May 1862. B: 4 June 1820, Guernsey Co., OH, carpenter. Grey eyes, brown hair, sallow complexion, 5'9¼. Disability discharge at Washington D.C. Dropped 31 December 1862 by G.O. Mustered: Pvt. Co. D, 88th OH Inf. 10 October 1862. Mustered out 3 July 1865 at Camp Chase, OH.

Babb, John H. Mustered: Pvt. Co. D, 34th PA Inf. 21 June 1861–25 September 1861. Disability discharge. Enlisted: Pvt. Cos. C, L, 6th U.S. Cav. 2 December 1861 (age 30 at Washington, DC)–19 December 1864. B: 28 April 1837, Penobscot, ME, millwright. Grey eyes, brown

hair, ruddy complexion, 5'7¾. POW, Fairfield, 3 July 1863–26 May 1864. Paroled, reported at Fredericksburg. Discharged at Winchester, VA. D: 3 September 1901.

Babcock, Perry E. Mustered: Pvt. Co. C, 7th MI Inf. 9 August 1861. Transferred: Pvt. Co. H, 6th U.S. Cav. 27 October 1862 (age 25 at Knoxville, MD)–28 August 1864. B: Launcy, MI. Blue eyes, dark hair, light complexion, 5'5½. Discharged at Lighthouse Point, VA.

Babler, William. Pvt. Co. H, 5 August 1861 (age 26 at Philadelphia, PA)–5 August 1864. B: Schwandon, SWZ, machinist. Blue eyes, light hair, fair complexion, 5'7. MIA, Fairfield. Discharged in the field, VA.

Baer, Ephraim D. Mustered: Pvt. Co. G, 37th PA Inf. 24 May 1861–29 October 1862. Transferred: Co. K, 6th U.S. Cav. 28 October 1862 (age 20 at Knoxville, MD)–28 April 1864. B: 1843, Adamstown, MD, wagoner. Grey eyes, brown hair, fair complexion, 5'5. Discharged at 6th CAV Camp. D: 1880.

Bailey, Cloyed. Pvt. Co. F, 10 December 1864 (age 23 at Cincinnati, OH)–31 January 1865. B: 10 May 1842, Wyoming, WV (although enlistment documents say Essex, CAN), farmer. Hazel eyes, brown hair, fair complexion, 5'5¾. Deserted.

Bailey, David. Mustered: Pvt. Co. A, 45th PA Inf. 16 August 1861. Transferred: Pvt. Co. D, 6th U.S. Cav. 28 October 1862 (age 21 at Knoxville, MD)–9 November 1866. B: Lycoming Co., PA. Grey eyes, dark hair, dark complexion, 5'6. Reenlisted: 9 February 1864 at Brandy Station, VA. D: of consumption at Sherman, TX, 9 November 1866.

Bailey, George. Pvt. Co. F, 16 December 1864 (age 21 at Cincinnati, OH)–29 January 1865. B: St. Catharine, CAN, farmer. Grey eyes, brown hair, fair complexion, 5'5. Deserted.

Bailey, Samuel. Enlisted: Saddler. Cos. I, B, 2nd U.S. Cav. 27 April 1855–1 April 1860. Reenlisted (Camp Colorado, TX). Transferred: Co. D, 6th U.S. Cav. By S.O. 92, A.G.O., 21 April 1861. (age 30). B: Richmond, VA, saddler. Blue eyes, brown hair, dark complexion, 5'8¾. Deserted 1 May 1861. Surrendered 25 June 1869. Discharged 25 May 1873 at Ft. Wallace, KS.

Bakeley, Joseph H. Pvt. Co. D, 21 August 1861 (age 21 at Pittsburgh, PA)–5 December 1861. B: Crawford Co., PA, boatman. Brown eyes, light hair, dark complexion, 5'10¾. D: of fever at Circle Hospital, Washington D.C., 5 December 1861.

Baker, Archibald. Pvt. Co. F, 27 October 1864

(age 21 at Cincinnati, OH)–10 December 1865. B: New Richmond, Clermont, OH, laborer. Blue eyes, dark hair, sallow complexion, 5'8. Deserted.

Baker, Ira David. Mustered: Pvt. Co. A, 13th OH Inf. Discharged 18 June 1861 at Camp Dennison, OH. Enlisted: Rct. 6th U.S. Cav. 18 September 1861 (age 22 at Cleveland, OH)–10 October 1861. B: Zoar, Stark Co., OH, machinist. Black eyes, brown hair, ruddy complexion, 5'11. Disability discharge at Camp near Bladensburg, MD. Enlisted: Pvt. 18th U.S. Inf. 10 June 1862. Disability discharge 1 January 1863 at Louisville, KY. Enlisted: Pvt. Co. B, 177th OH Inf. Discharged 26 June 1865 at Pittsburg, PA. Enlisted: Co. M, 8th U.S. Cav. 27 October 1866, Cincinnati, OH. Deserted 18 March 1867. Apprehended 13 November 1867. Disability discharged 14 February 1868 at Angel Island, CA.

Baker, William H. Pvt. Co. G, 1 August 1861 (age 35 at Cleveland, OH)–1 August 1864. B: Benson, OH, farrier. Blue eyes, sandy hair, ruddy complexion, 5'8½. Discharged at Lighthouse Point, VA.

Balder, Christian. Enlisted: Pvt. Co. A, 1st U.S. Cav. 13 April 1855. Promoted to Sgt. Co. A, 14 February 1860 (age 28 at Ft. Arbuckle)–23 October 1861. B: Leeham, GER. Grey eyes, brown hair, fair complexion, 5'6. Promoted 23 October 1861 to 2nd Lt., 6th U.S. Cav. at Washington, D.C. Promoted to 1st Lt. 23 December 1862. KIA, Fairfield.

Balk, Stephen S. Enlisted: Musician, Co. A, 2nd U.S. Art. 15 February 1845–15 February 1850 at Ft. McHenry, MD. Reenlisted (McHenry, MD) 13 September 1850–13 September 1855. Enlisted: Pvt.-Sgt., GMS, 21 June 1856–21 June 1861. Enlisted: Sgt. 6th U.S. Cav. 1 July 1861 (age 36 at Pittsburgh, PA)–24 August 1861. B: Hull, ENG, soldier. Hazel eyes, brown hair, sallow complexion, 5'6½. Promoted to 2nd Lt., 6th U.S. Cav. 20 August 1861. MIA/WIA, Gaines Mill 27 June 1862. Promoted to 1st Lt. 17 July 1862. Wholly retired 4 May 1864. Enlisted (Alcatraz Island, CA) Sgt. Cos. G, B, 2nd U.S. Art. 20 September 1867. Discharged 30 October 1868 by S.O. 186, Dept. of CA at Alcatraz Island, a Sgt.

Ball, John. Rct. 15 September 1864 (age 24 at Harrisburg, PA)–14 October 1864. B: Westmouth, IRE, laborer. Grey eyes, fair hair, sallow complexion, 5'6. Deserted.

Ball, John A. Pvt. Co. B, 19 July 1861 (age 18 at Columbus, OH)–19 January 1863. B: Franklin Co., OH, saddler. Hazel eyes, brown hair, fair

complexion, 5'9. Disability discharge at Frederick, MD.

Ballard, Lamont D. Mustered: Lapeer, MI as a Pvt. Co. G, 7th MI Inf. 12 August 1861. Transferred: Pvt. Co. E, 6th U.S. Cav. 26 October 1862 (age 30 at Knoxville, MD)–22 August 1864. B: February 1835 Albany, NY. Blue eyes, dark hair, dark complexion, 5'9½. Discharged at Camp in the field, VA.

Ballinger, Joseph William. Pvt. Co. A, 20 September 1861 (age 24 at Columbus, OH)–31 January 1862. B: Franklin Co., OH, farmer. Blue eyes, brown hair, ruddy complexion, 5'3½. Deserted.

Balmer, William H. Mustered: Pvt. Co. E, 10th PA Inf. 29 April 1861–31 July 1861 (3 months). Mustered out at Harrisburg, PA. Enlisted: Pvt. Cos. C & L, 6th U.S. Cav. 15 October 1861 (age 24 at Mount Joy, PA)–30 December 1862. B: Elizabethtown, Lancaster Co., PA, carpenter. Grey eyes, brown hair, ruddy complexion, 5'4½. Disability discharge at Camp Convalescent, VA. D: 3 October 1916.

Banker, John Wesley. Pvt.-Cpl. Cos. G, A: 1 August 1861 (age 21 at Erie, PA)–1 August 1864. B: Seneca Falls, Seneca, NY, cooper. Grey eyes, light hair, fair complexion, 5'9¼. WIA in the field. POW, 7 May to 28 September 1863. Paroled, reported 28 September 1863 at Annapolis, MD. Discharged at Lighthouse Point, VA.

Banks, Michael. Pvt. Co. E, 16 September 1861 (age 18 at Cleveland, OH)–1 September 1864. B: Toledo, OH, sailor. Blue eyes, brown hair, fair complexion, 5'5¼. Discharged at Berryville, VA. Break in service. Enlisted: 12th U.S. Inf. 10 May 1867–12 May 1868.

Barbeau, Peter (alias Goyette, Louis). Farrier. Co. A, 19 July 1864 (age 44 at Rochester, NY)–19 July 1867. B: Sopprary, NY, blacksmith. Grey eyes, dark hair, dark complexion, 5'6½. Discharged at Buffalo Springs, TX.

Barker, Cyrus J. Pvt. Mustered: Pvt. Co. H, 34th PA Inf. 21 June 1861. Transferred: Pvt. Co. A, 6th U.S. Cav. 28 October 1862 (age 18 at Knoxville, MD)–22 June 1864. B: IN. Grey eyes, light hair, light complexion, 5'5. MIA/POW, Funkstown, 7 July–24 December 1863. Paroled, reported at Annapolis, MD. Discharged at White House, VA. Mustered: Pvt. Co. A, 100th Pa. Inf., 12 January 1865. KIA, Ft. Stedman, VA, 25 March 1865.

Barker, William B. Rct. Enlisted: Pvt. Co. D, 14th IN Inf. 7 June 1861. Transferred: Pvt. 6th U.S. Cav. 23 October 1862 (age 20 at Knoxville,

MD)–December 1862. B: Green Co., IN. Grey eyes, brown hair, fair complexion, 5'6½. Returned to the U.S.V. Discharged 8 June 1864.

Barkley, William J. Enlisted (Monroe, MI): Pvt. Co. D, 7th MI Inf. 28 August 1861–23 October 1862. Transferred: Co. K, 6th U.S. Cav. 27 October 1862 (age 26 at Knoxville, MD)–27 August 1863. B: Madrid, NY, farmer. Grey eyes, brown hair, light complexion, 5'4½. Discharged at City Point, VA. Enlisted: Co. K, 14th OH Inf.

Barlow, George "Billy." Pvt. Co. F, 3 July 1861 (age 27 at Pittsburgh, PA)–3 July 1863. B: Aldenberg, GER, laborer. Blue eyes, light hair, dark complexion, 5'8. Discharged at Lighthouse Point, VA. Mustered: Pvt. Co. A, 47th OH Inf. 1 October 1864–31 May 1865. Mustered out at Washington, D.C.

Barnard, Silas Wright. Rct. 19 August 1861 (age 19 at Rochester, NY)–22 August 1861. B: Rochester, Monroe, NY, brush maker. Hazel eyes, brown hair, dark complexion, 5'6¼. Discharged for "General unfitness for the Service." Enlisted: Co. H, 3rd NY Cav. 26 August 1861. Promoted to Cpl. 28 March 1865. Transferred: Pvt. Co. L, 1st NY Cav. 21 July 1865. Mustered out 1 August 1865 at Portsmouth, VA. D: 14 November 1906, Los Angeles, CA.

Barnard, William. Mustered: Pvt. Co. B, 110th PA Inf. Transferred: Pvt. Co. D, 28 October 1862 (age 21 at Knoxville, MD)–28 August 1864. B: Mifflin Co., PA. Grey eyes, sandy hair, light complexion, 5'7. Discharged near Halltown, VA.

Barnes, Adolphus M. Pvt. Co. A, 24 September 1861 (age 22 at Philadelphia, PA)–17 October 1864. B: Philadelphia, PA, dentist. Hazel eyes, light hair, light complexion, 5'11½. Deserted 27 April 1862. Apprehended 23 November 1863. Discharged 17 October 1864 at Greensboro Hospital. D: 3 March 1871, Philadelphia, PA.

Barnes, Conrad. Pvt. Co. H, 31 July 1861 (age 21 at Philadelphia, PA)–22 December 1861. B: Fermanagh, IRE, laborer. Blue eyes, dark hair, light complexion, 5'6¾. Disability discharge at Washington D.C. Enlisted: Pvt. U.S.M.C. 2 June 1862 at Philadelphia, PA. D: 15 January 1892.

Barnett, John R. Pvt. Co. M, 12 December 1861 (age 24 at Columbus, OH)–14 June 1862. B: Delaware, OH, blacksmith. Hazel eyes, light hair, light complexion, 5'8. Deserted.

Barnett, Robert. Pvt.-Sgt. Cos. C, L, 21 October 1861 (age 33 at Philadelphia, PA)–21 October 1864. B: 12 October 1825, Londonderry, IRE, clerk. Hazel eyes, brown hair, ruddy complex-

ion, 5'4. WIA, Fairfield. Discharged at Cedar Creek, VA. D: 20 March 1906, Philadelphia, PA.

Barns, Thomas. Rct. 25 November 1864 (age 19 at Harrisburg, PA)–1864. B: Co. Roscommon, IRE, laborer. Grey eyes, light hair, light complexion, 5'3. Deserted.

Barnum, William. Pvt. Co. K, 16 July 1861 (age 24 at Franklin, PA)–29 December 1863. B: New York, NY, cooper. Hazel eyes, black hair, olive complexion, 5'7. POW, Fairfield. Paroled, reported by hospital at Annapolis, MD on 22 December 1863 as having died 29 November 1863 from diarrhea.

Barr, Benjamin Franklin. Musician 2nd Class. Co. F&S, 15 October 1861 (age 23 at Mount Joy, PA)–15 October 1864. B: 1837, Columbia, Lancaster, PA, musician. Grey eyes, black hair, light complexion, 5'5. Discharged at Strausburg, VA. D: 1912.

Barr, Lewis. Sgt. Cos. F, I, 10 August 1861 (age 22 at Rochester, NY)–7 August 1864. B: 15 November 1838, GER, mechanic. Blue eyes, brown hair, fair complexion, 5'6. WIA, Brandy Station. Discharged in the field.

Barr, Thomas. Pvt. Co. L, 18 May 1864 (age 24 at Rochester, NY)–15 November 1866. B: Glasgow, SCO, laborer. Grey eyes, brown hair, ruddy complexion, 5'6. Deserted 20 August 1864. Apprehended 6 May 1865. Deserted 27 June 1865. Surrendered 6 June 1866. D: 15 November 1866 of cholera at Wakeford, TX.

Barr, William T. Pvt. Co. I, 9 August 1861 (age 29 at Indiana, PA)–11 June 1862. B: Indiana Co., PA, farmer. Grey eyes, brown hair, florid complexion, 5'6¾. Deserted.

Barry, James. Pvt. 22 August 1861 (age 21 at Pittsburgh, PA)–30 August 1861. B: Allegheny Co., MD, coal miner. Blue eyes, brown hair, dark complexion, 5'6½. Deserted.

Barry, William J. Pvt. Co. A, 6 January 1865 (age 32 at Carlisle, PA)–6 December 1865. B: Wakeford, IRE. Tried by GCMO 28 September 1865 at Frederick, MD. Deserted 18 October 1865. Surrendered 6 November 1865. Deserted 6 December 1865.

Bartlett, Emerson. Musician 2nd Class. Band, F&S. 7 March 1865 (age 37 at NY)–10 April 1867. B: 14 September 1827, Conway, Franklin Co., MA. Blue eyes, brown hair, fair complexion, 5'6. Discharged by Special Order 153, AGO 67, Austin, TX. D: 5 May 1898, NY.

Bartlett, George D. Pvt. Co. B, 1 August 1861 (age 21 at Cleveland, OH)–5 August 1862. B: Brockville, OH, farmer. Grey eyes, brown hair, ruddy complexion, 5'10½. D: 5 August 1862 from wounds received near Malvern Hill, VA.

Bartlett, Marcus B. Bugler. Co. B, 3 August 1861 (age 15 at Cleveland, OH)–3 August 1864. B: Grangeville, OH, farmer. Grey eyes, light hair, fair complexion, 5'4. Discharged at Lighthouse Point, VA. Reenlisted: Co. K, 18th OH Inf., 30 March 1865–9 October 1865. D: 12 October 1928.

Barton, Philander. Mustered: Pvt. Co. K, 38th PA Inf. 4 May 1861. Transferred: Co. M, 6th U.S. Cav. 28 October 1862 (age 25 at Knoxville, MD)–6 June 1865. B: Pittsburgh, Allegheny, PA, carpenter. Hazel eyes, dark hair, fair complexion, 5'5½. Deserted 22 June 1863. Apprehended 16 July 1864. Gained from desertion 6 February 1865 at Winchester, VA. Tried by GCMO May 1865 at Blandensburg, MD. Discharged 6 June 1865 at Alexandria, VA.

Barton, Samuel. Rct. 11 November 1864 (age 19 at Harrisburg, PA)–21 November 1864. B: Scioto Co., OH, painter. Hazel eyes, brown hair, dark complexion, 5'3½. Deserted.

Bartung, Charles. Rct. 24 November 1861 (age 35 at Pittsburgh, PA)–20 December 1861. B: Prussia, GER, carpenter. Grey eyes, brown hair, light complexion, 5'8. Disability discharge at Washington, D.C.

Bascom, Levi B. Pvt. Co. B, 27 July 1861 (age 22 at Columbus, OH)–11 October 1862. B: 27 July 1839, Clarkson, Monroe, NY, clerk. Grey eyes, sandy hair, light complexion, 5'7¾. Deserted. D: 7 July 1926, Decatur, Macon, IL.

Bateman, James E. Pvt. 26 August 1864 (age 22 at Harrisburg, PA)–23 August 1864. B: Co. Dublin, IRE, laborer. Grey eyes, brown hair, ruddy complexion, 5'9½. Register says deserted 23 August 1864. Sub.

Bates, Alphord (Alphred) H. Pvt. 3 October 1864 (age 24 at Harrisburg, PA)–1864. B: Philadelphia, PA, machinist. Grey eyes, brown hair, ruddy complexion, 5'6½. Deserted.

Bates, Butler H. Mustered: Pvt. Co. E, 3rd WI Inf. Transferred: Pvt. Co. F, 6th U.S. Cav. 25 October 1862 (age 19 at Knoxville, MD)–29 June 1864. B: Erie Co., NY, farmer. Blue eyes, light hair, light complexion, 5'9. POW (captured by guerrillas), Warrenton, 21 January–6 April 1864. Paroled, reported at Annapolis, MD. Discharged at 6th Cav. Camp, VA.

Bates, George Parmly. Pvt. Co. G, 1 August 1861 (age 19 at Erie Co., PA)–13 August 1861. B: Erie Co., PA, farmer. Grey eyes, light hair, fair complexion, 5'8. Disability discharge. Mustered: Co. C, 83rd PA Inf. 29 August 1861–30 September 1862. Disability discharge. D: 18 August 1866.

Battersby, George Lorce. Pvt. Co. H, 16 July 1861 (age 21 at Philadelphia, PA)–2 February 1863. B: 18 June 1841, Philadelphia, PA, carver. Blue eyes, dark hair, ruddy complexion, 5'6. Disability discharge at Convalescent Camp, VA. D: 27 August 1898, Philadelphia, PA.

Bauerman, Ignatius. Pvt. Co. I, 7 September 1861 (age 25 at Rochester, NY)–1 July 1862. B: GER, farmer. Grey eyes, light hair, florid complexion, 5'9¼. Deserted.

Baughton, James. Pvt. 6 October 1864 (age 23 at Harrisburg, PA)–1864. B: Co. Tipperary, IRE, shoemaker. Blue eyes, dark hair, dark complexion, 5'9. Deserted.

Baum, George. Pvt.-Saddler. Co. M, 14 October 1861 (age 35 at Pittsburgh, PA)–14 September 1864. B: Franklin Co., OH, saddler. Hazel eyes, brown hair, light complexion, 5'8. WIA, Williamsburg, VA. POW at Richmond, VA and Salisbury, NC. Left Salisbury May 1862 and arrived at New York 9 June 1862 via steamer "Guide." Gained 16 July 1862 from parole. Discharged at Berryville, VA.

Bauman, Jacob K. Pvt. Co. G, 7 August 1861 (age 29 at Rochester, NY)–7 August 1864. B: 26 May 1831, SWZ, farmer. Blue eyes, brown hair, florid complexion, 5'5½. Discharged at Lighthouse Point, VA. Enlisted in the General Mounted Service. D: 21 August 1936, KS.

Baxter, James M. Pvt. Co. K, 9 August 1861 (age 18 at Pittsburgh, PA)–31 January 1862. B: Westmoreland Co., PA, printer. Hazel eyes, dark hair, fair complexion, 5'7½. D: of disease at Camp east of Capitol, Washington D.C. on 31 January 1862.

Bayette, Joseph. Mustered (De Kalb, St. Lawrence, NY): Pvt. Co. F, 60th NY Inf. 12 September 1861. Transferred: Pvt. Co. A, 6th U.S. Cav. 25 October 1862 (age 20 at Knoxville, MD)–28 October 1864. B: May 1843, Ogdensburg, NY. Grey eyes, dark hair, light complexion, 5'5. POW, Fairfield, 3 July to 5 October 1863. Paroled, reported at Culpepper, VA. Discharged near Middletown, VA. Enlisted as a Pvt. Co. B. 193rd NY Inf. 20 February 1865 at Hermon, St. Lawrence, NY. Note: Served with brothers Stephen and Louis, Jr. in Co. F, 60th NY Inf.

Beach, Edward. Pvt. Co. E, 14 September 1861 (age 25 at Adrian, MI)–14 September 1864. B: Berlin, OH, farmer. Grey eyes, brown hair, sallow complexion, 5'8½. Discharged in the field. Invalid pension filed 28 June 1880

(394848/371238). Widow (Margaret) pension filed 18 February 1918, OH (1115255/877486). D: 6 February 1918, Huron, Erie, OH.

Beach, Ephraim Mansfield. Mustered: Pvt. Co. D, 106th PA Inf. 27 August 1861. Transferred: Pvt. Co. B, 6th U.S. Cav. 28 October 1862 (age 22 at Knoxville, MD)–28 July 1865. B: 31 December 1840, Troy, Bradford, PA. Dark eyes, dark hair, dark complexion, 5' 8. Reenlisted: 8 February 1864 at 6th Cav. Camp, VA. Deserted 28 July 1865.

Beal, William R. Mustered: Pvt. Co. D, 14th IN Inf. 6 July 1861. Transferred: Rct. 6th U.S. Cav. 23 October 1862 (age 20 at Knoxville, MD)–December 1862. B: 25 January 1842, Green Co., IN. Grey eyes, brown hair, florid complexion, 5' 7½. Returned to U.S.V. November/December 1862. Promoted to Cpl. and Sgt. Transferred: Co. B, 20th IN Inf. 21 December 1863. Mustered out 21 July 1865, Louisville, KY. D: 16 May 1920, Mangrum, Durham, NC.

Beath, David S. Mustered: Pvt. Co. K, 28th PA Inf. 20 July 1861–5 November 1862. Transferred: Pvt. Cos. D, K, 25 October 1862 (age 18 at Knoxville, MD)–26 June 1868. Promoted to Cpl. B: Philadelphia, PA, teamster. Blue eyes, light hair, fair complexion, 5' 4½. WIA, Beverly Ford. Discharged 26 May 1864 near Milford, VA. Reenlisted 26 June 1865. Discharged 26 June 1868 at Ft. Richardson, TX. D: 30 April 1880, Philadelphia, PA.

Beaver, Charles. Sgt. Co. M, 1 October 1861 (age 32 at Pittsburgh, PA)–17 September 1864. B: London, ENG, laborer. Hazel eyes, brown hair, light complexion, 5' 7½. Discharged in the field.

Beavington, John G. Pvt. Co. E, 11 September 1861 (age 21 at Adrian, MI)–3 May 1862. B: Starkton, OH, engineer. Hazel eyes, brown hair, ruddy complexion, 6' 2. Deserted.

Becher, Louis. Pvt. Co. E, 22 July 1861 (age 21 at Columbus, OH)–22 July 1864. B: Columbus, OH, farmer. Hazel eyes, brown hair, sallow complexion, 5' 5¼. Deserted 31 July 1861. Apprehended 12 September 1861. Discharged 22 July 1864 at Lighthouse Point, VA.

Beck, Christopher F. (alias Frederick). Cpl.-Sgt.-1st Sgt. Co. B, 19 July 1861 (age 22 at Columbus, OH)–19 July 1864. B: Columbus, OH, painter. Grey eyes, brown hair, sallow complexion, 5' 9. MIA, Fairfield. Discharged at Lighthouse Point, VA. Enlisted: Sgt. Co. G, 185th OH Inf. 31 January 1865. Mustered out on 26 September 1865 at Lexington, KY.

Beck, Conrad. Bugler. Co. B, 7 August 1861 (age 16 at Cleveland, OH)–7 August 1864. B: Little

York, PA, butcher. Blue eyes, light hair, fair complexion, 5' 7¾. Discharged at Lighthouse Point, VA. D: 10 November 1929, Cleveland, Cuyahoga, OH.

Beck, Martin. Mustered: Sgt. Co. E, 8th OH Inf. 25 June 1861. Transferred: Pvt. Co. C, 6th U.S. Cav. 24 October 1862 (age 20 at Knoxville, MD)–25 June 1864. B: Baden, GER. Hazel eyes, black hair, florid complexion, 5' 3. POW, Funkstown, 7 July 1863–7 January 1864. Paroled, reported at Annapolis, MD. Discharged at Camp in the field, VA.

Beckert, George. Pvt. Co. D, 12 August 1861 (age 21 at Pittsburgh, PA)–6 June 1864. B: Rochelle, FRA, rope maker. Brown eyes, brown hair, dark complexion, 5' 8. D: 6 June 1864, Stevensville, VA.

Beckman, Francis. Pvt. Cos. A, B, 9 October 1861 (age 32 at Philadelphia, PA)–26 March 1862. B: Baden, Baden, GER, blacksmith. Hazel eyes, light hair, fair complexion, 5' 6. Deserted.

Beeler, Charles. Cpl.-Sgt. Co. M, 17 September 1861 (age 21⅔ at Pittsburgh, PA)–17 September 1864. B: 1840, Beaver Co., PA, farmer. Blue eyes, brown hair, florid complexion, 5'10½. POW, Fairfield. Prisoner at Belle Island. Discharged in the field, VA. D: 1924, Beaver, PA.

Beeman, Adelbert. Pvt. Co. G, 14 August 1861 (age 21 at Rochester, NY)–2 June 1864. B: Monroe Co., NY, farmer. Blue eyes, brown hair, florid complexion, 5' 8½. D: of disease while on a march from Bottoms Bridge to Old Church, VA, 2 June 1864.

Bell, James A. Pvt. Co. L, 2 April 1862 (age 23 at Bellafontaine, PA)–1 May 1862. B: Northumberland Co., PA, tailor. Grey eyes, light hair, fair complexion, 5' 4½. Deserted.

Belote, James. Mustered (Elysian, Le Seuer, MN): Pvt. Co. G, 1st MN Inf. 23 May 1861. Transferred: Pvt. Co. 6th U.S. Cav. F, 24 October 1862 (age 26 at Knoxville, MD)–19 May 1864. B: Newaygo Co., MI, engineer. Hazel eyes, dark hair, dark complexion, 5' 8. POW, Fairfield, 3 July 1863–19 February 1864. Paroled, reported at Camp Parole. Discharged at 6th Cav. Camp. D: 28 March 1899, Centreville, St. Joseph, MI.

Bemis, Joseph G. Mustered (Morristown, Rice, MN): Pvt. Co. G, 1st MN Inf. 23 May 1861. Transferred: Pvt. Co. F, 6th U.S. Cav. 25 October 1862 (age 18 at Knoxville, MD). B: Schulsberry, MA, student. Grey eyes, sandy hair, fair complexion, 6'. KIA, Fairfield.

Benedict, Olascon M. Rct. 6 August 1861 (age 18 at Cleveland, OH)–12 August 1861. Deserted.

Benford, George Leroy. QM Sgt. Co. H, 12 August 1861 (age 21 in Philadelphia, PA)–12 August 1864. B: Somerset Co., PA, clerk. Blue eyes, light hair, fair complexion, 5' 8. Discharged at Geisboro Point. D: 17 October 1922, Soldiers House, Washington, D.C.

Bennet, Thomas. Rct. 4 November 1864 (age 19 at Cincinnati, OH)–21 November 1864. B: Windsor, CAN, hostler. Dark eyes, brown hair, dark complexion, 5' 6. Deserted.

Bennett, Cyrus R. Pvt. Co. I, 1 September 1861 (age 30 at Rochester, NY)–16 November 1862. B: 1831, Nova Scotia, CAN, engineer. Blue eyes, brown hair, ruddy complexion, 5' 9½. Disability discharge at Washington, D.C. D: 7 December 1919, Livingston Co., NY.

Benson, Nelson. Pvt. Co. E, 14 September 1861 (age 18 at Adrian, MI)–3 May 1862. B: Cayuga Co., NY, farmer. Grey eyes, light hair, ruddy complexion, 5'10. Deserted.

Benson, Thomas H. Pvt. 26 September 1864 (age 20 at Rochester, NY)–27 September 1864. B: Co. Longford, IRE, laborer. Blue eyes, light hair, light complexion, 5' 6½. Deserted.

Benson, William. Pvt. Co. M, 17 September 1864 (age 18 at Rochester, NY)–1864. B: Saratoga, NY, farmer. Blue eyes, light hair, sallow complexion, 5' 5½. Deserted.

Benton, Alfred. Rct. 13 August 1861 (age 18 at Columbus, OH)–21 August 1861. B: Delaware Co. OH, farmer. Grey eyes, sandy hair, ruddy complexion, 5' 8½. Rejected recruit. Disability discharge. Rejected. Enlisted (Westorville, OH): Pvt. Cos. D, C, 5th U.S. Inf. 16 September 1861–16 September 1864. Received a gunshot wound to right thigh which resulted to paralysis of lower limbs. D: 18 December 1918, Hughes Co., SD.

Berbrick, Frederick. Saddler. Co. D, 8 August 1861 (age 23 at Pittsburgh, PA)–8 August 1864. B: Baden, GER, shoemaker. Blue eyes, sandy hair, light complexion, 5' 7. Discharge at Camp in the field, VA.

Bergner, Louis F. Pvt. Co. B, 30 July 1861 (age 21 at Cleveland, OH). Deserted 17 February 1863. B: Saxony, GER, stone cutter. Hazel eyes, brown hair, ruddy complexion, 5' 4½. Enlisted: Pvt. Co. H, 1st MD Cav. 21 December 1863. Deserted 21 March 1864.

Berry, Allen. Rct. Mustered (Monroe Co., IN): Pvt. Co. K, 14th IN Inf. 7 July 1861. Transferred: Rct. 6th U.S. Cav. 23 October 1862 (age 21 at Knoxville, MD)–December 1862. B: Sarahsville, Noble, OH. Blue eyes, black hair, florid complexion, 5' 8½. Returned to U.S.V.

November/December 1862. Mustered out of Co. K. 14th IN Inf. 6 June 1864 at Indianapolis, IN. Enlisted: Cpl. Co. G, 176th OH Inf. 15 September 1864. Promoted to Sgt. 12 March 1865. Mustered out 14 June 1865 at Nashville, TN.

Besk, John. Pvt. Co. F, 14 December 1864 (age 26 at Philadelphia, PA)–24 January 1865. B: Bedford Co., PA, teamster. Blue eyes, brown hair, fair complexion, 5' 6½. Deserted.

Besser, Adam. Pvt. Co. F, 15 July 1861 (age 23 at Pittsburgh, PA)–25 July 1864. B: Gahaus, GER, gardener. Lt. grey eyes, lt. brown hair, fair complexion, 5' 5½. POW, Fairfield, 3 July– 3 November 1863. Paroled, reported at Annapolis, MD. Discharged at Lighthouse Point, VA. D: 15 February 1916, PA.

Bestor, Nelson Henry. Pvt. Co. B, 31 July 1861 (age 23 at Cleveland, OH)–31 July 1864. B: 26 August 1839, Bainbridge, Geauga, OH, carpenter. Blue eyes, light hair, ruddy complexion, 5' 4¾. Discharged at Lighthouse Point, VA. D: 9 September 1899, Inglewood, Los Angeles, CA. Note: Nelson and William were brothers.

Bestor, William Henry. Pvt. Co. B, 1 August 1861 (age 20 at Cleveland, OH)–1 August 1864. B: 28 September 1841, Bainbridge, Geauga, OH, blacksmith. Grey eyes, light hair, ruddy complexion, 5' 6¾. Discharged in the field, VA. Enlisted: Pvt. Cos. C, B, 38th OH Inf. 28 September 1864. Mustered out 12 July 1865 at Louisville, KY. D: 12 March 1899.

Betz, Charles W. Pvt. Co. E, 16 September 1861 (age 19 at Norton, OH)–1 May 1862. B: Norton, OH, farmer. Hazel eyes, brown hair, fair complexion, 5' 8½. D: 1 May 1862, Yorktown.

Bickford, George. Rct. 8 November 1861 (age 21 at Cleveland, OH)–1 January 1862. B: Monroe, NY, farmer. Blue eyes, brown hair, ruddy complexion, 5' 6½. Deserted 1 January 1862 at Cleveland, OH.

Biehler, Thomas. Pvt. Co. F, 11 July 1861 (age 35 at Pittsburgh, PA)–11 July 1864. B: Freeberge, GER, butcher. Grey eyes, brown hair, dark complexion, 5' 7¼. Discharged at Lighthouse Point, VA. D: 11 November 1904, Western Branch Hospital, Leavenworth, KS.

Bigelow, Jonas A. Pvt. Co. B, 26 July 1861 (age 25 at Columbus, OH)–26 July 1864. B: 1836, Greenport, OH, farmer. Blue eyes, sandy hair, ruddy complexion, 5' 7¾. POW, Funkstown, 7 July–13 November 1863. Paroled, reported at Camp 6th Cav. Discharged at Camp in the field, VA. Enlisted: Pvt. Co. K, 14th OH Inf. 28 September 1864. Mustered out 3 June 1865. D: 20 June 1877, Columbus, Franklin, OH.

Bilger, Anton. Pvt. Co. I, 5 August 1861 (age 23 at Rochester, NY)–5 August 1864. B: GER, butcher. Blue eyes, brown hair, fair complexion, 5' 6. Discharged in the field, VA. Mustered: Pvt. Co. B, 140th NY Inf. D: October 1904, Rochester, Monroe, NY.

Billings, William H. Pvt.-Cpl. Co. M, 28 October 1861 (age 23 at Pittsburgh, PA)–2 December 1862. B: New York, NY, painter. Hazel eyes, brown hair, dark complexion, 5' 9½. Deserted at Knoxville, MD.

Binger, John. Pvt. Co. I, 7 September 1861 (age 30 at Rochester, NY)–30 September 1862. B: GER, farmer. Hazel eyes, light hair, florid complexion, 5' 6¾. D: 30 September 1862 at Ft. Ellsworth, VA.

Bird, John W. Pvt. Co. D, 31 August 1861 (age 36 at Pittsburgh, PA)–31 August 1864. B: Nottingham, ENG, machinist. Blue eyes, black hair, light complexion, 5' 7. Discharged at Halltown, VA.

Bird, Morris H. Pvt. Co. E, 28 October 1862 (age 22 at Knoxville, MD)–23 August 1864. B: East Indies, farmer. Grey eyes, dark hair, fair complexion, 5' 9¾. POW (captured by guerrillas), Warrenton, 21 January–23 August 1864. D: of disease (anasarca) as POW at Andersonville, GA. 23 August 1864.

Bishop, Philip. Pvt.-Cpl. Cos. E, C, 19 September 1861 (age 20 at Cleveland, OH)–19 September 1864. B: Bern, GER, teamster. Blue eyes, brown hair, ruddy complexion, 5' 3½. Discharged in the field. Mustered: Pvt. Co. C, 6th OH Cav. 11 March 1865–17 June 1865. Mustered out at Petersburg, VA. D: 29 December 1914, Cleveland, Cuyahoga, OH.

Black, Henry M. Pvt. Cos. C, L, 20 December 1861 (age 28 at Philadelphia, PA)–29 December 1864. B: Bucks Co., PA, carpenter. Grey eyes, brown hair, fair complexion, 5' 5. Discharged at Winchester, VA.

Black, John M. Rct. 15 August 1861 (age 25 at Indiana, PA). B: Indiana Co., PA, blacksmith. Hazel eyes, brown hair, dark complexion, 5' 6¾.

Blacksmith, Andrew. Mustered (Pittsburgh, PA): Pvt. Co. G, 38th PA Inf. WIA (shell wound to left thigh). Transferred: Pvt. Co. F, 6th U.S. Cav. 28 October 1862 (age 22 at Knoxville, MD)–15 October 1866. B: 4 July 1841, Pittsburgh, Allegheny Co., PA, laborer. Blue eyes, sandy hair, light complexion, 5' 8. MIA, Fairfield. Discharged 24 July 1864 at Lighthouse Point, VA. Enlisted: Pvt. Co. D, 67th PA Inf. 29 November 1864. Mustered out 30 May 1865. Reenlisted: Pvt., 6th U.S. Cav. 13

June 1865 at Pittsburgh, PA. Deserted 15 October 1866. D: 19 September 1912.

Blain, John. Pvt. Co. D, 26 August 1861 (age 27 at Pittsburgh, PA)–9 October 1862. B: Galloway, SCO, stone mason. Blue eyes, light hair, light complexion, 5' 8½. Disability discharge at Ft. Monroe, VA. Mustered: Cpl. Co. K, 104th PA Inf. Mustered out 25 August 1865. Note: Thomas and John were brothers.

Blain, Thomas A. Pvt. Co. D, 26 August 1861 (age 23 at Pittsburgh, PA)–10 March 1865. B: December 1836, Galoway, SCO, farmer. Blue eyes, light hair, light complexion, 5' 7. Discharged at Baltimore, MD. D: 17 September 1917, MO.

Blanchard, James. Pvt. Co. M, 11 September 1861 (age 28 at Pittsburgh, PA)–11 September 1864. B: 2 June 1835, Berks Co., PA, farmer. Blue eyes, brown hair, light complexion, 5'10. Discharged at Berryville, VA. D: 17 December 1904, PA.

Blank, Albert. Mustered: Pvt. Co. F, Erie, PA Rgt. 21 April 1861–21 July 1861. Enlisted: Pvt. Co. G, 6th U.S. Cav. 6 August 1861 (age 18 at Erie, PA). B: Caelin, Prussia, GER, musician. Blue eyes, white hair, fair complexion, 5' 6. Sick in hospital at Pittsburgh, PA, 27 August–September 1861. Muster roll for September/October 1862 report him as deserted. Note: Albert and Aurelius were brothers.

Blank, Aurelius. Mustered: Pvt. Co. F, Erie, PA Rgt. 21 April 1861–21July 1861. Enlisted: Pvt. Co. G, 6th U.S. Cav. 6 August 1861 (age 16 at Erie, PA). No further information. B: Caelin, Prussia, GER, musician. Blue eyes, white hair, fair complexion, 5'¼.

Blank, Johann (a.k.a. Gottlieb). Mustered: Saddler (as Gottlieb), Co. M., 2nd CA Cav. Transferred: Pvt. Co. G, 6th U.S. Cav. 5 August 1861 (age 48 at Erie, PA)–No further information. Mustered: Pvt., Cos. D, E., 5th U.S.V.V. Inf. Mustered: General Mounted Service. B: Boblitz, Prussia, GER, musician. Blue eyes, dark hair, fair complexion, 5' 8. D: 27 September 1902.

Blasy, Paul. Pvt. Co. M, 19 October 1861 (age 21 at Pittsburgh, PA)–26 February 1862. B: SWZ, teamster. Hazel eyes, brown hair, light complexion, 5' 8. Deserted.

Blossom, Charles. Pvt. Co. E, 16 September 1861 (age 24 at Adrian, MI)–22 May 1864. B: Clinton, MI, carpenter. Blue eyes, light hair, fair complexion, 5' 5. POW, Brandy Station, 11 October 1863–22 May 1864. D: of disease as POW at Andersonville, GA, 22 May 1864.

Blush, Edward C. Sgt. Co. L, 16 July 1861 (age 24

at Columbus, OH)–4 October 1862. B: Burlington, VT, engineer. Grey eyes, brown hair, sallow complexion, 5' 8. Disability discharge at Washington, D.C. D: 12 September 1916.

Boal, David Craig. Pvt. Co. K, 17 July 1861 (age 23 at Franklin, PA)–17 July 1864. B: September 1838, Jackson Township, PA, carpenter. Blue eyes, brown hair, fair complexion, 5' 7. Discharged at Lighthouse Point, VA. D: 1903, PA.

Bock, Jacob. Pvt. Co. F, 15 July 1861 (age 33 at Pittsburgh, PA). B: Wurttemberg, GER, carpenter. Blue eyes, sandy hair, ruddy complexion, 5' 6. D: of disease (pithias pulmonalis) at Washington, D.C., 23 November 1862.

Bockes, William H. Mustered: Pvt. Co. K, 8th OH Inf. Transferred: Pvt. Co. C, 6th U.S. Cav. 23 October 1862 (age 20 at Knoxville, MD)–26 May 1864. B: 1842, Medina Co., OH. Blue eyes, brown hair, florid complexion, 5' 8. Discharged at 6th Cav. Camp, VA. Mustered: Pvt. Co. B, 2nd OH Cav., 14 February 1865–11 September 1865. Mustered out at St. Louis, MO. D: 1933.

Bogert, John. Mustered: Drummer, Co. I, 8th OH Inf. 10 August 1861. Discharged as a bugler. Transferred: Bugler, Co. C, 6th U.S. Cav. 22 October 1862 (age 18 at Knoxville, MD)–8 August 1865. B: Erie Co., OH. Hazel eyes, brown hair, dark complexion, 5' 3. Reenlisted: 10 February 1864 at Brandy Station, VA. Deserted 8 August 1865.

Boles, William. Pvt. Co. B, 5 August 1861 (age 22 at Cleveland, OH)–8 November 1862. B: Newburgh, Cuyahoga, OH, farmer. Hazel eyes, brown hair, ruddy complexion, 5' 7½. D: of typhoid fever at Bakersville, MD, on 8 November 1862.

Bonner, James. Mustered: Pvt. Co. B, 6th PA Cav. (unassigned "not accounted for"). Enlisted: Pvt. Co. A, 6th U.S. Cav. 22 August 1861 (age 18 at Philadelphia, PA)–22 August 1864. B: Philadelphia, PA, butcher. Grey eyes, brown hair, freckled complexion, 5' 5. WIA, Williamsburg. Brought to the Seminary Hospital, Hampton, VA, 11 May 1862. Discharged at Harper's Ferry, VA.

Booth, John T. Mustered: Pvt., Co. G. 37th PA Inf., 24 May 1861. Transferred: Pvt. Co. K, 6th U.S. Cav. 27 October 1862 (age 19 at Knoxville, MD). B: West Brownsville, Washington Co., PA, blacksmith. Hazel eyes, black hair, dark complexion, 5' 7¾. Reenlisted: 11 February 1864 at Brandy Station, VA. Deserted 24 July 1865. Discharged 6 April 1889 at Washington, D.C. without character (backdate 24 July 1865).

Booz, Martin V. Pvt. Co. H, 5 August 1861 (age 32 at Philadelphia, PA)–8 December 1862. B: Bristol, Bucks Co., PA, carpenter. Brown eyes, black hair, dark complexion, 5' 7¾. POW, Coal Harbor, 27 June 1862. Disability discharge at Bellevue Hospital, NY. D: 9 January 1900, Philadelphia, PA.

Borden, Henry. Pvt. Co. G, 23 July 1861 (age 30 at Columbus, OH)–3 July 1863. B: Red Bank, Monmouth Co., NJ, cooper. Hazel eyes, black hair, sallow complexion, 5' 7. KIA, Fairfield.

Bordy, Albert Peter. Pvt. Co. H, 8 August 1861 (age 21 at Philadelphia, PA)–8 August 1864. B: March 1843, Jersey Shore, Sullivan Co., PA, boatman. Blue eyes, light hair, fair complexion, 5' 6. WIA/POW, Malvern Hill, 6 August 1862. POW at Libby Prison. WIA/POW, Fairfield. POW at Libby Prison. Discharged at Lighthouse Point, VA. D: 27 January 1930.

Bould, Joseph. Pvt.-Cpl.Sgt.-1st Sgt. Co. A, 29 August 1861 (age 26 at Philadelphia, PA)–9 July 1863. B: 3 December 1838, Walsall, Staffordshire, ENG, collar maker. Blue eyes, brown hair, light complexion, 5' 6½. 2nd Lt. 6th U.S. Cav. 1 June 1863. Resigned: 25 February 1865. D: 1888, St. Luke's Cannock, ENG.

Bousman, Henry. Pvt. Co. M, 15 October 1861 (age 21 at Pittsburgh, PA). B: St. Lawrence Borough, Berks, PA, farmer. Hazel eyes, brown hair, dark complexion, 5' 8. Reenlisted: 17 February 1864 at Brandy Station, VA. Deserted 29 July 1865. Note: Surname also spelled Bausman.

Bower, Charles. Rct. 23 December 1861 (age 34 at Pittsburgh, PA)–14 January 1862. B: GER, gunsmith. Hazel eyes, dark hair, dark complexion, 5' 5½. Disability discharge at Washington, D.C.

Bowers, Isaac. Pvt. Co. G, 29 July 1861 (age 34 at Erie Co., PA)–6 November 1862. B: 1827, Rensselaer Co., NY, ship carpenter. Blue eyes, dark hair, light complexion, 5' 9½. Disability discharge at Alexandria, VA. Enlisted: Pvt. Co. K, 145th PA Inf. 22 April 1864. Mustered out 30 May 1865. Transferred: 1 June 1865, Co. C, 53rd PA Inf. Mustered out 30 June 1865, Washington, D.C. D: 21 February 1903, Erie, PA.

Bowman, William. Pvt. Co. L, 26 August 1864 (age 19 at Harrisburg, PA)–15 November 1864. B: Port Hope, CAN, laborer. Blue eyes, light hair, ruddy complexion, 5' 5½. Deserted.

Boyce, Elijah. Pvt. Co. M, 20 October 1861 (age 31 at Pittsburgh, PA)–11 October 1863. B: 1828, Allegheny Co., PA, farmer. Hazel eyes, brown hair, light complexion, 5' 8. MIA, Culpepper

Station, VA. December casualty list says "Brandy Station." D: 1904, Allegheny, PA.

Boyd, Hugh. Pvt. Co. M, 14 December 1861 (age 34 at Pittsburgh, PA)–14 January 1862. B: Westmoreland Co., PA, farmer. Blue eyes, brown hair, light complexion, 6'1. Disability discharge at Washington, D.C.

Boyd, John. Pvt. Co. D, 20 August 1861 (age 24 at Pittsburgh, PA)–24 November 1861. B: Lanarkshire Co., SCO, coal miner. Blue eyes, light hair, light complexion, 5' 8. Deserted.

Boyd, Robert. Cpl. Co. D, 22 August 1861 (age 25 at Pittsburgh, PA)–28 August 1864. B: Co. Londonderry, IRE, oil miner. Blue eyes, light hair, light complexion, 6'½. Discharged in the field, VA.

Boyer, Andrew. Pvt. Co. K, 16 July 1861 (age 17 at Franklin, PA). B: Butler Co., PA, farmer. Grey eyes, brown hair, brown complexion, 5' 6¾. Reenlisted: 10 February 1864 at Brandy Station, VA. Deserted 16 October 1865.

Boyle, Matthew. Pvt. Co. A, 2 December 1864 (age 20 at Philadelphia, PA)–2 December 1867. B: IRE, laborer. Hazel eyes, brown hair, light complexion, 5' 6. Discharged at Buffalo Springs, TX.

Boyle, Owen. Pvt. Co. M, 1 June 1863 (age 29 at Cincinnati, OH)–21 September 1866. B: Rochester, Monroe Co., NY, clerk. Hazel eyes, brown hair, ruddy complexion, 5'11. Discharged at Austin, TX, by Special Order 435, AGO '66. Reenlisted: Pvt. Cos. I, D, 1st U.S. Inf. 8 October 1866 (Rochester, NY). Drowned 2 July 1867 at New Orleans, LA.

Boynton, William A. Pvt. Co. G, 8 August 1861 (age 29 at Rochester, NY)–4 September 1862. B: Allegheny Co., NY, laborer. Grey eyes, brown hair, dark complexion, 5' 5. D: 4 September 1862. Fall's Church.

Bracker, Reid Graham. Pvt. Co. K, 13 August 1861 (age 22 at Butler, PA)–13 August 1864. B: Butler Co., PA, tanner. Blue eyes, light hair, fair complexion, 5' 7. Discharged in the field, VA.

Brackin, John. Pvt.-Sgt. Co. H, 7 August 1861 (age 23 at Philadelphia, PA)–7 August 1864. B: Philadelphia, PA, carpenter. Brown eyes, brown hair, fair complexion, 5' 7½. Discharged in the field, VA.

Bradish, John E. Pvt. Co. G, 26 July 1861 (age 21 at Rochester, NY)–26 July 1864. B: Crafton, Monroe Co., NY, laborer. Blue eyes, brown hair, fair complexion, 6'¼. Discharged in the field, VA.

Bradish, Warner C. Pvt. Cos. E, C, 17 September 1861 (age 24 at Adrian, MI)–31 January 1862.

B: Madison, MI, farmer. Grey eyes, light hair, ruddy complexion, 5' 8¾. D: 31 January 1862 at Camp east of Capitol, Washington, D.C.

Bradley, William. Mustered: Pvt. Co. C, 37th PA Inf. 17 April 1861. Transferred: Pvt. Co. D, 6th U.S. Cav. 28 October 1862 (age 20 at Knoxville, MD)–28 April 1864. B: SCO, miner. Blue eyes, brown hair, dark complexion, 5'11. Discharged at 6th Cav. Camp, VA. WIA (GSW through left breast).

Bradley, Zalmon C. Pvt. Co. I, 27 July 1861 (age 32 at Rochester, NY)–27 April 1863. B: at Regi, Monroe Co., NY, blacksmith. Grey eyes, brown hair, fair complexion, 6'. Deserted.

Bradly, Joseph. Pvt. Co. L, 7 December 1862 (age 32)–28 March 1863. Deserted.

Bradly, Merrick. Pvt. Co. G, 25 July 1861 (age 26 at Rochester, NY)–27 March 1862. B: Onondaga Co., NY, farmer. Blue eyes, brown hair, fair complexion, 5'1½. Deserted.

Bradmon, Alvah M. Sgt.-1st Sgt. Co. M, 26 September 1861 (age 22 at Pittsburgh, PA)–23 August 1864. B: Fayette Co., PA, carpenter. Grey eyes, light hair, light complexion, 6' 2½. WIA/POW, Beverly Ford. D: 23 August 1864 from chronic diarrhea as POW at Andersonville, GA.

Bradt, Louis. Pvt. Cos. C, L, 15 December 1861 (age 23 at Little Rock, PA)–2 December 1864. B: Hesse, GER, physician. Brown eyes, dark hair, fair complexion, 5' 4½. Discharged at Winchester, VA.

Bradt, Michael. Pvt. Co. I, 26 August 1861 (age 21 at Rochester, NY)–26 August 1864. B: Albany, NY, farmer. Blue eyes, brown hair, florid complexion, 5'11¼. Discharged in the field, VA.

Brady, John. Pvt. Co. A, 24 October 1864 (age 23 at NY)–27 May 1867. B: Canan, IRE, brick layer. Blue eyes, brown hair, ruddy complexion, 5' 8½. Tried by GCMO 3 October 1865 at Frederick, MD. D: of accidental gunshot wound at Austin, TX, on 27 May 1867.

Brady, Thomas. Rct. 16 November 1864 (age 22 at Harrisburg, PA)–21 November 1864. B: Co. Roscommon, IRE, boatman. Grey eyes, dark hair, ruddy complexion, 5' 4½. Deserted.

Brandt, Henry. Pvt. Co. I, 11 September 1861 (age 33 at Rochester, NY)–11 November 1867. B: Hanover, GER, tailor. Blue eyes, brown hair, brown complexion, 5' 4. Reenlisted: 11 November 1864 at Rochester, NY. Deserted 24 September 1865. Surrendered 17 October 1865. Discharged 11 November 1867 at Camp Wilson, TX.

Brantingham, Edward. Pvt. Co. G, 21 July 1861 (age 22 at Columbus, OH)–21 January 1865.

B: Columbus, OH, laborer. Blue eyes, light hair, ruddy complexion, 5' 5. Discharged at 6th Cav. Camp, VA.

Breen, Jeremiah. Pvt. Co. G, 16 August 1861 (age 19 at Rochester, NY)–5 June 1863. B: CAN, hostler. Grey eyes, black hair, dark complexion, 5' 7. Deserted.

Brenan, James. Pvt.-Farrier. Co. A, 28 September 1861 (age 30 at Pottsville, PA)–30 January 1863. B: Tolert(?), IRE, farmer. Blue eyes, light hair, dark complexion, 5' 5½. WIA, New Bridge. Disability discharge at Alexandria, VA.

Brennan, James. Mustered: Pvt. 3rd WI Inf. 1 June 1861. Transferred: Pvt. Co. C, 24 October 1862 (age 21 at Knoxville, MD)–2 June 1864. B: Co. Kilkenny, IRE. Blue eyes, sandy hair, florid complexion, 5' 8. WIA, Beverly Ford. Discharged at Camp 6th Cav., VA.

Brennan, Thomas. Pvt. Co. A, 15 November 1864 (age 21 at NY)–21 November 1864. B: Brandling, NY, seaman. Grey eyes, light hair, fair complexion, 5' 8. Deserted.

Breno, Louis (alias Greeno, Louis). Mustered: Pvt. Co. E, 60th NY Inf. 18 September 1861. Transferred: Pvt. Co. L, 6th U.S. Cav. 23 October 1862 (age 19 at Knoxville, MD)–11 February 1867. B: 1846, Franklin Co., NY. Hazel eyes, black hair, dark complexion, 5' 3. Returned to duty 8 August 1863. Reenlisted: 10 February 1864 at Brandy Station, VA. Discharged at Jacksboro, TX. D: 1908, Middlesex, Washington, VT.

Brethauer, Fred. Pvt. Co. H, 5 August 1861 (age 19 at Philadelphia, PA)–5 August 1864. B: Capel, GER, confectioner. Blue eyes, light hair, ruddy complexion, 5' 5¾. Discharged in the field, VA.

Brewster, Carlton. Pvt. Co. I, 4 September 1861 (age 18 at Rochester, NY)–6 September 1864. B: Wayne Co., NY, farmer. Grey eyes, brown hair, florid complexion, 5' 9½. Disability discharge at Carlisle Barracks, PA.

Bright, Joseph C. Pvt. Cos. H, I, 2 August 1861 (age 21 at Philadelphia, PA)–10 March 1863. B: Montgomery, Lycoming Co., PA, grocer. Grey eyes, light hair, fair complexion, 5' 5. POW, Coal Harbor, 27 June 1862. Disability discharge at Camp near Falmouth, VA.

Brison, David. Pvt. 16 August 1861 (age 21 at Indiana, PA)–No further information. B: Indiana Co., PA, laborer. Black eyes, black hair, dark complexion, 5'10.

Britton, Thomas B. Pvt. Co. G, 5 August 1861 (age 24 at Columbus, OH)–17 February 1863. B: Franklin Co., OH, farmer. Blue eyes, brown

hair, ruddy complexion, 6'. Disability discharge at Camp Convalescent.

Brock, Andrew J. (alias Brock, Harold B.). Mustered: Pvt. 1st MN Inf. 23 May 1861. Transferred: Pvt. Co. B, 6th U.S. Cav. 26 October 1862 (age 19 at Knoxville, MD)–26 May 1864. B: Cincinnati, Hamilton Co., OH. Dark eyes, dark hair, dark complexion, 5' 7. MIA, Youngville (Stoneman's Raid), 11 May 1863. Reported from MIA 24 September 1863 at Culpepper, VA. Discharged at 6th Cav. Camp, VA. Mustered: Pvt. Co. E, 1st MN (H) Art. 4 February 1865–27 September 1865. D: 27 March 1919.

Brocker, Samuel. Pvt. Co. D, 9 August 1861 (age 24 at Pittsburgh, PA)–10 November 1861. B: Shaftland, SWZ, carpenter. Blue eyes, auburn hair, sallow complexion, 5' 6. D: of disease at Camp east of Capitol, Washington, D.C., 10 November 1861.

Brooks, Robert T. Pvt. Cos. C, F, F&S, 6 July 1861 (age 21 at Pittsburgh, PA)–16 August 1868. B: Brownsville, Washington Co., PA, trunk maker. Grey eyes, brown hair, dark complexion, 5' 5. Reenlisted: 8 February 1864 at 6th Cav. Camp, VA. Transferred to F&S 12 July 1864. Deserted 17 October 1865. Apprehended 20 April 1867. Discharge 16 August 1868 at Ft. Richardson, TX.

Brosman, John. Mustered: Pvt. Co. D, 14th IN Inf. 7 June 1861. Transferred: Rct. 6th U.S. Cav. 23 October 1862 (age 22 at Knoxville, MD)–December 1862. B: Myerstown, Lebanon Co., PA, plasterer. Blue eyes, brown hair, florid complexion, 5'11. Returned to USV. Transferred: Pvt. Cos. B, E, 20th IN Inf. 6 June 1864–23 April 1865. Transferred: Pvt. Co. A, 17th V.R.C. 23 April 1865.

Brown, George H. Mustered: Pvt. Co. D, 37th PA Inf. Transferred: Pvt. Co. D, 25 October 1862 (age 29 at Knoxville, MD)–26 June 1864. B: Glasgow, SCO, miner. Blue eyes, light hair, fair complexion, 5' 9. Deserted 12 July 1862. Apprehended 24 September 1863. Discharged 26 June 1864 at Nelson's Landing, VA.

Brown, George W. Co. E, 16 September 1861 (age 28 at Columbus, OH)–3 March 1862. B: Sussex Co., NJ, farmer. Grey eyes, sandy hair, ruddy complexion, 5' 6½. Disability discharge at Washington, D.C.

Brown, George W. Pvt. Co. G, 18 July 1861 (age 18 at Columbus, OH)–18 July 1864. B: Licking Co., OH, painter. Grey eyes, brown hair, sallow complexion, 5' 5. Deserted 26 November 1862. Apprehended. Deserted 8 January 1863. Surrendered 1 April 1863. POW, ?–20 December

1863. Discharged 18 July 1864 at Lighthouse Point.

Brown, Henry. Pvt. Co. I, 16 September 1861 (age 29 at Rochester, NY)–9 July 1862. B: GER, farmer. Blue eyes, light hair, fair complexion, 5' 7½. Deserted.

Brown, James. Pvt. Co. F, 22 November 1864 (age 26 at Harrisburg, PA)–19 July 1865. B: London, ENG, sailor. Dark eyes, dark hair, ruddy complexion, 5'10½. Deserted.

Brown, John C. Pvt. Co. F, 16 December 1864 (age 28 at Cincinnati, OH)–26 January 1865. B: Windsor, CAN, farmer. Light eyes, light hair, fair complexion, 5' 7. Deserted.

Brown, John M. Pvt.-Sgt. Co. F, 1 July 1861 (age 23 at Pittsburgh, PA)–1 July 1864. B: Blairesville, Indiana, Co., PA, machinist. Blue eyes, sandy hair, light complexion, 5' 7½. MIA, Fairfield. Discharged at Lighthouse Point.

Brown, Joseph. Pvt. Co. D, 29 August 1861 (age 27 at Pittsburgh, PA)–29 August 1864. B: Co. Down, IRE, miner. Blue eyes, light hair, dark complexion, 5' 4½. Discharged at Halltown, VA.

Brown, William James. Pvt.-1st Sgt. Cos. K, L, 16 July 1861 (age 24 at Franklin, PA)–25 June 1866. B: Onondaga Co., NY, farmer. Hazel eyes, lt. brown hair, dark, complexion, 5' 7½. Reenlisted: 10 February 1864 at Brandy Station, VA. WIA, Kernstown 19 August 1864. Gained from MIA 31 March 1865. Disability discharge at Austin, TX.

Brownholtz, George W. Sgt. Co. H, 6 August 1861 (age 21 at Philadelphia, PA)–6 August 1864. B: Montgomery, Lycoming Co., PA, book keeper. Brown eyes, dark hair, dark complexion, 5' 8¾. Discharged in the field, VA.

Brownwell, John W. (alias, Kingston, J. Wade). Sgt. Co. H, 9 August 1861 (age 21 at Philadelphia, PA)–8 August 1864. B: Cumberland Co., PA, book keeper. Blue eyes, brown hair, ruddy complexion, 5' 9. Discharged in the field, VA. Mustered (under Brownwell): Pvt. Co. L, 13th OH Cav. 10 March 1865. Promoted to Q.M. Sgt. 24 April 1865. Mustered out 10 August 1865 at Petersburg, VA.

Brubaker, William W. Mustered: Pvt. Co. E, 38th PA Inf. 1 May 1861. Transferred: Pvt. Co. A, 28 October 1862 (age 19 at Knoxville, MD)–29 July 1864. B: Allegheny Co., PA. Grey eyes, light hair, light complexion, 5' 7¼. POW, Fairfield, 3 July 1863–8 April 1864. Paroled, reported at Annapolis, MD. Discharged at Lighthouse Point. Mustered: Pvt., Co. G, 87th Pa. Inf. 18 February 1865. Promoted to Sgt. 7 March 1865. Mustered out at Alexandria, VA.

Bruce, William F. (T). Pvt. Co. A, 8 December 1864 (age 23 at Philadelphia, PA)–16 June 1865. B: Concord, NH, sailor. Brown eyes, dark hair, dark complexion, 5' 6. Deserted.

Buchmyer, Henry A. Musician 1st Class. Co. F&S, 15 October 1861 (age 24 at Mount Joy, PA)–15 October 1864. B: Graceland, MD, musician. Hazel eyes, brown hair, fair complexion, 5' 6. Discharged at Strausburg, VA.

Buck, George. Pvt. Co. F, 26 July 1861 (age 22 at Pittsburgh, PA)–23 November 1862. B: Carbon Co., PA, farmer. Blue eyes, dark hair, ruddy complexion, 5'10½. D: of disease at Washington, D.C., 23 November 1862.

Buck, Thomas. Pvt. Co. L, 27 February 1862 (age 18 at Bellafontaine, PA)–24 February 1863. B: Centre Co., PA. No further information. D: of typhoid fever at Falmouth, VA., 24 February 1863.

Buckton, John. Sgt. Co. F, 10 July 1861 (age 21 at Pittsburgh, PA)–10 July 1864. B: Darlington, ENG, laborer. Blue eyes, sandy hair, ruddy complexion, 5' 8. Discharged at Lighthouse Point, VA.

Budrough, Charles L. Mustered (Mexico, NY): Pvt. Batt. G, 1st NY Light Art. 9 October 1861. Transferred: Pvt. Co. H, 28 October 1862 (age 19 at Knoxville, MD)–16 June 1863. B: Oswego, NY. Blue eyes, light hair, light complexion, 5' 8. Deserted.

Bulkley, Charles A. Pvt. Co. G, 8 August 1861 (age 19½ at Columbus, OH)–8 August 1864. B: Litchfield, Litchfield Co., CT, tailor. Grey eyes, brown hair, light complexion, 5' 5½. MIA in the field 7 May 1863. Discharged at Lighthouse Point, VA.

Bullard, Lorenzo D. Pvt. Co. B, 10 August 1861 (age 23 at Cleveland, OH)–25 November 1863. B: Berkshire Co., PA, machinist. Blue eyes, brown hair, fair complexion, 5' 7½. Disability discharge at Ft. Monroe.

Bulle, Frederick. Pvt. Co. L, 15 May 1862 (at Washington, D.C.)–29 October 1862. Deserted.

Bunn, Philip A. (alias Barker, Peter A.) Pvt. Co. B. No further information. Mustered: Co. F, 1st NY Vet Cav. 31 August 1864 to 7 June 1865. Reenlisted: Co. H, 3rd U.S. Art., 08 August 1867–8 August 1870, GA.

Burch (Birch), Stephen. Pvt. Co. M, 16 September 1864 (age 18 at Rochester, NY)–4 January 1865. B: Toronto, CAN, farmer. Blue eyes, light hair, fair complexion, 5' 6. D: of disease at Winchester, VA. 4 January 1865.

Burdick, William. Pvt.-Cpl. Co. A, 24 September

1861 (age 33 at Cleveland, OH)–7 October 1867. B: Summit Co., OH, painter. Blue eyes, brown hair, ruddy complexion, 5'4½. POW, Fairfield, 3 July–24 December 1863. Paroled, reported at Annapolis, MD. Discharged 24 September 1864 at Harrisonburg, VA. Reenlisted: 6 October 1864 at Cleveland, OH. Discharged 7 October 1867 at Buffalo Springs, TX.

Burge, Theodore M. Pvt. Co. E, 1 September 1861 (age 19 at Columbus, OH)–1 September 1864. B: Union Co., OH, farmer. Hazel eyes, brown hair, ruddy complexion, 5'9½. Disability discharge at Falmouth, VA.

Burk, Cyrus. Pvt. Co. L, 28 October 1862 (age 28 at Knoxville, MD)–27 June 1864. B: Dauphin Co., PA, shoemaker. Grey eyes, auburn hair, fair complexion, 5'8. MIA, Fairfield. Discharged at Camp in the field, VA.

Burk, Henry. Pvt. Co. L, 6 October 1864 (age 23 at Cleveland, OH)–1864. B: Co. Dublin, IRE, laborer. Blue eyes, brown hair, ruddy complexion, 5'7. Deserted.

Burns, Ashbury Thompson. Pvt. Co. K, 19 July 1861 (age 21 at Franklin, PA)–19 July 1864. B: German Twp., Fayette Co., PA, farmer. Blue eyes, red hair, sallow complexion, 5'9½. Discharged at Lighthouse Point, VA.

Burns, John. Pvt. Cos. L, M, 31 August 1864 (age 31 at Rochester, NY)–29 July 1865. B: Co. Fermanagh, IRE, blacksmith. Brown eyes, dark hair, dark complexion, 5'11. Deserted.

Burns, William. Pvt. Co. L, 14 December 1864 (age 21 at Cincinnati, OH)–2 February 1865. B: IN, boatman. Blue eyes, brown hair, fair complexion, 5'5¾. Deserted.

Burns, William. Pvt. Co. M, 13 October 1864 (age 31 at Rochester, NY)–13 October 1867. B: Co. Dublin, IRE, boatman. Blue eyes, brown hair, fair complexion, 5'5¾. Discharged at Mt. Pleasant, TX.

Burns, William H. Mustered: Sgt. Co. A, 3rd WI Inf. 18 April 1861. WIA (GSW, right leg), Antietam. Transferred: Pvt.-Cpl. Co. C, 6th U.S. Cav. 23 October 1862 (age 23 at Knoxville, MD)–26 December 1863. B: Toronto, CAN, painter. Hazel eyes, brown hair, florid complexion, 5'6. WIA (GSW, left breast), Beverly Ford. Disability discharged at Lincoln Hospital, Washington, D.C. D: Milwaukee, WI.

Burr, Benjamin Franklin. Musician 2nd Class. Co. F&S, 15 October 1861 (age 23 at Mount Joy, PA)–15 October 1864. B: Columbia, Lancaster Co., PA, musician. Grey eyes, black hair, light complexion, 5'5. Discharged at Strausburg, VA.

Burroughs, Levi S. Pvt. Co. B, 1 August 1861 (age 23 at Cleveland, OH)–18 February 1865. B: Cuyahoga Falls, OH, blacksmith. Hazel eyes, black hair, ruddy complexion, 5'5. POW, Fairfield, 3 July–24 September 1863. POW, Brandy Station, 11 October 1863–? Paroled and reported at Culpepper, VA. Discharged at Baltimore, MD.

Burrows, James. Pvt. Co. G, 12 August 1861 (age 22 at Rochester, NY)–1 February 1862. B: CAN, sailor. Hazel eyes, brown hair, florid complexion, 5'8. Deserted.

Burt, Byron C. Mustered: Pvt. Co. K, 8th OH Inf. 6 May 1861. Transferred: Cpl. Co. C, 6th U.S. Cav. 23 October 1862 (age 19 at Knoxville, MD)–26 May 1864. B: 1843, Medina Co., OH. Blue eyes, light hair, fair complexion, 5'8. Discharged at 6th Cav. Camp, VA. Mustered: Pvt., Co. B, 2nd OH Cav. 14 February 1865–11 September 1865. D: 1921, NB.

Burton, Frank. Pvt. Co. L, 13 December 1864 (age 18 at Harrisburg, PA)–14 September 1866. B: Gallia, Euclid Co., OH, farmer. Black eyes, dk. Brown hair, dark complexion, 5'5½. Deserted.

Butler, Samuel. Pvt. Co. B, 18 July 1861 (age 24 at Columbus, OH)–9 October 1863. B: Franklin Co., OH, carpenter. Grey eyes, brown hair, ruddy complexion, 5'8. Disability discharge at Mower Hospital, Philadelphia, PA.

Button, Japhet H. Enlisted: Pvt. Co. K, 19 August 1861 (age 21 at Rochester, NY)–19 August 1864. B: Oswego Co., NY, chair maker. Hazel eyes, light hair, brown complexion, 5'7. Discharged in the field, VA. Mustered (Rochester, NY): Pvt. Co. E, 111th NY Inf. 3 August 1864. Transferred: Co. E, 4th NY Heavy Art. 4 June 1865.

Caffrey, Thomas. Rct. 23 July 1861 (age 31 at Warren, OH)–No further information. B: Kingstown, IRE, laborer. Hazel eyes, brown hair, ruddy complexion, 5'7¾.

Caityr, John. Pvt. Co. L, 30 November 1864 (age 33 at Cincinnati, OH)–22 January 1865. B: IRE, boatman. Grey eyes, dark hair, dark complexion, 6'2. Deserted.

Calbert, William J. Pvt. Co. M, 15 November 1864 (age 24 at Harrisburg, PA)–21 November 1864. B: Tazewell, VA, laborer. Hazel eyes, dark hair, dark complexion, 5'7. Deserted.

Callan, Samuel. Pvt. Co. H, 12 July 1861 (age 21 at Philadelphia, PA)–12 July 1864. B: Philadelphia, PA, carpenter. Hazel eyes, light hair, ruddy complexion, 5'6¼. Discharged at Dismounted Camp, VA.

Callender, William V. E. Cpl. Co. B, 21 July 1861 (age 22 at Cleveland, OH)–28 October 1862.

B: Fayette Co., OH, Farmer. Hazel eyes, brown hair, ruddy complexion, 5'11¼. Disability discharge at Governers Island, New York Harbor. Mustered: Pvt. 9th Indep. Bat., OH Light Art. 24 September 1863–25 July 1865. Promoted to Cpl. 11 July 1864.

Calvert, James. Rct. 30 November 1864 (age 28 at Cincinnati, OH)–18 December 1864. B: Manchester, ENG, laborer. Grey eyes, brown hair, fair complexion, 5'5½. Deserted.

Cameron, John. Pvt. Co. A, 28 November 1864 (age 25 at Cincinnati, OH)–28 November 1867. B: CAN, farmer. Blue eyes, brown hair, fair complexion, 6'1. Discharged at Buffalo Springs, TX.

Cameron, Joseph. Pvt. Co. H, 10 July 1861 (age 21 at Philadelphia, PA)–10 July 1864. B: Boston, MA, fisherman. Blue eyes, brown hair, ruddy complexion, 5'6¼. MIA in the field April 1863. Discharged at Lighthouse Point, VA.

Cameron, Thomas. Pvt. Co. M, 26 September 1864 (age 21 at Cleveland, OH)–11 October 1866. B: New London, CAN, farmer. Black eyes, brown hair, dark complexion, 5'8. Deserted 31 December 1864. Apprehended 14 October 1865. Dropped from rolls as per instructions AGO, 11 October 1866.

Camp, Henry. Mustered: Sgt.-Pvt. Co. G, 50th PA Inf. 26 September 1861. Transferred: Pvt. Co. H, 28 October 1862 (age 22 at Knoxville, MD)–24 March 1864. B: 22 January 1840 Camptown, Bradford Co., PA. Blue eyes, light hair, light complexion, 5'4. Discharged at 6th Cav. Camp, VA, by S. O. 122, AGO 64.

Camp, Hezekiah. Rct. 8 July 1861 (age 21 at Philadelphia, PA)–22 July 1861. B: Delaware Co., PA, farmer. Grey eyes, brown hair, ruddy complexion, 5'7. Discharged by Civil Authority on assault of a minority at Philadelphia, PA area. Mustered: Co. L, 15th PA Cav. D: 5 April 1863, Murfreesboro, TN.

Campbell, Bernard. Pvt. Co. F, 9 November 1864 (age 23 at Cincinnati, OH)–3 December 1865. B: IRE, laborer. Grey eyes, light hair, fair complexion, 5'4. D: 3 December 1865 of tuberculosis at Baltimore, MD.

Campbell, James Potts. Cpl. Co. E, 14 September 1861 (age 23 at Adrian, MI)–14 September 1864. B: 11 January 1837 Newburgh, NY, farmer. Grey eyes, sandy hair, fair complexion, 5'9½. POW, Fairfield, 3 July 1863–26 May 1864. Paroled, reported at Annapolis, MD. Discharged in the field, VA. D: 28 April 1908.

Cannon, John. Pvt. Co. L, 25 November 1864 (age 21 at Harrisburg, PA)–10 October 1865.

B: Co. Donegal, IRE, boatman. Dark eyes, brown hair, ruddy complexion, 5'7½. Deserted.

Capan, David. Pvt. Co. L, 7 November 1861 (age 16 at Galion, OH)–16 February 1867. B: Marion, OH, mason. Hazel eyes, red hair, yellow complexion, 5'7¼. Reenlisted: 16 February 1864, Brandy Station, VA. Discharged 16 February 1867 at Jacksboro, TX.

Caragan, William. Rct. 4 November 1864 (age 26 at Harrisburg, PA)–21 November 1864. B: Co. Tipperary, IRE, laborer. Grey eyes, brown hair, ruddy complexion, 5'10½. Deserted.

Carel, John H. Pvt. Co. A, 3 December 1864 (age 31 at Cleveland, OH)–4 January 1865. B: Toronto, CAN, engineer. Grey eyes, brown hair, dark complexion, 5'10½. Deserted.

Carey, Michael. Sgt. Co. A, 25 November 1864 (age 25 at Cincinnati, OH)–23 November 1867. B: Manchester, ENG, soldier. Blue eyes, brown hair, fair complexion, 6'1. Deserted 19 October 1865. Apprehended 6 January 1866. Discharged 23 November 1867 at Buffalo Springs, TX.

Carey, William. Mustered: Cpl. Co. G, 50th PA Inf. 26 September 1861. Transferred: Pvt. Co. H, 28 October 1862 (age 20 at Knoxville, MD)–28 August 1864. B: Lawrenceville, Tioga Co., PA. Grey eyes, dark hair, dark complexion, 5'6. Discharged at Sandy Hook, MD.

Carl, Daniel A. Mustered: Co. A, 3rd MD Inf. Transferred: Pvt. Co. K, 27 October 1862 (age 22 at Knoxville, MD)–15 July 1864. B: Gettysburg, Adams Co., PA, harness maker. Light eyes, light hair, fair complexion, 5'6½. Discharged at Jordan's Point, VA.

Carman, George. Rct. 19 August 1861 (age 18 at Rochester, NY)–22 August 1861. B: Tompkins Co., NY, shoemaker. Hazel eyes, light hair, light complexion, 5'5¾. Discharged for general unfitness for service at Pittsburgh, PA.

Carns, William H. Mustered: Pvt. Co. B, 8th OH Inf. 5 June 1861. Transferred: Pvt. Cos. C, E, 6th U.S. Cav. 22 October 1862 (age 22 at Knoxville, MD)–22 August 1864. B: Romney, WAL, heater. Blue eyes, brown hair, light complexion, 5'10½. POW, Funkstown, 7 July–8 August 1863.

Carothers, Alpheus. Pvt. Co. K, 31 July 1861 (age 27 at Pittsburgh, PA)–4 February 1863. B: Carrol Co., OH, brakeman. Grey eyes, brown hair, sandy complexion, 5'11¾. Disability discharge at Convalescent Camp, VA.

Carpenter, David P. Pvt. Co. L, 29 October 1862 (age 18 at Knoxville, MD)–4 April 1865. B: Bedford Co., PA, tanner. Grey eyes, dark hair, fair complexion, 5'7. POW, Fairfield, 3 July 1863–27 February 1864. Paroled. POW, 21 June 1864–16 August 1864. Paroled, reported at Camp Parole. Discharged at Camp Parole, MD.

Carpenter, George. Pvt. Co. L, 1 November 1864 (age 26 at Rochester, NY)–21 November 1864. B: Mexico, Oswego Co., NY, sailor. Blue eyes, light hair, fair complexion, 5'7. Deserted.

Carpenter, Louis Henry. Sgt. Cos. C, L, 1 November 1861 (age 22 at Philadelphia, PA)–20 September 1862. B: Carpenter Landing, NJ, student. Hazel eyes, black hair, light complexion, 5'9. Discharged 20 September 1862 upon commission as 2nd Lt. 6th U.S. Cav. at Antietam, MD.

Carr, James. Pvt. Co. G, 22 August 1861 (age 22 at Columbus, OH)–27 July 1863. B: Dublin, IRE, painter. Blue eyes, brown hair, ruddy complexion, 5'5¼. D: from disease at Carver Hospital, Washington, D.C., 27 July 1863. (RR says he died 20 August 1863.)

Carrigan, William H. H. Pvt.-Cpl. Co. K, 16 July 1861 (age 21 at Franklin, PA)–3 August 1865. B: KY, teamster. Grey eyes, brown hair, brown complexion, 5'4¼. R: 10 February 1864 at Brandy Station, VA. Deserted 3 August 1865. Discharged 2 January 1890 (backdated 3 August 1865) at Washington, D.C., without character.

Carroll, Hercules C. G. Sgt.-Sgm.-Pvt.-Sgt. Cos. B, F&S, 5 August 1861 (age 32 at Columbus, OH)–1 April 1864. B: 2 November 1828 Painsville, Geauga Co., OH, tailor. Grey (bl.) eyes, brown hair, sallow (fair) complexion, 5'8 (5'8½). Appointed Sgt. Maj. 1 December 1862. POW, Aldie, 23 June–7 November 1863 (Libby Prison). Paroled, reported at Washington, D.C. Transferred: AGO, General Service, 9 November 1863. Reenlisted (by Maj. Williams, Washington, D.C.): Sgt. 18 February 1864. by G. O. 25 AGO 64. Appt. Clerk Class 1, AGO, General Service, 1 April 1864. Discharged a Sgt. D: 7 May 1906.

Carroll, John P. Pvt. Co. A, 13 December 1864 (age 27 at Philadelphia, PA)–27 January 1865. B: Philadelphia, PA, painter. Brown eyes, dark hair, dark complexion, 5'9. Deserted.

Carson, Thomas C. (also William). Rct. 4 August 1861 (age 18 at Warren, OH)–No further information. B: Newton Falls, OH, farmer. Blue eyes, light hair, light complexion, 5'9.

Carter, George W. Pvt. Co. I, 27 October 1862 (age 34 at Knoxville, MD)–27 August 1864. B: Bucks Co., PA, carpenter. Blue eyes, brown hair, ruddy complexion, 5'8. Discharged at Harper's Ferry, VA.

Carty, John M. Pvt. Co. A, 3 October 1861 (age 30 at Cleveland, OH)–3 January 1862. B: Co. Cork, IRE, laborer. Grey eyes, brown hair, ruddy complexion, 5'3½. Discharged at Camp east of Capitol, Washington, D.C. D: 16 February 1878.

Case, John F. (T.). Pvt. Co. A, 28 December 1864 (age 18 at Cincinnati, OH)–23 January 1865. B: Chili, OH, boatman. Hazel eyes, brown hair, ruddy complexion, 5'7¼. Deserted 23 January 1865 at Carlisle Barracks, PA.

Casey, Martin. Cpl. Co. A, 2 October 1861 (age 24 at Philadelphia, PA)–2 October 1864. B: Luzerne Co., PA, painter. Brown eyes, black hair, dark complexion, 5'4½. Discharged at Harrisonburg, VA.

Casker, Richard. Pvt. Co. M, 14 November 1864 (age 22 at Harrisburg, PA)–29 July 1865. B: Montreal, Quebec, CAN, brick maker. Grey eyes, dark hair, ruddy complexion, 5'8. Deserted.

Cassady, Park H. Sgt. Cos. A, M, 23 August 1861 (age 21 at Philadelphia, PA)–23 August 1864. B: Philadelphia, PA, baker. Blue eyes, sandy hair, fair complexion, 5'6¼. POW, Fairfield, 3 July 1863–18 January 1864. Paroled, reported at Annapolis, MD. Discharged at Geisboro Point, Washington, D.C.

Cassady, William M. Mustered: Pvt. Co. K, 110th PA Inf. 19 December 1861. Transferred: Pvt. Co. I, 6th U.S. Cav. 27 October 1862 (age 22 at Knoxville, MD)–27 September 1865. B: Centre Co., PA, collier. Grey eyes, red hair, ruddy complexion, 5'8. Discharged in the field, VA.

Cassidy, Peter. Pvt. Co. L, 22 December 1864 (age 18 at Cincinnati, OH)–25 May 1865. B: Pittsburgh, Allegheny Co., PA, laborer. Grey eyes, dark hair, ruddy complexion, 5'6. Deserted 5 February 1865. Gained from desertion 6 February 1865 at Winchester, VA. Apprehended 18 February 1865. Deserted 25 May 1865.

Catteson, William. Pvt. Co. M, 15 November 1861 (age 21 at New Castle, PA)–15 November 1864. B: New Castle, Lawrence Co., PA, farmer. Grey eyes, dark hair, dark complexion, 5'9½. MIA, Fairfield. Discharged in the field, VA.

Cavanagh, James. Rct. 25 November 1864 (age 21 at Harrisburg, PA)–1864. B: Athton, IRE, painter. Grey eyes, light hair, fair complexion, 5'10. Deserted.

Cawley, Francis. Pvt. Co. G, 5 August 1861 (age 30 at Columbus, OH)–10 August 1864. B: Co. Sligo, IRE, carpenter. Blue eyes, sandy hair, ruddy complexion, 5'6½. WIA/POW, Fairfield,

3 July–11 August 1863. Paroled, reported at Annapolis, MD. Discharged at Lighthouse Point, VA. D: 30 March 1867.

Center, Charles Wesley. Mustered (NYC): Pvt. Co. A, 78th NY Inf. 10 April 1861. Transferred: Pvt. Co. F, 6th U.S. Cav. 22 October 1862 (age 22 at Knoxville, MD)–11 May 1863. B: 17 November 1843 Mount Vernon, OH, machinist. Blue eyes, light hair, florid complexion, 5' 4½. Deserted to the enemy. Worked for the Confederates at Libby Prison.

Chaffee, Adna Romanza. Pvt.-1st Sgt. Co. K, 22 July 1861 (age 19 at Warren, OH)–12 May 1863. B: 14 April 1842, Orwell, Ashtabula, OH, farmer. Grey eyes, brown hair, ruddy complexion, 5' 7¾. WIA, Fairfield and Culpepper. Promoted to 2nd LT, 6th U.S. Cav.

Chalfant, Joseph. Pvt. Co. L, 1 February 1862 (at Cleveland, OH)–30 January 1864. Disability discharge at Carlisle Barracks, PA.

Champlavski, Stephen. Pvt. Co. G, 26 July 1861 (age 33 at Erie Co., PA)–5 August 1863. B: Poland, POL, shoemaker. Blue eyes, dark hair, fair complexion, 5' 7½. Transferred: Pvt. 2nd Bn. V.R.C.

Chapin, Charles H. Pvt. Co. G, 7 August 1861 (age 18 at Rochester, NY)–26 March 1863. B: Ontario, NY, farmer. Blue eyes, black hair, ruddy complexion, 5' 6. D: of disease at camp near Falmouth, VA, on 26 March 1863.

Chapin, Edward. Mustered: Co. K, 8th OH Inf. 1 January 1862. Transferred: Pvt. Co. C, 6th U.S. Cav. 22 October 1862 (age 18 at Knoxville, MD)–28 January 1865. B: Brunswick, OH, teamster. Blue eyes, light hair, fair complexion, 5' 7. Discharged at Carlisle Barracks, PA.

Chapman, Francis Riggs. Pvt. Co. B, 5 August 1861 (age 23 at Columbus, OH)–5 August 1864. B: Dublin, OH, clerk. Grey eyes, brown hair, sallow complexion, 5' 8. Discharged in the field, VA.

Chapman, Pulaski. Sgt. Co. D, 2 August 1861 (age 24 at Pittsburgh, PA)–2 August 1864. B: Rochester, Monroe Co., NY, machinist. Blue eyes, brown hair, dark complexion, 5' 8. Discharged in the field, VA.

Chapman, Thomas L. Mustered: Pvt. Co. F, 84th PA Inf. Transferred: Pvt. Co. A, 6th U.S. Cav. 28 October 1862 (age 22 at Knoxville, MD)–28 September 1864. B: Lycoming Co., PA. Hazel eyes, light hair, light complexion, 5' 9½. POW, Fairfield, 3 July 1863–18 January 1864. Paroled, reported at Annapolis, MD. Discharged at Harrisonburg, VA.

Charlton, Joseph, Jr. Pvt. Co. F, 11 July 1861 (age

20 at Pittsburgh, PA)–29 July 1864. B: New Castle, ENG, farmer. Blue eyes, light hair, fair complexion, 5' 9. WIA, Fairfield. Disability discharge at West Philadelphia, PA. Mustered: Pvt. Co. G, 14th PA Cav. 12 September 1864. POW, Berry's Ford, near Millford, VA, 17 December 1864 (Libby Prison). Paroled 15 February 1865. Discharged 30 May 1865.

Chase, George William. Pvt. Co. G, 28 October 1862 (age 28 at Knoxville, MD)–22 June 1864. B: Bedford Co., PA, stone mason. Hazel eyes, dark hair, ruddy complexion, 5' 8. POW, Fairfield, 3 July–10 November 1863. Paroled, reported at Camp 6th Cav. Discharged at White House, VA.

Chase, Oliver. Pvt. Co. L, 4 December 1862 (age 28 at Knoxville, MD)–4 March 1863. Deserted from confinement near Falmouth, VA. For history of this man see 4048-P.R.D. 1891.

Chasi, William. Pvt. Co. I, 27 January 1864 (age 33 at Cleveland, OH)–29 January 1864. B: Corsica, FRA, mould maker. Grey eyes, brown hair, dark complexion, 5' 6. Deserted.

Cheeney, George. Mustered (Ogdensburg, NY): Pvt. Co. E, 60th NY Inf. 10 September 1861. Transferred: Pvt. Co. K, 6th U.S. Cav. 28 October 1862 (age 18 at Knoxville, MD)–10 March 1863. B: Franklin Co., NY. Blue eyes, light hair, light complexion, 6'. Deserted. Mustered (listing himself as a veteran): Pvt. Co. E, 60th NY Inf. 14 December 1863–17 July 1865. Mustered out at Alexandria, VA. Note: Surname also spelled Cheany, Chaney, Cheney.

Chilcoat, Allen Edward. Mustered: Pvt. Co. B, 110th PA Inf. Transferred: Pvt.-Sgt. Co. B, 6th U.S. Cav. 22 October 1862 (age 18 at Knoxville, MD)–12 February 1867. B: Scottsville, Mifflin Co., PA, Brown eyes, auburn hair, light complexion, 5' 8. MIA, Fairfield. Reenlisted: 8 February 1864, 6th Cav. Camp, VA. Discharged 12 February 1867 at Austin, TX.

Christ, Jacob W. Pvt. Co. H, 14 August 1861 (age 18 at Philadelphia, PA)–14 August 1864. B: Bucks Co., PA, tailor. Hazel eyes, brown hair, fair complexion, 5' 9. Discharged at Sandy Hook, MD.

Clark, Charles. Mustered (Russia, NY): Pvt. Co. C, 60th NY Inf. 24 October 1861. Transferred: Pvt. Co. A, 6th U.S. Cav. 25 October 1862 (age 22 at Knoxville, MD)–30 October 1864. B: St. Lawrence Co., NY, lawyer. Blue eyes, dark hair, fair complexion, 5' 5½. Discharged at Middletown, VA.

Clark, Jacob S. Mustered: Pvt. Co. B, 110th PA Inf. 24 October 1861. Transferred: Pvt. Co. D, 6th

U.S. Cav. 28 October 1862 (age 24 at Knoxville, MD)–28 August 1864. B: Huntington Twp., PA. Grey eyes, dark hair, dark complexion, 5' 5½. Discharged at Halltown, VA. Mustered: Pvt. Co. F, 12th PA Cav. 12 October 1864–20 July 1865. Mustered out at Winchester, VA.

Clark, James H. Pvt. Co. L, 12 August 1864 (age 25 at NY)–13 April 1866. B: Melbourne, CAN, soldier. Blue eyes, brown hair, ruddy complexion, 6'1½. Deserted.

Clark, John. Co. E, 6 December 1864 (age 19 at Carlisle, PA)–15 August 1865. B: Liverpool, ENG, sailor. Grey eyes, sandy hair, ruddy complexion, 5' 7. Deserted 29 December 1864. Apprehended 10 January 1865. Gained from desertion 1 February 1865 at Winchester, VA. Deserted 15 August 1865.

Clark, John. Enlisted: Co. K, 1st U.S. Art. 2 January 1862–24 January 1864. Transferred: Reg. Vet. Surg. Co. F&S, 6th U.S. Cav. 24 January 1864 (age 29 at Camp Duncan)–2 January 1865. B: Oxford, ENG, vet. surgeon. Blue eyes, auburn hair, fair complexion, 5' 7.

Clarke, Thomas. Rct. 13 September 1864 (age 20 at Harrisburg, PA)–1864. B: Co. Tipperary, IRE, laborer. Grey eyes, brown hair, ruddy complexion, 5' 5½. Deserted.

Clay, Phillip. Cpl. Co. A, 16 December 1864 (age 20 at Cincinnati, OH)–16 December 1867. B: Toronto, CAN, farmer. Blue eyes, light hair, fair complexion, 6'. Discharged at Buffalo Springs, TX.

Clay, Robert H. Rct. 7 December 1864 (age 21 at Cincinnati, OH)–December 1864. B: New York, NY, farmer. Blue eyes, brown hair, dark complexion, 5' 7¼. Deserted.

Clayton, George. Rct. 10 November 1864 (age 22 at Harrisburg, PA)–21 November 1864. B: Liverpool, ENG, farmer. Blue eyes, dark hair, sallow complexion, 5'10. Deserted.

Cleland, George. Mustered: Pvt. Co. F, 60th NY Inf. 14 October 1861. Transferred: Pvt. Co. A, 6th U.S. Cav. 25 October 1862 (age 19 at Knoxville, MD)–13 December 1864. B: St. Lawrence Co., NY, farmer. Blue eyes, light hair, light complexion, 5' 7½. MIA, Morrisonville, 26 May 1864. WIA, Beverly Ford. Discharged 22 February 1865 (backdated to 13 December 1864), Baltimore, MD.

Clemens, Jacob. Bugler. Cos. I, G, 22 July 1861 (age 16 at Columbus, OH)–22 July 1864. B: Baden, GER, gardener. Blue eyes, sandy hair, fair complexion, 5' 4½. MIA, Fairfield. Discharged in the field, VA.

Clifford, Charles. Pvt. Co. M, 8 September 1864

(age 41 at Rochester, NY)–25 July 1865. B: Manchester, ENG, carpenter. Blue eyes, brown hair, ruddy complexion, 5' 8. Disability discharge at Carlisle Barracks, PA.

Clifford, Jeremiah. Mustered: Pvt. Co. B, 1st MN Inf. Transferred: Pvt. Co. B, 6th U.S. Cav. 26 October 1862 (age 20 at Knoxville, MD)–17 September 1864. B: Bosquine, MA. Grey eyes, dark hair, light complexion, 5' 7. POW at Andersonville. D: from scorbutus, Andersonville, GA., 17 September 1864.

Cline, Joseph J. Mustered: Pvt. Co. A, 45th PA Inf. 16 August 1861. Transferred: Pvt. Co. L, 6th U.S. Cav. 27 October 1862 (age 25 at Knoxville, MD)–29 August 1864. B: Cenre Co., PA, miller. Brown eyes, black hair, fair complexion, 6'. Discharged at Harper's Ferry, VA.

Clinton, Henry. Rct. 29 September 1864 (age 24 at Rochester, NY)–1864. B: Toronto, CAN, laborer. Hazel eyes, brown hair, sallow complexion, 5' 8½. Deserted.

Closz, Jacob. Pvt. Co. F, 22 July 1861 (age 21 at Pittsburgh, PA)–25 August 1861. B: Sharpsburg, Allegheny Co., PA, musician. Blue eyes, brown hair, light complexion, 5' 4½. Deserted.

Closz, John. Pvt. Band, Co. F&S, 22 July 1861 (age 23 at Pittsburgh, PA)–22 July 1864. B: Sharpsburg, Allegheny Co., PA, musician. Dark. Grey eyes, black hair, dark complexion, 5' 8¼. Discharged at 6th Cav. Camp.

Coats, Haskell. Mustered: Pvt. Co. G, 3rd WI Inf. 21 May 1861. Transferred: Pvt. Co. G, 6th U.S. Cav. 28 October 1862 (age 21 at Knoxville, MD)–26 April 1864. B: St. Lawrence Co., NY, farmer. Hazel eyes, light hair, fair complexion, 5'10. WIA, Beverly Ford. Disability discharge at Carlisle Barracks, PA. Mustered: Pvt. Co. B, 1st WI Cav. 30 August 1864–19 July 1865. Mustered out at Edgefield, TN.

Cocker, John J. Pvt.-Sgt. Co. B, 29 July 1861 (age 23 at Cleveland, OH)–29 July 1864. B: Lancashire, ENG, horse breaker. Blue eyes, light hair, ruddy complexion, 5' 9. POW, Funkstown, 7 July–19 November 1863. Paroled, reported at Camp 6th Cav. Discharged at Lighthouse Point, VA.

Coffin, Albert B. Cpl. Co. H, 6 August 1861 (age 22 at Philadelphia, PA)–6 August 1864. B: Philadelphia, PA, clerk. Grey eyes, auburn hair, ruddy complexion, 5' 7. Discharged in the field, VA.

Cokely, Patrick. Mustered: Pvt. Co. H, 81st PA Inf. 22 August 1861. Transferred: Pvt. Co. D, 25 October 1862 (age 19 at Knoxville, MD)–25 August 1864. B: Cook Co., IN, laborer. Blue eyes, light hair, light complexion, 5'9. Discharged at Halltown, VA.

Cole, Henry. Pvt. Co. M, 11 November 1864 (age 28 at NY)–8 August 1865. B: South Reading, MA, shoemaker. Hazel eyes, brown hair, ruddy complexion, 5'5. Deserted.

Cole, John W. Sgt. Co. A, 26 August 1861 (at Columbus, OH)–26 August 1864. Discharged at Halltown, VA.

Cole, Johnathan. Pvt.-Sgt.-Band Ldr. A, F&S, 10 October 1862 (age 41 at Knoxville, MD)–10 October 1865. B: Cheshire Co., NH, musician. Blue eyes, dark hair, fair complexion, 5'10. Discharged at Frederick, MD, as the band leader.

Cole, Thomas J. Mustered: Pvt. Co. D, 106th PA Inf. 27 August 1861. Transferred: Cpl. Co. G, 6th U.S. Cav. 28 October 1862 (age 18 at Knoxville, MD)–25 August 1864. B: Bradford Co., PA, farmer. Blue eyes, fair hair, fair complexion, 5'7. Discharged at Harper's Ferry, VA.

Collins, Homer S. Pvt. Co. K, 20 August 1861 (age 25 at Rochester, NY)–7 February 1863. B: Erie Co., NY, farmer. Blue eyes, light hair, fair complexion, 5'6¼. Disability discharge at Ft. Monroe, VA.

Collins, John D. Pvt.-Wagoner. Co. M, 4 September 1861 (age 22 at Pittsburgh, PA)–4 September 1864. B: Venango Co., PA, shoemaker. Grey eyes, light hair, light complexion, 5'9. Discharged in the field, VA.

Collins, Joseph. Pvt. 1 November 1864 (age 24 at Cleveland, OH)–21 November 1864. B: Harrisburg, Dauphin Co., PA, carpenter. Blue eyes, black hair, dark complexion, 5'5. Deserted.

Collins, Levin J. Mustered: Drummer/fifer, 1st DE Inf. Transferred: Bugler, Cos. K, F&S, 6th U.S. Cav. 25 October 1862 (age 18 at Knoxville, MD)–30 April 1865. B: Kent Co., DE. Blue eyes, brown hair, fair complexion, 5'6. Reenlisted: 10 February 1864, Brandy Station, VA. Deserted 30 April 1865. Enlisted: Pvt. Co. I, 25th U.S. Inf. 1 June 1867–14 September 1867. Deserted. Enlisted: Chief Trumpeter, F&S, 3rd U.S. Cav. 14 August 1875 (Ft. D.A. Russell, WY)–13 August 1880. Discharged with character excellent. Reenlisted: 3rd U.S. Cav. 14 August 1880. Transferred: Sgt. Co. B, 4th U.S. Inf. Discharged 13 August 1885. Enlisted: Musician, Co. G, 4th U.S. Art. 12 September 1893–3 June 1895. Retired, S.O. 125, A.G.O. 95.

Collins, Patrick F. Enlisted: Pvt. Co. I, 1st U.S. Art. 23 November 1857. Transferred: Cpl. Co. D, 6th U.S. Cav. 15 November 1862 (age 23 in the field, VA)–23 November 1862. B: Co. Cork, IRE, laborer. Blue eyes, brown hair, ruddy complexion, 5'7. Discharged (a Cpl.) in the field, VA.

Collins, Robert. Pvt. Co. Det., 23 July 1861 (age 25 at Pittsburgh, PA)–5 August 1861. B: Bristol, ENG, puddler. Blue eyes, sandy hair, ruddy complexion, 5'7. Deserted.

Collins, William. Rct. 18 November 1864 (age 22 at Harrisburg, PA)–22 November 1864. B: Co. Galway, IRE, laborer. Dark eyes, brown hair, fair complexion, 5'2½. Deserted.

Combs, Alfred. Mustered: Pvt. Co. H, 7th OH Inf. 25 April 1861–20 June 1861. Reenlisted. Transferred: Pvt. Co. K, 6th U.S. Cav. 24 October 1862 (age 22 at Knoxville, MD)–24 April 1864. B: Hartford, OH, farmer. Blue eyes, brown hair, light complexion, 5'9. Discharged at 6th Cav. Camp, VA. Mustered: Pvt. Co. D, 39th OH Inf.6 April 1865. Sub.

Comstock, James. Rct. 3 December 1864 (age 25 at Carlisle, PA)–December 1864. B: Windsor, CAN, boatman. Blue eyes, black hair, ruddy complexion, 5'8. Deserted.

Conley, James. Pvt. Co. F, 9 November 1864 (age 24 at Cincinnati, OH)–1 July 1865. B: IRE, machinist. Grey eyes, dark hair, ruddy complexion, 5'7. Deserted 18 December 1864. Apprehended 23 December 1864. Deserted 1 July 1865.

Conner, John. Rct. 14 November 1864 (age 24 at Harrisburg, PA)–21 November 1864. B: Coban, IRE, boatman. Grey eyes, brown hair, ruddy complexion, 5'5½. Deserted.

Conners, Michael. Pvt. Co. G, 5 August 1861 (age 22 at Rochester, NY)–7 September 1862. B: New Ross, IRE, boatman. Black eyes, dark brown hair, ruddy complexion, 5'4¾. Deserted at Rockville, MD, with arms.

Conners, Samuel. Pvt. Co. A, 19 November 1864 (age 23 at Cincinnati, OH)–19 November 1867. B: Co, Tipperary, IRE, laborer. Grey eyes, light hair, fair complexion, 5'6. Deserted 11 December 1864. Apprehended 13 December 1864. Discharge 19 November 1867 at Buffalo Springs, TX.

Connor, Patrick. Rct. 29 November 1864 (age 21 at Harrisburg, PA)–December 1864. B: Co. Tyrone, IRE, teamster. Hazel eyes, brown hair, ruddy complexion, 5'6. Deserted.

Conway, Michael. Pvt. Co. F, 3 July 1861 (age 32 at Pittsburgh, PA)–1 January 1862. B: Co. Kerry, IRE, wagon maker. Grey eyes, light hair, fair complexion, 5'8½. D: 1 January 1862 from disease at Camp east of Capitol, Washington, D.C.

Conway, Michael. Pvt. Co. M, 1 September 1864 (age 23 at Harrisburg, PA)–1864. B: Co. Tyrone, IRE, laborer. Hazel eyes, brown hair, ruddy complexion, 5' 9½. Deserted. Dropped from the rolls 11 October 1866.

Cook, Emmit. Pvt. Co. M, 20 July 1861 (age 21 at Columbus, OH)–21 August 1861. B: Franklin Co., OH, farmer. Grey eyes, sandy hair, ruddy complexion, 5' 8. Disability discharge (a rejected recruit). Mustered: Pvt. Co. D, 20th OH Inf. 24 September 1861–23 April 1862. Disability discharged.

Cook, George H. Saddler. Co. B, 5 August 1861 (at Columbus, OH)–5 August 1864. Discharged in the field, VA.

Cook, James. Pvt. Co. F, 23 December 1864 (age 21 at NY)–27 January 1865. B: Co. Sligo, IRE, teamster. Blue eyes, sandy hair, fair complexion, 5' 5. Deserted.

Cook, Lawrence. Sgt.-Blacksmith. Co. D, 9 August 1861 (age 20 at Pittsburgh, PA)–9 August 1864. B: Baden, GER, canal hand. Blue eyes, light hair, light complexion, 5' 4½. Discharged in the field, VA.

Cook, Philip. Pvt. Co. H, 14 August 1861 (age 21 at Philadelphia, PA)–3 August 1865. B: Frankeuthal, GER, farmer. Blue eyes, brown hair, ruddy complexion, 5' 6½. Reenlisted: 5 February 1864 in the field, VA. Deserted 3 August 1865.

Cook, Valentine. Pvt. Co. K, 21 July 1861 (age 15 at Columbus, OH)–31 March 1865. B: Darmstadt, Bundesland, Hesse, GER, clerk. Grey eyes, brown hair, fair complexion, 5'. Discharged at Washington, D.C. D: 13 June 1916.

Cooke, Edson S. Bugler. Co. I, 22 July 1861 (age 16 at Columbus, OH)–3 July 1863. B: Circleville, Pickaway Co., OH, confectioner. Hazel eyes, brown hair, ruddy complexion, 5'1¾. KIA, Fairfield.

Cooley, Michael. Bugler. Co. I, 13 September 1864 (age 24 at Harrisburg, PA)–1864. B: Brooklyn, NY, sailor. Hazel eyes, brown hair, ruddy complexion, 5' 3½. Deserted.

Cooney, Michael. Enlisted: Sgt. Co. A, 1st U.S. Cav. 4 December 1857–4 December 1861. QM Sgt.-1st Sgt. Cos. M, F&S, 18 December 1861 (age 24 at Washington, DC)–28 July 1866. B: 1 May 1837, Co. Limerick, IRE. Blue eyes, red hair, fair complexion, 5' 9. Reenlisted: Sgt. 22 March 1864, 6th Cav. Camp. Promoted to Cpt., 5th U.S. Col. Cav. 30 December 1864–16 March 1866. Discharged from 6th Cav. 28 July 1866. D: 10 September 1928.

Coonrod, John. Mustered: Pvt. Co. H, 8th OH Inf. 6 June 1861. Transferred: Pvt. Co. C, 6th U.S. Cav. 23 October 1862 (age 19 at Knoxville, MD)–23 December 1862. B: Wayne Co., OH. Hazel eyes, black hair, florid complexion, 5' 6. Disability discharge at Washington, D.C. Mustered: Pvt. Co. A, 48th OH Inf. Mustered out at Columbus, OH. Mustered: Pvt. Co. C, 96th OH Inf. 17 February 1864–1 August 1865. Transferred: Pvt. Co. A, 77th OH Inf. 1 August 1865.

Coontz, John. Cpl. Co. E, 14 August 1861 (age 23 at Columbus, OH)–14 August 1864. B: Pickaway Co., OH, farmer. Hazel eyes, brown hair, sallow complexion, 5' 9. Discharged at Washington, D.C.

Cooper, Albert. Pvt. Co. K, 22 August 1861 (age 24 at Rochester, NY)–4 May 1865. B: SWZ, laborer. Hazel eyes, brown hair, ruddy complexion, 5' 8½. Reenlisted: 10 February 1864, Brandy Station, VA. D: 4 May 1865 of pneumonia at Washington, D.C.

Cooper, George W. Pvt. Co. E, 5 September 1861 (age 23 at Columbus, OH)–1 April 1864. B: Hancock Co., OH, farmer. Hazel eyes, black hair, ruddy complexion, 5' 8¾. MIA, Fairfield. Reported in hospital 30 August 1863. Disability discharge at Carlisle Barracks, PA.

Copeland, George B. Mustered Co. K, 110th PA Inf. Transferred: Pvt. Co. I, 6th U.S. Cav. 26 October 1862 (age 18 at Knoxville, MD)–27 September 1864. B: Mifflin Co., PA, teamster. Hazel eyes, brown hair, fair complexion, 5' 8. Discharged in the field, VA.

Coplin, Hugh F. Pvt.-Cpl. Co. I, 19 July 1861 (age 18 at Tyrone City, PA)–19 July 1864. B: Lewistown, Mifflin Co., PA, wagoner. Grey eyes, light hair, fair complexion, 5' 5¾. POW, Funkstown, 7 July 1863–17 August 1863 (Libby Prison). Paroled, reported at Annapolis, MD. Discharged in the field, VA.

Corban, Isaiah. Rct. Mustered (Putnam Co., IN): Pvt. Co. D, 14th IN Inf. 7 June 1861. Transferred: Pvt. 6th U.S. Cav. 23 October 1862 (age 28 at Knoxville, MD). B: Fayette Co., IN. Hazel eyes, black hair, florid complexion, 5' 6. Returned to U.S.V. Transferred: Co. B, 20th IN Inf. 6 June 1864. Mustered out 12 July 1865 at Louisville, KY.

Corbitt, Patrick. Pvt. Co. M, 8 September 1864 (age 19 at NY)–1864. B: Limirick Co., IN, brick layer. Grey eyes, sandy hair, fair complexion, 5' 8½. MIA in the field 29 November 1864. Deserted.

Corrigheen, Eugene J. Pvt. Co. H, 3 August 1861 (age 28 at Philadelphia, PA)–29 July 1865. B:

Co. Tyrone, IRE, laborer. Brown eyes, black hair, dark complexion, 5' 6½. Reenlissted: 19 March 1864, Brandy Station, VA. Deserted 29 July 1865.

Cory, James H. Pvt. Co. E, 17 September 1861 (age 18 at Adrian, MI)–3 June 1862. B: 1842 Lenawee Co., MI, farmer. Hazel eyes, brown hair, ruddy complexion, 5'11. Disability discharge at Washington, D.C.

Cosgrove, Martin J. Rct. 10 October 1864 (age 43 at Harrisburg, PA)–1864. B: Co. Tyrone, IRE, machinist. Blue eyes, fair hair, florid complexion, 5' 8½. Deserted.

Cotton, Zera Lucerne. Mustered: Hughes Co. D.C. & MD Vols. (Mexican War). Mustered: Pvt. Co. D, 3rd MI Inf. Enlisted: Pvt. Co. B, 6th U.S. Cav. 1 December 1862 (at Falmouth, VA)–13 April 1864. B: 9 May 1834 Fayetteville, Onondaga Co., NY. POW, Fairfield, 3 July–6 August 1863. Reported at Convalescent Hospital. Discharged at 6th Cav. Camp, VA. D: 4 September 1905.

Couch, Warren Jr. Sgt. Co. G, 12 August 1861 (age 24 at Rochester, NY)–13 August 1864. B: Chautaugua Co., NY, salesman. Grey eyes, light hair, fair complexion, 5' 7¼. Discharged at Lighthouse Point, VA.

Couse, James. Pvt. Co. F, 24 December 1864 (age 20 at NY)–9 February 1865. B: Co. Waterford, IRE, boatman. Blue eyes, brown hair, fair complexion, 5' 8. Deserted 31 January 1865. Apprehended 5 February 1865. Deserted 9 February 1865.

Cousins, Frank. Pvt. Co. M, 22 September 1864 (age 18 at Cleveland, OH)–19 December 1864. B: Co. Wexford, IRE, ship carpenter. Blue eyes, brown hair, fair complexion, 5' 4½. MIA, 29 November 1864. MIA, Gordonsville 19 December 1864. No further information.

Cousins, William. Pvt. Co. I, 7 September 1861 (age 24 at Rochester, NY)–7 September 1864. B: ENG, farmer. Blue eyes, black hair, florid complexion, 5' 4¾. Discharged in the field, VA.

Couts, Jacob. Mustered: Pvt. Co. C, 8th OH Inf. 6 January 1861. Transferred: Pvt. Co. G, 6th U.S. Cav. 27 October 1862 (age 19 at Knoxville, MD)–25 June 1864. B: Bucyrus, OH, plasterer. Blue eyes, light hair, light complexion, 5'10. WIA, Beverly Ford, 9 June 1863. WIA (slightly), Upperville, 21 June 1863. Discharged at Wyanoke, VA. Mustered: Pvt. Co. B, 179th OH Inf.

Cowhen, David. Pvt.-Blacksmith. Co. D, 16 August 1861 (age 21 at Pittsburgh, PA)–16 August 1864. B: Co. Cork, IRE, blacksmith. Grey eyes, light hair, light complexion, 5' 9. Discharged in the field, VA.

Cox, Michael L. Pvt. Co. I, 13 August 1861 (age 25 at Rochester, NY)–8 January 1862. B: IRE, shoemaker. Grey eyes, brown hair, fair complexion, 5' 7½. Deserted.

Crager, Samuel E. Mustered: Pvt. Co. C, 14th IN Inf. Transferred: Rct. 6th U.S. Cav. 24 October 1862 (age 25 at Knoxville, MD). B: Vanderburgh, IN, carpenter. Black eyes, black hair, fair complexion, 5' 8. Returned to U.S.V. Mustered: Pvt. Co. C, 143rd IL Inf. 14 May 1864–24 September 1864. Mustered out at Mattoon, IL.

Craig, Charles. Pvt. Co. E, 17 September 1861 (age 23 at Adrian, MI)–17 September 1864. B: Co. Louth, IRE, farmer. Blue eyes, light hair, ruddy complexion, 5' 5¾. Discharged in the field, VA.

Craig, Louis Y. Pvt. Co. F, 7 November 1864 (age 23 at Philadelphia, PA)–26 May 1865. B: Nashville, TN, blacksmith. Grey eyes, fair hair, dark complexion, 5' 8. Deserted.

Craig, Robert. Pvt. Co. E, 17 September 1861 (age 19 at Adrian, MI)–17 September 1864. B: Co. Louth, IRE, farmer. Grey eyes, light hair, ruddy complexion, 5' 6. MIA, Fairfield. Discharged in the field, VA.

Craven, John. Pvt. Co. F, 8 July 1861 (age 20 at Pittsburgh, PA)–30 July 1863. B: Co. Galway, IRE, moulder. Blue eyes, brown hair, fair complexion, 5' 6. Disability discharge at Washington, D.C.

Cray, William H. Mustered (Blue Earth, MN): Pvt. Co. B, 3rd WI Inf. 21 April 1861. Transferred: Pvt. Co. B, 6th U.S. Cav. 28 October 1862 (age 20 at Knoxville, MD)–10 November 1865. B: NYC, (also Clinton Co.), NY. Hazel eyes, dark hair, dark complexion, 5' 8¾. MIA, Fairfield. Reenlisted: 13 February 1864 at 6th Cav. Camp, VA. Deserted 10 November 1865.

Creery, Edward. Cpl.-Sgt. Co. H, 10 August 1861 (age 23 at Philadelphia, PA)–31 December 1864. B: Co. Tyrone, IRE, shoemaker. Blue eyes, brown hair, fair complexion, 5' 6½. POW, Funkstown, 7 July–24 August 1863. Paroled at Annapolis, MD. Reenlisted: 19 March 1864, Brandy Station, VA. Discharged 31 December 1864, by appointment as 1st Lt. 5th U.S.C. Cav. Enrolled at Louisville, KY, 1 January 1865. Promoted to Cpt. Mustered out 27 December 1865. Reenlisted: 1st Sgt. Co. H, 6th U.S. Cav. 18 September 1866. KIA at Sulpher Springs, TX, 14 August 1868.

Crist, Daniel. Pvt. Co. A, 23 September 1861 (age 22 at Columbus, OH)–23 September 1864. B: York Co., PA, farmer. Hazel eyes, black hair, yellow complexion, 5'9. POW, Fairfield, 3 July–22 October 1863. Paroled, reported at Hospital, Annapolis, MD. Discharged at Harper's Ferry, VA.

Croft, Thomas G. Cpl. Co. M, 1 October 1861 (age 23 at Waynesburg, PA)–7 November 1862. B: New York, NY, machinist. Hazel eyes, brown hair, dark complexion, 5'5½. Disability discharge at Washington, D.C.

Croihsant, Charles. Pvt.-Sgt. Co. B, 24 July 1861 (age 21 at Columbus, OH)–5 August 1862. B: Bavaria, GER, baker. Blue eyes, sandy hair, florid complexion, 5'8. MIA/WIA, Malvern Hill. D: 5 August 1862.

Crooker, Epaphio S. Pvt. Co. K, 8 August 1861 (age 22 at Warren, OH)–8 August 1864. B: Denmark Twp., Ashtabula Co., OH, farmer. Grey eyes, light hair, light complexion, 5'3¼. POW, Fairfield, 3 July–22 December 1863. Paroled, reported at Annapolis, MD. Discharged in the field, VA. Note: Epaphio and Herman were brothers.

Crooker, Herman Doolittle. Pvt. Co. K, 8 August 1861 (age 21 at Warren, OH)–8 August 1864. B: Denmark Twp., Ashtabula Co., OH, farmer. Hazel eyes, brown hair, brown complexion, 5'4½. Discharged in the field, VA.

Crowley, Thomas. Pvt. Co. A, 21 November 1864 (age 24 at Harrisburg, PA)–6 January 1865. B: Co. Dublin, IRE, boatman. Grey eyes, brown hair, ruddy complexion, 5'4½. Deserted.

Croy, Levi B. Sgt. Co. F, 3 July 1861 (age 34 at Pittsburgh, PA)–3 July 1864. B: Butler Co., PA, salesman. Grey eyes, light hair, fair complexion, 5'10. MIA, Fairfield. Discharged in the field, VA.

Cruse, Henry. Pvt. Co. B, 5 August 1861 (age 22 at Cleveland, OH)–5 August 1864. B: Hanover, GER, moulder. Hazel eyes, brown hair, ruddy complexion, 5'5¼. MIA, Beverly Ford 9 June 1863. Discharged in the field, VA.

Cullen, Patrick. Pvt. Co. G, 13 August 1861 (age 26 at Rochester, NY)–10 August 1864. B: IRE, laborer. Blue eyes, fair hair, fair complexion, 5'4½. MIA, Fairfield. Discharged at Lighthouse Point, VA.

Cullen, William. Mustered: 14th IN Inf. 7 June 1861. Transferred: Pvt. Co. B, 6th U.S. Cav. 22 October 1862 (age 22 at Knoxville, MD). B: Washington Co., IN. Blue eyes, light hair, fair complexion, 5'8. Returned to U.S.V., November/December 1862. Transferred: Pvt. Co. B, 20th IN Inf. 21 December 1863. Mustered out on 12 July 1865 at Louisville, KY.

Culver, Anthony A. Mustered: Pvt. Co. F, 8th OH Inf. 24 April 1861–5 June 1861. Transferred:

Pvt. Co. L, 6th U.S. Cav. 27 October 1862 (age 23 at Knoxville, MD)–5 June 1864. B: Morris Co., NJ, farmer. Dark eyes, dark hair, dark complexion, 5'9. POW, Fairfield, 3 July 1863–27 February 1864. Paroled, reported at Camp Parole. Discharged in the field, VA.

Cummins, John D. Mustered: Pvt. Co. K, 110th PA Inf. 19 December 1861. Transferred: Pvt. Co. I, 6th U.S. Cav. 27 October 1862 (age 18 at Knoxville, MD)–21 November 1864. B: Mifflin Co., PA, farmer. Hazel eyes, dark hair, fair complexion, 5'8. POW, Funkstown, 7 July 1863–18 June 1864. Paroled. Discharged at 6th Cav. Camp, VA.

Curren, John. Pvt. Co. I, 1 September 1864 (age 40 at Harrisburg, PA)–7 August 1865. B: Co. Galway, IRE, laborer. Grey eyes, grey hair, ruddy complexion, 5'7. Disability discharge at U.S. General Hospital, Frederick, MD.

Curthin, John. Bugler. Co. F, 22 July 1861 (age 18 at Pittsburgh, PA)–22 July 1864. B: Allegheny Co., PA, musician. Blue eyes, light hair, light complexion, 5'7½. POW, Fairfield, 7 July–3 November 1863. Paroled, reported at Annapolis, MD. Discharged in the field, VA.

Curtis, William H. Mustered: Pvt. Co. I, 60th NY Inf. 24 September 1861. Transferred: Pvt. Co. A, 6th U.S. Cav. 28 October 1862 (age 24 at Knoxville, MD)–28 October 1864. B: 1837, Colchester, VT. Blue eyes, light hair, dark complexion, 5'5. Discharged at Middletown, VA. D: 1905, Cambridge, Lamoille, VT.

Cusack, Patrick. Enlisted: Pvt. Co. K, 4th U.S. Art. 8 April 1855–9 July 1860. Reenlisted: 9 July 1860. Promoted to Pvt.-Cpl.-Sgt. Transferred: Sgt.-Sgt. Maj. Cos. B, F&S, 6th U.S. Cav. 23 June 1863 (age 30)–19 January 1865. B: Co. Donegal, IRE. Hazel eyes, dark hair, dark complexion, 5'7¼. Discharged 19 January 1865 by appointment as Cpt. 6th U.S.C. Cav. 1 March 1865–15 April 1866. 2nd Lt. 9th U.S. Cav. 7 March 1867. 1st Lt. 31 July 1867. Cpt. 20 January 1883. Bvt. Cpt. 12 September 1868 for conspicuous gallantry in engagement with Indians at Horse Head Hill, TX, 12 September 1868. Bvt. Maj. 27 February 1890 for gallant service in action against Indians in the San Andreas Mountains, NM, 7 April 1880. Retired 21 April 1891. D: 9 January 1894.

Cypher, John. Pvt. Cos. M, C, 11 December 1861 (age 34 at Butler Co., PA)–29 January 1862. B: Butler Co., PA, farmer. Grey eyes, brown hair, light complexion, 5'6½. Deserted.

Dailey, James T. Mustered (Canton, NY): Pvt. Co. A, 60th NY Inf. 9 September 1861. Transferred: Pvt. Co. M, 6th U.S. Cav. 23 October 1862 (age 20 at Knoxville, MD)–23 August 1864. B: Lisbin, Co., NY. Blue eyes, brown hair, light complexion, 5'9. Discharged at Harper's Ferry, VA. D: 16 February 1892.

Dailey, Rowland Hatch Mustered: Pvt. Co. K, 60th NY Inf. 12 August 1861. Transferred: Pvt.-Cpl. Co. M, 6th U.S. Cav. 23 October 1862 (age 22 at Knoxville, MD)–23 August 1864. B: 2 October 1840, Lisbon, St. Lawrence, NY. Hazel eyes, light hair, light complexion, 5'3. POW, Fairfield, 3 July 1863–30 August 1863. Paroled at Annapolis, MD. Discharged at Harper's Ferry, VA.

Daily, Patrick. Pvt. Co. F, 12 November 1864 (age 23 at Harrisburg, PA)–27 May 1865. B: Co. Tyrone, IRE, stone cutter. Dark eyes, dark hair, ruddy complexion, 5'7½. Deserted.

Daily, Samuel. Mustered: Pvt. Co. B, 60th NY Inf. 9 October 1861. Transferred: Pvt. Co. M, 6th U.S. Cav. 22 October 1862 (age 21 at Knoxville, MD)–23 September 1864. B: St. Lawrence Co., NY, farmer. Blue eyes, brown hair, fair complexion, 5'7. Attached to Co. I, 1st Art. Discharged at City Point, VA.

Dalby, John, Pvt. Co. A, 9 November 1864 (age 26 at NY)–30 May 1865. B: Hull, ENG, laborer. Grey eyes, brown hair, fair complexion, 5'8. Deserted 24 November 1864. Apprehended 28 November 1864. Deserted 30 May 1865.

Danaly, Michael. Rct. 1 November 1861 (age 36 at Philadelphia, PA)–25 November 1861. B: Co. Tyrone, IRE, laborer. Blue eyes, brown hair, fair complexion, 5'3. Accidentally drowned at Philadelphia, PA, on 25 November 1861.

Daniels, Taylor Eugene. Pvt. Co. K, 19 August 1861 (age 19 at Rochester, NY)–19 August 1864. B: Genesee Co., NY, farmer. Blue eyes, light hair, fair complexion, 5'3½. Discharged at Harper's Ferry, VA.

Dann, Almond C. Mustered: Pvt. Co. D, 106th PA Inf. 3 February 1862. Transferred: Pvt. Co. G, 6th U.S. Cav. 28 October 1862 (age 22 at Knoxville, MD)–28 February 1865. B: 11 September 1840, Darke Co., OH, farrier. Blue eyes, light hair, fair complexion, 5'10. Transferred: Co. F, 10 November 1864 by R.O. 97. Discharged at Winchester, VA. D: 13 April 1890, PA.

Dare, Thomas E. Pvt. Co. A, 15 December 1864 (age 23 at Cleveland, OH)–15 October 1865. B: Albany, NY, soldier. Grey eyes, brown hair, florid complexion, 6'1. Deserted.

Dassey, John. Pvt. Co. K, 27 July 1861 (age 25 at Pittsburgh, PA)–11 February 1867. B: Co. Cork, IRE, laborer. Blue eyes, brown hair, medium complexion, 5'4½. Reenlisted: 11 February 1864, Brandy Station, VA. D: in hospital 12 October 1867 of yellow fever, LA.

Daved, John. Rct. 17 November 1864 (age 33 at Harrisburg, PA)–21 November 1864. B: Co. Cork, IRE, mason. Hazel eyes, brown hair, dark complexion, 5'6. Deserted.

Davies, Joseph. Pvt. Co. A, 30 September 1861 (age 28 at Pottsville, PA)–30 September 1864. B: Oswestry, ENG, miner. Blue eyes, brown hair, fair complexion, 5'6½. POW, Fairfield, 3 July 1863–18 January 1864. Paroled, reported at Annapolis, MD. Discharged at Harrisonburg, VA.

Davis, Calvin L. Mustered: Pvt. Co. C, 41st PA Inf. 26 July 1861. Transferred: Pvt. Co. G, 28 October 1862 (age 25 at Knoxville, MD)–28 July 1864. B: Bradford Co., PA, teamster. Blue eyes, fair hair, fair complexion, 6'. MIA, Fairfield. Discharged at Lighthouse Point, VA.

Davis, Charles. Pvt. Co. F, 16 November 1864 (age 23 at Harrisburg, PA)–27May 1865. B: Co. Donegal, IRE, laborer. Grey eyes, brown hair, ruddy complexion, 5'4½. Deserted. Sub for Raymond.

Davis, Charles. Sgt. Co. M, 12 September 1864 (age 20 at Harrisburg, PA)–12 September 1867. B: Bremen, GER, sailor. Blue eyes, fair hair, ruddy complexion, 5'3½. Discharged at Mt. Pleasant, TX.

Davis, Evan. Pvt. Co. F, 9 July 1861 (age 27 at Pittsburgh, PA)–9 July 1864. B: WAL, coal miner. Brown eyes, auburn hair, dark complexion, 5'5½. Discharged at Lighthouse Point, VA.

Davis, Fletcher. Rct. 5 August 1861 (age 21 at Columbus, OH)–19 August 1861. B: Franklin Co., OH, farmer. Grey eyes, light hair, light complexion, 5'8½. Rejected for disability.

Davis, Francis M. Rct. 20 July 1861 (age 21 at Columbus, OH)–21 August 1861. B: Rappahannock Co., PA, farmer. Blue eyes, brown hair, ruddy complexion, 5'10¼. Rejected for disability.

Davis, George T. Pvt. Co. H, 25 July 1861 (age 21 at Philadelphia, PA)–3 July 1863. B: Montgomery Co., PA, spinner. Blue eyes, sandy hair, ruddy complexion, 5'7½. KIA, Fairfield.

Davis, Harvey. Rct. 5 November 1864 (age 19 at Harrisburg, PA)–21 November 1864. B: Galt, Ontario, CAN, farmer. Blue eyes, sandy hair, fair complexion, 5'7. Deserted.

Davis, James T. Pvt. Co. D, 23 August 1861 (age 19 at Pittsburgh, PA)–3 August 1862. B: Allegheny Co., PA, farmer. Blue eyes, light hair, light complexion, 5'8. Disability discharge at Baltimore, MD.

Davis, John B. Mustered: Pvt.-Cpl. Co. F, 8th OH Inf. 5 June 1861. Transferred: Sgt. Co. C, 6th U.S. Cav. 23 October 1862 (age 21 at Knoxville, MD)–7 June 1864. B: Lawrence Co., PA, shoemaker. Blue eyes, dark hair, fair complexion, 5'9. POW, Fairfield, 3 July 1863–7 January 1864. Paroled, reported at Annapolis, MD. Discharged in the field, VA.

Davis, Sidney Morris. Pvt. Co. F, 8 July 1861 (age 20 at Pittsburgh, PA)–8 July 1864. B: Mobile, AL, printer. Hazel eyes, brown hair, dark complexion, 5'8. POW, Fairfield, 3 July 1863–August 1864 (Belle Isle Prison). Paroled, discharged at Camp 6th Cav. D: 1 December 1899.

Davis, William. Rct. 2 November 1864 (age 24 at Cleveland, OH)–21 November 1864. B: Co. Kilkenny, IRE, moulder. Blue eyes, brown hair, florid complexion, 5'6½. Deserted.

Davis, Winfield S. Pvt. Co. L, 21 March 1862 (at Bellefonte, Centre, PA)–15 May 1862. Discharged.

Dawson, William I. Mustered: Pvt. Co. H, 28th PA Inf. 11 July 1861. Transferred: Pvt. Co. F, 28 October 1862 (age 19 at Knoxville, MD)–16 July 1864. B: Pittsburgh, Allegheny Co., PA, surveyor. Blue eyes, light hair, fair complexion, 5'8. POW, Fairfield, 3 July 1863–6 April 1864. Paroled, reported at Annapolis, MD. Discharged at Lighthouse Point, VA.

Day, Edward. Rct. 17 September 1864 (age 18 at Rochester, NY)–8 October 1864. B: Co. Cork, IRE, farmer. Blue eyes, light hair, fair complexion, 5'5½. Deserted, Carlisle Barracks, PA.

Day, Michael O. Mustered: Sgt. Co. F, 84th PA Inf. Transferred; Pvt. Co. A, 6th U.S. Cav. 28 October 1862 (age 18 at Knoxville, MD)–12 April 1864. B: Dauphin Co., PA. Grey eyes, dark hair, light complexion, 5'4. POW, Fairfield, 3 July–5 October 1863. Paroled, reported at Culpepper, VA. Reenlisted: 13 February 1864, Warrenton, VA. Transferred: Pvt. Co. I, 1st U.S. Art. 12 April 1864–22 July 1865. Deserted.

Deamer, Dudley Allen. Rct. 31 July 1861 (age 24 at Erie Co., PA)–6 August 1861. B: Crawford Co., PA, teamster. Blue eyes, dark hair, fair complexion, 5'9½. Deserted from Erie Co., PA.

Dean, John. Pvt. Co. A, 5 December 1864 (age 18 at Cleveland, OH)–24 January 1865. B: Hamilton, West Can., CAN, laborer. Grey eyes, brown hair, sallow complexion, 5'9. Deserted.

Dean, John. Pvt.-Cpl. Co. M, 13 September 1861 (age 22 at Pittsburgh, PA)–13 September 1864.

B: Co. Antrim, IRE, farmer. Blue eyes, auburn hair, fair complexion, 5'10½. WIA/POW, Fairfield, 3 July–24 August 1863. Paroled at Annapolis, MD. Sick in hospital. Discharged at Berryville, VA.

Deegan, William. Pvt. Cos. C, L, 20 August 1861 (age 33 at Philadelphia, PA)–20 August 1864. B: Kings Co., IRE, clerk. Hazel eyes, brown hair, florid complexion, 5'5½. WIA, Haskins Crossroads/Barber's Crossroads, VA, 6 November 1862. Discharged at Charleston, VA.

Deery, James. Pvt. Co. A, 8 October 1861 (age 21 at Philadelphia, PA)–28 November 1862. B: Co. Donegal, IRE, laborer. Hazel eyes, black hair, dark complexion, 5'4½. Disability discharge at Alexandria, VA.

Degnon, Patrick. Pvt. Co. M, 8 August 1864 (age 37 at Cincinnati, OH)–10 August 164. B: Co. Roscommon, IRE, soldier. Hazel eyes, light hair, ruddy complexion, 5'6. Deserted.

[De]Groff, Harmon. Mustered: Pvt. Co. E, 8th OH Inf. 25 June 1861. Transferred: Pvt. Co. C, 24 October 1862 (age 20 at Knoxville, MD)–25 June 1864. B: Baden, GER. Grey eyes, light hair, florid complexion, 5'8½. WIA/POW, Brandy Station, 11 October–30 November 1863. Paroled, reported at Annapolis, MD. Discharged in the field, VA.

Deitrich, Peter. Mustered: Co. K, 110th PA Inf. Transferred: Pvt. Co. I, 6th U.S. Cav. 27 October 1862 (age 24 at Knoxville, MD)–12 June 1864. B: Blair Co., PA, farmer. Grey eyes, brown hair, fair complexion, 6'2. POW, Trevilion Station, 12 June 1864 –? No further information.

Delamarter, Lewis. Mustered: Pvt. Co. G, 50th PA Inf. September 1861. Transferred: Pvt. Co. H, 6th U.S. Cav. 28 October 1862 (age 23 at Knoxville, MD)–28 February 1865. B: 5 December 1838, Binghamton, NY. Blue eyes, dark hair, light complexion, 5'4½. Discharged at Winchester, VA. D: 15 February 1908, Hagerstown, Washington, MD.

Demay, Francis. Pvt. Co. D, 27 August 1861 (age 31 at Pittsburgh, PA)–24 July 1863. B: Durham, CAN, axe maker. Brown eyes, black hair, dark complexion, 5'9¾. Disability discharge at Douglas Hospital, Washington, D.C.

Deneif, James D. Pvt. Mustered: Pvt. Co. B, 8th OH Inf. 18 April 1861. Transferred: Co. C, 6th U.S. Cav. 22 October 1862 (age 30 at Knoxville, MD)–26 May 1864. B: Ross, IRE, teamster. Blue eyes, brown hair, dark complexion, 5'5. POW, ?–7 January 1864. Paroled, reported at Annapolis, MD. Discharged at Camp 6th Cav., VA.

Denicore, Michael. Mustered: Pvt. Co. H, 60th NY Inf. 22 October 1861–24 October 1862. Reported deserted. Transferred: Pvt. Co. L, 6th U.S. Cav. 16 October 1862 (age 21 at Knoxville, MD)–15 April 1864. B: Clinton Co., NY. Grey eyes, dark hair, light complexion, 5' 8. MIA, Fairfield. Reenlisted: 27 February 1864 at Brandy Station, VA. Deserted 15 April 1864.

Denn, James. Pvt. Co. D, 12 August 1861 (age 21 at Pittsburgh, PA)–8 August 1864. B: Co. Tipperary, IRE, puddler. Blue eyes, red hair, light complexion, 5' 5½. Discharged at City Point, VA.

Dennis, Selby. Saddler. Cos. B, A, 23 July 1861 (age 26 at Columbus, OH)–21 July 1864. B: Pickaway Co., OH, harness maker. Blue eyes, auburn hair, florid complexion, 5' 4½. Discharged at Lighthouse Point, VA.

Dennison, William. Pvt. Co. A, 25 November 1864 (age 26 at Harrisburg, PA)–30 May 1865. B: Co. Cork, IRE, laborer. Hazel eyes, brown hair, ruddy complexion, 5'10. Deserted. Sub.

DeRemer (DeRoemer), Jared Russell. Mustered: Pvt. Co. N, 28th PA Inf. 30 August 1861. Transferred: Co. C, 147th PA Inf. Transferred: Pvt. Co. B, 6th U.S. Cav. 25 October 1862 (age 19 at Knoxville, MD)–18 December 1863. B: 2 July 1844, Milesburg, PA, machinist. Blue eyes, light hair, light complexion, 5'10. Disability discharge at McClellan Hospital, Philadelphia, PA. D: 3 January 1917, Newark, NJ.

Dermody, Patrick. Rct. 28 November 1864 (age 20 at Harrisburg, PA)–12 December 1864. B: Co. Tipperary, IRE, teamster. Blue eyes, auburn hair, fair complexion, 5' 6½. Deserted from Carlisle Barracks, PA. Sub. for C. Miller.

Dervin, John C. Mustered: Pvt. Co. A, 3rd WI Inf. 18 April 1861. Transferred: Pvt. Co. F, 25 October 1862 (age 20 at Knoxville, MD)–29 June 1864. B: Juniata Co., PA, store keeper. Hazel eyes, light hair, ruddy complexion, 5' 5. Discharged at Camp 6th Cav., VA. Mustered: Batt. C, D, 1st MO Light Art.

Derwin, Thomas. Rct. 28 July 1864 (age 18 at Providence, NJ)–5 August 1864. B: Dublin, IRE, hatter. Grey eyes, brown hair, fair complexion, 5' 5. Deserted. Sub for G. Manchester.

Dessum, Adam. Pvt. Co. G, 6 August 1861 (age 23 at Columbus, OH)–9 June 1862. B: 1837, Chambersburg, Franklin Co., PA, laborer. Grey eyes, black hair, ruddy complexion, 5' 4½. Disability discharge at Washington D.C. D: 13 January 1902.

Dewoody, Mortimer L. Pvt. Co. M, 9 November

1861 (age 26 at Franklin Co., PA)–18 January 1864. B: Franklin Co., PA, shoemaker. Hazel eyes, dark hair, dark complexion, 5' 7½. Deserted 5 February 1862. Enlisted: Pvt. Co. C, 18th Inf. 19 April 1862. Deserted 27 November 1862. Joined 6th Cav. 8 January 1864. Disability discharge 18 January 1864 at Convalescent Camp, VA. Enlisted: Pvt. Co. B, 23rd OH Inf. 18 July 1864. Also served in Co. K, 13th V.R.C. Enlisted: 10 April 1869 at Carlisle, PA. Deserted 25 April 1869.

Diamon, James. Rct. 7 October 1861 (age 24 at Philadelphia, PA)–7 October 1861. B: Co. Derry, IRE, shoemaker. Blue eyes, light hair, fair complexion, 5' 8. Deserted the same day at Philadelphia, PA.

Diamond, James F. Co. M, 22 October 1861 (age 25 at Pittsburgh, PA)–No further information. B: Co. Galway, IRE, peddler. Blue eyes, brown hair, dark complexion, 5' 3½.

Dickey, Nuton. Pvt. Co. A, 10 December 1864 (age 25 at Cincinnati, OH)–26 September 1865. B: CAN, farmer. Blue eyes, light hair, fair complexion, 5'10. Deserted.

Dickson, James. Pvt. Co. M, 22 October 1861 (age 22 at Pittsburgh, PA)–27 September 1864. B: Pittsburgh, Allegheny Co., PA, soldier. Grey eyes, light hair, light complexion, 5' 6½. POW, Fairfield, 3 July–20 August 1863. Paroled at Annapolis, MD. Discharged at Strasburg, VA.

Dickson, William. Pvt. Cos. A, M, 28 August 1861 (age 26 at Philadelphia, PA)–28 August 1864. B: Bedford, IRE, gardener. Blue eyes, light hair, light complexion, 5' 5½. MIA, Fairfield. WIA, New Bridge. Discharged at Halltown, VA.

Diem, William F. Pvt. Co. M, 19 September 1861 (age 21 at Pittsburgh, PA)–19 September 1864. B: 1843 Beaver Co., PA, farmer. Grey eyes, light hair, florid complexion, 5' 6½. POW, Fairfield, 3 July–20 August 1863. Paroled at Annapolis, MD. Discharged at Berryville, VA. D: 1895.

Dierdorff, Jonas. Pvt. Co. E, 17 September 1861 (age 26 at Adrian, MI)–17 September 1864. B: Westfield, OH, farmer. Hazel eyes, brown hair, ruddy complexion, 6'1. Discharged at Berryville, VA.

Dies, Richard. Pvt. Co. D, 23 August 1861 (age 22 at Pittsburgh, PA)–26 August 1863. B: Indiana Co., PA, miner. Brown eyes, black hair, dark complexion, 6' 3. D: from typhoid fever at Convalescent Camp, VA, 26 August 1863.

Dietz, Frank A. Bugler. Co. F, 23 July 1861 (age 24 at Pittsburgh, PA)–12 January 1863. B: Rattelsdorf, Bavaria, GER, butcher and bugler. Lt.

grey eyes, light hair, sallow complexion, 5'11. Disability discharge at Washington, D.C.

Dignian, Michael. 15 September 1864 (age 29 at Harrisburg, PA)–No further information. B: Co. Roscommon, IRE, laborer. Blue eyes, auburn hair, florid complexion, 5'9.

Dille, Thomas C. Pvt. Co. I, 15 August 1861 (age 21 at Cleveland, OH)–3 January 1862. B: Euclid, OH, farmer. Blue eyes, brown hair, ruddy complexion, 6'. D: of disease at Camp 6th Cav., Washington D.C., 3 January 1862.

Diller, Francis M. Pvt. Mustered: Pvt. Co. C, 8th OH Inf. 24 June 1861. Transferred: Co. G, 6th U.S. Cav. 28 October 1862 (age 22 at Knoxville, MD)–25 June 1864. B: 1841, Middlesex Co., PA, painter. Blue eyes, light hair, fair complexion, 5'4. WIA/MIA, Beverly Ford, 9 June 1863. Discharged at Wyanoke, VA. Enlisted: Pvt.-Cpl. Co. A, 1st U.S.V.V. Inf. 19 December 1864–18 December 1865. D: 1908, Wyandot, OH.

Dimeling, Milton. Mustered: Pvt. Co. K, 110th PA Inf. 19 December 1861. Transferred: Pvt. Co. I, 6th U.S. Cav. 26 October 1862 (age 18 at Harper's Ferry, VA)–17 September 1864. B: Venango Co., PA, laborer. Hazel eyes, dark hair, fair complexion, 5'8. Discharged at Camp 6th Cav.

Dinan, John. Rct. 16 November 1864 (age 21 at Harrisburg, PA)–25 November 1864. B: Co. Clare, IRE, laborer. Grey eyes, dark hair, fair complexion, 5'7. Deserted. D: 5 January 1923.

Dingman, Bruce. Mustered (Memphis, MI), Pvt. Co. H, 7th MI Inf. 3 August 1861. Transferred: Pvt. Co. E, 6th U.S. Cav. 27 October 1862 (age 25 at Knoxville, MD)–No further information. B: Westminster Co., CAN, saddler. Grey eyes, black hair, dark complexion, 5'9½. WIA, Beverly Ford.

Dix, Leander Vaughn. Pvt. Co. I, 5 August 1861 (age 18 at Rochester, NY)–5 August 1864. B: Oneida Co., NY, farmer. Hazel eyes, black hair, fair complexion, 5'9¼. Discharged at Harper's Ferry, VA.

Dixon, Jasper. Pvt. Co. L, 31 December 1864 (age 20 at NY)–31 March 1865. B: Philadelphia, PA, farmer. Hazel eyes, brown hair, fair complexion, 5'9. Deserted.

Dodd, Thomas. Sgt. Co. B, 30 July 1861 (age 20 at Cleveland, OH)–30 July 1864. B: Leeds, ENG, farmer. Grey eyes, light hair, ruddy complexion, 5'8¼. WIA/MIA, Funkstown. Discharged at Lighthouse Point, VA.

Dodds, George. Mustered: Pvt. Co. D, 34th NY Inf. 14 October 1861. Transferred: Pvt. Co. L,

6th U.S. Cav. 27 October 1862 (age 18 at Knoxville, MD)–27 October 1864. B: Champlain, NY. Blue eyes, light hair, light complexion, 5'6½. POW, Fairfield, 3 July–7 November 1863. Paroled, reported at Auburn, VA. Discharged at Camp Stoneman, Washington, D.C. Enlisted: Pvt. Co. G, 26th NY Cav. 1 June 1865–6 July 1865. Promoted to Sgt. 30 June 1865. Mustered out at Plattsburg, NY.

Doherty, William H. Pvt. Co. G, 12 August 1861 (age 19 at Columbus, OH)–12 August 1864. B: 1842 Franklin Co., OH, farmer. Hazel eyes, brown hair, ruddy complexion, 5'11. POW, Fairfield, 3 July 1863–17 February 1864. Paroled, reported at Camp Parole. Discharged at Washington, D.C. D: January 1913.

Dolan, William. Cpl. Co. M, 13 September 1864 (age 21 at Harrisburg, PA)–13 September 1867. B: Co. Limerick, IRE, laborer. Grey eyes, brown hair, ruddy complexion, 5'6. Deserted 16 October 1864. Apprehended October 1864. Deserted 1 January 1865. Apprehended 1 January 1865. Deserted 19 October 1865. Apprehended 6 November 1865. Discharged upon expiration of service.

Dolton, James. 12 September 1864 (age 22 at Harrisburg, PA)–No further information. B: Co. Tipperary, IRE, blacksmith. Blue eyes, auburn hair, florid complexion, 5'3.

Donagin, Thomas. Pvt. Co. A, 6 December 1864 (age 27 at Cincinnati, OH)–10 November 1865. B: CAN, laborer. Grey eyes, brown hair, fair complexion, 5'7½. Deserted.

Donaldson, James. Pvt.-Cpl. Co. F, 29 July 1861 (age 23 at Pittsburgh, PA)–29 July 1864. B: Zelienople, Butler Co., PA, blacksmith. Blue eyes, light hair, fair complexion, 5'10½. MIA, Funkstown. Discharged at Lighthouse Point, VA.

Doney, John W. Mustered: Cpl. Co. D, 14th IN Inf. 6 July 1861. Transferred: Sgt. Co. C, 6th U.S. Cav. 24 October 1862 (age 23 at Knoxville, MD)–21 May 1864. B: Coshocton Co., OH. Blue eyes, light hair, dark complexion, 5'8. POW, Fairfield, 3 July 1863–21 May 1864. D: from chronic diarrhea as a POW at Andersonville, GA., 21 May 1864.

Donley, Upton. Mustered: Pvt. Co. L, 1st MN Inf. Assigned to the 2nd Co. MN Sharpshooters. Transferred: Pvt. Co. B, 6th U.S. Cav. 28 October 1862 (age 19 at Knoxville, MD)–8 October 1864. B: Chambersburg, Franklin Co., PA. Blue eyes, light hair, light complexion, 5'10. POW (captured while on picket), Richard's Ford, 14 February–24 September 1863. Paroled at Culpepper, VA. Discharged at Cedar Creek, VA. D: ID.

Donneld, Samuel B. Rct. 2 August 1861 (age 24 at Pittsburgh, PA)–26 August 1861. B: Germantown, PA, teamster. Blue eyes, brown hair, light complexion, 5'6. Deserted.

Donnelly, Henry H. Pvt. Co. M, 10 September 1861 (age 21 at Pittsburgh, PA)–15 June 1865. B: Allegheny Co., PA, farmer. Grey eyes, brown hair, fair complexion, 5'7. MIA (while on the march), 24 June 1864, VA. Discharged at Frederick, MD. D: 9 February 1904.

Donnelly, Martin. Pvt. Co. M, 28 November 1861 (age 21 at Pittsburgh, PA)–20 September 1862. B: New York, NY, painter. Blue eyes, brown hair, dark complexion, 5'10. Deserted.

Donoghue, Thomas. Rct. 26 August 1864 (age 19 at Harrisburg, PA)–1864. B: Dublin, IRE, sailor. Grey eyes, light hair, ruddy complexion, 5'5. Deserted.

Donohue, John. Pvt. Co. L, 21 December 1861 (age 33 at Cleveland, OH)–19 December 1862. B: Co. Tyrone, IRE, sailor. Grey eyes, brown hair, ruddy complexion, 5'5. Disability discharge at Falmouth, VA.

Donovan, Jeremiah. Pvt. Co. L, 14 January 1862 (age 18 at Cleveland, OH)–1 July 1862. B: Co. Cork, IRE, sailor. Grey eyes, brown hair, ruddy complexion, 5'4. Deserted.

Donson, Daniel. Mustered: Pvt. Co. G, 84th PA Inf. Transferred: Pvt. Co. I, 6th U.S. Cav. 27 October 1862 (age 22 at Knoxville, MD)–9 December 1862. B: York Co., PA, laborer. Brown eyes, brown hair, light complexion, 5'9. Returned to USV.

Dorn, John F. Enlisted: Pvt. G.M.S. 17 August 1859–20 January 1865. Reenlisted: Musician 2nd Class. Cos. M, F&S, 6th U.S. Cav. 20 January 1864 (age 24 at Carlisle, PA)–10 September 1866. B: Chambersburg, Franklin Co., PA, musician. Hazel eyes, brown hair, sallow complexion, 5'6. Transferred: Co. F&S, 17 August 1865. D: from cholera at Austin, TX, 10 September 1866.

Dort, Lewis. Mustered: Pvt. Co. E, 3rd DE Inf. Transferred: Pvt. Co. K, 6th U.S. Cav. 24 October 1862 (age 22 at Knoxville, MD). B: GER, farmer. Blue eyes, brown hair, dark complexion, 5'6. Reenlisted: 10 February 1864 at Brandy Station, VA.

Doty, Vinton. Pvt. Co. E, 21 August 1861 (abt age 24 at Columbus, OH)–10 October 1862. B: 1837, no further information. Disability discharge at Washington, D.C. D: 28 November 1898, St. Louis, MO.

Dougherty, John A. Rct. 14 November 1864 (age 19 at Harrisburg, PA)–21 November 1864. B: Co. Donegal, IRE, laborer. Hazel eyes, brown hair ruddy complexion, 5'3½. Deserted.

Dougherty, Patrick. Pvt. Co. A, 8 October 1861 (age 21 at Philadelphia, PA)–8 October 1864. B: Co. Roscommon, IRE, laborer. Hazel eyes, black hair, dark complexion, 5'8. Discharged at Navy Yard Hospital, Annapolis, MD.

Dougherty, Robert. Enlisted: Pvt. Cos. E, G, Regiment of Mounted Riflemen, 26 June 1857–26 June 1862. Discharged at Ft. Union, NM. Enlisted: Sgt.-1st Sgt. Cos. L, M, 6th U.S. Cav. 11 December 1862 (age 26 at NYC, NY)–17 January 1869. B: Co. Derry, IRE. Blue eyes, brown hair, ruddy complexion, 5'8½. Discharged at Austin, TX. Reenlisted: 11 December 1865 at Austin, TX. Discharged 11 December 1868 at Ft. Richardson, TX. Reenlisted: 17 December 1868. Deserted 17 January 1869.

Dougherty (Doherty), William. Pvt. Co. M, 9 November 1861 (age 21 at Pittsburgh, PA)–13 February 1867. B: St. John's, New Brunswick, CAN, mule driver. Hazel eyes, dark hair, dark complexion, 5'4½. Reenlisted: 13 February 1864 at Brandy Station, VA. Discharged 13 February 1867 at Austin, TX.

Douglas, William. Pvt. Cos. C, L, 8 January 1862 (age 21 at Philadelphia, PA)–18 June 1863. B: Bucks Co., PA, lock tender. Hazel eyes, brown hair, ruddy complexion, 5'4½. Deserted 8 March 1862. Apprehended 4 September 1862. D: from typhoid fever at Columbia Hospital, Washington D.C., 18 June 1863.

Douglass, Edward E. Mustered (Meadville, PA): Pvt. Co. I, 10th PA Inf. 18 July 1861. Transferred: Pvt. Co. A, 6th U.S. Cav. 28 October 1862 (age 20 at Knoxville, MD)–1 August 1863. B: Crawford Co., PA. Grey eyes, dark hair, dark complexion, 5'6. Transferred: Invalid Corps. Disability discharge, Alexandria, VA.

Dowling, John. Mustered: Pvt. Co. B, 14th IN Inf. 7 June 1861. Transferred: Rct. 6th U.S. Cav. 23 October 1862 (age 19 at Knoxville, MD)–November/December 1862. B: Tuscarawas Co., OH. Grey eyes, light hair, florid complexion, 5'9½. Returned to USV. Discharged 9 April 1863.

Downs, William A. Pvt. Co. H, 10 August 1861 (age 23 at Philadelphia, PA)–19 October 1861. B: Philadelphia, PA, brush maker. Brown eyes, brown hair, fair complexion, 5'9½. Disability discharge at Washington, D.C.

Doyle, Denis. Pvt. Cos. I, C, 9 September 1861 (age 30 at Rochester, NY)–28 October 1862.

B: IRE, farmer. Blue eyes, brown hair, florid complexion, 5'11½. Deserted.

Doyle, John D. Rct. 28 November 1864 (age 22 at Harrisburg, PA)–13 December 1864. B: Liverpool, ENG, laborer. Grey eyes, brown hair, ruddy complexion, 5'5½. Deserted at Carlisle Barracks, PA.

Doyle, Patrick. Pvt. Co. A, 5 October 1861 (age 25 at Cleveland, OH)–25 June 1863. B: Co. Tipperary, IRE, peddler. Blue eyes, brown hair, ruddy complexion, 5'11. WIA/POW, Beverly Ford. D: 25 June 1863 from wounds received in action while a prisoner at Libby Prison, Richmond, VA.

Drake, Ellis. Pvt. Co. F, 25 July 1861 (age 25 at Pittsburgh, PA)–25 July 1864. B: Halifax, ENG, laborer. Blue eyes, light hair, light complexion, 5'6. Discharged at Lighthouse Point, VA. D: 10 April 1898.

Drake, George W. Pvt. Co. B, 12 August 1861 (age 28 at Columbus, OH)–12 August 1864. B: Herkimer Co., NY, engineer. Blue eyes, brown hair, ruddy complexion, 5'8. Discharged at Geisboro Point, Washington D.C.

Draker, Christian. Pvt. Co. F, 16 July 1861 (age 31 at Pittsburgh, PA)–16 July 1864. B: Hanover, GER, farmer. Lt. blue eyes, lt. brown hair, dark complexion, 5'4½. Discharged at Lighthouse Point, VA. Mustered (Pittsburgh, PA): Pvt. Co. C, 12th PA Cav. 27 August 1864–1 June 1865. D: 11 October 1907, OH.

Dreiblebis, Peter. Mustered: Pvt. Co. A, 45th PA Inf. 12 March 1862. Transferred: Pvt. Co. I, 6th U.S. Cav. 27 October 1862 (age 25 at Knoxville, MD)–27 August 1864. B: Bucks Co., PA, miller. Brown eyes, brown hair, dark complexion, 5'5. MIA, Funkstown. Discharged at Harper's Ferry, VA.

Driscoll, John. Rct. 7 December 1864 (age 20 at Cincinnati, OH)–December 1864. B: Cork, IRE, miner. Grey eyes, dark hair, fair complexion, 5'10. Deserted.

Dryden, William A. Rct. 12 December 1864 (age 19 at Cincinnati, OH)–26 December 1864. B: Hocking Co., OH, boatman. Blue eyes, brown hair, fair complexion, 5'6½. Deserted.

Dryett, Edward A. Pvt. Co. B, 1 August 1861 (age 20 at Cleveland, OH)–1 August 1864. B: Cleveland, Cuyahoga Co., OH, laborer. Grey eyes, light hair, ruddy complexion, 5'4¾. Discharged.

Dubois, Ezekiel. Pvt. Co. E, 18 September 1861 (age 26 at Columbus, OH)–23 December 1862. B: Lancaster Co., PA, farmer. Black eyes, black hair, ruddy complexion, 5'8¼. Disability discharge at Providence, RI.

Dubois, Joshua W. Pvt. Co. E, 18 September 1861 (age 29 at Columbus, OH)–18 September 1864. B: Salem, NY, farmer. Hazel eyes, sandy hair, ruddy complexion, 5'10. POW, Upperville, 21 June–11 November 1863. Paroled, reported at Camp 6th Cav. Discharged at Berryville, VA.

Duffy, James. Rct. 24 October 1862 (age 30 at Knoxville, MD)–No further information. B: IRE, laborer. Blue eyes, brown hair, dark complexion, 5'5½.

Duffy, Peter. Pvt. Co. A, 14 December 1864 (age 21 at Cincinnati, OH)–16 February 1866. B: IRE, boatman. Hazel eyes, dark hair, fair complexion, 5'7. Deserted.

Duly, George. Pvt. Co. L, 11 October 1861 (age 24 at Cleveland, OH)–29 March 1862. B: Oswego Co., NY, ferryman. Black eyes, dark hair, ruddy complexion, 5'5. Deserted.

Dumas, Joseph. Pvt. Co. M, 28 September 1864 (age 27 at Rochester, NY)–11 October 1866. B: Three Rivers, CAN, sailor. Hazel eyes, brown hair, sallow complexion, 5'3½. MIA. Dropped from rolls as per letter, A.G.O. dated October 1866.

Duncan, Howard. Farrier. Co. I, 8 August 1861 (age 35 at Rochester, NY)–16 July 1862. B: IRE, Vet. Surgeon. Blue eyes, brown hair, fair complexion, 5'6. Discharged at hospital at Ft. Monroe, VA.

Duncan, Samuel. Pvt. Co. D, 20 July 1861 (age 21 at Pittsburgh, PA)–20 August 1864. B: Westmoreland Co., PA, farmer. Grey eyes, red hair, light complexion, 5'8½. Discharged at Bolivar Heights, VA.

Dunmore, John. Pvt. Cos. E, C, 18 September 1861 (age 21 at Adrian, MI)–14 April 1862. B: Hillsdale Co., MI, farmer. Grey eyes, light hair, ruddy complexion, 5'8½. Deserted 3 May 1862 and 14 April 1862. Register states he was assigned to Co. E, yet attached to Co. C.

Dunn, George. Pvt. Co. M, 12 September 1861 (age 21 at Pittsburgh, PA)–12 September 1864. B: SCO, teamster. Hazel eyes, light hair, fair complexion, 5'7. Discharged at Berryville, VA.

Dunn, James. Pvt. Co. D, 29 August 1861 (age 35 at Pittsburgh, PA)–29 August 1864. B: Berwickshire, SCO, laborer. Grey eyes, black hair, dark complexion, 5'7½. Discharged in the field, VA.

Dunn, John. Mustered: Pvt. Co. G, 34th PA Inf. Transferred: Pvt. Cos. A, B, 6th U.S. Cav. 28 October 1862 (age 18 at Knoxville, MD)–6 May 1864. B: IRE. Blue eyes, dark hair, light complexion, 5'5. D: 6 May 1864 of dysentery as a POW at Andersonville, GA.

Dunn, John. Rct. 21 November 1864 (age 30 at Harrisburg, PA). B: Co. Tyrone, IRE, laborer. Grey eyes, brown hair, ruddy complexion, 5'7. Deserted. Sub for Blackburn.

Dunn, Thomas. Pvt. Co. M, 3 November 1864 (age 20 at NYC, NY). B: Dublin, IRE, laborer. Blue eyes, light hair, ruddy complexion, 5'9. Deserted 24 November 1864. Apprehended 28 November 1864. No further information.

Dunne, Charles. Pvt. Co. M, 22 October 1864 (age 35 at NYC, NY)–22 October 1867. B: Co. Tipperary, IRE, soldier. Hazel eyes, light hair, fair complexion, 5'6. Discharged at New Orleans, LA.

Durant, George. Co. M, 26 September 1864 (age 41 at Cleveland, OH)–19 May 1865. B: Norwich, ENG, laborer. Grey eyes, brown hair, dark complexion, 6'. Disability discharge at Carlisle Barracks, PA.

Durboraw, John F. Pvt. Co. M, 30 September 1861 (age 22 at Pittsburgh, PA)–3 January 1863. B: Chambersburg, Franklin Co., PA, miner. Blue eyes, brown hair, dark complexion, 5'8. Deserted.

Durling, George W. Mustered: Pvt. Co. H, 8th OH Inf. 6 June 1861. Transferred: Pvt. Co. C, 6th U.S. Cav. 24 October 1862 (age 20 at Knoxville, MD)–24 April 1864. B: Cayuga Co., NY. Brown eyes, black hair, florid complexion, 5'11. Discharged at Camp 6th Cav., VA.

Durluef, Frederick. Pvt.-Cpl. Co. E, 26 August 1861 (age 20 at Columbus, OH)–3 July 1863. B: Barren, SWZ, farmer. Hazel eyes, sandy hair, light complexion, 5'4½. Paroled at City Point, VA, 22 November 1862. Sent to Army of the Potomac 19 February 1863. MIA, Fairfield.

Durst, Lewis. Mustered: Pvt. Co. B, 148th PA Inf. Mustered: Cos. B, D, 19th V.R.C. Enlisted: Pvt. Co. K, 6th U.S. Cav. 10 February 1864 (age 24 at Brandy Station, VA)–16 October 1865. B: GER. Black eyes, brown hair, dark complexion, 5'6. Deserted.

Duzett, Edward A. Pvt. Co. B, 1 August 1861 (age 20 at Cleveland, OH)–1 August 1864. B: Cleveland, Cuyahoga Co., OH, laborer. Grey eyes, light hair, ruddy complexion, 5'4¾. POW, Coal Harbor, 27 June 1862–? POW, Malvern Hill, 6 August 1862–? Discharged at Lighthouse Point, VA.

Dyer, James. Rct. 28 November 1864 (age 29 at Harrisburg, PA)–12 December 1864. B: Quebec, CAN, sailor. Dark eyes, dark hair, ruddy complexion, 5'6½. Deserted at Carlisle Barracks, PA.

Eakerman, Henry L. Pvt.-Sgt. Co. L, 23 October 1861 (age 23 at Cleveland, OH)–23 October 1864. B: Hanover, GER, carpenter. Blue eyes, light hair, ruddy complexion, 5'9. POW, Fairfield, 3 July–12 November 1863. Paroled, reported at Brandy Station. Discharged in the field, VA.

Earhart, Eli Irwin. Rct. 30 July 1861 (age 21 at Columbus, OH)–No further information. B: Franklin Co., OH, farmer. Blue eyes, light hair, light complexion, 5'7¼. See 459–2300 P.R.D. 90.

Earl, William W. Mustered (Youngtown, OH): Pvt. Co. I, 7th OH Inf. 19 June 1861. Transferred: Pvt. Co. K, 6th U.S. Cav. 27 October 1862 (age 21 at Knoxville, MD)–27 April 1864. B: Butler Co., IA, boatman. Grey eyes, brown hair, light complexion, 6'1. Discharged at Camp 6th Cav., VA. Mustered (New Castle, PA): Pvt. Co. H, 77th PA Inf. 14 February 1865–6 December 1865. Mustered out at Victoria, TX.

Earnest, Isaac. Pvt. Co. M, 19 September 1864 (age 42 at Rochester, NY)–29 August 1865. B: Berlin, GER, farmer. Grey eyes, black hair, sallow complexion, 5'4¼. Disability discharge at Carlisle Barracks, PA.

Eaton, William. Mustered: Pvt. Co. H, 1st MN Inf. 22 May 1861. Transferred: Pvt. Co. B, 6th U.S. Cav. 26 October 1862 (age 19 at Knoxville, MD)–22 May 1864. B: Spencer Co., IN. Blue eyes, dark hair, light complexion, 6'. MIA, Funkstown. Discharged in the field, VA.

Eberle, Adam. Pvt. Co. G, 13 August 1861 (age 35 at Erie Co., PA)–19 August 1861. B: Bayern, GER, laborer. Blue eyes, light hair, light complexion, 5'7¾. D: 19 August 1861, Erie Co., PA.

Eckerman, Lewis H. Cpl. Cos. B, L, 7 August 1861 (age 19 at Cleveland, OH)–7 August 1864. B: Hanover, GER, laborer. Grey eyes, light hair, ruddy complexion, 5'4½. POW, Funkstown, 7 July 1863–21 June 1864. Paroled. Discharged at Washington, D.C.

Edwards, Franklin. Pvt. Co. I, 24 August 1861 (age 22 at Rochester, NY)–3 January 1862. B: Addison Co., VT, painter. Hazel eyes, brown hair, fair complexion, 5'9¼. Disability discharge at Washington, D.C.

Edwards, John. Rct. 1 December 1862 (age 26 at St. Hamilton, NY)–No further information. B: ENG, laborer. Dark eyes, brown hair, light complexion, 5'7.

Edwards, William H. Mustered: Pvt. Co. K, 14th IN Inf. 7 June 1861. Transferred: Pvt. Co. C, 6th U.S. Cav. 23 October 1862 (age 19 at

Knoxville, MD)–1 June 1864. B: NC. Black eyes, black hair, florid complexion, 5' 8. POW, Funkstown, 7 July–1 November 1863. Paroled, reported at Annapolis, MD. Discharged in the field, VA.

Eisle, Henry. Mustered: Pvt. Co. F, 41st PA Inf. 8 January 1861. Transferred: Pvt. Co. H, 6th U.S. Cav. 28 October 1862 (age 19 at Knoxville, MD)–19 October 1863. B: Westmoreland Co., PA, fisherman. Hazel eyes, dark hair, ruddy complexion, 5' 4. WIA, Catlett Station, VA, 13 October 1863. D: 19 October 1863 from wounds at CCHQ, VA.

Eligot, Patrick. Pvt. Co. M, 27 October 1864 (age 25 at NYC, NY)–30 August 1865. B: Co. Limerick, IRE, laborer. Hazel eyes, brown hair, ruddy complexion, 5' 3½. Deserted.

Ellicott, George W. Pvt. Cos. C, L, 11 January 1862 (age 21 at Philadelphia, PA)–11 January 1865. B: Hunterdon, NJ, engineer. Hazel eyes, brown hair, sallow complexion, 5' 4½. Discharged at Winchester, VA.

Elliott, Daniel D. Cpl.-Sgt. Co. B, 1 August 1861 (age 19 at Cleveland, OH)–1 April 1864. B: Cleveland, Cuyahoga Co., OH, farmer. Grey eyes, brown hair, ruddy complexion, 5' 6. Reenlisted: 8 February 1864 in the field, VA. Transferred: U.S. Navy, 1 April 1864 by S.O. 108.

Elliott, James S. Mustered: Pvt. Co. H, 11th PA Inf. (3 months). Enlisted: Pvt.-Sgt.-1st Sgt. Co. H, 14 August 1861 (age 21 at Philadelphia, PA)–31 December 1864. B: Williamsport, Lycoming Co., PA, laborer. Blue eyes, light hair, ruddy complexion, 5' 6½. Reenlisted: 5 February 1864 at Camp 6th Cav., Brandy Station, VA. Discharged: 31 December 1864 by appointed Cpt., Co. H, 5th U.S. Cav. At Winchester, VA. Note: James and Thomas were brothers.

Elliott, Thomas T. Enlisted: Pvt. Co. H, 5th U.S. Inf. 1 October 1856–20 March 1857. Discharged by order, AGO. Enlisted: Pvt. Co. A, Cav. 9 December 1857–13 July 1859. Deserted. Mustered: 1st Sgt., Co. A, 11th PA Inf. (3 months). Enlisted: Sgt.-1st Sgt. Co. H, 14 August 1861 (age 23 at Philadelphia, PA)–14 August 1864. B: Williamsport, Lycoming Co., PA, carpenter. Blue eyes, light hair, fair complexion, 5' 7 ½. POW, Fairfield, 3 July–24 August 1863. Paroled at Annapolis, MD., 24 August 1863. Discharged at Lighthouse Point, VA.

Ellis, Elisha J. Pvt. Co. E, 16 September 1861 (age 22 at Adrian, MI)–9 May 1862. B: Sandwich, Barnstable Co., MA, farmer. Grey eyes, brown hair, ruddy complexion, 5' 6½. MIA, Slaterville.

Ellis, Franklin. Pvt. Co. K, 19 August 1861 (age 18 at Rochester, NY)–19 August 1864. B: Athens, Bradford Co., PA, farmer. Hazel eyes, brown hair, sandy complexion, 5' 8. Discharged at Lighthouse Point, VA.

Ellis, J. Sgt. Co. K, 31 July 1861 (age 18 at Warren, OH)–31 July 1864. B: Kinsman, Trumbull Co., OH, farmer. Blue eyes, brown hair, light complexion, 5' 6½. Discharged at Lee's Mills, VA.

Ellsworth, Alonzo. Cpl. Co. I, 23 September 1861 (age 23 at Rochester, NY)–7 July 1863. B: Erie Co., NY, farmer. Grey eyes, brown hair, fair complexion, 5' 9¾. KIA, Funkstown.

Ellsworth, William. Sgt. Co. I, 27 August 1861 (age 22 at Rochester, NY)–11 October 1863. B: Batavia, NY, farmer. Hazel eyes, sandy hair, ruddy complexion, 6'1¼. KIA, Brandy Station, 11 October 1863.

Elmer, Henry A. Pvt. Co. F, 24 December 1864 (age 20 at Cincinnati, OH)–22 April 1865. B: Philadelphia, PA, laborer. Hazel eyes, brown hair, fair complexion, 5' 7. Deserted.

Elwanger, Francis. Pvt. Co. G, 28 July 1861 (at Rochester, NY)–4 July 1862. D: from fever at Davids Island, NY, 4 July 1862.

Emsley, Emanuel T. Pvt. Co. L, 10 February 1862 (at Cleveland, OH)–23 April 1862. Deserted.

English, Charles. Co. B, 8 August 1861 (age 21 at Cleveland, OH)–23 March 1862. B: Adrian, MI, shoemaker. Blue eyes, brown hair, sallow complexion, 5' 6¾. Deserted.

Ensign, Austin. Mustered: Pvt. Co. K, 38th PA Inf. 5 April 1861. Transferred: Pvt. Co. E, 6th U.S. Cav. 28 October 1862 (age 23 at Knoxville, MD)–28 July 1864. B: Fairfield, OH, tinsmith. Blue eyes, light hair, fair complexion, 5' 7½. Discharged at Lighthouse Point, VA. D: 11 May 1883.

Ent, Henry. Pvt. Co. C, 4 January 1862 (age 26 at Philadelphia, PA)–4 January 1865. B: New Hope, Bucks Co., PA, carpenter. Grey eyes, black hair, sallow complexion, 5' 6¾. Discharged at Winchester, VA.

Erb, John H. Cpl. Co. D, 16 August 1861 (age 26 at Pittsburgh, PA)–7 October 1862. B: Westmoreland Co., PA, boatman. Grey eyes, brown hair, dark complexion, 5' 6. D: KIA near Charleston, VA, 7 October 1862.

Erhardt, Gustav W. Pvt. Cos. E, C, 19 August 1861 (age 23 at Cleveland, OH)–22 January 1862. B: Berlin, Prussia, GER, clerk. Hazel eyes, brown hair, ruddy complexion, 5' 8½. Deserted.

Ernst, Carl (alias Arnst, Carl). Pvt. Co. I, 9 September 1861 (age 25 at Rochester, NY)–9 September 1864. B: GER, farmer. Blue eyes, light hair, florid complexion, 5' 7¼.

Espy, Frederick R. Mustered: Pvt. Co. A, 37th PA Inf. 22 April 1861. Transferred: Pvt. Co. H, 6th U.S. Cav. 28 October 1862 (age 18 at Knoxville, MD)–28 July 1864. B: MI, farmer. Blue eyes, brown hair, fair complexion, 5' 8. WIA/POW, Fairfield, 3 July–10 November 1863. Paroled, reported at Camp 6th Cav. Discharged in the field, VA. Mustered: Co. H, 8th MD Inf. D: 6 June 1885, KY.

Estlow, Jacob. Pvt. Co. A, 19 September 1861 (age 25 at Philadelphia, PA)–23 September 1864. B: Weymouth, NJ, moulder. Grey eyes, brown hair, light complexion, 5' 6½. WIA, Beverly Ford. Discharged at Harper's Ferry, VA.

Evans, James. Pvt. Co. F, 22 July 1861 (age 19 at Pittsburgh, PA)–7 July 1863. B: Allegheny Co., PA, glass blower. Grey eyes, grey hair, light complexion, 5' 6½. KIA, Funkstown.

Evans, William H. Pvt. Co. G, 19 July 1861 (age 21 at Columbus, OH)–19 July 1864. B: Georgetown, Washington, D.C., cooper. Blue eyes, light hair, ruddy complexion, 5' 9. POW, Fairfield, 3 July 1863–17 February 1864. Paroled, reported at Camp Parole. Discharged at Harper's Ferry, VA.

Everson, Richard. Sgt. Co. F, 3 July 1861 (age 40 at Pittsburgh, PA)–3 July 1864. B: Newport Co., ENG, mechanic. Grey eyes, grey hair, fair complexion, 5' 5. Discharged at Lighthouse Point, VA.

Everts, William W. Mustered: Pvt. Co. H, 1st MN Inf. 29 April 1861. WIA, Antietam. Transferred: Pvt. Co. C, 6th U.S. Cav. 26 October 1862 (age 23 at Knoxville, MD)–at least 29 April 1864. B: St. Lawrence Co., NY. Blue eyes, sandy hair, light complexion, 5' 5. POW, Fairfield, 3 July–24 August 1863. Paroled at Annapolis, MD. Reenlisted: 29 April 1864 at 6th Cav. Camp near Brandy Station, VA.

Ewart, Robert H. Pvt. Co. M, 2 September 1861 (age 20 at Pittsburgh, PA)–9 September 1864. B: Allegheny Co., PA, farmer. Blue eyes, light hair, light complexion, 5'11. WIA/POW, Aldie, 22 June 1863–? Paroled, reported at Annapolis, MD. POW, Fairfield, 3 July 1863–18 July 1864. Discharged at Carlisle Barracks, PA.

Ewing, John. Pvt. Co. F, 14 December 1864 (age 19 at Cincinnati, OH)–14 December 1867. B: CAN, farmer. Grey eyes, dark hair, sallow complexion, 5' 9. Discharged at Camp Wilson, TX.

Faas, Jacob. Pvt. Co. E, 27 August 1861 (age 26 at Columbus, OH)–31 December 1862. B: Columbiana Co., OH, carpenter. Hazel eyes,

red hair, ruddy complexion, 5' 9½. Dropped 31 December 1862 as per General Order.

Falkins, John. Mustered: U.S.V. Transferred: Pvt. Co. D, 6th U.S. Cav. 25 October 1862 (age 22 at Knoxville, MD)–28 June 1864. B: Nova Scotia, CAN. Blue eyes, light hair, light complexion, 5' 6½. Discharged at Well's Landing, VA.

Falkner, Edward. Pvt. Co. I, 7 September 1861 (age 23 at Rochester, NY)–9 June 1863. B: ENG, farmer. Grey eyes, brown hair, fair complexion, 5' 8. KIA, Beverly Ford.

Farquhar, Thomas. Pvt. Co. M, 6 December 1861 (age 21 at Pittsburgh, PA)–6 December 1864. B: Washington Co., PA, farmer. Grey eyes, light hair, light complexion, 5' 9½. Discharged at Stephenson Station, VA.

Farrell, James. Pvt. Co. L, 19 December 1864 (age 19 at Cincinnati, OH)–No further information. B: IRE, laborer. Blue eyes, dark hair, fair complexion, 5' 5½.

Farrell, Joseph Peter. Pvt. Co. H, 20 July 1861 (age 26 at Philadelphia, PA)–20 July 1864. B: Philadelphia, PA, moulder. Blue eyes, brown hair, ruddy complexion, 5' 6½. MIA, Fairfield. Discharged in the field, VA.

Farrell, Thomas. Pvt. Co. L, 23 September 1864 (age 20 at Harrisburg, PA)–13 April 1866. B: New Haven, CT, rubber maker. Blue eyes, fair hair, fair complexion, 5' 7. Deserted 27 July 1865. Joined 2 August 1865. Deserted 6 November 1865. Apprehended 19 January 1866. Deserted 13 April 1866.

Farris, Joseph. Rct. 2 November 1864 (age 27 at Harrisburg, PA)–22 November 1864. B: Co. Armagh, IRE, harness maker. Blue eyes, auburn hair, ruddy complexion, 5' 8. Deserted 11 November 1864. Apprehended same day. Deserted 22 November 1864.

Farrow, William. Mustered: Pvt. Co. N, 28th PA Inf. 20 August 1861. Transferred: Pvt. Co. B, 6th U.S. Cav. 25 October 1862 (age 25 at Knoxville, MD)–8 August 1864. B: Pottsville, Schuylkill Co., PA, boiler maker. Blue eyes, brown hair, light complexion, 5' 8½. D: 8 August 1864 of acute dysentery at Cavalry Corps hospital, City Point, VA.

Faucett, George W. Mustered: Pvt. Co. D, 14th IN Inf. 6 July 1861. Transferred: Rct. 6th U.S. Cav. 23 October 1862 (age 22 at Knoxville, MD) Returned to USV. B: Green Co., IN. Blue eyes, black hair, light complexion, 5' 6. Promoted to Sgt. D: from wounds, 10 May 1864.

Faulkner, Frederick. Pvt. Co. M, 23 September 1861 (age 18 at Pittsburgh, PA)–23 September 1864. B: ENG, coal miner. Grey eyes, light hair, light complexion, 5' 6½. WIA, Fairfield. Discharged at Berryville, VA. Note: Frederick and Robert were brothers.

Faulkner, Robert. Pvt. Co. M, 23 September 1861 (age 21 at Pittsburgh, PA)–23 September 1864. B: ENG, coal miner. Grey eyes, light hair, dark complexion, 5' 8½. Discharged at Berryville, VA.

Feely, Martin. Pvt.-Cpl. Cos. L, C, 5 November 1861 (age 34 at Edwina, PA)–16 October 1865. B: Co. Galway, IRE, boatman. Grey eyes, brown hair, dark complexion, 5' 8. Reenlisted: 16 February 1864 at Brandy Station, VA. Deserted 16 October 1865.

Feigels, John. Mustered: Pvt. Co. H, 34th PA Inf. Transferred: Pvt. Co. A, 6th U.S. Cav. 28 October 1862 (age 19 at Knoxville, MD)–23 July 1864. B: Lycoming Co., PA. Grey eyes, light hair, light complexion, 5' 7. POW, Fairfield, 3 July 1863–18 January 1864. Paroled, reported at Annapolis, MD. Discharged at Lighthouse Point, VA.

Felmlee, Jacob R. Pvt. Co. I, 30 July 1861 (age 24 at Indiana, PA)–3 September 1862. B: Centre Co., PA, teamster. Grey eyes, black hair, dark complexion, 5' 8. D: 3 September 1862 at Ft. Monroe, VA.

Feranbach, Ansalem. (Prior service). Pvt. Co. I, 30 July 1861 (age 21 at Indiana, PA)–21 June 1862. B: Baden, GER, stone mason. Blue eyes, light hair, fair complexion, 5' 7¾. Deserted.

Ferguson, John. Pvt. Co. B, 9 August 1861 (age 27 at Columbus, OH)–2 November 1862. B: Boston, MA, blacksmith. Grey eyes, black hair, dark complexion, 5' 6¼. According to Pvt. Sidney M. Davis, deserted to the enemy at Philomont.

Ferguson, Joseph. Mustered: Pvt. Co. F, 3rd WI Inf. Transferred: Pvt. Co. E, 6th U.S. Cav. 28 October 1862 (age 18 at Knoxville, MD)–13 March 1864. B: Lafayette Co., WI, farmer. Blue eyes, light hair, fair complexion, 5'10. POW, Funkstown, 7 July 1863–13 March 1864. D: of pneumonia as a POW at Andersonville, GA, 13 March 1864.

Ferguson, Robert A. Mustered: Co. H, 1st MN Inf. Rct. 24 October 1862 (age 19 at Knoxville, MD)–No further information. B: Fredericksburg, IN, farmer. Blue eyes, light hair, light complexion, 5' 6.

Ferguson, William. Pvt. Co. F, 3 July 1861 (age 32 at Pittsburgh, PA)–3 July 1864. B: Indiantown, Lebanon Co., PA, coach maker. Brown eyes, black hair, dark complexion, 5' 9½. Discharged at Lighthouse Point, VA.

Ferry, Lemuel Austin. Sgt. Co. K, 22 July 1861 (age 18 at Warren, OH)–22 July 1864. B: Bloomfield, OH, farmer. Grey eyes, brown hair, brown complexion, 6'1¼. Discharged at White House Point, VA.

Ficht, George. Pvt. Co. M, 20 November 1861 (age 19 at Pittsburgh, PA)–17 February 1867. B: Allegheny Co., PA, farmer. Greyish eyes, light hair, light complexion, 5' 8. Reenlisted: 17 February 1864 at Brandy Station, VA. Discharged at Austin, TX.

Fields, Henry. Pvt. Co. A, 30 September 1861 (age 30 at Pottsville, PA)–30 September 1864. B: Paulton, ENG, miner. Blue eyes, brown hair, florid complexion, 5' 6½. POW, Fairfield, 3 July–5 October 1863. Paroled, reported at Culpepper, VA. Discharged at Harrisonburg, VA.

Fillmore, James. Rct. 27 October 1864 (age 32 at Cleveland, OH)–November 1864. B: Hamilton, West Can, CAN, laborer. Blue eyes, light hair, sallow complexion, 5' 7½. Deserted.

Finch, Philetus. Pvt. Co. E, 10 September 1861 (age 19 at Adrian, MI)–1 January 1863. B: Rome, MI, farmer. Blue eyes, light hair, fair complexion, 5' 4½. Discharged 3 September 1869 to date 1 January 1863 per S. O. 125, HQ, Dept. of the Lakes, Detroit, MI.

Finnam, John. Pvt. Cos. L, C, 12 November 1861 (age 25 at Cleveland, OH)–3 January 1862. B: Co. Galway, IRE, laborer. Blue eyes, light hair, ruddy complexion, 5'10. Disability discharge at Washington, D.C.

Finney, Charles John. Pvt. Cos. C, L, 4 September 1861 (age 25 at Philadelphia, PA)–4 September 1862. B: Gateshead, ENG, nursery man. Brown eyes, brown hair, dark complexion, 5'11½. Deserted at camp near Alexandria, VA.

Fischer, Domanikus. Pvt. Co. D, 12 August 1861 (age 20 at Pittsburgh, PA)–12 August 1864. B: Baden, GER, farmer. Brown eyes, brown hair, light complexion, 5' 9. Discharged at Geisboro Point, Washington, D.C.

Fischer, John Paul. Pvt. Co. D, 19 August 1861 (age 19 at Rochester, NY)–No further information. B: Cleveland, Cuyahoga Co., OH, brushmaker. Chestnut eyes, black hair, ruddy complexion, 5' 5¾.

Fisher, George Jr. Pvt. Co. C, 17 October 1861 (age 33 at Philadelphia, PA)–13 April 1862. B: Rapho Township, Lancaster Co., PA, laborer. Hazel eyes, brown hair, light complexion, 5' 5. Deserted.

Fisher, John. Mustered: Pvt. Co. F, 8th OH Inf. 6 May 1861. Transferred: Pvt. Co. C, 6th U.S.

Cav. 23 October 1862 (age 20 at Knoxville, MD)–7 July 1863. B: Wayne Co., OH. Grey eyes, light hair, light complexion, 5'10. KIA, Funkstown.

Fisher, William. Pvt. Co. F, 10 December 1864 (age 22 at Cleveland, OH)–26 January 1865. B: St. Catharina, CAN, auctioneer. Grey eyes, black hair, dark complexion, 5'9. Deserted.

Fisk, Andrew Murry. Pvt. Co. I, 22 August 1861 (age 21 at Rochester, NY)–4 September 1863. B: Genesee Co., NY, farmer. Grey eyes, brown hair, brown complexion, 5'8¾. Disability discharge at Convalescent Camp, VA.

Fitch, Samuel DeWolf. Pvt. Co. K, 8 August 1861 (age 22 at Warren, OH). B: Vienna Co., OH, clerk. Black eyes, black hair, olive complexion, 5'8. MIA, Beverly Ford, 9 June 1863. Reenlisted: 10 February 1864 at Brandy Station, VA, a Sgt. Transferred: Co. F&S, 24 August 1864. Discharged: 14 November 1864 at Winchester, VA by appointment as Cpt. Co. C, 6th U.S.C. Cav. (appointment backdated to 21 October 1864), a 1st Sgt.. Dismissed 10 May 1865. Enlisted: Cos. K, L, 6th U.S. Cav. 23 August 1865–23 August 1868, Discharged at Ft. Griffin, TX. Reenlisted: Pvt. Co. G, 6th U.S. Cav. 20 September 1868. Deserted 10 December 1868. Enlisted 14 December 1868 in Co. E, Eng. Under the name "Samuel De-Wolff." Deserted 29 May 1869. Apprehended 18 February 1870. Deserted 21 September 1870. Apprehended 23 September 1870. Deserted 26 November 1870. Surrendered 4 December 1873. Deserted 11 March 1874.

Fitzgerald, Thomas. Enlisted: Pvt. Cos. H, D, Regiment of Mounted Riflemen, 10 January 1848. Deserted: 11 June 1850. Apprehended: 27 February 1855. Reenlisted: Pvt. Cos. E, C, Regiment of Mounted Riflemen, 1 August 1858–1 August 1863. Discharged at Camp McRae, Memphis, TN. Enlisted: Sgt. Cos. L, H, 6th U.S. Cav. 14 October 1863 (age 35 at Washington, DC)–14 October 1868. B: Albany, NY. Grey eyes, brown hair, fair complexion, 5'7½. Discharged at Sulpher Springs, TX. Enlisted (Carlisle Barracks, PA): Pvt. Co. H, 1st U.S. Cav. 25 March 1869. Discharged 1 October 1870 by section 10, Act of Congress, 15 July 1870, at Camp Harney, OR, a Cpl. Reenlisted at Portland, OR, Co. F, 23rd Inf. 25 October 1870. Deserted 8 June 1871.

[Fitz]Henry, Edwin Sawtell. Farrier. Co. B, 5 August 1861 (age 25 at Columbus, OH)–5 August 1864. B: 24 July 1835, Dublin, Franklin, OH, blacksmith. Grey eyes, black hair, sallow complexion, 5'6½. WIA, Hanover Courthouse. Discharged at Lighthouse Point, VA. D: 12 January 1884, Fairbury, Jefferson, NB.

Fitzpatrick, Edward. Pvt. Co. B, 1 August 1861 (age 19 at Cleveland, OH)–1 August 1864. B: Pittsburgh, Allegheny Co., PA, blacksmith. Grey eyes, light hair, ruddy complexion, 5'8¾. Discharged at Lighthouse Point, VA.

Fitzsimmons, Peter. Pvt. Co. A, 8 October 1861 (age 27 at Cleveland, OH)–26 January 1862. B: Montreal, CAN, runner. Blue eyes, brown hair, ruddy complexion, 5'3. Deserted.

Flack, Alexander. Served both Pvt. Co. B, 6th U.S. Cav. and Batt. F, 5th U.S. Light Art. 25 March 1864 (age 26 at Pittsburgh, PA)–14 May 1867. B: Allegheny Co., PA, printer. Blue eyes, brown hair, fair complexion, 5'7. Deserted (Batt. F) 12 June 1866. Surrendered: 27 July 1866. Discharged at Austin, TX, with 6th U.S. Cav. Note: was assigned to the 5th U.S. Art at least by 25 December 1863, as per a discovered news article.

Flannagan, John. Rct. 14 November 1864 (age 29 at Cincinnati, OH)–Never joined. B: IRE, shoemaker. Hazel eyes, brown hair, dark complexion, 5'6½.

Flansburgh, Parker. Pvt. Co. G, 31 July 1861 (age 24 at Erie Co., PA)–10 May 1862. B: East Davenport, Delaware Co., NY, farmer. Blue eyes, dark hair, dark complexion, 5'5¼. WIA, Williamsburg. Brought North from Baltimore to New York. Deserted.

Flater, James M. Mustered: Pvt. Co. D, 14th IN Inf. 6 July 1861. Transferred: Pvt. Co. C, 6th U.S. Cav. 24 October 1862 (age 20 at Knoxville, MD)–1 June 1864. B: 1842, Carroll Co., MD. Brown eyes, brown hair, florid complexion, 5'5. MIA, Fairfield. Discharged at Camp 6th Cav., in the field, VA. Mustered: Cos. H, F, 6th IN Cav. 23 October 1864–15 September 1865. Mustered out at Mufreesboro, TN. D: 1918, Cedar Co., IA.

Fleischer, Mathias. Farrier. Co. F, 3 July 1861 (age 32 at Pittsburgh, PA)–3 July 1864. B: 6 April 1829, Konigsfeld, GER, blacksmith. Brown eyes, brown hair, dark complexion, 6'. Deserted. Joined 27 October 1862 at Knoxville. Discharged at Lighthouse Point, VA. Enlisted: Pvt. Co. A, 1st U.S.V.V. Inf. D: 6 April 1910, MI.

Fleming, S. Lloyd. Sgt. Co. H, 29 July 1861 (age 30 at Philadelphia, PA)–29 July 1864. B: Williamsport, Lycoming Co., PA, clerk. Hazel eyes, light hair, fair complexion, 5'8. Discharged in the field, VA. D: 21 March 1907, Erie, PA.

Fleming, William A. Enlisted: Rct. 1 June 1857–27 June 1857. Discharged by order, AGO. Enlisted: Cpl. Co. I, 6th U.S. Cav. 15 August 1861 (age 23 at Lock Haven, PA)–30 June 1863. B: Clinton Co., PA, farmer. Grey eyes, light hair, fair complexion, 5' 8. D: of disease at hospital, Acquia Creek, VA, 30 June 1863.

Fletcher, William P. Pvt. Co. B, 5 August 1861 (age 20 at Cleveland, OH)–30 October 1862. B: Washington Co., VT, farmer. Hazel eyes, brown hair, ruddy complexion, 5' 9¼. Disability discharge at Cincinnati, OH.

Flinn, Francis. Pvt. Co: A, 10 December 1864 (age 22 at Carlisle, PA)–6 November 1867. B: Co. Antrim, IRE, laborer. Brown eyes, black hair, ruddy complexion, 5'10. Discharged at New Orleans, LA.

Flory, Peter. Pvt.-Cpl. Cos. C, L, 21 November 1861 (age 21 at Philadelphia, PA)–3 July 1863. B: Lancaster Co., PA, miller. Grey eyes, brown hair, ruddy complexion, 5' 9. KIA, Fairfield.

Floyd, Wilson. Mustered: Pvt. Co. F, 38th PA Inf. Transferred: Pvt. Co. A, 6th U.S. Cav. 28 October 1862 (age 24 at Knoxville, MD)–28 June 1864. B: Crawford Co., PA, farmer. Hazel eyes, dark hair, fair complexion, 5'11. WIA, Beverly Ford. Discharged at Wincock Landing, VA.

Foley, Thomas. Rct. 26 September 1864 (age 26 at Rochester, NY)–Never joined. B: Co. Kildare, IRE, boatman. Blue eyes, brown hair, florid complexion, 6'½.

Foller, John M. Saddler. Co. E, 14 August 1861 (age 24 at Columbus, OH)–14 August 1864. B: Emmitsburg, MD, shoemaker. Hazel eyes, black hair, ruddy complexion, 5' 4½. Discharged.

Forbes, Washington. Mustered: Pvt. Co. K, 8th OH Inf. 6 May 1861. Transferred: Pvt. Co. C, 6th U.S. Cav. 23 October 1862 (age 23 at Knoxville, MD)–3 June 1864. B: Medina Co., OH, teamster. Blue eyes, black hair, florid complexion, 5'10½. Discharged in the field, VA. Mustered: Pvt. Co. C, 176th OH Inf. 21 August 1864–14 June 1865. Mustered out at Nashville, TN.

Forrey, John J. Pvt. Co. A, 8 December 1864 (age 21 at Philadelphia, PA)–8 December 1867. B: Lancaster Co., PA, carpenter. Blue eyes, brown hair, fair complexion, 5' 5. Discharged at Buffalo Springs, TX.

Fouse, Nerva. Pvt. Co. H, 29 July 1861 (age 19 at Philadelphia, PA)–29 July 1864. B: Philadelphia, PA, carter. Blue eyes, light hair, ruddy complexion, 5' 6¾. WIA/POW, Fairfield, 3 July 1863–27 February 1864. Paroled, reported at Camp Parole. Discharged in the field, VA.

Fowler, Benjamin Jr. Pvt. Co. K, 30 July 1861 (age 16 at Warren, OH)–17 January 1862. B: Champion, Trumbull Co., OH, farmer. Grey eyes, light hair, light complexion, 5' 8. D: from typhoid fever at Camp east of Capitol, Washington D.C., 17 January 1862.

Fox, George. Pvt. Co. A, 25 November 1864 (age 24 at Harrisburg, PA)–31 May 1865. B: Co. Cork, IRE, sailor. Grey eyes, auburn hair, florid complexion, 5'1. Deserted 11 December 1864. Apprehended 13 December 1864. Deserted 7 March 1865. Deserted 31 May 1865.

Fox, John W. Mustered: Pvt. Co. F, 12th PA Inf. Transferred: Pvt. Co. A, 6th U.S. Cav. 28 October 1862 (age 24 at Knoxville, MD)–23 August 1864. B: West Newton, Westmoreland Co., PA, painter. Blue eyes, dark hair, fair complexion, 5' 3. POW, Fairfield, 3 July–23 December 1863. Paroled, reported at Harrisburg, PA. Discharged at Harper's Ferry, VA.

Fox, Samuel A. Mustered: Pvt. Co. D, 14th IN Inf. Transferred: Pvt. Co. C, 6th U.S. Cav. 14 October 1862 (age 22 at Knoxville, MD)–1 June 1864. B: Cambury Co.(?), PA, farmer. Dark eyes, dark hair, dark complexion. WIA, Beverly Ford. Discharged.

Fox, Theodore. Pvt.-Sgt. Co. E, 13 September 1861 (age 21 at Adrian, MI)–10 December 1863. B: Richland Co., OH, clerk. Grey eyes, light hair, ruddy complexion, 5'7. WIA/POW, Fairfield, 3 July–24 August 1863. Reported to hospital 24 August 1863. Disability discharge at Carlisle Barracks, PA.

Francis, Abraham. Rct. 26 September 1864 (age 19 at Cleveland, OH)–Never joined. B: Richland, NY, sailor. Brown eyes, brown hair, dark complexion, 5'10. Sub.

Francis, William T. Mustered: Musician, Co. K, 14th IN Inf. 7 June 1861. Transferred: Pvt. Co. L, 6th U.S. Cav. 28 October 1862 (age 21 at Knoxville, MD)–5 June 1864. B: Bedford Co., PA, soldier. Dark eyes, dark hair, light complexion, 5' 5½. POW, Brandy Station, 11 October 1863–27 February 1864. Paroled, reported at Camp Parole. Discharged at Old Church, VA.

Frank, Julius. Pvt. Co. I, 2 August 1861 (age 25 at Rochester, NY)–9 July 1862. B: GER, laborer. Grey eyes, sandy hair, fair complexion, 5'10¾. Deserted.

Frank, Rufus R. Pvt. Co. C, 1 November 1861 (age 19 at Elizabethtown, PA)–29 September 1862. B: Elizabethtown, Lancaster Co., PA, clerk. Blue eyes, sandy hair, fair complexion, 5' 8½. Disability discharge at Philadelphia, PA.

Fratcher, David. Mustered (Utica, NY): Pvt. Co. D, 78th NY Inf. 26 November 1861. Transferred: Pvt. Co. M, 20 October 1862 (age 19 at Knoxville, MD)–4 December 1864. B: New York, NY. Blue eyes, light hair, ruddy complexion, 5' 9½. POW, Fairfield, 3 July–20 August 1863. Paroled at Annapolis, MD. Discharged in the field, VA.

Frazer, Peter B. Enlisted: Pvt. Co. D, 1st U.S. Cav. 10 March 1855–10 March 1860. Discharged at Ft. Cobb, KS. Enlisted: Pvt. Cos. B, F, 6th U.S. Cav. 18 July 1861 (age 28 at Columbus, OH)–16 July 1864. B: Lancaster Co., PA, shoemaker. Hazel eyes, brown hair, ruddy complexion, 5' 7. Discharged at Carlisle Barracks, PA. D: Milton, Northumberland, PA.

Freaney, Thomas. Pvt. Co. A, 25 October 1862 (age 20 at Knoxville, MD)–10 September 1865. B: IRE, soldier. Blue eyes, brown hair, light complexion, 5' 9. POW, Fairfield, 3 July 1863–23 May 1864. Paroled, reported at Charlesport, VA. Discharged near Frederick, MD.

Frederick, Joseph. Mustered: Pvt. Co. C, 37th PA Inf. 17 April 1861. Transferred: Pvt. Co. G, 6th U.S. Cav. 28 October 1862 (age 23 at Knoxville, MD)–29 July 1864. B: Pittsburgh, Allegheny Co., PA, barber. Blue eyes, light hair, light complexion, 5' 9. POW, Beverly Ford, 9 June 1863. POW, Andersonville, GA. Left at Trevilion Station, VA as a hospital attendant, 12 June 1864. Discharged at Baltimore, MD, 29 July 1864.

Freeman, Allen. Pvt. Co. I, 12 July 1861 (age 22 at Clearfield, PA)–12 July 1864. B: ME, farmer. Hazel eyes, brown hair, florid complexion, 5' 8. Discharged in the field, VA.

Freese, Henry Harry. Pvt. Co. K, 3 August 1861 (age 21 at Warren, OH)–3 August 1864. B: Warren, OH, hostler. Grey eyes, brown hair, red complexion, 5' 6¾. Discharged at Harper's Ferry, VA.

French, John C. Pvt. Co. I, 2 August 1861 (age 24 at Indiana, PA)–28 October 1863. B: Wykertown, Sussex Co., NJ, clerk. Grey eyes, brown hair, fair complexion, 5' 7. Deserted.

Frick, Christian G. Mustered: Pvt. Co. E, 163rd NY Inf. 25 August 1862 (Brooklyn, NY). Transferred: Rct. 6th U.S. Cav. 21 October 1862 (age 22 at Knoxville, MD). B: Württemberg, GER, shoemaker. Blue eyes, light hair, fair complexion, 5' 3. Returned to USV. Transferred: Pvt. Co. C, 73rd NY Inf. 18 January 1863.

Frutchey, Moses. Mustered: Pvt. Co. G, 50th PA Inf. 24 September 1861. Transferred: Pvt. Co. E, 6th U.S. Cav. 28 October 1862 (age 18 at Knoxville, MD)–12 February 1863. B: 20 January 1846, Bradford Co., PA. Blue eyes, light hair, light complexion, 5' 4. Deserted 25 December 1862 with rifle from Vol. unit. Apprehended 16 January 1863. Deserted 10 February 1863. Apprehended 12 February 1863. Deserted 12 February 1863. D: 7 March 1922, Wilmot, Bradford, PA.

Fry, Norbert. Pvt. Co. I, 22 August 1861 (age 23 at Rochester, NY)–1 July 1862. B: GER, farmer. Grey eyes, black hair, dark complexion, 5' 7½. D: 1 July 1862 near Richmond, VA.

Fuller, James. Rct. 5 November 1861 (age 28 at Pittsburgh, PA)–5 December 1861. B: Westmoreland Co., PA, cook. Hazel eyes, brown hair, light complexion, 5' 8. Disability discharge at Washington, D.C.

Fulton, David. Mustered: Co. C, 12th PA Inf. 25 April–5 August 1861 (Harrisburg, PA). Enlisted: Cpl. Co. D, 16 August 1861 (age 23 at Pittsburgh, PA)–13 January 1865. B: Pittsburgh, Allegheny, PA, miner. Grey eyes, brown hair, sandy complexion, 5' 8½. POW, Brandy Station, 11 October 1863–? Discharged at Camp Russell, VA.

Fulton, Harrison P. Sgt. Co. D, 19 August 1861 (age 18 at Pittsburgh, PA)–19 August 1864. B: Allegheny Co., PA, miner. Grey eyes, light hair, dark complexion, 5' 7. Discharged at Boliver Heights, VA.

Funk, John. Cpl. Co. C, 18 December 1861 (age 34 at Philadelphia, PA)–12 June 1862. B: Lancaster Co., PA, carpenter. Hazel eyes, black hair, dark complexion, 6' 2. Disability discharge at Washington, D.C.

Furl, George W. Mustered: Pvt. Co. B, 110th PA Inf. Transferred: Pvt. Co. D, 6th U.S. Cav. 28 October 1862 (age 18 at Knoxville, MD)–7 July 1864. B: Blair Co., PA. Blue eyes, dark hair, light complexion, 5' 9. D: from chronic diarrhea as a POW at Andersonville, GA, 7 July 1864.

Gabler, George. Pvt. Co. L, 14 November 1861 (Cleveland, OH)–19 January 1863. B: Columbiana Co., OH, shoemaker. Light eyes, brown hair, ruddy complexion, 5' 3. D: 19 January 1863 from typhoid fever at Washington D.C.

Gadbow, Peter William. Mustered: Pvt. Co. D, 34th NY Inf. 22 May 1861. Transferred: Pvt. Co. L, 6th U.S. Cav. 28 October 1862 (age 19 at Knoxville, MD)–1 May 1863. B: 5 March 1842, Massena, NY, farmer. Grey eyes, fair hair, fair complexion, 5' 4. Discharged. Mustered:

Pvt. Co. U, 14th NY Heavy Art. 23 December 1863–10 May 1864. Transferred: 6th NY Heavy Art. D: MN.

Gainer, Thomas D. Mustered: Pvt. Co. K, 110th PA Inf. 19 December 1861. Transferred: Pvt. Co. I, 6th U.S. Cav. 19 October 1862 (age 19 at Knoxville, MD)–27 October 1864. B: 1845, Lewistown, Mifflin Co., PA, farmer. Hazel eyes, dark hair, fair complexion, 5'8. Discharged in the field, VA. D: 25 July 1924, Oklahoma City, Oklahoma, OK.

Gains, Benjamin F. Pvt. Co. L, 11 March 1864 (age 20 at Washington, D.C.)–11 March 1867. B: Madison Co., NY, farmer. Grey eyes, brown hair, fair complexion, 5'6. Discharged at Jacksboro, TX.

Gallagher, Charles. Mustered: Pvt. Co. B, 8th OH Inf. 11 June 1861. Transferred: Pvt. Co. C, 6th U.S. Cav. 22 October 1862 (age 18 at Knoxville, MD)–17 February 1863. B: Cobourg, CAN, butcher. Blue eyes, brown hair, fair complexion, 5'11. Deserted.

Gallagher, Daniel. Enlisted: Co. E, Signal Corps, USA. Enlisted: Pvt. Cos. M, C, L, 6th U.S. Cav. 7 September 1861 (age 20 at Pittsburgh, PA)–7 September 1864. B: SCO, miner. Grey eyes, brown hair, dark complexion, 5'10. POW, ?–21 June 1864. Paroled. Discharged at Baltimore, MD. Enlisted: Pvt. Co. G, 2nd U.S. Cav. 15 March 1865 (Pittsburgh, PA)–25 September 1865. Deserted.

Gallagher, Hugh. Mustered: Pvt. Co. A, 37th PA Inf. 23 April 1861. Transferred: Cpl. Co. G, 6th U.S. Cav. 28 October 1862 (age 23 at Knoxville, MD)–29 July 1864. B: Moers(?), IRE, teamster. Blue eyes, fair hair, fair complexion, 6'. POW, Fairfield, 3 July 1863–8 April 1864. Paroled, reported at Annapolis, MD. Discharged in the field, VA.

Gallagher, Hugh. Pvt. Co. H, 5 August 1861 (age 25 at Philadelphia, PA)–5 August 1864. B: Co. Donegal, IRE, farmer. Blue eyes, light hair, ruddy complexion, 5'6½. Discharged at Lighthouse Point, VA.

Gallonough, William. Pvt. Co. M, 23 September 1864 (age 42 at Rochester, NY)–23 August 1865. B: IRE, vet. surgeon. Grey eyes, brown hair, florid complexion, 5'6½. Disability discharge at Carlisle Barracks, PA.

Galy, Christian. Pvt. Co. D, 8 August 1861 (age 29 at Pittsburgh, PA)–20 February 1863. B: Wesenberg, GER, butcher. Blue eyes, sandy hair, dark complexion, 5'7. Deserted.

Ganon, Michael. Rct. 17 September 1864 (age 35 at Harrisburg, PA)–Never joined. B: Co. Langford, IRE, laborer. Dark eyes, dark hair, ruddy complexion, 5'7.

Ganson, Charles. Pvt. Co. H, 12 August 1861 (age 34 at Philadelphia, PA)–9 January 1863. B: Co. Down, IRE, porter. Brown eyes, dark hair, dark complexion, 5'10. Disability discharge at camp near Falmouth, VA.

Gantey, Frederick U. Pvt. Cos. C, L, 2 December 1861 (age 21 at Philadelphia, PA)–2 December 1864. B: Lancaster Co., PA, farmer. Grey eyes, brown hair, fair complexion, 5'11. Discharged at Winchester, VA.

Gardner, Theodore C. Mustered: Pvt. Co. K, 8th OH Inf. 27 April–5 June 1861. Reenlisted. Transferred: Sgt. Co. C, 6th U.S. Cav. 23 October 1862 (age 19 at Knoxville, MD)–26 June 1864. B: 1843, Medina Co., OH. Blue eyes, light hair, fair complexion, 5'9½. Discharged in the field, VA. D: 24 July 1908, Big Rapids, Mecosta, MI.

Gargan, James "Jim." Pvt. Co. F, 6 July 1861 (age 29 at Pittsburgh, PA)–3 December 1861. B: Co. Kilkenny, IRE, coal miner. Grey eyes, sandy hair, fair complexion, 5'6. D: 3 December 1861 of fever. Note: James and Peter were brothers.

Gargan, Peter. Pvt. Co. F, 6 July 1861 (age 34 at Pittsburgh, PA)–27 January 1862. B: Co. Kilkenny, IRE, coal miner. Grey eyes, light hair, fair complexion, 5'7. Deserted.

Garrard, Charles T. Mustered: Pvt. Co. H, 7th OH Inf. Transferred: Cpl.-QM Sgt. Cos. K, F&S, 6th U.S. Cav. 23 October 1862 (age 19 at Knoxville, MD)–12 October 1865. B: Portage Co., OH. Brown eyes, black hair, florid complexion, 6'. Reenlisted: 10 February 1864 at Brandy Station, VA. Deserted 12 October 1865. Discharged at Washington, D.C. under Act of Congress, approved 1 August 1892.

Garrington, James C. Pvt. Co. M, 29 December 1861 (age 23 at Pittsburgh, PA)–5 April 1865. B: Coburgh, CAN, boatman. Blue eyes, sandy hair, light complexion, 5'5½. Reported MIA 16 February 1865 at Annapolis, MD. Discharged at Annapolis, MD.

Gates, Emanuel E. Musician-Band Leader. Co. F&S, 15 October 1861 (age 48 at Mount Joy, PA)–31 July 1862. B: SWZ, musician. Hazel eyes, black hair, ruddy complexion, 5'5. Disability discharge. Note: Emmanuel and John were father and son.

Gates, John L. Musician. Co. F&S, 15 October 1861 (age 24 at Mount Joy, PA)–15 October 1864. B: Cape May Co., NJ, musician. Grey eyes, brown hair, sallow complexion, 5'8½. Discharged at Strausburg, VA.

Gaunt, Benjamin E. Pvt. Co. A, 23 September

1861 (age 21 at Philadelphia, PA)–18 June 1865. B: Milford, NJ, laborer. Lt. blue eyes, light hair, light complexion, 5'7½. Deserted 26 March 1862. Apprehended 8 July 1864. Deserted 18 June 1865.

Gaynor, Thomas. Rct. 25 November 1864 (age 21 at Harrisburg, PA)–No further information. B: Liverpool, ENG, painter. Grey eyes, brown hair, fair complexion, 5'8.

Gebhardt, Friedrich. Pvt. Co. D, 7 August 1861 (age 33 at Pittsburgh, PA)–7 August 1864. B: Zoewlanger(?), GER, laborer. Grey eyes, brown hair, dark complexion, 5'7. Discharged at City Point, VA.

Gehrke, William. Pvt. Co. M, 12 September 1864 (age 19 at Harrisburg, PA)–16 October 1865. B: Bremen, GER, sailor. Blue eyes, fair hair, fair complexion, 5'7¾. Deserted.

Geissinger, John R. Mustered: Pvt. Co. B, 110th PA Inf. 24 October 1861. Transferred: Cpl. Co. D, 6th U.S. Cav. 28 October 1862 (age 19 at Knoxville, MD)–28 September 1864. B: Aug 1844, Huntingdon Twp., Huntingdon, PA. Grey eyes, dark hair, dark complexion, 5'8. Discharged in the field, VA. D: 7 February 1907, Dayton, Montgomery, OH.

George, C. W. Pvt. Co. I, 23 August 1861 (age 23 at Rochester, NY)–23 August 1864. B: Livingston Co., NY, farmer. Grey eyes, brown hair, brown complexion, 5'4½. Discharged at Harper's Ferry, VA.

Geould, William C. Pvt. Co. B, 6 August 1861 (age 23 at Cleveland, OH)–20 February 1862. B: Summit Co., OH, farmer. Blue eyes, brown hair, fair complexion, 5'4¾. Deserted.

Geritt, Stafford. Pvt. Co. L, 17 December 1861 (age 34 at Cleveland, OH)–22 July 1869. B: Cobert, CAN, carpenter. Grey eyes, brown hair, ruddy complexion, 5'5. Deserted 24 June 1862. Apprehended 28 February 1867. Joined 26 July 1867. Discharged 22 July 1869 at Pilot Grove, TX.

Gerlach, Conrad F. (alias Guardlock, Conrad). Mustered: Pvt. Co. I, 125th PA Inf. 13 August 1862–18 May 1863 (Harrisburg, PA). Mustered: Pvt. Co. A, 46th PA Inf. 8 March 1861. Enlisted: Chief Musician. Co. F&S, 6th U.S. Cav. 20 March 1865 (age 20 at NYC, NY)–10 April 1867. B: Frankfort, GER, musician. Hazel eyes, light hair, light complexion, 5'8½. Discharged by S. O. 153 at Austin, TX. Also served: 149th Co., 2nd Bn. VRC.

Geyer, John Jr. Musician. Co. F&S, 15 October 1861 (age 26 at Mount Joy, PA)–15 October 1864. B: Mount Joy, Lancaster Co., PA, musi-

cian. Blue eyes, brown hair, ruddy complexion, 5'10. Discharged at Strausburg, VA.

Gibbey, Marshall H. Pvt. Co. B, 2 August 1861 (age 22 at Columbus, OH)–11 October 1862. B: Washington Co., PA, farmer. Grey eyes, brown hair, sallow complexion, 5'7½. WIA (right arm during a skirmish), Sugar Loaf Mountain. Deserted.

Gibbons, Edward. Mustered: Pvt. Co. B, 8th OH Inf. 14 June 1861. Transferred: Pvt. Co. E, 6th U.S. Cav. 22 October 1862 (age 18 at Knoxville, MD)–14 June 1864. B: Cleveland, Cuyahoga Co., OH, painter. Blue eyes, light hair, florid complexion, 5'9½. Discharged in the field, VA.

Gibbons, Edward. Pvt. Cos. C, L, 16 December 1861 (age 21 at Philadelphia, PA)–20 August 1862. B: Chicago, IL, teamster. Grey eyes, brown hair, fair complexion, 5'11. Deserted.

Giberson, John. Pvt. Co. C, 6 January 1862 (age 21 at Philadelphia, PA)–25 March 1862. B: Berks Co., PA, farmer. Grey eyes, lt. brown hair, ruddy complexion, 5'8½. Deserted.

Gibson, Frederick G. Jr. Pvt. Co. I, 5 September 1861 (age 32 at Rochester, NY)–1 May 1862. B: Genesee Co., NY, farmer. Blue eyes, brown hair, dark complexion, 5'9¾. Deserted.

Gibson, William. Pvt. Co. I, 5 September 1861 (age 34 at Rochester, NY)–5 September 1864. B: Genesee Co., NY, farmer. Grey eyes, red hair, florid complexion, 5'10. Discharged in the field, VA.

Giel, Peter. Pvt. Cos. E, M, 3 September 1861 (age 35 at Cleveland, OH)–3 September 1864. B: Cleveland, Cuyahoga Co., OH, farmer. Blue eyes, brown hair, ruddy complexion, 5'7½. Discharged in the field, VA.

Giesecke, Franz. Emigrated: 10 May 1864 aboard the ship *Hansa*. Enlisted: Musician 1st Class. Co. F&S; 16 January 1865 (age 30 at NYC, NY)–10 April 1867. B: Ringelheim, Hanover, GER, musician. Grey eyes, brown hair, fair complexion, 5'3½. Discharged by S. O. 153 at Austin, TX.

Gilbert, Aaron. Pvt. Co. K, 5 August 1861 (age 19 at Warren, OH)–5 August 1864. B: Jackson Co., OH, farmer. Grey eyes, light hair, light complexion, 5'8½. Discharged at City Point, VA.

Gilbert, Hiram. Pvt. Co. K, 8 August 1861 (age 21 at Warren, OH)–8 August 1864. B: Jackson Co., OH, farmer. Blue eyes, light hair, light complexion, 5'8. MIA, Fairfield. Returned the same day. Discharged at City Point, VA.

Gilbreath, Joseph S. Cpl. Co. B, 29 July 1861 (age 31 at Columbus, OH)–29 July 1864. B: Portage

Co., OH, farrier. Blue eyes, brown hair, sallow complexion, 5'6. Discharged at Lighthouse Point, VA.

Gillen, Jacob. Pvt. Cos. C, L, 14 December 1861 (age 22 at York Co., PA)–8 January 1863. B: Lancaster Co., PA, miller. Black eyes, dark hair, ruddy complexion, 5'6. D: 8 January 1863 from consumption at Belle Plain, VA.

Gillespie, James W. Pvt. Co. A, 25 November 1864 (age 23 at Harrisburg, PA)–25 April 1865. B: Toronto, CAN, cord wounder. Grey eyes, brown hair, ruddy complexion, 5'6½. D: 25 April 1865, from accidental GSW at Washington, D.C.

Gilliams, Charles. Bugler, Co. F, 2nd U.S. Cav. 23 August 1856 (Philadelphia, PA)–23 August 1861 (Hyattsville, MD). Enlisted: 1st Sgt.-Chief Bugler–Pvt. Cos. M, F&S, M, 6th U.S. Cav. 18 September 1861 (age 23 at Pottsville, PA)–26 December 1862. B: 14 February 1838, Philadelphia, PA. Blue eyes, lt. brown hair, florid complexion, 5'6. Disability discharge at NYC. Mustered: Bugler, Co. L, 7th PA Cav. 8 February 1864–23 August 1865. D: 29 September 1896, Reading, Berks, PA. He is buried beneath the soldiers monument for which he posed.

Ginnis, Charles. Pvt. Co. M, 13 September 1864 (age 19 at Harrisburg, PA)–October 1864. B: Washington, D.C., boatman. Blue eyes, brown hair, ruddy complexion, 5'6. Deserted 16 October 1864. Apprehended October 1864. Deserted.

Gipson, Samuel F. Pvt. Co. F, 26 October 1864 (age 21 at Cincinnati, OH)–7 January 1865. B: ENG, coal miner. Blue eyes, light hair, fair complexion, 5'4. Deserted. Sub.

Glazier, Jabez. Mustered: Pvt. Co. C, 60th NY Inf. 28 September 1861. Transferred: Pvt. Co. H, 6th U.S. Cav. 28 October 1862 (age 21 at Knoxville, MD)–20 September 1863. B: Fowler, NY, farmer. Blue eyes, brown hair, fair complexion, 5'8. D: 20 September 1863 from chronic diarrhea at U.S. Army General Hospital, Alexandra, VA.

Glenn, William. Pvt. Co. A, 17 September 1861 (age 21 at Philadelphia, PA)–September 17, 1864. B: Philadelphia, PA, shoemaker. Hazel eyes, brown hair, dark complexion, 5'8. POW, Funkstown, 7 July 1863–18 January 1864. Paroled, reported at Annapolis, MD. Discharged at Harper's Ferry, VA.

Gliby, Frederick. Pvt. Co. C, 5 December 1861 (age 29 at Bristol, PA)–24 March 1862. B: Saxony, GER, farmer. Grey eyes, brown hair, dark complexion, 5'3½. Deserted.

Gloor, Jacob. Pvt. Co. I, 24 September 1861 (age 25 at Rochester, NY)–13 September 1862. B: SWZ, barber. Brown eyes, brown hair, light complexion, 5'3. Deserted.

Glyn, John. Rct. 9 June 1864 (age 24 at Groveland, NY)–11 June 1864. B: Toronto, CAN, cooper. Brown eyes, brown hair, ruddy complexion, 5'5¼. Deserted.

Goen, Joseph A. Pvt. Co. L, 2 January 1865 (age 21 at Cincinnati, OH)–25 September 1865. B: Augusta Co., VA, farmer. Hazel eyes, brown hair, fair complexion, 5'7¾. Deserted.

Goffield, Vord. Pvt. Co. D, 24 August 1861 (age 24 at Pittsburgh, PA)–24 August 1864. B: Madison Co., NY, miner. Hazel eyes, black hair, dark complexion, 5'5. Discharged at Bolivar Heights, VA.

Goist, George W. Pvt. Co. K, 30 July 1861 (age 20 at Warren, OH)–27 June 1862. B: Liberty Twp., Butler Co., OH, farmer. Black eyes, black hair, dark complexion, 5'9½. Disability discharge at Annapolis, MD.

Golaspie, John. Pvt. Co. L, 10 December 1864 (age 23 at Cincinnati, OH)–29 January 1865. B: Toronto, CAN, farmer. Hazel eyes, brown hair, fair complexion, 5'7½. Deserted. Sub.

Gordon, George F. Pvt. Co. D, 29 July 1861 (age 21 at Warren, OH)–No further information. B: Lancashire, ENG, farmer. Blue eyes, light hair, sandy complexion, 5'9½.

Gordon, Thomas W. Mustered: Pvt. Co. F, 8th OH Inf. 5 June 1861–16 October 1862. Discharged. Enlisted: Pvt. Co. B, 6th U.S. Cav. 28 October 21 1862 (age 35 at Knoxville, MD)–28 April 1864. B: Boston, MA. Grey eyes, light hair, light complexion, 5'7½. Discharged in the field, VA.

Gorman, Michael C. O. Pvt.-Sgt. Co. I, 26 August 1861 (age 21 at Rochester, NY)–26 August 1864. B: Essex Co., NY, farmer. Blue eyes, black hair, florid complexion, 5'11. WIA, Brandy Station. Extracted an officer from the hands of the enemy at Funkstown, 7 July 1863. Discharged in the field, VA.

Gorman, Patrick. Mustered: Pvt. Co. A, 3rd WI Inf. 16 April 1861. Transferred: Pvt. Co. F, 6th U.S. Cav. 24 October 1862 (age 20 at Knoxville, MD)–8 February 1867. B: Northampton, MA. Blue eyes, brown hair, florid complexion, 5'3. WIA, Five Forks, 30 March 1865. Reenlisted: 9 February 1864 at Camp 6th Cav., VA. Discharged at Jackson, TX.

Gormley, Frank P. RQM. Sgt.-Pvt. Cos. F&S, E, 23 July 1861 (age 22 at Pittsburgh, PA)–31 May

1862. B: Brownsville, Fayette Co., PA, steamboat clerk. Hazel eyes, black hair, ruddy complexion, 5'9. Transferred from being the RQM Sgt. to being a Pvt., Co. E on 1 March 1862. He deserted days later.

Gosney, John W. Pvt. Co. M, 31 October 1861 (age 30 at Pittsburgh, PA)–26 January 1862. B: Allegheny Co., PA, cook. Hazel eyes, brown hair, florid complexion, 5'8. Deserted.

Goss, John. Mustered: Pvt. Co. K, 110th PA Inf. 19 December 1861. Transferred: Pvt. Co. C, 6th U.S. Cav. 24 October 1862 (age 20 at Knoxville, MD)–24 October 1864. B: Clearfield Co., PA. Blue eyes, black hair, fair complexion, 5'8. Discharged in the field, VA.

Goss, Richard A. Mustered: Pvt. Co. K, 110th PA Inf. 19 December 1861. Transferred: Pvt. Co. I, 6th U.S. Cav. 27 October 1862 (age 23 at Knoxville, MD)–27 October 1864. B: 1836, Clearfield Co., PA, farmer. Hazel eyes, brown hair, dark eyes, 5'8. Discharged in the field, VA. D: 1897, Sanborn, Clearfield, PA

Gould, George. Pvt. Co. A, 26 November 1864 (age 18 at Cincinnati, OH)–8 February 1869. B: Cayuga Co., NY, farmer. Blue eyes, brown hair, fair complexion, 5'11. Deserted 17 February 1866. Apprehended 23 May 1867. Discharged 8 February 1869 at Pilot Grove, TX.

Goultsch, David. Pvt.-Sgt. Co. D, 7 August 1861 (age 29 at Pittsburgh, PA)–7 August 1864. B: 1831, Mersin(?), GER, moulder. Brown eyes, brown hair, sallow complexion, 5'5. Discharged at City Point, VA. D: 9 June 1901, Erie, Erie, PA.

Gourley, James G. Pvt. Co. M, 18 November 1861 (age 26 at Pittsburgh, PA)–1 June 1864. B: Allegheny City, PA, stone cutter. Grey eyes, light hair, light complexion, 5'6. POW, Fairfield. Paroled at Annapolis, MD, 20 August 1863. Disability discharge at Judiciary Square Hospital, Washington D.C.

Graf, John C. Pvt. Co. I, 25 September 1861 (age 18 at Rochester, NY)–11 June 1862. B: GER, butcher. Grey eyes, brown hair, dark complexion, 5'5. Deserted.

Graham, William. Pvt. Co. A, 16 September 1861 (age 30 at Philadelphia, PA)–16 September 1864. B: Bainbridge, IRE, book keeper. Hazel eyes, light hair, fair complexion, 6'½. Discharged at Harper's Ferry, VA.

Gramlich, Francis Joseph. Mustered: Pvt. Co. H, 34th PA Inf. 21 June 1861. Transferred: Pvt. Co. A, 6th U.S. Cav. 29 October 1862 (age 22 at Knoxville, MD)–22 June 1864. B: 1840, Northumberland Co., PA. Blue eyes, light hair, light complexion, 5'5½. WIA, Beverly Ford. Discharged at White House Landing, VA. Reenlisted: Clerk, GS, 5 July 1864–17 August 1865. Discharged by appointment as a clerk, AGO. Orderly Sgt. (Clerk), AGO, 17 August 1865 (Washington, D.C.)–17 August 1868. D: 2 April 1896, Prince George's Co., MD.

Gramm, George W. Mustered: Pvt. Co. C, 14th IN Inf. 7 June 1861. Transferred: Pvt. Co. C, 6th U.S. Cav. 23 October 1862 (age 20 at Knoxville, MD)–23 November 1863. B: Tuscarawas Co., OH, farmer. Hazel eyes, light hair, fair complexion, 5'9. POW, Fairfield. D: 24 November 1863 of chronic diarrhea in General Hospital No. 21, Richmond, VA.

Gray, John. Pvt. Co. C, 13 September 1864 (age 19 at Rochester, NY)–Never joined. B: Mitchell, West Can., CAN, teamster. Grey eyes, brown hair, fair complexion, 5'6.

Green, Dick. Pvt. Co. A, 27 October 1864 (age 19 at Rochester, NY)–24 January 1865. B: Albany, NY, boatman. Grey eyes, light hair, fair complexion, 5'9. Deserted.

Green, James T. Mustered: Pvt. Co. K, 8th OH Inf. 27 April–5 June 1861. Reenlisted. Transferred: Pvt. Co. 6th U.S. Cav. E, 22 October 1862 (age 21 at Knoxville, MD)–26 May 1864. B: Ball, OH, farmer. Blue eyes, light hair, light complexion. 5'8. POW, Fairfield, 3 July–11 November 1863. Paroled, reported at Camp 6th Cav. Discharged in the field, VA.

Green, John. Mustered: Pvt. Co. C, 3rd WI Inf. 27 May 1861. Transferred: Pvt. Co. C, 6th U.S. Cav. 24 October 1862 (age 21 at Knoxville, MD). B: Bronson, Branch, MI, farmer. Grey eyes, brown hair, dark complexion, 5'10½. Returned to USV. D: 14 April 1864 of disease at Fayetteville, TN.

Green, Luke. Pvt. Co. L, 6 November 1861 (age 32 at Cleveland, OH)–9 June 1862. B: Co. Roscommon, IRE, laborer. Grey eyes, sandy hair, ruddy complexion, 5'10. Disability discharge at Washington, D.C.

Greene, Thomas. Bugler. Co. A, 7 July 1864 (age 19 at NYC, NY)–7 July 1867. B: Co. Kilkenny, IRE, clerk. Blue eyes, brown hair, fair complexion, 5'9½. Discharged at Buffalo Springs, TX.

Greener, Adolph. Pvt. Co. F, 15 July 1861 (age 26 at Pittsburgh, PA)–17 April 1862. B: Oekran, GER, coal miner. Grey eyes, brown hair, dark complexion, 5'8. Disability discharge at Washington, D.C. Mustered: Pvt. Co. D, 5th PA Cav. 12 July 1864–7 August 1865 (Richmond, VA).

Greenwood, Thomas J. Pvt. Co. B, 5 August 1861 (age 21 at Cleveland, OH)–5 August 1864. B: Girard Twp., Erie Co., PA, harness maker. Grey eyes, light hair, sallow complexion, 5' 4½. Discharged at Lighthouse Point, VA.

Grey, James. Pvt. Co. L, 17 June 1864 (age 18 at Brighton, NY)–18 August 1864. B: Columbiana Co., OH, clerk. Blue eyes, light hair, ruddy complexion, 5'10. Discharged.

Grieble, Henry. Pvt. Co. B, 13 August 1861 (age 21 at Columbus, OH)–13 August 1864. B: Hanover, GER, farmer. Grey eyes, brown hair, sallow complexion, 5' 8. MIA, Funkstown. Discharged at Washington, D.C.

Griffin, Benjamin. Mustered: Pvt. Co. A, 82nd OH Inf. 8 November 1861–20 August 1862. Disability discharged. Enlisted: Pvt. Co. C, 6th U.S. Cav. 28 October 1862 (age 22 at Knoxville, MD)–17 September 1864. B: Bradford Co., PA. Grey eyes, dark hair, light complexion, 5'11½. POW, Fairfield, 3 July 1863–7 January 1864. Paroled, reported at Annapolis, MD. Discharged at Berryville, VA.

Grinnell, George William. Mustered: Pvt. Co. F, 1st MN Inf. 24 May 1861. Transferred: Cpl. Co. B, 26 October 1862 (age 22 at Knoxville, MD)–26 April 1864. B: Baltimore, MD. Blue eyes, light hair, light complexion, 5' 8½. Discharged in the field, VA. D: SD

Grisom, Franklin. Pvt. Co. F, 10 November 1864 (age 19 at Cincinnati, OH)–30 July 1865. B: Hendrick Co., IN, farmer. Grey eyes, brown hair, dark complexion, 5' 6. Deserted.

Grogan, William W. Pvt. Co. L, 17 June 1864 (age 27 at Spartan, NY)–17 June 1867. B: Edinburgh, SCO, laborer. Grey eyes, brown hair, ruddy complexion, 5' 8. Discharged at Ft. Belknap, TX.

Groomes, Morris. Pvt. Co. K, 21 July 1861 (age 15 at Columbus, OH)–5 June 1862. B: Clinton Co., OH, teamster. Blue eyes, black hair, ruddy complexion, 5' 4. Disability discharge at camp near Richmond, VA.

Groomes, Thomas C. Pvt. Co. B, 18 July 1861 (age 28 at Columbus, OH)–8 February 1867. B: Clinton/Chester Co., OH, tailor. Grey eyes, black hair, ruddy complexion, 5' 6. Reenlisted: 8 February 1864 at Camp 6th Cav., VA. Discharged at Jackson, TX. D: 9 July 1892, Cedar Vale, Chautauqua, KS.

Gross, James L. Mustered: Pvt. Co. G, 42nd PA Inf. 27 July 1861. Transferred: Pvt. Co. E, 6th U.S. Cav. 28 October 1862 (age 22 at Knoxville, MD)–15 February 1864. B: Elk Co., PA, farmer. Blue eyes, light hair, ruddy complexion, 6' 2. POW, Fairfield, 3 July 1863–15 February 1864. D: 15 February 1864 from chronic diarrhea as a POW at Richmond, VA.

Gross, Sebastian. Pvt. Co. F, 9 July 1861 (age 22 at Pittsburgh, PA)–29 July 1864. B: Merzhausen, GER, blacksmith. Grey eyes, black hair, dark complexion, 5' 8. WIA, Fairfield. Disability discharge at West Philadelphia, PA.

Grover, Philo. Mustered: Pvt. Co. E, 8th OH Inf. 25 June 1861. Transferred; Pvt. Co. G, 27 October 1862 (age 19 at Knoxville, MD)–25 June 1864. B: Bellevue, OH, farmer. Hazel eyes, light hair, light complexion, 5' 9. MIA, Fairfield. Discharged at Wyanoke, VA. Enlisted. Pvt. Co. H, 6th U.S.V.V. Inf.

Grunsteidel, Karl. Immigrated: 20 June 1861 aboard the ship *Germanic*. Enlisted: Pvt. Cos. C, L, 2 November 1861 (age 22 at Philadelphia, PA)–11 July 1862. B: Wurttemberg, GER, miller. Blue eyes, light hair, fair complexion, 5' 4½. D: 11 July 1862 from typhoid fever at Washington, D.C.

Grush, Andrew. Mustered: Pvt. Co. A, 3rd MD Inf. Transferred: Pvt. Co. K, 6th U.S. Cav. 26 October 1862 (age 20 at Knoxville, MD)–27 August 1864. B: Lancaster Co., PA. Dark eyes, dark hair, dark complexion, 5' 8. Discharged in the field, VA.

Gushard, Peter D. (alias Gushart, Deader; alias Gushart, Peter; alias Miller, John H.). Mustered: Pvt. Co. G, 26th OH Inf. 18 July 1861 (unknown service time). Enlisted: Pvt. Co. L, 6th U.S. Cav. 19 November 1861 (age 17 at Cleveland, OH)–13 April 1862. B: Sinton, OH, painter. Light eyes, light hair, ruddy complexion, 5' 3. Deserted. Mustered: Pvt. Batt. M, 1st MI Light Art. 11 August–10 September 1863. Deserted. Enlisted: U.S.N., served on the S.S. *Fairplay*, 1863–1864.

Hackett, Andrew. Pvt. Co. A, 20 September 1861 (age 34 at Philadelphia, PA)–26 January 1863. B: Wolverhampton, Staffordshire, ENG, blacksmith. Blue eyes, light hair, light complexion, 5' 8½. D: 26 January 1863 of disease at Belle Plain, VA.

Hadden, Samuel. Pvt. Co. B, 26 July 1861 (age 26 at Columbus, OH)–24 July 1864. B: Putnam Valley, Putnam Co., NY, carpenter. Grey eyes, brown hair, ruddy complexion, 5' 8. Discharged at Lighthouse Point, VA.

Haffner, Louis. Pvt. Co. F, 7 July 1861 (age 23 at Pittsburgh, PA)–6 August 1862. B: Wurttemberg, GER, butcher. Grey eyes, brown hair, ruddy complexion, 5' 6½. Disability discharge at Washington, D.C. Reenlisted: Pvt. Co. F,

13th U.S. Inf. 28 June 1869. Discharged 28 June 1874. Reenlisted: Pvt. Co. E, 13th U.S. Inf. 26 July 1879. Discharged: 25 July 1884. Reenlisted: 26 July 1884. Disability discharged 23 July 1888.

Hagan, James. Pvt. Co. A, 9 December 1864 (age 26 at Carlisle, PA)–3 January 1865. B: Co. Kilkenny, IRE, painter. Grey eyes, light hair, ruddy complexion, 5' 9½. Deserted. Sub.

Haight, George W. Pvt. Co. E, 9 September 1861 (age 18 at Adrian, MI)–31 January 1863. B: Adrian, MI, farmer. Hazel eyes, brown hair, ruddy complexion, 5' 8. Disability discharge at Convalescent Camp, VA.

Haines, Theodore C. Pvt. Co. H, 2 August 1861 (age 19 at Philadelphia, PA)–2 August 1864. B: Gloucester, Camden Co., NJ, farmer. Hazel eyes, brown hair, ruddy complexion, 5' 6½. Discharged at Sandy Fork, MD.

Hale, Lyman W. Pvt. Co. E, 2 September 1861 (age 19 at Cleveland, OH)–August 1862. B: Summit Co., OH, farmer. Blue eyes, light hair, ruddy complexion, 5' 7½. WIA, Malvern Hill, 6 August 1862. Sick from wounds. D: on his way from Ft. Monroe to New York City.

Hall, George. Pvt. Co. L, 9 December 1864 (age 37 at Cincinnati, OH)–31 March 1865. B: Essex Co., CAN, farmer. Hazel eyes, dark hair, ruddy complexion, 5' 6½. Deserted.

Hall, Henry. Mustered: Pvt. Co. B, 8th OH Inf. 17 June 1861. Transferred: Pvt. Co. C, 6th U.S. Cav. 22 October 1862 (age 21 at Knoxville, MD)–16 June 1864. B: Gowanda, NY. Hazel eyes, brown hair, dark complexion, 5' 3½. Discharged in the field, VA. D: 8 October 1924, Los Angeles, CA.

Hall, John. Pvt. Co. L, 22 October 1861 (age 18 at Cleveland, OH)–22 October 1864. B: GER, laborer. Grey eyes, brown hair, ruddy complexion, 5' 3. Discharged at Cedar Creek, VA.

Hall, John. Rct. 7 October 1864 (age 25 at Harrisburg, PA)–No further information. B: New York City, NY, boatman. Blue eyes, dark hair, ruddy complexion, 5' 6.

Hamiel, Benjamin. Pvt. Co. A, 28 November 1864 (age 18 at Cincinnati, OH)–2 January 1866. B: Boone Co., KY, farmer. Blue eyes, light hair, fair complexion, 5' 3¾. Deserted 31 March 1865. Surrendered 8 May 1865. Deserted 2 January 1866. Sub.

Hamilton, John. Pvt. Co. A, 8 December 1864 (age 23 at Carlisle, PA)–30 May 1865. B: Cayuga, CAN, sailor. Blue eyes, light hair, ruddy complexion, 5'10. Deserted. Sub.

Hamilton, Samuel. Pvt. Co. F, 14 August 1861 (age

23 at Pittsburgh, PA)–20 November 1863. B: Allegheny Co., PA, corker. Grey eyes, light hair, light complexion, 5' 8½. Disability discharge at Convalescent Camp, Alexandria, VA.

Hamilton, Samuel M. Pvt. Co. E, 16 September 1861 (age 34 at Adrian, MI)–16 September 1864. B: Perinton, Monroe Co., NY, farmer. Blue eyes, light hair, sallow complexion, 5' 9. Discharged at Berryville, VA.

Hamilton, Thomas J. Pvt. Co. A, 27 July 1861 (age 26 at Columbus, OH)–No further information. B: Co. Londonderry, IRE, soldier. Grey eyes, brown hair, sallow complexion, 5'10½.

Hanland, James. Pvt. Co. D, 30 August 1861 (age 30 at Pittsburgh, PA)–31 August 1864. B: Co. Louth, IRE, laborer. Blue eyes, brown hair, light complexion, 5'11½. Discharged at Charlestown, VA.

Hannah, Wesley. Pvt. Co. D, 9 August 1861 (age 23 at Pittsburgh, PA)–9 August 1864. B: Erie Co., PA, baker. Grey eyes, red hair, light complexion, 5' 4½. Discharged at City Point, VA.

Happersett, William H. Rct. 5 November 1864 (age 19 at Cincinnati, OH)–21 November 1864. B: Evansville, Vanderburgh Co., IN, engineer. Grey eyes, brown hair, fair complexion, 5' 4½. Deserted.

Hardee, John. Pvt. Co. M, 16 September 1864 (age 29 at Harrisburg, PA). B: Glasgow, SCO, miner. Hazel eyes, fair hair, florid complexion, 5'10. Deserted.

Hardy, Harrison N. Pvt. Co. B, 8 August 1861 (age 22 at Cleveland, OH)–13 December 1861. B: Buford Co., OH, farmer. Grey eyes, black hair, ruddy complexion, 5' 9. D: 13 December 1861 of smallpox at Kalorama Hospital, Washington, D.C.

Hare, John W. Cpl. Co. B, 5 August 1861 (age 26 at Columbus, OH)–5 August 1864. B: Chester Co., PA, carpenter. Hazel eyes, black hair, sallow complexion, 5' 7. MIA, Fairfield. Discharged at Lighthouse Point, VA.

Hargr[e]aves, Henry. Pvt. Co. F, 8 July 1861 (age 33 at Pittsburgh, PA). B: Lancashire Co., ENG, coal miner. Lt. grey eyes, sandy hair, ruddy complexion, 5' 8. Deserted to the enemy.

Hariel, Isam. Rct. 28 November 1864 (age 20 at Cincinnati, OH)–? B: KY, farmer. Blue eyes, light hair, fair complexion, 5' 8. Deserted.

Harigon, James. Pvt. Co. L, 19 December 1864 (age 19 at Cincinnati, OH)–27 July 1865. B: CAN, teamster. Grey eyes, brown hair, fair complexion, 5' 5½. Deserted.

Harrel, James. Mustered: Pvt. Co. D, 14th IN Inf. 7 June 1861. Transferred: Rct. 6th U.S. Cav. 22

October 1862 (age 23 at Knoxville, MD)–November/December 1862. B: Greene Co., IN. Hazel eyes, brown hair, dark complexion, 5' 6½. Returned to USV. Discharged: 16 July 1864, Indianapolis, IN.

Harrel, John M. Mustered: Pvt. Co. D, 14th IN Inf. 7 June 1861. Transferred: Rct. 6th U.S. Cav. 23 October 1862 (age 21 at Knoxville, MD)–November/December 1862. B: 4 December 1840, Greene Co., IN, farmer. Black eyes, black hair, florid complexion, 5' 8½. Returned to USV. Disability discharged 20 February 1863. D: 27 October 1897, Perkins, Payne, OK.

Harrington, John. Mustered: Pvt. Co. E, 1st MN Inf. 23 May 1861. Transferred: Pvt. Co. C, 6th U.S. Cav. 28 October 1862 (age 28 at Knoxville, MD)–June 1864. B: New Brunswick, CAN. Grey eyes, red hair, light complexion, 6'. POW (captured by guerrillas), Auburn, VA, 9 November 1863–7 January 1864. Paroled, reported at Annapolis, MD. Discharged in the field, VA.

Harris, Amos Eugene. Mustered: Pvt. Co. H, 3rd WI Inf. 27 March 1862. Transferred: Pvt. Co. B, 6th U.S. Cav. 28 October 1862 (age 19 at Knoxville, MD)–27 March 1865. B: 16 November 1844, Cottage Grove, Dane, WI. Blue eyes, brown hair, ruddy complexion, 5' 5½. POW, Fairfield, 3 July 1863–? (Libby Prison). POW, Charlestown, 17 September 1864–? (Libby Prison). Discharged at Petersburg, VA. D: 12 December 1924, Worthing, Lincoln, SD.

Harris, Charles. Pvt. Co. A, 6 December 1864 (age 20 at Cincinnati, OH)–30 May 1865. B: Steubenville, Jefferson Co., OH, laborer. Blue eyes, brown hair, fair complexion, 5' 6. Deserted.

Harris, Thomas L. Pvt. Co. A, 17 November 1864 (age 35 at Cincinnati, OH)–1 February 1865. B: SCO, mason. Blue eyes, dark hair, ruddy complexion, 5' 7½. Deserted.

Harrison, Cornelius D. Pvt. Co. K, 22 July 1861 (age 21 at Franklin, PA)–27 July 1864. B: Ulster Co., NY, farmer. Dk. hazel eyes, dk. brown hair, dark complexion, 5' 9¾. Discharged in the field, VA.

Harrison, James. Pvt. Cos. C, L, 4 January 1862 (age 21 at Philadelphia, PA). B: Belfast, IRE, boatman. Grey eyes, light hair, fair complexion, 6'. Deserted 23 March 1862. Apprehended 27 October 1863.

Harrown, George T. Mustered: Pvt. Co. H, 1st MN Inf. 29 April 1861. Pvt. Co. B, 28 October 1862 (age 19 at Knoxville, MD)–26 May 1864.

B: IL, farmer. Grey eyes, auburn hair, light complexion, 5' 5. POW, Fairfield, 3 July 1863–22 May 1864. Paroled, reported at Camp 6th Cav. Discharged at Camp 6th Cav., VA. Mustered: Pvt. Co. I, 22nd WI Inf. 30 September 1864–24 June 1865. D: 19 March 1887, St. Louis, MO.

Hart, Henry. Rct. 13 September 1864 (age 23 at Harrisburg, PA)–Never joined. B: Manson, IRE, laborer. Grey eyes, dark hair, fair complexion, 5' 11½. Sub.

Hart, William. Pvt. Co. K, 5 August 1861 (age 19 at Warren, OH)–26 October 1862. B: Niagra Co., PA, boatman. Hazel eyes, brown hair, brown complexion, 5' 7¾. Deserted.

Hart, William. Rct. 13 September 1864 (age 23 at Harrisburg, PA)–Never joined. B: Manaen, IRE, tobacconist. Blue eyes, auburn hair, florid complexion, 5' 9.

Hartman, Henry. Mustered: Pvt. Co. N, 28th PA Inf. 26 August 1861. Transferred: Pvt. Co. B, 6th U.S. Cav. 25 October 1862 (age 23 at Knoxville, MD)–23 December 1862. B: Espy, Columbia, PA, boatman. Black eyes, brown hair, dark complexion, 5' 8¾ D: 23 December 1862 at Belle Plain near Falmouth, VA.

Hartman, James. Pvt.-Sgt. Cos. B, H, 7 August 1861 (age 21 at Cleveland, OH)–11 February 1864. B: Brock, SWZ, teamster. Hazel eyes, black hair, ruddy complexion, 5' 6¾. Spent some time in Co. K, 4th Art. Reenlisted (Brandy Station): Sgt. Co. K, 4th U.S. Art. 11 February 1864. Discharged: 11 February 1867 at Ft. Delaware, DE.

Hartzel, Lewis H. Pvt. Co. M, 19 September 1861 (age 21 at Pittsburgh, PA)–12 April 1864. B: Beaver Co., PA, farmer. Hazel eyes, brown hair, dark complexion, 5' 6½. D: 12 April 1864 from chronic dysentery at Douglas Hospital, Washington, D.C.

Hartzell, Henry W. Pvt. Co. B, 29 July 1861 (age 19 at Columbus, OH)–29 July 1864. B: Westmoreland Co., PA, laborer. Grey eyes, brown hair, ruddy complexion, 5' 7½. Discharged at Lighthouse Point, VA.

Harvey, Alexander A. Mustered: Pvt. Co. F, 16th NY Inf. Transferred: Bugler, Co. A, 6th U.S. Cav. 25 October 1862 (age 21 at Knoxville, MD)–24 October 1864. B: 15 March 1843, Selkirkshire, SCO, druggist. Grey eyes, fair hair, fair complexion, 5' 5. Discharged at Middletown, VA. Reenlisted: U.S.M.C. Reenlisted: Co. G, 6th U.S. Cav., 13 February 1867–13 February 1872. Discharged, Ft. Dodge, KS, a 1st Sgt. D: 1917, Panama City, Bay, FL.

Harvey, Patrick. Rct. 19 August 1861 (age 19 at Rochester, NY)–22 August 1861. B: IRE, farmer. Grey eyes, light hair, light complexion, 5' 6. Disability discharge at Pittsburgh, PA. A rejected recruit.

Hase, Solomon. Pvt. Co. A, 20 September 1861 (age 17 at Columbus, OH)–24 March 1862. B: Franklin Co., OH, farmer. Blue eyes, brown hair, sallow complexion, 5' 8¼. Disability discharge at camp near Alexandria, VA.

Haskins, William H. Cpl. Co. G, 8 August 1861 (age 22 at Rochester, NY)–24 January 1863. B: Genesee Co., NY, laborer. Hazel eyes, brown hair, florid complexion, 5' 2½. Disability discharge at Convalescent Camp, VA.

Haslett, William. Pvt. Co. I, 5 August 1861 (age 28 at Indiana, PA)–24 February 1866. B: Indiana Co., PA, stone mason. Grey eyes, light hair, fair complexion, 5' 6. Reenlisted: 8 February 1864 at Brandy Station, VA. Discharged 24 February 1866.

Hastings, Norman L. Pvt. Co. M, 10 September 1861 (age 27 at Pittsburgh, PA)–22 November 1861. B: KY, soldier. Blue eyes, brown hair, light complexion, 5' 9. Deserted.

Hatch, Samuel G. Cpl. Co. B, 1 August 1861 (age 22 at Cleveland, OH)–1 August 1864. B: Aurora, OH, carpenter. Hazel eyes, brown hair, ruddy complexion, 5' 6¼. Discharged at Charlestown, VA.

Hattabough, Andrew J. Mustered: Pvt. Co. D, 14th IN Inf. 7 June 1861. Transferred: Pvt. Co. C, 6th U.S. Cav. 21 October 1862 (age 24 at Knoxville, MD)–June 1864. B: 1838, Greene Co., IN, farmer. Dark eyes, dark hair, dark complexion, 5' 4. POW, Fairfield, 3 July 1863–7 January 1864. Paroled, reported at Annapolis, MD. Discharged in the field, VA. D: 28 October 1924, Marco, Greene, IN.

Haulton, Daniel. Pvt. Cos. C, L, 20 October 1861 (age 30 at Philadelphia, PA)–7 August 1865, B: Carnaville, Co. Meath, IRE, laborer. Grey eyes, brown hair, florid complexion, 5' 4. MIA, Fairfield. Reenlisted: 15 February 1864 at Brandy Station, VA. Deserted.

Havens, Elias. Pvt. Co. E, 3 September 1861 (age 23 at Columbus, OH)–24 November 1862. B: Columbus, OH, teamster. Grey eyes, brown hair, ruddy complexion, 5' 9. D: 24 November 1862 from chronic diarrhea at Alexandria, VA.

Havens, George. Pvt. Co. E, 23 August 1861 (age 34 at Columbus, OH)–23 August 1864. B: Morris Co., OH, farmer. Hazel eyes, black hair, sallow complexion, 5' 7½. Discharged at Washington, D.C.

Havens, Silas N. Pvt. Co. G, 10 August 1861 (age 18 at Rochester, NY)–10 August 1864. B: Genesee Co., NY, laborer. Blue eyes, fair hair, fair complexion, 5' 5½. Discharged at Washington, D.C.

Hawkins, John. Rct. 6 June 1864 (age 20 at Avon, NY)–11 June 1864. B: Kinston, West, CAN, boatman. Grey eyes, lt. brown hair, fair complexion, 5' 8. Deserted.

Hayden, James. Sgt. Cos. D, L, 30 July 1861 (age 26 at Pittsburgh, PA)–30 July 1864. B: IRE, laborer. Blue eyes, brown hair, fair complexion, 5' 8¾. MIA/WIA, Fairfield. Discharged at Lighthouse Point, VA.

Heakin, Edward. Pvt. Co. D, 27 August 1861 (age 23 at Pittsburgh, PA)–26 November 1861. B: Staffordshire, ENG, miner. Brown eyes, dark hair, light complexion, 5' 7. Deserted.

Heakin, Joshua. Pvt. Co. D, 23 August 1861 (age 20 at Pittsburgh, PA)–21 June 1864. B: Staffordshire, ENG, miner. Blue eyes, light hair, light complexion, 5' 7. Right leg amputated at Stanton Hospital, Washington, D.C. D: 21 June 1864 from wounds.

Heck, Abraham. Pvt. Co. A, 2 October 1861 (age 21 at Pottsville, PA)–3 October 1864. B: Pine Grove, PA, boatman. Hazel eyes, sandy hair, fair complexion, 5' 4½. POW, Fairfield, 3 July–1 November 1863. Paroled, reported at Annapolis, MD. Discharged at Harrisonburg, VA.

Heckert, John. Mustered: Pvt. Co. K, 38th PA Inf. 4 May 1861. Transferred: Cpl. Co. M, 6th U.S. Cav. 28 October 1862 (age 23 at Knoxville, MD)–28 July 1864. B: Butler Co., PA, carpenter. Grey eyes, brown hair, fair complexion, 5' 9. Discharged in the field, VA.

Heckman, John. Pvt. Co. E, 13 September 1861 (age 22 at Adrian, MI)–13 September 1864. B: Mercer Co., PA, carpenter. Hazel eyes, brown hair, ruddy complexion, 5' 7. POW (captured while on duty), Madison Court-House, 25 September 1863–14 June 1864. Paroled, reported at White House. Discharged at Berryville, VA.

Hefler, Charles. Pvt. Co. F, 13 July 1861 (age 22 at Pittsburgh, PA)–13 July 1864. B: Ottobarian, Bavaria, GER, hostler. Black eyes, black hair, dark complexion, 5' 7. Discharged at Lighthouse Point, VA.

Hehn, Hyram. Pvt. Co. H, 12 August 1861 (age 22 at Philadelphia, PA)–12 August 1864. B: Schuylkill Co., PA, boatman. Blue eyes, light hair, fair complexion, 5'10¾. MIA in the field, April 1863. Discharged at Harper's Ferry, VA.

Heinberger, Phillipp. Pvt. Co. G, 2 August 1861

(age 23 at Erie Co., PA)–26 June 1862. B: Haslach, SWZ, farmer. Grey eyes, light hair, fair complexion, 6'. D: 26 June 1862 from fever at Hospital near Coal Harbor, VA.

Heinecke, Charles. Pvt. Co. A, 7 September 1861 (age 33 at Philadelphia, PA)–7 September 1864. B: Hanover, GER, soldier. Blue eyes, hazel hair, light complexion, 5'8. POW, Fairfield, 3 July 1863–18 January 1864. Paroled, reported at Annapolis, MD. Discharged at Halltown, VA.

Held, Charles. Musician. Co. F&S, 12 November 1861 (age 21 at Pittsburgh, PA)–15 December 1864. B: Wurttemberg, GER, musician. Brown eyes, brown hair, ruddy complexion, 5'5. Discharged at Carlisle Barracks, PA.

Hellings, Jesse. Q.M. Sgt.-Vet. Surg. Co. C, 18 November 1861 (age 22 at Bristol, PA)–14 January 1863. B: Berks Co., PA, farrier. Hazel eyes, brown hair, ruddy complexion, 5'10½. Disability discharge at Frederick, MD.

Helm, Edward R. Mustered: Pvt. Co. C, D, 110th PA Inf. 19 December 1861. Transferred: Pvt. Co. I, 6th U.S. Cav. 27 October 1862 (age 20 at Knoxville, MD). B: 21 September 1844, Union Co, PA, farmer. Blue eyes, light hair, fair complexion, 5'7. Dropped from 6th Cav. Ordered to report to Co. C, 110th Pa. Vols. by order of Gen. Hooker. Deserted Co. C, 14 March 1864. Mustered: Pvt. Co. I, 97th PA Inf. 22 February 1865–6 June 1865. D: 4 October 1940, PA.

Helmut, George. Pvt. Co. I, 12 August 1861 (age 30 at Cincinnati, OH)–12 August 1864. B: Ottenberg, GER, farmer. Blue eyes, brown hair, ruddy complexion, 5'5¾. Discharged at Harper's Ferry, VA.

Hemphill, James. Pvt.-Sgt. Co. H, 12 August 1861 (age 21 at Philadelphia, PA)–27 February 1867. B: Co. Tyrone, IRE, laborer. Hazel eyes, brown hair, ruddy complexion, 5'9. Reenlisted: 27 February 1864 at Camp 6th Cav., VA. Discharged at Austin, TX. D: 22 March 1880.

Hendershot, Martin V. Pvt. Co. L, 9 November 1861 (age 18 at Cleveland, OH)–14 May 1864. B: Cleveland, Cuyahoga Co., OH, butcher. Hazel eyes, brown hair, ruddy complexion, 5'6¼. Disability discharge at Camp east of Capitol, Washington, D.C. D: 1895, OH.

Hendershot, Sutton H. Pvt. Co. L, 6 November 1861 (age 21 at Cleveland, OH)–23 May 1862. B: Cleveland, Cuyahoga Co., OH, h"unr." Blue eyes, light hair, ruddy complexion, 5'8. Disability discharge at Washington, D.C. Mustered: Pvt. Cos. E, I, 10th OH Cav. 10 September 1862–3 May 1863 (died of disease).

Henry, Matthew. Pvt. Co. F, 9 December 1864 (age 20 at Cincinnati, OH)–24 January 1865. B: IRE, laborer. Blue eyes, brown hair, fair complexion, 5'7. Deserted.

Hensel, Benjamin F. Pvt. Co. H, 12 July 1861 (age 24 at Philadelphia, PA)–14 January 1862. B: Philadelphia, PA, saddler. Blue eyes, black hair, dark complexion, 5'4¾. Disability discharge at Washington, D.C. Mustered: Cpl. 118th PA Inf., 8 February 1862. Transferred: Co. A. 2 August 1862–31 October 1863. D: 25 December 1893, PA.

Henson, Joseph (alias Anson, Joseph). Pvt. Co. K, 19 August 1861 (age 17 at Rochester, NY)–4 May 1865. B: 1844. ENG, farmer. Blue yes, light hair, light complexion, 5'6½. POW (captured while on picket), White House, VA, 23 June 1864 and dropped from the rolls. Record also records discharged at Petersburg, VA upon expiration of service on 4 May 1865. D: 28 April 1897, Jackson, Jackson, MI.

Heres, Peter. Pvt. Co. M, 7 October 1864 (age 28 at Harrisburg, PA)–17 October 1867. B: Copenhagen, DEN, stone mason. Blue eyes, light hair, light complexion, 5'5½. Discharged at Mt. Pleasant, TX.

Herrmann, Louis. Pvt. Co. A, 11 October 1861 (age 22 at Philadelphia, PA)–11 October 1864. B: Casel, Brandenburg, GER, cabinet maker. Blue eyes, light hair, fair complexion, 5'8½. POW, Fairfield, 3 July–5 October 1863. Paroled, reported 5 October 1863 at Culpepper, VA. Discharged at Middleton, VA.

Hess, Charles Philip. Pvt.-Sgt.-1st. Sgt. Cos. A, C, 10 October 1861 (age 23 at Philadelphia, PA)–10 October 1864. B: 9 September 1837, Langenlonsheim, Prussia, GER, wheel wright. Blue eyes, black hair, dark complexion, 5'7. WIA (left knee dislocated by a horse falling on him after it had been shot), Fairfield. Discharged at Cedar Creek, VA. Appointed a 2nd Lt. in the 27th U.S. Reserves. D: 26 August 1925, Macon, Macon, MO.

Hessom, Charles H. Mustered: Pvt. Co. E, 37th PA Inf. 24 April 1861. Transferred: Pvt. Co. E, 6th U.S. Cav. 28 October 1862 (age 22 at Knoxville, MD)–26 April 1863. B: 4 February 1840, Philadelphia, PA. Black eyes, black hair, dark complexion, 5'11. Deserted. Mustered: Pvt. Co. A, 51st IL Inf. 28 September 1864–16 June 1865. D: 5 June 1892, Pittsburgh, Allegheny, PA.

Heverin, Thomas. Pvt. Cos. F, B, 30 December 1861 (age 18 at Cincinnati, OH)–10 February 1867. B: Lawrence, IRE, laborer. Blue eyes, brown hair, ruddy complexion, 5'5. MIA, Fairfield. Reenlisted (Camp 6th Cav.): 9 February 1864. Discharged at Austin, TX. Reenlisted: 2nd U.S. Cav. 25 June 1868. Discharged 25 June 1873. Reenlisted: 20th U.S. Inf. 21 June 1873–14 November 1874. Discharged by S. O.

Hewett, William A. Pvt. Co. E, 13 September 1861 (age 18 at Cleveland, OH)–30 December 1862. B: Medina Co., OH, fisherman. Black eyes, brown hair, ruddy complexion, 5'6¼. D: 30 December 1862 at camp near Falmouth, VA.

Hewitt, James (alias Truesdal, Nathaniel). Rct. 19 August 1861 (age 18 at Rochester, NY)–22 August 1861. B: Binghamton, Broome Co., NY, farmer. Hazel eyes, light hair, dark complexion, 5'6. Rejected recruit at Pittsburgh, PA. Mustered: Pvt. Co. H, 3rd NY Cav. 26 August 1861 (Rochester, NY)–16 October 1861. Deserted at Dawsonville. Enlisted: Pvt. 33rd Batt. NY Art. 20 July 1863–18 January 1866. Deserted the same day he enlisted. Arrested 15 November 1863. Tried by GCM and sentenced to Ft. Delaware.

Heyse, Julius. Pvt. Co. F, 6 July 1861 (age 19 at Pittsburgh, PA)–8 July 1862. B: Berlin, Prussia, GER, cook and confectioner. Brown eyes, black hair, dark complexion, 5'8½. Deserted.

Hibbs, William. Pvt. Cos. C, L, 1 December 1861 (age 21 at Bristol, PA)–22 May 1865. B: Bucks Co., PA, farmer. Grey eyes, auburn hair, ruddy complexion, 5'4. Deserted 8 March 1862. Apprehended 9 December 1864. Deserted 22 May 1865. Gained from desertion 4 January 1864 from Philadelphia.

Hick, Joseph C. Mustered: Co. E, 163rd NY Inf. 27 August 1862. Transferred: Rct. 6th U.S. Cav. 21 October 1862 (age 19 at Knoxville, MD)–November/December 1862. B: Puchen, Baden, GER, founder. Blue eyes, brown hair, fair complexion, 5'6. Returned to USV. Transferred: Pvt. Co. B, 73rd NY Inf. 18 January 1863.

Hickey, Edward H. Pvt. Co. L, 7 December 1861 (age 34 at Cleveland, OH). B: Co. Limerick, IRE, laborer. Grey eyes, brown hair, ruddy complexion, 6'1. WIA, Fairfield. POW, Funkstown, 7 July 1863–31 August 1863. Paroled, reported at Fredericksburg. POW, Berryville, VA, 26 May 1864 and 16 August 1864 to ?

Higgins, James. Pvt. Co. L, 20 November 1861 (age 21 at Cleveland, OH)–31 January 1863. B: Cleveland, Cuyahoga Co., OH, cook. Grey eyes, light hair, sallow complexion, 5'11½. Disability discharge at Camp near Falmouth, VA.

Higgins, John. Pvt. Co. L, 7 December 1861 (age 34 at Cleveland, OH)–Not enough information. B: Belfast, IRE, laborer. Grey eyes, sandy hair, ruddy complexion, 5'10.

Higgins, Josephus. Rct. 1 November 1864 (age 24 at Rochester, NY)–21 November 1864. B: Yanceyville, NY, blacksmith. Hazel eyes, brown hair, dark complexion, 6'. Deserted.

Higgins, Michael. Pvt. Co. L, 7 December 1861 (age 21 at Cleveland, OH)–24 June 1862. B: Co. Dublin, IRE, railroad man. Blue eyes, sandy hair, ruddy complexion, 5'6½. Deserted.

Higgins, Webster R. Pvt. Co. L, 6 November 1861 (age 20 at Galion, OH)–19 February 1967. B: Washington Co., MD, cook. Grey eyes, light hair, sallow complexion, 5'11½. Reenlisted: 18 February 1864 at Brandy Station, VA. Discharged at Jacksboro, TX.

Hiland, John. Pvt. Co. D, 26 August 1861 (age 26 at Pittsburgh, PA)–26 August 1864. B: Co. Meath, IRE, laborer. Blue eyes, light hair, dark complexion, 5'5½. Discharged at Hillsboro, VA.

Hildenbrand, Christian F. Pvt. Co. M, 30 October 1861 (age 25 at Pittsburgh, PA)–3 July 1863. B: GER, baker. Hazel eyes, dark hair, dark complexion, 5'5½. KIA, Fairfield.

Hill, Adin. Mustered: Pvt. Co. C, 8th OH Inf. 23 April–22 June 1861. Reenlisted. WIA, Antietam. Transferred: Pvt. Co. G, 6th U.S. Cav. 28 October 1862 (age 23 at Knoxville, MD)–22 June 1863. B: February 1839, Buckeye, OH, farmer. Blue eyes, light hair, fair complexion, 5'9. Deserted.

Hill, Hiram. Pvt. Co. L, 8 June 1864 (age 19 at Avon, NY)–No further information. B: Le Ray, NY, farmer. Brown eyes, dark hair, fair complexion, 5'5.

Hill, John C. 1st Sgt. Co. M, 13 September 1861 (age 22 at Pittsburgh, PA)–13 September 1864. B: Westmoreland Co., PA, machinist. Blue eyes, brown hair, fair complexion, 5'10. Discharged at Berryville, VA.

Hill, John H. Pvt. Co. H, 5 August 1861 (age 18 at Philadelphia, PA)–21–31 August 1863. B: Philadelphia, PA, farmer. Grey eyes, light hair, fair complexion, 5'8. MIA, Fairfield. Deserted between 21–31 August at Camp Parole, MD.

Hill, Michael. Rct. 17 November 1864 (age 18 at Harrisburg, PA)–21 November 1864. B: Co. Dublin, IRE, sailor. Dark eyes, brown hair, fair complexion, 5'4¼. Deserted. Sub.

Hill, Pliny E. Mustered: Pvt. Co. B, 7th OH Inf. 20 June 1861. Transferred: Pvt. Co. L, 6th U.S. Cav. 27 October 1862 (age 18 at Knoxville, MD)–27 April 1864. B: Wayne Co., NY, farmer. Blue eyes, brown hair, fair complexion,

5' 8. WIA, Fairfield. Discharged at Brandy Station, VA.

Hillebolt, August. Pvt.-Chief Bugler. Co. F&S, 10 August 1861 (age 29 at Rochester, NY)–9 February 1863. B: Prussia, GER, bugler. Hazel eyes, brown hair, dark complexion, 5' 8¾. Deserted.

Hilles, Charles H. Pvt. Co. L, 14 November 1864 (age 19 at Cincinnati, OH)–14 November 1867. B: Cincinnati, Hamilton Co., OH, farmer. Hazel eyes, brown hair, fair complexion, 5' 4½. Discharged at Camp Wilson, TX.

Hillman, Arthur. Pvt. Co. M, 9 November 1861 (age 22 at Pittsburgh, PA)–31 March 1862. B: Allegheny Co., PA, farmer. Blue eyes, dark hair, light complexion, 5' 7½. Deserted.

Hines, James A. Mustered: Pvt. Co. G, 11th PA Inf. 24 April–31 July 1861 (Harrisburg, PA). Mustered: Co. F, 84th PA Inf. (unaccounted for). Transferred: Pvt. Co. A, 6th U.S. Cav. 28 October 1862 (age 21 at Knoxville, MD)–28 October 1864. B: Chester Co., PA. Blue eyes, light hair, light complexion, 5' 9. POW, Fairfield, 3 July 1863–2 February 1864. Paroled, reported at Baltimore, MD. Discharged near Middletown, VA.

Hiney, Matthew. Mustered: Pvt. Co. G, 50th PA Inf. 26 September 1861. Transferred: Pvt. Co. E, 6th U.S. Cav. 28 October 1862 (age 31 at Knoxville, MD)–2 October 1864. B: Bradford Co., PA. Brown eyes, grey hair, light complexion, 5'10. Deserted 20 December 1862. Apprehended 20 January 1863. WIA/POW, Fairfield, 3 July–30 August 1863. Reported in hospital 30 August 1863. Discharged 2 October 1864 in the field, VA.

Higley, John. Mustered: Pvt. Co. A, 11th PA Inf. 24 April–31 July 1861 (Harrisburg, PA). Enlisted: Pvt.-Cpl.-Pvt. Co. H, 6th U.S. Cav. 14 August 1861 (age 21 at Philadelphia, PA)–7 October 1866. B: Wurttemberg, GER, brick moulder. Hazel eyes, brown hair, fair complexion, 5' 9. WIA/MIA, Fairfield. Reenlisted: 19 March 1864 at Brandy Station, VA. Tried by GCM 26 September at Frederick, MD. Deserted.

Hinkel, Franz (Frank). Pvt. Co. M, 23 September 1864 (age 43 at Rochester, NY)–14 October 1865. B: 20 March 1820, Cowlden(?), GER, farmer. Grey eyes, light hair, florid complexion, 5' 6½. Disability discharge at Baltimore, MD. D: 16 December 1912, Chadwick, Carroll, IL.

Hinman, Benjamin. Mustered: Pvt. Co. E, 60th NY Inf. 20 September 1861. Transferred: Pvt. Co. M, 6th U.S. Cav. 19 October 1862 (age 23

at Knoxville, MD)–22 October 1864. B: December 1838, Franklin Co., NY. Blue eyes, light hair, fair complexion, 6'. Discharged in the field, VA. D: 9 March 1904, Bangor, Franklin, NY.

Hippard, Emanuel. Pvt. Co. C, 4 January 1862 (age 19 at Philadelphia, PA)–13 April 1862. B: Lancaster Co., PA, cabinet maker. Hazel eyes, brown hair, fair complexion, 5' 6½. Deserted.

Hitchcock, William. Pvt. Co. C, 29 July 1864 (age 18 at Providence, RI)–Not enough information. B: Newport, RI, operator. Blue eyes, auburn hair, light complexion, 5' 7.

Hoadley, Edward J. Pvt. Co. B, 5 August 1861 (age 22 at Cleveland, OH)–24 October 1862. B: Burton, OH, horseshoer. Hazel eyes, brown hair, florid complexion, 5' 8½. POW, Coal Harbor 27 June 1862–? Disability discharge at Ft. Monroe, VA.

Hoffman, Abraham. Pvt. Cos. C, L, 21 November 1861 (age 19 at Philadelphia, PA)–21 November 1864. B: Lancaster Co., PA, farmer. Brown eyes, brown hair, ruddy complexion, 5' 7½. Discharged near Winchester, VA.

Hoffman, Christian B. Pvt. Cos. C, L, 12 November 1861 (age 30 at Pittsburgh, PA)–16 February 1867. B: Lancaster Co., PA, miller. Grey eyes, brown hair, ruddy complexion, 5' 5. POW, ?–21 December 1863. Reported at Brandy Station. Reenlisted: 15 February 1864 at Brandy Station, VA. Discharged at Jacksboro, TX.

Hoffman, Daniel. Pvt. Co. H, 8 August 1861 (age 21 at Philadelphia, PA)–8 August 1864. B: Philadelphia, PA, boatman. Hazel eyes, dark hair, dark complexion, 5' 4¾. MIA, Fairfield. Discharged at Harper's Ferry, VA.

Hoffman, Lewis. Pvt. Co. F, 7 July 1861 (age 23 at Pittsburgh, PA)–6 August 1862. B: Wurttemberg, GER, butcher. Grey eyes, brown hair, ruddy complexion, 5' 6½. Disability discharge at Washington, D.C.

Hoffman, Samuel G. Pvt. Co. G, 8 August 1861 (age 18 at Rochester, NY)–26 June 1862. B: Genesee Co., NY, farmer. Grey eyes, light hair, florid complexion, 5' 9¾. Disability discharge at Convalescent Camp, VA.

Hoffner, Peter. Pvt. Co. I, 4 September 1861 (age 21 at Rochester, NY)–1 May 1863. B: Rochester, Monroe Co., NY, farmer. Grey eyes, brown hair, florid complexion, 5' 1¾. Deserted. Enlisted: 5 January 1864 in violation of the articles of war, in Co. E, 4th MI Cav. as Wm. P. Hopkins.

Hoffrichter, George A. Pvt.-Bugler. Cos. H, I, 22

July 1861 (age 17 at Columbus, OH)–22 July 1864. B: St. Louis, MO, shoemaker. Blue eyes, light hair, fair complexion, 5'2. Transferred: Co. I, 8 March 1864. Discharged in the field, VA.

Hogan, John. Mustered: Pvt. Co. B, 8th OH Inf. 5 June 1861. Transferred: Pvt. Co. C, 6th U.S. Cav. 22 October 1862 (age 25 at Knoxville, MD)–6 June 1864. B: Co. Limerick, IRE. Grey eyes, brown hair, dark complexion, 5'8½. Discharged in the field, VA.

Hogan, Richard. Pvt. Co. K, 8th OH Inf. 5 June 1861. Transferred: Pvt.-Cpl. Co. C, 6th U.S. Cav. 22 October 1862 (age 19 at Knoxville, MD)–26 May 1864. B: Co. Roscommon, IRE. Grey eyes, brown hair, dark complexion, 6'. MIA, Funkstown. Discharged in the field, VA.

Hogue, John C. Mustered: Pvt. Co. K, 14th IN Inf. 7 June 1861. Transferred; Pvt. Co. C, 6th U.S. Cav. 23 October 1862 (age 22 at Knoxville, MD)–10 April 1864. B: Putnam Co., IN, carpenter. Blue eyes, black hair, florid complexion, 5'9½. WIA, Funkstown. Disability discharge at Carlisle Barracks, PA.

Holbert, Freeland. Mustered: Pvt. Co. D, 32nd PA Inf. May 1861. POW, Gaine's Mill, 27 June 1862. Paroled, 6 August 1862. Transferred: Pvt. Co. C, 6th U.S. Cav. 28 October 1862 (age 26 at Knoxville, MD)–6 January 1864. B: Chautauqua Co., NY, lumber man. Blue eyes, light hair, ruddy complexion, 5'7¾. POW, Fairfield. D: 6 January 1864 from typhoid fever and diarrhea while a POW at Richmond, VA.

Holley, John. Pvt. Co. A, 19 December 1864 (age 23 at Cleveland, OH)–1 February 1865. B: Portage Co., OH, laborer. Hazel eyes, black hair, dark complexion, 5'6. Deserted.

Hollister, George Newton. Pvt. Co. E, 1st MN Inf. 29 April 1861. Transferred: Pvt. Co. F, 6th U.S. Cav. 28 October 1862 (age 19 at Knoxville, MD)–29 April 1864. B: 27 September 1843, Glastonbury, Hartford, CT, clerk. Hazel eyes, dark hair, dark complexion, 5'6. Discharged at Camp 6th Cav. D: 30 November 1926, Lewiston, Nez Pierce, ID.

Holm, Henry M. Pvt. Co. M, 26 October 1864 (age 31 at Harrisburg, PA)–19 October 1865. B: Hamburg, GER, brewer. Blue eyes, sandy hair, ruddy complexion, 5'8. Deserted.

Holmes, Calvin T. Pvt. Co. M, 1 October 1861 (age 34 at Waynesburg, PA)–31 July 1865. B: Fayette Co., PA, farmer. Hazel eyes, brown hair, dark complexion, 5'10½. WIA/POW, Fairfield, 3 July–28 September 1863. Paroled, reported at Annapolis, MD. Reenlisted: 10 March

1864 at Brandy Station, VA. Deserted 31 July 1865. Released from service 31 March 1891 under Act of Congress. Approved 11 April 1890.

Holmes, Charles. Rct. 16 November 1864 (age 22 at Harrisburg, PA)–21 November 1864. B: Co. Tyrone, IRE, carpenter. Blue eyes, auburn hair, fair complexion, 5'11½. Deserted. Sub.

Homan, William H. Mustered: Pvt. Co. A, 110th PA Inf. 24 October 1861. Transferred: Pvt. Co. D, 6th U.S. Cav. 28 October 1862 (age 20 at Knoxville, MD)–9 February 1867. B: 1841, Centre Co., PA. Grey eyes, dark hair, dark complexion, 5'7. Reenlisted: 9 February 1864 at Brandy Station, VA. Discharged at Jacksboro, TX. D: 1923, Williamsburg, Blair, PA.

Honey, James. Pvt. Co. D, 18 October 1861 (age 18 at Cleveland, OH)–No further information. B: Rochester, Monroe Co., NY, machinist. Grey eyes, brown hair, fair complexion, 5'9.

Honeywell, George C. Mustered: Pvt. Co. F, 38th PA Inf. 1 July 1861. Transferred: Pvt. Co. M, 6th U.S. Cav. 28 October 1862 (age 21 at Knoxville, MD)–29 June 1864. B: Crawford Co., PA, laborer. Grey eyes, dark hair, fair complexion, 5'5. POW, Fairfield. Paroled at Annapolis, MD 20 August 1863. Discharged at Lighthouse Point, VA. D: Meadville, Crawford, PA.

Hood, Malcome. Pvt. Co. A, 5 December 1864 (age 31 at Philadelphia, PA)–22 July 1865. B: Co. Donegal, IRE, soldier. Hazel eyes, fair hair, fair complexion, 5'9½. Disability discharge at Frederick, MD. Sub.

Hood, Thomas. Mustered: Pvt. Co. K, 38th PA Inf. 4 May 1861. Transferred: Pvt. Co. E, 6th U.S. Cav. 28 October 1862 (age 22 at Knoxville, MD)–28 July 1864. B: Allegheny Co., PA. Dark eyes, light hair, light complexion, 5'9. Discharged in the field, VA.

Hopfengarten, Christian. Pvt. Co. F, 7 August 1861 (age 25 at Pittsburgh, PA)–26 October 1862. B: Bavaria, GER, hostler. Grey eyes, brown hair, ruddy complexion, 5'8¼. POW, Savage Station, 1 July 1862. D: 26 October 1862 of disease at Washington, D.C.

Hopkins, David Henry. Pvt. Co. K, 13 July 1861 (age 23 at Franklin, PA)–13 July 1864. B: Carmarthenshire, South Wales, WAL, coal miner. Hazel eyes, brown hair, light complexion, 5'11. Discharged in the field, VA.

Horner, Jeremiah. Rct. 27 July 1861 (age 21 at Warren, OH)–13 August 1861. B: Cambria Co., PA, carpenter. Blue eyes, light hair, light complexion, 5'10¾. Disability discharge.

Hoster, Samuel. Musician 2nd Class. Co. F&S,

15 October 1861 (age 22 at Mount Joy, PA)–15 October 1864. B: Mount Joy, Lancaster Co., PA, musician. Blue eyes, brown hair, ruddy complexion, 5'7. Discharged Strausburg, VA.

House, Wesley L. Pvt. Co. A, 16 July 1861 (age 31 at Columbus, OH)–16 July 1864. B: Hartford, Hartford Co., CT, carpenter. Blue eyes, brown hair, ruddy complexion, 5'6¾. Discharged at Lighthouse Point, VA.

Howard, Cornelius. Rct. 7 December 1864 (age 31 at Philadelphia, PA)–No further information. B: Fishkill, Dutchess, NY, sailor. Grey eyes, fair hair, ruddy complexion, 5'6.

Howard, John. Mustered: Pvt. Co. E, 8th OH Inf. 25 June 1861. Transferred: Pvt. Cos. F, E, 6th U.S. Cav. 22 October 1862 (age 19 at Knoxville, MD)–26 May 1864. B: Buffalo, NY. Grey eyes, light hair, dark complexion, 5'3½. POW, Funkstown, 7 July 1863–19 May 1864. Paroled, reported at Annapolis, MD. Discharged at Hospital, Richmond, VA.

Howard, John H. Pvt. Co. F, 30 December 1864 (age 28 at Cincinnati, OH)–27 January 1865. B: Lewis Co., KY, farmer. Hazel eyes, dark hair, dark complexion, 5'6. Deserted.

Howard, John W. Rct. 5 November 1864 (age 24 at Harrisburg, PA)–21 November 1864. B: Liverpool, ENG, laborer. Blue eyes, light hair, florid complexion, 5'6½. Deserted. Sub.

Howell, Charles. Pvt. Co. L, 24 October 1861 (age 35 at Cleveland, OH)–4 March 1862. B: New York Co., NY, boiler maker. Grey eyes, brown hair, ruddy complexion, 6'3¼. Disability discharge at Falmouth, VA.

Howenstein, George W. Mustered: Pvt. Co. G, 38th PA Inf. 5 April 1861. Transferred: Pvt. Co. F, 6th U.S. Cav. 28 October 1862 (age 21 at Knoxville, MD)–4 May 1864. B: Pittsburgh, Allegheny, PA, nail cutter. Grey eyes, black hair, swarthy complexion, 5'6. Discharged in the field, VA. D: 29 December 1921.

Hubbard, Robert A. Cpl. Co. M, 4 September 1861 (age 29 at Pittsburgh, PA)–4 September 1864. B: Johnstown, Cambria Co., PA, silversmith. Blue eyes, light hair, light complexion, 5'6. Discharged at Charlestown, VA.

Huber, John. Mustered: Pvt. Co. G, 3rd WI Inf. Transferred: Pvt. Co. L, 6th U.S. Cav. 28 October 1862 (age 22 at Knoxville, MD)–28 April 1864. B: Breuberg, HUN, cooper. Brown eyes, sandy hair, ruddy complexion, 5'5½. Discharged at Brandy Station, VA.

Huber, Noah N. Mustered: Pvt. Co. A, 45th PA Inf. 16 August 1861. Transferred: Pvt. Co. I, 6th U.S. Cav. 27 October 1862 (age 22 at Knox-

ville, MD)–27 August 1864. B: Centre Co., PA, wheelwright. Grey eyes, brown hair, dark complexion, 6'1. MIA, Fairfield. Discharged in the field, VA.

Hudson, Ephraim A. Mustered: Pvt. Co. B, 110th PA Inf. 24 October 1861. Transferred: Pvt. Co. D, 6th U.S. Cav. 28 October 1862 (age 21 at Knoxville, MD)–20 February 1864. B: Scottsville, Wyoming Co., PA. Grey eyes, dark hair, dark complexion, 5'7. Disability discharge at Carlisle Barracks, PA.

Huff, Thomas. Pvt.-Teamster. Co. I, 15 August 1861 (age 20 at Lock Haven, PA)–15 August 1864. B: Clinton Co., PA, farmer. Blue eyes, light hair, light complexion, 5'8. Discharged at Harper's Ferry, VA.

Hughes, David. Rct. 6 August 1861 (age 18 at Cleveland, OH)–Not enough information. B: Cleveland, Cuyahoga Co., OH, boiler maker. Blue eyes, brown hair, ruddy complexion, 5'8.

Hughes, James M. Mustered: Pvt. Co. K, 14th Ind. Inf. 7 June 1861. Transferred: Rct. 6th U.S. Cav. 23 October 1862 (age 20 at Knoxville, MD)–November/December 1862. B: Bloomington, IN. Blue eyes, light hair, florid complexion, 5'6½. Returned to USV. KIA, Wilderness, VA, 5 May 1864.

Hughes, Napoleon Bonaparte. Mustered: Pvt. Cos. A, C, 50th NY Eng. 13 August 1861. Transferred: Pvt. Co. A, 6th U.S. Cav. 28 October 1862 (age 22 at Knoxville, MD)–28 August 1864. B: Springfield Twp., Bradford Co., PA, farmer. Grey eyes, dark hair, florid complexion, 5'10. Discharged at Halltown, VA.

Hull, Henry. Pvt. Co. A, 16 August 1861 (age 25 at Cleveland, OH). B: Copley, Summit Co., OH, farmer. Hazel eyes, brown hair, ruddy complexion, 5'6. Deserted.

Hull, Joseph. Mustered: Pvt. Co. B, 4th OH Inf. 20 August 1861. Transferred: Pvt. Co. A, 6th U.S. Cav. 28 October 1862 (age 22 at Knoxville, MD)–19 October 1864. B: Knox Co., OH. Black eyes, dark hair, dark complexion, 5'8½. Discharged near Middletown, VA.

Hults, William. Pvt. Co. B, 5 August 1861 (age 21 at Cleveland, OH)–22 November 1861. B: Huron Co., OH, machinist. Blue eyes, light hair, ruddy complexion, 5'9½. Deserted.

Humphet, Daniel. Rct. 4 November 1864 (age 27 at Cincinnati, OH)–21 November 1864. B: Montreal, Quebec, CAN, farmer. Hazel eyes, brown hair, dark complexion, 5'3. Deserted.

Hunley, Thomas. Pvt. Co. L, 12 November 1864 (age 21 at Cincinnati, OH)–22 January 1865.

B: Grayson Co., KY, farmer. Grey eyes, light hair, fair complexion, 5'7. Deserted.

Hunt, Alonzo F. Rct. 25 July 1861 (age 33 at Rochester, NY)–31 August 1861. B: Johnston, NY, carpenter. Grey eyes, brown hair, dark complexion, 5'8½. Disability discharge at Rochester, NY.

Hunt, John. Rct. 22 July 1861 (age 23 at Philadelphia, PA)–19 August 1861. B: Philadelphia, PA, gas fitter. Blue eyes, light hair, ruddy complexion, 5'5. Disability discharge.

Hunter, Robert. Pvt. Co. A, 25 November 1864 (age 20 at Harrisburg, PA)–30 May 1865. B: Co. Antrim, IRE, boatman. Grey eyes, light hair, light complexion, 5'7. Deserted. Sub.

Hurley, Joseph T. Musician 1st Class Co. F&S, 14 March 1865 (age 35 at NYC, NY)–10 April 1867. B: Co. Dublin, IRE, musician. Blue eyes, dark hair, light complexion, 5'5. Discharged by S. O. 153 at Austin, TX.

Hurley, Thomas. Mustered: Pvt. Co. H, 82nd NY Inf. 8 August 1861. Transferred: Pvt. Co. C, 6th U.S. Cav. 23 October 1862 (age 27 at Knoxville, MD)–8 August 1864. B: Co. Clare, IRE, painter. Blue eyes, brown hair, fair complexion, 5'8½. Discharged in the field, VA.

Huston, Charles C. Sr. Mustered: Pvt. Co. U, 32nd MA Inf. 27 September 1862. Mustered out 9 February 1863. Enlisted: Pvt. Cos. H, F, 6th U.S. Cav. 10 February 1863 (age 21 at Boston, MA)–27 September 1865. B: New York, NY, clerk. Blue eyes, light hair, fair complexion, 5'5. MIA on the march. POW Andersonville, 23 June 1864–? Also served, 2nd Sqd. 4th MA. Sent to Millen, 11 November. Discharged at camp near Frederick, MD.

Hutchens, John E. Mustered: Pvt. Co. B, 14th IN Inf. 6 June 1861. Transferred: Pvt. Co. H, 6th U.S. Cav. 28 October 1862 (age 21 at Knoxville, MD)–November/December 1862. B: Hamilton, OH. Black hair, dark hair, dark complexion, 5'7½. Returned to USV. KIA, 19 December 1862.

Hutchinson, William. Mustered: Pvt. Co. A, 3rd WI Inf. 18 April 1861. Transferred: Pvt.-Sgt. Co. F, 6th U.S. Cav. 28 October 1862 (age 19 at Knoxville, MD)–8 February 1867. B: Walworth Co., WI. Blue eyes, light hair, light complexion, 5'5½. Reenlisted: 9 February 1864 at Camp 6th Cav., VA. Discharged at Jacksboro, TX.

Hyland, James. Rct. 3 November 1864 (age 22 at Harrisburg, PA)–21 November 1864. B: Co. Dublin, IRE, porter. Grey eyes, brown hair, ruddy complexion, 5'10½. Deserted. Sub.

Ingrenthron, Jacob. Pvt. Co. A, 30 November 1864 (age 31 at Cincinnati, OH)–30 May 1865. B: GER, soldier. Brown eyes, brown hair, dark complexion, 5'7¾. Deserted.

Ireton, Franklin. Cpl. Co. H, 12 August 1861 (age 22 at Philadelphia, PA)–12 August 1864. B: Burlington Twp., Burlington Co., NJ, farmer. Brown eyes, brown hair, ruddy complexion, 5'7. MIA, Fairfield. Discharged at Lighthouse Point, VA.

Irish, Abel A. Pvt. Co. E, 10 September 1861 (age 21 at Adrian, MI)–9 May 1862. B: Logan Co., OH, clerk. Hazel eyes, brown hair, fair complexion, 5'10½. WIA, Slatersville. D: 9 May 1862.

Irons, James A. Pvt. Co. F, 25 July 1861 (age 24 at Pittsburgh, PA)–No further information. B: Phillipsburg, Centre Co., PA, blacksmith. Blue eyes, sandy hair, light complexion, 5'10½.

Irwin, John A. "Redhead." Enlisted: Pvt.-1st Sgt. Co. C, 1st U.S. Cav. 16 February 1857 (St. Louis, MO)–16 February 1862 (Sedalia, MO). Enlisted: 1st Sgt. Co. E, 6th U.S. Cav. 21 May 1862 (age 22 at New York, NY)–21 September 1862. B: 1 July 1839, Co. Monaghan, IRE, clerk. Grey eyes, sandy hair, fair complexion, 5'6½. Discharged by appointment to 2nd Lt., 6th Cav. at Sharpsburg, MD, dated 17 July 1862. Dismissed: 27 July 1875. D: 11 December 1901, Los Angeles, CA.

Iverson, John. Rct. 25 July 1864 (age 19 at Rochester, NY)–30 July 1864. B: Co. Kildare, IRE, sailor. Brown eyes, brown hair, sallow complexion, 5'8½. Deserted from Carlisle Barracks, PA.

Ives, John. Pvt. Co. M, 13 September 1864 (age 21 at Harrisburg, PA)–Not further information. B: Co. Wexford, IRE, laborer. Hazel eyes, black hair, dark complexion, 5'8. Deserted. Dropped from rolls per letter, dated AGO, 11 October 1866.

Jack, Gavin. Mustered: Pvt. Co. B, 7th OH Inf. Transferred: Pvt. Co. B, 6th U.S. Cav. 28 October 1862 (age 35 at Knoxville, MD)–22 June 1864. B: 19 June 1827 Larnkashire, SCO, puddler. Blue eyes, dark hair, dark complexion, 5'6. MIA, Fairfield. Discharged at Camp 6th Cav., VA. D: 2 September 1921.

Jackson, James. Mustered: Pvt. Co. D, 14th IN Inf. 7 June 1861. Transferred: Pvt. Co. C, 6th U.S. Cav. 24 October 1862 (age 24 at Knoxville, MD)–1 June 1864. B: Davis, IN. Black eyes, brown hair, florid complexion, 5'9. Discharged in the field, VA.

Jackson, James. Pvt. Co. B, 6 October 1864 (age 26 at Harrisburg, PA)–No further information.

B: Co. Louth, IRE, blacksmith. Blue eyes, brown hair, ruddy complexion, 5' 6.

Jackson, James F. (aka Charles). Pvt.-Sgt.-Sgt. Maj.. Cos. D, F&S, K, L, 30 August 1861 (age 26 at Pittsburgh, PA)–1 October 1862. B: Co. Dublin, IRE, clerk. Hazel eyes, brown hair, ruddy complexion, 5' 6. Enlisted: G.M.S., 4 May 1860 as James Jackson. Deserted 21 August. Enlisted: Co. D, 6th U.S. Cav. Enlistment was cancelled by S.O 189, Army of the Potomac. Reorganized date not dated, as "Charles" Jackson, a deserter from General Mounted service. Assigned to Co. K, 1 December 1861 after apprehension at Camp East of Capitol. Returned to duty without trial. Deserted 1 October 1862.

Jackson, William. Rct. 20 September 1864 (age 20 at Rochester, NY)–20 September 1864. B: Co. Cork, IRE, laborer. Grey eyes, brown hair, light complexion, 5' 6½. Deserted same day. Sub.

Jacobs, Abram B. Mustered: 20 April 1861 (Jersey City, NJ), Pvt. Co. A, 34th PA Inf. Transferred: Pvt. Co. H, 6th U.S. Cav. 28 October 1862 (age 24 at Knoxville, MD)–23 April 1864. B: RUS, laborer. Dark eyes, dark hair, dark complexion, 5' 6. MIA/WIA, Fairfield. Discharged at Camp 6th Cav., VA. D: 26 September 1898, Los Angeles, CA.

James, David. Pvt. Co. D, 16 August 1861 (age 26 at Pittsburgh, PA)–16 June 1865. B: Merther(?), PA, miner. Brown eyes, brown hair, light complexion, 5' 9. Discharged at Camp Sheridan, Frederick, MD.

James, David B. Pvt. Co. B, 17 July 1861 (age 17 at Columbus, OH)–2 March 1864. B: Winchester Co., NY, farmer. Grey eyes, brown hair, fair complexion, 5' 7¼. POW (captured while on picket), Richard's Ford, 14 February 1863. Paroled. WIA/POW, Funkstown. D: 2 March 1864 of pneumonia while a POW at Richmond, VA.

Jamison, Robert. Pvt. Co. A, 16 September 1861 (age 31 at Philadelphia, PA)–26 May 1864. B: Co. Antrim, IRE, leather dresser. Grey eyes, brown hair, fair complexion, 5' 3½. Deserted 24 March 1862. Apprehended 29 September 1862 at Philadelphia. Deserted 26 May 1864.

Jasson, Anton. Rct. 19 August 1861 (age 19 at Rochester, NY)–22 August 1861. B: CAN, farmer. Grey eyes, black hair, dark complexion, 5' 9. Rejected recruit at Pittsburgh, PA.

Jay, John C. Pvt. Co. E, 14 September 1861 (age 27 at Columbus, OH)–30 October 1862. B: Washington Co., PA, farmer. Grey eyes, sandy hair, sandy complexion, 5' 5½. Deserted.

Jeffcoat, Emanuel. Pvt. Co. F, 30 September 1864 (age 37 at NYC, NY)–27 September 1865. B: Lexington Co., SC, farmer. Hazel eyes, brown hair, sallow complexion, 5' 6. Deserted 27 September 1865. Second record states he enlisted on 31 December 1864.

Jefferson, Rufus Horatio. Mustered: Pvt. Co. E, 1st MN Inf. 29 April 1861. WIA, Bull Run. Transferred: Pvt. Co. F, 6th U.S. Cav. 28 October 1862 (age 22 at Knoxville, MD)–24 July 1864. B: 6 May 1840, IL, trapper. Grey eyes, dark hair, light complexion, 5'10. Discharged in the field, VA. D: 24 August 1932, Windom, Cottonwood, MN.

Jewell, Benjamin H. Mustered: Pvt. Co. G, 1st MN Inf. 29 April 1861. Transferred: Pvt. Co. F, 6th U.S. Cav. 25 October 1862 (age 22 at Knoxville, MD)–16 November 1863. B: 19 July 1840, Whitingham, Windham Co., VT, farmer. Dark eyes, black hair, dark complexion, 5' 9½. POW, Funkstown, 7 July–16 November 1863. D: of dysentery at General Hospital No. 21, Richmond.

Jimmison, John. Pvt. Co. A, 9 October 1861 (age 33 at Cleveland, OH)–9 October 1864. B: CAN, laborer. Blue eyes, light hair, ruddy complexion, 5' 5½. POW, Funkstown, 7 July 1863–25 February 1864. Paroled, reported at Baltimore, MD. Discharged at Harrisonburg, VA.

Johnson, Edward P. 31 August 1864 (age 23 at Cleveland, OH)–No further information. B: Kingston, CAN, engineer. Grey eyes, brown hair, dark complexion, 5'10.

Johnson, James. Cpl. Co. I, 22 August 1861 (age 22 at Rochester, NY)–22 August 1864. B: IRE, farmer. Blue eyes, light hair, light complexion, 5' 8. Discharged at Harper's Ferry, MD.

Johnson, James. Pvt. Co. L, 7 November 1864 (age 23 at Cincinnati, OH)–27 February 1865. B: Woodford Co., KY, painter. Hazel eyes, dark hair, fair complexion, 5' 7. Deserted.

Johnson, James A. Cpl. Co. M, 11 October 1861 (age 25 at Pittsburgh, PA)–8 August 1865. B: Harrisburg, Dauphin Co., PA, shoemaker. Grey eyes, brown hair, light complexion, 5' 6½. Deserted 26 June 1864. Joined 24 May 1865. Discharged 8 August 1865 at Frederick, MD.

Johnson, James W. 18 November 1864 (age 18 at Harrisburg, PA)–No further information. B: Clark Co., MA, farmer. Grey eyes, brown hair, ruddy complexion, 5' 5.

Johnson, John. Rct. 22 June 1864 (age 24 at Clarkson, NY)–19 July 1864. B: Co. Cork, IRE, student. Hazel eyes, black hair, dark complexion, 5' 8. Deserted at Carlisle Barracks, PA.

Johnson, Peter. Mustered: Pvt. Co. K, 8th OH Inf. 5 June 1861. Transferred: Pvt. Co. C, 6th U.S. Cav. 28 October 1862 (age 26 at Knoxville, MD)–15 May 1864. B: Medina Co., OH, farmer. Grey eyes, dark hair, fair complexion, 5'11. POW, Brandy Station, 11 October 1863–15 May 1864. D: 15 May 1864 from chronic diarrhea as a POW at Andersonville, GA.

Johnson, William, Mustered: Pvt. Co. D, 3rd MD Inf. 1 October 1861. Transferred: Pvt. Co. K, 6th U.S. Cav. 26 October 1862 (age 19 at Knoxville, MD)–10 March 1863. B: New York, NY. Blue eyes, dark hair, dark complexion, 5'8½. Deserted near Falmouth, VA.

Johnson, William. 31 October 1864 (age 30 at Cincinnati, OH)–No further information. B: Co. Belfast, IRE, laborer. Hazel eyes, brown hair, fair complexion, 5'5½.

Johnston, John. Pvt. Co. M, 4 December 1861 (age 21 at Pittsburgh, PA)–28 December 1861. B: Trumbull Co., OH, farmer. Hazel eyes, brown hair, light complexion, 5'7. Rejected recruit. Deserted before discharge.

Jones, Daniel H. Pvt.-Sgt. Co. L, 28 January 1862 (age 26 at Cleveland, OH)–3 July 1863. B: Coshocton Co., OH, carpenter. Hazel eyes, black hair, sallow complexion, 5'8. WIA, Uniontown. Deserted, Fairfield.

Jones, Daniel W. Cpl. Co. E, 7 September 1861 (age 26 at Cleveland, OH)–7 September 1864. B: Brecon, WAL, cooper. Grey eyes, brown hair, ruddy complexion, 5'4½. MIA at Funkstown. Discharged at Berryville, VA.

Jones, Edward E. Pvt. Cos. C, L, 14 December 1861 (age 25 at Cleveland, OH)–3 January 1862. B: Pittsburgh, Allegheny Co., PA, shoemaker. Black eyes, brown hair, ruddy complexion, 5'10½. Disability discharge at Washington, D.C.

Jones, Henry. Rct. 8 November 1864 (age 27 at Rochester, NY)–16 November 1864. B: London, CAN, cooper. Hazel eyes, brown hair, dark complexion, 5'8. Deserted.

Jones, Howard S. Saddler Sgt. Cos. D, F&S, 2 August 1861 (age 21 at Pittsburgh, PA)–2 August 1864. B: Winfield, Herkimer Co., NY, machinist. Dark eyes, dark hair, dark complexion, 5'7. MIA, Fairfield. WIA, Five Forks, 2 April 1865. Discharged at Lighthouse Point, VA.

Jones, Isaac. Pvt. Co. B, 27 July 1861 (age 22 at Columbus, OH)–27 August 1861. B: Perry Co., PA, farmer. Grey eyes, dark hair, ruddy complexion, 5'7½. Deserted.

Jones, James. Pvt. Co. D, 7 August 1861 (age 26 at Pittsburgh, PA)–20 March 1862. B: Carmarthenshire, South Wales, WAL, blacksmith. Black eyes, black hair, dark complexion, 5'9. Disability discharge at Alexandria, VA.

Jones, John. Rct. 17 September 1864 (age 41 at Rochester, NY)–No further information. B: Montreal, CAN, farmer. Hazel eyes, black hair, sallow complexion, 5'9. Sub.

Jones, John Wheldon. Pvt. Co. G, 3 August 1861 (age 24 at Erie Co., PA)–18 March 1862. B: South Trenton, Oneida Co., NY, farmer. Blue eyes, dark hair, fair complexion, 5'5½. D: 18 March 1862 of disease at General Hospital Mansion House, Alexandria, VA.

Jones, Joseph R. Musician 2nd Class. Co. F&S, 15 October 1861 (age 26 at Mount Joy, PA)–15 October 1864. B: Harrisburg, Dauphin Co., PA, musician. Grey eyes, sandy hair, light complexion, 5'8. Discharged at Strausburg, VA.

Jones, Lyman L. Cpl. Co. B, 17 July 1861 (age 22 at Columbus, OH)–17 July 1864. B: Coshocton, OH, boatman. Grey eyes, brown hair, sallow complexion, 5'6¾. Discharged at Lighthouse Point, VA. D: 23 January 1919.

Jones, Reese. Pvt. Co. D, 27 August 1861 (age 29 at Pittsburgh, PA)–22 September 1864. B: Carmarthenshire, South Wales, WAL, fireman. Black eyes, black hair, dark complexion, 5'7. WIA, Beverly Ford. Disability discharge at West Philadelphia, PA.

Jones, Samuel. Mustered: Cpl. Co. E, 3rd DE Inf. Transferred: Pvt. Co. I, 6th U.S. Cav. 25 October 1862 (age 21 at Knoxville, MD)–28 December 1864. B: Luzerne Co., PA, clerk. Blue eyes, dark hair, fair complexion, 5'5½. Discharged at Winchester, VA. by G.C.M.O.

Jones, Thomas W. Pvt. Co. A, 9 November 1864 (age 26 at Cincinnati, OH)–30 May 1865. B: Bedford Co., PA, farmer. Blue eyes, brown hair, fair complexion, 5'9½. Deserted 24 November 1864. Apprehended 28 November 1864. Deserted 30 May 1865.

Jones, Vian J. Rct. 24 September 1864 (age 27 at Cleveland, OH)–No further information. B: Port Hope, CAN, printer. Grey eyes, brown hair, dark complexion, 5'9. Sub.

Jones, William. Pvt. Cos. C, L, 14 November 1861 (age 34 at Bristol, PA)–25 June 1864. B: Queens, IRE, boatman. Brown eyes, black hair, light complexion, 5'8½. Disability discharge at Carlisle Barracks, PA.

Jones, William A. Pvt. Cos. A, B, 7 August 1861 (age 22 at Cleveland, OH)–7 August 1864. B: Wadsworth, Medina Co., OH, farmer. Hazel eyes, brown hair, sallow complexion, 5'8. Discharged at Lighthouse Point, VA.

Joralemon, David. Rct. 23 September 1864 (age 19 at Rochester, NY)–23 September 1864. B: Saratoga, Saratoga County, NY, laborer. Hazel eyes, light hair, fair complexion, 5'4 ½. Deserted same day. Reenlisted: 20 September 1870, 12th U.S. Inf. Discharged 20 September 1875. Reenlisted: 18 October 1875, 12th U.S. Inf. Disability discharge 16 December 1877. D: 5 December 1878, Washington, D.C.

Jordan, William. Mustered: Pvt. Co. K, 8th OH Inf. 27 April–5 June 1861. Reenlisted: 5 June 1861. Transferred: Cpl. Co. C, 23 October 1862 (age 18 at Knoxville, MD)–26 May 1864. B: Medina Co., OH. Blue eyes, brown hair, florid complexion, 5'8. Discharged at Camp 6th Cav., VA.

Joseph, Henry. Mustered: Pvt. Co. B, 14th IN Inf. 7 June 1861. Transferred: Pvt. Co. I, 6th U.S. Cav. 23 October 1862 (age 19 at Knoxville, MD)–1 January 1865. B: GER. Hazel eyes, black hair, dark complexion, 5'5. MIA, Brandy Station. Discharged in the field, VA.

Judd, Henry C. Cpl. Co. I, 23 September 1861 (age 19 at Rochester, NY)–23 September 1864. B: Genesee Co., NY, farmer. Grey eyes, sandy hair, fair complexion, 5'10½. Discharged in the field, VA.

K[a]elber, Gustav. Pvt. Co. B, 26 July 1861 (age 22 at Columbus, OH)–26 December 1865. B: Prussia, GER, farmer. Blue eyes, light hair, ruddy complexion, 5'7½. Reenlisted: 8 February 1864 at Camp 6th Cav. Deserted 26 December 1865.

Kain, John. 24 October 1862 (age 24 at Knoxville, MD)–Not enough information. B: IRE, soldier. Blue eyes, brown hair, dark complexion, 5'7¾. See 43403, P.R.D. 92.

Kaler, Henry. Pvt. Co. C, 22 October 1861 (age 21 at Mount Joy, PA)–26 April 1862. B: Lancaster Co., PA, carpenter. Grey eyes, light hair, light complexion, 5'4½. Deserted.

Kaltenbacher, Joseph. Pvt. Co. G, 30 July 1861 (age 21½ at Erie Co., PA)–30 July 1864. B: 17 February 1841, Louderbach, Württemberg, GER, cooper. Hazel eyes, light hair, light complexion, 5'6¾. Discharged in the field, VA. D: 20 July 1906, Erie, PA.

Kane, Henry. Pvt. Co. M, 10 October 1861 (age 31 at Pittsburgh, PA)–10 October 1864. B: Co. Derry, IRE, coal miner. Hazel eyes, sandy hair, light complexion, 5'7¼. WIA/POW, Fairfield, 3 July 1863–22 February 1864. Paroled, reported at Camp Parole. Discharged in the field, VA.

Kane, John. Pvt. Co. F, 26 August 1864 (age 23 at Harrisburg, PA)–5 June 1865. B: Liverpool, ENG, bartender. Grey eyes, light hair, florid complexion, 5'6½. Deserted. Sub.

Kane, John. Rct. 24 September 1861 (age 21 at Columbus, OH)–30 October 1861. B: Co. Cork, IRE, farmer. Blue eyes, ruddy complexion, 5'8½. Deserted.

Kane, Michael. Cpl. Co. H, 25 July 1861 (age 27 at Philadelphia, PA)–9 January 1863. B: Co. Londonderry, IRE, soldier. Blue eyes, brown hair, dark complexion, 5'7½. Disability discharge at Camp near Falmouth, VA.

Karhoff, Joseph A. Pvt. Co. L, 14 October 1861 (age 39 at Cleveland, OH)–1 July 1862. B: Oldenburg, Lower Saxony, GER, porter. Grey eyes, brown hair, ruddy complexion, 5'6. Deserted. D: 8 September 1912, Yeadon, Delaware, PA.

Kasson, William Otis. Pvt. Co. E, 18 September 1861 (age 21 at Adrian, MI)–18 September 1864. B: 1841, Hewlett Hill, Nassau, NY, farmer. Grey eyes, brown hair, ruddy complexion, 6'. POW, Fairfield, 3 July 1863–12 March 1864. Paroled, reported at Annapolis, MD. Discharged in the field, VA. D: 1914, Pompey, Onondaga, NY.

Keenan, Denis. Rct. 10 August 1861 (age 25 at Cleveland, OH)–14 August 1861. B: Dublin, IRE, laborer. Blue eyes, black hair, ruddy complexion, 5'7¼. Deserted at Columbus, OH.

Keenan, Isaac. Pvt. Co. D, 8 August 1861 (age 30 at Pittsburgh, PA)–8 August 1864. B: Washington Co., PA, boat builder. Brown eyes, black hair, sandy complexion, 6'3. Discharged at City Point, VA.

Keene, Henry F. Mustered: Philadelphia, PA, Pvt. Co. H, 23rd PA Inf. 18 April 1861–20 July 1861 (3 months). Enlisted: Pvt. Co. H, 9 August 1861 (age 21 at Philadelphia, PA)–30 April 1864. B: London, ENG, cordwainer. Hazel eyes, dark hair, dark complexion, 5'8. WIA (GSW, right hand), Catlett's Station, 13 October 1863. Disability discharge at Carlisle Barracks, PA, 10 May 1864.

Keene, Samuel. Pvt. Co. F, 16 December 1864 (age 18 at Cincinnati, OH)–31 January 1865. B: Union Co., VA, laborer. Grey eyes, dark hair, fair complexion, 5'6. Deserted.

Kelley, James. Pvt.-Bugler. Cos. H, K, 6 August 1861 (age 21 at Philadelphia, PA)–27 January 1862. B: Philadelphia, PA, musician. Blue eyes, light hair, fair complexion, 5'3. Transferred to Co. K, 9 September 1861. Deserted.

Kellogg, Cassius A. Pvt. Co. M, 3 October 1864 (age 18 at Cleveland, OH)–3 October 1867. B: 1845, Hinckley, Medina Co., OH, farmer. Grey eyes, brown hair, ruddy complexion, 5'10½. MIA on Raid to Gordonsville 30 December 1864. Sub. Discharged 3 October 1867, Mt. Pleasant, TX. D: 1920, Hinckley, Medina Co., OH.

Kelly, Francis. Mustered: Pvt. Co. B, 8th OH Inf. June 1861. Transferred: Pvt. Co. C, 6th U.S. Cav. 22 October 1862 (age 26 at Knoxville, MD)–11 June 1864. B: Charlestown, MA. Grey eyes, light hair, light complexion, 5'4. Discharged at Camp 6th Cav., VA. D: 2 October 1895, Hampton City, VA.

Kelly, James. 12 September 1864 (age 19 at Harrisburg, PA)–Not enough information. B: Co. Tyrone, IRE, laborer. Grey eyes, dark hair, ruddy complexion, 5'8.

Kelly, John. Pvt. Co. F, 1 September 1864 (age 21 at Harrisburg, PA)–10 December 1865. B: Montreal, Quebec, CAN, butcher. Grey eyes, brown hair, fair complexion, 5'6. Sub. Deserted 10 September 1864. Apprehended 11 September 1864. Deserted 10 December 1865.

Kelly, John. Rct. 31 October 1864 (age 27 at Cincinnati, OH)–21 November 1864. B: ENG, laborer. Hazel eyes, dark hair, ruddy complexion, 5'9½. Deserted.

Kelly, Levi. Mustered: Pvt. Co. B, 110th PA Inf. 24 October 1861. Transferred: Pvt. Co. D, 6th U.S. Cav. 28 October 1862 (age 21 at Knoxville, MD)–1 September 1863. B: Huntington Twp., PA. Grey eyes, dark hair, dark complexion, 6'4½. D: 1 September 1863 from dysentery and pneumonia at General Hospital, Frederick, MD.

Kelly, Martin. Rct. 13 June 1864 (age 22 at North Danville, NY)–14 June 1864. B: Dublin, IRE, sailor. Grey eyes, dark hair, ruddy complexion, 5'10. Deserted.

Kelly [Kelley], Michael. 1 December 1864 (age 21 at NYC, NY)–Not enough information. B: Frankfort, IRE, laborer. Grey eyes, black hair, ruddy complexion, 5'5.

Kelly, Patrick. Pvt. Co. H, 29 July 1861 (age 22 at Philadelphia, PA)–29 July 1864. B: Co. Donegal, IRE, coal heaver. Blue eyes, brown hair, dark complexion, 5'8. On 3 July 1863 made a desperate effort to capture one of the enemy's standards. Discharged in the field, VA.

Kelly, William. Pvt. Co. M, 17 September 1861 (age 21 at Pittsburgh, PA)–7 September 1864. B: Butler Co., PA, farmer. Hazel eyes, brown hair, hazel complexion, 5'10½. Discharged in the field, VA.

Kelsey, George B. Mustered: Pvt. Co. E, 1st MN Inf. 23 May 1861. Transferred: Pvt. Co. F, 6th U.S. Cav. 28 October 1862 (age 21 at Knoxville, MD)–23 May 1864. B: Pittsburgh, Allegheny Co., PA, moulder. Blue eyes, light hair, light complexion, 5'8. Discharged at Camp 6th Cav., VA.

Kennedy, Beach B. Pvt. Co. E, 13 September 1861 (age 19 at Adrian, MI)–23 March 1864. B: Adrian, MI, farmer. Blue eyes, light hair, ruddy complexion, 5'7½. Disability discharge at Camp 6th Cav., VA.

Kennedy, Daniel. 28 November 1864 (age 22 at Cincinnati, OH)–Not enough information. B: Co. Waterford, IRE, laborer. Grey eyes, red hair, fair complexion, 6'.

Kennedy, James. Co. H, 34th PA Inf. 21 June 1861. Transferred: Pvt. Co. E, 6th U.S. Cav. 28 October 1862 (age 21 at Knoxville, MD)–2 April 1863. B: Utica, Oneida Co., NY, lawyer. Hazel eyes, brown hair, ruddy complexion, 5'7. Disability discharge at Camp Distribution, VA.

Kenny, Thomas. Pvt. Co. G, 13 August 1861 (age 29 at Rochester, NY)–No further information. B: Ogdensburg, St. Lawrence Co., NY, teamster. Blue eyes, fair hair, fair complexion, 5'8.

Kepperd, Samuel. Pvt. 12 December 1861 (age 30 at Cleveland, OH)–25 December 1861. B: Franklin Co., OH, farmer. Black eyes, black hair, ruddy complexion, 5'10. Deserted.

Kerns, Patrick. Pvt. Co. L, 27 December 1864 (age 24 at NYC, NY)–21 March 1865. B: 1827 Co. Galway, IRE, laborer. Hazel eyes, auburn hair, fair complexion, 5'8. Deserted.

Kerns, Sylvester Yardley. Cpl. Co. A, 27 August 1861 (age 21 at Philadelphia, PA)–27 August 1864. B: 1840, Philadelphia, PA, grocer. Blue eyes, brown hair, light complexion, 5'5½. WIA, Beverly Ford. Discharged at Halltown, VA. D: 12 December 1890, Philadelphia, PA.

Kester, Stephen J. Mustered: Pvt. Co. C, 8th OH Inf. 23 April 1861–22 June 1861. Reenlisted 22 June 1861. Transferred: Pvt. Co. H, 6th U.S. Cav. 24 October 1862 (age 23 at Knoxville, MD)–23 April 1864. B: Crawford Co., OH, farmer. Blue eyes, light hair, fair complexion, 6'1. Discharged at Camp 6th Cav., VA.

Kettelburger, Jacob. Pvt. Co. F, 26 July 1861 (age 21 at Pittsburgh, PA)–18 November 1863. B: Altdorf, GER, farmer. Grey eyes, sallow hair, light complexion, 5'8. POW, Fairfield, 3 July 1863–18 November 1863. D: of pneumonia at General Hospital No. 21, Richmond, VA.

Key, John. Pvt. Co. K, 15 July 1861 (age 23 at Franklin, PA)–17 July 1862. B: Mercer Co., PA, carpenter. Grey eyes, brown hair, light complexion, 5'10½. Deserted. D: 13 December 1893.

Kier, John. Pvt. Co. D, 26 August 1861 (age 21 at Pittsburgh, PA)–12 January 1863. B: Armstrong Co., PA, coal miner. Blue eyes, light hair, dark complexion, 5' 6½. Disability discharge at Emory Hospital, Washington, D.C.

Kihn, Joseph Peter. Mustered: Pvt. Co. F, 8th OH Inf. 6 July 1861. Transferred: Pvt. Co. C, 6th U.S. Cav. 23 October 1862 (age 23 at Knoxville, MD)–7 June 1864. B: Folberesveler(?), FRA, porter. Blue eyes, dark hair, dark complexion, 5' 4½. POW, Fairfield, 3 July 1863–7 January 1864. Paroled, reported at Annapolis, MD. Discharged at Camp 6th Cav., VA. Mustered: Cpl. Co. E, 186th OH Inf. 27 February 1865. Promoted to Sgt. 1 July 1865. Mustered out 18 September 1865, Nashville, TN.

Kiley, James. Pvt. Co: M, 27 November 1861 (age 27 at Pittsburgh, PA)–27 November 1864. B: IRE, steam boatman. Blue eyes, brown hair, dark complexion, 5' 7. Discharged in the field, VA.

Kimbro, John. Pvt. Co. M, 14 September 1864 (age 23 at Rochester, NY)–17 August 1866. B: Atlanta, Fulton Co., GA, boot maker. Hazel eyes, light hair, fair complexion, 5'10½. Disability discharge at Austin, TX.

Kiner, John Stewart. Pvt. Co. G, 6 August 1861 (at Columbus, OH)–6 August 1864. B: 1843. No information available. Discharged at Lighthouse Point, VA.

Kiner, Joseph. Pvt. Co. G, 6 August 1861 (age 23 at Columbus, OH)–6 August 1864. B: 26 October 1837, Franklin Co., OH, teamster. Grey eyes, black hair, light complexion, 5' 7¼. Discharged at City Point, VA. D: 23 May 1899.

King, Benjamin F. Pvt. Co. D, 20 August 1861 (age 21 at Pittsburgh, PA)–20 August 1864. B: Armstrong Co., PA, boatman. Dark eyes, black hair, dark complexion, 5' 7½. Discharged at Charlestown, VA.

King, Charles. 7 December 1864 (age 21 at Cincinnati, OH)–Not enough information. B: Brooklyn, NY, engineer. Hazel eyes, light hair, fair complexion, 5' 7.

King, Frederick L. Rct. 4 November 1864 (age 23 at Cleveland, OH)–November 1864. B: Montreal, Quebec, CAN, waterman. Brown eyes, brown hair, sallow complexion, 5'10½. Deserted 13 November 1864. Apprehended same day. Deserted again in November 1864.

King, James. Pvt. Co. M, 29 September 1864 (age 18 at Rochester, NY)–6 April 1865. B: Lockport, NY, farmer. Blue eyes, auburn hair, florid complexion, 5'11. D: 6 April 1865 from effects of wounds received in action, Dinwiddie Courthouse.

King, James E. Chief Bugler. Cos. A, F&S, 2 November 1864 (age 17 at NYC, NY)–2 November 1867. B: Fort Monroe, VA, laborer. Grey eyes, brown hair, fair complexion, 5' 6. Discharged at Ft. Harker, KS.

King, John. Rct. 1 June 1864 (age 21 at North Danville, NY)–7 June 1864. B: Co. Derry, IRE, blacksmith. Brown eyes, brown hair, fair complexion, 5' 5. Deserted.

King, John W. Mustered: Pvt. Co. D, 106th PA Inf. 27 August 1861. Transferred: Pvt. Co. G, 6th U.S. Cav. 28 October 1862 (age 20 at Knoxville, MD)–25 August 1864. B: Pine Twp., PA, lumberman. Dark eyes, dark hair, fair complexion, 5' 6. Discharged at Harper's Ferry, VA.

King, Seymour D. Pvt. Co. G, 10 August 1861 (age 25 at Rochester, NY)–10 August 1864. B: Genesee Co., NY, painter. Grey eyes, brown hair, sandy complexion, 5' 9. Discharged at Harper's Ferry, VA. D: 11 December 1876.

King, William T. Bugler. Cos. C, L, 3 December 1861 (age 16 at Bristol, PA)–26 March 1863. B: Bristol, Bucks Co., PA, farm boy. Hazel eyes, brown hair, fair complexion, 5' 2½. Disability discharge at Convalescent Camp, VA.

Kingsley, Edwin M. Pvt. Co. H, 27 October 1862 (age 18 at Knoxville, MD)–16 June 1863. B: Liverpool, Onondaga Co., NY, farmer. Blue eyes, light hair, fair complexion, 5' 8. Deserted.

Kinney, John P. Pvt. Co. I, 26 October 1862 (age 22 at Knoxville, MD)–1 October 1865. B: Blair Co., PA, laborer. Brown eyes, brown hair, fair complexion, 5' 9. WIA, Beverly Ford. Reenlisted: 8 February 1864 at Brandy Station, VA. Deserted 1 October 1865. Released from service 11 December 1891 by Act of Congress.

Kinsler, Charles. Enlisted: Pvt. Co. F, 2nd U.S. Dragoons, 28 September 1848–28 September 1853. Discharged at Ft. Graham, TX. Enlisted: Ord. Dept., U.S.A. Enlisted: Sgt. Co. H, 6th U.S. Cav. 5 July 1861 (age 31 at Philadelphia, PA)–5 July 1864. B: September 1826, Stuttgart, Baden-Wurttemberg, GER, clerk. Brown eyes, dark hair, ruddy complexion, 5' 7½. Discharged at Lighthouse Point, VA. D: 3 May 1893, Augusta, Kennebec, ME.

Kipley, Joseph. Pvt. Co. L, 27 December 1864 (age 18 at Cleveland, OH)–27 February 1865. B: Baden, GER, farmer. Grey eyes, brown hair, dark complexion, 5' 3. Deserted.

Kirby, Byron. Sgt. Co. B, 6 December 1861 (age 20 at Bladensburg, MD)–1 December 1861. B: 8 September 1829, Cleveland, Cuyahoga Co., OH, attorney-at-law. Grey eyes, light hair, light complexion, 5' 7½. Discharged 1 December 1861. Appointed 2nd Lt., 6th U.S. Inf. at Washington, D.C. and subsequently to the rank of Brig. Gen. D: 29 November 1881, Cincinnati, Hamilton, OH.

Kirk, Hugh. Pvt. Co. F, 23 July 1861 (age 25 at Pittsburgh, PA)–17 January 1863. B: Belfast, IRE, teamster. Brown eyes, brown hair, fair complexion, 6'1¼. Deserted.

Kirk, Peter. Pvt. Co. F, 10 December 1864 (age 24 at Cincinnati, OH)–27 January 1865. B: Toronto, Ontario, CAN, farmer. Grey eyes, brown hair, dark complexion, 6½. Sub. Deserted.

Kirkendall, Newton G. Pvt. Co. L, 15 December 1864 (age 19 at Philadelphia, PA)–30 July 1865. B: Pittsburgh, Allegheny Co., PA, laborer. Brown eyes, fair hair, fair complexion, 5' 5. Sub. Deserted.

Kirkpatrick, James. Cpl. Co. M, 9 November 1861 (age 24 at Pittsburgh, PA)–9 November 1864. B: SCO, stone cutter. Blue eyes, light hair, light complexion, 5' 9½. Discharged in the field, VA.

Kirsch, Joseph. Pvt. Co. G, 1 August 1861 (age 21 at Erie Co., PA)–18 April 1862. B: Erie Co., PA, butcher. Blue eyes, light hair, light complexion, 5' 9¾. Disability discharge at Alexandria, VA.

Klein, Conrad. Pvt. Co. K, 15 August 1861 (age 22 at Rochester, NY)–9 May 1862. B: GER, farmer. Brown eyes, brown hair, fair complexion, 5' 8. KIA, Slatersville, 9 May 1862.

Kletsch, Fredrick John. Sgt. Co. G, 23 July 1861 (age 26 at Erie Co., PA)–22 July 1864. B: Bishofuerda, Saxony, GER, woolen manufacturer. Light eyes, light hair, fair complexion, 5' 4½. Discharged at City Point, VA. D: 16 August 1902.

Kline, Daniel J. Pvt. Co. E, 16 September 1861 (age 21 at Columbus, OH)–15 October 1861. B: Franklin Co., OH, blacksmith. Hazel eyes, ruddy complexion. Discharged 14 May 1880 to date 15 October 1861 at Washington, D.C. by order of Sec. of War.

Kling, Kaspar (Cling, Casper). Farrier. Co. M, 10 October 1861 (age 19 at Pittsburgh, PA)–10 October 1864. B: GER, blacksmith. Hazel eyes, brown hair, light complexion, 5' 8½. POW at Richmond from ?–16 July 1862. Gained from parole. WIA/POW, Fairfield, 3 July 1863–20 August 1863. Paroled at Annapolis, MD. Discharged in the field, VA.

Klingmann, Johann. Band. Co. F&S, 8 April 1865 (age 40 NYC, NY)–19 October 1865. B: Baden, GER, musician. Hazel eyes, dark hair, fair complexion, 5' 9. Deserted.

Knapp, Allen. Pvt. Co. L, 3 February 1862 (at Cleveland, OH)–19 May 1862. B: New York, NY, rail roader. Blue eyes, brown hair, sallow complexion, 5'10. Disability discharge at Washington, D.C.

Knapp, Andrew B. Musician 1st Class. Co. F&S, 7 March 1865 (age 39 at NYC, NY)–10 April 1867. B: Macomb Twp., Macomb Co., MI, musician. Blue eyes, brown hair, fair complexion, 5'11. Discharged by S. O. 153 at Austin, TX.

Knapp, Edgar R. Hospital Steward. Co. E, 10 September 1861 (age 27 at Adrian, MI)–10 September 1864. B: Tompkins Co., NY, medical doctor (M. D.). Grey eyes, light hair, sallow complexion, 5' 7¾. MIA, Funkstown. Discharged at Baltimore, MD.

Knapp, Frederick. Pvt. Co. E, 20 September 1861 (age 21 at Cleveland, OH)–25 January 1865. B: February 1842, Monroe, MI, farmer. Hazel eyes, light hair, ruddy complexion, 5' 6. POW, Fairfield. POW at Andersonville, GA. Discharged at Baltimore, MD. D: 31 January 1938.

Knapp, Randolph Richard. Pvt. Co. E, 10 September 1861 (age 21 at Adrian, MI)–10 September 1864. B: Brooklyn, MI, clerk. Grey eyes, light hair, fair complexion, 5' 6½. WIA/POW, Funkstown, 7 July–17 August 1863. Reported in hospital 17 August 1863. Discharged in the field, VA. D: 1 June 1902.

Knarr, George. Pvt. Co. H, 16 August 1861 (age 19 at Philadelphia, PA)–10 August 1864. B: 18 September 1844, Schuylkill Haven, Schuylkill Co., PA, boatman. Blue eyes, light hair, fair complexion, 5' 6. MIA, Fairfield. Discharged at Berlin, Worchester, MD. Mustered: Pvt. Co. C, 50th PA Inf. 21 January 1865–30 July 1865. Mustered out at Georgetown, D.C. D: 14 November 1889, Schuylkill Haven, Schuylkill, PA.

Knight, Robert B. 4 October 1864 (age 23 at Rochester, NY)–No further information. B: Savannah, GA, bar keeper. Grey eyes, brown hair, fair complexion, 5' 6.

Knouse, Benjamin M. Pvt. Co. A, 22 August 1861 (at Columbus, OH)–23 November 1863. No further information. POW, Fairfield. D: as POW, 23 November 1863 of pneumonia at Richmond, VA.

Knowles, Eugene. Pvt. Co. K, 19 August 1861 (age 17 at Rochester, NY)–No further information. B: Onondaga, NY, farmer. Blue eyes, light hair, dark complexion, 5' 5. MIA, Malvern Hill.

Knowles, Jacob. Pvt. Co. G, 2 August 1861 (age 20 at Erie Co., PA). B: Darmstadt, Bundesland, Hesse, GER, blacksmith. Black eyes, black hair, fair complexion, 5'9. Deserted 3 August 1862. Apprehended 28 October 1863. Originally sentenced to be shot to death. Remitted to imprisonment for the remainder of the war. Discharged 15 March 1864 at Camp 6th Cav. by GCM.

Kohler, Philipp. Rct. 22 July 1861 (age 21 at Columbus, OH)–26 July 1861. B: Bavaria, GER, farmer. Hazel eyes, brown hair, sallow complexion, 5'5¾. Deserted at Columbus, OH.

Kohlhapp, Wilhelm. Pvt. Co. F, 13 July 1861 (age 18 at Pittsburgh, PA)–25 November 1862. B: Hope Caste, GER, butcher. Grey eyes, light hair, dark complexion, 5'8½. Discharged by order of Sec. of War at Belle Plain, VA. Enlisted: Pvt. Co. H, 7th IA Cav. 27 August 1863–17 May 1866. Mustered out at Ft. Leavenworth, KS.

Kohlmeier, Karl (anglicized: Kohlmeyer, Charles (Carl) Adam) Saddler. Co. F, 23 July 1861 (age 23 at Pittsburgh, PA)–23 July 1864. B: 4 July 1838, Adenbach, Kusel, Rhineland-Palatinate, GER, shoemaker. Grey eyes, brown hair, ruddy complexion, 5'8. POW from ? to 3 November 1863. Paroled, reported at Annapolis, MD. Discharged in the field, VA. D: 31 January 1925, St. Omaha, Douglas, NB.

Konder, George. Pvt. Cos. L, C, 16 December 1861 (age 35 at Cleveland, OH)–3 January 1862. B: Southwick, Prussia, GER, moulder. Blue eyes, brown hair, ruddy complexion, 5'10. Disability discharge at Washington, D.C.

Koon, Henry Calvin. Mustered: Pvt. Co. K, 110th PA Inf. 19 December 1861. Transferred: Pvt. Co. I, 6th U.S. Cav. 27 October 1862 (age 19 at Knoxville, MD)–27 November 1864. B: 27 November 1844, Blair Co., PA, laborer. Grey eyes, light hair, fair complexion, 5'8. Discharged in the field, VA. D: 30 March 1897, Blair Co., PA.

Kopke, Hermann. Pvt. Co. B, 19 July 1861 (age 27 at Columbus, OH)–23 January 1862. B: Prussia, GER, clerk. Blue eyes, light hair, sallow complexion, 5'8¼. Deserted.

Kornhauer, Henry. Rct. 7 October 1864 (age 22 at Cleveland, OH)–No further information. B: Darmstadt, Bundesland, Hesse, GER, paper hanger. Grey eyes, brown hair, fair complexion, 5'5½.

Kraft, George. Pvt. Co. A, 5 September 1861 (age 21 at Philadelphia, PA)–15 December 1862. B: Cassel, Hessen, GER, farmer. Hazel eyes, brown hair, dark complexion, 5'9. WIA, Williamsburg. Disability discharge at Washington, D.C. D: 9 January 1891.

Kraft, William. Pvt. Co. B, 12 August 1861 (age 18 at Columbus, OH)–12 August 1864. B: Columbus, OH, laborer. Grey eyes, light hair, ruddy complexion, 5'8½. Deserted 1 February 1863. Discharged 12 August 1864 in the field, VA.

Kreps, John. Pvt.-Sgt. Co. M, 10 September 1861 (age 22 at Pittsburgh, PA)–10 September 1864. B: Butler Co., PA, farmer. Hazel eyes, dark hair, dark complexion, 6'½. Discharged at Berryville, VA. D: 19 August 1927. Note: John and Joshua were brothers.

Kreps, Joshua. Pvt.-Cpl. Co. M, 21 September 1861 (age 24 at Pittsburgh, PA)–15 July 1862. B: Butler Co., PA, farmer. Grey eyes, brown hair, florid complexion, 6'3½. WIA, Williamsburg. Brought to the Seminary Hospital, Hampton, VA, 11 May 1862. Disability discharge at Baltimore, MD.

Krouse, Samuel S. Pvt.-Sgt. Cos. C, L, 1 November 1861 (age 23 at Philadelphia, PA)–15 February 1867. B: Mount Joy, Lancaster Co., PA, miller. Brown eyes, brown hair, fair complexion, 5'6½. Reenlisted: 29 March 1864 at Huntsville, AL. Discharged 15 February 1867 at Jacksboro, TX.

Kuhn, Joseph. Pvt.-Sgt. Co. K, 15 August 1861 (age 19 at Rochester, NY)–10 February 1867. B: GER, farmer. Blue eyes, light hair, fair complexion, 5'5. Reenlisted: 11 February 1864 at Brandy Station, VA. Discharged at Jacksboro, TX.

Kuman, Michael. Pvt. Co. A, 27 October 1862 (age 19 at Knoxville, MD)–28 September 1864. B: Philadelphia, PA, member USV. Blue eyes, light hair, light complexion, 5'6. WIA (slightly), Upperville, 21 June 1863. Discharged at Harrisonburg, VA.

Kuppisch, Rudolph. Pvt. Co. I, 31 July 1861 (age 25 at Rochester, NY)–9 February 1862. B: Prussia, GER, farmer. Hazel eyes, brown hair, florid complexion, 5'8½. Deserted.

Lablue, Alexander. Mustered: Pvt. Co. H, 60th NY Inf. 21 September 1861. Deserted 24 October 1862 at Loudon Heights, VA. Transferred: Pvt. Co. E, B, 6th U.S. Cav. 28 October 1862 (age 18 at Knoxville, MD)–23 April 1864. B: Champlain, NY. Blue eyes, light hair, dark complexion, 5'9½. Reenlisted: 10 March 1864 at Brandy Station, VA. Deserted 23 April 1864.

Ladd, Frederick S. Pvt. Co. E, 9 September 1861 (age 20 at Adrian, MI)–12 April 1863. B: Jackson Co., MI, clerk. Blue eyes, light hair, fair complexion, 5'9. Listed as deserted. Commissioned 2nd Lt., 9th Michigan Cavalry 3 April

1863; 1st Lt. 5 November 1863; Cpt. 5 February 1864. KIA 7 December 1864, Sister's Ferry or Cypress Swamp, GA.

Ladd, Henry J. Sgt. Co. E, 14 August 1861 (age 29 at Cleveland, OH)–19 July 1862. B: Rome, NY, conductor. Hazel eyes, brown hair, ruddy complexion, 6'¾. Discharged to accept appointment as a 2nd Lt. with 8th Pa. Cav. at Harrison's Landing, VA.

Lafountain, William. Pvt.-Cpl. Co. H, 60th NY Inf. 21 September 1861. Transferred: Pvt. Co. A, 6th U.S. Cav. 28 October 1862 (age 23 at Knoxville, MD)–3 March 1865. B: 15 October 1841, Champlain, NY. Blue eyes, light hair, light complexion, 5'6. POW (captured by guerrillas), Germantown, 10 March 1864. Discharged at Camp Parole, MD.

Lafre, Nicholas. Pvt. Co. K, 15 August 1861 (age 19 at Rochester, NY)–27 March 1862. B: GER, farmer. Blue eyes, light hair, fair complexion, 5'5. Deserted.

Lafross, Charles W. Mustered: Pvt. Co. H. 1st PA Cav. Enlisted: Pvt. Cos. D, B, F&S; 29 August 1861 (age 27 at Pittsburgh, PA)–22 August 1865. B: Erie City, Erie Co., PA, paper hanger. Blue eyes, light hair, dark complexion, 5'4½. Reenlisted: 9 February 1864 at Brandy Station, VA. Deserted 22 August 1865.

Laird, William. Pvt. Co. A, 6 December 1864 (age 20 at Cincinnati, OH)–28 March 1865. B: IN, farmer. Grey eyes, brown hair, fair complexion, 5'7. D: 28 March 1865 from accidental gunshot at Pleasant Valley, MD.

Lallin, Clark. Pvt. Co. K, 5 August 1861 (age 20 at Warren, OH)–28 April 1862. B: Bagetta, OH, farmer. Blue eyes, brown hair, fair complexion, 5'7¾. Disability discharge at Convalescent Hospital at Washington, D.C.

Lammel, James. Pvt. Co. M, 12 November 1861 (age 19 at Pittsburgh, PA)–12 April 1865. B: Austria, GER, mule driver. Blue eyes, brown hair, light complexion, 5'6. Discharged at Annapolis, MD.

Lanning, Millard F. Band. Co. F&S, 23 January 1865 (age 30 at NYC, NY)–21 August 1865. B: New York City, NY. Deserted.

Larimore, John. Mustered: Pvt. Co. B, 3rd WI Inf. 22 April 1861. Transferred: Pvt. Co. F, 6th U.S. Cav. 25 October 1862 (age 20 at Knoxville, MD)–29 January 1864. B: Centre Co., PA, farmer. Brown eyes, brown hair, fair complexion, 5'9½. Discharged at Camp 6th Cav., VA.

Larkin, John. Pvt. Co. A, 26 November 1864 (age 21 at Cincinnati, OH)–26 November 1867. B: Kings, IRE, laborer. Hazel eyes, dark hair, fair complexion, 5'6¼. Discharged at Buffalo Springs, TX.

Larkin, William. Pvt. Co. F, 28 November 1864 (age 18 at Cincinnati, OH)–7 January 1865. B: Manhattan, IL, laborer. Blue eyes, light hair, ruddy complexion, 5'7¼. Deserted.

Larmore, George. Pvt. Co. I, 7 September 1861 (age 21 at Rochester, NY)–10 August 1863. B: Niagara Co., NY, farmer. Brown eyes, brown hair, fair complexion, 5'11¾. D: 10 August 1863 from chronic diarrhea at Middleburg, Wyoming Co., NY.

Larochefoucault, Charles George. Rct. 16 November 1864 (age 22 at NYC, NY)–22 November 1864. B: Montreal, CAN, jeweler. Hazel eyes, brown hair, sallow complexion, 5'5. Deserted.

Lathrop, James R. Pvt. Co. G, 19 August 1861 (age 18 at Rochester, NY)–19 August 1864. B: Dutchess Co., NY, sailor. Blue eyes, black hair, dark complexion, 5'9. Appointed a Hospital Steward 4 March 1864. Discharged at Lincoln Hospital, Washington, D.C.

Lauderbach, Andrew. Pvt. Co. D, 7 August 1861 (age 31 at Pittsburgh, PA)–7 August 1864. B: Washington Co., PA, miner. Black eyes, black hair, dark complexion, 5'10½. Discharged at City Point, VA. D: 10 May 1919, Washington Co., PA.

Lauer, Benjamin. Cpl. Co. B, 27 July 1861 (age 21 at Columbus, OH)–26 July 1864. B: Lehigh Co., PA, carpenter. Grey eyes, sandy hair, ruddy complexion, 5'9¼. Discharged.

Laughlin, Elias. Pvt. Co. D, 8 August 1861 (age 25 at Pittsburgh, PA)–8 August 1864. B: Allegheny Co., PA, miner. Blue eyes, brown hair, sandy complexion, 5'10. Discharged at City Point, VA.

Laughlin, Washington. Mustered: Pvt. Co. A, 12th PA Inf. 25 April 1861–5 August 1861. Mustered out at Harrisburg, PA. Enlisted: Pvt. Co. D, 6th U.S. Cav. 20 August 1861 (age 27 at Pittsburgh, PA)–24 November 1861. B: Armstrong Co., PA, miner. Black eyes, black hair, dark complexion, 5'8. Deserted.

Lawler, Martin. Pvt. Co. I, 28 September 1861 (age 21 at Pottsville, PA)–28 September 1864. B: Tolert, IRE, miner. Hazel eyes, brown hair, fair complexion, 5'6½. Discharged at Harrisonburg, VA.

Lawrence, Charles W. Pvt. Co. L, 3 July 1864 (age 19 at Rochester, NY)–24 June 1865. B: Adrian, MI, laborer. Blue eyes, light hair, light complexion, 5'7¾. Deserted 24 June 1865 at Frederick City, MD. AGO released from service 8 February 1892 under Act of Congress.

Leach, Francisco. Pvt. Co. B, 5 August 1861 (age 21 at Cleveland, OH)–5 August 1864. B: Burton, Geauga Co., OH, carpenter. Grey eyes, light hair, ruddy complexion, 5'9¼. MIA, Youngsville (Stoneman's Raid), 11 May 1863. Reported 24 September 1863 at Culpepper, VA. Discharged at Lighthouse Point, VA. Mustered: Pvt.-Cpl. Co. F, 5th OH Inf. 30 August 1864.

Leach, Henry. Pvt. Co. E, 19 August 1861 (age 18 at Cleveland, OH)–12 January 1863. B: Hudson, Summit Co., OH, farmer. Grey eyes, light hair, ruddy complexion, 5'4½. Disability discharge at Washington, D.C.

Leach, Oscar. Pvt. Co. I, 23 September 1861 (age 24 at Rochester, NY)–1 May 1862. B: Cortland Co., NY, farmer. Blue eyes, light hair, dark complexion, 5'6½. Deserted.

Leader, George W. Mustered: Pvt. Co. F, 37th PA Inf. 11 June 1861. Transferred: Pvt. Co. B, 6th U.S. Cav. 27 October 1862 (age 19 at Knoxville, MD)–27 April 1864. B: Hopewell, PA, farmer. Grey eyes, light hair, dark complexion, 5'6. POW (captured while on picket), Richard's Ford, 14 February 1863. Discharged at Camp 6th Cav., VA.

Leathers, William Thomas. Mustered: Pvt. Co. A, 45th PA Inf. 16 August 1861. Transferred: Pvt. Co. I, 6th U.S. Cav. 27 October 1862 (age 19 at Knoxville, MD)–27 August 1864. B: Centre Co., PA, farmer. Brown eyes, brown hair, sandy complexion, 5'10. WIA (both hips). Discharged at Harper's Ferry, VA. Mustered: Pvt. Co. I, 210th PA Inf. September 1864. D: 1904, Curtin, Centre, PA.

Leavey, Brian. Pvt. Co. M, 7 September 1864 (age 19 at Floyd, NY)–29 July 1865. B: Co. Longford, IRE, laborer. Grey eyes, sandy hair, fair complexion, 5'8½. Deserted.

Lechner, Lorenz. Mustered: Pvt. Co. I, McLane's Erie Inf. Rgt. 21 April 1861–21 Jul 1861. Mustered out at Erie, PA. Enlisted: Pvt. Co. G, 6th U.S. Cav. 8 August 1861 (age 35 at Erie Co., PA)–8 August 1864. B: Wurzburg, GER, laborer. Brown eyes, black hair, fair complexion, 5'5½. Discharged at Lighthouse Point, VA.

Lee, John. Enlisted: Pvt.-Cpl. Co. I, 2nd U.S. Dragoons, 12 August 1850–12 August 1855. Discharged at Ft. Belknap, TX. Enlisted: Pvt. G.M.S., 21 November 1855–10 October 1860, Albany, NY. Reenlisted: 10 October 1861, G.M.S. Transferred: Sgt.-Sgm.-1st Sgt. Cos. K, F&S, K, 6th U.S. Cav. 10 October 1860 (age 30 at Albany, NY)–21 September 1862. Discharged by appointment as 2nd Lt. 6th U.S.

Cav., Harpers Ferry, VA. B: Co. Tipperary, IRE, painter. Grey eyes, light hair, fair complexion, 5'9. D: 24 April 1890.

Lee, Thomas. Mustered: Pvt. Co. D, 8th OH Inf. 6 June 1861. Transferred: Pvt. Co. C, 6th U.S. Cav. 24 October 1862 (age 18 at Knoxville, MD)–23 June 1863. B: Harm Co., OH. Blue eyes, light hair, light complexion, 5'9. WIA, Beverly Ford. D: 23 June 1863 from wounds received in action at hospital in Alexandria, VA.

Lee, William H. Mustered: Pvt. Co. B, 110th PA Inf. 24 October 1861. Transferred: Farrier–Pvt. Co. B, 6th U.S. Cav. 28 October 1862 (age 21 at Knoxville, MD)–23 September 1865. B: Berkley Co., VA, blacksmith. Grey eyes, light hair, light complexion, 5'10. POW (captured while on picket), Richard's Ford, 14 February 1863. Reenlisted: 14 February 1864 at Camp 6th Cav. Deserted 28 July 1865. Apprehended 3 August 1865. Deserted 23 September 1865.

Lees, John. Bugler. Co, K, 20 August 1861 (age 18 at Rochester, NY)–20 August 1864. B: GER, farmer. Black eyes, black hair, florid complexion, 5'2¾. Discharged at City Point, VA.

Lego, Martin W. Mustered: Pvt. Co. K, 110th PA Inf. 19 December 1861. Transferred: Pvt. Co. I, 6th U.S. Cav. 26 October 1862 (age 22 at Knoxville, MD)–24 September 1864. B: 17 July 1840, Blair Co., PA, teamster. Blue eyes, brown hair, ruddy complexion, 5'8. Discharged in the field, VA. D: 28 May 1867, Tyrone, PA.

LeMotte, John O. Cpl. Cos. I, K, 7 August 1861 (age 24 at Rochester, NY)–19 December 1862. B: Bern, SWZ, harness maker. Blue eyes, brown hair, florid complexion, 5'5. Disability discharge at Falmouth, VA. Note: Enlisted in Co. I, appointed to Co. K.

Lenix, Simon. Pvt. Cos. C, L, 22 October 1861 (age 23 at Mount Joy, PA)–22 October 1864. B: Mount Joy, Lancaster Co., PA, musician. Grey eyes, light hair, light complexion, 5'7. Deserted 26 April 1862. Apprehended 20 March 1863. Discharged 22 October 1864 at Cedar Creek, VA. D: 22 February 1882, Toledo, OH.

Lenox, Jacob. Pvt. Co. K, 26 July 1861 (age 34 at Warren, OH)–26 July 1864. B: Geauga Co., OH, furnace man. Blue eyes, brown hair, brown complexion, 5'7. Discharged in the field, VA. Mustered: Pvt. Co. K, 29th OH Inf. 24 August 1864–13 July 1865.

Leonard, Frederick. Rct. 10 July 1864 (age 21 at Meadon, NY)–11 August 1864. B: Hinsdale, NY, farmer. Brown eyes, dark hair, dark complexion, 5'8½. Deserted 4 August 1864. Apprehended. Discharged 11 August 1864 for disability at Carlisle Barracks, PA.

Leonard, John. Pvt. Co. F, 10 July 1861 (age 22 at Pittsburgh, PA)–15 July 1865. Bo: Staffordshire, ENG, puddler. Grey eyes, auburn hair, dark complexion, 5' 4¼. WIA, Five Forks, 30 March 1865. Discharged at Lighthouse Point, VA. Reenlisted: 10 August 1864. Disability discharge 15 July 1865 at Carlisle Barracks, PA.

Leonard, Wells. Pvt. Co. E, 14 September 1861 (age 23 at Cleveland, OH)–4 April 1865. B: Syracuse, NY, teamster. Blue eyes, dark hair, fair complexion, 5' 9. POW, Madison Court-House, 25 September 1863 to 22 February 1864. Paroled, reported at NYC in confinement. Discharged at Camp Parole, Annapolis, MD. D: 24 October 1909.

Leonard, William Webster. Cpl. Co. E, 9 September 1861 (age 26 at Columbus, OH)–6 December 1862. B: St. Lawrence Co., NY, clerk. Hazel eyes, sandy hair, ruddy complexion, 5' 9. Disability discharge at Florence, RI. Dropped from rolls 31 December 1862. D: 1914.

Leony, Arthur. Pvt. Co. A, 15 November 1864 (age 24 at Cincinnati, OH)–30 May 1865. B: Marseilles, FRA, fruit dealer. Black eyes, black hair, dark complexion, 5' 8. Deserted.

Lepper, John. Cpl. Co. B, 7 August 1861 (age 20 at Cleveland, OH)–7 August 1864. B: 1841 London, ENG, engineer. Grey eyes, brown hair, ruddy complexion, 5' 6½. POW, Coal Harbor, 27 June 1862–? Discharged at Washington, D.C. Afterward, served in the General Service, USA. D: 6 July 1911.

Lepper, William M. Cpl.-Sgt. Co. B, 7 August 1861 (age 18 at Cleveland, OH)–10 April 1863. B: London, ENG, clerk. Blue eyes, brown hair, fair complexion, 5' 7½. POW (captured while on picket), Richard's Ford, 14 February 1863. Paroled. WIA (left arm), Upperville. Disability discharge at Baltimore, MD. D: 28 December 1908.

Letsinger, William G. Mustered: Pvt. Co. G, 14th IN Inf. 7 June 1861. Transferred: Pvt. Co. C, 6th U.S. Cav. 24 October 1862 (age 27 at Knoxville, MD)–1 June 1864. B: 24 April 1844, Knox Co., TN, farmer. Dark eyes, dark hair, florid complexion, 5' 9. Discharged in the field, VA. D: 12 January 1924.

Lewis, Evan. Pvt. Co. D, 28 August 1861 (age 29 at Pittsburgh, PA)–1 July 1863. B: Merthyr Tydfil, South Wales, WAL, coal miner. Black eyes, black hair, dark complexion, 5' 5½. Deserted.

Lewis, Harry W. Sgt.-1st Sgt. Co. G, 29 July 1861

(age 21 at Erie Co., PA)–29 July 1864. B: 30 August 1840, Harborcreek Twp., Erie Co., PA, farmer. Grey eyes, light hair, fair complexion, 5' 5½. POW, Fairfield, 3 July 1863–17 February 1864. Paroled, reported at Camp Parole. Discharged. D: 9 March 1912, Erie, Erie, PA.

Lewis, James. Mustered: Unknown NY USV unit, 30 September 1861. Transferred: Pvt. Co. I, 6th U.S. Cav. 27 October 1862 (age 21 at Knoxville, MD)–29 July 1865. B: 3 September 1840, Orange Co., NY, laborer. Grey eyes, dark hair, ruddy complexion, 6'1. MIA, Funkstown. Discharged at Frederick, MD. Mustered: Pvt. Co. H, 2nd NY Cav. (Provisional), 17 June–9 August 1865 (Louisville, KY). D: 1 January 1919.

Lewis, James T. Pvt. Co. F, 13 December 1864 (age 26 at Philadelphia, PA)–26 January 1865. B: Houonduler, Sandwich Islands, CAN, sailor. Grey eyes, brown hair, dark complexion, 5' 6. Deserted 14 December 1864. Apprehended 16 December 1865. Deserted.

Lewis, John. Pvt. Cos. K, F, 15 August 1861 (age 21 at Rochester, NY)–20 April 1862. B: Long Island, NY, copper. Grey eyes, brown hair, fair complexion, 5' 7¼. Deserted. AGO charge removed.

Lewis, Lewis. Pvt. Cos. C, L, D, 2 December 1861 (age 18 at Columbia, PA)–2 December 1864. B: South Wales, Great Britain, WAL, rolling mill man. Hazel eyes, brown hair, fair complexion, 5' 3. Discharged in the field, VA.

Lewis, Ramsy J. Mustered: USV. Transferred: Pvt. Co. I, 6th U.S. Cav. 27 October 1862 (age 20 at Knoxville, MD)–10 May 1863. B: Passaic Co., NJ, blacksmith. Blue eyes, light hair, fair complexion, 5'10. Deserted.

Lewis, Royal P. Mustered: Pvt. Co. D, 3rd WI Inf. 13 May 1861. Transferred: Pvt. Co. B, 6th U.S. Cav. 1 December 1862 (age 26 at Falmouth, VA)–20 January 1864. B: 30 November 1835, Loraine, OH. Grey eyes, light hair, dark complexion, 6'. MIA, Funkstown. D: 20 January 1864 of disease at Camp 6th Cav., VA.

Lewis, William. Pvt. Co. F, 6 July 1861 (age 28 at Pittsburgh, PA)–10 May 1863. B: Carmody, WAL, coal miner. Blue eyes, brown hair, fair complexion, 5' 8¾. Deserted.

Lewis, William. Pvt. Co. F, 13 November 1864 (age 22 at Harrisburg, PA)–7 January 1865. B: Co. Derry, IRE, seaman. Blue eyes, sandy hair, florid complexion, 5' 8. Deserted 1 January 1865. Apprehended 7 January 1865. Deserted the same day.

Light, Isaac Newton. Bugler. Co. C, 29 March

1864 (age 14 at Washington, DC)–25 February 1866. B: Frederick, VA, musician. Blue eyes, brown hair, fair complexion, 4'8. Gained from recruit depot. Deserted from Waco, TX.

Light. William H. Pvt. Co. C, 26 March 1864 (age 28 at Washington, DC)–26 March 1867. B: Hardy, VA, miller. Blue eyes, brown hair, fair complexion, 5'10. Gained from recruit depot. Discharged at Waco, TX.

Lightcap, James Sanford. Mustered: Pvt. Co. A, 8th OH Inf. 6 February 1861. Transferred: Pvt. Co. L, 6th U.S. Cav. 26 October 1862 (age 19 at Knoxville, MD)–25 May 1864. B: 1842 Fremont Co., OH. Blue eyes, light hair, light complexion, 5'10. POW, Fairfield, 3 July 1863–? POW (captured by guerrillas), Warrenton, 21 January–26 May 1864. Paroled, reported at Fredericksburg. Discharged at Camp 6th Cav., VA. D: 15 May 1883.

Linch, James. Mustered: Pvt. Co. C, 8th OH Inf. 19 August 1861. Disability discharge 6 October 1862. Enlisted: Pvt. Co. B, 6th U.S. Cav. 24 October 1862 (age 19 at Knoxville, MD)–24 January 1864. B: Philadelphia, PA, boatman. Blue eyes, sandy hair, light complexion, 5'5½. Discharged at Headquarters, Middle Military Division. Alternate surname: Lynch.

Lindley, Martha Parks (alias Smith, James). Pvt. Co. D, 12 August 1861 (age 27 at Pittsburgh, PA)–12 August 1864. B: Co. Derry, IRE, soldier (homemaker). Brown eyes, black hair, dark complexion, 5'8. Discharged in the field, VA. Note: Martha and William were married.

Lindley, William D. Pvt. Co. D, 16 August 1861 (age 27 at Pittsburgh, PA)–17 January 1863. B: Portage, Cambria Co., PA, boatman. Blue eyes, black hair, sandy complexion, 5'10. Accidentally shot himself in the ankle. Disability discharged at Emory Hospital, Washington, D.C.

Lindsley, Charles Jr. Pvt. Cos. C, L, 4 January 1862 (age 21 at Philadelphia, PA)–4 January 1865. B: 1842, Mercer Co., NJ, farmer. Grey eyes, brown hair, ruddy complexion, 5'6¾. Discharged at Camp Russell, VA. D: 1923, Titusville, Mercer, NJ.

Lines, William N. Mustered: Pvt. Co. G, 50th PA Inf. 26 September 1861. Transferred: Pvt. Co. H, 6th U.S. Cav. 28 October 1862 (age 18 at Knoxville, MD)–28 July 1864. B: Bradford Co., PA. Black eyes, black hair, dark complexion, 5'9. Discharged in the field, VA.

List, Thomas R. Musician 3rd Class. Co. F&S, 15 October 1861 (age 18 at Mount Joy, PA)–15 October 1864. B: Columbia, Lancaster Co., PA, musician. Grey eyes, brown hair, light complexion, 5'9. Discharged at Strausburg, VA.

Littell, John. Pvt. Co. D, 14 August 1861 (age 22 at Pittsburgh, PA)–14 August 1864. B: Pittsburgh, Allegheny Co., PA, painter. Grey eyes, brown hair, sallow complexion, 5'6½. Discharged at Washington, D.C.

Little, Christopher P. Pvt. Co. I, 19 September 1861 (age 34 at Rochester, NY)–9 January 1862. B: Co. Meath, IRE, farmer. Blue eyes, brown hair, sandy complexion, 5'8. Disability discharged at Washington, D.C.

Little, R.J.M. 15 October 1861 (age 22 at Mount Joy, PA)–15 October 1861. B: LaHines Twp., PA, musician. Grey eyes, sandy hair, light complexion, 5'7. Deserted the same day he enlisted.

Livingston, Francis Marion. Mustered: Pvt. Co. K, 14th IN Inf. 7 June 1861. Transferred: Pvt. Co. C, 6th U.S. Cav. 23 October 1862 (age 19 at Knoxville, MD)–7 June 1865. B: 9 February 1842 Greene Co., IN. Blue eyes, light hair, fair complexion, 5'9½. POW, Brandy Station, 11 October 1863–? (Andersonville). Discharged at Carlisle Barracks, PA. D: 17 August 1922.

Lloyd, Joseph Paxton. Pvt.-Sgt.-Cpl. Co. H, 19 March 1862 (at Alexandria, VA)–1 April 1865. No other information provided. MIA, Funkstown. Discharged at Washington, D.C.

Lloyd, William. Pvt.-1st Sgt. Co. H, 29 July 1861 (age 23 at Philadelphia, PA)–25 September 1867. B: Williamsport, Lycoming Co., PA, clerk. Blue eyes, brown hair, ruddy complexion, 5'11. Discharged 29 July 1864 in the field, VA. Reenlisted: 23 January 1865 at NYC. Discharged by SO 421 on 25 September 1867 at Mt. Pleasant, TX.

Long, John B. Musician, 2nd Class. Co. F&S; 15 October 1861 (age 21 at Mount Joy, PA)–15 October 1864. B: Spring Mills, Centre Co., PA, musician. Grey eyes, brown hair, light complexion, 5'8. Discharged at Strausburg, VA.

Looney, Daniel. Rct. 15 August 1864 (age 29 at Cincinnati, OH)–16 August 1864. B: Hamilton, CAN, boatman. Blue eyes, brown hair, fair complexion, 5'8¾. Deserted.

Loop, Francis M. Mustered: Pvt. Co. E, 14th IN Inf. 6 July 1861. WIA (saber wound to right arm). Transferred: Co. C, 4th U.S. Art. 20 October 1862–19 April 1864. Discharged at Brandy Station, VA. Enlisted: Rct. 6th U.S. Cav. 15 June 1864 (age 25 at Washington, DC)–19 June 1864. B: Williamsburg, OH. Grey eyes, brown hair, sallow complexion, 6'½. Deserted at Washington, D.C. Enlisted: Co. F, 5th U.S. Art. 4 October 1867. Discharged 4

October 1870, Ft. Adams, RI. D: 13 November 1910.

Losey, Henry N. (alias Losey, Nicholas). Pvt. Cos. G, C, 1 August 1861 (age 21 at Rochester, NY)–24 May 1865. B: November 1839 Orleans Co., NY, farmer. Blue eyes, black hair, florid complexion, 5' 5¼. MIA, Fairfield. Reenlisted: 10 February 1864 at Brandy Station, VA.

Loughery, John. Pvt. Co. A, 24 September 1861 (age 25 at Philadelphia, PA)–24 September 1864. B: IRE, laborer. Blue eyes, brown hair, light complexion, 5'11. Discharged at Harrisonburg, VA.

Louther, Adam. Pvt. Co. C, 28 October 1862 (age 23 at Knoxville, MD)–8 September 1864. B: Jefferson Co., OH, farmer. Hazel eyes, brown hair, light complexion, 5' 8. POW, Fairfield, 3 July 1863–7 January 1864. Paroled, reported at Annapolis, MD. Discharged in the field, VA.

Lowden, James J. Enlisted: Marine Corps, 1859–1861. Enlisted: Pvt. Cos. I, M, 9 July 1861 (age 24 at Tyrone City, PA)–9 July 1864. B: New York, NY, moulder. Grey eyes, light hair, fair complexion, 5' 7½. Captured at Williamsburg, VA. POW at Richmond, VA and Salisbury, NC. Paroled May 1862 and arrived in New York 9 June 1862 via steamer "Guide." Gained 16 July 1862 from parole. MIA at Fairfield. Discharged in the field, VA.

Loyd, Adolphus W. Enlisted (Confederacy): Wagoner, Co. D, 4th VA Cav. 2 January 1863–1 March 1864. Deserted. Enlisted (Union): Pvt. Co. L, 11 March 1864 (age 20 at Washington, DC)–11 March 1867. B: Culpepper, VA, farmer. Grey eyes, brown hair, fair complexion, 5' 7. On detached service at Gen. Meade's HQ since 12 March 1864. Dropped by expiration of service. Pension denotes he also served in Co. B, Powell's Det. U.S.C. Inf. And Co. K, 49th U.S.C. Inf. Filed in AR.

Loyd, William. Pvt.-1st Sgt.-Pvt. Co. H, 8 August 1861 (age 26 at Philadelphia, PA)–8 August 1864. B: Schuylkill Co., PA, boatman. Hazel eyes, brown hair, ruddy complexion, 5' 8½. POW, Coal Harbor, 27 June 1862. Discharged at Harper's Ferry, VA.

Lucas, Charles. Sgt. Co. A, 4 November 1861 (age 20 at Pottsville, PA)–4 November 1864. B: Manchester, ENG, moulder. Brown eyes, black hair, dark complexion, 5' 6. Discharged at Cedar Creek, VA.

Lucas, Robert. Pvt. Co. D, 27 August 1861 (age 32 at Pittsburgh, PA)–27 August 1864. B: Indiana Co., PA, miner. Brown eyes, black hair,

dark complexion, 5'11½. Discharged at Halltown, VA.

Luce, William W. Pvt. Co. D, 12 September 1863 (age 27 at Rockville, MD)–17 March 1865. B: Warren Co., PA, farmer. Blue eyes, light hair, light complexion, 5' 8¾. Disability discharge at Philadelphia, PA.

Luckett, John W. Mustered: Co. A, 3rd MD Inf. 13 August 1861. Transferred: Pvt. Co. K, 6th U.S. Cav. 28 October 1862 (age 32 at Knoxville, MD)–30 April 1865. B: Fauquier Co., VA, boatman. Grey eyes, dark hair, florid complexion, 5' 8½. Reenlisted: 11 February 1864 at Brandy Station, VA. Deserted 30 April 1865. AGO released from service 8 February 1893 by Act of Congress, approved 11 April 1890.

Ludwick, Charles. Pvt. Co. M, 7 November 1864 (age 19 at Cincinnati, OH)–26 December 1865. B: Midway, KY, laborer. Blue eyes, light hair, fair complexion, 5' 4. Deserted 3 February 1865. Apprehended 7 February 1865. Deserted 26 December 1865.

Luh, Casper. Pvt. Cos. F, M, 3 July 1861 (age 25 at Pittsburgh, PA)–3 July 1864. B: Nordshausen, GER, laborer. Blue eyes, light hair, fair complexion, 5' 5. MIA, Fairfield. Discharged at Lighthouse Point, VA.

Lukeman, Michael. Pvt. Co. E, 24 August 1861 (at Cleveland, OH)–30 January 1864. WIA, Upperville. Disability discharge at Carlisle Barracks, PA.

Luse, John. Pvt. Co. B, 27 July 1861 (age 27 at Columbus, OH)–27 July 1864. B: Baden, GER, farmer. Grey eyes, light hair, ruddy complexion, 5' 9. Discharged at Hospital, Washington, D.C.

Lynch, Michael. Mustered: Pvt. Co. C, 14th IN Inf. 7 June 1861. Transferred: Pvt. Co. C, 6th U.S. Cav. 23 October 1862 (age 27 at Knoxville, MD)–23 February 1866. B: Co. Limerick, IRE. Blue eyes, light hair, fair complexion, 5' 5½. Discharged at Waco, TX.

Lynders, John. Pvt. Co. A, 7 December 1864 (age 28 at Philadelphia, PA)–23 May 1865. B: Milwaukee, WI, ferryman. Brown eyes, dark hair, dark complexion, 5' 7. Deserted.

Lynn, Eli C. Pvt. Co. H, 14 August 1861 (age 24 at Philadelphia, PA)–16 October 1862. B: Summit Co., OH, lumberman. Blue eyes, brown hair, ruddy complexion, 5' 5. D: 16 October 1862 at Hospital, Washington, D.C.

Lytle, A. G. Pvt. Co. K, 11 July 1861 (age 21 at Franklin, PA)–16 July 1864. B: Rockland Twp., PA, clerk. Hazel eyes, brown hair, light complexion, 5' 3½. Discharged in the field, VA.

Mack, Thomas. Pvt. Co. D, 16 August 1861 (age 19 at Pittsburgh, PA)–27 March 1862. B: Brooke Co., VA (WV), farmer. Black eyes, brown hair, sandy complexion, 5' 7½. Deserted.

Mack, Thomas. Pvt. Co. L, 7 October 1861 (age 18 at Cleveland, OH)–2 March 1863. B: Clan, IRE, laborer. Blue eyes, brown hair, ruddy complexion, 5' 6¼. Disability discharge at Falmouth, VA.

MacKelvey, John W. Pvt. Co. B, 6 August 1861 (age 18 at Cleveland, OH)–8 August 1862. B: Williams Co., OH, farmer. Blue eyes, light hair, fair complexion, 5' 6½. D: 8 August 1862 from typhoid fever at Harrison's Landing, VA.

Mackley, Thomas J. Pvt. Co. M, 8 October 1864 (age 35 at NYC, NY)–8 October 1867. B: Attica, NY, carriage trimmer. Blue eyes, black hair, dark complexion, 6'. Discharged at Mt. Pleasant, TX.

Madden, Daniel. Pvt. Co. E, 2nd U.S. Dragoons, 9 December 1850 (Boston). Also served with HQ, 1st U.S. Dragoons. Discharged: 9 December 1855, Ft. Leavenworth, Kansas Territory. Enlisted: Co. B, 2nd U.S. Dragoons, 1 May 1856–28 April 1861. Discharged at Ft. Critten-den, Utah Territory, by order, AGO, a 1st. Sgt. Enlisted: Comm. Sgt. Co. F&S, 6th U.S. Cav. 14 August 1861 (age 27 at Pittsburgh, PA)–4 November 1861. B: Liverpool, ENG. Blue eyes, brown hair, fair complexion, 5' 7½. Discharged by appointment to 2nd Lt., 6th Cav., at Washington, D.C. WIA, Beverly Ford. Promoted to Cpt. 10 May 1867; Maj. 7th U.S. Cav. 21 May 1886. Retired: 5 October 1887.

Maenner, Charles. Pvt. Co. F, 15 July 1861 (age 26 at Pittsburgh, PA)–15 July 1864. B: Zweibrucken, GER, saddler. Grey eyes, brown hair, dark complexion, 5' 8. POW from ?–8 January 1864. Paroled, reported at Annapolis, MD. Discharged at Lighthouse Point, VA. Enlisted: Cpl. Co. F, 50th PA Inf. 28 September 1864–1 June 1865.

Magill, James. Pvt. Co. C, 14 October 1861 (age 21 at Philadelphia, PA)–24 March 1862. B: Co. Donegal, IRE, clerk. Blue eyes, light hair, fair complexion, 5' 6½. Deserted.

Maglet, John. Pvt. Co. A, 1 October 1861 (age 19 at Cleveland, OH)–1 October 1864. B: GER, bartender. Black eyes, brown hair, fair complexion, 5' 7½. WIA, Williamsburg. Discharged at Strausburg, VA.

Maguire, Edward. Pvt. Co. I, 3 September 1861 (age 25 at Rochester, NY)–3 September 1864. B: Co. Tyrone, IRE, shoemaker, Grey eyes, brown hair, dark complexion, 5'11½. Discharged at Camp 6th Cav., in the field, VA.

Maguire, James. 5 November 1864 (age 21 at Harrisburg, PA)–1864. B: Toronto, CAN, waiter. Grey eyes, fair hair, fair complexion, 5' 6½. Deserted.

Maguire, Walter H. Cpl. Co. H, 6 August 1861 (age 21 at Philadelphia, PA)–26 January 1863. B: Philadelphia, PA, book keeper. Grey eyes, brown hair, fair complexion, 5' 8½. Disability discharge at Philadelphia, PA.

Mahar, Phillip (alias Meagher, Phillip). Mustered: Pvt. Co. E, 60th NY Inf. 16 September 1861. Transferred: Cpl. Co. M, 6th U.S. Cav. 23 October 1862 (age 18 at Knoxville, MD)–26 September 1864. B: 1 May 1845, Malone, NY. Grey eyes, brown hair, light complexion, 5' 6. WIA (neck)/POW, Fairfield, 3 July–24 August 1863. Paroled at Annapolis, MD. Discharged at Berryville, VA. Mustered: Pvt. Co. B, 43rd OH Inf. 4 March 1865–13 July 1865 (Louisville, KY). D: 6 June 1916, Centralia, Lewis, WA.

Mahoney, Denis W. Pvt. Co. A, 26 November 1864 (age 28 at Cincinnati, OH)–8 November 1865. B: Co. Kilkenny, IRE, laborer. Hazel eyes, dark hair, dark complexion, 5' 6. Deserted.

Mahoney, John. Pvt. Co. I, 28 September 1861 (age 27 at Rochester, NY)–2 January 1864. B: IRE, laborer. Blue eyes, brown hair, florid complexion, 5' 7½. Disability discharge at Lincoln General Hospital, Washington, D.C.

Mahoney, Peter. Mustered: Pvt. Co. F, 60th NY Inf. 9 July 1861. Transferred: Pvt. Co. A, 6th U.S. Cav. 25 October 1862 (age 21 at Knoxville, MD)–24 September 1863. B: Ramsey, NY. Dark eyes, light hair, light complexion, 5' 3½. WIA, Beverly Ford. Disability discharge at Division Hospital No. 2 at Annapolis, MD.

Maier, Albert. Pvt. Cos. C, L, 19 November 1861 (age 22 at Philadelphia, PA)–14 March 1863. B: Um, GER, soldier. Grey eyes, brown hair, light complexion, 5'10. Disability discharge at Hospital, Frederick, MD.

Malmesbury, Joel B. Pvt.-Sgt. Cos. C, L, 1 December 1861 (age 21 at Philadelphia, PA)–21 November 1864. B: Falls Twp., Bucks Co., PA, farmer. Hazel eyes, light hair, light complexion, 5' 6. Reenlisted: 16 February 1864, Brandy Station, VA. Discharged 21 November 1864 near Winchester, VA, by promotion to Cpt., Co. D, 6th U.S.C. Cav.

Malone, Martin. Pvt. Co. K, 14 August 1861 (age 25 at Rochester, NY)–14 May 1862. B: IRE, carpenter. Blue eyes, black hair, florid complexion, 5' 5¾. Disability discharge at Camp east of Capitol, Washington, D.C.

Malony, Patrick. 22 November 1864 (age 34 at Cincinnati, OH)–Not enough information. B: Dublin, IRE, laborer. Hazel eyes, brown hair, ruddy complexion, 5'7.

Maloy, Thomas. Pvt. Cos. C, L, 19 October 1861 (age 22 at Cleveland, OH)–1 July 1862. B: Dublin, IRE, moulder. Blue eyes, brown hair, ruddy complexion, 5'4. Deserted.

Manahan, Cornelius. Pvt. Co. G, 12 August 1861 (age 21 at Columbus, OH)–12 August 1864. B: London, ENG, boatman. Blue eyes, brown hair, ruddy complexion, 5'6¼. MIA, Fairfield. Discharged at Lighthouse Point, VA. Mustered: Co. I, 193rd OH Inf. March 1865–4 August 1865.

Mandry, George A. Pvt. Co. L, 15 December 1864 (age 21 at Philadelphia, PA)–31 March 1865. B: Wurttemberg, GER, farmer. Brown eyes, dark hair, dark complexion, 5'5½. Deserted.

Manehan, Patrick F. Pvt. Co. A, 16 September 1861 (age 21 at Philadelphia, PA)–26 January 1862. B: Philadelphia, PA, brick maker. Blue eyes, brown hair, light complexion, 5'9½. Deserted.

Manell, Mathias. Pvt. Co. F, 28 October 1862 (age 21 at Knoxville, MD)–29 June 1864. B: Koeln, Prussia, GER, carpenter. Grey eyes, dark hair, swarthy complexion, 5'9. POW, Fairfield, 3 July 1863–19 February 1864. Paroled, reported at Camp Parole. Discharged at Camp 6th Cav., VA.

Mangle, Nicholas. Pvt. Co. L, 2 February 1864 (age 23 at NYC, NY)–2 February 1867. B: IRE, shoemaker. Blue eyes, black hair, ruddy complexion, 5'6. Discharged at Jacksboro, TX.

Manhon, Joseph. Pvt. Co. E, 6 September 1861 (age 18 at Columbus, OH)–6 September 1864. B: Licking Co., OH, farmer. Grey eyes, brown hair, sallow complexion, 5'10¾. Discharged at Berryville, VA.

Manice, John. Cpl. Co. A, 17 September 1861 (age 23 at Philadelphia, PA)–20 May 1862. B: Co. Tyrone, IRE, wheel wright. Grey eyes, dark hair, dark complexion, 5'7½. KIA, New Bridge, 20 May 1862.

Mann, George W. Mustered: Pvt. Co. C, 1st MO Cav. Transferred: Pvt. Co. G, 6th U.S. Cav. 28 October 1862 (age 19 at Knoxville, MD)–26 January 1863. B: Montreal, Quebec, CAN, shoemaker. Blue eyes, light hair, light complexion, 5'5. Deserted. D: 22 February 1898.

Manson, John Woods. Pvt. Co. K, 16 July 1861 (age 23 at Franklin, PA)–6 November 1861. B: Sandy Creek Twp., Mercer Co., PA, farmer. Grey eyes, black hair, light complexion, 5'8.

D: 6 November 1861 from typhoid fever at Hospital at Camp east of Capitol, Washington, D.C.

Manville, John S. D. Mustered: Pvt. Co. F, 84th PA Inf. Transferred: Pvt. Co. A, 6th U.S. Cav. 28 October 1862 (age 18 at Knoxville, MD)–28 September 1864. B: 1845, Lycoming Co., PA. Blue eyes, dark hair, light complexion, 5'5. POW, Fairfield, 3 July 1863–18 January 1864. Paroled, reported at Annapolis, MD. Discharged at Harrisonburg, VA. Enlisted: Sgt. Maj. Co. H, 5th U.S.V.V. Inf. D: 1913, Boise, Ada, ID.

Marchland, Henry. Rct. 19 August 1861 (age 20 at Rochester, NY)–22 August 1861. B: Ogdensburg, St. Lawrence Co., NY, shoemaker. Brown eyes, black hair, dark complexion, 5'2½. Rejected recruit at Pittsburgh, PA.

Marion, Eugene. Pvt. Co. F, 23 November 1864 (age 27 at Cincinnati, OH)–31 May 1865. B: Troy, FRA, carpenter. Blue eyes, light hair, fair complexion, 5'6. Deserted.

Marrylees, John. Sgt. Co. A, 17 September 1861 (age 21 at Philadelphia, PA)–26 May 1864. B: Philadelphia, PA, teamster. Grey eyes, brown hair, florid complexion, 5'5. Deserted 26 May 1864. Discharged 3 January 1888 at Washington, D.C. to date to 26 May 1864 by reason of desertion.

Marshall, Andrew. Rct. 1 September 1861 (age 33 at Cleveland, OH)–2 September 1861. B: Manchester, ENG, musician. Blue eyes, light hair, sallow complexion, 5'7. Deserted.

Marshall, James. Pvt. Co. E, 1 September 1861 (age 15 at Cleveland, OH)–1 September 1864. B: Quebec, CAN, teamster. Blue eyes, brown hair, ruddy complexion, 5'4. MIA, Fairfield. Discharged at Berryville, VA.

Marshall, Lloyd. Mustered: Pvt. Co. E, 50th NY Eng. 3 September 1861. Transferred: Pvt. Co. E, 6th U.S. Cav. 28 October 1862 (age 19 at Knoxville, MD)–1 September 1864. B: Addison Co., NY. Blue eyes, dark hair, dark complexion, 5'10.

Marshall, Milo A. Pvt. Co. B, 16 August 1861 (age 22 at Columbus, OH)–19 May 1862. B: Randolph, OH, farmer. Brown eyes, black hair, sandy complexion, 5'10. D: 19 May 1862 from typhoid fever at Yorktown Hospital, VA.

Marshel, John Jr. Sgt. Co. D, 21 July 1861 (age 32 at Pittsburgh, PA)–20 July 1861. B: Washington Co., PA, printer. Grey eyes, light hair, sallow complexion, 5'8. Discharged.

Marshell, George. Rct. 20 November 1861 (age 30 at Pittsburgh, PA)–20 December 1861. B:

GER, farmer. Grey eyes, brown hair, light complexion, 5'5½. Disability discharge at Washington, D.C.

Marshman, Eli. 3 October 1864 (age 19 at Rochester, NY)–No further information. B: Wiltshire, ENG, farmer. Hazel eyes, brown hair, florid complexion, 5'10.

Martin, Charles. Pvt. Co. F, 16 December 1864 (age 18 at Cincinnati, OH)–31 March 1865. B: Washington Co., OH, boatman. Dark eyes, brown hair, dark complexion, 5'5. Deserted.

Martin, Henry. Pvt. Co. M, 25 August 1864 (age 21 at Harrisburg, PA)–29 July 1865. B: Morington, IRE, laborer. Blue eyes, brown hair, fresh complexion, 5'7½. Deserted.

Martin, James. Pvt. Co. M, 19 September 1861 (age 22 at Pittsburgh, PA)–6 December 1861. B: SCO, baker. Hazel eyes, sandy hair, light complexion, 5'5. Disability discharge at Washington, D.C.

Martin, Jerima. Mustered: Mayville, WI, Pvt. Co. E, 3rd WI Inf. April 1861. Transferred: Pvt. Co. C, 6th U.S. Cav. 24 October 1862 (age 22 at Knoxville, MD)–24 April 1864. B: Allegheny Co., NY. Black eyes, black hair, dark complexion, 5'7. Discharged at Camp 6th Cav., VA.

Martin, John M. Mustered: Pvt. Co. D, 8th OH Inf. Transferred: Pvt. Co. H, 6th U.S. Cav. 24 October 1862 (age 25 at Knoxville, MD)–1 June 1864. B: Cayuga Co., NY, farmer. Blue eyes, light hair, fair complexion, 5'8. POW, Fairfield, 3 July–30 December 1863. Paroled, reported at Camp 6th Cav. Discharged at Camp 6th Cav., VA.

Martin, Marquis Lafayette. Mustered: Co. C, 14th IN Inf. 7 June 1861. Transferred: Pvt. Co. K, 6th U.S. Cav. 24 October 1862 (age 23 at Knoxville, MD)–24 April 1864. B: 1838, Salem, IN, farmer. Blue eyes, dark hair, dark complexion, 5'9. Discharged at Camp 6th Cav., VA. D: 1901, Rantoul, Champaign, IL.

Martin, Peter. 15 November 1864 (age 21 at Harrisburg, PA)–21 November 1864. B: Co. Antrim, IRE, baker. Grey eyes, light hair, fair complexion, 5'7. Deserted. Sub For S. Jones.

Mason, John. 14 November 1864 (age 18 at Harrisburg, PA)–21 November 1864. B: Co. Tyrone, IRE, boatman. Brown eyes, brown hair, ruddy complexion, 5'7½. Deserted. Sub.

Mason, John C. Mustered: Pvt. Co. F, 8th OH Inf. 5 June 1861. Transferred: Pvt. Co. C, 6th U.S. Cav. 23 October 1862 (age 20 at Knoxville, MD)–24 April 1864. B: Cohocton Co., NY, carpenter. Hazel eyes, dark hair, fair complexion, 5'7. Discharged at Camp 6th Cav., VA.

Masters, William D. Mustered: Cpl. Co. D, 8th OH Inf. 24 June 1861. Transferred: Pvt. Co. C, 6th U.S. Cav. 23 October 1862 (age 22 at Knoxville, MD)–3 July 1863. B: Cuyahoga Co., OH. Grey eyes, brown hair, florid complexion, 5'10. KIA, Fairfield.

Mathews, Edward. Rct. 7 December 1864 (age 24 at Cincinnati, OH)–Not enough information. B: Delaware Co., CAN, carpenter. Hazel eyes, dark hair, fair complexion, 5'7¾.

Mattern, William L. Pvt. Co. H, 12 August 1861 (age 28 at Philadelphia, PA)–3 July 1863. B: Berks Co., PA, boatman. Blue eyes, light hair, fair complexion, 5'6½. WIA, Fairfield. D: 3 July 1863 of wounds received at Fairfield, VA.

Maurer, David. Pvt. Co. D, 8 August 1861 (at Pittsburgh, PA)–8 August 1864. Discharged.

Mayhoin, Isaac. Pvt. Co. A, 28 October 1862 (age 20 at Knoxville, MD)–29 July 1864. B: James Island, VA, farmer. Brown eyes, fair hair, fair complexion, 5'6. POW, Fairfield, 3 July 1863–18 January 1864. Paroled, reported at Annapolis, MD. Discharged at Lighthouse Point, VA.

McAdams, John (alias Marvin, John). Mustered: Pvt. Co. D, 8th OH Inf. Transferred: Pvt. Co. G, 6th U.S. Cav. 27 October 1862 (age 18 at Knoxville, MD)–24 June 1864. B: Poughkeepsie, NY. Hazel eyes, dark hair, dark complexion, 5'4. POW, Fairfield, 3 July 1863–17 February 1864. Paroled, reported at Camp Parole. Discharged at City Point, VA. Mustered: Co. I, 1st U.S.V.V. Inf.

McAlligott, Charles. Pvt. Co. F, 9 July 1861 (age 25 at Pittsburgh, PA)–9 July 1864. B: Co. Kerry, IRE, laborer. Blue eyes, brown hair, dark complexion, 5'8. Deserted 19 July 1863. Apprehended 6 October 1863. Discharged at expiration of service at Lighthouse Point, VA.

McAnale, Robert. Musician 3rd Class. Co. F&S, 15 October 1861 (age 28 at Mount Joy, PA)–15 October 1864. B: Morris Twp., PA, musician. Brown eyes, brown hair, light complexion, 5'11. Discharged at Strausburg, VA.

McBride, George. Mustered: Cpl. Co. D, 14th IN Inf. 7 June 1861. Transferred: Pvt. Co. C, 6th U.S. Cav. 23 October 1862 (age 21 at Knoxville, MD)–Never joined. B: Green Co., IN, farmer. Hazel eyes, brown hair, florid complexion, 5'7. Returned to USV. Transferred: 20th IN Inf. 21 December 1863–6 June 1864 (Louisville, KY).

McBride, James. Pvt. Co. M, 6 September 1861 (age 21 at Pittsburgh, PA)–10 April 1862. B: McKeesport, Allegheny Co., PA, soldier. Dark eyes, brown hair, dark complexion, 5'8. Deserted.

McBride, Robert. Pvt. Co. M, 14 October 1861 (age 20 at Pittsburgh, PA)–17 January 1863. B: McKeesport, Allegheny Co., PA, farmer. Dark eyes, brown hair, fair complexion, 5' 7½. WIA, Williamsburg. Brought to the Seminary Hospital, Hampton, VA, 11 May 1862. Disability discharge at Baltimore, MD.

McCabe, Patrick. Mustered: Pvt. 140th NY Inf. Transferred: Pvt. Co. D, 25 October 1862 (age 18 at Knoxville, MD)–10 June 1863. B: CAN, brushmaker. Blue eyes, light hair, fair complexion, 5' 3. Disability discharge at St. Mary's Hospital, Rochester, NY. Mustered: Pvt. Co. H, 14th NY Heavy Art. 19 October 1863 (Rochester, NY)–14 October 1864. Disability discharged at Ft. Trumbull, CT.

McCaffrey, John. Sgt.-1st Sgt. Co. A, 31 August 1861 (age 26 at Philadelphia, PA)–31 August 1864. B: Kings Co., IRE, shoemaker. Blue eyes, brown hair, dark complexion, 5' 9¾. 7 July 1863: Funkstown: shot the enemy's standard bearer. Discharged at Charlestown, VA.

McCale, Thomas. Rct. 21 July 1861 (age 16 at Columbus, OH)–Not enough information. B: Albany, NY, dyer. Blue eyes, brown hair, fair complexion, 5' 4.

McCallister, James. Sgt. Co. A, 5 October 1861 (age 23 at Pottsville, PA)–9 June 1863. B: Bedfordshire, SCO, laborer. Blue eyes, brown hair, florid complexion, 5' 4. WIA, Beverly Ford. D: from wounds, 9 June 1863.

McCarrell, William. Pvt. Co. M, 11 September 1861 (age 25 at Pittsburgh, PA)–10 September 1864. B: IRE, farmer. Grey eyes, brown hair, fair complexion, 5' 8. WIA/POW, Fairfield, 3 July–24 August 1863. Paroled at Annapolis, MD. Discharged at Berryville, VA.

McCarrick, Neil. Blacksmith-Farrier. Co. H, 13 August 1861 (age 24 at Philadelphia, PA)–14 March 1867. B: Co. Antrim, IRE, blacksmith. Blue eyes, black hair, dark complexion, 5' 7½. MIA/WIA, Fairfield. Reenlisted: 14 March 1864 at Camp 6th Cav., VA. Discharged 14 March 1867 at Austin, TX.

McCarty, Daniel S. Pvt. Co. A, 4 October 1861 (age 21 at Philadelphia, PA)–7 July 1862. B: Philadelphia, PA, printer. Blue eyes, dark hair, fair complexion, 5' 9½. Deserted.

McCarty, John. Pvt. Cos. K, H, 14 August 1861 (age 23 at Rochester, NY)–27 July 1865. B: IRE, farmer. Grey eyes, brown hair, fair complexion, 5' 7¼. Reenlisted: 10 February 1864 at Brandy Station, VA. Deserted 27 July 1865. Released from service 13 November 1891.

McCasey, Patrick. Pvt. Co. B, 1 January 1862 (age 28 at Washington, DC)–1 January 1865. B: Queens Co., IRE, soldier. Blue eyes, brown hair, fair complexion, 5' 6. Discharged at Winchester, VA.

McCauslin, William. Mustered: Pvt. Co. I, 60th NY Inf. 12 October 1861. Transferred: Pvt. Co. M, 6th U.S. Cav. 25 October 1862 (age 22 at Knoxville, MD)–29 September 1864. B: 1840, Co. Tyrone, IRE, farmer. Blue eyes, light hair, light complexion, 5' 6½. POW, Fairfield. Paroled at Annapolis, MD, 20 August 1863. Discharged at Berryville, VA. D: 1895, Utica, IL.

Mc[C]Lain, Henry B. Pvt. Co. G, 7 August 1861 (age 19 at Columbus, OH)–31 December 1862. B: Posey Co., IN, blacksmith. Black eyes, black hair, ruddy complexion, 5' 7½. Deserted.

McClain, James. Pvt. Co. A, 8 October 1861 (age 22 at Philadelphia, PA)–9 August 1862. B: Philadelphia, PA, teamster. Blue eyes, black hair, dark complexion, 5'11½. Deserted.

McClanathan, William A. Pvt. Co. M, 26 August 1864 (age 23 at Harrisburg, PA)–30 July 1865. B: Mifflin Co., PA, farmer. Hazel eyes, dark hair, fresh complexion, 5' 6½. Deserted. Released from service 21 April 1891.

McClaskey, Patrick. Pvt. Co. C, 21 November 1861 (age 34 at Philadelphia, PA)–27 January 1862. B: Co. Derry, IRE, paper maker. Grey eyes, black hair, ruddy complexion, 5'10. Discharged per instruction from AGO dated 24 January 1862 east of Capitol, Washington, D.C.

McClay, Alexander. Sgt. Co. A, 18 September 1861 (age 21 at Philadelphia, PA)–18 September 1864. B: Belfast, IRE, seaman. Hazel eyes, dark hair, florid complexion, 5' 5½. POW, Fairfield, 3 July–24 December 1863. Paroled, reported at Annapolis, MD. Discharged at Harper's Ferry, VA.

McClay, James. Pvt. Co. G, 3 August 1861 (age 18 at Columbus, OH)–19 November 1864. B: Franklin Co., OH, farmer. Hazel eyes, brown hair, light complexion, 5' 5¼. MIA in the field. POW, 7 May–20 December 1863. Paroled, reported at Camp 6th Cav. Discharged 10 January 1865 to date 19 November 1864 at Lighthouse Point, VA.

McClelland, John. Pvt. Co. B, 9 August 1861 (age 22 at Cleveland, OH)–13 November 1861. B: Co. Antrim, IRE, horsehoer. Hazel eyes, brown hair, ruddy complexion, 5' 6. Deserted.

McClelland, John. Sgt. Co. H, 13 August 1861 (age 21 at Philadelphia, PA)–13 August 1864. B: Co. Tyrone, IRE, clerk. Blue eyes, brown hair, ruddy complexion, 5'6. Discharged at Lighthouse Point, VA.

McClelland, Johnathan. Pvt. Co. D, 19 August 1861 (age 21 at Pittsburgh, PA)–31 March 1864. B: Allegheny Co., PA, broom maker. Blue eyes, light hair, sandy complexion, 5'8. POW, Brandy Station, 11 October 1863–31 March 1864. D: 31 March 1864 from typhoid fever as a POW at Andersonville, GA. Register of enrollments states death date as 20 March 1864.

McCombs, David. Pvt. Co. M, 22 October 1861 (age 27 at Pittsburgh, PA)–3 January 1863. B: Allegheny Co., PA, painter. Hazel eyes, brown hair, dark complexion, 5'7½. Disability discharge at Ft. Monroe, VA. D: 30 August 1890.

McCormick, Daniel. Pvt. Co. H, 22 July 1861 (age 18 at Philadelphia, PA)–28 July 1864. B: Philadelphia, PA, laborer. Hazel eyes, brown hair, fair complexion, 5'6½. MIA, Fairfield. Discharged in the field, VA.

McCormick, James. Pvt. Co. I, 28 September 1861 (age 22 at Rochester, NY)–6 March 1862. B: IRE, farmer. Hazel eyes, brown hair, florid complexion, 5'6¼. D: 6 March 1862 from measles in the hospital at Camp east of Capitol, Washington, D.C.

McCoy, Augustus G. Pvt. Co. M, 18 October 1861 (age 24 at Pittsburgh, PA)–26 March 1864. B: Westmoreland Co., PA, shoemaker. Grey eyes, brown hair, fair complexion, 5'10½. POW, Fairfield. D: 26 March 1864 from diarrhea as a POW at Andersonville, GA.

McCoy, Jacob. Pvt. Co. M, 3 October 1864 (age 18 at Harrisburg, PA)–3 October 1867. B: Cumberland Co., PA, laborer. Grey eyes, light hair, fair complexion, 5'4. Discharged at Austin, TX.

McCoy, James A. Mustered: Sgt. Co. C, 14th IN Inf. 7 June 1861. Transferred: Pvt. Co. C, 6th U.S. Cav. 23 October 1862 (age 28 at Knoxville, MD)–30 November 1863. B: Carroll Co., OH. Grey eyes, brown hair, florid complexion, 5'3. POW, Fairfield. D: 30 November 1863 of pneumonia at General Hospital at Richmond, VA.

McCoy, Miles B. Pvt. Co. I, 15 July 1861 (age 26 at Clearfield, PA)–17 May 1862. B: PA, school teacher. Grey eyes, brown hair, light complexion, 5'10½. Deserted.

McCoy, Thomas B. Pvt. Co. I, 5 September 1861 (age 23 at Rochester, NY)–5 September 1864. B: IRE, miller. Grey eyes, black hair, florid complexion, 5'8¼. Attached to 1st U.S. Art. Discharged at City Point, VA.

McCracken, James. Pvt. Co. D, 27 August 1861 (age 25 at Pittsburgh, PA)–27 August 1864. B: Washington Co., PA, coal miner. Blue eyes, light hair, dark complexion, 5'7½. Deserted 30 October 1862. Apprehended 8 April 1863. Discharged at Halltown, VA. D: 16 March 1901.

McCracken, Samuel. Pvt. Co. K, 13 August 1861 (age 22 at Butler, PA)–13 August 1864. B: Lawrence Co., PA, farmer. Grey eyes, light hair, fair complexion, 5'5½. WIA, Gaines Mill, 27 June 1862. Discharged at Lighthouse Point, VA.

McCrehon, Alexander. Rct. Co. I, 2 August 1861 (age 21 at Rochester, NY)–6 August 1861. B: NJ, fireman. Blue eyes, brown hair, fair complexion, 5'5. Discharged by Civil Authority being a minor.

McCruden, James. Rct. 15 November 1864 (age 22 at Harrisburg, PA)–21 November 1864. B: Co. Donegal, IRE, weaver. Hazel eyes, brown hair, ruddy complexion, 5'9. Deserted.

McCullough, Albert. Pvt. Cos. C, L, 13 November 1861 (age 19 at Philadelphia, PA)–3 July 1863. B: Philadelphia, PA, farmer. Hazel eyes, light hair, light complexion, 5'6½. MIA, Fairfield.

McCullough, John. Mustered: Pvt. Batt. E, (Knap's PA Independent), 20 July 1861. Transferred: Pvt. Co. K, 6th U.S. Cav. 26 October 1862 (age 19 at Knoxville, MD)–17 December 1864. B: Wilmington, DE. Blue eyes, dark hair, light complexion, 5'5. Discharged on or about 15 January 1865 to date 17 December 1864 at Camp Russell, VA.

McDerment, James H. Pvt. Co. M, 23 August 1864 (age 23 at Harrisburg, PA)–15 August 1865. B: Co. Donegal, IRE, laborer. Blue eyes, brown hair, fair complexion, 5'6. MIA in the field 29 November 1864. Gained from MIA 31 March 1865. Deserted.

McDermott, Edward. Pvt. Co. A, 28 September 1861 (age 22 at Philadelphia, PA)–28 September 1864. B: Co. Derry, IRE, boatman. Grey eyes, sandy hair, light complexion, 5'8. POW, Fairfield, 3 July 1863–18 January 1864. Paroled, reported at Annapolis, MD. Discharged at Harrisonburg, VA.

McDermott, Edward. 16 October 1861 (age 32 at Philadelphia, PA)–25 October 1861. B: Co. Roscommon, IRE, laborer. Blue eyes, brown hair, ruddy complexion, 5'3. Deserted.

McDonald, Charles Jr. Mustered: Pvt. Co. E, 1st MN Inf. 29 April 1861. Transferred: Saddler. Co. C, 6th U.S. Cav. 28 October 1862 (age 46 at Knoxville, MD)–28 April 1864. B: CAN East, CAN, saddler. Grey eyes, dark hair, dark complexion, 5'7. Discharged at Brandy Station, VA.

McDonald, Samuel. Mustered: Pvt. Co. D, 110th PA Inf. 19 December 1861. Transferred: Pvt. Co. E, 6th U.S. Cav. 28 October 1862 (age 21 at Knoxville, MD)–25 August 1864. B: Bedford Co., PA. Blue eyes, dark hair, dark complexion, 5'11. Discharged at Washington, D.C. Substitute: Pvt. Co. A, 97th PA Inf. 3 March 1865–28 August 1865 (Weldon, NC).

McDonel, Patrick. Pvt. Co. L, 9 December 1861 (age 35 at Cleveland, OH)–29 January 1863. B: Co. Kildare, IRE, laborer. Grey eyes, sandy hair, ruddy complexion, 5'5. Disability discharge at Convalescent Camp, VA.

McDonell, Henry. Mustered: Pvt. Co. E, 8th OH Inf. 25 June 1861. Transferred: Cpl. Co. C, 6th U.S. Cav. 24 October 1862 (age 19 at Knoxville, MD)–25 June 1864. B: Cincinnati, Hamilton Co., OH, blacksmith. Grey eyes, black hair, florid complexion, 5'6½. POW, Funkstown, 7 July 1863–7 January 1864. Paroled, reported at Annapolis, MD. Discharged in the field, VA. Alternate surname: McDonald.

McDonell, James. Pvt. Co. H, 8 July 1861 (age 18 at Philadelphia, PA)–8 July 1864. B: Co. Antrim, IRE, laborer. Grey eyes, sandy hair, fair complexion, 5'8. WIA/MIA, Fairfield. Discharged in the field, VA. Alternate surname: McDowell.

McDonnell, Andrew. Pvt. Co. M, 11 September 1861 (age 22 at Pittsburgh, PA)–11 September 1864. B: Co. Cavan, IRE, teamster. Hazel eyes, auburn hair, florid complexion, 5'7. WIA/POW, Fairfield, 3 July–24 August 1863. Paroled at Annapolis, MD. Discharged at Berryville, VA.

McDowel, Thomas. Pvt. Co. A, 17 September 1861 (age 28 at Philadelphia, PA)–17 September 1864. B: Bucks Co., OH, wheel wright. Hazel eyes, brown hair, florid complexion, 5'5½. Discharged at Harper's Ferry, VA.

McDowell, William A. Pvt. Co. E, 19 August 1861 (age 23 at Columbus, OH)–3 January 1863, B: Uniontown, Fayette Co., PA, clerk. Blue eyes, brown hair, ruddy complexion, 5'7½. Disability discharge at Washington, D.C.

McElrath, Robert W. Lance Sgt. Co. L, 16 August 1861 (age 22 at Cleveland, OH)–19 July 1862. B: Cleveland, Cuyahoga Co., OH, farmer. Hazel eyes, brown hair, ruddy complexion, 5'10. Disability discharge at Emory Hospital, Washington, D.C.

McElroy, Robert. Saddler. Cos. C, L, 28 October 1861 (age 28 at Philadelphia, PA)–5 September 1862. B: Philadelphia, PA, saddler. Black eyes, brown hair, dark complexion, 5'6½. KIA near Falls Church, VA, 5 September 1862.

McFadden, John E. Pvt. Co. C, 11 December 1861 (age 22 at Columbia, PA)–23 May 1862. B: Lancaster Co., PA, railroader. Grey eyes, dark hair, dark complexion, 5'7. Disability discharge at Camp east of Capitol, Washington, D.C.

McFarland, Peter. Pvt. Co. L, 19 December 1864 (age 35 at Cleveland, OH)–20 June 1865. B: Co. Armagh, IRE, laborer. Blue eyes, brown hair, ruddy complexion, 5'6. Disability discharge at Carlisle Barracks, PA.

McFurlong, Thomas E. Pvt. Co. I, 7 February 1862 (at Washington, DC)–24 March 1862. Apprehended 24 March 1862 as a deserter from 1st Pa. Rifles. Transferred to that organization as Edward McFurlong.

McGarvey, James. Mustered: Pvt. Co. B, 9th PA Inf. 22 April–29 July 1861 (Harrisburg, PA). Enlisted: Pvt. Co. M, 6th U.S. Cav. 20 September 1861 (age 28 at Pittsburgh, PA)–20 September 1864. B: IRE. Grey eyes, brown hair, florid complexion, 5'6½. POW, Fairfield. Paroled at Annapolis, MD, 20 August 1863. Discharged at Berryville, VA.

McGee, George. Pvt. Co. L, 14 June 1864 (age 20 at Washington, DC)–16 October 1865. B: Fairfax, VA, farmer. Grey eyes, brown hair, sallow complexion, 5'3½. Deserted.

McGee, Henry K. Musician 3rd Class. Co. F&S, 15 October 1861 (age 27 at Mount Joy, PA)–15 October 1864. B: Chillisguagua, PA, musician. Hazel eyes, brown hair, ruddy complexion, 5'4. Discharged at Strausburg, VA.

McGee, Robert. Pvt. Cos. E, B, E, 11 March 1864 (age 24 at Washington, DC)–12 March 1867. B: Spotsylvania Co., VA, farmer. Grey eyes, brown hair, fair complexion, 5'5. Gained from MIA on 31 March 1865 at Annapolis, MD. Discharged at Austin, TX.

McGinley, Bernard (Barney). Pvt. Co. M, 9 September 1861 (age 22 at Pittsburgh, PA)–5 August 1865. B: IRE, teamster. Black eyes, black hair, florid complexion, 5'4. Discharged at Fredericksburg, MD. Second record states dropped 11 July 1865 from rolls for expiration of service. Substitute: Pvt. Co. D, 97th PA Inf. 27 February–28 August 1865 (Weldon, NC).

McGinley, James. Cpl. Cos. C, L, 28 October 1861 (age 21 at Philadelphia, PA)–15 April 1864. B: Chester Co., PA, laborer. Grey eyes, brown hair, light complexion, 5'8. MIA, Fairfield. Reenlisted: 16 February 1864 at Camp 6th Cav., VA. Deserted 14 April 1864.

McGinn, John. Pvt. Co. H, 30 July 1861 (age 18 at Philadelphia, PA)–7 March 1864. B: Philadelphia, PA, school teacher. Blue eyes, black hair, ruddy complexion, 5'8. MIA, Fairfield. Disability discharge at Carlisle Barracks, PA.

McGinnigle, James. Sgt. Co. M, 16 September 1861 (age 29 at Pittsburgh, PA)–16 September 1864. B: Co. Monaghan Co., IRE, coal miner. Grey eyes, brown hair, dark complexion, 5'8½. MIA, Fairfield. Paroled at Annapolis, MD, 25 August 1863. Sick in hospital. Discharged at Berryville, VA.

McGinnis, Philip. Rct. 19 August 1861 (age 18 at Rochester, NY)–22 August 1861. B: IRE, shoemaker. Grey eyes, dk. brown hair, dark complexion, 5'6½. Rejected recruit. Discharged at Pittsburgh, PA.

McGitigan, John. Pvt. Co. A, 22 August 1861 (age 19 at Philadelphia, PA)–22 August 1864. B: Philadelphia, PA, huckster. Hazel eyes, brown hair, florid complexion, 5'7½. Discharged at Harper's Ferry, VA.

McGiven, Robert. Pvt. Co. A, 5 December 1864 (age 20 at Cincinnati, OH)–30 May 1865. B: Washington, NY, saddler. Grey eyes, brown hair, dark complexion, 5'7. Deserted.

McGovern, Owen. Mustered: Co. N, 28th PA Inf. 20 August 1861. Transferred: Pvt. Co. B, 6th U.S. Cav. 25 October 1862 (age 22 at Knoxville, MD)–17 August 1864. B: IRE, laborer. Blue eyes, brown hair, ruddy complexion, 5'6½. MIA at Fairfield. Discharged at Knoxville, MD.

McGraw, Michael. Rct. Co. I, 5 August 1861 (age 21 at Rochester, NY)–16 August 1861. B: NYC, NY, farmer. Blue eyes, brown hair, fair complexion, 5'9½. Discharged by Civil Authority being a minor.

McGrew, Benjamin D. Sgt. Co. L, 2 January 1862 (age 23 at Cleveland, OH)–14 November 1862. B: Jefferson Co., OH, farmer. Grey eyes, sandy hair, ruddy complexion, 5'9½. Disability discharge at Baltimore, MD.

McGuire, James. Rct. 19 August 1861 (age 18 at Rochester, NY)–22 August 1861. B: Rome, NY, shoemaker. Grey eyes, brown hair, fair complexion, 5'5¼. Rejected recruit. Discharged at Pittsburgh, PA.

McGuire, John. Mustered: Pvt. Co. D, 14th IN Inf. 8 March 1862. Transferred: Rct. 6th U.S. Cav. 22 October 1862 (age 21 at Knoxville, MD)–Never joined regiment/returned to USV. B: Greene Co., IN. Blue eyes, light hair, light complexion, 5'6½. Transferred: U.S.V.R.C. 15 November 1863.

McHarnas, William. Pvt. Co. F, 11 July 1861 (age 23 at Pittsburgh, PA)–11 July 1864. B: Lincolnshire, ENG, boatman. Lt. grey eyes, black hair, dark complexion, 5'6. Discharged at Lighthouse Point, VA.

McHenry, Thomas. Mustered: Pvt. Co. D, 8th OH Inf. Transferred: Pvt. Co. C, 6th U.S. Cav. 23 October 1862 (age 20 at Knoxville, MD)–25 June 1864. B: Hamilton, West Can, CAN. Dark eyes, dark hair, dark complexion, 5'5. Discharged in the field, VA. Enlisted: Pvt. Co. H, 2nd U.S. Cav. 16 May 1866 (Cincinnati, OH)–11 October 1866. Deserted.

McIlwaine, John. Sgt. Co. M, 5 February 1862 (at Philadelphia, PA)–5 February 1865. Discharged at Camp Russel, VA.

McInness, Dongald J. Musician. Band, Co. F&S, 20 January 1865 (age 31 at NYC, NY)–3 August 1865. B: Edinburgh, SCO, musician. Blue eyes, light hair, fair complexion, 5'8. Deserted.

McIntyre, Michael. 1st Sgt. Co. A, 11 October 1861 (age 20 at Philadelphia, PA)–11 October 1864. B: Ballinastoe, IRE, stone cutter. Blue eyes, light hair, fair complexion, 5'8½. Discharged at Middleton, VA.

McIntyre, Robert. Pvt. Co. M, 30 November 1861 (age 27 at Pittsburgh, PA)–30 November 1864. B: IRE, painter. Grey eyes, sandy hair, light complexion, 5'7½. WIA/POW, Fairfield, 3 July–24 August 1863. Paroled at Annapolis, MD. Discharged at Kernstown, VA.

McKean, William. Pvt. Co. H, 1 August 1861 (age 24 at Philadelphia, PA)–10 December 1862. B: Co., Donegal, IRE, carpenter. Hazel eyes, brown hair, fair complexion, 5'9. Disability discharge at Philadelphia, PA.

McKee, Thomas Joseph. Sgt.-Comm. Sgt. Cos. K, F&S, 16 July 1861 (age 18 at Franklin, PA)–14 November 1864. B: Pittsburgh, Allegheny Co., PA, nail maker. Grey eyes, reddish hair, sandy complexion, 5'4¾. Reenlisted: 10 February 1864 at Camp 6th Cav., VA. Transferred to F&S as Comm. Sgt. on 24 August 1864. Discharged 14 November 1864 by appointment as Cpt., 6th U.S.C. Cavalry.

McKeefrey, Thomas. Pvt. Co. F, 8 July 1861 (age 21 Pittsburgh, PA)–8 July 1864. B: Coleraine, Co. Tipperary, IRE, teamster. Blue eyes, sandy hair, ruddy complexion, 5'6. WIA/POW, Upperville, 21 June–13 November 1863. Libby Prison. Paroled, reported at Annapolis, MD. Discharged at Lighthouse Point, VA.

McKenna, James. Rct. 24 September 1861 (age 22 at Philadelphia, PA)–26 September 1861. B: Dragheda, IRE, shoemaker. Blue eyes, black hair, dark complexion, 5'5. Deserted.

McKibbin, John W. Pvt. Co. F, 6 July 1861 (age

21 at Pittsburgh, PA)–6 July 1864. B: Linntown, Union Co., PA, farmer. Grey eyes, black hair, dark complexion, 5' 8. MIA, Fairfield. Discharged at Lighthouse Point, VA. Tended to Lt. Chaffee at Fairfield.

McLaughlin, John. Pvt. 4 November 1861 (age 34 at Philadelphia, PA)–1 November 1861. B: Co. Wexford, IRE, laborer. Blue eyes, light hair, ruddy complexion, 5' 3. Deserted. Probable error with the dates recorded.

McLelland, Reed. Sgt. Co. D, 19 August 1861 (age 20 at Pittsburgh, PA)–19 August 1864. B: Allegheny Co., PA, moulder. Blue eyes, sandy hair, dark complexion, 5' 8½. Discharged at Bolivar Heights, VA.

McMahon, William. Mustered: Pvt. 2nd MN Sharpshooters (1st MN Inf.), 10 February 1862. Transferred: Pvt. Co. B, 6th U.S. Cav. 28 October 1862 (age 21 at Knoxville, MD)–15 May 1863. B: IRE. Blue eyes, light hair, light complexion, 5'10. POW (captured while on picket), Richard's Ford, 14–20 February 1863. Paroled. Army of the Potomac 15 May 1863. No further record.

McMartin, Robert. Pvt. Co. K, 14 August 1861 (age 19 at Rochester, NY)–14 August 1864. B: Genesee Co., NY, farmer. Blue eyes, light hair, fair complexion, 5' 4. Discharged at City Point, VA.

McMasters, Robert H. Sgt. Co. F, 6 July 1861 (age 25 at Pittsburgh, PA)–6 July 1864. B: Upper Can., CAN, coal miner. Grey eyes, brown hair, fair complexion, 5' 8½. Discharged at Lighthouse Point, VA.

McMichael, Abraham M. Mustered: Pvt. Co. G, 30th PA Inf. Transferred: Pvt. Co. D, 6th U.S. Cav. 28 October 1862 (age 21 at Knoxville, MD)–28 January 1864. B: Allegheny Co., PA. Grey eyes, dark hair, light complexion, 5' 9. Discharged at Wells Landing, VA. Mustered: Pvt. Cos. I, D, 14th PA Cav. 8 September 1864–28 May 1865.

McMiller, Alexander. Pvt. Co. M, 3 October 1864 (age 28 at NYC, NY)–18 August 1865. B: Co. Antrim, IRE, laborer. Grey eyes, brown hair, dark complexion, 5'11. Deserted.

McMillion, Michael. Sgt. Co. A, 31 October 1864 (age 25 at Cincinnati, OH)–31 October 1867. B: Greenbrier, Charlottesville, VA (WV), farmer. Hazel eyes, brown hair, fair complexion, 6'. Discharged at Buffalo Springs, TX.

McMunn, Anthony W. Pvt. Co. H, 8 July 1861 (age 21 at Philadelphia, PA)–8 July 1864. B: Delaware Co., PA, farmer. Grey eyes, brown hair, fair complexion, 5' 7. MIA, Warrenton, 18 November 1862. Discharged in the field, VA.

McMunn, Archibald. Pvt. Co. H, 8 July 1861 (age 27 at Philadelphia, PA)–8 July 1864. B: Delaware Co., PA, farmer. Blue eyes, light hair, fair complexion, 5' 5½. Discharged in the field, VA.

McNair, Alvan. Pvt. Co. D, 31 August 1861 (age 21 at Pittsburgh, PA)–31 August 1864. B: Middletown, PA, painter. Blue eyes, brown hair, light complexion, 5' 8. Discharged.

McNickel, Robert. Enlisted: Pvt. Co. E, 3rd U.S. Art. 1 September 1853 (Philadelphia, PA)–1 September 1858 (Ft. Leavenworth, K.T.). Reenlisted: 15 November 1858–24 September 1863 (Carlisle Barracks, PA). Reenlisted: Pvt. 6th U.S. Cav. 15 September 1863 (age 32 at Carlisle Barracks, PA)–8 August 1864. B: Co. Londonderry, IRE. Grey eyes, brown hair, fair complexion, 5' 8. D: 8 August 1864 of (unreadable cause) at Carlisle Barracks, PA.

McNite, John. Mustered: Pvt. Co. B, 110th PA Inf. 24 October 1861. Transferred: Pvt. Co. D, 6th U.S. cav. 28 October 1862 (age 21 at Knoxville, MD)–28 August 1864. B: Schuylkill Co., PA. Blue eyes, auburn hair, light complexion, 5' 6. Discharged at Halltown, VA.

McQuirk, William. Pvt. Co. A, 29 November 1864 (age 26 at NYC, NY)–6 August 1865. B: Co. Tipperary, IRE, sailor. Grey eyes, auburn hair, fair complexion, 5' 8. Deserted.

McQuiston, Henry. 1st Sgt. Co. K, 31 July 1861 (age 22 at Warren, OH). B: November 1839, Warren, OH, physician. Blue eyes, brown hair, brown complexion, 5' 7¾. WIA, Upperville. Discharged 21 September 1862 for appointment as 2nd Lt. 6th U.S. Cav. dated 17 July 1862. Retired (from wounds received): 26 September 1863. D: 13 February 1903, Pasadena, CA.

McQuiston, Hiram. Mustered: Pvt. Co. H, 7th OH Inf. 20 June 1861. Transferred: Pvt. Co. K, 6th U.S. Cav. 23 October 1862 (age 25 at Knoxville, MD)–23 April 1864. B: 1837 at Warren, OH. Blue eyes, brown hair, florid complexion, 5' 5½. Discharged at Camp 6th Cav., VA. D: 1918.

McQuiston, Ulysses. Pvt. Co. K, 5 September 1861 (age 18 at Bladensburg, MD)–15 October 1862. B: Warren, OH, butcher. Blue eyes, light hair, light complexion, 5' 9½. Disability discharge at Harewood Hospital, Washington, D.C. D: 1863.

McSherer, Ruben. Mustered: Pvt. Co. B, 41st PA Inf. 15 May 1861. Transferred: Pvt. Co. L, 6th U.S. Cav. 27 October 1862 (age 21 at Knoxville, MD)–27 April 1864. B: Apollo, Armstrong, PA, shoemaker. Blue eyes, light hair, light complexion, 5'6. Discharged at Camp 6th Cav., VA.

McSweeney, Edward. Pvt. Co. L, 28 March 1862 (age 25 at Philadelphia, PA)–15 May 1862. B: Co. Longford, IRE, saddler. Grey eyes, brown hair, ruddy complexion, 5'5¾. Disability discharge at Camp east of Capitol, Washington, D.C.

McTammany, Francis. Mustered: Pvt. Co. F, 28th PA Inf. 6 July 1861. Transferred: Pvt. Batt. E, (Knap's PA Independent), 5 October 1861. Transferred: Pvt. Co. K, 6th U.S. Cav. 27 October 1862 (age 23 at Knoxville, MD)–24 December 1864. B: 1839, Maghera, Co. Londonderry, IRE. Blue eyes, brown hair, light complexion, 5'6. POW (captured by the enemy), Wilderness, 13 May 1864. POW, Andersonville, GA. Delivered on parole at Florence, SC, 9 December 1864. Reported from Annapolis, MD 24 December 1864. Reported deserter 7 February 1865. Charge of desertion removed. D: 30 October 1866, Rapides Parish, LA.

McWilliams, Denis. Mustered: Pvt. Co. D, 37th PA Inf. 21 June 1861. Transferred: Pvt. Co. I, 6th U.S. Cav. 27 October 1862 (age 22 at Knoxville, MD)–27 July 1864. B: SCO, miner. Hazel eyes, brown hair, fair complexion, 5'7. D: 9 May 1863 from wounds received.

Meach, William S. Mustered: Pvt. Co. E, 3rd WI Inf. 10 June 1861. Transferred: Farrier. Co. C, 6th U.S. Cav. 24 October 1862 (age 20 at Knoxville, MD)–5 July 1864. B: Cuyahoga Co., OH. Grey eyes, brown hair, florid complexion, 5'9. Discharged at Lighthouse Point, VA. Reenlisted: Pvt. Co. C, 9th U.S. Inf. Unknown dates. D: 22 December 1881, Unity, Marathon, WI.

Meade, Levant. Mustered: Pvt. Co. F, 38th PA Inf. 9 July 1861. Transferred: Pvt. Co. M, 6th U.S. Cav. 28 October 1862 (age 25 at Knoxville, MD)–13 January 1865. B: Livingston Co., NY, engineer. Hazel eyes, dark hair, fair complexion, 5'11½. POW (captured by guerrillas), Warrenton 21 January 1864. Discharged at Winchester, VA.

Meagher, Edward. Mustered: Pvt. Co. E, 60th NY Inf. Transferred: Pvt. Co. M, 6th U.S. Cav. 20 October 1862 (age 21 at Knoxville, MD)–24 May 1864. B: Montreal, Quebec, CAN. Grey eyes, brown hair, ruddy complexion, 5'6. POW, Fairfield. Paroled at Annapolis, MD, 24 August 1863. Disability discharge at Carlisle Barracks, PA.

Mealheim, Frederick. Bugler. Co. E, 21 July 1861

(age 14 at Columbus, OH)–15 February 1864. B: Columbus, OH, laborer. Blue eyes, light hair, fair complexion, 5'½. POW, Fairfield. D: 15 February 1864 from diarrhea as a POW at Richmond, VA.

Meany, James. Pvt. Co. H, 12 July 1861 (age 18 at Philadelphia, PA)–23 March 1863. B: Philadelphia, PA, laborer. Blue eyes, brown hair, fair complexion, 5'6¼. Disability discharge at Philadelphia, PA.

Mecum, Charles William. Mustered: Pvt. Co. F, 84th PA Inf. Transferred: Pvt. Co. A, 6th U.S. Cav. 24 October 1862 (age 19 at Knoxville, MD)–7 October 1864. B: 15 January 1843 Muncy, Lycoming Co., PA. Hazel eyes, dark hair, dark complexion, 5'4½. Discharged at Harrisonburg, VA. D: 25 May 1926.

Mecum, Jared M. Mustered: Pvt. Co. H, 34th PA Inf. 21 June 1861. Transferred: Pvt. Co. A, 6th U.S. Cav. 28 October 1862 (age 22 at Knoxville, MD)–22 June 1864. B: 1839 Muncy, Lycoming Co., PA. Hazel eyes, dark hair, light complexion, 5'6. Discharged at White House, VA. D: 4 April 1901.

Mecum, Robert H. Mustered: Pvt.-Sgt. Co. G, 11th PA Inf. Mustered: Sgt. Co. F, 84th PA Inf. Transferred: Pvt. Co. L, 6th U.S. Cav. 25 October 1862 (at Knoxville, MD)–25 October 1864. B: 6 April 1839, Lycoming Co., PA. Discharged at Cedar Creek, VA. D: 18 May 1909, La Porte, IN.

Meizer, John B. Pvt. Cos. C, L, 11 December 1861 (age 34 at Lancaster, PA)–23 March 1863. B: Minster, Prussia, GER, tailor. Grey eyes, light hair, light complexion, 5'10½. MIA, Malvern Hill. Disability discharge at Convalescent Camp, VA.

Melloy, Peter. 14 November 1864 (age 22 at Harrisburg, PA)–21 November 1864. B: Queens Co., IRE, boatman. Grey eyes, light hair, fair complexion, 5'8. Deserted. Sub.

Melvin, Michael. 18 November 1864 (age 26 at Harrisburg, PA)–21 November 1864. B: Co. Sligo, IRE, boatman. Grey eyes, brown hair, ruddy complexion, 5'6. Deserted. Sub.

Merican, George. Pvt. Co. L, 17 October 1864 (age 24 at Cincinnati, OH)–31 March 1865. B: Baltimore, MD, brick layer. Blue eyes, brown hair, sallow complexion, 5'7. Deserted.

Merkle, Frederick. Pvt. Co. E, 28 August 1861 (age 24 at Cleveland, OH)–28 August 1864. B: Württemberg, GER, stonecutter. Blue eyes, light hair, ruddy complexion, 5'4½. Discharged at Washington, D.C.

Merkle, Suel. Pvt. Co. E, 11 September 1861 (age

19 at Cleveland, OH)–4 May 1862. B: Württemberg, GER, laborer. Grey eyes, light hair, ruddy complexion, 5' 9½. WIA, Williamsburg. D: 4 May 1862, Williamsburg.

Merritt, George. Mustered: Pvt. Co. H, 8th OH Inf. 6 June 1861. Transferred: Pvt. Co. G, 6th U.S. Cav. 24 October 1862 (age 22 at Knoxville, MD)–25 June 1864. B: Medina Co., OH, farmer. Grey eyes, brown hair, fair complexion, 5' 8. POW, Fairfield, 3 July 1863–17 February 1864. Paroled, reported at Camp Paroled. Discharged at Wyanoke, VA.

Merryman, George W. M. Enlisted: Pvt.-1st Sgt. Co. G, 1st U.S. Dragoons, 8 February 1858 (Baltimore, MD)–8 February 1863 (Ft. Union, NM). Reenlisted: Sgt. Co. D, 6th U.S. Cav. 7 August 1863 (age 27 at Washington, DC)–8 August 1866 (Sherman, TX). B: St. Marys Co., MD, stage driver. Hazel eyes, brown hair, fair complexion, 6'1. WIA, Five Forks, 2 April 1865. Reenlisted: Sgt. Co. I, 2nd U.S. Cav. 1 November 1866 (St. Louis, MO)–1 November 1871 (Medicine Bow, W.T.): Reenlisted: Co. F, 2nd U.S. Cav. 20 November 1871–20 November 1876. Reenlisted: Pvt. Cos. F, F&S, 2nd U.S. Cav. 20 November 1876 (Ft. Sanders, A.T.)–9 November 1881 (Ft. Custer, M.T.). Reenlisted: Sgt. Cos. F, F&S (Band), 2nd U.S. Cav. 20 November 1881 (Ft. Clark, M.T.)–19 November 1881 (Ft. Walla Walla, W.T.). Reenlisted: Band, 2nd U.S. Cav. 20 November 1886–21 January 1890. Retired per SO 17, AGO 90, a Saddler Sgt.

Merworth, John. Pvt.-Cpl. Co. C, 7 May 1864 (age 21 at Washington, DC)–7 May 1867. B: Leigh, PA, laborer. Blue eyes, brown hair, fresh complexion, 5' 6. WIA, Cedar Creek. Discharged at Austin, TX. Pension filed in TX denotes he was assigned to the 2 NY Heavy Art.

Meyer, Edward. Mustered: Pvt. Co. E, 163rd NY Inf. 8 August 1862. Transferred: Pvt. Co. M, 6th U.S. Cav. 21 October 1862 (age 25 at Knoxville, MD)–Never joined. B: Württemberg, GER, shoemaker. Hazel eyes, brown hair, dark complexion, 5' 8. Returned to USV. Discharged for desertion 21 January 1863. Alternate surname: Mayer.

Middaugh, Avery. Mustered: Pvt. Co. G, 50th PA Inf. 26 September 1861. Transferred: Pvt. Co. E, 6th U.S. Cav. 28 October 1862 (at Knoxville, MD)–25 June 1864. Deserted 25 December 1862. Apprehended 7 January 1863. MIA, Beverly Ford. POW, Brandy Station, 11 October 1863–25 June 1864. D: 25 June 1864 from scorbutus at Andersonville Prison, GA.

Might, John. Mustered: Pvt. Co. A, 12th PA Inf. 25 April–5 August 1861. Mustered out at Harrisburg, PA. Mustered: PA Independent Batt. C, Light Art. 6 November 1861. Transferred: Pvt. Co. E, 6th U.S. Cav. 28 October 1862 (age 19 at Knoxville, MD)–24 August 1864. B: Pittsburgh, Allegheny Co., PA. Blue eyes, dark hair, dark complexion, 5' 7½. WIA/MIA, Upperville. Record indicates discharged 24 August 1864 at Harper's Ferry, VA. Mustered: 5th PA Art. (H), 12 January 1865.

Miller, Abel S. Pvt. Co. H, 29 July 1861 (age 19 at Philadelphia, PA)–29 July 1864. B: Philadelphia, PA, carter. Grey eyes, light hair, fair complexion, 5' 7½. Discharged in the field, VA.

Miller, Charles F. Pvt. Cos. L, F, 5 April 1862 (age 27 at Carlisle Barracks, PA)–22 April 1865. B: Prussia, GER, soldier. Hazel eyes, brown hair, fair complexion, 5' 7. WIA, Beverly Ford. Discharged at Annapolis, MD.

Miller, Charles F. Sgt. Co. I, 11 September 1861 (age 20 at Rochester, NY)–11 September 1864. B: Wyoming Co., NY, farmer. Blue eyes, brown hair, fair complexion, 5' 9¼. POW, Fairfield, 3 July 1863–18 June 1864. Paroled. Discharged in the field, VA.

Miller, Charles H. Pvt. Co. E, 12 September 1861 (age 19 at Adrian, MI)–5 July 1864. B: Pittsford, NY, farmer. Grey eyes, light hair, ruddy complexion, 5' 9¾. MIA, Fairfield. POW (captured by guerrillas), Warrenton, 21 January–5 July 1864. D: 5 July 1864 from scorbutus as a POW at Andersonville, GA.

Miller, Francis M. Pvt. Co. I, 25 September 1861 (age 25 at Rochester, NY)–3 July 1863. B: Wyoming Co., NY, farmer. Grey eyes, brown hair, dark complexion, 5' 7¾. WIA/POW, Fairfield. D: from wounds received at Fairfield, 3 July 1863.

Miller, Frederick. Pvt. Co. D, 13 August 1861 (age 26 at Pittsburgh, PA)–20 October 1862. B: Buckswiler, GER, moulder. Grey eyes, black hair, dark complexion, 5' 5. Deserted.

Miller, Fritz. Rct. 26 October 1864 (age 37 at Rochester, NY)–21 November 1864. B: GER, teamster. Grey eyes, brown hair, sallow complexion, 5'10. Deserted.

Miller, Herman. Cpl.-Sgt. Co. H, 19 July 1861 (age 24 at Philadelphia, PA)–1 August 1865. B: Prussia, GER, clerk. Blue eyes, black hair, florid complexion, 5' 9. MIA, Sheridan's Raid, 16 June 1864. Reenlisted: 9 February 1864 at Camp 6th Cav., VA. Discharged 1 August 1865 per SO 370, AGO, 14 July 1865 at Ft. Delaware.

Miller, John. Rct. 4 November 1864 (age 32 at Harrisburg, PA)–21 November 1864. B: Yorkshire, ENG, laborer. Blue eyes, fair hair, fair complexion, 5' 6½. Deserted.

Miller, John W. Mustered: Pvt. Co. A (PA) Inf. Transferred: Pvt. Co. I, 6th U.S. Cav. 27 October 1862 (age 24 at Knoxville, MD)–14 July 1863. B: Centre Co., PA, forgeman. Dark eyes, dark hair, fair complexion, 5'10. Deserted from detached service.

Miller, Joseph. Mustered: Pvt. Co. H, 28th PA Inf. 11 July 1861. Transferred: Sgt. Cos. I, F, 6th U.S. Cav. 25 October 1862 (age 20 at Knoxville, MD)–29 April 1867. B: Malin, IRE, farmer. Blue eyes, dark hair, fair complexion, 5' 7. Discharged 25 April 1864 at Lighthouse Point, VA. Reenlisted: 29 April 1864 at NYC. WIA, Five Forks 30 March 1865. Discharged 29 April 1867.

Miller, Robert J. Pvt. Co. E, 11 September 1861 (age 23 at Cleveland, OH)–17 February 1863. B: Prussia, GER, book keeper. Grey eyes, brown hair, ruddy complexion, 5' 7. D: 17 February 1863 from typhoid fever at Stanton Hospital, Washington, D.C.

Miller, William John. Bugler. Cos. K, A, 20 August 1861 (age 25 at Rochester, NY)–20 August 1864. B: Darlington, CAN, carpenter. Grey eyes, light hair, brown complexion, 5' 3. POW, Fairfield, 3 July–23 December 1863. Paroled, reported at Annapolis, MD. Discharged at Charleston, VA.

Milligan, Edward T. Mustered: Pvt. Co. A, 37th PA Inf. 23 April 1816. Transferred: Pvt. Co. K, 6th U.S. Cav. 27 October 1862 (age 23 at Knoxville, MD)–27 April 1864. B: Pittsburgh, Allegheny Co., PA, nailor. Dark eyes, brown hair, dark complexion, 5' 8½. Discharged at Camp 6th Cav., VA.

Millington, John. Pvt. Co. A, 2 October 1861 (age 30 at Cleveland, OH)–2 October 1864. B: Durham, ENG, machinist. Blue eyes, light hair, ruddy complexion, 5' 6. POW, Fairfield. Paroled, reported 5 October 1863 at Culpepper, VA. Discharged at Harrisonburg, VA.

Mills, Benjamin. Pvt. Co. A, 30 September 1861 (age 27 at Pottsville, PA)–4 February 1862. B: Oldham, ENG, miner. Blue eyes, lt. brown hair, florid complexion, 5' 5. Disability discharge at Camp east of Capitol, Washington, D.C.

Mills, Henry S. Pvt. Co. I, 16 September 1861 (age 35 at Rochester, NY)–31 July 1862. B: Genesee Co., NY, farmer. Blue eyes, light hair, fair complexion, 5' 9. D: 31 July 1862 from disease at General Hospital, Philadelphia, PA.

Miner, Henry. Pvt. Co. F, 31 October 1864 (age 18 at Cincinnati, OH)–24 April 1865. B: Toronto, CAN, laborer. Brown eyes, black hair, sallow complexion, 5' 7. Deserted.

Minor, Wells C. Rct. 15 August 1861 (age 21 at Cleveland, OH)–24 August 1861. B: Cleveland, Cuyahoga Co., OH, farmer. Blue eyes, brown hair, ruddy complexion, 6'. Discharged by Civil Authority at Columbus, OH.

Mitchell, John. 16 November 1864 (age 20 at Harrisburg, PA)–21 November 1864. B: Cavan, IRE, laborer. Blue eyes, sandy hair, fair complexion, 5' 6. Deserted. Sub for J. F. Hutton.

Mitchell, Thomas Emmons. Sgt. Co. I, 25 July 1861 (age 22 at Rochester, NY)–28 January 1862. B: Mexico, NY, drover. Hazel eyes, brown hair, fair complexion, 5'10. Deserted.

Mittelstetter, John. Pvt. Co. F, 5 July 1861 (age 22 at Pittsburgh, PA)–5 July 1864. B: Darmstadt, GER, laborer. Blue eyes, light hair, fair complexion, 5' 7. MIA at Funkstown. Discharged.

Mockbee, Daniel K. Pvt. Co. M, 3 September 1861 (age 35 at Pittsburgh, PA)–22 December 1862. B: Fayette Co., PA, clerk. Dark eyes, dark hair, dark complexion, 5' 9. WIA near Uniontown. Disability discharge at Washington, D.C.

Moench, Jacob. Pvt. Co. I, 21 September 1861 (age 22 at Rochester, NY)–24 June 1862. B: GER, farmer. Blue eyes, flaxen hair, ruddy complexion, 5' 6. Deserted.

Molkey, Michael. Sgt. Co. L, 13 January 1862 (age 23 at Cleveland, OH)–13 January 1865. B: Co. Cork, IRE, laborer. Hazel eyes, black hair ruddy complexion, 5' 7¼. Discharged at Winchester, VA.

Moller, Thomas. 30 July 1861 (age 21 at Cleveland, OH)–12 August 1861. B: Dublin, IRE, musician. Blue eyes, black hair, ruddy complexion, 5' 4½. Deserted.

Monroe, Alfred. Pvt. Co. A, 24 December 1864 (age 21 at NYC, NY)–4–6 January 1865. B: Datson, OH, farmer. Grey eyes, sandy hair, fair complexion, 5' 4. Deserted.

Montag, Konrad. Pvt. Co. D, 2 August 1861 (age 25 at Pittsburgh, PA)–2 August 1864. B: Prussia, GER, iron worker. Brown eyes, brown hair, dark complexion, 5' 6. Discharged at City Point, VA.

Montgomery, Thomas. Mustered: Pvt. Co. G, 38th PA Inf. 13 July 1861. Transferred: Pvt.-Bugler. Co. F, 6th U.S. Cav. 28 October 1862 (age 22 at Knoxville, MD)–11 September 1865. B: London, ENG. Grey eyes, light hair, ruddy complexion, 5' 5. Reenlisted: 9 February 1864 at Camp 6th Cav., VA. Deserted 11 September 1865. Released from USA, 2 August 1891, AGO.

Moody, William H. Mustered: Pvt. Batt. E, (Knap's PA Independent), 6 July 1861. Transferred: Pvt. Co. K, 6th U.S. Cav. 27 October 1862 (age 26 at Knoxville, MD)–27 June 1864. B: Philadelphia, PA, stone cutter. Blue eyes, light hair, light complexion, 5'7. Discharged in the field, VA.

Moore, Benjamin F. Mustered: Pvt. Batt. E, (Knap's PA Independent), 3 May 1861. Transferred: Cpl. Co. K, 6th U.S. Cav. 26 October 1862 (age 24 at Knoxville, MD)–26 April 1864. B: Huntington, PA. Blue eyes, dark hair, light complexion, 5'8½. Discharged at Camp 6th Cav., VA.

Moore, George G. 1st Sgt. Co. E, 9 September 1861 (age 23 at Columbus, OH)–9 September 1864. B: Huron Co., OH, clerk. Grey eyes, sandy hair, sallow complexion, 5'10. Discharged at Berryville, VA.

Moore, Perry R. Pvt. Co. A, 18 September 1861 (at Columbus, OH)–25 January 1862. Disability discharge at Camp east of Capitol, Washington, D.C.

Moore, Sheldon. Pvt. Co. B, 30 July 1861 (age 18 at Cleveland, OH)–8 December 1862. B: Kirtland, OH, farmer. Grey eyes, light hair, fair complexion, 5'8. D: 8 December 1862 from typhoid fever at Berketsville, MD.

Moran, Thomas. 18 November 1864 (age 21 at Harrisburg, PA)–21 November 1864. B: Stockport, ENG, boatman. Blue eyes, light hair, fair complexion, 5'6½. Deserted. Sub.

Morehouse, Adonijah. Mustered: Pvt. Co. A, 42nd PA Inf. 21 August 1861. Transferred: Pvt. Co. A, 6th U.S. Cav. 28 October 1862 (age 21 at Knoxville, MD)–21 August 1864. B: Steuben Co., NY, farmer. Grey eyes, dark hair, florid complexion, 5'8. Discharged at Charlestown, VA.

Morfoot, Byron. Pvt. Co. B, 1 August 1861 (age 20 at Cleveland, OH)–23 October 1862. B: Plymouth, OH, printer. Grey eyes, black hair, ruddy complexion, 5'7. Disability discharge at Philadelphia, PA.

Morgan, Andrew J. Mustered: Pvt. Co. D, 14th IN Inf. 7 June 1861. Transferred: Pvt. Co. C, 6th U.S. Cav. 24 October 1862 (age 22 at Knoxville, MD)–5 June 1864. B: Venango Co., PA, farmer. Blue eyes, dark hair, fair complexion, 5'8½. POW, Funkstown, 7 July–30 November 1863. Paroled, reported at Annapolis, MD. Discharged at Camp 6th Cav., VA.

Morgan, John. Pvt. Co. A, 24 October 1864 (age 20 at Rochester, NY)–3 August 1865. B: Winslow, CAN, laborer. Grey eyes, light hair, fair complexion, 5'5. Deserted.

Morgan, William. Pvt. Co. A, 7 December 1864 (age 21 at Cincinnati, OH)–28 February 1866. B: CAN, farmer. Grey eyes, brown hair, ruddy complexion, 5'6. Deserted.

Morgan, William. Pvt. Co. B, 17 July 1861 (age 22 at Columbus, OH)–13 September 1862. B: Columbus, OH, boatman. Hazel eyes, brown hair, ruddy complexion, 5'7¾. Discharged at Philadelphia, PA.

Morris, John G. Mustered: Pvt. Co. A, 37th PA Inf. 23 April 1861. Transferred: Pvt. Co. H, 6th U.S. Cav. 28 October 1862 (age 23 at Knoxville, MD)–28 July 1864. B: Allegheny Co., PA, laborer. Blue eyes, brown hair, ruddy complexion, 5'9. Discharged in the field, VA.

Morris, Richard. Pvt. Co. E, 20 August 1861 (at Columbus, OH)–28 October 1862. Deserted. No further information.

Morrison, George W. Pvt. Cos. D, L, 20 August 1861 (age 21 at Pittsburgh, PA)–27 February 1865. B: Washington Co., PA, farmer. Grey eyes, brown hair, light complexion, 5'9½. Discharged 20 August 1864 at Charlestown, VA. Reenlisted: 24 October 1864. Deserted 27 February 1865.

Morrison, James. Rct. 15 November 1864 (age 34 at Harrisburg, PA)–1864. B: Co. Antrim, IRE, farmer. Blue eyes, brown hair, fair complexion, 5'5. Deserted. Sub for J. Kelly.

Morrissey, Thomas. 11 November 1864 (age 21 at Harrisburg, PA)–21 November 1864. B: St. John's, New Foundland, CAN, sailor. Blue eyes, dark hair, fair complexion, 5'7½. Deserted. Sub.

Morrow, Robert. Pvt. Co. C, 11 December 1861 (age 32 at Columbia, PA)–7 May 1862. B: York Co., PA, blacksmith. Blue eyes, brown hair, ruddy complexion, 5'10. Disability discharge at Washington, D.C.

Morton, David. Pvt. Co. D, 13 August 1861 (age 28 at Pittsburgh, PA)–13 August 1864. B: Yorkshire, ENG, coal miner. Blue eyes, sandy hair, light complexion, 5'7. Discharged.

Motts, Phillip. Mustered: Pvt. Co. H, 28th PA Inf. 11 July 1861. Transferred: Pvt. Co. F, 6th U.S. Cav. 28 October 1862 (age 21 at Knoxville, MD)–16 July 1864. B: Pittsburgh, Allegheny Co., PA, tobacconist. Grey eyes, black hair, ruddy complexion, 5'10. Discharged at Lighthouse Point, VA.

Mountain, Francis. Mustered: Pvt. Co. D, 110th

PA Inf. 19 December 1861. Transferred: Pvt. Co. D, 6th U.S. Cav. 28 October 1862 (age 21 at Knoxville, MD)–19 February 1867. B: Blair Co., PA. Grey eyes, dark hair, dark complexion, 5' 5½. Reenlisted: 9 February 1864 at Brandy Station, VA. Discharged 19 February 1867 at Jacksboro, TX.

Mowery, Jacob A. Mustered: Pvt. Co. C, 8th OH Inf. 22 June 1861. Transferred: Pvt. Co. C, 6th U.S. Cav. 22 October 1862 (age 23 at Knoxville, MD)–22 April 1864. B: Butler Co., PA, farmer. Hazel eyes, black hair, light complexion, 5' 7. POW, Funkstown. Paroled at Annapolis, MD, 24 August 1863. Discharged at Camp 6th Cav., VA. D: 22 April 1910, Dayton, Montgomery, OH.

Moyer, George. Pvt. Co. H, 2 August 1861 (age 21 at Philadelphia, PA)–2 August 1864. B: Slaven, Schuylkill, PA, boatman. Hazel eyes, black hair, dark complexion, 5' 7½. MIA, Fairfield. Discharged at Harper's Ferry, VA.

Muler, Anton. Rct. 7 October 1861 (age 28 at Cleveland, OH)–30 October 1861. B: Bremen, Prussia, GER, finisher. Grey eyes, brown hair, ruddy complexion, 6'. Deserted.

Mullen, Patrick. Rct. 15 November 1864 (age 22 at Harrisburg, PA)–22 November 1864. B: Dublin, IRE, laborer. Grey eyes, brown hair, ruddy complexion, 5'10. Deserted. Sub.

Muller, Gottlieb. Pvt. Co. F, 16 July 1861 (age 22 at Pittsburgh, PA)–16 July 1864. B: Barkhausen, Prussia, GER, farmer. Blue eyes, red hair, ruddy complexion, 5' 7. MIA, Fairfield. Discharged.

Mulloney, John. Pvt. Co. K, 16 July 1861 (age 24 at Franklin, PA)–30 July 1863. B: Co. Kilkenny, IRE, coal miner. Blue eyes, auburn hair, fair complexion, 5' 6½. Disability discharge at Washington, D.C.

Murphy, Frederick. Pvt. Co. F, 22 November 1864 (age 21 at Harrisburg, PA)–3 March 1865. B: Liverpool, ENG, boatman. Grey eyes, brown hair, ruddy complexion, 5'11½. Deserted 27 January 1865. Was shot dead for desertion at Harper's Ferry, VA, 31 March 1865, GO 20, Middle Military Division, 28 February 1865. Another record states he enlisted 27 December 1864.

Murphy, James J. Pvt. Co. A, 17 September 1861 (age 24 at Philadelphia, PA)–3 December 1862. B: Dublin, IRE, wheel wright. Grey eyes, light hair, light complexion, 5' 5½. Disability discharge at Belle Plain, VA.

Murphy, John. Pvt. Co. A, 12 December 1864 (age 27 at Cincinnati, OH)–30 May 1865. B: IRE,

laborer. Blue eyes, light hair, fair complexion, 5' 9. Deserted.

Murray, Peter. Pvt. Co. L, 26 October 1864 (age 40 at NYC, NY)–26 October 1867. B: Belfast, IRE, laborer. Brown eyes, dark hair, dark complexion, 5' 6. Discharged at Camp Wilson, TX.

Murray, William H. Pvt. Co. B, 6 August 1861 (age 22 at Cleveland, OH)–28 August 1866. B: Houston, ENG, sailor. Blue eyes, light hair, ruddy complexion, 5' 4½. WIA (right hand), Upperville. MIA, Fairfield. Reenlisted: 8 February 1864 at Camp 6th Cav., VA. Transferred to Navy on 30 April 1864. Gained from MIA 31 March 1865 at Annapolis, MD. Deserted 28 August 1866. Surrendered 29 November 1877. Dishonorable discharge by GCM at Newport Barracks, NY.

Murry, Andrew. Pvt. Co. F, 15 November 1864 (age 22 at Harrisburg, PA)–30 July 1865. B: Co. Mayo, IRE, boatman. Hazel eyes, brown hair, ruddy complexion, 5' 7½. Deserted.

Murry, James. Cpl.-Sgt. Co. M, 10 October 1861 (age 34 at Pittsburgh, PA)–10 October 1864. B: Co. Tyrone, IRE, blacksmith. Grey eyes, brown hair, light complexion, 5' 8½. MIA, Fairfield. Discharged at Strausburg, VA.

Murry, Thomas. Pvt. Co. M, 7 September (age 29 at Pittsburgh, PA)–7 September 1864. B: IRE, coal miner. Grey eyes, light hair, light complexion, 5' 9. WIA, Upperville. Discharged at Berryville, VA.

Myers, David. Rct. 22 October 1862 (age 30 at Knoxville, MD)–Never joined. B: Holton, Muskegon Co., MI, member USV. Blue eyes, sandy hair, ruddy complexion, 5' 3½. Returned to USV.

Myers, Frederick. Mustered: Pvt. Co. H, 1st MN Inf. 29 April 1861. Transferred: Pvt. Co. B, 6th U.S. Cav. 26 October 1862 (age 22 at Knoxville, MD)–26 February 1864. B: Prussia, GER. Blue eyes, light hair, light complexion, 5' 6. POW, Brandy Station, 11 October 1863–26 February 1864. D: 26 February 1864 from chronic diarrhea while a POW at Richmond, VA.

Myers, George. Pvt. Co. G, 13 August 1861 (age 23 at Rochester, NY)–13 August 1864. B: CAN, laborer. Grey eyes, light hair, fair complexion, 5' 6. POW, Fairfield, 3 July 1863–17 January 1864. Paroled, reported at Annapolis, MD. Discharged at Lighthouse Point, VA.

Myers, Henry. Pvt. Co. L, 21 May 1861 (age 19 at Champlaiyn, NY)–22 May 1863. B: St. Lawrence Co., NY, farmer. Blue eyes, brown hair, light complexion, 5' 5½. Discharged at

Brooks Station, VA. Register denotes he was a transfer from Co. D, 34th NY Inf. Officially mustered out of USV 23 November 1861.

Myers, Joseph. 1st Sgt. Co. C, 13 October 1864 (age 19 at Cleveland, OH)–13 October 1867. B: New York City, NY, farmer. Grey eyes, brown hair, sallow complexion, 5'8. Discharged at Buffalo Springs, TX.

Nafe, Samuel. Mustered: Pvt., Co. G, 8th OH Inf. 24 April 1861 (Fremont, OH)–4 June 1861. Reenlisted: 5 June 1861–4 November 1862. Transferred: Pvt. Co. K, 6th U.S. Cav. 27 October 1862 (age 24 at Knoxville, MD)–29 May 1864. B: 1839, Perry Co., PA, farmer. Blue eyes, black hair, fair complexion, 5'7½. Discharged at Camp 6th Cav., VA. D: 1904, IN. Another record states he transferred to 6th Cav. 20 December 1862.

Neal, Louis W. Rct. Co. C, 25 January 1862 (age 22 at Philadelphia, PA)–14 February 1862. B: Trenton, NJ, hostler. Grey eyes, black hair, fair complexion, 5'8. Disability discharge at Camp east of Capitol, Washington, D.C.

Neff, Emanuel, Jr. Mustered: Pvt. Co. F, 41st PA Inf. 30 July 1861. Transferred: Pvt. Co. E, 6th U.S. Cav. 28 October 1862 (age 19 at Knoxville, MD)–10 August 1864. B: 1844, West Chester, Chester Co., PA, shoemaker. Blue eyes, light hair, ruddy complexion, 5'4. POW, Funkstown, 7 July 1863–14 June 1864. Paroled, reported at White House. Discharged at Washington, D.C. D: 1925, PA. Note: He served alongside his father and brother John in the U.S.V.

Neff, Isaac T. Pvt. Co. E, 1 September 1861 (age 18 at Columbus, OH)–24 November 1862. B: 3 February 1843, Prairie Twp., Franklin, OH, farmer. Black eyes, brown hair, ruddy complexion, 5'8¼. Disability discharge at New York. D: 19 January 1912, Florissant, Teller, Co.

Neff, John H. Mustered: Pvt. Co. F. 41st PA Inf. 1 August 1861. Transferred: Pvt. Co. A, 28 October 1862 (age 21 at Knoxville, MD)–10 August 1864. B: West Chester, Chester, Co., PA, farmer. Blue eyes, light hair, fair complexion, 5'8. POW, Fairfield, 3 July 1863–18 January 1864. Paroled, reported at Annapolis, MD. Discharged at Lighthouse Point, VA.

Negler, Louis. Pvt. Co. A, 17 September 1861 (age 19 at Philadelphia, PA)–16 August 1864. B: Salon, Baden, GER, frame guilder. Grey eyes, brown hair, florid complexion, 5'5. KIA 16 August 1864 by guerrillas near Charlestown, VA.

Neill, William. Pvt. Co. H, 13 August 1861 (age 21 at Philadelphia, PA)–13 August 1864. B: Co.

Tyrone, IRE, laborer. Blue eyes, brown hair, ruddy complexion, 5'9¾. Discharged at Harper's Ferry, VA.

Nell, Isaac. Pvt. Co. K, 26 July 1861 (age 23 at Warren, OH)–26 July 1864. B: Beaver Co., PA, teamster. Black eyes, black hair, olive complexion, 5'4½. Discharged in the field.

Nellis, Dennis. Pvt. Co. F, F&S, B, 13 July 1861 (age 21 at Pittsburgh, PA)–8 February 1867. B: Co. Donegal, IRE, teamster. Lt. grey eyes, auburn hair, ruddy complexion, 5'7. Reenlisted: (teamster) 9 February 1864 at Camp 6th Cav. near Brandy Station, VA. Discharged at Jacksboro, TX upon expiration of service. D: 2 September 1900.

Nellis, Samuel. Pvt. Co. H, 10 August 1861 (age 22 at Philadelphia, PA)–1 May 1862. B: Co. Tyrone, IRE, laborer. Blue eyes, black hair, dark complexion, 5'7¼. Disability discharge at Camp before Yorktown, VA.

Nelson, Augustus B. Pvt. Co. E, 19 August 1861 (age 19 at Columbus, OH)–3 July 1863. B: Newburgh, Cuyahoga, OH, printer. Blue eyes, light hair, fair complexion, 5'7. KIA, Fairfield.

Nelson, Robert. Pvt. Co. A, 27 October 1864 (age 22 at NYC, NY)–25 September 1866. B: Bolton, ENG, clerk. Blue eyes, sandy hair, fair complexion, 5'6½. D: 25 September 1866 from cholera at Austin, TX.

Newell, Alonzo. Mustered: Pvt. Co. K, 3rd WI Inf. 18 April 1861. Transferred: Pvt. Co. F, 6th U.S. Cav. 28 October 1862 (age 19 at Knoxville, MD)–29 June 1864. B: Lagrange, WI, farmer. Blue eyes, light hair, fair complexion, 5'10. MIA, Funkstown. Discharged at Camp 6th Cav., VA.

Newell, Warren. Sgt. Co. I, 11 September 1861 (age 21 at Rochester, NY)–11 September 1864. B: Wyoming Co., NY, hotel keeper. Blue eyes, light hair, fair complexion, 5'8. MIA, Fairfield. Paroled at Annapolis, MD, 28 September 1863. Discharged in the field, VA.

Newman, David. Pvt. Co. L, 13 December 1864 (age 19 at Cleveland, OH)–23 May 1865. B: Queenstown, Ontario, CAN, butcher. Blue eyes, auburn hair, fair complexion, 5'3¼. Deserted 13 March 1865. Apprehended 6 May 1865. D: 23 May 1865 at Lincoln Hospital, Washington, D.C.

Newman, John. Rct. 3 October 1864 (age 23 at Rochester, NY)–Never joined. B: London, ENG, laborer. Grey eyes, brown hair, sallow complexion, 5'7.

Newton, Clement. Sgt. Co. M, 28 October 1861 (age 31 at Pittsburgh, PA)–28 October 1864.

B: ENG, coal miner. Grey eyes, brown hair, light complexion, 5' 8½. Discharged at Strasburg, VA.

Newton, James R. Pvt. Co. B, 30 July 1861 (age 18 at Cleveland, OH)–30 March 1865. B: Freedom, OH, farmer. Hazel eyes, brown hair, ruddy complexion, 5'11. Discharged at Camp Parole, Annapolis, MD. An exchanged POW.

Nicholas, Joseph. Pvt. Co. A, 7 December 1864 (age 21 at Cincinnati, OH)–23 March 1866. B: Yorkshire ENG, laborer. Blue eyes, brown hair, fair complexion, 5' 6. Deserted.

Nicholson, Thomas. Pvt. Co. D, 13 August 1861 (age 29 at Pittsburgh, PA)–12 August 1864. B: Durham, ENG, coal miner. Brown eyes, auburn hair, dark complexion, 5' 9. Discharged in the field, VA.

Nicol, David. Pvt. Co. A, 10 September 1864 (age 43 at Rochester, NY)–30 July 1865. B: Aberdeen, SCO, tailor. Blue eyes, brown hair, dark complexion, 5' 8. Deserted.

Nixon, Simon. Mustered: Pvt. Co. H, 13th Pa. Inf. 25 April 1861. Enlisted: Pvt. Co. G, 6th U.S. Cav. 22 August 1861 (age 24 at Pittsburgh, PA)–22 August 1864. B: 11 December 1836, Butler Co., PA, farmer and teacher. Hazel eyes, dark hair, dark complexion, 5'10. MIA, Beverly Ford, 9 June–11 December 1863. Discharged at Lighthouse Point, VA. D: 9 November 1902.

Noble, John. Cpl.-Sgt. Co. M, 27 November 1861 (age 26 at Pittsburgh, PA)–27 November 1864. B: IRE, miner. Hazel eyes, light hair, light complexion, 5' 6. WIA, Beverly Ford. Discharged in the field, VA.

Noble, Richard. Pvt. Co. L, 3 November 1864 (age 26 at NYC, NY)–6 July 1867. B: New York City, NY, laborer. Grey eyes, brown hair, ruddy complexion, 5' 8½. Not further information.

Nolan, Nicholas Murdock. Pvt.-Cpl. Co. M, 4th U.S. Art. 9 December 1852 (New York)–9 October 1857. Discharged at Ft. Leavenworth, KS. Reenlisted: 9 October 1857. Promoted to 1st Sgt. Served with Co. K, 2nd U.S. Dragoons. Transferred: Sgt.-1st Sgt. Co. B, 6th U.S. Cav. 5 September 1861 (age 25 at Pittsburgh, PA)–17 July 1862. Discharged 22 September 1862 to accept a commission as 2nd Lt. 6th U.S. Cav. (dated 17 July 1862). B: 10 March 1835, Co. Kilkenny, IRE, laborer. Brown eyes, black hair, fair complexion, 5'10. WIA (while carrying a dispatch), 13 October 1863. Bvt. 1st Lt. 1 August 1863 for Brandy Station. 1st Lt. on 5 July 1864. Bvt. Cpt. on 31 March 1865 Dinwiddie Court-House; Cpt. for 10th U.S. Cav. on 28 July 1866.

Maj., 3rd U.S. Cav. on 19 December 1882. D: 25 October 1883, TX.

Nold, Frank H. Pvt. Co. F, 24 July 1861 (age 23 at Pittsburgh, PA)–24 July 1864. B: Otigheim, Baden, GER, coal miner. Brown eyes, light hair, ruddy complexion, 5' 6½. MIA, Youngsville 12 May 1863. Discharged at Lighthouse Landing, Va. D: 3 May 1906.

Nollen, Mike. Pvt. Cos. C & L, 2 December 1861 (age 26 at Cleveland, OH)–3 January 1862. B: Co. Kildare, IRE, laborer. Grey eyes, sandy hair, ruddy complexion, 5' 6. Disability discharge at Washington, D.C.

Noon, Martin. Pvt. Co. F, 11 November 1864 (age 18 at Cincinnati, OH)–30 July 1865. B: Co. Cork, IRE, laborer. Grey eyes, brown hair, ruddy complexion, 5'1½. Deserted.

Norris, James. Pvt. Cos. M, F, 29 August 1864 (age 40 at Harrisburg, PA)–31 August 1865. B: Rochdale, ENG, clerk. Dark eyes, brown hair, ruddy complexion, 5' 6. Deserted.

Norris, Joseph. Pvt. Co. G, 1 August 1861 (age 22 at Columbus, OH)–1 August 1864. B: Massilon, OH, printer. Grey eyes, auburn hair, fair complexion, 5' 9. Discharged at Lighthouse Point, VA.

Northrop, Charles W. Pvt. Co. G, 24 July 1861 (age 22 at Rochester, NY)–10 October 1861. B: Oneida Co., NY, clerk. Grey eyes, brown hair, fair complexion, 5'11. Deserted.

Northrop, Doctor F. Pvt. Co. L, 21 March 1864 (age 22 at Washington, DC)–1 August 1865. B: New Hartford, CT, farmer. Black eyes, black hair, dark complexion, 5' 5. Deserted.

Northrop, Edward B. Pvt. Co. E, 17 September 1861 (age 28 at Columbus, OH)–29 December 1861. B: Cuyahoga Co., OH, clerk. Blue eyes, light hair, sallow complexion, 5' 4¾. D: 29 December 1861 of Brights Disease at the General Hospital at Annapolis, MD.

Norton, Edgar J. Pvt. Co. I, 2 September 1861 (age 21 at Rochester, NY)–2 September 1864. B: Livingston Co., NY, broom maker. Hazel eyes, brown hair, florid complexion, 5' 8. Deserted 25 November 1862. Apprehended 13 May 1863. Discharged 2 September 1864 in the field, VA.

Norton, Michael. Rct. 10 October 1864 (age 22 at Harrisburg, PA)–Never joined. B: Co. Fermanagh, IRE, soldier. Hazel eyes, fair hair, ruddy complexion, 5' 5.

Nugent, James C. Rct. 11 November 1864 (age 22 at NYC, NY)–21 November 1864. B: Long Island, NY, silver plater. Hazel eyes, brown hair, fair complexion, 5' 9. Deserted.

Nugent, James G. Mustered: Pvt. Co. K, 42nd NY Inf. 29 November 1861. Transferred: Pvt. Co. A, 6th U.S. Cav. 28 October 1862 (age 23 at Knoxville, MD)–10 November 1865. B: Kiltealy, IRE. Blue eyes, light hair, light complexion, 5'10. Reenlisted: 9 February 1864 at Camp 6th Cav., VA. Tried by GCMO 28 September 1865 at Frederick, MD. Deserted 10 November 1865.

Oakes, Gardner. Mustered: Pvt. Co. B, 8th OH Inf. 14 June 1861. Transferred: Sgt. Co. C, 6th U.S. Cav. 22 October 1862 (age 19 at Camp 6th Cav.)–1 June 1864. B: 1843, Cleveland, Cuyahoga Co., OH. Grey eyes, light hair, light complexion, 5'7½. Discharged in the field, VA. D: 1 May 1869, Cleveland, Cuyahoga, OH.

Oakley, Walter W. Pvt. Co. B, 10 December 1864 (age 23 at Cincinnati, OH)–26 December 1865. B: Queens Co., IRE, baker. Blue eyes, dark hair, fair complexion, 5'8¾. Deserted.

O'Brian, John. Co. F, 3 December 1864 (age 23 at Cleveland, OH)–12 January 1865. B: Co. Waterford, IRE, sailor. Hazel eyes, black hair, dark complexion, 5'3. Deserted. Note: Another record states he enlisted 21 November 1864.

O'Brien, James. Pvt. Co. L, 8 August 1864 (age 27 at NYC, NY)–8 July 1867. B: Dublin, IRE, soldier. Blue eyes, light hair, light complexion, 5'8½. Discharged at Camp Wilson, TX.

O'Brien, James. Rct. 18 November 1864 (age 19 at Harrisburg, PA)–21 November 1864. B: Co. Tipperary, IRE, farmer. Blue eyes, light hair, fair complexion, 5'5½. Deserted.

O'Brien, John. Pvt. Co. M, 8 September 1864 (age 28 at NYC, NY)–5 October 1866. B: Co. Roscommon, IRE, laborer. Blue eyes, brown hair, ruddy complexion, 5'5. D: 5 October 1866 from cholera at Austin, TX.

Oby, David E. Cpl. Co. B, 31 July 1861 (age 18 at Cleveland, OH)–7 July 1863. B: Clayton, Jefferson Co., NY, sailor. Hazel eyes, brown hair, ruddy complexion, 5'8¼. KIA, Funkstown, 7 July 1863.

Oby, George W. Sgt. Co. B, 29 July 1861 (age 21 at Cleveland, OH)–29 July 1864. B: January 1841 Clayton, Jefferson Co., NY, sailor. Hazel eyes, black hair, fair complexion, 5'8¾. MIA, Malvern Hill and Funkstown. Discharged at Lighthouse Point, VA. D: 7 February 1915.

O'Connell, James. Pvt. Co. F, 11 July 1861 (age 26 at Pittsburgh, PA)–29 February 1864. B: Co. Cork, IRE, laborer. Blue eyes, reddish hair, ruddy complexion, 5'5. Deserted 18 October 1861. Apprehended 4 September 1863. Discharged 29 February 1864 per G. C. M. O. #1, HQ, Res. Cav. Corps at camp of 6th Cav., VA.

O'Conner, Joseph. Pvt. Cos. G, F, 31 July 1861 (age 21 at Rochester, NY)–9 September 1867. B: Green Mt., IRE, wagon maker. Hazel eyes, brown hair, fair complexion, 5'4⅜. Transferred: Invalid Corps 17 December 1863. Discharged 17 August 1864 at Harper's Ferry, VA. Reenlisted: 9 September 1864 at Rochester, NY. Discharged 9 September 1867 at New Orleans, LA.

O'Connor, Pat. Rct. 24 September 1864 (age 26 at Carlisle Barracks, PA)–Never joined. B: Galway, IRE, soldier. Grey eyes, brown hair, ruddy complexion, 5'9¼.

O'Connor, Stephen. Pvt. Co. M, 5 September 1864 (age 30 at NYC, NY)–5 September 1867. B: Co. Cork, IRE, laborer. Grey eyes, brown hair, ruddy complexion, 5'7. Discharged at Mt. Pleasant, TX.

O'Harra, Charles. Pvt. Co. E, 9 September 1861 (age 18 at Columbus, OH)–9 May 1862. B: Pickaway Co., OH, farmer. Blue eyes, brown hair, light complexion, 5'9. WIA, Slatersville. D: 9 May 1862.

Oldham, David. Pvt. Co. D, 9 August 1861 (age 33 at Pittsburgh, PA)–11 February 1867. B: Cookstown, Huntingdon, PA, glass blower. Brown eyes, black hair, sandy complexion, 5'5. Reenlisted: 11 February 1864 at Brandy Station, VA. Discharged at Jacksboro, TX.

Olsen, Gilbert. Sgt. Cos. C, L, 16 December 1861 (age 27 at Philadelphia, PA)–20 December 1864. B: Christiana, NOR, sailor. Blue eyes, brown hair, ruddy complexion, 5'9½. POW from ? to 30 April 1864. Paroled, reported (Co. K) at Annapolis, MD. Discharged at Carlisle Barracks, PA.

O'Neil, Charles. Mustered: Pvt. Co. F, 110th PA Inf. 30 August 1861. Transferred: Pvt.-Cpl. Co. L, 6th U.S. Cav. 25 October 1862 (age 18 at Knoxville, MD)–10 August 1865. B: Bathurst, CAN. Grey eyes, black hair, dark complexion, 5'7. Reenlisted: 16 February 1864 at Brandy Station, VA. Deserted 10 August 1865. Released from service 29 December 1890.

O'Neil, Patrick. Pvt. Co. L, 14 January 1865 (age 22 at NYC, NY)–27 February 1865. B: Dublin, IRE, printer. Blue eyes, brown hair, fair complexion, 5'8. Deserted.

Ong, John. Cpl. Co. L, 21 March 1862 (age 24 at Bellafontaine, PA)–14 November 1862. B: Jefferson Co., OH, farmer. Black eyes, black hair, ruddy complexion, 5'9. Disability discharge at Baltimore, MD.

Opie, George Winfield. Pvt. Co. A, 22 December 1864 (age 19 at Cincinnati, OH)–30 May 1865. B: New York City, NY, laborer. Dark eyes, brown hair, ruddy complexion, 5' 6½. Deserted. D: 1901.

Oriel, Christopher. Mustered: Pvt. Co. H, 60th NY Inf. 19 October 1861. Transferred: Pvt. Co. M, 6th U.S. Cav. 23 October 1862 (age 19 at Knoxville, MD)–25 April 1864. B: Clinton Co., NY. Grey eyes, black hair, dark complexion, 5' 7. POW, Fairfield. Paroled at Annapolis, MD 20 August 1863. Reenlisted: 10 March 1864 at Brandy Station, VA. Deserted 25 April 1864.

Orme, Andrew J. Mustered: Co. A, 8th OH Inf. 17 June 1861. Transferred: Bugler. Co. I, 6th U.S. Cav. 22 October 1862 (age 25 at Knoxville, MD)–23 May 1864. B: Tiffin, OH. Hazel eyes, black hair, dark complexion, 5'10½. POW, Fairfield. Paroled at Annapolis, MD 28 September 1863. Discharged at Camp 6th Cav., VA, near Lighthouse Point.

Orr, Robert. Pvt. Co. I, 3 July 1861 (age 19 at Indiana, PA)–11 June 1862. B: Indiana Co., PA, carpenter. Hazel eyes, brown hair, florid complexion, 5'8. Deserted.

Orsay, Henry. Sgt.-Sgm. Cos. M, F&S, 12 April 1862 (age 27 at NYC, NY)–12 April 1868. B: Montreal, CAN, clerk. Blue eyes, auburn hair, ruddy complexion, 5'6. Discharged 1 June 1865 at Alexandria, VA (Sgt.). Reenlisted: 12 April 1865 at Alexandria, VA. Discharged 12 April 1868 at Austin, TX.

Ortt, James H. Pvt. Co. A, 18 September 1861 (age 19 at Pottsville, PA)–18 September 1864. B: Kutztown, Berks Co., PA, carpenter. Blue eyes, dk. brown hair, dark complexion, 5' 7½. WIA, Williamsburg. Discharged at Harper's Ferry, VA.

Otstoff, William. Pvt. Co. E, 24 August 1861 (age 20 at Columbus, OH)–3 July 1863. B: Columbus, OH, blacksmith. Hazel eyes, brown hair, sallow complexion, 5' 4¾. MIA, Fairfield.

Otten, Michael. Pvt. Co. L, 14 March 1864 (age 15 at Carlisle Barracks, PA)–27 March 1872. B: Ennis, Co. Clare, IRE, clerk. Grey eyes, brown hair, fair complexion, 5' 6. Discharged at Jacksboro, TX. Reenlisted: 18 November 1867 (New Orleans, LA)–27 March 1872. Deserted.

Owens, John. Pvt. Co. A, 21 November 1864 (age 31 at Harrisburg, PA)–12 January 1865. B: Co. Tyrone, IRE, laborer. Grey eyes, light hair, fair complexion, 5' 6½. Deserted.

Owens, Nathaniel B. Pvt. Co. I, 7 September 1861 (age 18 at Rochester, NY)–13 June 1863. B: Karen Co., IL, printer. Hazel eyes, black hair, dark complexion, 5'11. WIA (shot while on picket), Thoroughfare Gap, VA. D: 13 June 1863.

Owry, John. Pvt. Co. K, 22 July 1861 (age 24 at Warren, OH)–18 April 1862. B: Warren, OH, farmer. Grey eyes, brown hair, brown complexion, 5'11½. Discharged at Washington, D.C.

Paddock, George H. Pvt. Co. B, 2 August 1861 (age 28 at Cleveland, OH)–1 January 1862. B: Wyoming Co., NY, butcher. Hazel eyes, brown hair, ruddy complexion, 5' 6¼. Disability discharge at Washington, D.C.

Page, Frank S. Pvt. Co. A, 25 October 1861 (at Knoxville, MD)–30 October 1864. POW, Fairfield. Paroled, reported 22 October 1863 at Hospital, Annapolis, MD. Discharged at Middletown, VA.

Page, James G. Pvt. Co. E, 19 August 1861 (age 33 at Cleveland, OH)–10 April 1862. B: Faversham, ENG, mason. Blue eyes, light hair, ruddy complexion, 5' 9. Disability discharge at Washington, D.C.

Palmer, Gratz H. Mustered: Pvt. Co. B, 110th PA Inf. 24 October 1861. Transferred: Pvt. Co. B, 6th U.S. Cav. 28 October 1862 (age 19 at Knoxville, MD)–10 June 1865. B: Mount Union, Huntingdon Co., PA. Blue eyes, brown hair, light complexion, 5' 4½. Reenlisted: 8 February 1864 at Camp 6th Cav., VA. Disability discharge at Carlisle Barracks, PA. D: Huntingdon, PA.

Palmer, Myron S. Pvt.-Sgt.-Sgm.-1st Sgt. Co. B, 31 July 1861 (age 21 at Cleveland, OH)–28 July 1865. B: Ridgeville, OH, farmer. Hazel eyes, black hair, ruddy complexion, 5'11½. Reenlisted: 8 February 1864 at Brandy Station, VA. Deserted 28 July 1865.

Palmer, William. Pvt. Co: E, 9 September 1861 (age 28 at Adrian, MI)–31 December 1862. B: Dover, ENG, blacksmith. Blue eyes, brown hair, ruddy complexion, 5' 6. Disability discharge at Camp Banks, VA.

Palmer, William M. Pvt. Co. E, 10 September 1861 (age 21 at Columbus, OH)–29 January 1863. B: Fairfield Co., OH, farmer. Grey eyes, brown hair, sallow complexion, 5' 9½. Disability discharge at Camp Convalescent, VA.

Papke, Carle. Pvt. Co. K, 14 August 1861 (age 28 at Rochester, NY)–14 August 1864. B: GER, farmer. Blue eyes, fair hair, fair complexion, 5' 8½. Discharged in the field, VA.

Pardonner, Johnathan E. Mustered: Pvt. Co. B, 110th PA Inf. 24 October 1861. Transferred: Pvt. Co. B, 6th U.S. Cav. 28 October 1862 (age 20 at Knoxville, MD)–28 August 1864. B: Cassville, Huntington Co., PA, blacksmith. Dark eyes, dark hair, fair complexion, 5' 7½. MIA, Fairfield. Discharged in the field, VA.

Park, Henry W. Pvt. Co. M, 22 October 1861 (age 22 at Pittsburgh, PA)–9 November 1864. B: Pittsburgh, Allegheny Co., PA, blacksmith. Blue eyes, brown hair, florid complexion, 5' 6½. POW (captured by guerrillas), Germantown, 10 March 1864. Discharged at Annapolis, MD.

Parker, John. Pvt. Co. E, 9 September 1861 (age 21 at Adrian, MI)–9 September 1864. B: Cartwright, CAN, tinner. Hazel eyes, brown hair, ruddy complexion, 5' 6½. Discharged at Berryville, VA.

Parkhurst, Edwin. Mustered: Pvt. Co. H, 8th OH Inf. 6 June 1861. Transferred: Pvt. Co. C, 6th U.S. Cav. 26 October 1862 (age 21 at Knoxville, MD)–4 November 1863. B: Granger, Summit Co., OH, cooper. Blue eyes, light hair, fair complexion, 5' 9. POW, Fairfield. D: 4 November 1863 from pneumonia while a POW at Richmond, VA. Note: Listed on rolls as Edwin Parkers.

Parkhurst, Hugh C. Mustered: Pvt. Co. H, 8th OH Inf. 6 June 1861. Transferred: Pvt. Co. C, 6th U.S. Cav. 23 October 1862 (age 19 at Knoxville, MD)–19 November 1863. B: Medina Co., OH. Grey eyes, brown hair, florid complexion, 5' 9. MIA, Fairfield. D: 19 November 1863 from diarrhea at Annapolis, MD.

Parks, Henry. Pvt. Co. M, 21 September 1861 (at Pittsburgh, PA)–4 November 1864. WIA, Williamsburg. WIA/POW, Beverly Ford. Discharged at Camp Parole, Annapolis, MD.

Parrington, Daniel. Rct. 3 October 1864 (age 25 at Harrisburg, PA)–1864. B: Co. Tipperary, IRE, tailor. Brown eyes, light hair, fair complexion, 5' 5. Deserted.

Patterson, George. Pvt. Co. H, 1 August 1861 (age 22 at Philadelphia, PA)–1 August 1864. B: Philadelphia, PA, carver. Grey eyes, dark hair, fair complexion, 5' 8. Discharged in the field, VA

Patterson, George W. Mustered: Cpl. Co. K, 8th OH Inf. 27 April 1861. Transferred: Sgt. Co. C, 6th U.S. Cav. 23 October 1862 (age 21 at Knoxville, MD)–5 June 1864. B: Medina Co., OH. Blue eyes, brown hair, florid complexion, 5' 4½. POW, Funkstown, 7 July 1863–7 January 1864. Paroled, reported at Annapolis, MD. Discharged at James River, VA.

Pattinson, John. Sgt. Co. M, 23 September 1861 (age 22 at Pittsburgh, PA)–3 July 1863. B: Westmoreland Co., ENG, farmer. Grey eyes, brown hair, florid complexion, 5' 7½. WIA, Williamsburg. Brought to the Seminary Hospital, Hampton, VA, 11 May 1862. KIA, Fairfield, PA.

Patton, William. Pvt. Co. H, 30 July 1861 (age 19 at Philadelphia, PA)–27 May 1862. B: Philadelphia, PA, wheel wright. Blue eyes, red hair, ruddy complexion, 5' 6½. MIA, Hanover Court-House, VA.

Pauli, Henry A. 1st Sgt. Co. A, 24 August 1861 (age 19 at Philadelphia, PA)–25 August 1864. B: Philadelphia, PA, clerk. Grey eyes, brown hair, fair complexion, 5' 5. WIA, Williamsburg. Brought to the Seminary Hospital, Hampton, VA, 11 May 1862. WIA, Gettysburg 1 July 1863. Discharged at Halltown, VA.

Pearing, John. Pvt. Co. M, 15 November 1861 (age 21 at Pittsburgh, PA)–6 February 1868. B: New York City, NY, farmer. Blue eyes, brown hair, light complexion, 5' 4½. Reenlisted: 14 February 1864 at Brandy Station, VA. Deserted 29 July 1865. Surrendered 24 July 1866. Discharged 6 February 1868 at Fort Fetterman, D. T. Enlisted: Pvt. Co. C, F&S (Band), 3rd U.S. Art. 6 September 1870–6 September 1875. Discharged at Ft. Hamilton, NY. Reenlisted: 6 September 1875–5 September 1880. Discharged at Ft. Hamilton, NY (character excellent). Reenlisted: 6 September 1880–5 September 1885 (served with the 3rd and 5th U.S. Art.). Discharged at Ft. Hamilton, NY (character: see roll). Reenlisted: 5th U.S. Art. 6 September 1885–5 September 1890. Discharged at the Presidio of San Francisco, CA (character excellent). Reenlisted: 6 September 1890–1 October 1891. Retired by S.O. 221, AGO, 91, a Pvt. Note: Also served in Co. I, 18th U.S. Inf.

Pearsall, John. Rct. 8 November 1864 (age 22 at NYC, NY)–24 November 1864. B: New York City, NY, printer. Hazel eyes, black hair, ruddy complexion, 5' 6. Deserted.

Pearson, Richard. Cos. A, I, 3rd MD Inf. Transferred: Pvt. Co. K, 6th U.S. Cav. 27 October 1862 (age 19 at Knoxville, MD)–27 August 1864. B: Cambridgeshire, ENG, farmer. Dark eyes, dark hair, light complexion, 5' 5. Discharged in the field, VA.

Peffer, John. Mustered: Pvt. Co. F, 8th OH Inf. 6 July 1861. Transferred: Pvt. Co. B, 6th U.S. Cav. 28 October 1862 (age 21 at Knoxville, MD)–22 June 1864. B: Buffalo, NY. Dark eyes, dark hair, light complexion, 5' 7½. Discharged in the field, VA.

Pelton, Edward E. 1st Sgt. Cos. B, E, 9 February 1865 (age 23 at NYC, NY)–9 February 1868. B: Sheffield, MA, clerk. Blue eyes, black hair, fair complexion, 5' 7½. Discharged at Buffalo Springs, TX. D: 24 September 1924.

Penn, George. Mustered: Pvt. Co. C, 37th PA

Inf., 1 July 1861. Transferred: Cpl. Co. D, 6th U.S. Cav. 28 October 1862 (age 19 at Knoxville, MD)–28 June 1864. B: Allegheny Co., PA. Grey eyes, light hair, light complexion, 5' 6. Discharged at Wells Landing, VA. Note: George and William Williams were brothers.

Penn, William Williams. Mustered: Pvt. Co. C, 37th PA Inf. 1 July 1861. Transferred: Pvt. Co. D, 6th U.S. Cav. 28 October 1862 (age 22 at Knoxville, MD)–26 May 1864. B: Allegheny Co., PA. Blue eyes, dark hair, dark complexion, 5' 7. POW, Fairfield, 3 July 1863–21 May 1864 at Belle Isle Prison. Paroled, reported at Camp 6th Cav. Discharged at Melford, VA. Reenlisted: Co. D, 14th PA Cav. 14 August 1864–28 May 1865. D: 9 September 1911, Elizabeth Borough, Allegheny, PA.

Penney, Samuel E. Pvt. Co. D, 19 August 1861 (age 19 at Pittsburgh, PA)–19 August 1864. B: 1842, Allegheny Co., PA, farmer. Blue eyes, red hair, light complexion, 5'11. WIA, near Warrenton 16 October 1863. Discharged in the field, VA. D: 15 January 1912, McKeesport, Allegheny, PA. Note: Samuel and William were brothers.

Penney, William S. Pvt. Co. D, 17 August 1861 (age 21 at Pittsburgh, PA)–17 August 1864. B: Allegheny Co., PA, farmer. Grey eyes, light hair, light complexion, 5' 8. WIA near Rappahannock 12 November 1863. Discharged in the field, VA. D: 12 June 1900, McKeesport, Allegheny, PA.

Penrod, Henry Clay. Mustered: Pvt. Co. F, 37th PA Inf., 6 November 1861. Transferred: Pvt. Co. K, 6th U.S. Cav. 27 October 1862 (age 20 at Knoxville, MD)–29 April 1864. Grey eyes, light hair, dark complexion, 6' 2. Discharged in the field, VA. Enlisted: Pvt. Co. I, 194th PA Inf., 21 June 1864–6 September 1864 (mustered out). Transferred: Pvt. 97th PA Inf. (Independent Company), 6 September 1864–17 July 1865. B: Woodberry, PA, farmer. D: 1906, Tatesville, Bedford, PA. Note: Henry and John were brothers.

Penrod, John B. Jr. Mustered: Pvt., Co. F, 37th PA Inf. 11 June 1861. Transferred: Pvt. Co. K, 27 October 1862 (age 21 at Knoxville, MD)–29 April 1864. Dark eyes, dark hair, dark complexion, 5'11½. Discharged in the field, VA. Mustered: Cpl. Co. I, 194th PA Inf. 21 June 1864–6 September 1864. Transferred: Cpl. 97th PA Inf., 6 September 1864–17 July 1865. B: Martinsburg, Blair Co., PA, farmer. D: 17 October 1884, Everett, Bedford, PA.

Perveil, Leighton M. (alias Hunt, Charles H.). B: October 1842, Maryland. Enlisted: Harpers Ferry, VA as Pvt., Co. F, 2nd VA Inf. (C.S.A.), 1 May 1861. Enlisted as Pvt., Co. F, 1st MD Cav. (C.S.A.) Captured at Baltimore and thence confined as POW at Louisville, KY. Administered oath of allegiance September 1864 and released north of the Ohio River. Enlisted (Union): Pvt. Co. F, 6th U.S. Cav. 22 October 1864 (age 23 at Cleveland, OH)–24 April 1865. Record denotes born Toronto, CAN, tobacconist. Hazel eyes, brown hair, dark complexion, 5' 4¼. Deserted. Enlisted: Pvt., U.S.M.C., 12 June 1865, stationed at the Naval Yard, Washington, D.C. Joined the S.S. Princeton 23 October 1865 from Washington Navy Yard. "Awaiting court martial." Enlisted as "Charles H. Hunt" at Baltimore, MD, 17 November 1866 as Pvt. Co. K, 23rd U.S. Inf. Discharged 17 November 1869 upon expiration of service. Enlisted (Hunt): Pvt. Co. K, 2nd U.S. Art. 27 October 1872 (San Francisco, CA). Deserted 11 October 1873. Surrendered 30 December 1873 under G.O. 102, AGO 73 as Charles H. Hunt while serving in Marine Corps. Discharged as of date of surrender in Marine Corps. Granted pension in 1903. Note: His pension record says he also served in Co. K, 14th U.S. Inf.

Peterman, Thomas J. Pvt. Co. H, 6 August 1861 (age 28 at Philadelphia, PA)–6 August 1862. B: Philadelphia, PA, clerk. Brown eyes, brown hair, ruddy complexion, 5' 6. WIA/MIA, Malvern Hill. D: 6 August 1862.

Peters, Frank. Rct. 7 December 1864 (age 19 at Carlisle Barracks, PA)–Never joined. B: Baden, GER, carpenter. Grey eyes, fair hair, ruddy complexion, 5'10.

Petran, Christian. Mustered: Pvt.-Cpl. Co. E, 3rd WI Inf. 22 April 1861. Transferred: Pvt. Co. D, 6th U.S. Cav. 25 October 1862 (age 25 at Knoxville, MD)–4 March 1867. B: 1835, Farnstein, GER, farmer. Blue eyes, light hair, light complexion, 5' 9½. WIA, Beverly Ford. Reenlisted: 9 February 1864 at Brandy Station, VA. Deserted 27 July 1865. Apprehended 8 August 1865. Deserted 13 December 1865. Apprehended 7 January 1866. Discharged 4 March 1867 at Sherman, TX. Reenlisted: Pvt. Co. B, 21st U.S. Inf. 29 July–3 December 1867. Deserted. D: 1884, Outagamie Co., WI.

Pettit, George W. Pvt. Cos. C, L, 1 January 1862 (age 26 at Philadelphia, PA)–1 November 1862. B: Bucks Co., PA, farmer. Hazel eyes, brown hair, ruddy complexion, 5' 8. Deserted 23 March 1862. Apprehended 4 September 1862. D: 1 November 1862 from typhoid fever at Burkittsville, MD. Note: George and James were brothers.

Pettit, James A. Pvt. Cos. C, L, 1 January 1862 (age 21 at Philadelphia, PA)–22 February 1863. B: Bucks Co., PA, farmer. Hazel eyes, brown hair, fair complexion, 5' 7½. Deserted 24 March 1862. Apprehended 4 September 1862. Deserted 5 December 1862. Apprehended 17 January 1863. D: 22 February 1863 from typhoid fever at Falmouth, VA.

Peyton, Nathan. Rct. 12 October 1864 (age 25 at NYC, NY)–12 October 1864. B: Staunton, VA, blacksmith. Hazel eyes, black hair, dark complexion, 5' 8½. Deserted same day.

Pfaff, Frederick. Bugler. Co. A, 5 October 1861 (age 24 at Philadelphia, PA)–8 January 1863. B: Grebenstein, GER, door keeper. Hazel eyes, fair hair, light complexion, 5'. Disability discharge at Washington, D.C. D: 1886, Washington, D.C.

Pfeifer, Jacob. Rct. 26 November 1864 (age 22 at Cincinnati, OH)–Never joined. B: Baden, GER, boatman. Hazel eyes, brown hair, fair complexion, 5' 6.

Pfulf, Gustavus. Served in the U.S.M.C. from at least 1848–1863. Enlisted: Pvt. Co. M, 6th U.S. Cav. 1 October 1864 (age 39 at NYC, NY)–21 October 1866. B: PA, soldier. Hazel eyes, brown hair, light complexion, 5' 8½. D: 21 October 1866 from cholera at Austin, TX.

Phalor, Phillip. Rct. Co. F&S, 9 August 1861 (age 21 at Columbus, OH). B: 11 March 1841, Les Laseel, FRA, farmer. Grey eyes, brown hair, ruddy complexion, 5' 6½. Transferred to Rgt. HQ 12 August 1861 at Pittsburgh, PA. D: 1870.

Phalor, Tubalt. Pvt. Co. B, 6 August 1861 (age 18 at Columbus, OH)–6 August 1864. B: 23 December 1842 Les Sorte, FRA, teamster. Hazel eyes, light hair, light complexion, 5' 7¼. Discharged in the field, VA. D: 18 August 1888.

Phillips, John. Pvt. Co. M, 22 October 1861 (age 32 at Pittsburgh, PA)–21 December 1862. B: Warren Co., POL, machinist. Hazel eyes, black hair, dark complexion, 5' 4. Disability discharge at Washington, D.C.

Phillips, Thomas. Rct. Co. K, 6 August 1861 (age 18 at Warren, OH)–27 March 1862. B: Wales, Great Britain, WAL, coal miner. Grey eyes, light hair, light complexion, 5' 4½. Deserted.

Pickett, Syrrell S. Pvt. Co. G, 3rd WI Inf. Transferred: Pvt. Co. G, 6th U.S. Cav. 28 October 1862 (age 20 at Knoxville, MD)–29 June 1864. B: Cattaraugus Co., NY, farmer. Hazel eyes, dark hair, fair complexion, 5' 6. POW, Fairfield, 3 July 1863–17 February 1864. Paroled, reported at Camp Parole. Discharged at Wyanoke, VA.

Piedfort, Albert. Sgt. Co. A, 15 August 1863 (age 27 at NYC, NY)–15 August 1868. B: Havre, FRA, musician. Hazel eyes, brown hair, fair complexion, 6'. Reenlisted: Co. F, I , F&S, I, 7th U.S. Cav. 1 September 1868 to August 1872. Reenlisted: GS, 5 August 1878–4 September 1883. Note: Enlisted with brother in 1878.

Pierce, Francis H. Pvt. Co. L, 6 November 1861 (age 23 at Cleveland, OH)–6 November 1864. B: Liverpool, OH, blacksmith. Black eyes, dark hair, ruddy complexion, 5' 6½. Discharged at Cedar Creek, VA.

Pierce, William A. Pvt. Co. F, 4 July 1861 (age 21 at Pittsburgh, PA)–4 July 1864. B: Allegheny Co., PA, wagon maker. Blue eyes, light hair, fair complexion, 6'1⅜. POW, Fairfield, 3 July 1863–3 February 1864. Paroled, reported at Washington, D.C. Discharged in the field, VA.

Pifer, John. Pvt. Cos. M, L, 16 October 1861 (age 32 at Cleveland, OH)–16 October 1864. B: Bavaria, GER, farmer. Blue eyes, brown hair, ruddy complexion, 5' 6. Attached to Co. I, 1st U.S. Art. Discharged at Petersburg, VA.

Pike, Benjamin. Pvt. Co. K, 16 July 1861 (age 18 at Franklin, PA)–21 August 1863. B: Niagra Co., PA, farmer. Grey eyes, light hair, reddish complexion, 5' 4¾. Disability discharge at Philadelphia, PA.

Pike, William H. Sgt.-1st Sgt. Cos. B, C, 18 January 1862 (age 26 at Washington, DC)–18 January 1865. B: Middlesex, MA, soldier. Hazel eyes, brown hair, fair complexion, 5' 7½. POW, Fairfield, 3 July 1863–7 January 1864. Paroled, reported at Annapolis, MD. Discharged at Camp Russell, VA. D: 16 October 1915.

Pinkerton, Eli J. Pvt. Co. F, 21 November 1861 (age 23 at Pittsburgh, PA)–31 May 1865. B: Allegheny Co., PA, farmer. Black eyes, black hair, dark complexion, 5'11. Deserted 30 November 1861. Apprehended 2 December 1864. D: 31 May 1865 from typhoid fever at Judiciary Square Hospital, Washington, D.C.

Piper, John. Mustered: Pvt. Co. E, 37th PA Inf. 5 June 1861. Transferred: Pvt. Co. C, 6th U.S. Cav. 27 October 1862 (age 22 at Knoxville, MD)–29 July 1864. B: Jefferson Co., PA, boatman. Blue eyes, sandy hair, florid complexion, 5' 7. Discharged in the field, VA.

Place, Hiram. Mustered: Pvt. Co. E, 60th NY Inf. 10 August 1861. Transferred: Pvt. Cos. M, C, 6th U.S. Cav. 20 October 1862 (age 20 at Knoxville, MD)–25 October 1864. B: Franklin Co., NY. Blue eyes, light hair, fair complexion, 5' 6½. POW (captured by guerrillas), Auburn, VA. 9 November 1863–7 January 1864.

Paroled, reported at Annapolis, MD. Discharged in the field, VA.

Platt, George Crawford. Pvt.-Sgt. Co. H, 5 August 1861 (age 18 at Philadelphia, PA)–5 August 1864. B: 17 February 1842 Co. Londonderry, IRE, farmer. Blue eyes, brown hair, ruddy complexion, 5' 6½. WIA, Fairfield. Discharged in the field, VA. D: 20 June 1912.

Platt, Henry. Pvt. Co. F, 3 July 1861 (age 22 at Pittsburgh, PA)–November 1862. B: Hanover, GER, carriage driver. Grey eyes, light hair, fair complexion, 5'10. Deserted to the Confederates around November 1862.

Plumb, Charles R. Sgt. Co. G, 22 July 1861 (age 20 at Erie Co., PA)–22 July 1864. B: Bennington, VT, potter. Grey eyes, light hair, light complexion, 5' 8. Discharged at City Point, VA. Mustered: Co. C, 3rd VT Inf. 9 September 1864 (Rutland, VT)–25 May 1865. WIA (G.S.W. to left thigh), unknown date.

Pneumire, Peter. Rct. 4 October 1861 (age 25 at Pittsburgh, PA)–1 November 1861. B: Prussia, GER, farmer. Hazel eyes, black hair, dark complexion, 5' 5½. Deserted at Pittsburgh, PA.

Poel, William. Pvt. Co. L, 15 May 1862 (age 22 at Washington, DC)–15 May 1865. B: Odessa, RUS. Hazel eyes, dark hair, light complexion, 5'10. Discharged at Alexandria, VA. Reenlisted: dates between 1865–1868. Reenlisted: Cpl. 17 June 1868, Ft. Griffin, TX. D: 17 July 1868 at Washington, D.C.

Poet, Jacob. Pvt. Co. G, 20 July 1861 (age 32 at Columbus, OH)–9 June 1863. B: Birmingham, PA, engineer. Blue eyes, brown hair, ruddy complexion, 5' 9. WIA, Beverly Ford. D: 9 June 1863.

Poll, Andrew. Pvt. Co. D, 6 August 1861 (age 21 at Pittsburgh, PA)–6 August 1864. B: Coal Hill, PA, miner. Brown eyes, brown hair, sallow complexion, 5' 7. Discharged in the field, VA.

Poppenhager, August. Pvt. Co. F, 3 July 1861 (age 21⅚ at Pittsburgh, PA)–3 July 1863. B: Hesse Castle, GER, porter. Grey eyes, light hair, fair complexion, 5' 7¾. MIA, Funkstown. Discharged at Lighthouse Point, VA. Note: His surname is spelled with many variations.

Porter, Franklin H. Mustered: Pvt. Co. B, 3rd WI Inf. Transferred: Pvt. Co. B, 6th U.S. Cav. 28 October 1862 (age 19 at Knoxville, MD)–29 June 1864. B: New York City, NY. Hazel eyes, dark hair, dark complexion, 5' 6¾. POW, Fairfield. POW at Libby Prison. Discharged in the field, VA. Mustered: Pvt. Co. K, 4th MA Cav. 13 September 1864. Promoted to Cpl. 9 October 1864. Mustered out 22 May 1865 at Richmond, VA. D: 18 June 1920.

Portland, Michael. Rct. 7 October 1861 (age 18 at Cleveland, OH)–31 October 1861. B: Toledo, OH, printer. Grey eyes, brown hair, ruddy complexion, 5' 5. Deserted at Cleveland, OH.

Post, Parley P. Mustered: Pvt. Co. K, 110th PA Inf. 19 December 1861. Transferred: Pvt. Co. I, 6th U.S. Cav. 26 October 1862 (age 21 at Knoxville, MD)–16 September 1864. B: August 1842 Crawford Co., PA, laborer. Hazel eyes, black hair, fair complexion, 5' 9. Discharged in the field, VA. D: 11 February 1922.

Post, Theodore H. (alias Borst, Henry A.) Pvt. Co. K, 22 August 1861 (age 28 at Rochester, NY)–22 April 1862. B: GER, butcher. Blue eyes, light hair, light complexion, 5' 5¼. Deserted. Enlisted (Post, Theodore W.): Pvt. Co. H, 2nd U.S. Inf. 18 September 1863 (at Washington, D.C.). Enlistment records state he was born in ENG, carpenter, blue eyes, light hair, fair complexion, 5' 5. Discharged by disability 18 February 1864, Washington, D.C. Lost left leg below knee and right eye blinded (1890 Vet. Schedule). D: 30 November 1896, Camden, Camden, NJ.

Potter, Joseph. Pvt. Co. H, 2 August 1861 (age 21 at Philadelphia, PA)–1 May 1864. B: New York City, NY, boatman. Hazel eyes, light hair, fair complexion, 5' 9. Deserted 26 June 1863. Apprehended July/August 1863. Reenlisted: 19 March 1864 at Brandy Station, VA. Deserted 1 May 1864.

Powell, Patrick. Pvt. Co. F, 4 July 1861 (age 23 at Pittsburgh, PA)–4 July 1864. B: Co. Clare, IRE, teamster. Grey eyes, light hair, fair complexion, 5'10⅜. Deserted 18 August 1863. Apprehended 18 October 1863. Discharged 4 July 1864 in the field, VA.

Powers, Michael. Pvt. Co. A, 16 December 1864 (age 26 at Cincinnati, OH)–30 March 1865. B: Co. Tipperary, IRE, laborer. Grey eyes, brown hair, fair complexion, 5' 7¾. Deserted.

Powers, Patrick. Rct. 10 November 1864 (age 22 at NYC, NY)–20 November 1864. B: Co. Waterford, IRE, laborer. Blue eyes, brown hair, fair complexion, 5' 6. Deserted.

Powers, Thomas. Pvt. Co. I, 5 September 1861 (age 24 at Rochester, NY)–26 November 1861. B: IRE, farmer. Grey eyes, black hair, florid complexion, 5' 6. Deserted.

Praff, Frederick W. Pvt. Co. L, 29 March 1862 (at Washington, DC)–Not further information. B: about 1831, Prussia. 1870 Census denotes residence as NYC, NY

Prairie, Oliver. Mustered: Pvt. Co. E, 60th NY Inf. 9 October 1861. Transferred: Pvt. Co. M,

6th U.S. Cav. 19 October 1862 (age 21 at Knoxville, MD)–15 August 1865. B: CAN. Blue eyes, brown hair, dark complexion, 5' 3½. MIA, Fairfield. Discharged at Frederick, MD. Enlisted: G.M.S., 6 February 1866. Recognized as a deserter from the 6th U.S. Cav. 11 February 1866 at Carlisle Barracks, PA.

Pratt, Salem. Pvt. Co. K, 17 August 1861 (age 18 at Rochester, NY)–17 August 1864. B: Erie Co., NY, farmer. Blue eyes, light hair, fair complexion, 5' 8¾. Discharged in the field, VA.

Prestage, Daniel. Mustered: Pvt. Co. G, 7th MI Inf. 8 August 1861. Transferred: Pvt. Co. K, 6th U.S. Cav. 27 October 1862 (age 22 at Knoxville, MD)–14 April 1864. B: St. Lawrence Co., NY. Blue eyes, dark hair, dark complexion, 5' 6. Reenlisted 11 February 1864 at Brandy Station, VA. Deserted 14 April 1864.

Preston, Elijah L. Pvt. Co. G, 13 August 1861 (age 22 at Erie Co., PA)–14 October 1862. B: Poland, NY, farmer. Black eyes, black hair, fair complexion, 5' 8. Left sick in hospital at Yorktown, VA 1 September 1862. D: 14 October 1862. Term expired 13 August 1864.

Price, Edwin E. Pvt. Co. K, 16 July 1861 (age 27 at Franklin, PA)–16 July 1864. B: Williamsport, OH, cart & joiner. Grey eyes, light hair, fair complexion, 5' 9½. Discharged in the field, VA.

Price, Howard. Mustered: Co. G, 1st PA Inf. Transferred: Pvt. Co. E, 28 October 1862 (age 18 at Knoxville, MD)–21 June 1864. B: Centre Co., PA, laborer. Grey eyes, light hair, fair complexion, 5' 4. Discharged in the field, VA.

Price, Joseph. Pvt. Co. A, 18 September 1861 (age 21 at Philadelphia, PA)–9 February 1862. B: Bavaria, GER, glass blower. Brown eyes, light eyes, light complexion, 5' 6. Deserted.

Prichard, John W. Pvt. Co. G, 5 August 1861 (age 21 at Columbus, OH)–5 August 1864. B: Columbus, OH, farmer. Blue eyes, brown hair, sallow complexion, 5' 8. Discharged at Lighthouse Point, VA.

Prindwill, Edward. Rct. 28 October 1864 (age 23 at NYC, NY)–October 1864. B: Co. Kerry, IRE, laborer. Blue eyes, black hair, dark complexion, 5' 7½. Deserted.

Proper, Eli A. Pvt. Co. D, 12 September 1862 (age 27 at Rockville, MD)–12 August 1865. B: Pleasant Twp., Warren Co., PA, mill wright. Blue eyes, dark hair, sallow complexion, 5' 11½. Discharged at Frederick, MD. D: 20 December 1908, Bradford, PA.

Proper, Joseph M. Pvt. Co. D, 20 August 1861 (age 30 at Pittsburgh, PA)–20 August 1864. B: Venango Co., PA, farmer. Grey eyes, black hair,

light complexion, 6'. Discharged in the field, VA. Injured by falling horse (1890 Vet. Schedule).

Proper, Peter C. Pvt. Co. D, 20 August 1861 (age 23 at Pittsburgh, PA)–20 August 1864. B: Venango Co., PA, farmer. Brown eyes, black hair, sandy complexion, 5' 8. Discharged in the field, VA.

Prosser, Daniel. Pvt. Cos. C, L, 2 December 1861 (age 18 at Columbia, PA)–3 April 1865. B: South Wales, Great Britain, WAL, rolling mills man. Grey eyes, sandy hair, light complexion, 5' 3. WIA, Fairfield. POW, Funkstown, 7 July 1863–21 June 1864. POW, Berryville, VA, 16 August 1864–3 April 1865. Discharged at Camp Parole, Annapolis, MD.

Purath, August. Mustered: Pvt. Co. B, 3rd WI Inf. 21 April 1861. Transferred: Pvt. Co. F, 6th U.S. Cav. 25 October 1862 (age 25 at Knoxville, MD)–29 June 1864. B: Prussia, GER, laborer. Brown eyes, brown hair, fair complexion, 5' 8. POW, Fairfield, 3 July 1863–19 February 1864. Paroled, reported at Camp Parole. Discharged in the field, VA.

Purcell, John. Pvt. Co. F, 3 July 1861 (age 28 at Pittsburgh, PA)–1 September 1861. B: Lockport, NY, machinist. Brown eyes, brown hair, sandy complexion, 5' 7½. Confined on 27 July 1861 at Camp Scott, PA. Deserted.

Purcell, Patrick. Pvt. Cos. E, I, 3rd U.S. Inf. 1 June 1858–1 June 1863. While serving in the infantry, enlisted: Pvt. Co. F, 6th U.S. Cav. 26 July 1861 (age 29 at Pittsburgh, PA)–3 December 1861. B: Co. Kilkenny, IRE. Blue eyes, sandy hair, fair complexion, 6'. Deserted.

Purdy, Samuel Lewis P. Mustered: Pvt. Co. D, 110th PA Inf. 19 December 1861. Transferred: Pvt. Co. D, 6th U.S. Cav. 27 October 1862 (age 19 at Knoxville, MD)–27 August 1864. B: 1843, Blair Co., PA. Blue eyes, dark hair, dark complexion, 5' 6. Discharged in the field, VA. D: 1921, Palisade, Mesa, CO.

Pyle, John W. Sgt. Co. A, 23 August 1861 (age 20 at Philadelphia, PA)–23 August 1864. B: Reading Co., PA, baker. Blue eyes, sandy hair, fair complexion, 5' 5½. POW, Fairfield, 3 July 1863–18 January 1864. Paroled, reported at Annapolis, MD. Discharged at Harper's Ferry, VA.

Quick, Charles E. Mustered (Pontiac, MI): Pvt. Co. H, 7th MI Inf. 8 July 1861. Transferred: Pvt. Co. H, 6th U.S. Cav. 27 October 1862 (age 19 at Knoxville, MD)–23 April 1863. B: Ashtabula Co., OH, farmer. Blue eyes, light hair, fair complexion, 5' 5. Deserted.

Quiggin, Wilson. Cpl. Co. A, 3 October 1861 (age

20 at Cleveland, OH)–3 October 1864. B: Newberg, OH, farmer. Blue eyes, dark hair, fair complexion, 5'8. POW, Fairfield, 3 July 1863–19 February 1864. Paroled, reported at Camp 6th Cav. Discharged at Harrisonburg, VA.

Quigley, James. Mustered: USV. Enlisted: 6th U.S. Cav. 24 October 1862 (age 20 at Knoxville, MD)–No further information. B: CAN, mason. Blue eyes, brown hair, fair complexion, 5'7¼.

Quigley, Thomas. Pvt. Co. M, 15 November 1861 (age 21 at New Castle, PA)–15 November 1864. B:New Castle, Lawrence Co., PA, farmer. Grey eyes, brown hair, dark complexion, 6'. MIA, Fairfield. Discharged in the field, VA.

Quillen, William R. Mustered: Pvt. Co. D, 14th IN Inf. 6 July 1861. Transferred: Pvt. Co. C, 6th U.S. Cav. 23 October 1862 (age 21 at Knoxville, MD)–1 June 1864. B: Green Co., IN. Blue eyes, black hair, florid complexion, 5'11½. Discharged in the field, VA.

Quilligan, Thomas. Pvt. Co. H, 30 November 1861 (age 32 at Washington, DC)–4 November 1865. B: Co. Sligo, IRE, laborer. Blue eyes, brown hair, fair complexion, 5'7. Reenlisted: 29 February 1864 at Brandy Station, VA. Deserted 4 November 1865.

Quinn, James. Pvt. Co. A, 5 December 1864 (age 28 at Cincinnati, OH)–5 December 1867. B: Co. Dublin, IRE, laborer. Blue eyes, brown hair, sallow complexion, 5'5½. Deserted 12 December 1864. Apprehended 24 December 1864. Discharged at Buffalo Springs, TX.

Quinn, John G. Cpl. Co. M, 30 November 1861 (age 22 at Pittsburgh, PA)–30 November 1864. B: IRE, carriage driver. Blue eyes, light hair, light complexion, 5'7. WIA, Fairfield. Discharged in the field, VA.

Race, Abraham Vivian. Cos. I, K, 42nd NY Inf. 26 June 1861. Transferred: Pvt. Co. K, 6th U.S. Cav. 24 October 1862 (age 24 at Knoxville, MD)–24 April 1864. B: 2 February 1838, Belfast, Allegheny Co., NY, farmer. Blue eyes, brown hair, dark complexion, 5'6½. Discharged at Camp 6th Cav., VA. Reenlisted: Co. K, 1st NY Cav. 1 October 1864–30 June 1865. D: 24 November 1916, Bath, Steuben, NY.

Rae, Thomas. Rct. 5 November 1864 (age 20 at Harrisburg, PA)–21 November 1864. B: Toronto, CAN, farmer. Hazel eyes, light hair, fair complexion, 5'7. Deserted.

Rae, William. Pvt. Co. K, 30 July 1861 (age 31 at Warren, OH)–29 July 1864. B: Dumfries, SCO, soldier. Blue eyes, brown hair, fair com-

plexion, 5'10. Discharged at Carlisle Barracks, PA.

Ragan, John. Pvt. Co. L, 10 December 1864 (age 21 at Cincinnati, OH). B: Dublin, IRE, barber. Hazel eyes, dark hair, fair complexion, 5'5. Deserted 19 March 1865. Apprehended 26 March 1865. Dropped 13 December 1867 by expiration of service. Another record states he was captured 13 March 1865. Dropped from rolls 6 July 1867.

Ramhart, John. 27 September 1864 (age 29 at Rochester, NY)–20 October 1864. B: Baden, GER, cigar maker. Black eyes, black hair, sallow complexion, 5'8. Deserted.

Ramlow, Wilhelm (William). Musician. Cos. G, F&S, 5 August 1861 (age 27 at Erie Co., PA)–28 February 1867. B: 5 February 1834 Boblitz, Prussia, GER, musician. Blue eyes, light hair, fair complexion, 5'6. Reenlisted: 29 February 1864 at Brandy Station, VA. Discharged at Austin, TX. D: 16 January 1868, Columbus, Franklin, OH.

Ramsey, Sylvester S. Com. Sgt. Cos. K, F&S, 20 July 1861 (age 23 at Franklin, PA)–20 July 1864. B: Olean, NY, blacksmith. Hazel eyes, brown hair, light complexion, 5'5¾. Discharged at Lighthouse Point, VA.

Rau, Louis. Bugler. Co. M, 20 July 1861 (age 16 at Columbus, OH)–4 November 1863. B: Darmstadt, GER, laborer. Hazel eyes, brown hair, sallow complexion, 5'4½. D: 4 November 1863 of disease at hospital at Annapolis, MD.

Ray, Daniel T. Mustered: Pvt. Co. K, 100th PA Inf. Transferred: Pvt. Co. K, 6th U.S. Cav. 27 October 1862 (age 26 at Knoxville, MD)–27 August 1864. B: 16 September 1836, Philadelphia, PA, nailer. Grey eyes, dark hair, dark complexion, 5'6. Discharged at Lighthouse Point, VA. D: 19 February 1907, New Castle, PA.

Ray, Thomas B. Cpl.-Sgt. Co. K, 8 August 1861 (age 21 at Warren, OH)–8 August 1864. B: Bagetta, OH, cooper. Blue eyes, light hair, light complexion, 5'9¼. MIA, Watertown, 12 November 1862. Discharged at Lighthouse Point, VA.

Raymond, Matthew. Pvt. Co. L, 14 September 1864 (age 20 at Rochester, NY)–13 March 1865. B: Co. Cork, IRE, painter. Blue eyes, light hair, ruddy complexion, 5'8. Deserted.

Read, James P. Mustered: Co. I, 84th PA Inf. 14 October 1861. Transferred: Pvt. Co. A, 6th U.S. Cav. 28 October 1862 (age 19 at Knoxville, MD)–18 October 1864. B: Clearfield Co., PA. Blue eyes, sandy hair, light complexion, 5'8.

MIA 6–8 March 1863? Discharged at Middletown, VA.

Reader, Charles E. Cpl. Cos. C, L, 29 October 1861 (age 18 at Cleveland, OH)–21 December 1862. B: Cleveland, Cuyahoga Co., OH, stone cutter. Grey eyes, sandy hair, sallow complexion, 5'6. WIA, Uniontown. Disability discharge at Baltimore, MD. Mustered: Pvt. Co. K, 195th OH Inf. 6 March 1865–18 December 1865. Mustered out at Washington, D.C.

Readdy, John C. Mustered: Pvt. Co. B, 8th OH Inf. 18 April 1861. Transferred: Pvt. Co. C, 6th U.S. Cav. 22 October 1862 (age 19 at Knoxville, MD)–25 June 1864. B: Co. Mayo, IRE. Grey eyes, dark hair, dark complexion, 5'5. MIA, Funkstown. Discharged at Camp 6th Cav., VA. D: 15 July 1918, Cook Co., IL.

Reddon, John. Rct. 16 November 1864 (age 21 at Harrisburg, PA)–21 November 1864. B: Kingston, CAN, cook. Grey eyes, brown hair, ruddy complexion, 5'8. Deserted.

Redfield, Melvin S. Pvt. Co. I, 8 August 1861 (age 18 at Rochester, NY)–8 August 1864. B: Genesee Co., NY, farmer. Blue eyes, light hair, florid complexion, 5'5½. Discharged in the field, VA.

Redfield, Norton Daniel. Pvt. Co. I, 8 August 1861 (age 35 at Rochester, NY)–8 August 1864. B: 23 December 1822, LeRoy, Genesee Co., NY, constable. Grey eyes, lt. brown hair, florid complexion, 5'7½. Discharged at Harper's Ferry, VA.

Reed, Archibald. Mustered: Pvt. Co. A, 37th PA Inf. 23 April 1861. Transferred: Pvt. Co. H, 6th U.S. Cav. 28 October 1862 (age 17 at Knoxville, MD). B: Armstrong Co., PA, farmer. Blue eyes, brown hair, fair complexion, 5'6. POW (captured during Sheridan's Raid), Gordonsville, 16 June 1864.

Reed, Henry A. Mustered: Pvt. Co. D, 14th IN Inf. 7 June 1861. Transferred: 23 October 1862 (age 19 at Knoxville, MD)–Enlistment cancelled. B: Cumberland Co., PA. Blue eyes, light hair, light complexion, 5'4½. Returned to USV. Mustered out 6 June 1864, Indianapolis, IN.

Reed, William. Pvt.-Sgt. Co. G, 10 August 1861 (age 26 at Rochester, NY)–10 August 1864. B: New York City, NY, carpenter. Blue eyes, brown hair, fair complexion, 6'1½. POW, Fairfield, 3 July 1863–17 January 1864. Paroled, reported at Annapolis, MD. Discharged at Lighthouse Point, VA.

Rees, Abel P. Rct. 19 July 1861 (age 22 at Columbus, OH)–13 August 1861. B: Ross Co., OH, farmer. Blue eyes, sandy hair, ruddy complexion, 5'8. Deserted at Columbus, OH.

Reese, Benjamin F. Pvt.-Regt. Hospital Steward. Co. F&S, 6 July 1861 (age 26 at Pittsburgh, PA)–6 July 1864. B: Huntington Co., PA, clerk. Grey eyes, brown hair, dark complexion, 5'3¾. Appointed Regt. Hosp. Steward by Reg. Order No. 39, 25 October 1861 to rank from 1 September 1861. MIA at Fairfield. Discharged at City Point, VA.

Reese, Charles. Pvt. Co. A, 10 September 1861 (age 21 at Philadelphia, PA)–10 September 1864. B: Brunswick, GER, confectioner. Grey eyes, light hair, fair complexion, 5'5½. POW, Fairfield, 3 July–5 October 1863. Paroled, reported at Culpepper, VA. Discharged at Berryville, VA.

Reese, George. Pvt. Co. I, 7 September 1861 (age 25 at Rochester, NY)–31 October 1862. B: Saratoga Co., NY, farmer. Grey eyes, black hair, dark complexion, 5'10½. Disability discharge at Washington, D.C.

Reid, Gilbert. Pvt. Co. F, 13 December 1864 (age 25 at Cincinnati, OH)–27 January 1865. B: ENG, moulder. Grey eyes, dark hair, dark complexion, 5'5. Deserted. Sub.

Reidel, Charles. Band Leader. Co. F&S, 18 March 1865 (age 27 at NYC, NY)–23 April 1867. B: Baden, GER, musician. Blue eyes, brown hair, dark complexion, 5'7½. Discharged by SO 153, AGO 67, Austin, TX.

Reiley, Michael. Rct. 16 November 1864 (age 21 at Harrisburg, PA)–21 November 1864. B: Co. Longford, IRE, boatman. Grey eyes, brown hair, ruddy complexion, 5'6. Deserted.

Reilly, James. Rct. 9 November 1861 (age 32 at Pittsburgh, PA)–3 December 1861. B: IRE, laborer. Blue eyes, dark hair, light complexion, 5'8½. Disability discharge at Washington, D.C.

Reinel, Henry. Pvt. Co. F, 19 July 1861 (age 25 at Pittsburgh, PA)–19 July 1864. B: Hanover, GER, laborer. Blue eyes, brown hair, light complexion, 5'5. Discharged in the field, VA. Enlisted: Cos. C, F, 2nd U.S.V.V. Inf.

Reinhard, Andrew. Pvt. Co. E, 12 August 1861 (age 21 at Cleveland, OH)–27 January 1862. B: New York City, NY, laborer. Blue eyes, brown hair, ruddy complexion, 5'6¾. Disability discharge at Washington, D.C.

Reiter, Charles. Rct. 29 September 1864 (age 21 at Cleveland, OH)–Never joined. B: Wurttemberg, GER, confectioner. Hazel eyes, brown hair, fair complexion, 5'5.

Remmington, Nelson. Pvt. Co. A, 22 October 1861 (age 22 at Columbus, OH)–2 August 1864. B: Licking Co., OH, carpenter. Grey eyes, brown hair, ruddy complexion, 5'8.

POW, Fairfield, 3 July–24 December 1863. Paroled, reported at Annapolis, MD. WIA, Snickers Gap, 1864. WIA, Winchester, 1864. D: 2 August 1864 from wounds received in action at Winchester, VA.

Reniff, Merritt. Rct. 19 August 1861 (age 20 at Rochester, NY)–22 August 1861. B: Kalamazoo, MI, farmer. Hazel eyes, light hair, light complexion, 5' 6¾. Rejected recruit at Pittsburgh, PA. Mustered: Pvt. Co. D, 111th NY Inf. 21 July 1862–21 September 1862. Deserted at Annapolis, MD.

Reynolds, James T. Pvt. Co. H, 7 August 1861 (Cleveland, OH)–2 November 1862. B: Portage, NY, farmer. Grey eyes, black hair, sallow complexion, 5' 7. Deserted to the enemy at Philomont.

Reynolds, John G. 2nd Class Musician. Co. F&S, 7 March 1865 (age 26 at NYC, NY)–10 April 1867. B: New York City, NY, musician. Hazel eyes, dark hair, fair complexion, 5' 6½. Discharged by SO 153, AGO 67, Austin, TX.

Reynolds, William. Pvt. Co. A, 20 December 1864 (age 23 at Cincinnati, OH)–25 July 1865. B: Detroit, MI, blacksmith. Hazel eyes, brown hair, fair complexion, 5' 8. Deserted.

Reynolds, William R. Mustered: Pvt. Co. D, 8th OH Inf. 19 June 1861. Transferred: Pvt. Co. C, 6th U.S. Cav. 23 October 1862 (age 25 at Knoxville, MD)–3 July 1863. B: La Porte, IN. Grey eyes, light hair, light complexion, 5' 7. WIA, Fairfield. D: 3 July 1863 from wounds.

Rice, Dorman. Pvt. Co. G, 30 July 1861 (age 25 at Rochester, NY)–22 June 1863. B: Franklin Co., VT, farmer. Hazel eyes, brown hair, florid complexion, 5' 4½. Deserted.

Rice, William R. Mustered: Pvt. Co. K, 14th IN Inf. 7 July 1861. Transferred: Pvt. Co. C, 6th U.S. Cav. 23 October 1862 (age 19 at Knoxville, MD)–15 November 1864. B: Monroe Co., IN. Hazel eyes. light hair, florid complexion, 5' 5. MIA, Fairfield. POW, Brandy Station, 11 October 1863–15 November 1864. D: 15 November 1864 of unknown cause as a POW at Millen, GA.

Rich, Anson. Wagoner. Co. B, 2 August 1861 (age 33 at Cleveland, OH)–2 August 1864. B: Livingston Co., NY, teamster. Blue eyes, brown hair, ruddy complexion, 5'11. Discharged in the field, VA. D: 28 October 1883, Cleveland, OH.

Richards, William. Rct. 19 August 1861 (age 18 at Rochester, NY)–22 August 1861. B: IRE, farmer. Blue eyes, light hair, light complexion, 5' 9. Rejected recruit at Pittsburgh, PA.

Richey, Andrew W. Pvt. Co. K, 17 July 1861 (age 21 at Franklin, PA)–17 July 1864. B: Plum Twp., Venango Co., PA, farmer. Grey eyes, lt. brown hair, sandy complexion, 5' 8½. Discharged at Jordan Point, VA.

Ries, Charles. Pvt. Co. G, 29 July 1861 (age 28 at Erie Co., PA)–4 July 1864. B: Warsaw, POL, laborer. Blue eyes, dark hair, dark complexion, 5' 9½. Transferred to Invalid Corps to date.

Riley, James. Mustered: Pvt. Co. C, 14th IN Inf. 6 June 1861. Transferred: Rct. 6th U.S. Cav. 23 October 1862 (age 22 at Knoxville, MD)–Returned to USV. B: Coshocton Co., OH. Grey eyes, light hair, light complexion, 5' 6. Mustered out 6 June 1864, Indianapolis, IN.

Riley, James. Pvt. Co. K, 15 August 1861 (age 23 at Rochester, NY)–15 August 1864. B: IRE, farmer. Blue eyes, brown hair, florid complexion, 5' 5½. Discharged in the field, VA.

Riley, John. Mustered: Pvt. Co. E, 60th NY Inf. 1 October 1861. Transferred: Pvt.-Cpl. Co. M, 6th U.S. Cav. 23 October 1862 (age 20 at Knoxville, MD)–23 August 1864. B: Franklin Co., NY. Blue eyes, brown hair, fair complexion, 5' 7½. POW, Fairfield. Paroled at Annapolis, MD, 20 August 1863. Discharged at Harper's Ferry, VA.

Riley, John. Pvt. Company M, 7 July 1864 (at NYC, NY)–15 August 1865. Deserted. No further information.

Riley, Thomas. Pvt. Co. C, 12 December 1861 (age 24 at Cleveland, OH)–3 January 1862. B: Hyde, ENG, laborer. Black eyes, dark hair, ruddy complexion, 5' 5¾. Disability discharge at Washington, D.C.

Ring, Noah. Mustered: Pvt. Co. D, 14th IN Inf. 6 July 1861. Transferred: Rct. 6th U.S. Cav. 27 October 1862 (age 27 at Knoxville, MD). Returned to USV. B: 21 October 1835, Sullivan Co., IN, farmer. Grey eyes, brown hair, fair complexion, 5' 5. Mustered: Sgt. Co. F, 13th IN Inf. 23 December 1864. Mustered out 5 September 1865 at Goldsboro, NC. D: 28 August 1906, Sullivan, IN.

Rissman, Julius. Pvt. Co. H, 9 July 1861 (age 22 at Philadelphia, PA)–9 July 1864. B: Prussia, GER, machinist. Blue eyes, light hair, fair complexion, 5' 7. Discharged in the field, VA.

Ritz, Henry. Pvt. Co. F, 6 July 1861 (age 21 at Pittsburgh, PA)–6 July 1864. B: Hesse Castle, GER, coal miner. Lt. grey eyes, light hair, fair complexion, 5' 4½. Discharged in the field, VA.

Roach, Michael T. Rct. 26 September 1864 (age 19 at Rochester, NY)–Never joined. B: Montreal, Quebec, CAN, butcher. Grey eyes, brown hair, fair complexion, 5' 6.

Roads, Isaac. Pvt. Co. L, 22 October 1864 (age 18 at Cincinnati, OH)–27 February 1865. B: Morgan Co., OH, farmer. Blue eyes, light hair, fair complexion, 5'4. Deserted.

Robbins, Francis. Pvt. Co. K, 31 July 1861 (age 21 at Warren, OH)–31 July 1864. B: Howland, OH, brick maker. Grey eyes, brown hair, freckled complexion, 5'4½. Discharged in the field, VA.

Robelen, William Mustered: Pvt. Co. C, 2nd OH Inf. 17 April 1861–31 July 1861. Mustered out at Columbus, OH. Enlisted: G. Pvt. Co. G, 6th U.S. Cav. 4 August 1861 (age 18 at Columbus, OH)–4 August 1864. B: Wurttemberg, GER. Blue eyes, brown hair, ruddy complexion, 5'6¼. MIA at Fairfield. Discharged at Lighthouse Point, VA. D: 8 September 1894, Wilmington, New Castle, DE.

Robertson, Roswell A. Pvt. Co. G, 10 August 1861 (age 33 at Erie Co., PA)–27 May 1862. B: Ripley, NY, carpenter. Grey eyes, black hair, light complexion, 5'8. Disability discharge at Washington, D.C.

Robinson, Alexander. Rct. 2 December 1864 (age 18 at Cleveland, OH)–Never joined. B: Norfolk, ENG, porter. Grey eyes, brown hair, sallow complexion, 5'4½.

Robinson, Alvin B. Musician, 1st Class. Co. F&S, 29 November 1862 (age 25 at Belle Plain, VA)–7 November 1863. B: Stratford, ME, musician. Grey eyes, black hair, dark complexion, 5'9½. D: 7 November 1863, Vienna.

Robinson, John M. Saddler. Co. G, 29 July 1861 (age 24 at Erie Co., PA)–29 July 1864. B: Wellsville, OH, harness maker. Blue eyes, dark hair, fair complexion, 5'5½. Discharged in the field, VA.

Robinson, William. Pvt. Co. E, 13 September 1861 (age 19 at Adrian, MI)–13 September 1864. B: Yorkshire, ENG, farmer. Grey eyes, light hair, ruddy complexion, 5'4½. WIA/POW, Fairfield, 3 July–30 August 1863. Reported in hospital 30 August 1863. Discharged in the field, VA.

Robinson, William J. Pvt. Co. K, 19 August 1861 (age 18 at Rochester, NY)–22 April 1862. B: Onondaga Co., NY, farrier. Brown eyes, black hair, dark complexion, 5'3½. Deserted.

Robinson, William R. Mustered: Pvt. Co. H, 7th MI Inf. 28 April 1861. Transferred: Pvt. Co. H, 6th U.S. Cav. 26 October 1862 (age 26 at Knoxville, MD)–30 July 1864. B: Orleans, Jefferson Co., NY. Dark eyes, black hair, dark complexion, 5'5½. POW (captured by guerrillas), Warrenton, April 1863. POW at Andersonville, 21 January–30 July 1864. D: from scorbutus as a POW at Andersonville, GA.

Robison, Henry M. Pvt. Co. G, 30 July 1861 (age 22 at Erie Co., PA)–30 July 1864. B: Erie Co., PA, blacksmith. Blue eyes, light hair, fair complexion, 5'4. POW, Fairfield, 3 July 1863–17 February 1864. Paroled, reported at Camp Parole. Discharged in the field, VA.

Roehl, Frank. Pvt. Co. F, 16 July 1861 (age 28 at Pittsburgh, PA)–16 July 1864. B: Aschaffenberg, Bavaria, GER, farmer. Blue eyes, lt. brown hair, ruddy complexion, 5'7. POW (captured while on duty as a messenger), Culpepper, 28 September 1863–8 January 1864. Paroled, reported at Annapolis, MD. Discharged in the field, VA.

Roemer, Charles F. H. Pvt. Co. A, 10 October 1861 (age 21 at Philadelphia, PA)–10 October 1864. B: Hornback, GER, farmer. Hazel eyes, light hair, fair complexion, 5'5. WIA, Williamsburg. WIA, Upperville. Discharged at Carlisle Barracks, PA. Mentioned as mortally wounded in Capt. Cram's report on 23 July 1863.

Rogers, Dudley H. Mustered: Pvt. Co. K, 14th IN Inf. 6 July 1861. Transferred: Pvt. Co. C, 6th U.S. Cav. 23 October 1862 (age 21 at Knoxville, MD)–1 June 1864. B: Monroe Co., IN, carpenter. Grey eyes, dark hair, dark complexion, 5'8½. Discharged at Camp 6th Cav., VA.

Rogers, Jeremiah. Mustered (Fentonville, MI): Pvt. Co. F, 7th MI Inf. 8 May 1861. Transferred: Pvt. Co. H, 6th U.S. Cav. 28 October 1862 (age 27 at Knoxville, MD)–3 November 1865. B: Oakland Co., MI, carpenter. Blue eyes, brown hair, fair complexion, 5'8. Deserted 27 June 1863. Apprehended 9 May 1865. Discharged 3 November 1865, sentenced by GCM 2 June 1864 per SO 560, AGO 1865, New Orleans, LA.

Roland, Silas. Pvt. Co. K, 9 July 1861 (age 28 at Pittsburgh, PA)–9 July 1864. B: Allegheny City, Allegheny Co., PA, painter. Brown eyes, brown hair, ruddy complexion, 5'10¼. Discharged in the field, VA.

Roller, Joseph T. Mustered: Cpl. Co. D, 110th PA Inf. 19 December 1861. Transferred: Pvt. Co. D, 6th U.S. Cav. 27 October 1862 (age 19 at Knoxville, MD)–27 August 1864. B: 6 October 1844 Blair Co., PA. Blue eyes, auburn hair, light complexion, 5'6. Discharged at Charlestown, VA. D: 18 March 1917.

Rose, George M. Pvt. Co. G, 20 July 1861 (age 19 at Columbus, OH)–20 July 1864. B: Franklin, OH, teamster. Blue eyes, light hair, ruddy complexion, 5'11. POW, Fairfield, 3 July–18

November 1863. Paroled, reported at Camp 6th Cav. Discharged at Lighthouse Point, VA.

Rose, Roswell B. Mustered: Co. C, 2nd OH Inf. 17 April 1861–31 July 1861. Mustered out at Columbus, OH. Enlisted: Pvt. Co. G, 6th U.S. Cav. 12 August 1861 (age 18 at Columbus, OH)–13 August 1864. B: Columbus, OH, teamster. Hazel eyes, brown hair, ruddy complexion, 5'11. Discharged at Lighthouse Point, VA.

Rosney, John. Pvt. Co. C, 13 January 1862 (age 25 at Philadelphia, PA)–25 March 1862. B: Tullamore, IRE, hostler. Grey eyes, light hair, fair complexion, 5'7½. Deserted.

Ross, George. Pvt. Co. M, 5 October 1861 (age 22 at Pittsburgh, PA)–5 October 1864. B: GER, farmer. Grey eyes, brown hair, dark complexion, 5'10. Discharged in the field, VA.

Ross, George W. Rct. 31 August 1864 (age 39 at Rochester, NY)–Never joined regiment. B: Co. Limerick, IRE, laborer. Grey eyes, brown hair, dark complexion, 5'11½. Sub for S. D. Jackson.

Ross, Robert. 7 September 1864 (age 43 at Harrisburg, PA)–No record. B: Dublin, IRE, shoemaker. Blue eyes, grey hair, ruddy complexion, 5'6½.

Roth, Christian. Pvt. Co. I, 26 September 1861 (age 30 at Rochester, NY)–26 September 1864. B: GER, farmer. Blue eyes, brown hair, brown complexion, 5'3¾. Discharged in the field, VA.

Roth, Frederick. Pvt.-Cpl. Co. G, 2 August 1861 (age 19 at Erie Co., PA)–2 August 1864. B: Hasloh, Bavaria, GER, machinist. Hazel eyes, black hair, fair complexion, 5'5½. POW (in the field), 7 May 1863. Paroled 28 September 1863 at Annapolis, MD. Discharged at Lighthouse Point, VA.

Roth, John. Pvt. Co. D, 23 August 1861 (age 34 at Pittsburgh, PA)–23 August 1864. B: Rutzmagh, GER, moulder. Grey eyes, brown hair, dark complexion, 5'6½. Discharged in the field, VA.

Rothfuss, William G. Pvt. Co. A, 10 October 1861 (age 21 at Philadelphia, PA)–22 February 1863. B: Nurtingen, GER, cabinet maker. Blue eyes, light hair, fair complexion, 5'6½. Deserted. Enlisted: Landsman, U.S. Navy, Savannah, North Carolina, Colorado, Olnesee? Also served as a Pvt. U.S.V.V. Inf.

Rothrock, Alexander. Pvt. Co. D, 27 August 1861 (age 39 at Pittsburgh, PA)–27 August 1864. B: Fayette Co., PA, farmer. Brown eyes, black hair, dark complexion, 5'6½. Discharged in the field, VA.

Rotier (Rotzier), Emil. Pvt. Co. L, 12 September 1864 (age 19 at NYC, NY)–30 June 1865. B: Hamburg, GER, merchant. Brown eyes, black hair, ruddy complexion, 5'6. Deserted.

Rounds, John B. Rct. 3 October 1864 (age 23 at Rochester, NY)–Never joined. B: Whitehall, NY, trainer. Blue eyes, brown hair, sallow complexion, 5'11.

Rounds, Ruel V. Pvt. Co. E, 17 September 1861 (age 22 at Adrian, MI)–1 May 1862. B: Medina Co., MI, mason. Blue eyes, brown hair, ruddy complexion, 5'6½. D: 1 May 1862 from brain fever at Yorktown, VA.

Rousseau, John C. QM Sgt. Cos. C, F&S, 18 October 1861 (age 23 at Philadelphia, PA)–23 September 1862. B: Bristol, Bucks, PA, civil engineer. Grey eyes, brown hair, ruddy complexion, 5'10. Appointed a 2nd Lt. at Harper's Ferry, VA.

Rowe, John. Pvt. Co. M, 23 September 1864 (age 29 at Rochester, NY)–30 May 1865. B: New Haven, NY, farmer. Grey eyes, brown hair, florid complexion, 5'9½. Deserted.

Rowe, Thomas. Pvt. Co. F, 6 December 1864 (age 22 at Cincinnati, OH)–31 May 1865. B: VA, farmer. Hazel eyes, brown hair, fair complexion, 5'8. Deserted.

Roy, Edward. Pvt. Co. M, 26 September 1864 (age 34 at Cleveland, OH)–? B: New London, CAN, farmer. Blue eyes, sandy hair, ruddy complexion, 5'6½. Deserted.

Ruble, John H. Pvt. Co. E, 14 September 1861 (age 21 at Cleveland, OH)–23 February 1864. B: Canton, OH, painter. Grey eyes, brown hair, fair complexion, 5'11. POW, Funkstown. D: 23 February 1864 from chronic diarrhea as a POW at Richmond, VA.

Ruddy, Henry. Rct. 11 June 1864 (age 19 at Avon, NY)–20 June 1864. B: Cobury, West Can., CAN, circus rider. Grey eyes, dark hair, fair complexion, 5'5. Deserted.

Rumsey, Alfred. Pvt. Co. K, 19 August 1861 (age 18 at Rochester, NY)–19 August 1864. B: Carters Co., NY, farmer. Hazel eyes, light hair, brown complexion, 5'5¾. Discharged at Lighthouse Point, VA. D: 16 June 1926, Leavenworth, KS.

Rumsey, Noah S. Mustered (Sullivan, NY): Pvt. Co. C, 50th NY Eng. 9 December 1861. Transferred: Pvt. Co. E, 6th U.S. Cav. 28 October 1862 (age 20 at Knoxville, MD)–22 November 1863. B: Tioga Co., PA, farmer. Grey eyes, brown hair, dark complexion, 5'8. POW, Funkstown, 7 July–9 November 1863. Paroled, reported at Annapolis, MD. D: 22 November 1863 from chronic diarrhea at Annapolis, MD.

Russell, Harry. Rct. 10 September 1864 (age 34 at Rochester, NY)–21 September 1864. B: London, CAN, harness maker. Grey eyes, dark hair, ruddy complexion, 5' 4½. Sub. Deserted.

Russell, James. Rct. 5 October 1864 (age 24 at Harrisburg, PA)–Never joined. B: New York City, NY, boatman. Blue eyes, light hair, fair complexion, 5' 4½.

Russell, Simon. Mustered (Bradford, PA): Sgt. Co. G, 50th PA Inf. 26 September 1861. Transferred: Pvt. Co. A, 6th U.S. Cav. 28 October 1862 (age 25 at Knoxville, MD)–28 August 1864. B: 13 January 1836, Bradford Co., PA. Grey eyes, light hair, light complexion, 5'11. Discharged at Halltown, PA. D: 3 March 1911, Rome, Bradford, PA.

Ryan, Edmund. Pvt. Co. A, 8 September 1864 (age 20 at NYC, NY)–8 September 1867. B: Co. Limerick, IRE, laborer. Blue eyes, brown hair, ruddy complexion, 5' 6½. Sub. Discharged at Buffalo Springs, TX.

Ryan, Edward. Mustered: Pvt. Co. A, 45th PA Inf. 16 August 1861. Transferred: Pvt. Co. I, 6th U.S. Cav. 27 October 1862 (age 21 at Knoxville, MD)–27 August 1864. B: Centre Co., PA, boatman. Blue eyes, sandy hair, light complexion, 5'11. Discharged at Harper's Ferry, VA.

Ryan, John. Pvt. Co. A, 1 October 1861 (age 21 at Philadelphia, PA)–1 October 1864. B: Marburg, IRE, iron moulder. Blue eyes, brown hair, light complexion, 5' 6. POW, Fairfield, 3 July 1863–18 January 1864. Paroled, reported at Annapolis, MD. Discharged at Harrisonburg, VA.

Ryan, John. Rct. 23 September 1864 (age 22 at Rochester, NY)–Never joined. B: New York City, NY, laborer. Blue eyes, light hair, light complexion, 5' 9½.

Ryan, John H. Pvt. Co. D, 20 May 1865 (age 28 at Cincinnati, OH)–18 November 1867. B: NYC, NY, harness maker. Grey eyes, dark hair, sallow complexion, 5' 8½. D: 18 November 1867 from congestion of the brain at Buffalo Springs, TX.

Ryan, Patrick. Pvt. Co. F, 16 November 1864 (age 33 at Cincinnati, OH)–1 May 1865. B: IRE, laborer. Grey eyes, grey hair, fair complexion, 6' 2. Sub. Deserted.

Ryan, Thomas. Rct. 26 September 1864 (age 22 at Rochester, NY)–Never joined. B: Co. Tipperary, IRE, boatman. Hazel eyes, dark hair, florid complexion, 5' 9. Sub.

Sabin, Charles Henry. Mustered: Pvt. Co. E, 60th NY Inf. Transferred: Pvt. Co. A, 6th U.S. Cav. 28 October 1862 (age 19 at Knoxville, MD)–28 August 1864. B: Westville, NY. Grey eyes,

light hair, light complexion, 5' 8½. POW, Fairfield, 3 July–24 December 1863. Paroled, reported at Annapolis, MD. Discharged at Harrisonburg, VA. Mustered: Pvt. Co. A, 1st WI Heavy Art.

Sailer, Lewis. Mustered: Pvt. Co. E, 17th PA Inf. 25 April 1861–2 August 1861. Mustered out at Philadelphia, PA. Enlisted: Sgt. Co. H, 6th U.S. Cav. 12 August 1861 (age 24 at Philadelphia, PA)–12 August 1864. B: Philadelphia, PA, butcher. Blue eyes, brown hair, ruddy complexion, 5' 5½. POW, Coal Harbor, 27 June 1862. Discharged at Lighthouse Point, VA.

St. John, Joseph. Rct. 16 November 1864 (age 22 at NYC, NY)–21 November 1864. B: Montreal, Quebec, CAN, brick layer. Blue eyes, brown hair, fair complexion, 5' 5. Deserted.

Sanders, Daniel J. Farrier. Co. A, 18 September 1861 (age 23 at Pottsville, PA)–18 September 1864. B: Kutztown, Berks Co., PA, coach maker. Hazel eyes, black hair, fair complexion, 5' 7¾. POW, Fairfield, 3 July 1863–18 January 1864. Paroled, reported at Annapolis, MD. Discharged at Harper's Ferry, VA.

Sanders, Joseph E. Rct. 18 September 1861 (age 27 at Pottsville, PA)–3 November 1861. B: Kutztown, Berks Co., PA, shoemaker. Hazel eyes, dk. brown hair, fair complexion, 6' 2. Disability discharge at Washington, D.C.

Sands, William L. Pvt.-Bugler. H, 9 August 1861 (age 25 at Philadelphia, PA)–18 March 1863. B: Philadelphia, PA, marble cutter. Grey eyes, light hair, fair complexion, 5' 4½. Deserted from hospital in Annapolis, MD.

Sautter, Frederick. Sgt. Cos. L, C, 15 May 1864 (age 18 at Rochester, NY)–15 May 1867. B: Sadonville, GER, carpenter. Hazel eyes, brown hair, light complexion, 5' 6. Discharged at Ft. Belknap, TX.

Sayers, Charles H. Pvt. Co. I, 16 August 1861 (age 33 at Harrisburg, PA)–26 April 1864. B: Huntersville, AL, clerk. Black eyes, black hair, dark complexion, 5' 8. Disability discharge at Carlisle Barracks, PA.

Schaefer, John. Rct. 7 December 1864 (age 19 at Carlisle Barracks, PA)–Never joined. B: Prussia, GER, laborer. Grey eyes, fair hair, ruddy complexion, 5'11.

Schafer, Sebastian. Pvt. Co. F, 16 July 1861 (age 18 at Pittsburgh, PA)–13 January 1862. B: Niederbilken, GER, blacksmith. Lt. grey eyes, light hair, fair complexion, 5' 9. D: 13 January 1862 of disease at Washington, D.C.

Scheib, Andrew. Pvt. Co. C, 19 July 1861 (age 18 at Columbus, OH)–7 August 1864. B: Columbus, OH, carpenter. Blue eyes, light hair, fair complexion, 5'5. Discharged at City Point, VA. Mustered: Pvt. Co. K, 186th OH Inf. 21 February 1865–28 September 1865. Mustered out at Nashville, TN.

Scheid, George. Pvt. Co. F, 6 July 1861 (age 23 at Pittsburgh, PA)–11 November 1861. B: Sharpsburg, Allegheny Co., PA, farmer. Blue eyes, light hair, fair complexion, 5'8. D: 11 November 1861 of disease.

Schilling, Jacob. Pvt. Co. F, 11 July 1861 (age 25 at Pittsburgh, PA)–11 July 1864. B: Wernersberg, GER, farmer. Blue eyes, red randy hair, lt. sandy complexion, 5'7. MIA, Youngsville, 12 May 1863. Discharged at Lighthouse Point, VA.

Schilling, John. Pvt. Co. F, 26 July 1861 (age 21 at Pittsburgh, PA)–26 July 1864. B: Dettighoffer, GER, farmer. Blue eyes, light hair, sallow complexion, 5'9. POW, Fairfield, 3 July 1863–8 January 1864. Paroled, reported at Annapolis, MD. Discharged at Lighthouse Point, VA.

Schilling, William H. Pvt. Co. F, 12 July 1861 (age 21 at Pittsburgh, PA)–12 July 1864. B: Wernersberg, GER, barber. Blue eyes, flaxen hair, fair complexion, 5'3. Discharged at Lighthouse Point, VA. D: 1898.

Schinamann, August. Pvt. Co. K, 14 August 1861 (age 25 at Rochester, NY)–31 March 1864. B: GER, tailor. Blue eyes, fair hair, fair complexion, 5'3. D: 17 March 1864, Tonawanda, Erie, NY. Listed as Deserted, 31 March 1864.

Schmeider, Leopold. Enlisted: Pvt. Co. B, 44th U.S. Inf. 9 April 1857. Enlisted: Pvt. Co. M, 6th U.S. Cav. 29 November 1861 (age 35 at Pittsburgh, PA)–20 December 1861. B: GER. Blue eyes, grey hair, light complexion, 5'7½. Disability discharge at Washington, D.C. Enlisted: Pvt. 44th U.S. Inf. Transferred from Co. G to B, 24 November 1869.

Schmidt, George. Pvt. Co. C, 7 December 1861 (age 23 at Philadelphia, PA)–13 April 1862. B: Carhessen, GER, farmer. Grey eyes, auburn hair, ruddy complexion, 5'4. Deserted.

Schmith, William Henry. Pvt.-Cpl. Co. B, 18 July 1861 (age 18 at Columbus, OH)–19 July 1864. B: 12 December 1842, Columbus, OH, carpenter. Grey eyes, light hair, sallow complexion, 5'3½. MIA, Fairfield. WIA, Brandy Station, 11 October 1863. Discharged at Lighthouse Point, VA. D: 18 February 1923, Columbus, Franklin, OH.

Schmukler, John. Pvt. Co. F, 9 July 1861 (age 39 at Pittsburgh, PA)–20 November 1861. B: Wurttemberg, GER, blacksmith. Lt. grey eyes, black hair, dark complexion, 5'11. Deserted.

Schnell, Augustus. Mustered: Pvt. Co. F, 7th PA Inf. Enlisted: Pvt. Co. F, 6th U.S. Cav. 18 July 1861 (age 21 at Pittsburgh, PA)–19 May 1865. B: Hesse Castle, GER, tinner. Brown eyes, black hair, dark complexion, 5'7. Disability discharge at Baltimore, MD. Reenlisted: 21 July 1863 at Harrisburg, PA. Disability discharge 19 May 1865 at Carlisle Barracks, PA. Invalid Corps. 46th Co., 2nd Bn., V.R.C.

Schoonover, William N. Mustered: Pvt. Co. K, 110th PA Inf. 19 December 1861. Transferred: Pvt. Co. I, 6th U.S. Cav. 27 October 1862 (age 21 at Knoxville, MD)–27 August 1864. B: 1840, Tioga Co., NY, laborer. Grey eyes, brown hair, fair complexion, 5'10. Discharged in the field, VA. D: 1920, Johnson, Broome, NY.

Schreffler, Solomon H. Pvt.-Sgt. Co. L, 18 December 1864 (age 19 at Cincinnati, OH)–15 April 1866. B: 8 January 1846 Schuylkill Co., PA, teamster. Hazel eyes, dark hair, fair complexion, 5'7. Deserted 15 April 1866. Charge removed. Discharged at Washington, D.C. 6 November 1891 to date to 15 April 1866 under Act of Congress. D: 9 November 1917, Wichita, Sedgwick, KS.

Schryver, Charles E. Pvt. Co. L, 2 August 1861 (age 18 at Cleveland, OH)–14 May 1862. B: Green Co., NY, clerk. Grey eyes, brown hair, ruddy complexion, 5'5. Disability discharge at Washington, D.C. Afterwards served in the GMS.

Schuck, Jacob K. Chief Bugler. Mustered: Musician, Co. A. 11th PA Inf. (3 months). Enlisted: Cos. H, F&S, 6th U.S. Cav. 9 August 1861 (age 19 at Philadelphia, PA)–14 November 1864. B: Williamsport, Lycoming Co., PA, soldier. Blue eyes, light hair, fair complexion, 5'6½. Reenlisted: 15 March 1864 at Camp 6th Cav., VA. Discharged 14 November 1864 by promotion to Cpt. Co. E, 5th U.S. Cav., to date 14 November 1864, Camp Nelson, KY. Enlisted: Co. I, 6th U.S. Cav. 23 August 1865, Fredericksburg, MD. D: 25 May 1866. Assassinated on duty at Weatherford, TX..

Schultz, Frederick. Pvt. Co. L, 8 September 1864 (age 19 at NYC, NY)–6 September 1867. B: GER, farmer. Blue eyes, light hair, fair complexion, 5'3½. Discharged at Camp Wilson, TX.

Schumacher, John M. Pvt. Co. F, 9 July 1861 (age 27 at Pittsburgh, PA)–3 March 1863. B: Kanthausen, GER, blacksmith. Brown eyes, dark hair, dark complexion, 5'9¾. Disability discharge at Falmouth, VA.

Schwab, John. Pvt. Co. F, 26 July 1861 (age 26 at

Pittsburgh, PA)–26 July 1864. B: Obenurgl, SWZ, carpenter. Blue eyes, brown hair, ruddy complexion, 5' 4½. Discharged in the field, VA.

Schwarz, Andrew. Bugler. Co. M, 20 July 1861 (age 15 at Columbus, OH)–20 July 1864. B: Bavaria, GER, hostler. Blue eyes, light hair, fair complexion, 5'1. WIA, Williamsburg. Brought to Seminary Hospital, Hampton, VA, 11 May 1862. MIA, Fairfield. Paroled at Annapolis, MD, 20 August 1863. Discharged in the field, VA.

Schweigus, Frank. Sgt. Co. K, 15 August 1861 (age 26 at Rochester, NY)–29 September 1863. B: GER, farmer. Grey eyes, brown hair, florid complexion, 5' 7½. WIA (mortally), Culpepper. D: 29 September 1863.

Schwenk, Martin P. Enlisted: Pvt. Co. E. 3rd U.S. Art., 29 December 1856–29 December 1861. Enlisted: Sgt. Co. B, 6th U.S. Cav. 6 January 1862 (age 26 at Washington, DC)–6 January 1865. B: 28 April 1839, Baden, GER. Grey eyes, brown hair, fair complexion, 5' 4½. Discharged at Camp Russell, VA. Enlisted: Co. H, 6th U.S. Cav. (Washington, D.C.) 10 December 1866. Deserted 7 January 1868. Apprehended 31 December 1868. Deserted 14 January 1869. Later anglicized his name as George P. Martin. Received the Congressional Medal of Honor for action during at Millerstown, PA, 3 July 1863. Date of issue, 23 April 1889. Citation: Bravery in attempt to carry a communication through the enemy's lines; also rescued an officer from the hands of the enemy. D: 20 June 1924.

Scomb, John. Rct. 26 November 1864 (age 23 at Cincinnati, OH)–No further information. B: Dublin, IRE, shoemaker. Blue eyes, light hair, fair complexion, 5' 5¾.

Scott, Joseph B. Pvt. Co. B, 29 July 1861 (age 30 at Columbus, OH)–9 June 1862. B: Manchester, ENG, machinist. Brown eyes, dark hair, light complexion, 5' 5½. Disability discharge at Washington, D.C. RR lists him as deserted 2 November 1862 at Washington.

Scott, Walter W. Pvt. Co. C, 20 December 1861 (age 25 at Philadelphia, PA)–26 February 1862. B: Chicago, IL, machinist. Hazel eyes, dark hair, dark complexion, 5' 6. Deserted.

Scullen, Patrick (alias Robinson, James). Pvt. Co. D, 12 August 1861 (age 30 at Pittsburgh, PA)–6 June 1862. B: Co. Antrim, IRE, laborer. Blue eyes, light hair, light complexion, 5' 9½. Disability discharge at Washington, D.C. Mustered: Hasting's Co. (Independent) Light Art. 7 August 1862–20 August 1863. Mustered: Pvt. Co. E, 147th PA Inf. 19 March 1864. Trans-

ferred: Co. M, 5th PA Heavy Art. Mustered out on 15 July 1865. D: 5 July 1890.

Sebolt, Lawrence M. (alias Sebolt, Michael). Pvt. Co. F, 15 August 1861 (age 21 at Pittsburgh, PA)–15 August 1864. B: Allegheny Co., PA, farmer. Blue eyes, lt. brown hair, ruddy complexion, 5' 6. Deserted 4 August 1863. Apprehended 28 February 1864. Discharged in the field, VA.

Sedgwick, Charles S. Pvt. Co. I, 13 August 1861 (age 16 at Indiana, PA)–6 September 1862. B: Hollidaysburg, Blair Co., PA, farmer. Grey eyes, light hair, light complexion, 5' 4. Disability discharge at General Hospital, Ft. Wood, NY.

Sedgwick, William. Pvt. Co. L, 22 June 1864 (age 18 at Rochester, NY)–20 March 1866. B: North Ferrisburgh, Addison Co., VT, clerk. Grey eyes, light hair, fair complexion, 5' 5. Deserted.

Sedwick, George Fletcher. Pvt.-Sgt. Co. K, 16 July 1861 (age 28 at Franklin, PA)–12 May 1862. B, 23 February 1833, Armstrong Co., PA, gunsmith. Hazel eyes, brown hair, ruddy complexion, 6'¾. D: 12 May 1862 from typhoid fever at Yorktown, VA.

Seldon, George Baldwin. Rct. 18 June 1864 (age 18 at Rochester, NY)–2 July 1864. B: Clarkson, Monroe Co., NY, student. Brown eyes, dark hair, ruddy complexion, 5' 7½. Discharged by SO 222 at Carlisle Barracks, PA.

Selick, Andrew. Mustered: Co. G, 7th WV Inf. Transferred: Pvt. Co. A, 6th U.S. Cav. 28 October 1862 (age 20 at Knoxville, MD)–28 August 1864. B: GER. Grey eyes, light hair, light complexion, 5' 5. Discharged at Halltown, VA.

Senn, Henry. Mustered: Pvt. Co. E, 28th PA Inf. 15 July 1861. Transferred: Pvt. Co. B, 6th U.S. Cav. 25 October 1862 (age 22 at Knoxville, MD)–15 July 1864. B: GER. Grey eyes, light hair, ruddy complexion, 6' 2. POW, Fairfield, 3 July–16 November 1863. Paroled, reported at Camp 6th Cav. Discharged at Carlisle Barracks, PA.

Serrill, Edwin. Pvt. Co. A, 1 December 1864 (age 19 at Cleveland, OH)–31 March 1865. B: Aylmer, Ontario, CAN, farmer. Grey eyes, dk. brown hair, dark complexion, 5' 8. Deserted.

Settele, John. Rct. 20 September 1861 (age 27 at Columbus, OH)–No further information. B: Wurttemberg, GER, farmer. Hazel eyes, black hair, ruddy complexion, 5' 4.

Shaner, John I. Mustered: Pvt. Co. E, 34th PA Inf. 25 July 1861. Transferred: Pvt. Co. L, 6th U.S. Cav. 28 October 1862 (age 23 at Knoxville, MD)–18 February 1867. B: Centre Co.,

PA, lumberman. Blue eyes, fair hair, fair complexion, 5'10. Reenlisted: 18 February 1864 at Camp 6th Cav., VA. MIA at unknown place. Gained from MIA 16 February 1865 at Annapolis, MD. Discharged 18 February 1867 at Jacksboro, TX, a Cpl.

Shank, Joseph. Pvt. Co. I, 13 August 1861 (age 26 at Indiana, PA)–12 July 1864. B: Indiana Co., PA, farmer. Hazel eyes, brown hair, dark complexion, 5'5. Discharged at Camp 6th Cav., VA. Enlisted: Co. F, 9th U.S.V.V. Inf.

Sharkey, Charles. Pvt. Co. F, 21 November 1864 (age 23 at Harrisburg, PA)–29 January 1865. B: Tyrone, ENG, farmer. Blue eyes, brown hair, light complexion, 5'3. Deserted.

Sharp, Augustus F. Rct. 26 November 1864 (age 18 at Cincinnati, OH)–Not enough information. B: Harrisburg, PA, laborer. Blue eyes, dark hair, fair complexion, 5'7¾.

Sharp, Edward. Pvt. Co. L, 23 August 1864 (age 36 at Rochester, NY)–8 August 1865. B: Co. Cavan, IRE, laborer. Grey eyes, brown hair, florid complexion, 5'6. Deserted.

Sharp, Joseph. Rct. 25 July 1861 (age 18 at Columbus, OH)–12 August 1861. B: Delaware Co., OH, farmer. Blue eyes, brown hair, ruddy complexion, 5'4¼. Rejected recruit for disability.

Sharpe, James. Rct. 5 September 1864 (age 24 at Harrisburg, PA)–Never joined. B: Co. Antrim, IRE, laborer. Hazel eyes, brown hair, ruddy complexion, 5'5½.

Shaw, James. Mustered: Pvt. Co. E, 37th PA Inf. 27 June 1861. Transferred: Pvt. Co. H, 6th U.S. Cav. 28 October 1862 (age 18 at Knoxville, MD)–28 July 1864. B: Allegheny Co., PA, farmer. Grey eyes, dark hair, ruddy complexion, 5'7. Discharged in the field, VA.

Shay, Lawrence. Pvt. Co. I, 5 September 1861 (age 24 at Rochester, NY)–December 1861. B: IRE, tailor. Blue eyes, brown hair, florid complexion, 5'4. Deserted. Mustered: Pvt. Co. E, 115th PA Inf. 16 December 1861. D: 15 March 1862.

Shearrow, William B. Mustered: Pvt. Co. C, 14th IN Inf. Transferred: Pvt. Co. C, 6th U.S. Cav. 23 October 1862 (age 23 at Knoxville, MD)– 4 June 1865. B: Orange Co., IN, painter. Blue eyes, light hair, fair complexion, 5'6½. MIA, Funkstown. MIA, Brandy Station. POW. Exchanged 15 April 1865. Discharged at Alexandria, VA.

Sheed, Harrison C. Rct. 26 November 1864 (age 18 at Cincinnati, OH)–No further information. B: Harrisburg, PA, laborer. Hazel eyes, brown hair, fair complexion, 5'10.

Sheridan, John. Mustered: Mustered: Pvt. Co. E, 8th OH Inf. 17 June 1861. Transferred: Pvt. Co. C, 6th U.S. Cav. 22 October 1862 (age 21 at Knoxville, MD)–7 June 1864. B: Co. McCaren, IRE, teamster. Blue eyes, brown hair, florid complexion, 5'4. MIA, Fairfield. Discharged in the field, VA.

Sherman, Augustus. Rct. 2 November 1861 (age 17 at Cleveland, OH)–No further information. B: Cleveland, Cuyahoga Co., OH, teamster. Black eyes, light hair, ruddy complexion, 5'8.

Sherman, Frank. Rct. 6 October 1864 (age 21 at Harrisburg, PA)–8 October 1864. B: Chicago, IL, student. Blue eyes, fair hair, fair complexion, 5'8. Deserted.

Sherman, Horatio W. Pvt. Cos. C, L, 2 November 1861 (age 18 at Cleveland, OH)–11 February 1863. B: Cleveland, Cuyahoga Co., OH, stone cutter. Black eyes, light hair, ruddy complexion, 5'7. WIA, Uniontown. Disability discharge at Convalescent Camp, VA.

Sherry, Hiram. Pvt. Co. A, 24 September 1861 (age 21 at Philadelphia, PA)–24 September 1864. B: Weymouth, Atlantic Co., NJ, laborer. Blue eyes, dk. brown hair, light complexion, 5'5. Discharged at Harrisonburg, VA. Mustered: Pvt. Co. B, 2nd NJ Vet. Inf. 10 Apr 1865. Promoted to Cpl. 6 July 1865. Mustered out 11 July 1865 at Hall's Hill, VA.

Sherry, John. Pvt. Co. M, 3 September 1861 (age 21 at Pittsburgh, PA)–1 September 1863. B: SCO, coal miner. Grey eyes, brown hair, light complexion, 5'9. POW, Williamsburg. POW at Richmond, VA and Salisbury, NC. Paroled May 1862 and arrived in New York 9 June 1862 via steamer "Guide." Gained 16 July 1862 from parole. Deserted.

Shields, Stephen. Rct. 26 September 1864 (age 22 at Rochester, NY)–Never joined. B: Co. Roscommon, IRE, laborer. Blue eyes, brown hair, sallow complexion, 5'8. Sub for John Cline.

Shields, William. Pvt. Co. A, 9 December 1864 (age 31 at Cincinnati, OH)–9 December 1867. B: IRE, boatman. Blue eyes, brown hair, ruddy complexion, 5'7. Discharged at Buffalo Springs, TX.

Shierdan, William. Rct. 3 November 1864 (age 22 at Harrisburg, PA)–21 November 1864. B: Co. Cork, IRE, boiler maker. Blue eyes, brown hair, fair complexion, 5'7¼. Deserted.

Shimer, George W. Mustered: Pvt. Co. E, 17th PA Inf. 25 April 1861–2 August 1861. Mustered out at Philadelphia, PA. Enlisted: Pvt. Co. H, 6th U.S. Cav. 19 August 1861 (age 23 at

Philadelphia, PA)–17 January 1863. B: 1837, Chester Co., PA, blacksmith. Blue eyes, light hair, dark complexion, 5'7. Disability discharge at Convalescent Camp, VA. D: 1863, Chester, PA.

Shipley, Samuel. Mustered: Pvt. Co. B, 5th PA Inf. April 1861. Enlisted: Sgt. Co. D, 6th U.S. Cav. 8 August 1861 (age 23 at Pittsburgh, PA)– 8 August 1864. B: Baden, GER, butcher. Blue eyes, auburn hair, light complexion, 5'7. Discharged at Light House Point, VA. D: 30 April 1904.

Shoemaker, Jacob. Rct. 8 August 1861 (age 21 at Columbus, OH)–21 August 1861. B: Stack Co., OH, painter. Blue eyes, light hair, sallow complexion, 5'9½. Rejected recruit for disability.

Short, Edmund W. Pvt. Co. B, 30 July 1861 (age 24 at Cleveland, OH)–14 August 1862. B: ENG, farmer. Blue eyes, brown hair, ruddy complexion, 6'. Disability discharge at Georgetown, D.C. D: 25 July 1903, MI.

Shortall, Christopher. Pvt. Co. I, 29 July 1861 (age 21 at Rochester, NY)–15 July 1864. B: Java, Wyoming Co., NY, farmer. Brown eyes, brown hair, fair complexion, 5'10. POW, Brandy Station, 11 October 1863–20 May 1864. Paroled, reported at Camp 6th Cav. Discharged in the field, VA. D: 13 February 1916, Danville, Vermillion, IL.

Shorts, William W. Pvt. Co. K, 16 July 1861 (age 28 at Franklin, PA)–22 March 1862. B: Sandy Creek Twp., Mercer Co., PA, farmer. Blue eyes, chestnut hair, dark complexion, 5'4½. Discharged by S. O., HQ, Army of the Potomac, Alexandria, VA.

Shortter, Daniel. Rct. 1 December 1864 (age 24 at Cleveland, OH)–Never joined. B: Sheffield, New Brunswick, CAN, farmer. Grey eyes, brown hair, fair complexion, 5'7½.

Shoup, John. Rct. 12 August 1861 (age 24 at Indiana, PA)–No further information. B: Clarion Co., PA, cooper. Hazel eyes, brown hair, florid complexion, 5'7¾.

Showalters, Simon Peter. Mustered: Pvt. Co. F, 37th PA Inf. 23 April 1861. Transferred: Pvt. Co. K, 6th U.S. Cav. 27 October 1862 (age 19 at Knoxville, MD)–5 February 1863. B: Bedford Co., PA, shingle maker. Dark eyes, light hair, dark complexion, 5'10½. Disability discharge at camp near Falmouth, VA. Mustered: 2nd Cpl. Co. H, 22nd PA Cav. 26 February 1864. Transferred: Co. H, 3rd PA (Provisional) Cav. 25 June 1865. Mustered out 31 October 1865 at Cumberland, MD. D: 9 January 1878, Schellsburg, Bedford, PA.

Shuster, Absalom. Cpl. Co. D, 20 August 1861 (age 22 at Pittsburgh, PA)–20 August 1864. B: Armstrong Co., PA, coal miner. Brown eyes, black hair, dark complexion, 5'8. Discharged in the field, VA.

Shutle, Henry. Pvt. Co. M, 4 November 1861 (age 33 at Pittsburgh, PA)–14 July 1865. B: GER, tailor. Grey eyes, sandy hair, light complexion, 5'4. Discharged at Frederick, MD.

Sibel, Henry T. Pvt. Co. G, 25 July 1861 (age 18 at Columbus, OH)–25 July 1864. B: Reynoldsburg, OH, farmer. Grey eyes, sandy hair, fair complexion, 5'4¾. MIA/WIA, Fairfield. Rejoined 9 August 1863 from hospital. Discharged at City Point, VA.

Simcox, Hugh M. Pvt. Co. K, 17 July 1861 (age 20 at Franklin, PA)–7 July 1864. B: 22 May 1841, Venango Co., PA, farmer. Blue eyes, brown hair, light complexion, 5'6. Discharged in the field, VA. D: 10 March 1907, Springfield, Greene, MO.

Simmer, John P. Pvt. Co. F, 6 July 1861 (age 31 at Pittsburgh, PA)–6 July 1864. B: Trier, GER, blacksmith. Grey eyes, black hair, dark complexion, 5'9. Discharged at Lighthouse Point, VA.

Simmons, William. Sgt. Co. L, 22 June 1864 (age 18 at Rochester, NY)–1 October 1865. B: Hastings, West, Ontario, CAN, lawyer. Grey eyes, brown hair, fair complexion, 6'. D: 1 October 1865 of disease at hospital at Camp 6th U.S. Cav. in Frederick, MD.

Simonet, Peter. Cpl. Co. F, 25 July 1861 (age 34 at Pittsburgh, PA)–25 July 1864. B: Galwitz, SWZ, butcher. Hazel eyes, black hair, ruddy complexion, 5'6. WIA, Beverly Ford. Discharged at Lighthouse Point, VA.

Simons, John. Rct. 3 November 1864 (age 23 at Elmira, PA)–Never joined. B: Chester, Cheshire Co., ENG, painter. Brown eyes, dark hair, dark complexion, 5'6.

Simpson, Charles. Mustered: Pvt. Co. E, 8th OH Inf. 25 June 1861. Promoted to Cpl. 20 November 1861. Transferred: Cpl. Co. C, 6th U.S. Cav. 24 October 1862 (age 22 at Knoxville, MD)–25 June 1864. B: Erie Co., OH, member USV. Grey eyes, black hair, florid complexion, 5'9. MIA, Fairfield. Discharged in the field, VA.

Simpson, George. Pvt. Co. L, 27 October 1864 (age 22 at Rochester, NY)–27 February 1865. B: Clonmel, Co. Tipperary, IRE, boatman. Grey eyes, auburn hair, ruddy complexion, 5'11. Deserted.

Singer, Erotus R. Pvt. Co. E, 23 August 1861 (age

21 at Cleveland, OH)–24 March 1862. B: Thompson Twp., OH, farmer. Grey eyes, light hair, ruddy complexion, 5'10½. Deserted.

Singer, Frank O. Sr. Pvt. Co. H, 9 August 1861 (age 21 at Philadelphia, PA)–9 August 1864. B: 17 June 1849, GER, barber. Blue eyes, light hair, fair complexion, 5'5. MIA, Union, 10 November 1862. Discharged at Lighthouse Point, VA. D: 29 November 1909, Pikesville, Baltimore, MD.

Sipe, Andrew. Pvt. Co. K, 15 August 1861 (age 24 at Rochester, NY)–11 February 1867. B: GER, teamster. Blue eyes, light hair, fair complexion, 5'9¾. Reenlisted: 11 February 1864, Brandy Station, VA. Deserted 30 April 1865. Apprehended 9 June 1865. Discharged 11 February 1867 at Jackson, TX.

Sisson, Benjamin F. Pvt. Co. G, 31 July 1861 (age 20½ at Erie Co., PA)–14 January 1863. B: McKean Twp., Erie Co., PA, farmer. Blue eyes, dark hair, dark complexion, 5'4¼. Disability discharge at Philadelphia, PA.

Skiff, Henry R. Pvt. Cos. B, A, F, 26 July 1861 (age 31 at Cleveland, OH)–8 September 1866. B: Reading, Schuyler Co., NY, farrier. Blue eyes, brown hair, ruddy complexion, 5'6. MIA, Fairfield. Reenlisted: 8 February 1864 at Brandy Station, VA. Reported on November roll as a gain 14 November 1864. Deserted 8 September 1866.

Slack, Charles A. Pvt.-Cpl. Co. G, 12 August 1861 (age 21 at Columbus, OH)–3 July 1863. B: 19 September 1841 Delaware Co., OH, farmer. Blue eyes, light hair, light complexion, 5'6¼. KIA, Fairfield.

Slattery, Michael A. Cpl. Co. F, 5 July 1861 (age 22 at Pittsburgh, PA)–5 July 1864. B: Co. Tipperary, IRE, boot maker. Grey eyes, lt. brown hair, fair complexion, 5'8¼. Discharged at Lighthouse Point, VA.

Slemer, Henry. Enlisted (Slemer, Herman): GMS, 23 December 1862 (Cincinnati, OH)–5 January 1863. Deserted at Cincinnati, OH. Enlisted (Henry): Rct. 6th U.S. Cav. 23 December 1864 (age 22 at Cincinnati, OH)–7 December 1864. B: Hanover, GER, moulder. Blue eyes, light hair, fair complexion, 5'8. Mustered: Pvt. Co. K, 5th OH Inf. 2 June 1865. Mustered out 30 October 1865 at Charlotte, NC. Reenlisted: Co. M, 5th U.S. Art. 19 April 1866–18 February 1867. Deserted.

Sligh, Jacob. Pvt. Co. L, 29 August 1864 (age 18 at Cleveland, OH)–1 May 1866. B: Erie Co., PA, laborer. Blue eyes, light hair, fair complexion, 5'9½. Deserted.

Smith, Charles. Mustered: Pvt. Co. K, 10th ME Inf. 6 August 1862. Transferred: Pvt. Co. C, L, 6th U.S. Cav. 24 October 1862 (age 21 at Knoxville, MD)–2 November 1864. B: Grand Isle Co., VT. Black eyes, black hair, dark complexion, 5'7. Discharged at Cedar Creek, VA.

Smith, Edwin M. Pvt. 2 June 1864 (age 18 at Aaron, NY)–22 November 1864. B: Charlemont, Franklin, MA, clerk. Grey eyes, brown hair, fair complexion, 5'10½. Discharged by SO 395, AGO 12 November 1864 at Kernstown, VA.

Smith, Frederick. Pvt. Co. H, 16 August 1861 (age 21 at Philadelphia, PA)–16 August 1864. B: Leicester, Leicestershire Co., ENG, tinsmith. Blue eyes, brown hair, florid complexion, 5'6. MIA, Fairfield. Discharged at Harper's Ferry, VA.

Smith, Hara. Pvt. Co. F, 9 December 1864 (age 25 at Carlisle Barracks, PA)–5 October 1865. B: ENG, sailor. Grey eyes, light hair, ruddy complexion, 5'8½. Deserted.

Smith, Harrison C. Pvt. Co. H, 14 August 1861 (age 21 at Philadelphia, PA)–9 March 1863. B: Oldtown, Penobscot Co., ME, lumberman. Brown eyes, dark hair, ruddy complexion, 5'6¾. WIA, Hanover Court-House. Discharged by order of the War Department, in the field, VA. (RR states discharge date 9 November 1863).

Smith, James. Pvt. Co. F, 11 November 1864 (at Cincinnati, OH)–12 January 1865. B: Middleton, CAN, farmer. Black eyes, black hair, dark complexion, 5'3½. Deserted.

Smith, James. Pvt. Co. F, 21 November 1864 (age 21 at Harrisburg, PA)–12 January 1865. B: Co. Tyrone, IRE, teamster. Blue eyes, auburn hair, fair complexion, 5'5½. Deserted.

Smith, James. Rct. 19 August 1861 (age 17 at Rochester, NY)–22 August 1861. B: Springfield, Hampden Co., MA, shoemaker. Blue eyes, light hair, sandy complexion, 5'5. Discharged for general unfitness for service.

Smith, James H. Mustered: Pvt. Co. C, 14th IN Inf. 7 June 1861. Transferred: Pvt. Co. C, 6th U.S. Cav. 23 October 1862 (age 22 at Knoxville, MD)–15 May 1864. B: Martin Co., IN, farmer. Dark eyes, brown hair, dark complexion, 6'½. WIA, Funkstown. Disability discharge at Finley General Hospital, Washington, D.C.

Smith, John. Pvt. Cos. A, F, 24 October 1864 (age 21 at Cleveland, OH)–16 October 1865. B: Perthshire, Perth Co., SCO, carpenter. Brown eyes, black hair, sallow complexion, 5'9. Deserted.

Smith, John. Pvt. Co. D, 24 August 1861 (age 25 at Pittsburgh, PA)–4 May 1865. B: Saarbrucken, Prussia, GER, farmer. Blue eyes, light hair, light complexion, 5'3. Discharged at Petersburg, VA.

Smith, John. Rct. 1 October 1864 (age 28 at Harrisburg, PA)–Never joined regiment. B: Co. Cork, IRE.

Smith, John F. Rct. 30 July 1861 (age 22 at Erie Co., PA)–13 August 1861. B: Berne, SWZ, laborer. Blue eyes, dark hair, light complexion, 5'7½. Rejected recruit for disability.

Smith, John H. Pvt. Co. B, 30 July 1861 (age 20 at Cleveland, OH)–30 July 1864. B: Washington Co., PA, clerk. Hazel eyes, brown hair, ruddy complexion, 5'8. Discharged at Lighthouse Point, VA.

Smith, John P. Pvt. Co. A, 6 December 1864 (age 22 at Cincinnati, OH)–31 January 1865. B: SCO, moulder. Hazel eyes, brown hair, fair complexion, 5'3. Deserted.

Smith, Josiah. Pvt. Co. D, 20 August 1861 (age 18 at Pittsburgh, PA)–20 August 1864. B: Allegheny Co., PA, blacksmith. Blue eyes, auburn hair, light complexion, 5'5½. Discharged in the field, VA.

Smith, Peter. Pvt. Co. M, 20 September 1864 (age 43 at Rochester, NY)–20 September 1867. B: Co. Kildare, IRE, laborer. Blue eyes, brown hair, florid complexion, 5'4. Discharged at Mt. Pleasant, TX.

Smith, Stephen. Pvt. Co. L, 18 August 1864 (age 20 at Rochester, NY)–25 September 1865. B: London, ENG, laborer. Brown eyes, brown hair, sallow complexion, 5'8½. Deserted.

Smith, Thomas. Pvt. Co. H, 26 July 1861 (age 22 at Philadelphia, PA)–26 July 1864. B: London, ENG, carpenter. Blue eyes, brown hair, ruddy complexion, 5'5. Discharged in the field, VA.

Smith, Thomas. Pvt. Co. M, 12 September 1864 (age 21 at Rochester, NY)–20 September 1867. B: Dublin, IRE, laborer. Brown eyes, dark hair, fair complexion, 5'11. Discharged at Mt. Pleasant, TX.

Smith, Thomas G. Mustered: Pvt. Co. B, 110th PA Inf. 24 October 1861. Transferred: Pvt. Co. D, 6th U.S. Cav. 28 October 1862 (age 21 at Knoxville, MD)–28 September 1864. B: 20 November 1840, Huntingdon, PA. Grey eyes, dark hair, dark complexion, 6'2. Discharged at Newton, VA. D: 28 August 1905, Huntingdon, PA.

Smith, Thomas J. Pvt. Co. K, 27 July 1861 (age 18 at Warren, OH)–15 January 1865. B: Aurora, Erie Co., NY, carpenter. Grey eyes, light hair, light complexion, 5'7. POW, 28 June 1862. WIA, Kernstown 19 August 1864. Reenlisted: 11 February 1864 at Brandy Station, VA. D: 15 January 1865 as POW at Salisbury, NC.

Snell, James. Pvt. Co. F, 5 July 1861 (age 22)–5 July 1864. No further information.

Snow, Richard H. Rct. 21 August 1861 (age 19 at Cleveland, OH)–27 August 1861. B: Summit Co., OH, farmer. Hazel eyes, brown hair, ruddy complexion, 5'6¾. Discharged by Civil Authority at Cleveland, OH.

Soetz, Henry. Cpl. Co. G, 1 August 1861 (age 26 at Erie Co., PA)–4 August 1864. B: York Co., PA, shoemaker. Blue eyes, light hair, fair complexion, 5'6¼. POW from ?–17 February 1864. Paroled, reported at Camp Parole. Discharged at Lighthouse Point, VA.

Sohier, Herrmann. Pvt. Co. H, 16 August 1861 (age 28 at Philadelphia, PA)–13 November 1862. B: Prussia, GER, tailor. Blue eyes, light hair, fair complexion, 5'4. Disability discharge at Baltimore, MD.

Solan, John. Pvt. Co. A, 11 November 1864 (age 25 at Cincinnati, OH)–30 May 1865. B: IRE, laborer. Blue eyes, black hair, dark complexion, 5'3½. Deserted 24 November 1864. Apprehended 28 November 1864. Deserted 30 May1865.

Sparrow, William. Pvt. Co. A, 16 November 1864 (age 23 at Cincinnati, OH)–30 May 1865. B: IRE, laborer. Grey eyes, brown hair, fair complexion, 5'6. Deserted 10 December 1864. Apprehended 24 December 1864. Deserted 30 May 1865.

Speck, Lewis. Pvt. Co. E, 28 August 1861 (age 28 at Cleveland, OH)–28 August 1864. B: Buffalo, Erie Co., NY, blacksmith. Black eyes, black hair, ruddy complexion, 5'4½. Discharged in the field, VA.

Speed, Frederick. Enlisted: Pvt. Co. H, 3rd U.S. Inf. 13 April 1855. Deserted 4 July 1858. Apprehended 5 July 1858. Discharged 13 April 1860 at Ft. Marcy, NM. Enlisted: Pvt.-1st Sgt. Cos. H, B, 6th U.S. Cav. 10 July 1861 (age 29 at Philadelphia, PA)–10 July 1864. B: Canterbury, Kent Co., ENG, gardener. Brown eyes, brown hair, dark complexion, 5'9. Discharged at Lighthouse Point, VA. Enlisted: Cos. L, B, 6th U.S. Cav. 19 January 1870–19 January 1875. Discharged at Washita River, TX.

Spence, Joseph J. Pvt. Co. E, 17 September 1861 (age 35 at Adrian, MI)–10 February 1862. B: New York City, NY, carpenter. Blue eyes, brown hair, sallow complexion, 5'8¼. Disability discharge at Washington, D.C.

Spofford, William P. Rct. 16 September 1861 (age 19 at Cleveland, OH)–20 September 1861. B: Olmsted, Cuyahoga Co., OH, farmer. Blue eyes, brown hair, ruddy complexion, 6' 3. Transferred to Civil Authority.

Spooner, William F. Mustered: Pvt. Co. I, 8th OH Inf. 10 August 1861. Transferred: Pvt. Co. C, 6th U.S. Cav. 26 October 1862 (age 40 at Knoxville, MD)–10 August 1864. B: Orleans, Jefferson Co., NY, farrier. Brown eyes, brown hair, fair complexion, 5' 5½. Transferred to F&S March 1864. Discharged at Lighthouse Point, VA.

Sprague, Charles H. Rct. 5 August 1861 (age 22 at Columbus, OH)–21 August 1861. B: Saugus, Essex Co., MA, shoemaker. Black eyes, black hair, light complexion, 5' 4½. Rejected recruit for disability.

Spurgeon, Edmond. Pvt.-Blacksmith. Co. E, 2 September 1861 (age 22 at Cleveland, OH)–6 March 1864. B: Bellevue, OH, blacksmith. Blue eyes, light hair, ruddy complexion, 5' 4½. POW, Funkstown. D: 6 March 1864 from chronic diarrhea as a POW at Richmond, VA.

Squires, Thomas. Mustered: Pvt. Co. B, 8th OH Inf. 10 June 1861. Transferred: Pvt. Co. C, 6th U.S. Cav. 22 October 1862 (age 22 at Knoxville, MD)–14 June 1864. B: Oxfordshire Co., ENG. Blue eyes, brown hair, light complexion, 5' 8½. Discharged in the field, VA.

Stafford, Mathew. Mustered: Co. C, 14th IN Inf. 7 June 1861. Transferred: Pvt. Co. K, 6th U.S. Cav. 24 October 1862 (age 24 at Knoxville, MD)–23 April 1864. B: Washington Co., IN, farmer. Black eyes, brown hair, dark complexion, 5' 7½. Discharged at Camp 6th Cav., VA. D: 20 November 1883, Chautauqua, KS.

Staley, Eli. Mustered: Pvt. Co. F, 8th OH Inf. 7 June 1861. Transferred: Pvt. Co. B, 28 October 1862 (age 22 at Knoxville, MD)–22 June 1864. B: 1841, Erie Co., NY. Blue eyes, dark hair, light complexion, 5' 8. POW (captured while on picket), Richard's Ford, 14 February 1863. Discharged at Camp 6th Cav., VA. D: 9 November 1924, Seneca Co., OH.

Staley, Samuel. Blacksmith. Co. D, 8 August 1861 (age 35 at Pittsburgh, PA)–31 December 1862. B:Baden, GER, blacksmith. Blue eyes, black hair, dark complexion, 6'. Disability discharge at Washington, D.C.

Stampfle, Nicholas. Pvt. Co. F, 23 July 1861 (age 33 at Pittsburgh, PA)–22 June 1864. B: Berne, SWZ, gardener. Blue eyes, light hair, fair complexion, 5' 7. Discharged at Lighthouse Point, VA. Mustered: Pvt. Co. I, 12th OH Cav. 1 Sep-

tember 1864–16 June 1865. Mustered out at Knoxville, TN.

Stanglin, Joseph. Pvt. Co. H, 3 August 1861 (age 18 at Philadelphia, PA)–3 August 1864. B: Stuttgart, Wurttemberg, GER, coppersmith. Blue eyes, light hair, fair complexion, 5' 5½. MIA, Union, 10 November 1862. Discharged in the field, VA.

Starks, Daniel. Mustered: Pvt. Co. D, 8th OH Inf. 6 June 1861. Transferred: Pvt. Co. C, 6th U.S. Cav. 24 October 1862 (age 22 at Knoxville, MD)–20 February 1863. B: Huron Co., OH, farmer. Grey eyes, light hair, light complexion, 5' 6½. D: 20 February 1863 from disease at camp near Falmouth, VA.

Starlin, Semour Thornton. Pvt. Co. K, 20 July 1861 (age 20 at Franklin, PA)–20 July 1864. B: 10 August 1840, Mercer Co., PA, blacksmith. Blue eyes, brown hair, dark complexion, 5'10¾. Discharged in the field, VA. D: 29 December 1921, Girton, Sandusky, OH.

Stearns, Samuel H. Pvt. Co. I, 5 September 1861 (age 21 at Rochester, NY)–10 September 1864. B: Cheshire Co., NH, salesman. Grey eyes, brown hair, dark complexion, 5'10. WIA/POW, Funkstown. Paroled at Annapolis, MD, 28 September 1863. Discharged at Annapolis, MD.

Steel, Michael. Pvt. Co. F, 29 July 1861 (age 21 at Pittsburgh, PA)–4 May 1865. B: Eppelsheim, Rhineland, GER, shoemaker. Brown eyes, brown hair, sallow complexion, 5'11½. MIA, Brandy Station. Discharged at Petersburg, VA.

Steel, Robert. Pvt. Co. M, 14 September 1861 (age 21 at Pittsburgh, PA)–27 November 1863. B: Beaver Co., PA. POW, Fairfield. D: 27 November 1863 from erysipelas while a POW at Richmond, VA.

Steen, Thomas. Pvt. Co. H, 31 July 1861 (age 21 at Philadelphia, PA)–31 July 1864. B: Philadelphia, PA, grocer. Hazel eyes, black hair, ruddy complexion, 6'1. Deserted 9 March 1861. Apprehended 25 January 1862.

Stettler, John. Musician 3rd Class. Co. F&S, 15 October 1861 (age 29 at Mount Joy, PA)–15 October 1864. B: Conestoga, Lancaster Co., PA, musician. Grey eyes, brown hair, ruddy complexion, 5' 6½. Discharged at Strausburg, VA.

Stevely, Samuel. Pvt. Co. K, 1 August 1861 (age 19 at Warren, OH)–27 April 1862. B: Wurttemberg, GER, farmer. Hazel eyes, light hair, brown complexion, 5' 6. D: 27 April 1862 from typhoid fever at Ship Point, VA.

Stevens, James P. Mustered: Pvt. Co. G, 38th PA Inf. 4 May 1861. Transferred: Pvt. Co. F, 6th

U.S. Cav. 28 October 1862 (age 23 at Knoxville, MD)–4 May 1864. B: Sharpsburg, Allegheny Co., PA, farmer. Grey eyes, dark hair, ruddy complexion, 5'8. Discharged at Camp 6th Cav., VA.

Stevens, William C. Pvt. Co. F, 12 July 1861 (age 19 at Pittsburgh, PA)–12 July 1864. B: Pittsburgh, Allegheny Co., PA, nail maker. Grey eyes, brown hair, dark complexion, 5'5½. Discharged at Lighthouse Point, VA.

Stevenson, John. Pvt. Co. M, 9 November 1864 (age 20 at Cleveland, OH)–22 March 1865. B: CAN, farmer. Grey eyes, brown hair, dark complexion, 5'5. D: 22 March 1865 from inflammation of lungs at Island Hospital, Harper's Ferry, VA.

Stevenson, William. Rct. Cos. L, C, 19 November 1861 (age 23 at Cleveland, OH)–3 January 1862. B: Isle of Man, ENG, plumber. Light eyes, light hair, ruddy complexion, 6'. Disability discharge at Washington, D.C.

Stevenson, William I. Pvt. Cos. M, F&S, 2 September 1861 (age 30 at Pittsburgh, PA)–2 September 1864. B: New York City, NY, type founder. Grey eyes, brown hair, light eyes, 5'10. Discharged in the field, VA. Rgt. Hospital Steward.

Stewart, James "Ole Blue." Pvt. Cos. F, I, 26 July 1861 (age 20 at Pittsburgh, PA)–8 February 1867. B: Williamsburg, Blair Co., PA, farmer. Brown eyes, black hair, ruddy complexion, 5'11¾. MIA, Fairfield. Reenlisted: 8 February 1864 in the field at Camp 6th Cav., VA. Discharged at Jackson, TX.

Stewart, John A. Pvt. Co. G, 1 August 1861 (age 24 at Erie Co., PA)–1 August 1864. B: Co. Armagh, IRE, farmer. Grey eyes, dark hair, fair complexion, 5'8¼. Discharged at Lighthouse Point, VA.

Stine, Joseph. Pvt. Co. A, 21 October 1861 (age 22 at Columbus, OH)–31 January 1862. B: Trenton, Mercer Co., NJ, blacksmith. Hazel eyes, brown hair, sallow complexion, 5'7. Deserted.

Stinson, Samuel F. Sgt. Co. F, 7 December 1864 (age 21 at Philadelphia, PA)–7 December 1867. B: Philadelphia, PA, stove moulder. Grey eyes, fair hair, fair complexion, 5'6. Discharged at Camp Wilson, TX.

Stoll, Andrew W. Enlisted: Pvt. Co. G, 4th U.S. Art. 21 October 1850–21 October 1855. Discharged at Ft. Laramie, NJ. Enlisted: Sgt. Co. K, 1st U.S. Cav. 1 May 1856–1 May 1861. Discharged at Ft. Wise, C.T. Reenlisted: 1st Sgt. 5 May 1861, Ft. Wise. Transferred: 6th U.S. Cav. Appointed 2nd Lt. 6th U.S. Cav. 5 No-

vember 1861. B: Frankford, Sussex Co., NJ. Grey eyes, brown hair, fair complexion, 5'10½. POW, Beverly Ford. D: as a POW at Libby Prison, VA.

Stone, Edward J. Farrier. Co. G, 25 July 1861 (age 24 at Columbus, OH)–25 July 1864. B: Madison Co., OH, blacksmith. Grey eyes, brown hair, sallow complexion, 5'11. Discharged at City Point, VA.

Stone, Elisha P. Mustered: Pvt. Co. B, 14th IN Inf. 6 June 1861. Transferred: Pvt. Co. C, 6th U.S. Cav. 24 October 1862 (age 22 at Knoxville, MD)–1 June 1864. B: 18 April 1840, Mineral City, Green Co., IN. Grey eyes, black hair, dark complexion, 5'6½. Discharged in the field, VA. D: 15 January 1870, Greene Co., IN.

Stonebraker, John. Mustered: Pvt. Co. K, 110th PA Inf. 19 December 1861. Transferred: Pvt. Co. I, 6th U.S. Cav. 27 October 1862 (age 21 at Knoxville, MD)–27 August 1864. B: Blair Co., PA, laborer. Brown eyes, dark hair, fair complexion, 5'8. Discharged in the field, VA.

Stonesifer, Jacob H. Mustered: Pvt. Co. G, 84th PA Inf. Transferred: Pvt. Co. I, 6th U.S. Cav. 27 October 1862 (age 35 at Knoxville, MD)–7 March 1864. B: 9 February 1827, Carroll Co., MD, miller. Blue eyes, light hair, fair complexion, 5'6. Suffered internal injuries when his horse fell on him at Fredericksburg, 13 December 1862. Disability discharge at Carlisle Barracks, PA. D: 30 September 1903, York, PA.

Stoppelbein, George C. Pvt. Co. K, 19 August 1861 (age 25 at Rochester, NY)–19 August 1864. B: 1834, GER, farmer. Blue eyes, brown hair, florid complexion, 5'5¾. Discharged in the field, VA. D: 1913, Le Roy, Genesee, NY.

Strain, Harvey. Rct. 25 July 1861 (age 25 at Columbus, OH)–13 August 1861. B: Madison Co., OH, miller. Blue eyes, brown hair, sallow complexion, 5'11½. Deserted at Columbus, OH.

Strine, Jeremiah. Mustered: Pvt. Co. M, 1st PA Cav. 5 August 1861–18 September 1861. Disability discharged. Mustered: Pvt. Co. C, 136th PA Inf. 29 August 1862–29 May 1863. Mustered out at Harrisburg, PA. Enlisted: Pvt. Co. F, 6th U.S. Cav. 12 November 1864 (age 19 at Harrisburg, PA)–12 November 1867. B: Dauphin Co., PA, laborer. Blue eyes, light hair, fair complexion, 5'7½. Discharged at Camp Wilson, TX.

Stroop, John W. Pvt. Co. M, 9 November 1861 (age 25 at Pittsburgh, PA)–9 June 1863. B: Wheeling, Ohio Co., VA, brick maker. Hazel eyes, dark hair, dark complexion, 5'9½. MIA, Beverly Ford. MIA, Fairfield.

Stroup, James. Mustered: Pvt. Co. H, 37th PA Inf. 30 April 1861. Transferred: Pvt. Co. B, 6th U.S. Cav. 28 October 1862 (age 23 at Knoxville, MD)–26 July 1864. B: Strattanville, Clarion Co., PA, farmer. Brown eyes, brown hair, sallow complexion, 5'10. WIA, Fairfield. WIA, Brandy Station. Deserted 25 December 1863. Apprehended 5 January 1864. Discharged 26 July 1864. Charge of desertion was removed by AGO.

Sturgeon, Edson. Mustered: Pvt. Co. H, 1st PA Cav. 9 June 1861–6 September 1861. Enlisted: Pvt.-Sgt. Co. G, 1 November 1861 (age 21 at Washington, DC)–1 November 1864. B: 26 April 1840, Fairview, Butler Co., PA, coach maker. Blue eyes, fair hair, fair complexion, 5'6. MIA (in the field), 7 May 1863. Discharged at Camp 6th Cav., VA. D: 8 October 1920, Kitsap, WA.

Sturgeon, James M. Cpl. Co. 6th U.S. Cav. G, 29 July 1861 (age 27½ at Erie Co., PA)–29 July 1864. B: Fairview, Erie, PA, farmer. Blue eyes, light hair, light complexion, 5'5. MIA, Fairfield. Discharged at City Point, VA. D: 30 May 1911, Los Angeles, CA.

Sturgeon, Mason K. Mustered: 3rd Cpl. Co. A, Erie PA Inf. 21 April 1861–21 July 1861. Mustered out at Erie, PA. Enlisted: Pvt. Co. G, 6th U.S. Cav. 29 July 1861 (age 25 at Erie Co., PA)–29 July 1864. B: 1835, Fairview, Erie, PA, farmer. Blue eyes, dark hair, light complexion, 5'5½. POW, Fairfield, 3 July 1863–17 February 1864. Paroled, reported at Camp Parole. Discharged at City Point, VA. D: 14 September 1896, Fairview, Erie, PA.

Sturgis, John C. Pvt. Co. L, 7 October 1861 (at Cleveland, OH)–4 April 1865. POW, Fairfield, 3 July 1863–28 February 1864. POW, Berryville, 16 August 1864–4 April 1865. Paroled, reported at Camp Parole. Discharged at Annapolis, MD, a paroled POW.

Styles, Alfred O. Mustered: Cpt. Cogswell's Independent Battery, IL Light Art. Enlisted: Pvt. Co. C, 6th U.S. Cav. 7 December 1861 (age 27 at Cleveland, OH)–3 January 1862. B: New Orleans, LA, printer. Hazel eyes, black hair, sallow complexion, 5'5¾. Disability discharge at Washington, D.C. D: 8 September 1894, New Orleans, LA.

Sulivan, Henry. Rct. 25 October 1864 (age 25 at Cincinnati, OH)–2 November 1864. B: IRE, laborer. Blue eyes, light hair, fair complexion, 5'10. Deserted.

Sullivan, Daniel. Rct. Co. L, 26 November 1861 (age 31 at Pittsburgh, PA)–4 December 1861. B: IRE, farmer. Grey eyes, brown hair, light complexion, 5'7. Deserted at Pittsburgh, PA.

Sullivan, Henry. Rct. 5 October 1864 (age 21 at Harrisburg, PA)–Never joined. B: New York City, NY, boatman. Grey eyes, brown hair, ruddy complexion, 5'7½.

Sullivan, Henry W. Pvt. Co. L, 16 June 1862 (age 28 at Washington, DC)–18 July 1864. B: Co. Waterford, IRE, carriage maker. Grey eyes, auburn hair, ruddy complexion, 5'4. POW, Brandy Station, 11 October–7 November 1863. Paroled, reported at Washington, D.C. Disability discharge at Carlisle Barracks, PA.

Sul[l]ivan, James. Mustered: Co. A, 184th PA Inf. Transferred: Pvt. Co. I, 6th U.S. Cav. 27 October 1862 (age 18 at Knoxville, MD)–28 August 1865. B: Orange Co., NY, farmer. Hazel eyes, brown hair, ruddy complexion, 5'8. WIA/POW, Funkstown, 7 July–28 September 1863. Paroled, reported at Annapolis, MD. Discharged at Frederick, MD.

Sullivan, John. Bugler. Co. D, 25 July 1861 (age 18 at Columbus, OH)–25 July 1864. B: New York City, NY, shoemaker. Grey eyes, red hair, fair complexion, 5'3½. POW, Charlestown, October 1862–11 March 1863. Returned. Discharged at City Point, VA.

Sullivan, John. Pvt. Co. F, 29 November 1864 (age 19 at Harrisburg, PA)–Never joined. B: Co. Kerry, IRE, farmer. Grey eyes, light hair, fair complexion, 5'7. Sub for E. W. Hollbrook.

Sullivan, Martin. Pvt. Co. A, 11 September 1861 (age 28 at Philadelphia, PA)–27 September 1862. B: Co. Kerry, IRE, tailor. Blue eyes, light hair, fair complexion, 5'6. Disability discharge at Philadelphia, PA.

Sullivan, Richard B. Mustered: Pvt. Co. A, 42nd PA Inf. 21 July 1861. Transferred: Farrier. Co. H, 6th U.S. Cav. 28 October 1862 (age 35 at Knoxville, MD)–2 December 1863. B: Allegheny Co., MD, blacksmith. Blue eyes, grey hair, fair complexion, 6'1. Disability discharge at Emory General Hospital, Washington, D.C.

Sullivan, Thomas. Co. F, 14 December 1864 (age 24 at Carlisle Barracks, PA)–31 May 1865. B: Montreal, Quebec, CAN, laborer. Grey eyes, dark hair, ruddy complexion, 5'10. Deserted 12 December 1864. Apprehended. Deserted 31 May 1865.

Sullivan, William. Rct. 27 September 1864 (age 24 at Cincinnati, OH)–Never joined. B: Co. Cork, IRE, blacksmith. Blue eyes, dark hair, fair complexion, 5'6¼.

Sulter, Christian. Pvt. Co. G, 2 August 1861 (age 34 at Rochester, NY)–16 October 1861. B:

GER, farmer. Blue eyes, black hair, florid complexion, 5'5¼. Disability discharge at Bladensburg, MD.

Surrener, Christopher C. Mustered: Pvt. Co. C, 8th OH Inf. 6 January 1861. Transferred: Pvt. Co. H, 6th U.S. Cav. 24 October 1862 (age 23 at Knoxville, MD)–1 June 1864. B: Sitzendorf, Thuringia, GER, farmer. Grey eyes, light hair, light complexion, 5'8. Discharged in the field, VA. Mustered: Pvt. Co. I, 175th OH Inf. 10 March 1864–27 June 1865. Mustered out at Nashville, TN.

Suter, John Henry. Bugler. Co. G, 8 August 1861 (age 32 at Rochester, NY)–12 January 1863. B: SWZ, gardener. Blue eyes, brown hair, florid complexion, 5'7. Disability discharge at Philadelphia, PA.

Swan, Andrew F. 1st Sgt. Co. G, 29 July 1861 (age 27 at Erie Co., PA)–22 May 1863. B: 16 October 1832, Fairview, Erie, PA, farmer. Grey eyes, dark hair, light complexion, 5'10. WIA, Williamsburg. Accepted commission as 2nd Lt., 16th PA Cav., Brooks Station, VA. Promoted to Lt. Col. D: 18 April 1876, Erie, PA.

Swartz, Emil. Enlisted: Pvt. Co. E, 1st U.S. Cav. 1 September 1860. Transferred: 1st Sgt. Co. F, 6th U.S. Cav. (age 31 at Cottonwood Creek, Berks, PA)–31 January 1863. B: Berks Co., PA, butcher. Blue eyes, auburn hair, fresh complexion, 5'8. Disability discharge 31 January 1863 at camp near Falmouth, VA. Enlisted: Pvt. GMS, HQ, Army (by Maj. Williams), 26 February 1863–6 February 1868. Promoted to Sgt. Mustered out at Washington, D.C. D: 8 September 1878, Washington, D.C.

Sweatland, George F. Mustered (Blackburn, RI): Pvt. Co. K, 15th MA Inf. 7 January 1861. Transferred: Pvt. Co. K, 6th U.S. Cav. 24 October 1862 (age 22 at Knoxville, MD)–20 July 1863. B: Glocester, Providence Co., RI, farmer. Blue eyes, brown hair, light complexion, 5'5. Enlisted: Co. D, 3rd U.S.V.V.C. 20 July 1863–24 July 1864. D: 26 February 1889, Dayton, OH.

Sweeney, Daniel. Pvt.-Cpl. Co. K, 13 July 1861 (age 27 at Franklin, PA)–13 July 1864. B: Butler Twp., PA, teamster. Blue eyes, dark hair, dark complexion, 5'9. MIA, Stuart's Raid. Discharged in the field, VA.

Sweeney, Frank. Pvt. Co. M, 9 November 1864 (age 29 at Harrisburg, PA)–12 June 1865. B: London, ENG, butcher. Grey eyes, sandy hair, ruddy complexion, 5'9. Disability discharge at Stone Hospital, Washington, D.C.

Sweeney, Thomas. Rct. 12 September 1864 (age 21 at Harrisburg, PA)–No further information. B: Co. Longford, IRE, teamster. Grey eyes, dark hair, ruddy complexion, 5'7.

Sweeny, John. Mustered (Ogdensburg, NY): Pvt. Co. I, 60th NY Inf. 15 October 1861. Transferred: Pvt. Co. C, 6th U.S. Cav. 28 October 1862 (age 20 at Knoxville, MD)–14 October 1864. B: St. Lawrence Co., NY. Black eyes, black hair, dark complexion, 5'6. POW (captured by guerrillas), Auburn, VA. 9 November 1863–7 January 1864. Paroled, reported at Annapolis, MD. Discharged in the field, VA. Alternate surname: Sweeney.

Sweet, Benjamin F. Rct. 12 September 1861 (age 28 at Adrian, MI)–10 October 1861. B: Wayne Co., NY, farmer. Blue eyes, light hair, fair complexion, 6'. Disability discharge at Bladensburg, MD.

Sweet, Henry L. Mustered: Pvt. Co. G, 7th MI Inf. 8 October 1861. Transferred: Pvt. Co. K, 26 October 1862 (age 22 at Knoxville, MD)–8 September 1863. B: Lapeer Co., MI. Blue eyes, light hair, light complexion, 5'8. D: 8 September 1863 from diarrhea at Annapolis, MD.

Swicker, Herman G. Rct. 23 July 1861 (age 21 at Columbus, OH)–21 August 1861. B: 1836, Saxony, GER, hostler. Grey eyes, brown hair, ruddy complexion, 5'8½. Rejected recruit for disability. D: 23 May 1918, Richmond, Wayne, IN.

Swift, Edward. Sgt. Cos. E, F&S, E, 12 August 1861 (age 30 at Cleveland, OH)–14 March 1864. B: Windham, Windham Co., CT, carriage maker. Blue eyes, light hair, fair complexion, 6'1. Transferred: GS, 9 November 1863. Reenlisted (Washington, D.C.): GS, 14 March 1864. Promoted to Sgt. Discharged 31 March 1864 by appointment as a clerk.

Swift, John. Rct. 1 October 1864 (age 28 at Harrisburg, PA)–Never joined. B: Co. Cork, IRE, laborer. Blue eyes, light hair, ruddy complexion, 5'5¼.

Swift, Moses A. Pvt. Co. B, 10 August 1861 (age 22 at Cleveland, OH)–10 August 1864. B: Brecksville, Cuyahoga Co., OH, farmer. Hazel eyes, black hair, ruddy complexion, 5'9. Discharged in the field, VA.

Switzer, Andrew W. Pvt. Co. K, 13 August 1861 (age 18 at Butler, PA)–13 August 1864. B: PA, shoemaker. Blue eyes, light hair, sandy complexion, 5'7½. MIA (in the field) April 1863. Discharged in the field, VA.

Symington, Thomas H. Mustered; Pvt-Cpl.-Sgt. Co. I, 110th PA Inf. 19 August 1861. Transferred:

Pvt. Co. I, 6th U.S. Cav. 27 October 1862 (age 22 at Knoxville, MD)–27 September 1864. B: Philadelphia, PA, carpenter. Blue eyes, dark hair, fair complexion, 5'8. Discharged in the field, VA.

Taber, Charles A. Pvt.-Bugler. Co. E, 10 August 1861 (age 18 at Columbus, OH)–4 December 1864. B: Auburn, Cayuga Co., NY, musician. Grey eyes, brown hair, light complexion, 5' 4½. POW, Fairfield. Furloughed 4 December 1864 at Camp Parole, MD.

Taggart, James. Mustered: Pvt. Co. D, 8th OH Inf. 6 June 1861. Transferred: Pvt. Co. C, 6th U.S. Cav. 23 October 1862 (age 28 at Knoxville, MD)–4 June 1865. B: Co. Armagh, IRE. Grey eyes, brown hair, florid complexion, 5' 7. POW, Fairfield (Andersonville). Discharged at Rgt. HQ, VA.

Taro, Alfred (Albert). Mustered: Pvt. Co. E, 60th NY Inf. Transferred: Pvt. Co. C, 6th U.S. Cav. 23 October 1862 (age 21 at Knoxville, MD)–18 April 1864. B: Three Rivers, Quebec, CAN. Blue eyes, sandy hair, light complexion, 5'1½. Reenlisted (Brandy Station, VA): 27 February 1864. Deserted 18 April 1864.

Tasker, Charles. Mustered: Pvt. Co. K, 4th VT Inf. 3 September 1861. Transferred: Pvt. Co. A, 6th U.S. Cav. 30 October 1862 (age 18 at Knoxville, MD)–7 September 1865. B: Claremont, Sullivan, NH. Blue eyes, black hair, light complexion, 5' 7. POW, Fairfield, 3 July–24 December 1863. Paroled, reported at Annapolis, MD. Discharged at Camp Sheridan, in the field, VA. Reenlisted (New Orleans, LA): Co. D, 4 November 1865. Deserted 13 December 1865. Apprehended 12 April 1866. Deserted 18 April 1866.

Taylor, Charles H. Pvt. Co. H, 12 August 1861 (age 23 at Philadelphia, PA)–12 August 1864. B: Philadelphia, PA, farmer, Blue eyes, light hair, fair complexion, 5' 8½. POW, Fairfield, 3 July 1863–27 February 1864. Paroled, reported at Camp Parole. Discharged at Harper's Ferry, VA.

Taylor, Lucius H. Pvt. Co. F, 21 November 1864 (age 20 at Cincinnati, OH) 4 November 1865. B: Montreal, Quebec, CAN, farmer. Hazel eyes, brown hair, dark complexion, 5'11. Deserted. Sub.

Taylor, William M. Mustered: Sgt. Co. F, 48th PA Inf. 1 October 1861. Transferred: Pvt. Co. A, 6th U.S. Cav. 28 October 1862 (age 23 at Knoxville, MD)–28 October 1864. B: Chester Co., PA. Hazel eyes, dark hair, light complexion, 5' 4½. POW, Fairfield, 3 July 1863–23 May

1864. Paroled, reported at Annapolis, MD. Discharged at Middletown, VA.

Tayman, Mortimer S. Enlisted (Washington, D.C.): 11–23 February 1864. B: Prince George's Co., MD, blacksmith. Deserted. Enlisted: Pvt. Co. F, 27 November 1864 (age 20 at Philadelphia, PA)–7 January 1865. B: Kingston, Ontario, CAN, sailor. Blue eyes, brown hair, fair complexion, 5' 9. Deserted 1 December 1864. Apprehended 3 December 1864. Deserted 7 January 1865. Enlisted (Washington, D.C.): Co. F, 5th U.S. Cav. 21–29 October 1865. Deserted. Note: Original enlistment paper filed with "B" 1864–Bradshaw (No. 413).

Teel, Alexander O Jr. Pvt. Co. G, 13 August 1861 (age 18⅝ at Erie Co., PA)–13 August 1864. B: 1845, Millcreek, Erie, PA, laborer. Blue eyes, red hair, freckled complexion, 5' 4½. Discharged at Lighthouse Point, VA. Enlisted (Erie, PA): Pvt. Co. E, 19th U.S. Inf. 9 June 1865. Transferred: Pvt. Co. E, 28th U.S. Inf. Discharged 9 June 1868 at Little Rock, AR. D: after 1919, Sawtelle, Los Angeles, CA.

Teneyck, Miles L. Mustered: Pvt. Co. K, 1st MI Inf. 18 April 1861–7 August 1861. Mustered out at Detroit, MI. Enlisted: Sgt. Co. E, 6th U.S. Cav. 14 September 1861 (age 23 at Adrian, MI)–6 July 1863. B: Benton, Yates Co., NY, farmer. Grey eyes, brown hair, ruddy complexion, 5' 8½. WIA, Williamsport, MD. D: 6 July 1863.

Teneyck, William. Farrier. Co. E, 16 September 1861 (age 30 at Adrian, MI)–16 September 1864. B: Vernon, Oneida Co., NY, blacksmith. Grey eyes, light hair, ruddy complexion, 5' 8. Discharged at Berryville, VA.

Termayne, William. Pvt. Co. F, 18 November 1864 (age 39 at Cincinnati, OH)–18 November 1867. B: Schuylkill Co., PA, miner. Grey eyes, sandy hair, fair complexion, 5' 7½. Discharged at Austin, TX.

Terry, Darius R. Mustered: Pvt. Co. D, 106th PA Inf. 27 August 1861. Transferred: Pvt. Co. G, 6th U.S. Cav. 28 October 1862 (age 21 at Knoxville, MD)–25 August 1864. B: Delaware Co., NY, farmer. Blue eyes, dark hair, fair complexion, 5' 7. WIA/MIA, Fairfield. Rejoined 9 August 1863 from hospital. Discharged at Harper's Ferry, VA. Transferred: Co. G, 6th U.S.V.R.C.

Thayers, Charles. Pvt. Co. F, 29 December 1864 (age 20 at Cincinnati, OH)–31 May 1865. B: Armstrong Co., PA, engineer. Blue eyes, brown hair, fair complexion, 5' 7½. Deserted.

Thoburn, David Andrew. Pvt. Co. K, 14 August 1861 (age 28 at Rochester, NY)–1 December

1862. B: ENG, farmer. Grey eyes, black hair, fair complexion, 5'7¾. KIA, Belle Plain.

Thomas, John. 28 August 1861 (age 35 at Pittsburgh, PA)–No further information. B: Mathertidet, Wales, WAL, soldier. Brown eyes, light hair, dark complexion, 5'6¾.

Thomas, John S. Pvt. Co. F, 6 July 1861 (age 21 at Pittsburgh, PA)–6 July 1864. B: Rockland Co., NY, iron puddler. Grey eyes, brown hair, dark complexion, 5'9¾. POW, Fairfield, 3 July 1863–19 February 1864. Paroled, reported at Camp Parole. Discharged at Lighthouse Point, VA.

Thomas, Robert. Pvt. Co. K, 15 August 1861 (age 22 at Rochester, NY)–15 August 1864. B: ENG, wagon maker. Blue eyes, light hair, fair complexion, 5'7½. Discharged at Lighthouse Point, VA.

Thomas, William H. Pvt. Co. I, 8 August 1861 (age 22 at Rochester, NY)–7 July 1863. B: ENG, farmer. Blue eyes, brown hair, florid complexion, 5'7½. KIA, Funkstown.

Thompson, Archibald. Pvt. Cos. K, D, 27 July 1861 (age 18 at Warren, OH)–1 June 1866. B: Trumbull Co., OH, farmer. Blue eyes, light hair, light complexion, 5'3½. Reenlisted: 10 February 1864 at Brandy Station, VA. Deserted 1 June 1866.

Thompson, John. Pvt. Co. M, 10 September 1864 (age 26 at NYC, NY)–15 September 1866. B: Derby, ENG, clerk. Grey eyes, brown hair, ruddy complexion, 5'8½. WIA, Five Forks, 30 March 1865. Deserted.

Thompson, John. Rct. 6 October 1864 (age 38 at Harrisburg, PA)–Never joined. B: Co. Longford, IRE, laborer. Blue eyes, light hair, sandy complexion, 5'7.

Thompson, Lorenzo. Mustered: Pvt. Co. G, 3rd WI Inf. 15 May 1861. Transferred: Sgt. Co. G, 6th U.S. Cav. 28 October 1862 (age 21 at Knoxville, MD)–29 June 1864. B: Jackson Co., MI, farmer. Blue eyes, light hair, fair complexion, 5'4. MIA, Beverly Ford, 9 June 1863. Discharged at Wyanoke, VA.

Thompson, William. Pvt. Co. A, 17 August 1864 (age 26 at NYC, NY)–30 May 1865. B: Co. Longford, IRE, soldier. Grey eyes, brown hair, ruddy complexion, 5'8. Deserted.

Thompson, William. Rct. 5 November 1864 (age 24 at Harrisburg, PA)–21 November 1864. B: Montreal, Quebec, CAN, boatman. Grey eyes, brown hair, ruddy complexion, 5'7½. Deserted. Sub.

Thorn, Gustave (August). Mustered: Pvt. Co. B, 3rd WI Inf. Transferred: Pvt. Co. F, 6th U.S. Cav. 25 October 1862 (age 22 at Knoxville, MD)–29 June 1864. B: Behli, Prussia, GER, boatman. Blue eyes, light hair, fresh complexion, 5'7. POW, Fairfield, 3 July 1863–19 February 1864. Paroled, reported at Camp Parole. Discharged at Camp 6th Cav., VA.

Thorne, Thomas. Rct. 25 November 1864 (age 22 at Harrisburg, PA)–Never joined. B: Toronto, Ontario, CAN, boatman. Hazel eyes, black hair, dark complexion, 5'6½.

Thorner, John F. Pvt. Co. H, 8 July 1861 (age 22 at Philadelphia, PA)–20 January 1863. B: Osnabruck, GER, miller. Blue eyes, brown hair, fair complexion, 5'8½. Disability discharged at Philadelphia, PA. Enlisted (Philadelphia, PA): Pvt. Cos. M, D, 1st U.S. Cav. 15 June 1869–15 June 1874. Discharged at Benicia Barracks, CA. D: 7 August 1896, San Francisco, CA.

Thorp, John J. Mustered: Pvt. Co. F, 7th MI Inf. 7 January 1861. Transferred: Pvt. Co. H, 6th U.S. Cav. 28 October 1862 (age 18 at Knoxville, MD)–28 August 1864. B: Fentonville, Genesee Co., MI, laborer. Blue eyes, light hair, fair complexion, 5'8. Discharged at Harper's Ferry, VA.

Thorp, William H. Mustered: Pvt. Co. E, 3rd WI Inf. 22 April 1862. Transferred: Pvt. Co. C, 6th U.S. Cav. 24 October 1862 (age 22 at Knoxville, MD)–24 April 1864. B: Wayne Co., NY. Blue eyes, black hair, florid complexion, 5'11. Discharged at Camp 6th Cav., VA.

Throop, John D. Mustered: Pvt. Co. H, 7th MI Inf. 28 August 1861. Transferred: Pvt. Co. C, 6th U.S. Cav. 20 October 1862 (age 26 at Knoxville, MD)–15 May 1863. B: Cayuga Co., NY, engineer. Blue eyes, brown hair, ruddy complexion, 5'3. D: 15 May 1863 from consumption at Aquia Creek, VA.

Tigent, Josias. Rct. 25 July 1861 (age 21 at Rochester, NY)–29 July 1861. B: Western Can., CAN, farmer. Blue eyes, sandy hair, fair complexion, 5'11½. Deserted from Philadelphia, PA.

Tillotson, Alvin W. Pvt. Co. G, 5 August 1861 (age 25 at Columbus, OH)–12 August 1864. B: 20 May 1836, Columbus, Warren, PA, boatman. Grey eyes, brown hair, sallow complexion, 5'6. Discharged at Washington, D.C. D: 22 November 1905, Billings, Yellowstone, MT.

Titchworth, George. Pvt. Co. M, 12 December 1863 (age 26 at Cleveland, OH)–12 December 1868. B: Paris, West Can. CAN, ship carpenter. Blue eyes, brown hair, ruddy complexion, 5'8. Discharged at Austin, TX. Transferred: GMS (Permanent Party Cav. Dept., U.S.A.)

Todd, James. Pvt. Co. F, 9 July 1861 (age 21 at Pittsburgh, PA)–9 July 1864. B: Charlestown, Clark, IN, trunk maker. Grey eyes, light hair, fair complexion, 5' 6½. MIA, Fairfield. Discharged in the field, VA.

Tolan, John. Rct. 15 November 1864 (age 22 at Harrisburg, PA)–21 November 1864. B: Co. Derry, IRE, boat maker. Grey eyes, brown hair, ruddy complexion, 5' 9½. Deserted.

Tole, Charles. Rct. 23 July 1861 (age 23 at Warren, OH)–8 August 1861. B: Co. Tyrone, IRE, teamster. Grey eyes, brown hair, ruddy complexion, 5' 5. Deserted.

Tomes, William. Bugler. Co. M, 29 July 1864 (age 18 at Rochester, NY)–26 July 1867. B: Chilton, ENG, painter. Brown eyes, brown hair, fair complexion, 5' 4. Discharged at Mt. Pleasant, TX.

Tompkins, John. Mustered: Pvt. Co. G, 7th MI Inf. 8 June 1861. Transferred: Pvt. Co. E, 6th U.S. Cav. 26 October 1862 (age 21 at Knoxville, MD)–22 August 1864. B: ENG. Grey eyes, light hair, light complexion, 5' 8½. Discharged at Washington, D.C.

Toomai, John. Rct. 25 October 1864 (age 25 at Cleveland, OH)–21 November 1864. B: Biscay, Basque, SPA, farmer. Hazel eyes, brown hair, dark complexion, 5' 6. Deserted.

Tooth, Samuel. Pvt. Co. I, 2 September 1861 (age 27 at Rochester, NY)–3 September 1864. B: ENG, moulder. Brown eyes, brown hair, fair complexion, 5' 9. Discharged in the field, VA. D: 25 July 1890, Brockport, Monroe, NY.

Tracy, William. Pvt. Co. M, 5 October 1861 (age 21 at Pittsburgh, PA)–5 September 1864. B: Allegheny Co., PA, farmer. Hazel eyes, brown hair, florid complexion, 5' 8½. Discharged in the field, VA.

Trainer, James W. Mustered: Pvt. Co. C, 14th IN Inf. 6 July 1861. Transferred: Cpl. Co. C, 6th U.S. Cav. 22 October 1862 (age 20 at Knoxville, MD)–5 June 1864. B: Bowling Green, Pike Co., MO. Grey eyes, light hair, light complexion, 5' 7½. POW, Fairfield, 3 July 1863–7 January 1864. Paroled, reported at Annapolis, MD. Discharged in the field, VA.

Travis, Charles Glaston. Mustered: Pvt. Co. F, 38th PA Inf. 1 July 1861. Transferred: Pvt. Co. A, 6th U.S. Cav. 28 October 1862 (age 21 at Knoxville, MD)–28 June 1864. B: Indiana Co., PA. Blue eyes, dark hair, light complexion, 5' 8. WIA, Beverly Ford. Discharged at Windock Landing, VA. D: 1934, Porter, Jefferson, PA.

Trudell, Royel. Mustered: USV. Transferred: Pvt. Co. E, 6th U.S. Cav. 28 October 1862 (age 19 at Knoxville, MD)–23 April 1864. B: Montreal, Quebec, CAN. Black eyes, auburn hair, light complexion, 5' 7½. Deserted 23 July 1863. An-

other record states he reenlisted 10 March 1864 at Brandy Station then deserted 23 April 1864.

Truett, Frederick. Pvt. Co. E, 22 July 1861 (age 22 at Columbus, OH)–22 July 1864. B: Columbus, Franklin Co., OH, farmer. Blue eyes, brown hair, fair complexion, 5' 4¾. Deserted 26 July 1861. Apprehended 11 September 1861. Discharged 22 July 1864 at Lighthouse Point, VA.

Tupper, Tullius Cicero. Sgm. Cos. E, F&S, 19 July 1861 (age 22 at Columbus, OH)–23 September 1862. B: Strongsville, Cuyahoga, OH, clerk. Hazel eyes, brown hair, ruddy complexion, 5' 9. Discharged. Appointed 2nd Lt. at Harper's Ferry, VA.

Turner, Charles. Pvt. Co. A, 31 July 1861 (age 23 at Cleveland, OH)–14 February 1862. B: Tompkins Co., NY, blacksmith. Grey eyes, black hair, sallow complexion, 5' 6½. Deserted.

Turner, Edward. Sgt. Co. A, 10 February 1865 (age 32 at NYC, NY)–10 February 1868. B: Co. Dublin, IRE, moulder. Hazel eyes, brown hair, dark complexion, 5'10½. Discharged at Buffalo Springs, TX.

Turner, James H. Pvt. Co. C, 6 May 1864 (age 37 at Washington, D.C.)–6 May 1867. B: Albany Co., NY, laborer. Grey eyes, black hair, fresh complexion, 5' 9. Discharged at Austin, TX.

Turner, Nelson H. Mustered: Pvt. Co. H, 3rd WI Inf. 22 April 1861. Transferred: Pvt. Co. B, 6th U.S. Cav. 28 October 1862 (age 21½ at Knoxville, MD)–29 June 1864. B: OH. Blue eyes, brown hair, dark complexion, 6' 2½. MIA, Upperville. Discharged at Camp 6th Cav., VA.

Turney, John B. Pvt. Co. G, 6 August 1861 (age 19 at Columbus, OH)–6 August 1864. B: 20 August 1842, Troy, Rensselaer, NY, blacksmith. Grey eyes, brown hair, light complexion, 5' 7¼. POW. Discharged at City Point, VA. D: 26 April 1899, Columbus, Franklin, OH.

Tush, Lewis. Pvt. Co. D, 28 August 1861 (age 21 at Pittsburgh, PA)–24 September 1862. B: Paris, FRA, farmer. Grey eyes, light hair, dark complexion, 5' 8¼. Disability discharge at hospital, NYC.

Uffelmann, Melchor (alias Upperman, Melchor, alias Michael). Pvt. Co. K, 19 July 1861 (age 21 at Pittsburgh, PA)–19 July 1864. B: Hohenzell, Austria, GER, hostler. Blue eyes, light hair, light complexion, 5' 6. Discharged at Ft. Adams, RI. Mustered: Pvt. Co. H, 83rd PA Inf. 16 February 1865–28 June 1865. Mustered out at Washington, D.C.

Uhl, Jacob. Pvt. Co. K, 20 August 1861 (age 18 at

Rochester, NY)–20 August 1864. B: GER, farmer. Blue eyes, brown hair, light complexion, 5' 6½. Discharged at Lighthouse Point, VA. Transferred: 2nd Bn. U.S.V.R.C. D: 30 December 1895, Flushing, Queens, NY.

Ulscht, Martin. Pvt. Co. K, 22 August 1861 (age 22 at Rochester, NY)–15 June 1864. B: GER, mason. Blue eyes, light hair, light complexion, 5' 7. Deserted.

Upham, Nathan G. Pvt. Co. G, 3 August 1861 (age 21 at Erie Co., PA) 3 August 1864. B: Harmonsburg, Crawford Co., PA, farmer. Hazel eyes, red hair, fair complexion, 5' 5½. POW, ?–26 April 1864. Paroled, reported at Annapolis, MD. Discharged at Harper's Ferry, VA.

Vail, William L. Rct. 24 September 1864 (age 18 at NYC, NY)–Never joined. B: New York City, NY, tailor. Brown eyes, black hair, sallow complexion, 5' 6½.

Valentine, Abraham H. Mustered: Pvt. Co. K, 8th OH Inf. 26 May 1861. Transferred: Pvt. Co. C, 6th U.S. Cav. 23 October 1862 (age 19 at Knoxville, MD)–26 May 1864. B: Medina Co., OH. Blue eyes, black hair, dark complexion, 5' 3½. Discharged at Camp 6th Cav., VA. Mustered: Pvt. Co. B, 2nd OH Cav. 14 February 1865–11 September 1865. Mustered out at St. Louis, MO.

Valentine, Henry L. Farrier. Co. I, 30 July 1861 (age 22 at Indiana, PA)–30 July 1864. B: Altoona, Blair Co., PA, blacksmith. Brown eyes, black hair, dark complexion, 5' 7½. Discharged in the field, VA. D: 26 February 1925, Sawtelle, Los Angeles, CA.

Valley, Peter. Mustered: Pvt. Co. B, 60th NY Inf. 14 September 1861. Transferred: Pvt.-Cpl. Co. M, 6th U.S. Cav. 25 October 1862 (age 28 at Knoxville, MD)–25 August 1864. B: Hoganburg, Lower Can., CAN, farmer. Hazel eyes, black hair, sallow complexion, 5' 5. WIA/POW, Fairfield, 3 July–24 August 1863. Paroled at Annapolis, MD. Discharged at Harper's Ferry, VA.

VanDerender, William. Mustered: Pvt. Co. B, 7th MI Inf. Transferred: Pvt. Company B, 6th U.S. Cav. 27 October 1862 (age 19 at Knoxville, MD)–15 March 1865. B: New York City, NY, farmer. Brown eyes, dark hair, light complexion, 5'11. POW, Fairfield, 3 July 1863–12 June 1864. Paroled, reported at Camp 6th Cav. Reenlisted: 8 February 1864 at Camp 6th Cav., VA. KIA, Hanover Junction, VA, 15 March 1865.

VanMoss, Henry. Pvt. Co. A, 24 September 1861 (age 21 at Cleveland, OH)–25 September 1864. B: SWZ, barber. Black eyes, dark hair, fair

complexion, 5' 6½. Discharged at Harrisonburg, VA.

VanReed, Mabury A. Mustered: Pvt. Co. G. 1st PA Cav. 20 April 1861–27 July 1861. Mustered out at Harrisburg, PA. Enlisted: Sgt. Cos. C, L, F&S, 18 October 1861 (age 21 at Philadelphia, PA)–18 October 1864. B: Reading, Berks Co., PA, paper maker. Hazel eyes, dark hair, sallow complexion, 5'10. Transferred to F&S, 24 July 1864. Discharged at Cedar Creek, VA.

VanSlack, James. Pvt. Co. M, 26 December 1861 (age 31 at Pittsburgh, PA)–26 January 1862. B: Mifflin Co., PA, boatman. Blue eyes, dark hair, dark complexion, 5' 8. Deserted.

Vantine, Charles A. Unknown Vol. Unit. Transferred: Pvt. Co. K, 6th U.S. Cav. 24 October 1862 (age 21 at Knoxville, MD)–15 October 1865. B: Philadelphia, PA, silver plater. Blue eyes, light hair, light complexion, 5' 5. Reenlisted: 10 February 1864 at Brandy Station, VA. Deserted 15 October 1865. Note: Pension denotes he also served in Co. H, 1st U.S. Cav.

VanWormer, Charles J. Pvt. Co. K, 15 August 1861 (age 21 at Rochester, NY)–13 December 1862. B: 22 November 1842, Monroe Co., NY, farmer. Grey eyes, black hair, florid complexion, 5' 9. Disability discharge at Ft. McHenry, MD. Mustered (Selby, NY): Pvt. Co. I, 90th NY Inf. 15 September 1864–3 June 1865. D: 7 February 1899, Hudsonville, Ottawa, MI.

VanZant, Joseph F. Pvt. Co. B, 19 August 1861 (age 27 at Cleveland, OH)–5 August 1862. B: Dryden, Tompkins Co., NY, farmer. Hazel eyes, black hair, ruddy complexion, 5'11¾. WIA/MIA, Malvern Hill. D: 5 August 1862.

Verbaum, Jacob. Pvt. Co. L, 16 May 1864 (age 18 at Rochester, NY)–16 May 1867. B: 1847 Rochester, Monroe Co., NY. Grey eyes, light hair, fair complexion, 5' 4. Discharged at Ft. Belknap, TX. D: 27 October 1925, Los Angeles, CA.

Versey, Felix. Rct. 24 April 1864 (age 22 at NYC, NY)–13 May 1864. B: Lyons, FRA, baker. Blue eyes, brown hair, ruddy complexion, 5' 6. Deserted.

Vialilake, Louis. Pvt. Co. G, 30 July 1861 (age 38 at Erie Co., PA)–7 February 1862. B: Chawrrd, HUN, hatter. Blue eyes, dark hair, dark complexion, 5' 6½. Deserted.

Viall, Spencer. Mustered: Pvt. Co. F, 3rd WI Inf. 22 April 1861. Transferred: Pvt. Co. F, 6th U.S. Cav. 25 October 1862 (age 33 at Knoxville, MD)–9 June 1863. B: Croydon, Bucks, PA, millwright. Blue eyes, black hair, fair complexion, 5'7¾. WIA, Brandy Station. KIA (a bouncing cannon ball decapitated him), Beverly Ford, VA.

Vick, Holland E. Pvt. Co. B, 5 August 1861 (age 18 at Cleveland, OH)–18 October 1862. B: 1842, Marlboro Twp., Stark, OH, farmer. Grey eyes, light hair, ruddy complexion, 5'11¼. Disability discharge at Ft. Monroe, VA. D: 1911, Alliance, Stark, OH.

Vickery, James. Pvt. Co. L, 2 January 1862 (age 32 at Cleveland, OH)–6 April 1862. B: Clifton Park, Saratoga Co., NY, corker. Black eyes, black hair, ruddy complexion, 6'1¾. Deserted.

Vining, Albert J. Mustered: Pvt. Co. E, 8th OH Inf. Transferred: Pvt. Co. C, 6th U.S. Cav. 24 October 1862 (age 19 at Knoxville, MD)–25 June 1864. B: Castalia, Erie, OH. Hazel eyes, black hair, florid complexion, 5'4½. POW, Fairfield, 3 July–30 November 1863. Paroled, reported at Annapolis, MD. Discharged in the field, VA. Mustered: Pvt. Co. I, 128th OH Inf. 22 August 1864–13 July 1865. Mustered out at Camp Chase, OH.

Von Froben, Louis. Cpl.-Hosp. Steward. Cos. F, F&S, F, 3 July 1861 (age 21 at Pittsburgh, PA)–3 July 1864. B: Karlsruhe, Bundesland, GER, moulder. Grey eyes, light hair, fair complexion, 5'7¾. MIA, Fairfield. Discharged at Lighthouse Point, VA. Reenlisted: Sgt. GMS, 10 August 1864–20 September 1866.

Vorderman, Andrew H. Pvt. Co. B, 5 August 1861 (age 22 at Cleveland, OH)–5 August 1864. B: 1838 Glarus, SWZ, moulder. Grey eyes, light hair, sallow complexion, 5'5¼. POW, White House Landing, 28 June 1862–? Discharged at Lighthouse Point, VA. D: 1917, Akron, Summit, OH.

Vought, Hugh L. Pvt. Co. A, 23 September 1861 (at Columbus, OH)–17 September 1862. B: 10 January 1842, OH. Discharged at Providence, RI. Mustered: Pvt. Co. C, 178th OH Inf. 23 September 1864–29 June 1865. Mustered out at Charlotte, NC. D: 10 April 1907, Tama Co., IA.

Wachter, Charles. Pvt. Co. D, 9 August 1861 (age 23 at Pittsburgh, PA)–9 August 1864. B: 1838, GER, canal hand,. Grey eyes, black hair, dark complexion, 5'5. Discharged at City Point, VA. D: 2 November 1917, Allegheny, PA.

Wadsworth, John. Pvt. Co. K, 15 July 1861 (age 19 at Franklin, PA)–9 January 1862. B: Cleveland, Cuyahoga, OH, lumberman. Hazel eyes, brown hair, light complexion, 5'6½. Disability discharge at Washington, D.C.

Waggoner, Albert C. Pvt. Co. E, 19 September 1861 (age 23 at Adrian, MI)–30 April 1863. B: 1837, Steuben Co., NY, farmer. Grey eyes, red hair, florid complexion, 5'9¼. WIA, Williamsburg. Brought to the Seminary Hospital, Hampton, VA, 11 May 1862. Disability discharge at convalescent camp, VA. D: 1914, Wayne, Steuben, NY.

Waggoner, Francis M. Mustered: Pvt. Co. K, 14th IN Inf. 7 June 1861. Transferred: Rct. 6th U.S. Cav. 23 October 1862 (age 21 at Knoxville, MD)–Returned to USV. B: Brown Co., IN, farmer. Blue eyes, sandy hair, florid complexion, 5'11½. Transferred: Pvt. Co. K, 20th IN Inf. 6 June 1864.

Waggoner, George W. Mustered: Pvt. Co. D, 14th IN Inf. Transferred: Pvt. 6th U.S. Cav. 23 October 1862 (age 26 at Knoxville, MD). B: Dubois Co., IN, farmer. Dark eyes, dark hair, dark complexion, 5'7. Returned to USV. Transferred: Pvt. Co. B, 20th IN Inf. 15 December 1863–12 July 1865. Mustered out at Louisville, KY.

Wagner, Gustavus. Pvt. Co. M, 21 December 1861 (age 34 at Pittsburgh, PA)–7 June 1867. B: Dresden, Saxony, GER, civil engineer. Hazel eyes, brown hair, dark complexion, 5'5. Deserted 14 June 1862. Apprehended 28 December 1864. Tried by GCMO 21 June 1865, VA. Discharged 7 June 1867 enroute to Mt. Pleasant, TX.

Waldruff, George. Mustered: Pvt. Co. D, 67th NY Inf. 18 May 1861–4 July 1864. Mustered out at Brooklyn, NY. Enlisted: Cpl. Co. M, 6th U.S. Cav. 29 August 1864 (at Buffalo, NY)–1 November 1867. Deserted 27 October 1864. Apprehended 30 November 1864. Discharged 1 November 1867 at Mt. Pleasant, TX.

Walker, Aaron. Pvt. Co. D, 20 August 1861 (age 24 at Pittsburgh, PA)–20 August 1864. B: Washington Co., PA, farmer. Brown eyes, black hair, dark complexion, 6'3. Discharged at City Point, VA. D: 1923, Pittsburgh, Allegheny, PA.

Walker, Charles. Pvt. 11 November 1864 (age 27 at Harrisburg, PA)–21 November 1864. B: Kent Co., IRE, sailor. Blue eyes, light hair, sallow complexion, 5'9. Deserted. Sub.

Walker, George. Rct. 6 December 1864 (age 22 at Cincinnati, OH)–Never joined. B: Toronto, Ontario, CAN, sailor. Blue eyes, dark hair, fair complexion, 5'7¾. Sub.

Walker, William B. Pvt. Co. E, 14 September 1861 (age 24 at Adrian, MI)–14 September 1864. B: Falls, OH, farmer. Blue eyes, brown hair, fair complexion, 5'7. Discharged at Berryville, VA.

Wallace, James. Mustered: Pvt. Co. C, 14th IN

Inf. Transferred: Rct. 6th U.S. Cav. 23 October 1862 (age 20 at Knoxville, MD)–Returned to USV. B: Columbiana Co., OH. Blue eyes, light hair, florid complexion, 5' 7½.

Wallace, John. Pvt. Co. H, 3 August 1861 (age 28 at Philadelphia, PA)–23 November 1861. B: Prussia, GER, hostler. Hazel eyes, brown hair, dark complexion, 5' 6. Disability discharge at Washington, D.C.

Wallace, Robert. 1st Sgt. Co. F, 6 July 1861 (age 28 at Pittsburgh, PA)–6 July 1864. B: Ayre, Isle of Man, SCO, teamster. Grey eyes, light hair, fair complexion, 5'10¾. Discharged at Light-house Point, VA.

Wallace, William. Mustered: Pvt. Co. K, 110th PA Inf. Transferred: Pvt. Co. L, 6th U.S. Cav. 27 October 1862 (age 18 at Knoxville, MD)–7 October 1864. B: Blair Co., PA, farmer. Hazel eyes, light hair, fair complexion, 5' 8. POW, Fairfield, 3 July 1863–21 June 1864. Paroled. Discharged at Cedar Creek, VA.

Wallace, William. Pvt. Co. K, 19 July 1861 (age 21 at Franklin, PA)–15 January 1862. B: SCO, carpenter & engineer. Hazel eyes, black hair, swarthy complexion, 5'10¼. Disability discharge at Washington, D.C.

Wallace, William H. Cpl. Co. H, 13 August 1861 (age 23 at Philadelphia, PA)–13 August 1864. B: Philadelphia, PA, pipe moulder. Hazel eyes, brown hair, ruddy complexion, 5' 7. MIA, Funkstown. Discharged at Lighthouse Point, VA.

Wallace, William L. Mustered: Pvt. Co. D, 8th OH Inf. 29 June 1861. Transferred: Pvt. Co. C, 6th U.S. Cav. 24 October 1862 (age 21 at Knoxville, MD)–20 April 1864. B: Essex Co., VT. Blue eyes, black hair, florid complexion, 5' 8½. Disability discharge at Carlisle Barracks, PA.

Wallman, Henry H. Pvt. Co. E, 16 August 1861 (age 33 at Columbus, OH)–16 August 1864. B: Prussia, GER, musician. Grey eyes, black hair, ruddy complexion, 5' 6¼. Discharged at Washington, D.C.

Walsh, John. Pvt. Co. L, 8 September 1864 (age 33 at Harrisburg, PA)–24 February 1866. B: Co. West Meath, IRE, laborer. Grey eyes, dark hair, ruddy complexion, 5' 6. Sub. Deserted.

Walsh, Michael. Sgt. Co. F, 4 July 1861 (age 23 at Pittsburgh, PA)–4 July 1864. B: Co. Cork, IRE, puddler of iron. Grey eyes, black hair, fair complexion, 5'10¾. Discharged at Lighthouse Point, VA.

Walsh, Richard. Rct. 17 September 1864 (age 32 at Harrisburg, PA)–Never joined. B: Co.

Kilkenny, IRE, miner. Blue eyes, sandy hair, sallow complexion, 5'11½.

Walter, Harry. Pvt. Co. F, 22 November 1864 (age 18 at Cincinnati, OH)–21 November 1867. B: Richmond, VA, printer. Hazel eyes, brown hair, ruddy complexion, 5' 7. Sub. Discharged at Camp Wilson, TX.

Walter, John H. H. Sgt. Cos. I, K, 21 August 1861 (age 3* at Pittsburgh, PA)–9 February 1863. B: Chenango Co., NY, clerk. Blue eyes, light hair, fair complexion. Disability discharge from Convalescent Camp, VA.

Walton, Charles P. Bugler. Cos. C, L, 1 November 1861 (age 16 at Philadelphia, PA)–9 August 1862. B: Londonderry, PA, farmer. Hazel eyes, light hair, light complexion, 5' 7½. D: 9 August 1862 from disease at Harrison's Landing, VA.

Ward, David O. Mustered: Pvt. Co. D, 8th OH Inf. 3 June 1861. WIA, Antietam. Transferred: Pvt. Co. C, 6th U.S. Cav. 23 October 1862 (age 20 at Knoxville, MD)–14 June 1864. B: 5 December 1842, Huron Co., OH, farmer. Blue eyes, light hair, fair complexion, 5' 7. Discharged in the field, VA. D: 14 January 1917, Freeport, Barry, MI.

Ward, Isaac M. Enlisted: Pvt.-Cpl.-Sgt.-1st Sgt. Co. A, 1st U.S. Cav. 26 January 1857 (age 24 at Decatur)–23 October 1861. B: Scott Co., KY, boot maker. Hazel eyes, light hair, fair complexion, 5' 6. Discharged by appointment as 2nd Lt. 6th U.S. Cav. 26 October 1861. KIA 9 June 1863, Beverly Ford, VA.

Ward, James W. Pvt. Co. E, 1 September 1861 (age 18 at Columbus, OH)–7 September 1864. B: Licking Co., OH, farmer. Hazel eyes, black hair, sallow complexion, 5' 9. Discharged at Berryville, VA.

Ward, Jeremiah. Rct. 7 September 1861 (age 26 at Rochester, NY)–19 September 1861. B: Cayuga Co., NY, farmer. Blue eyes, brown hair, fair complexion, 5' 5. Deserted.

Ward, John. Rct. 12 September 1864 (age 26 at Cleveland, OH)–Never joined. B: Windsor, Ontario, CAN, laborer. Grey eyes, brown hair, sallow complexion, 5' 7½. Sub.

Warl, Daniel L. Pvt. Co. E, 20 September 1861 (age 19 at Cleveland, OH)–23 January 1865. B: Clinton, Prince George's Co., MD, teamster. Grey eyes, black hair, ruddy complexion, 5' 4½. MIA, Brandy Station. MIA, while on duty at CCHQ. Discharged at Baltimore, MD.

Warner, Nelson E. Mustered: Pvt. Co. G, 50th PA Inf. 26 September 1861. Transferred: Pvt. Co. E, 6th U.S. Cav. 28 October 1862 (age 22 at Knoxville, MD)–18 September 1864. B: 8

April 1840, Bradford Co., PA. Blue eyes, dark hair, light complexion, 5' 7½. Discharged at Berryville, VA. D: 2 March 1914, Bunker Hill, Russell, KS.

Wasmuth, Henry. Pvt. Co. A, 5 October 1861 (age 23 at Philadelphia, PA)–12 February 1863. B: Pickelsheim, Prussia, GER, miner. Blue eyes, light hair, fair complexion, 5' 7½. Deserted from hospital.

Waters, William W. Mustered: Pvt. Co. D, 7th MI Inf. 8 March 1861. Transferred: Cpl.-1st Sgt.-Sgt. Co. K, 6th U.S. Cav. 27 October 1862 (age 21 at Knoxville, MD)–6 July 1865. B: Monroe City, Monroe Co., MI, carpenter. Blue eyes, dark hair, light complexion, 5' 7½. Reenlisted: 10 February 1864 at Brandy Station, VA. Disability discharge at Slough General Hospital, Alexandria, VA.

Wathey, Thomas. Mustered: Pvt.-1st Sgt. Co. H, 15th MA Inf. 25 May 1861. Transferred: Pvt.-Cpl. Co. M, 6th U.S. Cav. 24 October 1862 (age 22 at Knoxville, MD)–23 July 1866. B: 2 February 1841, New York City, NY. Blue eyes, brown hair, fair complexion, 5' 8½. POW, Fairfield. Paroled at Annapolis, MD 20 August 1863. Reenlisted: 8 February 1864 at Brandy Station, VA. Deserted. D: 3 March 1907, Winchester, VA.

Watson, Abraham. Mustered: Pvt. Co. C, 14th IN Inf. 6 July 1861. Transferred: Rct. 6th U.S. Cav. 24 October 1862 (age 24 at Knoxville, MD)–Returned to USV. B: Martin Co., IN, miller. Black eyes, brown hair, light complexion, 5' 7½. Promoted to Cpl. Mustered out 12 May 1864 at Spotsylvania Court-House, VA.

Watson, Alexander. Pvt. Co. D, 26 August 1861 (age 21 at Pittsburgh, PA)–6 February 1863. B: Galloway Co., SCO, farmer. Blue eyes, light hair, dark complexion, 5'10. Disability discharge at Chester Hill Hospital, Philadelphia, PA.

Watson, George. Pvt. Co. F, 21 November 1864 (age 22 at Harrisburg, PA)–7 January 1865. B: Watford, Hertfordshire, ENG, laborer. Blue eyes, light hair, fair complexion, 5' 8. Sub. Deserted.

Watson, James Inglis. Rct. 10 March 1862 (age 21 at Philadelphia, PA)–31 March 1862. B: Forfarshire, SCO, engineer. Hazel eyes, black hair, ruddy complexion, 6'. Deserted at Philadelphia, PA.

Watson, John W. Pvt. Co. F, 3 December 1864 (age 32 at Cleveland, OH)–12 January 1865. B: Hamilton, Ontario, CAN, brick layer. Blue eyes, brown hair, sallow complexion, 5' 6½. Sub. Deserted.

Watson, Oliver. Pvt. Co. M, 24 August 1864 (age 31 at Harrisburg, PA)–9 May 1865. B: St. Johns, New Brunswick, CAN, sailor. Grey eyes, fair hair, fair complexion, 5' 7½. Sub. Deserted.

Watterson, Alexander. Pvt. Co. M, 27 September 1861 (age 21 at Pittsburgh, PA)–22 June 1864. B: Beaver Co., PA, farmer. Hazel eyes, brown hair, dark complexion, 5'10. POW, VA, 22 June 1864.

Waxted, Hugh. Pvt. Co. G, 6 August 1861 (age 27 at Rochester, NY)–8 August 1864. B: IRE, laborer. Hazel eyes, brown hair, ruddy complexion, 5'5. MIA, Fairfield. Discharged at Lighthouse Point, VA.

Way, Benjamin Francis. Pvt. Co. I, 19 August 1861 (age 30 at Rochester, NY)–7 August 1862. B: Cayuga Co., NY, teamster. Blue eyes, light hair, fair complexion, 5' 4¾. MIA, Malvern Hill, VA.

Weaver, William. Pvt. Cos. L, M, 1 October 1864 (age 18 at NYC, NY)–21 July 1865. B: Geneva, NY, farmer. Blue eyes, light hair, ruddy complexion, 5' 4½. Disability discharge at Carlisle Barracks, PA.

Webb, Cornelius. Pvt. Co. M, 30 August 1864 (age 18 at NYC, NY)–17 September 1865. B: NY, laborer. Blue eyes, brown hair, fair complexion, 5' 4½. Sub.

Webb, Edward C. Pvt. Co. F, 7 November 1864 (age 19 at Cincinnati, OH)–7 November 1867. B: Independence, Warren, IN, laborer. Hazel eyes, dark hair, fair complexion, 5' 3½. Discharged at Camp Wilson, TX.

Webb, Leicester Austin. Mustered: Pvt. Co. F, 1st MN Inf. 29 April 1861. Transferred: Pvt. Co. B, 6th U.S. Cav. 26 October 1862 (age 19 at Knoxville, MD)–5 May 1864. B: 26 December 1842, Webb Settlement, Ridgefield, Huron, OH. Blue eyes, light hair, light complexion, 5' 8. POW (captured while on picket), Richard's Ford, 14 February 1863. Discharged at Ft. Snelling, MN. D: 27 August 1881, Ft. Buford, D.T.

Webster, Robert. Mustered: Pvt. Co. C, 147th PA Inf. 30 August 1861. Transferred: Pvt. Co. B, 6th U.S. Cav. 25 October 1862 (age 19 at Knoxville, MD)–28 August 1864. B: IRE, farmer. Blue eyes, light hair, fair complexion, 5' 7½. POW (captured while on picket), Richard's Ford, 14 February 1863. Paroled. POW, Fairfield. Paroled 24 September 1863 at Culpepper, VA. Discharged at Bolivar, VA.

Weeks, William H. Rct. 11 November 1864 (age 24 at Harrisburg, PA)–21 November 1864. B: Toronto, Ontario, CAN, boiler maker. Grey eyes, brown hair, fair complexion, 5' 9. Sub. Deserted.

Weigand, Jacob D. Musician 1st Class. Co. F&S, 15 October 1861 (age 23 at Mount Joy, PA)–1 December 1862. B: Elizabethtown, Lancaster Co., PA, musician. Hazel eyes, black hair, sallow complexion, 5'4. Disability discharge at camp near Belle Plain, VA.

Weigand, John. Pvt. Cos. C, L, 4 December 1861 (age 18 at Mount Joy, PA)–19 February 1867. B: 1842, New Holland, Lancaster Co., PA, farmer. Grey eyes, brown hair, ruddy complexion, 5'3½. Reenlisted: 19 February 1864 at Brandy Station, VA. Discharged at Jacksboro, TX, a Sgt. D: 1925, Mount Joy, Lancaster, PA.

Weimer, Gust. Rct. 30 August 1864 (age 35 at Carlisle Barracks, PA)–Never joined. B: Breston, Prussia, GER, miller. Grey eyes, brown hair, fair complexion, 5'4.

Weisenbiher, John. Pvt. Co. F, 15 July 1861 (age 24 at Pittsburgh, PA)–2 December 1862. B: Montbrun, FRA, butcher. Grey eyes, auburn hair, dark complexion, 5'2½. Disability discharge at Falmouth, VA.

Welch, Nicholas. Pvt. Co. M, 14 September 1864 (age 19 at Harrisburg, PA)–29 November 1864. B: Montreal, Quebec, CAN, boatman. Brown eyes, light hair, ruddy complexion, 5'11. MIA on a raid. Sub. No further information.

Weldele, Wendelin. Mustered: Pvt. Co. B, 140th NY Inf. 26 August 1862–18 March 1863. Disability discharge at convalescent camp, VA. Enlisted: Pvt. Co. M, 6th U.S. Cav. 28 September 1864 (age 35 at Rochester, NY)–16 August 1865. B: Baden, GER, lawyer. Grey eyes, light hair, sallow complexion, 5'6½. Disability discharge at U.S. General Hospital, Frederick, MD.

Welder, Joseph. Mustered: Co. K, 8th OH Inf. 26 May 1861. Transferred: Pvt. Co. C, 6th U.S. Cav. 22 October 1862 (age 19 at Knoxville, MD)–26 May 1864. B: Armstrong Co., PA, blacksmith. Hazel eyes, black hair, dark complexion, 6'. MIA, Fairfield. Discharged at Camp 6th Cav., VA.

Wells, Charles M. Pvt. Co. I, 3 September 1861 (age 21 at Rochester, NY)–30 October 1862. B: Steuben Co., NY, farmer. Blue eyes, red hair, sandy complexion, 5'4¼. Deserted.

Welsh, Daniel. Pvt. Co. M, 16 October 1861 (age 23 at Pittsburgh, PA)–18 October 1864. B: Co. Cork, IRE, coal miner. Hazel eyes, brown hair, dark complexion, 5'8. Discharged in the field, VA.

Welsh, James. Rct. 12 November 1861 (age 26 at Cleveland, OH)–No further information. B:

Casrant, IRE, laborer. Blue eyes, sandy hair, ruddy complexion, 5'7. See 43399 P.R.D. 1892.

Welsh, Thomas. Rct. 16 November (age 23 at Harrisburg, PA)–21 November 1864. B: Queens Co., IRE, laborer. Grey eyes, light hair, fair complexion, 5'5. Sub. Deserted.

Wenkstern, William. Pvt. Co. I, 26 August 1861 (age 29 at Rochester, NY)–26 August 1864. B: GER, farmer. Blue eyes, light hair, fair complexion, 5'4. Deserted 30 March 1863. Apprehended 17 August 1863. Discharged at Harper's Ferry, VA.

Werner, John. Pvt. Co. F, 11 July 1861 (age 19 at Pittsburgh, PA)–11 July 1864. B: Wurttemberg, GER, farmer. Grey eyes, auburn hair, ruddy complexion, 5'7. POW, Fairfield, 3 July 1863–19 February 1864. Paroled, reported at Camp Parole. Discharged at Lighthouse Point, VA.

Wernerut, James. Pvt. Co. H, 8 July 1861 (age 23 at Philadelphia, PA)–29 November 1861. B: Lehigh Co., PA, farmer. Blue eyes, dark hair, fair complexion, 5'6. Deserted.

West, John A. Enlisted: Pvt. Co. B, 1st U.S Dragoons, 10 June 1858. Transferred to F&S when unit redesignated as 1st U.S. Cav. Transferred: 6th U.S. Cav. Deserted 14 August 1861. Apprehended 17 August 1861. B: Olderburg, GER, tailor. Blue eyes, light hair, sandy complexion, 5'8⅛. Deserted 8 January 1862. Apprehended 20 February 1873. D: 8 October 1874 of cerebral apophy at Camp Supply, TX.

Weston, John. Pvt. Co. F, 8 December 1864 (age 36 at Cleveland, OH)–29 January 1865. B: Guelph, CAN, laborer. Hazel eyes, brown hair, ruddy complexion, 5'3. Sub. Deserted.

Wetherell, Harrison B. Rct. 21 September 1864 (age 25 at Rochester, NY)–Never joined. B: NY, brick maker. Blue eyes, light hair, florid complexion, 5'8.

Wetzel, Casper. Pvt. Co. I, 13 September 1861 (age 28 at Rochester, NY)–13 September 1864. B: GER, tailor. Blue eyes, brown hair, dark complexion, 5'7¾. POW, Funkstown, 7 July–18 December 1863. Paroled, reported at Annapolis, MD. Discharged in the field, VA. Enlisted: Pvt. Co. I, 4th U.S. Cav. 3 November 1864–3 November 1867. Discharged at Sparta, LA.

Wezel, John. Pvt. Co. M, 5 November 1861 (age 33 at Pittsburgh, PA)–15 August 1865. B: GER, blacksmith. Grey eyes, sandy hair, light complexion, 5'8½. Sick in hospital 28 May 1863. Honorably discharged at expiration of service.

Wheatley, Francis L. Mustered: Co. K, 37th PA Inf. 22 June 1861. Transferred: Pvt. Co. I, 6th U.S. Cav. 27 October 1862 (age 20 at Knoxville, MD)–5 June 1864. B: 1841, Green Co., PA, blacksmith. Brown eyes, brown hair, ruddy complexion, 5'7. POW, Funkstown, 7 July 1863–6 April 1864. Paroled, reported at Annapolis, MD. Discharged at Camp 6th Cav., VA. D: 1909, Sangamon, IL.

Wheeler, Julius M. Pvt. Co. E, 6 September 1861 (age 21 at Cleveland, OH)–5 September 1864. B: Manchester, Washtenaw Co., MI, painter. Hazel eyes, brown hair, ruddy complexion, 5'10. MIA, Fairfield. Discharged at Berryville, VA.

Whipp, Edward C. Pvt. Co. G, 8 August 1861 (age 21 at Columbus, OH)–29 September 1862. B: Columbus, Franklin, OH, blacksmith. Brown eyes, brown hair, ruddy complexion, 5'9½. Disability discharge at Philadelphia, PA.

Whitbeck, Abram (alias Smith, George). Pvt. Co. I, 29 September 1861 (age 30 at Rochester, NY)–15 April 1862. B: 21 March 1835, Montgomery Co., NY, mason. Blue eyes, sandy hair, florid complexion, 5'7. Deserted. D: 2 June 1925, Bridgeport, Saginaw, MI. Enlisted: Pvt. Co. C, 3rd Bn. 18th U.S. Inf. And also served in Co. B, 2nd Bn. 18th U.S. Inf. 16 May 1862. Deserted 15 November 1862. Joined 26 August 1863. Discharged 14 May 1865 at Lookout Mtn., TN. For illegal service see 14189 P.R.D. 90.

White, Frank. Pvt. Cos. F, L, 29 December 1864 (age 21 at Cincinnati, OH)–27 February 1865. B: KY, farmer. Hazel eyes, dark hair, dark complexion, 5'5. Deserted.

White, Franklin. Rct. 19 August 1861 (age 20 at Rochester, NY)–22 August 1861. B: Oswego Co., NY, farmer. Blue eyes, brown hair, sandy complexion, 5'5½. Rejected recruit at Pittsburgh, PA. Enlisted: Pvt. Co. H, 3rd NY Cav. 26 August 1861 (Rochester, NY)–18 November 1861. Deserted at Darnestown, MD.

White, George E. Enlisted: Pvt. GMS, 22 May 1860 (NYC, NY)–5 July 1864. Reenlisted: Commissary Sgt.-Sgt. Maj. Cos. F&S, M, 6th U.S. Cav. 5 July 1864 (age 24 at Harrisburg, PA)–5 July 1867. B: Southampton, Hampshire, ENG, hostler. Hazel eyes, brown hair, fair complexion, 6'. Discharged at Austin, TX. Reenlisted: 21 August 1868 (Austin, TX)–21 August 1873. Discharged at Ft. Hays, KS, the Reg. QM Sgt.

White, George S. (alias Young, Henry G., alias White, Henry G.) Mustered: Pvt. Co. F, 6th VT Inf. 3 October 1861. Transferred: Pvt. Co. H, 6th U.S. Cav. 25 October 1862 (age 20 at

Knoxville, MD)–25 April 1863. B: Manchester, Hillsborough, NH. Blue eyes, brown hair, light complexion, 5'11. Deserted 25 April 1863. Enlisted: 19 October 1863 (Pittsburgh, PA)–21 August 1865, Signal Corps (under alias). Enlisted: GS, Inf. 19 October 1866 (Hartford, CT)–"No information of disposition made of this man can be obtained." Enlisted: GS, Inf. 20 February 1867 (Ft. Du Lac, WI)–"Investigation fails to elicit information with regard to disposition of this man." Enlisted: Pvt. 1st U.S. Art. 1 November 1869 (Ft. Schuyler, NY)–14 July 1871. Disability discharge at Ft. Wood, NY.

Whitehouse, Henry. Pvt. Co. L, 16 February 1862 (at Cleveland, OH)–24 June 1862. Deserted.

Whiteside, Benjamin. Sgt. Co. I, 7 September 1861 (age 23 at Rochester, NY)–7 January 1863. B: IRE, farmer. Grey eyes, brown hair, fair complexion, 5'10. Discharged by appointment as 2nd Lt. 105th NY Vol. at Belle Plain, VA.

Whitmire, William. Pvt. Cos. M, E, 11 December 1861 (age 24 at Butler Co., PA)–11 October 1863. B: Butler Co., PA, farmer. Hazel eyes, brown hair, light complexion, 5'5. MIA, Brandy Station, VA.

Whitney, Henry M. Mustered: Pvt. Co. E, 20th IN Inf. 22 July 1861. Enlisted: Pvt. Co. F, 1st U.S. Cav. 13 February 1864 (age 21 at Camp near Mitchell's Station, VA)–4 March 1865. B: Chillicothe, Ross, OH. Grey eyes, light hair, light complexion, 5'4½. Transferred: Sgt. Co. B, 6th U.S. Cav. Disability discharge at Carlisle Barracks, PA.

Whitney, John C. Pvt.-Cpl. Co. K, 31 July 1861 (age 19 at Warren, OH)–31 July 1864. B: Trumbull Co., OH, farmer. Chestnut eyes, black hair, dark complexion, 5'8¾. Discharged at Lee's Mills, VA.

Whitside, Samuel Marmaduke. Enlisted: 10 October 1858. Transferred: Sgm. Co. F&S, 6th U.S. Cav. 27 July 1861 (at NYC, NY)–4 August 1861. B: Toronto, Ontario, CAN, book keeper. Blue eyes, light hair, fair complexion, 5'7¾. Discharged 4 November 1861 at Washington, D.C. by appoint as a 2nd Lt.

Wickham, George H. Pvt. Co. D, 8 August 1861 (age 21 at Pittsburgh, PA)–3 December 1863. B: Allegheny Co., PA, bill poster. Blue eyes, sallow hair, light complexion, 5'6. Deserted on the march.

Widdup, Joseph. Mustered: Pvt. Co. G, 37th PA Inf. 24 May 1861. Transferred: Pvt. Co. E, 6th U.S. Cav. 28 October 1862 (age 28 at Knoxville, MD)–24 November 1863. B: ENG, laborer. Blue eyes, light hair, fair complexion,

5'7. MIA, Fairfield. D: 24 November 1863 from bronchitis at General Hospital #21 at Richmond, VA.

Wiedel, Christian W. Mustered: Pvt. Co. E, 8th OH Inf. 25 June 1861. Transferred: Pvt. Co. C, 6th U.S. Cav. 24 October 1862 (age 27 at Knoxville, MD)–25 June 1864. B: Brunswieck, Lower Saxony, GER, sailor. Black eyes, black hair, dark complexion, 5'4. Discharged in the field, VA. Transferred: Pvt.-Cpl. Co. C, 9th Veterans Reserve Corps.

Wiederwax, Frank. Sgt. Cos. F, G, 8 August 1861 (age 32 at Rochester, NY)–1 February 1867. B: Schoharie Co., NY, carpenter. Hazel eyes, brown hair, dark complexion, 5'9. Reenlisted: 27 February 1864. Transferred to Co. G 10 November 1864 by R.O. 97. Disability discharge at New Orleans, LA.

Wier, John. Mustered: Pvt. Co. I, 7th OH Inf. 19 June 1861. Transferred: Pvt. Co. K, 6th U.S. Cav. 28 October 1862 (age 26 at Knoxville, MD)–27 May 1864. B: IRE, laborer. Grey eyes, dark hair, fair complexion, 5'7½. Discharged in the field, VA.

Wies, John. Pvt. Co. I, 26 August 1861 (age 21 at Rochester, NY)–26 August 1864. B: GER, farmer. Grey eyes, brown hair, florid complexion, 5'7¾. Discharged at Harper's Ferry, VA.

Wilkes, David. Pvt. Co. F, 21 November 1864 (age 29 at Cincinnati, OH)–8 August 1865. B: Kingston, Frontenac, CAN, laborer. Blue eyes, brown hair, fair complexion, 5'7¼. Deserted 12 January 1865. Apprehended. Disability discharge 8 August 1865 at U.S. General Hospital, Frederick, MD.

Williams, Andrew J. Pvt. Co. L, 13 September 1864 (age 28 at Harrisburg, PA)–April 1865. B: St. Mary's Co., MD, farmer. Blue eyes, black hair, florid complexion, 5'11. Deserted 23 May 1865. Apprehended April 1865. Investigation fails to furnish anything further.

Williams, Charles. Pvt. Co. A, 16 December 1864 (age 19 at Cincinnati, OH)–16 December 1867. B: Hamilton, Ontario, CAN, teamster. Grey eyes, light hair, fair complexion, 5'6½. Sub. Discharged at Galveston, TX.

Williams, Charles. Rct. 7 November 1864 (age 23 at Harrisburg, PA)–21 November 1864. B: Montreal, Quebec, CAN, cotton printer. Brown eyes, brown hair, fair complexion, 5'7. Sub. Deserted.

Williams, Evan B. Sgt.-1st Sgt. Co. H, 11 July 1861 (age 26 at Philadelphia, PA)–11 July 1864. B: Reading, Berks Co., PA, carpenter. Blue eyes, light hair, fair complexion, 5'8. MIA, Funkstown. Discharged in the field, VA.

Williams, Thomas. Pvt. Co. D, 27 August 1861 (age 21 at Pittsburgh, PA)–30 October 1862. B: Gemorganshire, South Wales, WAL, coal miner. Blue eyes, light hair, dark complexion, 5'7¼. Deserted.

Williams, Thomas. Rct. 9 August 1861 (age 24 at Pittsburgh, PA)–28 August 1861. B: Cookstown, PA, glass blower. Grey eyes, red hair, dark complexion, 5'6½. Deserted from rendezvous.

Williams, William. Pvt. Co. D, 27 August 1861 (age 29 at Pittsburgh, PA)–7 March 1864. B: Monmonshire, South Wales, WAL, coal miner. Blue eyes, red hair, light complexion, 5'6¾. WIA, Beverly Ford. Disability discharge at Carlisle Barracks, PA.

Williamson, John. Rct. 6 December 1864 (age 22 at Carlisle Barracks, PA)–Never joined. B: Co. Derry, IRE, sailor. Blue eyes, sandy hair, ruddy complexion, 5'7.

Wilson, Alexander. Mustered: Pvt. Co. G, 60th NY Inf. Transferred: Pvt. Co. M, 6th U.S. Cav. 20 October 1862 (age 21 at Knoxville, MD)–20 October 1864. B: Brogville, West Canada, CAN. Blue eyes, lt. brown hair, fair complexion, 5'6. POW, Fairfield, 3 July–20 August 1863. Paroled at Annapolis, MD. Discharged at Strasburg, VA.

Wilson, Benjamin H. Rct. 4 August 1861 (age 30 at Cleveland, OH)–No further information. B: Willet, Cortland Co., NY, carpenter. Blue eyes, black hair, ruddy complexion, 5'5¼.

Wilson, George. Pvt. Co. M, 6 September 1861 (at Pittsburgh, PA)–5 March 1863. B: Co. Monaghan, IRE, farmer. Blue eyes, light hair, light complexion, 5'3. Disability discharge at Ft. McHenry, MD.

Wilson, George. Rct. 6 October 1864 (age 23 at Harrisburg, PA)–Never joined. B: Cavan, PA, teamster. Blue eyes, brown hair, fair complexion, 6'1.

Wilson, James. Pvt. Co. L, 9 December 1864 (age 25 at Cincinnati, OH)–29 April 1868. B: ENG, laborer. Hazel eyes, brown hair, fair complexion, 5'9¾. Sub. Deserted 19 March 1865. Joined 22 August 1865. Discharged 29 April 1868 at Ft. Griffin, TX.

Wilson, James L. Rct. 17 July 1861 (age 23 at Pittsburgh, PA)–8 August 1861. B: Allegheny Co., PA, teamster. Grey eyes, brown hair, dark complexion, 6'½. Deserted.

Wilson, John. Pvt. Co. A, 26 November 1864 (age 26 at Cincinnati, OH)–10 February 1865. B: Co. Dublin, IRE, hostler. Blue eyes, light hair, fair complexion, 5'7. Deserted.

Wilson, John. Pvt. Co. H, 31 July 1861 (age 23 at Philadelphia, PA)–31 July 1864. B: Co. Londonderry, IRE, porter. Black eyes, black hair, dark complexion, 5' 9½. Discharged in the field, VA.

Wilson, John. Pvt. Co. M, 15 December 1861 (age 26 at Brownsville, PA)–4 May 1862. B: Brownsville, Fayette Co., PA, cook. Hazel eyes, light hair, light complexion, 5' 5½. POW, Williamsburg. POW at Richmond, VA and Salisbury, NC. Paroled May 1862 and arrived in New York 9 June 1862 via steamer "Guide." Gained 16 July 1862 from parole. See 3522-A-1874.

Wilson, Joshua L. Pvt. Co. E, 1 September 1861 (age 21 at Cleveland, OH)–1 September 1864. B: Harrison Co., OH, farmer. Blue eyes, brown hair, ruddy complexion, 5' 11¾. Discharged at Berryville, VA.

Wilson, Peter. Bugler. Co. M, 13 September 1864 (age 19 at Harrisburg, PA)–13 September 1867. B: Nova Scotia, New Brunswick, CAN, boatman. Grey eyes, brown hair, fair complexion, 5' 4½. Discharged at Mt. Pleasant, TX.

Wilson, Samuel. Pvt. Co. K, 12 July 1861 (age 19 at Franklin, PA)–9 June 1863. B: Mercer Co., PA, farmer. Grey eyes, brown hair, sandy complexion, 5' 4½. WIA (mortally), Beverly Ford.

Wilson, William H. Pvt. Co. B, 12 August 1861 (age 21 at Cleveland, OH)–12 August 1864. B: Portage Co., OH, farmer. Blue eyes, light hair, fair complexion, 5' 7. Discharged at Washington, D.C.

Winters, Horace. Mustered: Pvt. Co. H, 7th MI Inf. 19 August 1861. Transferred: Pvt. Co. H, 6th U.S. Cav. 27 October 1862 (age 23 at Knoxville, MD)–29 April 1864. B: Oswego Co., NY, farmer. Grey eyes, light hair, fair complexion, 5' 5½. Reenlisted: 12 March 1864 at Brandy Station, VA. Deserted. D: Bellaire, Antrim, MI.

Winters, James. Mustered: Pvt. Co. H, 7th MI Inf. 13 August 1861. Transferred: Pvt. Co. L, 6th U.S. Cav. 28 October 1862 (age 26 at Knoxville, MD)–29 August 1864. B: Onondaga Co., NY, farmer. Blue eyes, light hair, light complexion, 5' 6. MIA at Fairfield. Discharged at Harper's Ferry, VA.

Winters, John. Mustered: Pvt. Co. G, 38th PA Inf. 4 May 1861. Transferred: Pvt. Co. M, 6th U.S. Cav. 28 October 1862 (age 25 at Knoxville, MD)–28 May 1864. B: GER, fireman. Hazel eyes, brown hair, florid complexion, 5' 8½. Discharged at Camp 6th Cav., VA.

Wise, George B. Mustered: Pvt. Co. G, 38th PA Inf. 4 May 1861. Transferred: Pvt. Co. F, 6th U.S. Cav. 28 October 1862 (age 22 at Knoxville, MD)–15 November 1864. B: Allegheny Co., PA, farmer. Blue eyes, dark hair, dark complexion, 5' 9. POW (captured by guerrillas), Warrenton, 21 January–15 November 1864. D: from anasarca as a POW at Andersonville, GA.

Wise, John George. Pvt. Co. D, 13 August 1861 (age 19 at Pittsburgh, PA)–13 August 1864. B: Wurttemberg, GER, shoemaker. Grey eyes, light hair, sallow complexion, 5' 7. Discharged at Queens Ford, VA.

Wishart, Jacob H. Mustered: Pvt. Co. H, 60th NY Inf. Transferred: Pvt. Co. A, 6th U.S. Cav. 25 October 1862 (age 27 at Knoxville, MD)–25 April 1866. B: St. Albans, Franklin, VT, carpenter. Blue eyes, light hair, fair complexion, 5' 9. Reenlisted: 14 March 1864 at Camp 6th Cav., VA. Deserted 25 April 1866. Surrendered 4 September 1882. Note: RR lists more.

Withington, William W. Mustered: Pvt. Co. B, 110th PA Inf. 24 October 1861. Transferred: Pvt. Co. D, 6th U.S. Cav. 28 October 1862 (age 22 at Knoxville, MD)–28 August 1864. B: Clinton Co., PA. Blue eyes, light hair, light complexion, 5' 5. Discharged at Halltown, VA.

Witman, Cyrus. Pvt. Co. H, 9 August 1861 (age 22 at Philadelphia, PA)–23 November 1861. B: 21 September 1838, Schuylkill Co., PA, boatman. Blue eyes, light hair, ruddy complexion, 5' 5½. Disability discharge at Washington, D.C. D: 13 September 1920, Schuylkill Haven, Schuylkill, PA.

Witter, Almus B. Pvt. Cos. M, L, 4 October 1861 (age 18 at Cleveland, OH)–4 October 1864. B: 7 May 1843, Summit Co., OH, painter. Hazel eyes, brown hair, fair complexion, 5' 5. Discharged at Harrisburg, PA. D: 8 July 1905, Cleveland, Cuyahoga, OH.

Wolf, Joseph. Pvt. Co. C, 2 December 1861 (age 28 at Columbia, PA)–5 April 1862. B: York Co., PA, engineer. Grey eyes, brown hair, ruddy complexion, 5' 6½. Deserted.

Wolf[e], David H. Mustered: Pvt. Co. K, 72nd PA Inf. 10 August 1861–16 October 1862. Deserted. Enlisted: Pvt. Co. F, 1st U.S. Cav. 29 November 1862 (Philadelphia, PA)–13 February 1864. Reenlisted: Pvt. Co. B, 6th U.S. Cav. 13 February 1864 (age 22 at Mitchell Station, VA)–23 September 1867. B: Philadelphia, PA, barber. Black eyes, dark hair, fair complexion, 5' 4. Deserted 8 December 1865. Surrendered 18 July 1866. Discharged at Austin, TX.

Wolford, Albert. Pvt. Co. L, 20 December 1861

(age 28 at Cleveland, OH)–13 April 1862. B: Bourbon Co., KY, upholsterer. Blue eyes, brown hair, ruddy complexion, 5' 8¾. Deserted.

Womer, Porter. Mustered: Pvt. K, 110th PA Inf. 19 December 1861. Transferred: Pvt. Co. I, 6th U.S. Cav. 27 October 1862 (age 20 at Knoxville, MD)–27 October 1864. B: Blair Co., PA, farmer. Blue eyes, dark hair, fair complexion, 5'10. Discharged in the field, VA.

Wood, Daniel B. Mustered: Pvt. Co. G, 50th PA Inf. Transferred: Pvt. Co. H, 6th U.S. Cav. 28 October 1862–(age 20 at Knoxville, MD)–28 September 1864. B: Bradford Co., PA. Black eyes, light hair, light complexion, 5'11. WIA/POW, Fairfield, 3 July–30 December 1863. Reported at Camp 6th Cav. Discharged at Harper's Ferry, VA.

Wood, Henry B. Pvt. Co. H, 12 August 1861 (age 21 at Philadelphia, PA)–12 August 1864. B: Co. Tyrone, IRE, carter. Brown eyes, dark hair, dark complexion, 5'7. MIA, Fairfield. Discharged at Harper's Ferry, VA.

Wood, Leroy. Mustered: Pvt. Co. G, 3rd WI Inf. 1 May 1861. Transferred: Pvt. Co. G, 6th U.S. Cav. 27 October 1862 (age 19 at Knoxville, MD)–29 June 1864. B: Pompey, Onondaga Co., NY, carpenter. Brown eyes, dark hair, dark complexion, 5'9. Discharged at Wyanoke, VA.

Wood, William. Pvt. Co. B, 16 June 1864 (age 18 at Avon, NY)–16 March 1865. B: East Mendon, Monroe, NY, farmer. Grey eyes, light hair, fair complexion, 5'4. Deserted 28 August 1864. Apprehended 1 September 1864. Deserted 16 March 1865. Apprehended. Deserted.

Woods, Allen B. Sr. Pvt. Co. D, 31 August 1861 (age 18 at Pittsburgh, PA)–31 August 1864. B: Birmingham, PA. Blue eyes, light hair, light complexion, 5'9. Discharged at Charlestown, VA. D: Pittsburgh, Allegheny, PA.

Woods, Charles. Pvt. Co. L, 14 February 1862 (at Cleveland, OH)–14 February 1865. Discharged at Winchester, VA.

Woods, James R. Pvt. Co. B. 23 May 1861–23 May 1864. Discharged at Camp 6th Cav., VA.

Worman, John J. Mustered: Pvt. Co. B, 4th OH Inf. 20 April–21 August 1861. Enlisted: 1st Sgt. Co. E, 6th U.S. Cav. 27 August 1861 (age 22 at Columbus, OH)–27 August 1864. B: 7 November 1839, Frederick Co., MD, railroad man. Hazel eyes, brown hair, ruddy complexion, 5' 8¾. Discharged at Washington, D.C. D: 1 August 1922, Fostoria, Hancock, OH.

Worrell, Isaiah W. 1st Sgt. Co. I, 29 July 1861 (age 22½ at Indiana, PA)–29 July 1864. B: 1842, Chester Co., PA, school teacher. Grey eyes,

brown hair, florid complexion, 5' 8½. POW, Funkstown. Rejoined from parole at Annapolis, MD, 24 August 1863. Discharged in the field, VA. D: 1914, New Castle, Lawrence, PA.

Wright, Alfred L. Bugler-Pvt. Cos. C, L, 3 December 1861 (age 16 at Bristol, PA)–19 February 1867. B: Bristol, Bucks, PA, farm hand. Brown eyes, brown hair, dark complexion, 5' 2½. Reenlisted: 19 February 1864 at Brandy Station, VA. Discharged 19 February 1867 at Jacksboro, TX.

Wright, George. Pvt. Co. F, 7 December 1864 (age 19 at Philadelphia, PA)–7 December 1867. B: ENG, laborer. Grey eyes, fair hair, light complexion, 5' 4. Discharged at Camp Wilson, TX.

Wright, George. Pvt.-Sgt.-1st Sgt. Co. I, 28 August 1861 (age 22 at Rochester, NY)–9 February 1867. B: Rochester, Monroe, NY, farmer. Blue eyes, dark hair, florid complexion, 5' 8¾. Reenlisted: 8 February 1864 at Brandy Station, VA. Discharged 9 February 1867 at Jacksboro, TX.

Wright, George. Rct. 29 September 1864 (age 25 at Rochester, NY)–Never joined. B: Johnsville, New Brunswick, CAN, farmer. Blue eyes, auburn hair, fair complexion, 5'10. Sub.

Wright, Warner. Pvt. Cos. C, L, 25 November 1861 (age 22 at Bristol, PA)–10 April 1864. B: November, 1836, Bristol, Bucks, PA, blacksmith. Hazel eyes, lt. brown hair, fair complexion, 5' 5. Transferred: Co. H, 21st V.R.C. Transferred: Farrier, 17th Co. 2nd Bn. V.R.C. Disability discharge at Carlisle Barracks, PA. D: 10 August 1904, Bristol, Bucks, PA.

Wurm, Daniel. Pvt. Co. I, 21 September 1861 (age 22 at Rochester, NY)–23 September 1864. B: CAN, farmer. Hazel eyes, brown hair, dark complexion, 5' 8½. Discharged in the field, VA. Enlisted: Pvt. Co. H, 4th U.S. Cav. 3 November 1864 (Rochester, NY)–22 August 1867. KIA by hostile Comanche Indians near Mountain Pass, Ft. Chadbourne, TX.

Yochum, John. Pvt. Co. B, 22 July 1861 (age 19 at Columbus, OH)–13 November 1862. B: Columbus, Franklin, OH, tailor. Blue eyes, brown hair, fair complexion, 5' 7½. D: 13 November 1862 from typhoid fever at Washington, D.C.

Young, George. Pvt. Co. F, 9 December 1864 (age 21 at Philadelphia, PA)–1 May 1865. B: Sexton, ENG, sailor. Brown eyes, brown hair, fair complexion, 5' 5. Sub. Deserted.

Young, George. Rct. 22 November 1864 (age 27 at Harrisburg, PA)–20 January 1865. B: Co. Cork, IRE, soldier. Grey eyes, brown hair, fair complexion, 6'. Sub. Deserted.

Young, George W. Mustered: Pvt-Sgt. Co. A, 45th PA Inf. 16 August 1861. Transferred: Pvt. Co. I, 6th U.S. Cav. 27 October 1862 (age 21 at Knoxville, MD)–27 August 1864. B: Centre Co., PA, miller. Blue eyes, light hair, light complexion, 5'8. Discharged at Harper's Ferry, VA.

Young, John. Rct. 1 November 1864 (age 32 at Harrisburg, PA)–21 November 1864. B: Birkenhead, Wirral Borough, Merseyside, ENG, brick layer. Blue eyes, dark hair, ruddy complexion, 5'6. Sub. Deserted.

Young, John Daul. Pvt. Co. G, 19 August 1861 (age 21 at Rochester, NY)–19 August 1864. B: December 1840, SWZ, gardener. Brown eyes, brown hair, fair complexion, 5'6¼. Discharged at Lighthouse Point, VA. D: 28 September 1926, Clinton, Clinton, IA.

Young, Mathew. Cpl. Co. M, 26 September 1864 (age 22 at Rochester, NY)–11 October 1865. B: Montreal, Quebec, CAN, laborer. Blue eyes, brown hair, light complexion, 5'11. Disability discharge at Carlisle Barracks, PA.

Young, Robert. Mustered: Pvt. Co. D, 37th PA Inf. 21 June 1861. Transferred: Pvt. Co. I, 6th U.S. Cav. 27 October 1862 (age 27 at Knoxville, MD)–27 May 1864. B: Westmoreland Co., ENG, courier. Hazel eyes, sandy hair, florid complexion, 5'10. Discharged in the field, VA.

Zawadzky, Rudolph M. (alias Thauer, Mortimer). Enlisted (Richmond, VA): Pvt. Co. B, 2nd U.S. Cav. 8 October 1856–8 August 1861. Reenlisted (Camp Rucker, D.C.). Enlisted: 1st Sgt. Cos. C, L, 2 September 1861 (age 35 at Philadelphia, PA)–30 June 1862. B: Breslau, Prussia, GER, baker. Blue eyes, brown hair, fair complexion, 5'8. Discharged at Camp east of Capitol, Washington, D.C. Transferred: Co. F, 14th U.S.V.R.C. Enlisted (Carlisle Barracks, PA): Co. B, 6th U.S. Cav. 16 August 1871–17 January 1872. Deserted.

Zehfuss, Adam. (alias: Caffoot, Adam) Pvt. Co. M, 15 October 1861 (age 19 at Pittsburgh, PA)–15 October 1864. B: Washington Co., PA, barber. Grey eyes, brown hair, fair complexion, 5'5. WIA, Williamsburg. Brought North from Baltimore to New York. MIA, Fairfield. Discharged in the field, VA. D: 21 May 1868, Pittsburgh, Allegheny, PA.

Zell, John Jacob. Mustered: Pvt. Co. F, 2nd PA Inf. 20 April 1861–26 July 1861. Mustered out at Harrisburg, PA. Enlisted: Pvt. Cos. C, L, 6th U.S. Cav. 30 January 1862 (age 18 at Philadelphia, PA)–15 September 1863. B: Elizabethtown, Lancaster, PA, brick maker. Grey eyes, brown hair, fair complexion, 5'6. D: 15 September 1863 from typhoid fever at Lincoln General Hospital, Washington, D.C.

Zettle, John. Pvt. Co. A, 20 September 1861 (at Columbus, OH)–20 September 1864. B: GER, baker. Discharged at Harper's Ferry, VA. Alternate surname: Zittle.

Zimmer, Jacob (alias Simmer, Jacob). Pvt. Co. D, 9 August 1861 (age 21 at Pittsburgh, PA)–9 August 1864. B: Simmern, Prussia, GER, shoemaker. Brown eyes, brown hair, light complexion, 5'7. Discharged in the field, VA. Mustered: Pvt. Co. G, 91st PA Inf. 23 February 1865. Mustered out 10 July 1865 at Washington, D.C.

Zimmerman, Henry. Rct. 7 August 1861 (age 24 at Cleveland, OH)–12 August 1861. B: Alsace, FRA, wagon maker. Hazel eyes, light hair, ruddy complexion, 5'7. Deserted.

Epilogue

While the Grand Review marked the official end of the 6th U.S. Cavalry's participation in the war, President Lincoln's assassination the month before had resonating effects on some of the regiment's officers that lasted for months.

Doctor William M. Notson, who left service with the regiment after the battle of Fairfield, was residing in Washington, D.C. He was one of the officers who attended the president from the theater across the street to Mr. Petersen's house. After they laid him on a bed, Lt. MacLermont of the 11th New York Cavalry, one of the attendees recalled,

> He [Notson] sent for brandy to try and revive the dying man; I pulled off his boots and opened the back window for some fresh air. Mrs. Lincoln came in, and on beholding her suffering husband, she could not control herself, and finally swooned. I helped to take her into the next room, where we laid her on a sofa. When I returned to the room where the President lay gasping it was full of people, mostly officers. Dr. Notson ordered the room to be cleared of every one under the rank of major, and as I was only a lieutenant, I had to go out, although I had done much to assist the doctor. That was the last time I saw Mr. Lincoln, as he died the next morning.

Sometime during the night, Dr. Notson also treated Secretary of State William Seward and the wounded members in his chamber who had also been targets of assassination in the same plot. After President Lincoln passed away, Dr. Notson initially attended the president's autopsy at the White House, but his participation was interrupted to again attend Secretary Seward.

Maj. Gen. David Hunter was selected to lead the honor guard for the funeral train that took the president's body home to Springfield, Illinois. The assignment was entirely fitting, since he had escorted the president-elect to Washington, D.C. from Springfield in 1861.

On May 1st, President Johnson issued an order that the alleged conspirators be tried before a nine person military commission. Maj. Gen. Hunter and Maj. Gen. August V. Kautz were both appointed to the commission, with Hunter selected first officer of the tribunal. The commission ultimately sentenced four of the conspirators to death, and dissolved after the sentences had been executed on July 15, 1865. Gen. Hunter retired the following year.

While detailing the activities of all of the regiment's officers and enlisted men would fill volumes, it is entirely appropriate to examine those of considerable achievement.

Adna Romanza Chaffee became the first officer appointed from the ranks to subsequently rise to the rank of brigadier general in the regular army. He spent 27 years in the regiment during his long career. As a general, he commanded the China Relief Expedition, and later served as the second Army Chief of Staff.

Samuel Marmaduke Whitside earned the distinction of being the first of only three soldiers in American military history to have held the highest ranks within both the enlisted and officer corps, those of sergeant major and general.

James Franklin Wade eventually reached the rank of brigadier general in the regular army and major general of volunteers during the Spanish American War.

Louis Henry Carpenter also reached the rank of brigadier general in the regular army during the Spanish American War. He also earned the Congressional Medal of Honor while commanding a company in the 10th U.S. Cavalry "Buffalo Soldiers" during the Indian Wars.

Doctor William Forwood continued in service after the war, eventually rising to be selected as the nation's Surgeon General.

In 1875, Laurence A. Williams petitioned the Adjutant-General's Office in an effort to restore his name and return to the rolls of the army. Even with the evidence presented by him, to include an 1876 letter of endorsement from now retired Major-General George B. McClellan, it was to no avail.

Samuel H. Starr returned to command the regiment in Texas after the war, retiring in 1870.

August V. Kautz served briefly in July 1865 as the military governor of New Orleans to quell rioting there before returning to the western states, where he served the remainder of his career. He retired in 1892.

David McMurtie Gregg later served as the U.S. Consul to Prague, Bohemia. He was extremely active in veterans' activities, including the Grand Army of the Republic and the Military Order of the Loyal Legion of the United States.

George C. Cram later served with the regiment after the war in Texas. In 1868, he sought a brevet lieutenant colonelcy, citing his conduct in command of the regiment at Fairfield as justification. He was apparently unaware that such a request had to be endorsed by the regimental commander, who was Samuel Starr. In a rather heated letter, Col. Starr recommended disapproval of the request, and rebutted nearly every line of Cram's version of what happened during the battle. The brevet was denied, and Cram resigned the following year.

James S. Brisbin served for 25 years on the frontier in various cavalry regiments. He is perhaps best known for commanding the battalion of the 2nd U.S. Cavalry during the Centennial Campaign in 1876 that Gen. Custer refused to take with him to Little Big Horn. He was a prolific writer, and contributed many articles and letters to Eastern periodicals on many subjects throughout his career.

James Wade, Nicholas Nolan and L. Henry Carpenter served with distinction in the 9th and 10th U.S. Cavalry "Buffalo Soldier" regiments on the frontier following the war.

George Platt went on to be leader of the 6th U.S. Cavalry Association and a national leader in the Grand Army of the Republic.

Charles Gilliams, Co. M (public domain).

Former Chief Bugler Charles Gilliams was active in the Grand Army of the Republic, and later served as the model for the bugler topping the G.A.R. memorial at Charles Evans Cemetery in Reading, Pennsylvania.

After the war, veterans of the regiment formed the 6th U.S. Cavalry Association, and held numerous reunions at the battlefield outside of Fairfield. That battle became the hallmark of the regiment's Civil War service, and they paid to erect a memorial tablet in front of the Marshall House to commemorate the battle which can still be seen today. During the fifth such reunion, they invited Confederate veterans of the battle to attend as well.

The 6th U.S. Cavalry Association remains active today, supporting the regiment's active squadrons. The 6th U.S. Cavalry Museum, located near Chickamauga National Battlefield at Fort Oglethorpe, Georgia, preserves the regiment's rich heritage. The two are very active in their perpetual quest to restore and preserve the regiment's rich history.

The regiment itself has continued to serve the army and the nation with distinction in various conflicts since the Civil War. Four squadrons actively serve today, and continue to deploy overseas in ongoing conflicts. These active squadrons still carry on the traditions established by the regiment's initial soldiers over 150 years ago.

Appendices

A. Battles and Campaign Credit

In his history of the regiment, William H. Carter cites the following letter from Gen. Sheridan to the War Department concerning proper credit for the regiment's services in battle:

> I take this occasion to strongly urge that justice be done the Sixth Cavalry, and that the battles as given in the within order issued by me be credited to this regiment on the next Army Register, so that its record, or so much as it is permitted in the Army Register, may be in a measure correct and complete. In the following battles the Sixth Cavalry fought under my personal supervision, viz.: Wilderness, Todd's Tavern, Furnaces, Spotsylvania Court House, Yellow Tavern, Meadow Bridge, Winchester, Fisher's Hill, Cedar Creek, Five Forks, Dinwiddie Court House, Clover Hill, Sailor's Creek and Appomattox Court House.

Carter lists the regiment's participation in the following actions during the war:

Date	Place	Cos. Engaged
April 5–May 5, 1862	Yorktown, VA	Regiment
May 4–5, 1862	Williamsburg, VA	A,B,D,E,F,G,H,I,K,M
May 9, 1862	Slatersville, VA	A,E,K
May 20, 1862	New Bridge,	A,B,D,E,F,G,H,I,K,M
May 23–24, 1862	Ellison's Mills, VA	A,B,D,E,F,G,H,I,K,M
May 25–29, 1862	Hanover Ct. House	A,B,D,E,F,G,H,I,K,M
June 26, 1862	Black Creek, VA	A,B,D,E,F,G,H,I,K,M
June 27, 1862	Gaines' Mills, VA	Detachments
June 30–July 2, 1862	Malvern Hill, VA	A,B,D,E,F,G,H,I,K,M
August 4–6, 1862	Malvern Hill	A,B,D,E,F,G,H,I,K,L,M
September 4, 1862	Falls Church, VA	A,B,D,E,F,G,H,I,K,L,M
September 10, 1862	Sugar Loaf Mtn	A,B,D,E,F,G,H,I,K,L,M
September 16–17, 1862	Antietam, MD	A,B,D,E,F,G,H,I,K,L,M
October 7, 1862	Charlestown, VA	A,B,D,E,F,G,H,I,K,L,M
November 1, 1862	Philomont, VA	A,B,D,E,F,G,H,I,K,L,M
November 2, 1862	Union, VA	A,B,D,E,F,G,H,I,K,L,M
November 3, 1862	Upperville, VA	A,B,D,E,F,G,H,I,K,L,M
November 5, 1862	Barbee's Crossrds	A,B,D,E,F,G,H,I,K,L,M
November 8, 1862	Washington, VA	A,B,D,E,F,G,H,I,K,L,M
November 10, 1862	Corbin's Crossrds	A,B,D,E,F,G,H,I,K,L,M
December 11–15, 1862	Fredericksburg, VA	Regiment
February 14, 1863	Richard's Ford, VA	B
April 29–May 7, 1863	Stoneman's Raid, VA	Regiment
June 9, 1863	Beverly Ford, VA	Regiment
June 17, 1863	Benton's Mill, VA	Regiment
June 21–22, 1863	Upperville, VA	Regiment
July 1–3, 1863	Gettysburg, PA	Regiment
July 6, 1863	Williamsport, MD	Regiment

July 7, 1863	Funkstown, MD	Regiment
July 7–12, 1863	Boonsboro, MD	Regiment
July 9–11, 1863	Near Funkstown, MD	Regiment
September 12–15, 1863	Brandy Station, VA	Regiment
October 11, 1863	Culpeper/Brandy Station, VA	Regiment
Nov. 26–Dec. 2, 1863	Mine Run Campaign, VA	Regiment
May 5–7, 1864	The Wilderness, VA	Regiment
May 7–8, 1864	Todd's Tavern, VA	Regiment
May 9–12, 1864	Sheridan's expedition from Todd's Tavern to James River, VA	Regiment
May 11, 1864	Yellow Tavern, VA	Regiment
May 12, 1864	Meadow Bridge, VA	Regiment
May 12, 1864	Mechanicsville, VA	Regiment
May 22–June 1, 1864	North Anna, Pamunkey and Totopotomoy Rivers, VA	Regiment
May 27–28, 1864	Hawe's Shop, VA	Regiment
May 30, 1864	Old Church, VA	Regiment
May 31–June 1, 1864	Cold Harbor, VA	Regiment
June 11–13, 1864	Trevilian Station, VA	Regiment
June–August, 1864	Before Petersburg, VA	Regiment
June 29, 1864	Dabney's Mill, VA	Regiment
July 27–29, 1864	Deep Bottom, VA	Regiment
August 16, 1864	Berryville, VA	Regiment
September 19, 1864	Winchester, VA	A,B,C,D,F,G,H,I,K,L,M
September 20, 1864	Fisher's Hill, VA	A,B,C,D,F,G,H,I,K,L,M
September 20–30, 1864	Sheridan's Expedition in the Shenandoah Valley, VA	A,B,C,D,F,G,H,I,K,L,M
October 19, 1864	Cedar Creek, VA	A,B,C,D,F,G,H,I,K,L,M
November 29, 1864	Loudoun Valley	A,B,C,D,F,G,H,I,K,L,M
March 14, 1865	Taylorsville, VA	A,B,C,D,F,G,H,I,K,L,M
March 31, 1865	Dinwiddie Courthouse, VA	A,B,C,D,F,G,H,I,K,L,M
April 1, 1865	Five Forks, VA	A,B,C,D,F,G,H,I,K,L,M
April 2, 1865	Sutherland Station	A,B,C,D,F,G,H,I,K,L,M
April 6, 1865	Sailor's Creek, VA	A,B,C,D,F,G,H,I,K,L,M
April 8–9, 1865	Appomattox Court House, VA	A,B,C,D,F,G,H,I,K,L,M

While this is an impressive array of actions, it must also be said that during the Civil War there were periods when skirmishes were a daily occurrence. Yet they were considered so unimportant that, in many instances, they can only be traced by the casualty columns of the muster-rolls. For each battle fought, there were weeks and months of outpost duty, weary marches, and fruitless scouts that tried the strength and spirit of the troops. It is a marvel that any regiment could keep up its organization at all, under such service conditions, without a depot squadron from which to recruit its depleted ranks. All honor is due to the brave men of the 6th U.S. Cavalry who constantly rallied to the standard from dismounted camps, hospitals and Southern prisons.

Two of the regiment's soldiers, Pvt. George C. Platt and Sgt. Martin P. Schwenk (also known as George P. Martin), were later awarded the Congressional Medal of Honor for their actions during the Civil War.

The regulations guiding the display of streamers upon a regimental standard have changed numerous times over the army's history, mostly for the purpose of consolidating battles into a single campaign streamer for actions during a given campaign. Under the current regulations, dated January 2001, the 6th U.S. Cavalry is authorized to display the following 11 Civil War streamers upon its standard:

Peninsula 1862
Antietam 1862
Fredericksburg 1862
Chancellorsville 1863

Gettysburg 1863
Wilderness 1864
Spotsylvania 1864
Cold Harbor 1864
Petersburg 1864–1865
Shenandoah 1864
Appomattox 1865

B. Regimental Unique Facts

The 6th U.S. Cavalry Regiment was born a unique regiment in many ways. It was the only regular cavalry regiment formed during the Civil War. From its inception, it gave birth to the humble beginnings of the modern U.S. Army Veterinarian Corps. At the onset of the Peninsula Campaign, it was part of the initial cavalry force engaged, and was the last cavalry to leave the battlefields of the same campaign. During the Gettysburg Campaign, it was utterly decimated.

The largest of the regular cavalry regiments when active campaigning started in 1862, it was the smallest at the war's end, with only two officers and 61 enlisted men present for duty on the April 1865 muster roll.

The regiment has the unique distinction of having furnished from among its gallant soldiers the first officer ever promoted from the ranks who subsequently rose to the rank of brigadier-general in the regular army. Adna Romanza Chaffee enlisted as a private in Co. K, 6th U.S. Cavalry, on July 22, 1861, and was promoted to sergeant, first sergeant, and finally lieutenant in the regiment by the end of the war. He spent 27 years with the regiment before being promoted to major and transferring to the 9th U.S. Cavalry. As a general, he commanded the China Relief Expedition, and on August 19, 1904, he was appointed as the second U.S. Army chief of staff.

Samuel Marmaduke Whitside earned the distinction of being the first of only three soldiers in American military history to have held both of the highest ranks within both the enlisted and the officer corps, that being the ranks of sergeant-major and general. Additionally, he was the regiment's inaugural sergeant major.

The Civil War produced two Congressional Medal of Honor recipients in the regiment. Their modest citations read as follows:

> Platt, George C.: Pvt., Co H. Place and date: Fairfield, Pennsylvania, July 3, 1863. Issued: July 12, 1895. Citation: Seized the regimental flag upon the death of the standard-bearer in a hand-to-hand fight and prevented it from falling into the hands of the enemy.
>
> Schwenk, Martin: Sgt., Co B. Place and date: Millerstown, Pennsylvania, July 1863. Issued: April 23, 1889. Citation: Bravery in an attempt to carry a communication through the enemy's lines; also rescued an officer from the hands of the enemy.

Some other facts that may interest the reader and historians in general follow:

The regiment's first enlisted soldier: Pvt. Henry Myers, native of St. Lawrence Co, New York, enlisted at 19 years of age on May 21, 1861, in Co. L at Champlain, New York. He originally served with Co. D, 34th New York Infantry before transferring to the regular army, with the 6th U.S. Cavalry. While with the cavalry, he served during the Peninsula, Maryland, Fredericksburg, and Operations along the Rappahannock campaigns before being discharged on May 22, 1863, at Brooks Station, Virginia. He then joined the 14th New York Heavy Artillery as a private, serving in Cos. B and E, completing his enlistment as a corporal. His enlistment record is also unique in that during the Civil War he served in all three of the major branches of service — Infantry, Cavalry, and Artillery.

The regiment's youngest soldier: Many of the men who served the regiment during the Civil War were 17, 16, or even 15 years of age. Most of these young men were buglers for the various companies. Ultimately, two soldiers enlisted at 14 years of age: bugler Frederick Mealheim and bugler Isaac Newton Light.

Bugler Frederick Mealheim enlisted at 14 years of age on July 21, 1861, at his hometown of Columbus, Ohio, in Co. E, 6th U.S. Cavalry. He was captured on July 3, 1863, at the battle of Fairfield and died on February 15, 1864 as a prisoner of war at Richmond, Virginia.

The other 14-year-old trooper was bugler Isaac Newton Light. He enlisted as a bugler in Co. C on March 29, 1864. He served nearly two years before deserting after the war on February 25, 1866, at Waco, Texas.

The regiment's oldest soldier: This distinction belongs to Johann (a.k.a. Gottlieb) Blank and Emmanuel E. Gates; both of whom joined at 48 years of age. Johann had experienced prior service with the 2nd CA Cavalry before returning to Erie, PA, and joining the 6th U.S. Cavalry on August 5, 1861. He finished his military tour in the 5th U.S. Veteran Volunteers and the General Mounted Service. Emmanuel, along with his son John, were recruited from Mount Joy, PA, on October 15, 1861. Both were local musicians. Emmanuel also earned the distinction of becoming the regiment's inaugural band leader. He received a disability discharge on July 31, 1862.

The regiment's first death: Pvt. Adam Eberle, Co. G. Originally from Bayern, Germany. Enlisted at Erie County, Pennsylvania, on August 13, 1861. Died six day later on August 19, 1861, while still at Erie.

The regiment's first soldier wounded in battle: Two of the regiment's soldiers were wounded at the first battle of Bull Run, July 21, 1861, yet both while serving in the volunteer forces, neither having reported to the 6th U.S. Cavalry.

First, the inaugural regimental commander, Col. David Hunter, was wounded in the neck and cheek while detached on duty as brigadier general of volunteers commanding a division.

Second, Lt. Hugh McQuade, recently brevetted Cpt., Co. F, 38th New York Infantry (Scott Life Guard), was also wounded at the battle. He was severely wounded in the leg while cheering his men on, later requiring the leg to be amputated.

Future officer Lt. James Brisbin was also wounded during the battle but was not yet assigned to the regiment.

The regiment's first prisoner of war: Lt. Hugh McQuade. During the first battle of Bull Run, he was severely wounded and taken prisoner, held in Libby Prison, Richmond, Virginia. He died there on December 26, 1861, as a result of his wounds. This also earned him the unfortunate distinction of being the first trooper to die at the hands of the enemy and the first trooper to die while captured as a prisoner of war.

The regiment's first soldier killed in action: Pvt. Suel Merkle, a native of Württemberg, Germany, of Co. E. He served alongside his older brother Frederick, who enlisted 13 days prior to Suel. Suel was killed in action during the regiment's inaugural battle at Williamsburg, Virginia.

C. Key Regimental Positions

Regimental Commanders

Col. David Hunter was the official regimental commander from the initial appointment of its officers on May 14, 1861, to the date he retired from military service on July 31, 1866. However, because of his political ties with President Lincoln, he was brevetted brigadier-general of volunteers just three days after the appointment of the regiment's officers. He served his country through the entire war in the volunteer forces, never serving one day with the regular army regiment to which he was appointed. In his place a number of officers gallantly led the regiment to battle:

Emory, William H.	Lt.Col.	14MAY1861–27MAR1862
Williams, Lawrence A.	Maj.	27MAR1862–15MAY1862

Kautz, August V.	Cpt.	15MAY1862–17MAY1862
Williams, Lawrence A.	Maj.	17MAY1862–26JUN1862
Kautz, August V.	Cpt.	26JUN1862–02SEP1862
Sanders, William P.	Cpt.	02SEP1862–10NOV1862
Wade, James F.	1st Lt.	10NOV1862–12DEC1862
Cram, George C.	Cpt.	12DEC1862–02FEB1863
Brisbin, James S.	Cpt.	02FEB1863–31APR1863
Cram, George C.	Cpt.	31APR1863–12MAY1863
Brisbin, James S.	Cpt.	12MAY1863–02JUN1863
Cram, George C.	Cpt.	02JUN1863–29JUN1863
Starr, Samuel H.	Maj.	29JUN1863–03JUL1863
Carpenter, Louis H.	2nd Lt.	03JUL1863
Nolan, Nicholas M.	1st Lt.	03JUL1863
Claflin, Ira W.	Cpt.	03JUL1863–07JUL1863
Coats, Albert	1st Lt.	07JUL1863–01SEP1863
Morris, Robert M., Jr.	Maj.	01SEP1863–10FEB1864
Evans, Andrew W.	Cpt.	10FEB1864–15MAR1864
Tucker, Henry	1st Lt.	15MAR1864–21APR1864
Claflin, Ira W.	Cpt.	21APR1864–21NOV1864
Abert, William S.	Cpt.	21NOV1864–30NOV1864
McLean, Hancock T.	Cpt.	30NOV1864–mid DEC1864
Nolan, Nicholas M.	1st Lt.	mid DEC1864–28FEB1865
Morris, Robert M., Jr.	Maj.	28FEB1865–14OCT1865

Regimental Sergeants Major

The middle column indicates the rank and company appointed from:

Whitside, Samuel M.	Sgt. Maj., F&S	01AUG1861–04NOV1861
Jackson, James F.	Sgt., Co. D	04NOV1861–08DEC1861
Lee, John	Sgt., Co. K	08DEC1861–12MAY1862
Tupper, Tullius C.	Sgt., Co. E	12MAY1862–22SEP1862
Armstrong, Martin P.	Sgt., Co. M	01OCT1862–01DEC1862
Carroll, Hercules G.	Sgt., Co. B	01DEC1862–23JUN1863
Cusack, Patrick	Sgt., Co. B	23JUN1863–22JAN1865
Palmer, Myron S.	1st Sgt., Co. B	23JAN1865–24MAY1865

Note: During November of 1864, many soldiers were afforded the opportunity to take leave. Sgt. Maj. Cusack was one of these men, leaving regimental quartermaster sergeant Charles J. Garrard as acting sergeant major in his absence.

Regimental Adjutants

Spangler, John W.	2nd Lt.	01JUL1861–01OCT1861
McLellan, Curwen B.	2nd Lt.	01OCT1861–30NOV1861
Audenried, Joseph C.	2nd Lt.	01DEC1861–21JUL1862
Coats, Albert	2nd Lt.	21JUL1862–18MAY1863
Kerin, Joseph	2nd Lt.	18MAY1863–09JUN1863
Coats, Albert	2nd Lt.	09JUN1863–25OCT1863
Tupper, Tullius C.	2nd Lt.	25OCT1863–11NOV1864
Chaffee, Adna R.	2nd Lt.	11NOV1864–12DEC1866

Regimental Quartermasters

Hutchins, Benjamin T.	1st Lt.	01JUL1861–01OCT1861
Spangler, John W.	2nd Lt.	01OCT1861–01FEB1863
Irwin, John A.	2nd Lt.	01FEB1863–18MAY1863

Balk, Stephen S.	2nd Lt.	28JUN1863–22AUG1863
Irwin, John A.	2nd Lt.	22AUG1863–05NOV1865

Regimental Commissaries of Subsistence

Claflin, Ira W.	1st Lt.	27AUG1862–05SEP1862
Dodge, Frederick	1st Lt.	05SEP1862–20OCT1862
Tucker, Henry	1st Lt.	26OCT1862–06AUG1865

Company Officers

A

Sanders, William P.	Cpt.	14MAY1861–19NOV1863
Hutchins, Benjamin T.	Cpt.	19NOV1863–10SEP1869
Dodge, Frederick	1st Lt.	10DEC1861–20OCT1862
Ward, Isaac M.	1st Lt.	20OCT1862–09JUL1863
Vacant		09JUL1863–25JAN1864
Whitside, Samuel M.	1st Lt.	25JAN1864–20OCT1866
McGrath, Peter	2nd Lt.	14MAY1861–24OCT1861
Vacant		24OCT1861–17JUL1862
Rousseau, John C.	2nd Lt.	17JUL1862–13JAN1863
Tupper, Tullius C.	2nd Lt.	13JAN1863–25OCT1863

B

Kautz, August V.	Cpt.	14MAY1861–28JUL1866
Enos, Herbert M.	1st Lt.	14MAY1861–23DEC1862
Vacant		23DEC1862–03FEB1863
Spangler, John W.	1st Lt.	03FEB1863–05NOV1865
McQuade, Hugh	2nd Lt.	14MAY1861–26DEC1861

C

Evans, Andrew W.	Cpt.	14MAY1861–10MAY1867
Claflin, Ira W.	1st Lt.	14MAY1861–23DEC1862
Audenried, Joseph C.	1st Lt.	23DEC1862–01JUL1866
McLellan, Curwen B.	2nd Lt.	14MAY1861–17JUL1862
Carpenter, Henry L.	2nd Lt.	17JUL1862–28SEP1864

D

Abert, William S.	Cpt.	14MAY1861–08JUN1867
Brown, Sewell H.	1st Lt.	14MAY1861–18MAY1863
Coats, Albert	1st Lt.	18MAY1863–09JUN1863
Balk, Stephen S.	2nd Lt.	01NOV1861–17JUL1862
Vacant		17JUL1862–JUN1863
Irwin, John A.	2nd Lt.	JUN1863–

E

Gregg, David McM.	Cpt.	14MAY1861–03FEB1865
Johnson, John B.	Cpt.	03FEB1865–01JAN1871
Hutchins, Benjamin T.	1st Lt.	14MAY1861–19NOV1863
Coats, Albert	2nd Lt.	26OCT1861–21JUL1862
McQuiston, Henry	2nd Lt.	21JUL1862–26SEP1863

F

Taylor, Joseph H.	Cpt.	14MAY1861–28JUL1866
McLean, Hancock T.	1st Lt.	14MAY1861–05JUL1864
Ward, Isaac M.	2nd Lt.	26OCT1861–20OCT1862
Vacant		20OCT1862–01JUN1863
Bould, Joseph	2nd Lt.	01JUN1863–25FEB1865

G

Gregg, John I.	Cpt.	14MAY1861–28JUL1866
Paulding, Tatnall	1st Lt.	14MAY1861–20OCT1864
Balder, Christian	2nd Lt.	26OCT1861–23DEC1862

H

Savage, John	Cpt.	14MAY1861–23DEC1862
Dodge, Frederick	1st Lt.	14MAY1861–10DEC1861
Kerin, Joseph	1st Lt.	23DEC1862–JUN1863
Balder, Christian	1st Lt.	JUN1863–3JUL1863
Kerin, Joseph	2nd Lt.	26OCT1861–23DEC1862
Irwin, John A.	2nd Lt.	17JUL1862–28JUN1863
Chaffee, Adna R.	2nd Lt.	28JUN1863–22FEB1865

I

Cram, George C.	Cpt.	14MAY1861–12OCT1867
Johnson, John B.	1st Lt.	14MAY1861–03FEB1865
Stoll, Andrew	2nd Lt.	01NOV1861–19NOV1863

K

Lowell, Charles R., Jr.	Cpt.	14MAY1861–20OCT1864
Paulding, Tatnall	Cpt.	20OCT1864–01JUL1866
Wade, James F.	1st Lt.	14MAY1861–01MAY1866
Balk, Stephen S.	2nd Lt.	20AUG1861–01NOV1861
Whitside, Samuel M.	2nd Lt.	01NOV1861–25JAN1864

L

Brisbin, James S.	Cpt.	05AUG1861–28JUL1866
Leavenworth, Mark F.	1st Lt.	14MAY1861–06AUG1861
Tucker, Henry	1st Lt.	05AUG1861–26OCT1862
McLellan, Curwen B.	1st Lt.	26OCT1862–28JUL1866
Tupper, Tullius C.	2nd Lt.	17JUL1862–13JAN1863
Vacant		13JAN1863–13MAR1863
Chaffee, Adna R.	2nd Lt.	13MAR1863–28JUN1863

M

Hays, Henry B.	Cpt.	05AUG1861–05JUL1864
McLean, Hancock T.	Cpt.	05JUL1864–14MAY1868
Balk, Stephen S.	1st Lt.	17JUL1862–04MAY1864
Balder, Christian	2nd Lt.	26OCT1861–01NOV1861
Madden, Daniel	2nd Lt.	01NOV1861–04MAY1864

Chapter Notes

Chapter 1

1. Thomas O'Brien and Oliver Diefendorf, *General Orders of the War Department, Embracing the Years 1861, 1862 and 1863*, vol. 1, p. 37.

2. Ezra J. Warner, *Generals in Blue*, 243–244; Edward A. Miller, Jr., *Lincoln's Abolitionist General*, 63; George W. Cullum, *Biographical Register of the Officers and Graduates of the U.S. Military Academy*, vol. 1, pp. 290–291; Francis B. Heitman, *Historical Register and Dictionary of the United States Army*, vol. 1, p. 557 (all references are to volume 1 unless otherwise noted).

3. Heitman, 405–406, Cullum, vol. 1, pp. 481–483; Warner, *Generals in Blue*, 142–143; William Emory Papers, Special Collections, University of Maryland Libraries.

4. Emory papers

5. Ibid.

6. O'Brien and Diefendorf, *General Orders*, vol. 1, pp. 64–65.

7. Warner, *Generals in Blue*, 243.

8. Guy V. Henry, *Military Record of Civilian Appointments in the United States Army*, vol. 1, pp. 513–514.

9. Heitman, 1062; Henry, vol. 1, p. 221.

10. Cullum, 495–496; Heitman, 409; Henry, vol. 1, p. 53.

11. Heitman, 176.

12. Cullum, vol. 2, p. 673; Heitman, 407.

13. Heitman, 622.

14. Ibid, 681; Henry, vol. 2, p. 146.

15. Heitman, 667. Henry, vol. 2, p. 143.

16. Jeffry D. Wert, *Cavalryman of the Lost Cause*, 19.

17. Cullum, vol. 2, p. 668;

Heitman, 858; Warner, *Generals in Blue*, 419–420.

18. Cullum, vol. 2, pp. 504–506; Albert B. Faust, *The German Element in the United States*, 559–560; Heitman, 586; Lawrence G. Kautz, *August V. Kautz, USA: Biography of a Civil War General*, 16–18; Whitelaw Reid, *Ohio in the War: Her Statesmen, Generals and Soldiers*, vol. 1, pp. 844–848; Warner, *Generals in Blue*, 257–258.

19. Heitman, 133; Henry, vol. 1, p. 53; James L. Bowen, *Massachusetts in the War, 1861–1865*, 876.

20. *Book of Biographies, Biographical Sketches of Leading Citizens of Berks County, Pa.*, 11–15; Cullum, vol. 2, pp. 613–614; Heitman, 476–477; Warner, *Generals in Blue*, 187–188.

21. Cullum, vol. 2, pp. 660–661; Heitman, 947.

22. Heitman, 477; Henry, vol. 1, p. 155.

23. Heitman, 861; Henry, vol. 2, p. 184.

24. Heitman, 334; Henry, vol. 1, p. 285.

25. Bowen, *Massachusetts in the War*, 956–958; Heitman, 645; Henry, vol. 2, p. 132; Warner, *Generals in Blue*, 284–285.

26. Cullum, vol. 2, pp. 693–694; Heitman, 302.

27. Heitman, 253; Henry, vol. 2, p. 53.

28. Heitman, 560; Henry, vol. 2, p. 292.

29. Heitman, 675.

30. Ibid, 776; Henry, vol. 2, p. 165.

31. Heitman, 376.

32. Heitman, 576; Henry, vol. 1, pp. 351–352.

33. Heitman, 991; William H. Powell, *Powell's Records of Living*

Officers of the United States Army, 619.

34. James R. Arnold, *Jeff Davis's Own: Cavalry, Comanches, and the Battle for the Texas Frontier*, 203 and 245; Heitman, 909.

35. Heitman, 676; Henry, vol. 2, pp. 144–145; Powell, *Powell's Records of Living Officers of the United States Army*, 387–388.

36. O'Brien and Diefendorf, *General Orders of the War Department, Embracing the Years 1861, 1862 and 1863*, vol. 1, pp. 37–38.

37. Ibid. Due to the similarities between the letters I and J, no army regiments constituted a Company J in order to avoid confusion.

38. Ibid., 39.

39. Henry McQuiston memoir, McQuiston Papers, Special Collections, United States Military Academy Library, West Point, New York (hereafter cited as "McQuiston memoir").

40. Ibid.

41. *Philadelphia Press*, September 19, 1861.

42. *Pittsburgh Post*, June 28, 1861.

43. Arthur B. Fox, *Pittsburgh During the American Civil War 1860–1865*, 44.

44. Sidney Morris Davis, *Common Soldier Uncommon War, Life as a Cavalryman in the Civil War*, 18–19.

45. "Romance of an Ohio Woman Who Fought by Her Husband's Side as a Dare-devil Cavalry Man," *Cleveland Leader*, October 7, 1896; DeAnne Blanton and Lauren M. Cook, *They Fought Like Demons: Women Soldiers in the Civil War*, 30–31; National Archives, M233, *Register of Enlistments in the U.S. Army, 1798–1914* (hereafter cited as "Register of Enlistments").

46. Davis, *Common Soldier Uncommon War*, 21.
47. 1860 census information. The two cities had a combined population of 50,000 vs. 150,000 in Cincinnati.
48. Register of Enlistments.
49. Ibid.
50. Edward W. Emerson, *Life and Letters of Charles Russell Lowell*, 216.
51. William H. Carter, *Life of General Chaffee*, 11–12.
52. McQuiston memoir.
53. Ibid.
54. Register of Enlistments; *Wyoming County Mirror*, September 11, 1861.
55. *Lancaster Examiner and Herald*, October 30, 1861.
56. Register of Enlistments.
57. Ibid.
58. *Pittsburgh Evening Chronicle*, July 27, 1861, 3; Fox, *Pittsburgh During the American Civil War*, 44.
59. McQuiston memoir.
60. Davis, 23.
61. Ibid, 24.
62. Ibid.
63. McQuiston memoir.
64. Davis, 28.
65. Ibid, 30.
66. Ibid.
67. McQuiston memoir.
68. Ibid.
69. Ibid.
70. Davis, 29.
71. O'Brien and Diefendorf, *General Orders of the War Department*, vol. 1, pp. 100–101.
72. Davis, 29.
73. Cullum, vol. 2, pp. 824–825; Heitman, 175.
74. Heitman, 516; Henry, vol. 1, p. 106.
75. Henry, vol. 1, p. 140; Powell, *Powell's Records of Living Officers*, 86; Theophilus F. Rodenbough, *From Everglade to Canyon with the Second Dragoons*, 448; *The War of the Rebellion: Official Records of the Union and Confederate Armies*, vol. 4, p. 381 (hereafter cited as "OR"; all further references are to series 1, unless otherwise noted).
76. Heitman, 973; Henry, vol. 2, p. 347.
77. National Archives, *M744, roll 61: Monthly Return of the 6th Cavalry Regiment, August 1861–December 1869* (hereafter cited as "Monthly Returns").
78. McQuiston memoir.

Chapter 2

1. Davis, 35–38.
2. McQuiston memoir.
3. Davis, 39.
4. McQuiston memoir.
5. Ibid.
6. Davis, 42.
7. McQuiston memoir.
8. Ibid.
9. Heitman, 41; O'Brien and Diefendorf, 152.
10. Heitman, 281; Henry, vol. 1, pp. 141–142; Warner, *Generals in Blue*, 68–69.
11. Heitman, 1041.
12. McQuiston memoir.
13. Davis, 59.
14. McQuiston memoir.
15. Davis, 51.
16. L. Henry Carpenter Letters, Pennsylvania Historical Society (hereafter cited as "Carpenter letters").
17. Philip St. George Cooke, *Cavalry Tactics*.
18. McQuiston memoir.
19. Davis, 54; Monthly Returns.
20. McQuiston memoir.
21. Davis, 65; *New York Times*, October 10, 1861.
22. Carpenter letters.
23. McQuiston memoir.
24. Davis, 45. Author's note: Davis claims they received a ration per day, but we could not substantiate this claim, and it seems unlikely.
25. Ibid., 46.
26. Davis, 69–70.
27. Carpenter letters.
28. Ibid.
29. Davis, 75–76.
30. Ibid., 75.
31. Carpenter letters; McQuiston memoir.
32. Carpenter letters.
33. Monthly Returns.
34. Heitman, 1001; Henry, vol. 2, p. 215; Register of Enlistments.
35. Henry, vol. 2, p. 236.
36. Monthly Returns.
37. Heitman, 312; Henry, vol. 2, p. 254.
38. B. Nathaniel Owen letters, B. Conrad Bush Collection; Monthly Returns.
39. Henry, vol. 1, pp. 167–168; O'Brien and Diefendorf, 192; Powell, 364; Register of Enlistments.
40. Heitman, 928; Henry, vol. 2, p. 194.
41. O'Brien and Diefendorf, 192.

42. McQuiston memoir.
43. Carpenter letters.
44. Ibid.
45. Owen letters.
46. Monthly Returns.
47. Carpenter letters.
48. Davis, 81.
49. Monthly Returns.
50. Heitman, 791; Henry, vol. 1, p. 105; O'Brien and Diefendorf, 192.
51. Monthly Returns.
52. Robert Steel Letters, Beaver County Historical Society.
53. McQuiston memoir.
54. Davis, 82.
55. *Supplement to the Official Records of the Union and Confederate Armies*, ed. Janet B. Hewett, vol. 1, pp. 356–359 (hereafter cited as "SOR"; all further references are to part 1, unless otherwise noted).
56. Carter, 15.
57. SOR, vol. 1, p. 357.
58. Steel letters.
59. Edward W. Emerson, *The Life and Letters of Charles Russell Lowell*, 220–221.
60. SOR, vol. 1, p. 357.
61. Ibid., 355.
62. Carpenter letters.
63. James H. Cory Letters, Archives and Regional History Collections, Western Michigan University, December 13, 1861.
64. SOR, vol. 1, p. 359.
65. Carpenter letters.
66. SOR, vol. 1, p. 360.
67. Carpenter letters.
68. Monthly Returns.
69. Carpenter letters.
70. Carter, 19–20.
71. Carpenter letters.
72. Ibid.; Monthly Returns.
73. Carpenter letters.
74. Ibid.
75. Davis, 93.
76. Carpenter letters.
77. McQuiston memoir.
78. Davis, 94.
79. Carpenter letters.
80. Ibid.
81. Owen letters.
82. Davis, 98.
83. Kautz, *August V. Kautz*, 75.
84. SOR, vol. 2, p. 111.
85. Davis, 100.
86. Frederic Dennison, *Sabers and Spurs: The First Rhode Island Cavalry in the Civil War*, 43.
87. Carter, 23.
88. Davis, 110.
89. SOR, vol. 2, p. 112.
90. Ibid., 113.

91. Davis, 103.
92. SOR, vol. 2, p. 113.

Chapter 3

1. Davis, 104; Monthly Returns.
2. SOR, vol. 2, p. 113.
3. Davis, 108.
4. Ibid., 111.
5. Ibid., 111–112.
6. Carter, 24.
7. SOR, vol. 2, p. page 115.
8. Davis, 114.
9. OR, vol. 11, pt. 1, p. 423.
10. Ibid., 426; SOR, vol. 2, p. 116.
11. Ibid., 444.
12. Ibid., 442.
13. Ibid., 430.
14. Davis, 119.
15. Ibid., 442.
16. Ibid.
17. Ibid., 445.
18. Ibid., 439.
19. Ibid., 439–440.
20. Davis, 120.
21. Ibid., 122.
22. Monthly Returns, 1862 Annual Return. A list of the wounded follows: Co. A: Corp. Henry A. Pauli, Pvts. James Alexander, James Bonner, George Kraft, John Maglett, James H. Ortt, Charles F.H. Roemer and Henry Vanmoss; Co. G: Sgt. Martin Armstrong, Corp. James Allen, Bugler Andrew Schwartz, Pvts. George Baum, Adam Cafoot, Joshua Kreps, Robert McBride and Henry Parks; Co. G: 1st Sgt Andrew F. Swan and Pvt. Parker Flansburg.
23. OR, Vol. 11, pt. 1, p. 425.
24. Ibid., 428, 439–440.
25. Francis Colburn Adams, *The Story of a Trooper*, 393.
26. Davis, 127.
27. Carter, 30.
28. Emerson, *Life and Letters of Charles Russell Lowell*, 23–24.
29. Carter, 33.
30. Davis, 133.
31. Monthly Returns, May 1862.
32. *Western New Yorker*, May 22, 1862.
33. SOR, vol. 2, p. 117.
34. Davis, 135; Carter, 32; Heitman, 184; Monthly Returns.
35. Carter, 33.
36. Davis, 136–137.
37. *Western New Yorker*, May 29, 1862.
38. Carter, 33.

39. Ibid., 34.
40. Ibid.
41. SOR, vol. 2, pp. 117–118.
42. Ibid., 119.
43. Carter, 41; Monthly Returns.
44. Ibid.
45. SOR, vol. 2, p. 120.
46. Ibid., 121.
47. Davis, 147.
48. SOR, vol. 2, p. 121.
49. Owen letters.
50. OR, vol. 11, pt. 1, p. 693.
51. Ibid.
52. Ibid.
53. Ibid.
54. Davis, 152.
55. *Western New Yorker*, April 19, 1862.
56. Monthly Returns.
57. Davis, 152.
58. Carter, 42.
59. SOR, vol. 2, p. 123.
60. OR, vol. 11, pt. 1, p. 997.
61. Ibid.
62. SOR, vol. 2, p. 124.
63. Owen letters.
64. Carter, 46–50.
65. SOR, vol. 2, p. 125.
66. Owen letters.
67. SOR, vol. 2, p. 127.
68. Carter, 43. Williams was absent on sick leave from June 26 to October 5, then assigned on detached service in New York City. He was absent without leave from November 1862 until March 1863, then dismissed by the president on March 11, 1863. Williams attempted to clear his name and to be reinstated as an officer after the war but was unsuccessful. His brother, William Orton Williams, resigned his commission in 1861 and was later executed by Union authorities as a spy in the western theater of the war.
69. SOR, vol. 2, p. 127.
70. OR, vol. 11, pt. 2, p. 42.
71. SOR, vol. 2, p. 128; Carter, 51.
72. Davis, 162.
73. Carpenter letters.
74. Monthly Returns.
75. Carpenter letters.
76. Monthly Returns.
77. Carpenter letters.
78. SOR, vol. 2, p. 129; Carter, 52.
79. Davis, 185.
80. Carpenter letters.
81. Ibid.
82. Carter, 52.
83. SOR, vol. 2, p. 130.
84. Carter, 52.

85. SOR, vol. 2, p. 131.
86. Carpenter letters.
87. Ibid.
88. Monthly Returns.
89. SOR, vol. 2, p. 132.
90. Ibid.
91. Owen letters.
92. Davis, 192.
93. Carpenter letters.
94. Davis, 196.
95. Carpenter letters.
96. Davis, 198; Carpenter letters.
97. Carter, 52; Davis, 198; Monthly Returns. The casualties were Co. B: Pvts. Charles Croishant and Joseph Van Zant, killed, and George Bartlett, fatally wounded; Co. H: Pvts. Thomas Peterman, killed; and Albert Bordy, wounded. Pvt. Lyman Hall of Co. E was wounded during the artillery duel and died of his wounds en route from Fortress Monroe to New York City.
98. Davis, 201.
99. James Brisbin Letters, Gilder-Lehman Institute of American History
100. SOR, vol. 2, p. 134.
101. Ibid.
102. Ibid; Davis, 204.
103. Carter, 54.
104. SOR, vol. 2, p. 134.
105. Ibid; Carpenter letters.
106. Carpenter letters.
107. Owen letters.
108. SOR, vol. 2, pp. 136–137. The authors understand that Cpt. Kautz could be portrayed as intransigent and unsupportive of his superiors in some of the quotes used in this book. We have endeavored at all times to be fair to the truest information available. Although very critical in his discussion of Maj. Williams, our excerpts are from his diary, not the autobiography he published later for public consumption, which could have been abridged in hindsight. While he apparently disliked Pleasonton intensely, according to army regulations at the time, he was in the right on this matter. Interestingly, L. Henry Carpenter, while still a sergeant, wrote of Kautz the same month: "Captain Kautz is liked very much by the men and seems to be a very efficient officer."
109. Ibid., 138.
110. OR, vol. 11, pt. 2, p. 965
111. Ibid., 966.

Chapter 4

Note: The best coverage available of the Maryland Campaign is Thomas Clemens' *The Maryland Campaign of 1862.*

1. OR, vol. 19, pt. 2, p. 172; Davis, 258.
2. SOR, vol. 2, p. 139; Monthly Returns.
3. Monthly Returns.
4. Ibid. Thomas G. Clemens, ed., *The Maryland Campaign of September 1862*, vol. 1, p. 165; Davis, 211. According to Davis, Boynton was sick in the hospital and did not participate in the Peninsula Campaign. If this is true, he was killed in his first encounter with the enemy.
5. SOR, vol. 2, p. 139.
6. Ibid; Carter, 57; Davis, 218.
7. Clemens, 176.
8. *New York Times*, September 15, 1862; Monthly Returns; Carter, 58. It is fortunate the *Times* correspondent was present to record the fight, as Cpt. Sanders' report was not included in the *Official Records.*
9. Clemens, 177.
10. *New York Times*, September 15, 1862.
11. OR, vol. 19, pt. 1, p. 825.
12. OR, vol. 51, pt. 1, p. 824; Davis, 225–226.
13. Carter, 57.
14. Ibid., 58.
15. OR, vol. 19, pt. 1, p. 378.
16. Ibid., 212.
17. Davis, 229.
18. Monthly Returns; Heitman, 973–974; Henry, vol. 1, p. 184.
19. Monthly Returns; Heitman, 848.
20. Heitman, 750; Henry, vol. 2, p. 317.
21. Heitman, 565; Henry, vol. 2, pp. 115–116.
22. Heitman, 284; Henry, vol. 2, pp. 57–58; Carpenter letters.
23. Carter, 58–59; Davis, 231.
24. *Wyoming County Mirror,* October 8, 1862.
25. Davis, 232.
26. Carter, 59; Davis, 236–237.
27. OR, vol. 19, pt. 2, pp. 14–15.
28. Monthly Returns.
29. Davis, 234–235. Although Davis lists his name as Bappenger in his book, additional research in the enlistment records show the soldier's actual name as August Poppenhager.
30. OR, vol. 19, pt. 2, p. 96.
31. Ibid., 97.
32. Ibid.
33. Ibid., 92.
34. OR, vol. 19, pt. 2, p. 460.
35. Ibid., 476–478.
36. Carpenter letters.
37. Davis, 235–236; Monthly Returns; Register of Enlistments.
38. Carter, 61; Monthly Returns.
39. Ibid.
40. OR, Vol. 19, pt. 2, p. 125.
41. Monthly Returns. The wounded were Co. L: Sgt. Daniel H. Jones, Corp. Charles Reeves and Pvt. Horatio Sherman, and Co. M: Pvt. D.K. Mockbee.
42. Carter, 70.
43. Carpenter letters.
44. OR, vol. 19, pt. 2, p. 126; Monthly Returns. The wounded were Pvt. John Merrylees, Co. A, Pvt. Edward Addis, Co. B and Pvt. William Deagan, Co. L.
45. Ibid., 119; Davis, 277.
46. Ibid., 127.
47. Carpenter letters; Monthly Returns; Warner, *Generals in Blue,* 420.
48. Davis, 280–281.
49. Ibid.
50. Carpenter letters; Carter, 66.
51. Davis, 283.
52. George Platt Reminiscences, David E. Cronin Collection, Series II, New York Historical Society; Monthly Returns. The monthly returns support Platt's story in that he was one of a detail of ten men detailed to this battery during the Maryland Campaign.
53. Davis, 285.
54. OR, vol. 19, pt. 2, p. 128.
55. Monthly Returns.

Chapter 5

1. Carter, *From Yorktown to Santiago,* 67; Monthly Returns.
2. Warner, *Generals in Blue,* 420; Monthly Returns.
3. Carpenter letters.
4. Davis, 288–289.
5. Carter, 68.
6. Carpenter letters.
7. Carter, 70–71.
8. Monthly Returns.
9. Carter, 69.
10. Carpenter letters.
11. Davis, *Common Soldier, Uncommon War,* 288–289; McQuiston memoir.
12. McQuiston memoir.

13. Davis, 335; Monthly Returns.
14. Carpenter letters.
15. Ibid.
16. Davis, 307.
17. Carter, 67.
18. Carpenter letters; Carter, 68–69; Monthly Returns. Carter reports 2 men and 8 horses wounded and 2 horses killed, but the Monthly Returns show nothing for this engagement.
19. Frank A. O'Reilly, *The Fredericksburg Campaign,* 110.
20. OR, vol. 21, p. 220.
21. Ibid.
22. Carpenter letters.
23. Owen letters.
24. Davis, 322.
25. Ibid., 348.
26. Monthly Returns.
27. Carpenter letters.
28. Davis, 337.
29. Ibid., 338.
30. Carter, 71–72.
31. Carpenter letters.
32. Ibid.
33. Eric Wittenberg, *The Union Cavalry Comes of Age,* 46.
34. Carpenter letters.
35. Carter, 69–70.
36. Carpenter letters.
37. Carter, 71.
38. Carpenter letters.
39. Davis, 357.
40. Ibid., 349.
41. Owen letters.
42. Wittenberg, 26.
43. Ibid.
44. Owen letters.
45. Ibid.
46. Monthly Returns.

Chapter 6

Note: The most detailed account of the raid can be found in Eric Wittenberg's *The Union Cavalry Comes of Age.* Due to the multitude of moving pieces, it is a very difficult action to follow.

1. Theophilus F. Rodenbough, "Personal Recollections The Stoneman Raid of '63," in *From Everglade to Canyon with the Second Dragoons,* 270–273.
2. Carter, *From Yorktown to Santiago,* 77.
3. OR, vol. 25, pt. 1, p. 1088.
4. *Western New Yorker,* April 30, 1863.
5. Carter, 76.
6. OR, vol. 25, pt. 1, pp. 1067–1068.

7. Gracey, *Annals of the Sixth Pennsylvania Cavalry*, 137.

8. Rodenbough, "Personal Recollections," 278.

9. Gracey, 140.

10. Eric Wittenberg, *The Union Cavalry Comes of Age*, 191.

11. Ibid., 194.

12. Carter, 78.

13. OR, vol. 25, pt. 1, pp. 1060–1061.

14. Carpenter letters.

15. OR, vol. 25, pt. 1, pp. 1062, 1089; Carpenter letters.

16. OR, vol. 25, pt. 1, p. 1089.

17. Ibid. Wittenberg, 223.

18. Ibid., 225.

19. OR, vol. 25, pt. 1, p. 1063.

20. OR, vol. 25, pt. 1, p. 1090.

21. Carter, 79.

22. OR, vol. 25, pt. 1, p. 1090.

23. Carpenter letters.

24. Carter, 80.

25. Ibid.

26. James Brisbin letters, Iowa Historical Society.

27. Carpenter letters; Monthly Returns.

28. Ibid.

29. Carter, 82–83; Wittenberg, 246.

30. Carpenter letters.

31. Wittenberg, 249.

32. Carpenter letters.

33. Monthly Returns.

34. OR, Vol. 27, pt. 3, pp. 27–28.

35. Wittenberg, 255.

36. Davis, 391.

Chapter 7

1. Gracey, *Annals of the Sixth Pennsylvania Cavalry*, 157; Davis, *Common Soldier Uncommon War*, 391.

2. Of necessity, this chapter focuses on the regiment's participation in the battle. For a more comprehensive account of the entire battle, see Wittenberg, *The Battle of Brandy Station*, Downey, *Clash of Cavalry*, and Longacre, *The Cavalry at Gettysburg*.

3. John Buford to Lieutenant Colonel A.J. Alexander, June 13, 1863, Joseph Hooker Papers, Huntington Library, San Marino, CA. Buford's official report of the battle for some reason was not included in the *Official Records of the Civil War*.

4. Ibid.; McQuiston memoir.

5. Monthly Returns; Carpenter letters.

6. Ibid., Draft of Cram's official report contained in Carpenter letter to father, June 11, 1863.

7. Downey, *Clash of Cavalry*, 95.

8. William N. Pickerill, *History of the Third Indiana Cavalry*, 75–77.

9. Wittenberg, *The Battle of Brandy Station*, 89.

10. Buford to Alexander, June 13, 1863.

11. Ibid.

12. Gracey, 159.

13. Cram to Sir, June 11, 1863, Hooker Papers.

14. Wesley Merritt, "Personal Recollections — Beverly's Ford to Mitchell's Station, 1863," in *From Everglade to Canon with the Second Dragoons*, ed. Theophilus F. Rodenbough, 285–286.

15. Davis, 392.

16. Henry C. Whelan to Charles C. Cadwalader, June 11, 1863, Cadwalader Family Collection, Historical Society of Pennsylvania, Philadelphia.

17. Davis, 392.

18. Carpenter letters.

19. Robert Trout, *Memoirs of the Stuart Horse Artillery Battalion*, 206.

20. Gracey, 160.

21. Trout, 206.

22. Carpenter letters.

23. *New York Times*, June 11, 1863.

24. James F. Hart, in the *Philadelphia Weekly Times*, June 26, 1880, as quoted in Henry B. McClellan's *I Rode with Stuart*, 267–268.

25. Wise, *The Long Arm of Lee*, vol. 2, p. 587.

26. Gracey, 161.

27. Davis, 392. The *New York Times*, June 11, 1863, documents Miller's rank and wound.

28. Christian Balder to Tattnall Paulding, June 12, 1863, Tattnall Paulding Papers, Historical Society of Pennsylvania.

29. Ibid.

30. McQuiston memoir.

31. Wittenberg, *The Battle of Brandy Station*, 148.

32. Buford to Alexander, June 13, 1863.

33. Beale, *A Lieutenant of Cavalry in Lee's Army*, 96; Davis, 395.

34. William H. Carter, *From Yorktown to Santiago with the Sixth U.S. Cavalry*, 86.

35. Buford to Alexander, June 13, 1863.

36. Balder to Paulding, June 12, 1863.

37. Ibid.

38. McQuiston memoir.

39. Ibid.

40. Ibid. Casualty lists for the regiment show no one wounded in the head or killed from this squadron.

41. Carpenter letters.

42. Cram to Sir, June 11, 1863; Davis, 400.

43. Carpenter letters.

44. McQuiston memoir.

45. Cram to Sir, June 11, 1863; Carpenter letters.

46. Ibid.

47. McQuiston memoir.

48. Ibid.

49. Carpenter letters.

50. Cram to Sir, June 11, 1863, National Archives, M744, roll 61, *Monthly Return of the 6th Cavalry Regiment, August 1861-December 1869*. The regimental casualties for the battle in addition to the officers were Co. A: Sgt. James McAlister, killed, Corporal Wesley S. House, wounded, Pvts. Patrick Doyle, George Cleveland, Patrick Dougherty, Jacob Estlow, William Floyd, Charles G. Travis, and Peter Mahoney, wounded; Co. C: Corp. William Burns, wounded in side, Pvts. Thomas Lee, Alfred Taro, James Brennan, and Herman Groff, wounded; Co. D: Pvts. Christian Petzger, David S. Beach, William Williams, and Reese Jones, wounded; Co. E: Pvt. Bruce Dingman, wounded in hip; Co. F: Pvt. Spencer Viall, killed, Corp. Charles F. Miller, wounded in left breast, Corp. Peter Simonet, wounded; Co. G: Pvt. Jacob Palk, killed, Sgts. John F. Clark and Haskell Coats, wounded, Pvt. Jacob Couts, wounded; Co. I: Pvt. Edward Faulkner, killed, Pvt. John P. Kinney, wounded. Co. K: Pvt. Wilson, killed, Corp. Papke, wounded; Co. M: Sgt. Alvah Bradmon, Corp. John Noble and Pvt. Henry Parks, wounded.

51. Buford to Alexander, June 13, 1863.

52. Cram to Sir, June 11, 1863.

53. Ibid.

54. Carter, 90; Heitman, 594; Henry, vol. 2, pp. 119–120.

55. Heitman, 928; Henry, vol. 2, 194; *Official Army Register for 1865*, 94.

Chapter 8

1. Carter, *From Yorktown to Santiago*, 91; Carpenter letters; Monthly Returns.
2. Longacre, *The Cavalry at Gettysburg*, 92.
3. Davis, 420.
4. Ibid.
5. OR, vol. 27, pt. 1, 58.
6. Starr, *The Union Cavalry in the Civil War*, Vol. 1, p. 399.
7. Ibid., 64.
8. Wesley Merritt, "Personal Recollections: Beverly Ford to Mitchell's Station," in Theophilus F. Rodenbough's *From Everglade to Canyon with the Second Cavalry*, 294.
9. Longacre, *Lincoln's Cavalrymen*, 164.
10. Davis, 401.
11. Ibid., 403.
12. Monthly Returns.
13. *Western New Yorker*, July, 2, 1863.
14. Davis, 404.
15. Ibid.; McQuiston memoir.
16. Carter, 91; Monthly Returns.
17. Davis, 405.
18. McQuiston memoir.
19. Ibid.
20. Davis, 408; Monthly Returns.
21. Ibid., 409.
22. McQuiston memoir.
23. Ibid.
24. Longacre, *Lincoln's Cavalrymen*, 170.
25. McQuiston memoir.
26. OR, vol. 27, pt 1, p. 947.
27. Longacre, *Lincoln's Cavalrymen*, 171.
28. Davis, 411.
29. Ibid., 412.
30. McQuiston memoir.
31. Davis, 414.
32. McQuiston memoir.
33. Davis, 414.
34. McQuiston memoir.
35. OR, vol. 27, pt. 1, p. 947.
36. Longacre, *The Cavalry at Gettysburg*, 128.
37. McQuiston memoir.
38. Davis, 416.
39. Longacre, *The Cavalry at Gettysburg*, 128.
40. Davis, 419.
41. Carter, 93.
42. *New York Times*, June 26, 1863. The other wounded soldiers were all privates: Jacob Couts, Co. G; Robert H. Ewert, Co. M; Michael Kurnan, Co. A; Thomas Murray, Co. M; and John Wright, Co. E. Three privates were listed as missing: Joshua W. DuBois, Co. E; Thomas McKeffrey, Co. F; and Nelson H. Turner, Co. B; also Muster rolls.
43. OR, vol. 27, pt. 1, p. 947.
44. Muster rolls; family history of Hercules G. Carroll.
45. Davis, 420.
46. Longacre, *The Cavalry at Gettysburg*, 164.
47. Davis, 421.
48. Carter, 95.
49. McQuiston memoir.
50. Davis, 424.
51. Carter, 95; muster rolls.
52. Longacre, *The Cavalry at Gettysburg*, 169.
53. Ibid.
54. Longacre, *The Cavalry at Gettysburg*, 166.
55. Wittenberg, *Rush's Lancers*, 122.
56. Davis, 426. We were not able to determine the identity of the officer.

Chapter 9

1. James W. Milgram, "The Libby Prison Correspondence of Tattnall Paulding," *The American Philatelist* 89 (December 1975), 1114.
2. Charles F. Miller, "With the Sixth New York Cavalry in the Civil War," *Historical Wyoming* 19, no. 2 (January 1966), 38. Because this article is mistitled, it is largely unknown. Author Eric Wittenberg generously brought it to our attention and provided a partial copy of the article. The original article is available from the Wyoming County Historical Society in New York.
3. Milgram, "The Libby Prison Correspondence of Tattnall Paulding," 1115.
4. Monthly Returns.
5. Miller, "With the Sixth New York," 39.
6. Davis, *Common Soldier, Uncommon War*, 427.
7. Milgram, "The Libby Prison Correspondence of Tattnall Paulding," 1115.
8. Samuel Starr papers; Carter, *Yorktown to Santiago*, 95.
9. Davis, 428.
10. Milgram, "The Libby Prison Correspondence of Tattnall Paulding," 1115.
11. Davis, *Common Soldier, Uncommon War*, 428.
12. Ibid., 428–9.
13. OR, vol. 27, part 2, p. 752.
14. John W. Busey and David G. Martin, *Regimental Strengths and Losses at Gettysburg*, 2nd ed., 198.
15. Ibid., 201.
16. Ibid., 752.
17. T.J. Young, "The Battle of Fairfield, Pennsylvania," *Confederate Veteran* 5 (1897), 251.
18. Milgram, "The Libby Prison Correspondence of Tattnall Paulding," 1115.
19. Davis, 431.
20. OR, vol. 27, part 2, p. 752.
21. Ibid.
22. Ibid., 760.
23. William N. McDonald, *A History of the Laurel Brigade*, 155.
24. Davis, 431.
25. McDonald, *History of the Laurel Brigade*, 155.
26. Richard L. Armstrong, *Seventh Virginia Cavalry*, 57.
27. OR, vol. 27, part 2, p. 760.
28. John H. Connell, "A Cavalry Fight: A Confederate Tells of the Collision Between the 7th Va. and 6th U.S. Cavalry," *National Tribune*, April 30, 1891.
29. OR, vol. 27, part 2, p. 760.
30. Ibid., 752.
31. Connell, "A Cavalry Fight."
32. John Blue, *Hanging Rock Rebel: Lt. John Blue's War in West Virginia and the Shenandoah Valley*, 203.
33. Neese, *Three Years*, 188–189.
34. Miller, "With the Sixth New York," 39.
35. George W. Cooper, "That Cavalry Fight," *National Tribune*, May 28, 1891.
36. Carpenter letters.
37. Milgram, "The Libby Prison Correspondence of Tattnall Paulding," 1115.
38. Ibid., 300.
39. OR, vol. 27, part 2, p. 756.
40. McDonald, *History of the Laurel Brigade*, 155.
41. James J. Lowden, "Fight at Fairfield," *National Tribune*, June 18, 1891. This is most likely revisionist history. While survivors corroborated the story at a regimental reunion of the regiment's survivors after the war, it is very unlikely at this point in the battle that either side knew who their opponents were.

42. *Proceedings of the Fifth Annual Reunion,* 5.

43. OR, vol. 27, part 2, p. 756.

44. Starr papers; OR, vol. 27, part 2, p. 756.

45. Joseph Charlton pension file, RG 93, NARA.

46. Davis, 449–450.

47. Annual Return, 6th U.S. Cavalry, 1863. The other wounded members of Co. L were Sgt James Hayden, privates Benjamin Austin, Edward Hickey, Daniel Russell, Robert Barnett and Plericy E. Hill.

48. OR, vol. 27, part 1, p. 949; Davis, 432.

49. Milgram, "The Libby Prison Correspondence of Tattnall Paulding," 1115.

50. Connell, "A Cavalry Fight."

51. *Proceedings of the Fifth Annual Reunion,* 4.

52. Young, "The Battle of Fairfield, Pennsylvania," 251.

53. Davis, 433.

54. Blue, *Hanging Rock Rebel,* 203.

55. Ibid.

56. John N. Opie, *A Rebel Cavalryman with Lee, Stuart and Jackson* 178.

57. Ibid.

58. Blue, *Hanging Rock Rebel,* 203.

59. Ibid.

60. Paul Shevchuk, "Cut to Pieces: The Cavalry Fight at Fairfield, Pennsylvania, July 3, 1863," *Gettysburg* 1 (July 1989), 113.

61. Annual Return, 6th U.S. Cavalry, 1863. The other three wounded were Sgt. Thomas Fox, Pvt. George W. Cooper and Pvt. Matthew Hiney.

62. The War Department issued an order that no man captured by the enemy was to give his parole. Carter, *The Life of Lieutenant General Chaffee,* 31–32.

63. Davis, 435.

64. Ibid.

65. Milgram, "The Libby Prison Correspondence of Tattnall Paulding," 1115.

66. Carter, "The Sixth Regiment of Cavalry," 97.

67. O.W. Bennett to Louis H. Carpenter, April 4, 1895; Report of the Adjutant General's Office in the Case of George C. Platt, May 13, 1895, George C. Platt Medal of Honor File, NARA ("Platt MOH file").

68. James McDowell to Col.

Don Caldwell, April 6, 1895, Platt MOH file.

69. Annual Return, 6th U.S. Cavalry, 1863. The other wounded were Corporal John Higby, Farrier Neil McCarrick, privates James McDowell, Frederick Espy, Daniel B. Wood, George Davis and Abram B. Jacobs.

70. Regimental Returns; OR, vol. 27, part 1, p. 949.

71. Miller, "With the Sixth New York," 39.

72. Ibid., 40.

73. OR, vol. 27, part 1, p. 948.

74. Nicholas Nolan Appointments, Commissions, and Pension file, RG 94, NARA.

75. OR, vol. 27, part 1, p. 949.

76. OR, vol. 27, part 1, p. 948. Mechanicstown is known today as Thurmont, Maryland.

77. Charles W. McVicar Diary, Manuscript, Handley Regional Library, Winchester, VA.

78. Milgram, "The Libby Prison Correspondence of Tattnall Paulding," 1115.

79. Edward Carpenter and General Louis Henry Carpenter, *Samuel Carpenter and His Descendants,* 26–127.

80. Carpenter to his father, July 9, 1863.

81. Davis, 449.

82. Carpenter letters.

83. OR, vol. 27, part 2, pp. 756, 760.

84. "The Cavalry Fight at Fairfield," *Gettysburg Times,* June 30, 1958.

85. George W. Cooper, "That Cavalry Fight," *National Tribune,* May 28, 1891.

86. Samuel H. Starr to Susan Blythe, March 17, 1864, Civil War Miscellaneous Collection, Box 80, USAHEC.

87. Davis, 442–443.

88. John Krepps, "Regular Cavalry at Gettysburg," *National Tribune,* June 25, 1891.

89. Miller, "With the Sixth New York," 41. Miller states that the man was in fact the infamous Confederate spy William Richardson, whom John Buford captured and hanged in Frederick, Maryland, on July 7 during the retreat from Gettysburg. The author has been unable to confirm or deny this story, but it is very unlikely since it is apparent from several accounts that the Confederates did not know the regiment was in the area.

90. Davis, 436.

91. Samuel H. Starr to army headquarters, February 14, 1868.

92. Carter, *The Life of Lieutenant General Chaffee,* 31–32.

93. Medal of Honor citation of Sgt. Martin Schwenk, Martin Schwenk Medal of Honor file, NARA.

94. Medal of Honor citation of Sgt. George C. Platt, Platt MOH file.

Chapter 10

1. Davis, *Common Soldier, Uncommon War,* 442. Davis' book provides detailed coverage of the prisoners' march, as does Charles F. Miller's article, but it's much more difficult to find.

2. Miller, "With the Sixth New York Cavalry in the Civil War," 42.

3. Ibid., 45.

4. Davis, 465–467.

5. Monthly Returns.

6. Ibid.

7. Andersonville record—names?

8. William H. Carter, "The Sixth Regiment of Cavalry," *The Maine Bugle,* October 1896, p. 300; Monthly Returns.

9. OR, vol. 27, pt. 1, p. 948.

10. OR, vol. 27, pt. 2, p. 761.

11. Carpenter letters.

12. OR, vol. 27, pt. 1, p. 949.

13. OR, vol. 27, pt. 2, p. 761.

14. OR, vol. 27, pt. 1, p. 949.

15. Ibid and pt. 2, p. 761.

16. OR, vol. 27, pt. 1, p. 944.

17. Carpenter letters; Monthly Returns. Those killed were Cpls. David Oby, Co. B, and Alonzo Ellsworth, Co. I; and Pvts. James Evans, Co. F; John Fisher, Co. C; and William H. Thomas, Co. I. Oby's brother was killed at Fairfield four days earlier. In addition to Cpt. Claflin, the wounded were Co. B: Sgt. Thomas Dodd and Pvt. David Jones, Co. C: Pvts. James Smith and John C. Hogan, Co. E: Pvt. Randolph Knapp, Co. I: Pvts. John Albstag, Samuel Stearns and James Sullivan.

18. Monthly Returns.

19. Ibid; Carter, 102–103.

20. Carpenter letters.

21. Ibid.

22. Heitman, Balk.

23. Carpenter letters.

24. Ibid. The photo in this

book is believed to be of this second set of colors, now housed at the U.S. Cavalry Museum, Fort Riley, Kansas.

25. Monthly Returns.
26. Heitman, 889; Henry, vol. 2, p. 188.
27. Carpenter letters.
28. Monthly Returns.
29. Carpenter letters.
30. Carter, 103.
31. Monthly Returns.
32. Carpenter letters; Carter, "The Sixth Regiment of Cavalry,' 301.
33. Monthly Returns.
34. Carter, 103–104; Monthly Returns.
35. Monthly Returns.
36. Carpenter letters; Warner, *Generals in Blue*, 420.
37. Monthly Returns.
38. Carter, *From Yorktown to Santiago*, 105; Monthly Returns.
39. Ibid.
40. Henry, vol. 1, p. 140.
41. Monthly Returns.
42. Carpenter letters; Carter, 106; Monthly Returns.
43. Carter, 89–90.
44. Carpenter letters.
45. Ibid.

Chapter 11

Note: For detailed coverage of the Shenandoah Campaign, see Scott Patchan's *Shenandoah Sum-* mer and Jeffry Wert's *From Winchester to Cedar Creek*.

1. Philip H. Sheridan, *Personal Memoirs*, vol. 1, p. 353.
2. Edward Longacre, *Lincoln's Cavalry*, 250.
3. Carpenter letters.
4. Monthly Returns.
5. Starr, *The Union Cavalry in the Civil War*, vol. 2, pp. 97–113; Monthly Returns.
6. Carter, *From Yorktown to Santiago*, 112.
7. Heitman, xxx, 991.
8. Monthly Returns.
9. *New York Herald*, June 22, 1864.
10. Eric Wittenberg, *Glory Enough for All*, 231–232. Monthly Returns show Beckert killed on the 9th, but this does not correspond to other accounts of the campaign.
11. Carter, 114; Monthly Returns.
12. Monthly Returns.
13. Carter, 115.
14. Ibid., 116.
15. Monthly Returns.
16. Jeffry Wert, *From Winchester to Cedar Creek*, 40.
17. Ibid., 98.
18. Carter, 117.
19. Wert, 222.
20. Ibid.
21. OR, vol. 43, pt. 1, p. 450.
22. Wert, 249.
23. Monthly returns.
24. Hagemann, *Fighting Rebels and Redskins*, 304–306.

Chapter 12

Note: For detailed coverage of the Union cavalry in the final campaign, see Samuel Starr's *The Union Cavalry in the Civil War*, vol. 2, and Edward Longacre's *The Cavalry at Appomattox*.

1. Carter, *From Yorktown to Santiago*, 119.
2. Monthly Returns.
3. Sheridan, *Personal Memoirs*, vol. 2, p. 124.
4. Monthly returns.
5. OR, vol. 46, pt. 1, p. 499.
6. Ibid., 500.
7. Monthly Returns.
8. Carter, 122–123.
9. Longacre, *The Cavalry at Appomattox*, 71–73.
10. Gracey, *The Annals of the Sixth Pennsylvania Cavalry*, 150.
11. Starr, *The Union Cavalry in the Civil War*, vol. 2, pp. 469–472.
12. Carter, 124. There's no hard evidence to prove otherwise, but it seems more logical that this happened during the battle of Five Forks, perhaps following Lt. Nolan's capture.
13. Ibid; Monthly Returns.
14. Monthly Returns.
15. Ibid; Carter, 125.
16. OR, vol. 46, pt. 3, p. 1191.
17. Monthly Returns.

Bibliography

Newspapers

Army and Navy Journal
Cleveland Leader
Gettysburg Times
Harpers Weekly
Lancaster Examiner and Herald
National Tribune
New York Herald
New York Times
Philadelphia Press
Philadelphia Weekly Times
Pittsburgh Evening Chronicle
Pittsburgh Post
Western New Yorker
Wyoming County Mirror

Manuscript Collections

Archives and Regional History Collections, Western
   Michigan University
      James H. Cory Letters
      Randolph Knapp Papers
Archives, Historical Society of Pennsylvania, Philadel-
   phia, Pennsylvania
      Cadwallader Family Collection
      Louis Henry Carpenter Letters from the Field,
         1861–1865
      Tatnall Paulding Papers
Archives, Huntington Library, San Marino, Califor-
   nia
      Joseph Hooker Papers
Archives, New York Historical Society
      David E. Cronin Collection
Archives, United States Army History and Education
   Center, Carlisle, Pennsylvania
      Civil War Miscellaneous Collection
      Civil War Times Illustrated Collection
      James S. Brisbin Letters
      August V. Kautz Papers
B. Conrad Bush Collection
      B. Nathaniel Owen Letters
Beaver County Historical Society
      Robert Steel Letters
Gilder-Lehman Institute of American History, New
   York
      James Brisbin Letters
Harrisburg Civil War Roundtable Collection

Iowa Historical Society
      James Brisbin Letters
Manuscripts, Handley Regional Library, Winchester,
   Virginia
      Charles W. McVicar Diary
Michael Winey Collection
Montana Historical Society Library, Helena
      James Sanks Brisbin Papers
National Archives and Records Administration, Wash-
   ington, D.C.
      RG 94, Record of Enlistments in the U.S.
         Army, 1798–1914
      RG 94, Returns from Regular Cavalry Regi-
         ments, 1833–1916
Special Collections, United States Military Academy
   Library, West Point, New York
      Henry McQuiston Papers
Special Collections, University of Maryland Libraries
      William Emory Papers

Published Primary Sources

Articles

Averell, William W. "With the Cavalry on the Penin-
   sula." In *Battles and Leaders of the Civil War, Being
   for the Most Part Contributions by Union and Con-
   federate Officers Based upon "The Century War Series."*
   Vol. 2. Edited by Robert U. Johnson and Clarence
   C. Buel. New York: Thomas Yoseloff, 1956.
Connell, John H. "A Cavalry Fight." *National Tribune*,
   April 30, 1891.
Conrad, Holmes. "The Cavalry Corps of the Army of
   Northern Virginia." In *Photographic History of the
   Civil War*. Vol. 4. Edited by Theo. F. Rodenbough.
   New York: Review of Reviews, 1911.
Cooke, Philip St. George. "The Charge of Cooke's
   Cavalry at Gaines's Mill." In *Battles and Leaders of
   the Civil War, Being for the Most Part Contributions
   by Union and Confederate Officers Based upon "The
   Century War Series."* Vol. 2. Edited by Robert U.
   Johnson and Clarence C. Buel. New York: Thomas
   Yoseloff, 1956.
Cooper, George W. "That Cavalry Fight," *National
   Tribune*, May 28, 1891.
Davis, George B. "The Antietam Campaign." In *Pa-
   pers of the Military Historical Society of Massachusetts.*

Vol. 3, *Campaigns in Virginia, Maryland, and Pennsylvania, 1862–1863.* Boston: Griffith-Stilling, 1903. Reprint, Wilmington, NC: Broadfoot, 1989.

Gettysburg Times. "The Cavalry Fight at Fairfield," June 30, 1958.

Harris, Moses. "With the Reserve Brigade." *Journal of the United States Cavalry Association* 3 (1890).

_____. "With the Reserve Brigade." *Journal of the United States Cavalry Association* 4 (1891).

Krepps, John. "Regular Cavalry at Gettysburg," *National Tribune,* June 25, 1891.

Lowden, James J. "Fight at Fairfield," *National Tribune,* June 18, 1891.

Miller, Charles F. "With the Sixth New York Cavalry in the Civil War." *Historical Wyoming* 19, nos. 2 and 3 (January and March 1966).

Rea, D.B. "Cavalry Incidents of the Maryland Campaign." *The Maine Bugle,* January 1895.

Reno, Marcus A. "Boots and Saddles: The Cavalry of the Army of the Potomac." *National Tribune,* April 29, 1886.

Rhodes, Charles D. "The Mounting and Remounting of the Federal Cavalry," *The Photographic History of The Civil War.* Vol. 4, *The Cavalry.* Edited by Francis Trevelyan Miller. New York: Thomas Yoseloff, 1957.

Shevchuk, Paul. "Cut to Pieces: The Cavalry Fight at Fairfield, Pennsylvania, July 3, 1863." *Gettysburg* 1 (July 1989).

Waud, Alfred R. "The Cavalry Fight Near Culpeper." *Harper's Weekly,* July 10, 1863.

Young, T.J. "The Battle of Brandy Station." *Confederate Veteran* 23 (1915).

_____. "The Battle of Fairfield, Pennsylvania," *Confederate Veteran* 5 (1897).

Books

Adams, Francis Colburn. *The Story of a Trooper.* New York: Dick & Fitzgerald, 1865.

Baylor, George. *Bull Run to Bull Run; or, Four Years in the Army of Northern Virginia.* Richmond, VA: B.F. Johnson, 1900.

Beale, George William. *A Lieutenant of Cavalry in Lee's Army.* Boston: Gorham, 1918.

Beale, R.L.T. *History of the Ninth Virginia Cavalry in the War Between the States.* Richmond, VA: B.F. Johnson, 1899. Reprint, Salem, MA: Higginson, 1998.

Blackford, William W. *War Years with Jeb Stuart.* New York: Charles Scribner's Sons, 1945.

Blue, John. *Hanging Rock Rebel: Lt. John Blue's War in West Virginia and the Shenandoah Valley.* Edited by Dan Oates. Shippensburg, PA: Burd Street Press, 1994.

Brackett, Albert G. *History of the United States Cavalry, from the Formation of the Federal Government to the 1st of June 1863.* N.p., 1865.

Carpenter, Edward, and General Louis Henry. *Samuel Carpenter and His Descendants.* Philadelphia: J.B. Lippincott, 1912.

Carter, William R. *Sabres, Saddles, and Spurs.* Edited by Walbrook D. Swank. Shippensburg, PA: Burd Street Press, 1998.

Cooke, John Esten. *Wearing of the Gray, Being Personal Portraits, Scenes, and Adventures of the War.* New York: E.B. Treat, 1867. Reprint, Baton Rouge: Louisiana University Press, 1959.

Cooke, Phillip St. George. *Cavalry Tactics.* Washington: War Department, 1862.

Davis, Sidney Morris. *Common Soldier, Uncommon War: Life as a Cavalryman in the Civil War.* Edited by Charles F. Cooney. Bethesda, MD: SMD Group, 1994.

de Joinville, Prince. *The Army of the Potomac: Its Organization, Its Commander, and Its Campaign.* New York: Anson D.F. Randolph, 1863.

Dension, Rev. Frederic. *Sabres and Spurs: The First Rhode Island Cavalry in the Civil War, 1861–1865.* Providence: First Rhode Island Cavalry Veteran Association, 1876.

Emerson, Edward W., ed. *Life and Letters of Charles Russell Lowell.* Port Washington, NY: Kennikat Press, 1971.

Glazier, Willard. *Three Years in the Federal Cavalry.* New York: R.H. Ferguson, 1873.

Gracey, Samuel L. *Annals of the Sixth Pennsylvania Cavalry.* Philadelphia: E.H. Butler, 1868.

Grimsley, Daniel A. *Battles in Culpeper County, Virginia, 1861–1865.* Culpeper, VA: Raleigh Travers Green, 1900.

Hopkins, Luther W. *From Bull Run to Appomattox: A Boy's View.* Baltimore: Fleet-McGinley, 1908.

Hudgins, Robert S., II. *Recollections of an Old Dominion Dragoon: The Civil War Experiences of Sgt. Robert S. Hudgins II, Company B, 3rd Virginia Cavalry.* Edited by Garland C. Hudgins and Richard B. Kleese. Orange, VA: Publisher's Press, 1993.

McClellan, George B. *The Civil War Papers of George B. McClellan: Selected Correspondence, 1860–1865.* Edited by Stephen W. Sears. New York: Ticknor & Fields, 1989. Reprint, Cambridge, MA: Da Capo Press, 1992.

_____. *Report on the Organization and Campaigns of the Army of the Potomac.* New York: Sheldon, 1864.

McClellan, Henry B. *The Life and Campaigns of Major General J.E.B. Stuart.* Boston: Houghton-Mifflin, 1895.

McDonald, William N. *A History of the Laurel Brigade.* Baltimore: Sun Job Printing, 1907.

Miller, Charles H. *History of the 16th Regiment Pennsylvania Cavalry, for the Year Ending October 31st, 1863, Commanded by Colonel John Irvin Gregg, of Centre County, Pa.* Philadelphia: King & Baird, 1864.

Mitchell, Adele H., ed. *The Letters of Major General James E.B. Stuart.* Richmond, VA: Stuart-Mosby Historical Society, 1990.

Moore, Frank, ed. *The Rebellion Record: A Diary of American Events, with Documents, Narratives, Illustrative Incidents, Poetry, Etc.* 11 vols. New York: D. Van Nostrand, 1864–68.

Neese, George M. *Three Years in the Confederate Horse Artillery.* New York: Neale, 1911.

Newhall, Frederic C. *With General Sheridan in Lee's Last Campaign.* Philadelphia: J.B. Lippincott, 1866.

O'Brien, Thomas M., and Oliver Diefendorf. *General Orders of the War Department Embracing the Years 1861, 1862, and 1863.* 2 vols. New York: Derby & Miller, 1864.

Official Army Register for 1865. Washington: Adjutant General's Office, 1865.

Official Army Register for 1864. Washington: Adjutant General's Office, 1864.

Official Army Register for September, 1861. Washington: Adjutant General's Office, 1861.

Opie, John N. *A Rebel Cavalryman with Lee, Stuart, and Jackson*. Chicago: Charles Conkey, 1899.

Peck, Rufus H. *Reminiscences of a Confederate Soldier of Co. C, 2nd Va. Cavalry*. Fincastle, VA: privately published, 1913.

Pickerill, William N. *History of the Third Indiana Cavalry*. Indianapolis: Aetna, 1906.

Poinsett, J.R. *Cavalry Tactics, Second Part, School of the Trooper, of the Platoon and of the Squadron Mounted*. Washington, D.C.: J. and G.S. Gideon, 1841.

Proceedings from the Fifth Annual Reunion of the Survivors of the 6th U.S. Cavalry Reunion, Tuesday, July 3, 1888. 6th U.S. Cavalry Association.

Rawle, William B. *History of the Third Pennsylvania Cavalry, Sixtieth Regiment, Pennsylvania Volunteers in the American Civil War, 1861–1865*. Philadelphia: Franklin, 1905. Reprint, Salem, MA: Higginson, n.d.

Rodenbough, Theophilus F., ed. *From Everglade to Canon with the Second Dragoons*. New York: D. Van Nostrand, 1875.

Royall, William L. *Some Reminiscences*. New York: Neale, 1909.

Sanford, George B. *Fighting Rebels and Redskins: Experiences in Army Life of Colonel George B. Sanford, 1861–1892*. Edited by E.R. Hageman. Norman: University of Oklahoma Press, 1969.

Sheridan, Philip H. *Personal Memoirs of P.H. Sheridan*. 2 vols. New York: Charles L. Webster, 1888.

Supplement to the Official Records of the Union and Confederate Armies: Record of Events. Edited by Janet B. Hewett et al. Wilmington, NC: Broadfoot, 1994.

Swank, Walbrook D., ed. *Sabres, Saddles and Spurs*. Shippensburg, PA: Burd Street Press, 1998.

Thomas, Hampton S. *Some Personal Reminiscences of Service in the Cavalry of the Army of the Potomac*. Philadelphia: L.R. Hamersly, 1889.

Tobie, Edward P. *Service of the Cavalry in the Army of the Potomac*. Providence: N.B. Williams, 1882.

Tremain, Henry Edwin. *The Last Hours of Sheridan's Cavalry*. New York: Bonnell, Silver & Bowers, 1904.

Von Borcke, Heros. *Memoirs of the Confederate War for Independence*. Edinburgh: W. Blackwood, 1866. Reprint, Nashville: J.S. Sanders, 1999.

The War of the Rebellion: A Compilation of the Official Records of the Union and Confederate Armies. 128 vols., 3 series. Washington, D.C.: United States Government Printing Office, 1889.

Wise, Jennings Cropper. *The Long Arm of Lee; or, The History of the Artillery of the Army of Northern Virginia*. Vol. 1. Lynchburg, VA: J.P. Bell, 1915. Reprint, Lincoln: University of Nebraska Press, 1991.

Wright, Catherine M., ed. *Lee's Last Casualty: The Life and Letters of Sgt. Robert W. Parker, Second Virginia Cavalry*. Knoxville: University of Tennessee Press, 2008.

Secondary Sources

Articles

Barton, John V. "The Procurement of Horses. *Civil War Times Illustrated* 6, no. 8 (December 1967).

Carter, William H. "The Sixth Regiment of Cavalry." *The Maine Bugle*, October 1896.

Luvaas, Jay. "Cavalry Lessons of the Civil War." *Civil War Times Illustrated* 6, no. 9 (January 1968).

Milgram, James W. "The Libby Prison Correspondence of Tattnall Paulding." *American Philatelist* 89 (December 1975).

O'Neill, Robert. "Cavalry on the Peninsula: Fort Monroe to the Gates of Richmond, March to May, 1862." *Blue & Gray* 19, nos. 5, 6.

Books

Alberts, Don E. *Brandy Station to Manila Bay: A Biography of General Wesley Merritt*. Austin: Presidio Press, 1980.

Armstrong, Richard L. *7th Virginia Cavalry*. Lynchburg, VA: H.E. Howard, 1992.

Arnold, James R. *Jeff Davis's Own: Cavalry, Comanches, and the Battle for the Texas Frontier*. New York: John Wiley, 2000.

Bates, Samuel P. *Martial Deeds of Pennsylvania*. Philadelphia. T.H. Davis, 1875.

Beatie, Russel H. *Army of the Potomac: McClellan's First Campaign, March–May 1862*. New York: Savas Beatie, 2007.

Blanton, DeAnne, and Lauren M. Cook. *They Fought Like Demons: Women Soldiers in the Civil War*. New York: Random House, 2002.

Boatner, Mark N., III. *The Civil War Dictionary*. New York: David McKay, 1987.

Book of Biographies: Biographical Sketches of Leading Citizens of Berks County, PA. Buffalo: Biographical, 1898.

Bowen, James L. *Massachusetts in the Civil War, 1861–1865*. Springfield: Clark W. Bryan, 1889.

Busey, John W., and Martin, David G. *Regimental Strengths and Losses at Gettysburg*. Hightstown, NJ: Longstreet, 2005.

Carman, Ezra A. *The Maryland Campaign of September 1862*. Vol. 1, *South Mountain*. Edited by Thomas G. Clemens. New York: Savas Beatie, 2010.

Carter, William H. *From Yorktown to Santiago with the Sixth U.S. Cavalry*. Baltimore: Lord Baltimore Press; Friedenwald, 1900.

_____. *The Life of Lieutenant General Chaffee*. Chicago: University of Chicago Press, 1916.

Crouch, Richard E. *Brandy Station: A Battle Like None Other*. Westminster, MD: Willow Bend Books, 2002.

Cullum, George W. *Biographical Register of the Officers and Graduates of the U.S. Military Academy at West Point, N.Y., from Its Establishment in 1802 to 1890*. Boston and New York: Houghton, Mifflin, 1891.

Downey, Fairfax. *Clash of Cavalry: The Battle of Brandy Station, June 9, 1863*. New York: n.p., 1959.

Driver, Robert J. *5th Virginia Cavalry*. Lynchburg, VA: H.E. Howard, 1997.

_____. *1st Virginia Cavalry*. Lynchburg, VA: H.E. Howard, 1991.

Dyer, Frederick H. *A Compendium of the War of the*

Rebellion. 3 vols. Cedar Rapids: 1909. Reprint, New York: Thomas Yoseloff, 1959.

Eicher, John H., and David J. Eicher. *Civil War High Commands.* Stanford: Stanford University Press, 2001.

Faust, Albert B. *The German Element in the United States.* New York: Houghton Mifflin, 1909.

Fox, Arthur B. *Pittsburgh During the American Civil War, 1860–1865.* Pittsburgh: Mechling, 2004.

Fox, William F. *Regimental Losses in the American Civil War, 1861–1865.* Albany: Brandow, 1898. Reprint, Dayton: Morningside, 1985.

Furgurson, Earnest B. *Chancellorsville, 1863: The Souls of the Brave.* New York: Alfred A. Knopf, 1992.

Gray, Alonzo. *Cavalry Tactics as Illustrated by the War of the Rebellion, Together with Many Interesting Facts Important for Cavalry to Know.* Leavenworth: Ketcheson, 1910. Reprint, Whitefish, MT: Kessinger, n.d.

Griffith, Paddy. *Battle Tactics of the Civil War.* New Haven, CT: Yale University Press, 2001.

Hall, Hillman A. Chairman. *History of the Sixth New York Cavalry (Second Ira Harris Guard).* Worcester, MA: Blanchard, 1908. Reprint, Salem, MA: Higginson, n.d.

Heitman, Francis B. *Historical Register and Dictionary of the United States Army, from Its Organization, September 29, 1789, to March 2, 1902.* Vol. 1. Washington, D.C.: Government Printing Office 1903. Reprint, University of Illinois Press, Urbana: 1965.

Henry, Guy V. *Military Record of Civilian Appointments in the United States Army.* 2 vols. New York: D. Van Nostrand, 1873.

Heysinger, Isaac W. *Antietam and the Maryland and Virginia Campaigns of 1862.* New York: Neale, 1912.

Hopkins, Donald A. *The Little Jeff: The Jeff Davis Legion, Cavalry Army of Northern Virginia.* Shippensburg, PA: White Mane, 1999.

Kautz, Lawrence G. *August V. Kautz, USA: Biography of a Civil War General.* Jefferson, NC: McFarland, 2008.

Krick, Robert K. *9th Virginia Cavalry.* Lynchburg, VA: H.E. Howard, 1982.

Lambert, Joseph I. *One Hundred Years with the Second Cavalry.* Topeka: Press Caper, 1939.

Longacre, Edward G. *The Cavalry at Appomattox: A Tactical Study of Mounted Operations During the Civil War's Climactic Campaign, March 27–April 9, 1865.* Mechanicsburg: Stackpole Books, 2003.

———. *The Cavalry at Gettysburg: A Tactical Study of Mounted Operations During the Civil War's Pivotal Campaign, 9 June–14 June 1863.* Lincoln: University of Nebraska Press, 1993.

———. *Fitz Lee: A Military Biography of Major General Fitzhugh Lee, CSA.* Cambridge, MA: Da Capo, 2005.

———. *General John Buford: A Military Biography.* Cambridge, MA: Da Capo, 2003.

———. *Lincoln's Cavalrymen: A History of the Mounted Forces of the Army of the Potomac.* Mechanicsburg, PA: Stackpole Books, 2000.

McKinney, Joseph W. *Brandy Station, Virginia, June 9, 1863: The Largest Cavalry Battle of the Civil War.* Jefferson, NC: McFarland, 2006.

Moore, Robert H. *The 1st and 2nd Stuart Horse Artillery.* Lynchburg, VA: H.E. Howard Co., 1985.

Musick, Michael P. *6th Virginia Cavalry.* Lynchburg, VA: H.E. Howard, 1990.

Ness, George T., Jr. *The Regular Army on the Eve of the Civil War.* Baltimore: Toomey, 1990.

Newell, Clayton R., and Charles R. Shrader. *Of Duty Well and Faithfully Done: A History of the Regular Army in the Civil War.* Lincoln: University of Nebraska Press.

O'Reilly, Frank A. *The Fredericksburg Campaign.* Baton Rouge: University of Louisiana Press, 2006.

Patchan, Scott. *Shenandoah Summer: The 1864 Valley Campaign.* Lincoln: University of Nebraska Press, 2007.

Phisterer, Frederick. *New York in the War of the Rebellion, 1861–1865.* Albany: J.B. Lyon, 1912.

———. *Statistical Record of the Armies of the United States.* N.p., 1883. Reprint, Edison, NJ: Castle, 2002.

Powell, William H. *Powell's Records of Living Officers of the United States Army.* Philadelphia: L.R. Hamersly, 1890.

Price, George F. *Across the Continent with the Fifth Cavalry.* New York: Noble, 1883.

Reid, Whitelaw. *Ohio in the War: Her Statesmen, Generals and Soldiers.* Vol. 1. Cincinnati: Robert Clarke, 1872.

Rhodes, Charles D. *History of the Cavalry of the Army of the Potomac, Including That of the Army of Virginia (Pope's), and Also the History of the Operations of the Federal Cavalry in West Virginia During the War.* Kansas City: Hudson-Kimberly, 1900.

Starr, Stephen Z. *The Union Cavalry in the Civil War.* Vol. 1, *From Fort Sumter to Gettysburg, 1861–1863.* Baton Rouge: Louisiana State University Press, 1979.

Trout, Robert J. *Galloping Thunder: The Story of the Stuart Horse Artillery Battalion.* Mechanicsburg, PA: Stackpole Books, 2002.

———. *They Followed the Plume: The Story of J.E.B. Stuart and His Staff.* Mechanicsburg, PA: Stackpole Books, 1993.

———. *With Pen and Saber: The Letters and Diaries of J.E.B. Stuart's Staff Officers.* Mechanicsburg, PA: Stackpole Books, 1995.

Urwin, Gregory J.W. *The United States Cavalry: An Illustrated History.* Poole, England: Blandford Press, 1983.

Warner, Ezra J. *Generals in Blue: The Lives of the Union Commanders.* Baton Rouge: Louisiana State University Press, 1949.

———. *Generals in Gray: Lives of the Confederate Commanders.* Baton Rouge: Louisiana State University Press, 1949.

Welcher, Frank J. *The Union Army, 1861–1865: Organization and Operations.* Vol. 1, *The Eastern Theater.* Bloomington: Indiana University Press, 1989.

Wert, Jeffry D. *Cavalryman of the Lost Cause: A Biography of J.E.B. Stuart.* New York: Simon & Schuster, 2008.

———. *From Winchester to Cedar Creek: The Shenandoah Campaign of 1864.* Carlisle, PA: South Mountain Press, 1987.

Wittenberg, Eric J. *The Battle of Brandy Station.* Charleston: History Press, 2010.

———. *Gettysburg's Forgotten Cavalry Actions.* New York: Savas Beatie, 2011.

_____. *Glory Enough for All.* Washington, D.C.: Brassey's, 2002.

_____. *Rush's Lancers: The Sixth Pennsylvania Cavalry in the Civil War.* Yardley, PA: Westholme, 2006.

_____. *The Union Cavalry Comes of Age: Hartwood Church to Brandy Station, 1863.* Dulles, VA: Brassey's, 2002.

Wittenberg, Eric J., J. David Petruzzi and Michael F. Nugent. *One Continuous Fight: The Retreat from Gettysburg and the Pursuit of Lee's Army of Northern Virginia, July 4–14, 1863.* El Dorado Hills, CA: Savas-Beatie, 2008.

Index

Numbers in **_bold italics_** indicate pages with photographs.